PROGRESS IN BRAIN RESEARCH

VOLUME 149

CORTICAL FUNCTION:
A VIEW FROM THE THALAMUS

Other volumes in PROGRESS IN BRAIN RESEARCH

PROGRESS IN BRAIN RESEARCH

VOLUME 149

CORTICAL FUNCTION:
A VIEW FROM THE THALAMUS

EDITED BY

V.A. CASAGRANDE

*Department of Cell & Developmental Biology, Vanderbilt Medical School, Medical Center North,
Nashville, TN 37232, USA*

R.W. GUILLERY

Department of Anatomy, School of Medicine, University of Wisconsin, 1300 University Avenue, Madison, WI 53706, USA

S.M. SHERMAN

*Department of Neurobiology, Pharmacology & Physiology, The University of Chicago, 947 E. 58th Street, MC 0926, 316 Abbott,
Chicago, IL 60637, USA*

ELSEVIER

AMSTERDAM – BOSTON – HEIDELBERG – LONDON – NEW YORK – OXFORD
PARIS – SAN DIEGO – SAN FRANCISCO – SINGAPORE – SYDNEY – TOKYO

2005

Elsevier
Radarweg 29, PO Box 211, 1000 AE Amsterdam, The Netherlands
The Boulevard, Langford Lane, Kidlington, Oxford OX5 1GB, UK

First edition 2005
Reprinted 2006

Library of Congress Cataloging-in-Publication Data
A catalog record for this book is available from the Library of Congress

British Library Cataloguing in Publication Data
Cortical function : a view from the thalamus. – (Progress in brain research: v. 149)
 1. Thalamus   2. Cerebral cortex
 I. Casagrande. V. A.   II. Guillery, R. W.   III. Sherman, S. Murray
 612.8'262

ISBN–13: 978-0-444-51679-4
ISBN–10: 0-444-51679-4

For information on all Elsevier publications
visit our website at books.elsevier.com

Transferred to digital printing 2006
Printed and bound by CPI Antony Rowe, Eastbourne

Working together to grow
libraries in developing countries

www.elsevier.com | www.bookaid.org | www.sabre.org

ELSEVIER   BOOK AID International   Sabre Foundation

List of contributors

L.F. Abbott, Volen Center and Department of Biology, Brandeis University, Waltham, MA 02454-9110, USA

H.J. Alitto, Center for Neuroscience, University of California at Davis, Davis, CA 95616, USA

R.A. Berman, Department of Neuroscience, University of Pittsburgh, Center for the Neural Basis of Cognition, Mellon Institute, Room 115, 4400 Fifth Avenue, Pittsburgh, PA 15213-2683, USA

T. Bezdudnaya, Department of Psychology (U-20), The University of Connecticut, Storrs, CT 06269, USA

S. Blau, Department of Neuroscience, Brown University, 192 Thayer Street, Providence, RI 02912, USA

E.M. Callaway, Systems Neurobiology Laboratories, The Salk Institute for Biological Studies, 10010 North Torrey Pines Road, La Jolla, CA 92037, USA

V.A. Casagrande, Departments of Cell and Developmental Biology, Psychology and Ophthalmology & Visual Sciences, Vanderbilt Medical School, Medical Center North B2323, Nashville, TN 37232, USA

J. Cavanaugh, Laboratory of Sensorimotor Research, National Eye Institute, N.I.H., Building 49, Room 2A50, 9000 Rockville Pike, Bethesda, MD 20892, USA

F.S. Chance, Department of Neurobiology and Behavior, University of California at Irvine, 2205 McGaugh Hall, Irvine, CA 92697-4550, USA

P.S. Churchland, Philosophy Department 0119, University of California at San Diego, La Jolla, CA 92093, USA

C.L. Colby, Department of Neuroscience, University of Pittsburgh, Center for the Neural Basis of Cognition, Mellon Institute, Room 115, 4400 Fifth Avenue, Pittsburgh, PA 15213-2683, USA

B.W. Connors, Department of Neuroscience, Box 1953, Division of Biology & Medicine, Brown University, Providence, RI 02912, USA

S.J. Cruikshank, Department of Neuroscience, Box 1953, Division of Biology & Medicine, Brown University, Providence, RI 02912, USA

M. Deschênes, Centre de Recherche, Université Laval-Robert Giffard, 2601 de la Canardière, Quebec City, QC G1J 2G3, Canada

C. Dufresne, Centre de Recherche, Université Laval-Robert Giffard, 2601 de la Canardière, Quebec City, QC G1J 2G3, Canada

M. Fallah, Systems Neurobiology Laboratory, The Salk Institute for Biological Studies, 10010 North Torrey Pines Road, La Jolla, CA 92037-1099, USA

M.A. Goodale, Department of Psychology, University of Western Ontario, London, ON N6A 5C2, Canada

R.W. Guillery, Department of Anatomy, School of Medicine, University of Wisconsin, 1300 University Avenue, Madison, WI 53706, USA

A.G. Gusev, Institute of Higher Nervous Activity and Neurophysiology, Russian Academy of Medical Sciences, Moscow, 117865, Russia

J.A. Heimel, The Netherlands Ophthalmic Research Institute, Meibergdreef 47, 1105 BA Amsterdam ZO, The Netherlands

L.M. Heiser, Department of Neuroscience, University of Pittsburgh, Center for the Neural Basis of Cognition, Mellon Institute, Room 115, 4400 Fifth Avenue, Pittsburgh, PA 15213-2683, USA

X. Huang, VCL, The Salk Institute, 10010 North Torrey Pines Road, La Jolla, CA 92037-1099, USA

G. Króliczak, Neuroscience Program, Department of Psychology, University of Western Ontario, London, ON N6A 5C2, Canada

C.E. Landisman, Department of Neuroscience, Box 1953, Division of Biology & Medicine, Brown University, Providence, RI 02912, USA

P. Lavallée, Centre de Recherche, Université Laval-Robert Giffard, 2601 de la Canardière, Quebec City, QC G1J 2G3, Canada

S.P. MacEvoy, Duke University Medical Center, Bryan Research Building, Room 429, Research Drive, Durham, NC 27710, USA

J.G. Mancilla, Department of Otolaryngology, School of Medicine, University of North Carolina, Chapel Hill, NC 27599, USA

J.F. Mitchell, Systems Neurobiology Laboratory, The Salk Institute for Biological Studies, 10010 North Torrey Pines Road, La Jolla, CA 92037-1099, USA

S.B. Nelson, Brandeis University, 415 South Street, Waltham, MA 02454, USA

M.A. Paradiso, Department of Neuroscience, Brown University, 192 Thayer Street, Providence, RI 02912, USA

H.J. Ralston III, Department of Anatomy, W.M. Keck Foundation Center for Integrative Neuroscience, University of California at San Francisco, 515 Parnassus Avenue, San Francisco, CA 94143-0452, USA

J.H. Reynolds, Systems Neurobiology Laboratory, The Salk Institute for Biological Studies, 10010 North Torrey Pines Road, La Jolla, CA 92037-1099, USA

D. Royal, Center for Molecular Neuroscience, The Vanderbilt Vision Research Center, Vanderbilt University, Nashville, TN 37232, USA

O. Ruiz, Departments of Cell and Developmental Biology, Psychology and Ophthalmology & Visual Sciences, Vanderbilt Medical School, Medical Center North B2323, Nashville, TN 37232, USA

G. Sáry, Department of Physiology, University of Szeged, Szeged, Hungary

R.C. Saunders, Laboratory of Neuropsychology, National Institute of Mental Health, Room 1B80, Building 49, 49 Convent Drive, MSC 4415, Bethesda, MD 20892-4415, USA

P.H. Schiller, Department of Brain and Cognitive Sciences, Massachusetts Institute of Technology, 77 Massachusetts Avenue, E25-634, Cambridge, MA 02139, USA

J. Schummers, Department of Brain and Cognitive Sciences, Massachusetts Institute of Technology, E25-235, 45 Carleton Street, Cambridge, MA 02142, USA

J. Sharma, Department of Brain and Cognitive Sciences, Massachusetts Institute of Technology, E25-235, 45 Carleton Street, Cambridge, MA 02142, USA

S.M. Sherman, Department of Neurobiology, Pharmacology & Physiology, The University of Chicago, 947 E 58th Street, MC 0926, 316 Abbott, Chicago, IL 60637, USA

M.A. Sommer, Laboratory of Sensorimotor Research, National Eye Institute, N.I.H., Building 49, Room 2A50, 9000 Rockville Pike, Bethesda, MD 20892, USA

G.R. Stoner, Systems Neurobiology Laboratory, The Salk Institute for Biological Studies, 10010 North Torrey Pines Road, La Jolla, CA 92037-1099, USA

M. Sur, Department of Brain and Cognitive Sciences, Massachusetts Institute of Technology, E25-235, 45 Carleton Street, Cambridge, MA 02142, USA

H.A. Swadlow, Department of Psychology (U-20), The University of Connecticut, Storrs, CT 06269, USA

E.J. Tehovnik, Department of Brain and Cognitive Sciences, Massachusetts Institute of Technology, 77 Massachusetts Avenue, E25-634, Cambridge, MA 02139, USA

E. Timofeeva, Centre de Recherche, Université Laval-Robert Giffard, 2601 de la Canardière, Quebec City, QC G1J 2G3, Canada

W.M. Usrey, Center for Neuroscience, University of California at Davis, Davis, CA 95616, USA

D.C. Van Essen, Department of Anatomy & Neurobiology, Washington University School of Medicine, 660 South Euclid Avenue, St. Louis, MO 63110, USA

S.D. Van Hooser, Brandeis University, 415 South Street, Waltham, MA 02454, USA

D.A. Westwood, School of Health and Human Performance, Dalhousie University, Halifax, NS B3H 3J5, Canada

R.H. Wurtz, Laboratory of Sensorimotor Research, National Eye Institute, N.I.H., Building 49, Room 2A50, 9000 Rockville Pike, Bethesda, MD 20892-4435, USA

Preface

This book is a summary of talks given at a meeting held in Madison Wisconsin from 12–14 September 2004. This meeting was initiated by two of the editors (V.A.C. and S.M.S.) largely in recognition of the research career of the third editor, R.W. Guillery. Ray Guillery has enjoyed a long and productive career that is briefly summarized below. We thank the Provost's Office of the University of Wisconsin (P.D. Spear, Provost), the University of Wisconsin Center for Neuroscience (T.P. Sutula, Director), the Swartz Foundation, and the Zeiss Corporation for their generous support for this meeting.

The theme of the meeting

It was the purpose of the meeting to address specific issues concerning the communication between thalamus and cortex. Three areas were emphasized, all of which focus on the dynamic interdependence of thalamus and cortex in the construction of percepts and actions: (1) the role of thalamocortical communication in cognition and attention, (2) the role of the thalamus in communication between cortical areas, and (3) the role of thalamocortical interactions in relating motor control to perceptual processing. Each of the speakers was asked to produce a chapter in advance to focus on one of these issues. The chapters were available online before the meeting and this ensured a productive discussion at the end of each of the six planned sessions.

Almost all of the messages that are received by the cerebral cortex from the environment or from the body's internal receptors come through the thalamus. Much current thought about perceptual processing is based on sensory pathways that relay in the thalamus. These sensory pathways are represented as transferring information to the cerebral cortex with subsequent processing in the cortex for eventual passage to cortical areas that have motor outputs or pathways to memory. One part of the meeting was concerned with defining how the passage of sensory messages to cortex depends upon attentional state, considering particularly the neuronal properties of thalamic and cortical cells that play a role in the first entry of sensory messages to the cerebral cortex. A second part explored the extent to which higher cortical areas, which receive their inputs from other (lower) cortical areas, do so by direct corticocortical pathways or through a "higher order" thalamic relay that receives inputs from one cortical area and sends signals to other cortical areas. A third part of the meeting examined the relationship between the classical sensory pathways and the motor outputs of the brain. Many of the sensory pathways that are relayed to cortex by the thalamus, and many of the trans-thalamic corticocortical pathways mentioned above are made up of nerve fibers that also send branches to subcortical motor or premotor centers of the brain. That is, the messages that are passed through the thalamus to cortex represent copies of motor instructions (corollary discharges). Evidence for such patterns of corollary discharge were considered, and the significance of these early motor connections for understanding the role of cortical functions in motor control and in perceptual processing were discussed. Each of these areas, the dynamic role played by thalamic relays, the role of thalamus in corticocortical communications, and the thalamocortical pathways as copies of motor instructions represent some radical new concepts of thalamocortical functioning. The implications of the connectivity patterns that are important for understanding attentional mechanisms and also for new insights into perceptual mechanisms and their relationships to motor control.

V.A. Casagrande, R.W. Guillery, S.M. Sherman

The career of Ray Guillery (by Tom Sutula)

Ray Guillery was born in Greifswald, Germany, in 1929. His father was a pathologist in the Charité Hospital in Berlin, where his mother also worked as a technician. Ray's grandfather was an ophthalmologist who had published on the subject of visual acuity in 1931. His maternal great-uncle, Otto Deiters, was an early and eminent neuroanatomist who published some of the first accurate descriptions of nerve cells, including axons and dendrites, which were briefly called "Deiters' processes". During the 1930s and through the Second World War, Ray attended six different schools in Berlin, Switzerland, Holland, and England. He was in the last class of the Rudolph Steiner School in Berlin that was closed because of resistance to the Nazi movement. After attending schools in Holland, Switzerland, and

finally, a Quaker school in Oxfordshire, he emerged as an adolescent who, in his own words, "was able to think of (myself) proudly, as English".

Ray entered University College London (UCL) in 1948 on a scholarship to study medicine. By the end of the first year of medical school and later influenced by many discussions with J.Z. Young, he recognized that he preferred a career as a research scientist. He made a transition into Ph.D. training to pursue his interest in how morphology and connectivity could be informative about how the brain might work. As a graduate student he began a study on pathways of the hypothalamus, which evolved into a series of studies on connections of the fornix with the anterior thalamic nuclei.

Ray's interest in thalamocortical relationships developed during a sabbatical visit in Madison in 1960–61, where he collaborated with Jerzy Rose and Clinton Woolsey, who had proposed that a single thalamic nucleus might project to multiple cortical areas. After moving to the Department of Anatomy in Madison in 1964, he performed a series of pioneering experiments about the organization of inputs to the lateral geniculate nucleus and the effects of visual deprivation. In this work and in subsequent observations about the organization of chiasmatic projections in Siamese cats and animals with albinism, he produced a detailed characterization of the structural organization of the mammalian lateral geniculate nucleus and visual system and on the effects of monocular deprivation on the organization of geniculate inputs.

In 1977, Ray moved to Chicago, where he assumed the chairmanship of the Committee on Neurobiology at the University of Chicago. In 1984 he returned to Britain as Professor of Anatomy at Oxford, serving as the founding editor of the European Journal of Neuroscience, and continuing his studies on synaptic structure and the organization of the thalamus and visual system. After reaching mandatory retirement age at Oxford in 1996, he returned to Madison where he continues to pursue his interests in the organization of the thalamus, and contributes to teaching and mentoring graduate students. His career-long administrative wisdom and experience have had an ongoing influence on the development of neuroscience at the University of Wisconsin.

Ray Guillery's career, spanning continents and generations, has contributed to detailed understanding of the visual system, thalamus, and fine structure of the nervous system in more than 130 publications and books. He has been honored by election as a Fellow of the Royal Society and a Fellow of University College London.

Below are some of the publications that Ray himself deems the most interesting.

References

Adams, N.C., Lozsadi, D. and Guillery, R.W. (1997) Complexities of the thalamocortical and corticothalamic pathways. European J. Neurosci., 9: 204–209.

Bartlett, E.L., Stark, J.M., Guillery, R.W. and Smith, P.H. (2000) Comparison of the fine structure of cortical and collicular terminals in the rat medial geniculate body. Neuroscience, 100: 811–828.

Boycott, B.B., Gray, E.G. and Guillery, R.W. (1961) Synaptic structure and its alteration with environmental temperature: a study by light and electron microscopy of the central nervous system of lizards. Proc. Roy. Soc. B., 154: 151–172.

Chan, S.O., Baker, G.E. and Guillery, R.W. (1993) Differential action of the albino mutation on two components of the rat's uncrossed retinofugal pathway. J. Comp. Neurol., 336: 362–377.

Chan, S.O. and Guillery, R.W. (1993) Developmental changes produced in the retinofugal pathways of rats and ferrets by early monocular enucleations: the effects of age and the differences between normal and albino animals. J. Neuroscience, 13: 5277–5293.

Colello, R.J. and Guillery, R.W. (1992) Observations on the early development of the optic nerve and tract of the mouse. J. Comp. Neurol., 317: 357–378.

xii

Colello, S.J. and Guillery, R.W. (1998) The changing pattern of fibre bundles that pass through the optic chiasm of mice. Eur. J. Neurosci, 10: 3653–3663.

Colonnier, M. and Guillery, R.W. (1964) Synaptic organization in the lateral geniculate nucleus of the monkey. Z. Zellforsch., 62: 333–334.

Cucchiaro, J. and Guillery, R.W. (1984) The development of the retinogeniculate pathways in normal and albino ferrets. Proc. R. Soc. Lond. B., 223: 141–164.

Deiters, E. and Guillery, R.W. (1963) Otto Deiters, 1834–1863. Exptl. Neurol., 9: iii–vi iii–vi.

Feig, S.L. and Guillery, R.W. (2000) Corticothalamic axons contact blood vessels as well as nerve cells in the thalamus. Eur. J. Neurosci, 12: 2195–2198.

Gray, E.G. and Guillery, R.W. (1961) The basis of silver staining of synapses of the mammalian spinal cord: a light and electron microscope study. J. Physiol., 157: 581–588.

Gray, E.G. and Guillery, R.W. (1963) An electron microscopical study of the ventral nerve cord of the leech. Z. Zellforsch., 60: 826–849.

Gray, E.G. and Guillery, R.W. (1966) Synaptic morphology in the normal and degenerating nervous system. Intern. Rev. Cytol., 19: 111–182.

Guillery, R.W. (1955) A quantitative study of the mamillary bodies and their connexions. J. Anat. Lond., 89: 19–32.

Guillery, R.W. (1957) Degeneration in the hypothalamic connexions of the albino rat. J. Anat. Lond., 91: 91–115.

Guillery, R.W. (1965) Some electron microscopical observations of degenerative changes in central nervous synapses. Prog. Brain Res., 14: 57–76.

Guillery, R.W. (1966) A study of Golgi preparations from the dorsal lateral geniculate nucleus of the adult cat. J. Comp. Neurol., 128: 21–50.

Guillery, R.W. (1967) Patterns of fiber degeneration in the dorsal lateral geniculate nucleus of the cat following lesions in the visual cortex. J. Comp. Neurol., 130: 197–222.

Guillery, R.W. (1969) An abnormal retinogeniculate projection in Siamese cats. Brain Res., 14: 739–741.

Guillery, R.W. (1969) The organization of synaptic interconnections in the laminae of the dorsal lateral geniculate nucleus of the cat. Z. Zellforsch., 96: 1–38.

Guillery, R.W. (1969) A quantitative study of synaptic interconnections in the dorsal lateral geniculate nucleus of the cat. Z. Zellforsch., 96: 39–48.

Guillery, R.W. (1970) The laminar distribution of retinal fibers in the dorsal lateral geniculate nucleus of the cat: a new interpretation. J. Comp. Neurol., 138: 339–368.

Guillery, R.W. (1971) Survival of large cells in the dorsal lateral geniculate laminae after interruption of retino-geniculate afferents. Brain Res., 28: 541–544.

Guillery, R.W. (1971) An abnormal retino-geniculate projection in the albino ferret (Mustela furo). Brain Res., 33: 482–485.

Guillery, R.W. (1972) Experiments to determine whether retino-geniculate axons can form translaminar sprouts in the dorsal lateral geniculate nucleus of the cat. J. Comp. Neurol., 146: 407–420.

Guillery, R.W. (1972) Binocular competition in the control of geniculate cell growth. J. Comp. Neurol., 144: 117–130.

Guillery, R.W. (1973) The effect of lid suture upon the growth of cells in the dorsal lateral geniculate nucleus. J. Comp. Neurol., 148: 417–422.

Guillery, R.W. (1974) Visual pathways in albinos. Scientific American, 230: 44–45.

Guillery, R.W. (1979) A speculative essay on geniculate lamination and its development. Prog. Brain Res., 51: 403–418.

Guillery, R.W. (1989) Early monocular enucleations in fetal ferrets produce a decrease of uncrossed and an increase of crossed retinofugal components: a possible model for the albino abnormality. J. Anat., 164: 73–84.

Guillery, R.W. (1995) Anatomical evidence concerning the role of the thalamus in cortico-cortical communication. A Brief Review. J. Anat., 187: 583–592.

Guillery, R.W. (2000) Early electron microscopic observations on synaptic structures in the cerebral cortex: a view of the contributions made by George Gray (1924–1999). TINS, 23: 595–598.

Guillery, R.W. (2004) Observations of synaptic structures: origins of the neuron doctrine and its current status. Phi. Trans. Roy. Soc. B., Published Online.

Guillery, R.W. and August, B.K. (2002) Doubt and Certainty in Counting. Prog. Brain Res, 135: 25–42.

Guillery, R.W. and Casagrande, V.A. (1975) Adaptive synaptic connections formed in the visual pathways in response to congenitally aberrant inputs. Cold Spring Harbour Symp., 40: 611–617.

Guillery, R.W. and Casagrande, V.A. (1977) Studies of the modifiability of the visual pathways in Midwestern Siamese cats. J. Comp. Neurol., 174: 15–46.

Guillery, R.W. and Colonnier, M. (1970) Synaptic patterns in the dorsal lateral geniculate nucleus of the monkey. Z. Zellforsch., 103: 90–108.

Guillery, R.W., Casagrande, V.A. and Oberdorfer, M.D. (1974) Congenitally abnormal vision in Siamese cats. Nature, 252: 195–199.

Guillery, R.W., Feig, S.L. and Lozsádi, D. (1998) Paying attention to the thalamic reticular nucleus. Trends in Neurosci, 21: 28–32.

Guillery, R.W., Feig, S.L. and Van Lieshout, D.P. (2001) Connections of higher order visual relays in the thalamus: a study of corticothalamic pathways in cats. J. Comp. Neurol., 438: 66–85.

Guillery, R.W., Geisert, E.E. Jr., Polley, E.H. and Mason, C.A. (1980) An analysis of the retinal afferents to the cat's medial interlaminar nucleus and to its rostral thalamic extension, the "geniculate wing". J. Comp. Neurol., 194: 117–142.

Guillery, R.W. and Harting, J.K. (2003) Structure and connections of the thalamic reticular nucleus: advancing views over half a century. J. Comp. Neurol, 463: 360–371.

Guillery, R.W. and Herrup, K. (1997) Quantification without Pontification: choosing a method for counting objects in sectioned tissues. J. Comp. Neurol., 386: 2–7.

Guillery, R.W., Hickey, T.L., Kaas, J.H., Felleman, D.J., Debruyn, E.J. and Sparks, D.L. (1984) Abnormal central visual pathways in the brain of an albino green monkey (Cercopithecus aethiops). J. Comp. Neurol., 226: 165–183.

Guillery, R.W., Hickey, T.L. and Spear, P.D. (1981) Do blue-eyed white cats have normal or abnormal retinofugal pathways? Invest. Ophthal. Vis. Sci., 21: 27–33.

Guillery, R.W., Jeffery, G. and Cattanach, B.M. (1987) Abnormally high variability in the uncrossed retinofugal pathways of mice with albino mosaicism. Development, 101: 857–867.

Guillery, R.W. and Kaas, J.H. (1971) A study of normal and congenitally abnormal retino-geniculate projections in cats. J. Comp. Neurol., 143: 73–100.

Guillery, R.W. and Kaas, J.H. (1973) Genetic abnormality of the visual pathways in a "white" tiger. Science, 180: 1287–1289.

Guillery, R.W. and Kaas, J.H. (1974) The effects of monocular lid suture upon the development of the lateral geniculate nucleus in squirrels (Sciureus carolinensis). J. Comp. Neurol., 154: 433–442.

Guillery, R.W., LaMantia, A.S., Robson, J.A. and Huang, K. (1985) The influence of retinal afferents upon the development of layers in the dorsal lateral geniculate nucleus of mustelids. J. Neurosci., 5: 1370–1379.

Guillery, R.W., Mason, C.A. and Taylor, J.S.H. (1995) Developmental determinants at the mammalian optic chiasm. J. Neurosci., 15(7): 4727–4737.

Guillery, R.W., Okoro, A.M. and Witkop, C.J. (1975) Abnormal visual pathways in the brain of a human albino. Brain Res., 96: 373–377.

Guillery, R.W., Ombrellaro, M. and LaMantia, A.L. (1985) The organization of the lateral geniculate nucleus and of the geniculocortical pathway that develops without retinal afferents. Dev. Brain Res., 20: 221–233.

Guillery, R.W., Oberdorfer, M.D. and Murphy, E.H. (1979) Abnormal retino-geniculate and geniculo-cortical pathways in several genetically distinct color phases of the mink (Mustela vison). J. Comp. Neurol., 185: 623–656.

Guillery, R.W., Polley, E.H. and Torrealba, F. (1982) The arrangement of axons according to fiber diameter in the optic tract of the cat. J. Neurosci., 2: 714–721.

Guillery, R.W. and Ralston, H.J. (1964) Nerve fibers and terminals: electron microscopy after Nauta staining. Science, 143: 1331–1332.

Guillery, R.W. and Sherman, S.M. (2002) Thalamic relay functions and their role in corticocortical communica-tion: generalizations from the visual system. Neuron, 33: 163–175.

Guillery, R.W. and Sherman, S.M. (2003) The thalamus as a monitor of motor outputs. Phil. Trans. Roy. Soc. B., 357: 1809–1821.

Guillery, R.W. and Scott, G.L. (1971) Observations on synaptic patterns in the dorsal lateral geniculate nucleus of the cat: the C laminae and the perikaryal synapses. Exp. Brain Res., 12: 184–203.

Guillery, R.W. and Stelzner, D.J. (1970) The differential effects of unilateral lid closure upon the monocular and binocular segments of the dorsal lateral geniculate nucleus in the cat. J. Comp. Neurol., 139: 413–422.

Guillery, R.W. and Taylor, J.S.H. (1993) Different rates of axonal degeneration in the crossed and uncrossed retinofugal pathways of Monodelphis domestica.. J. Neurocytol., 22: 707–716.

Guillery, R.W. and Walsh, C. (1987) Changing glial organiza-tion relates to changing fiber order in the developing optic nerve of ferrets. J. Comp. Neurol., 265: 203–217.

Guillery, R.W., Scott, G.L., Cattanach, B.M. and Deol, D.L. (1973) Genetic mechanisms determining the central visual pathways of mice. Science, 179: 1014–1016.

Hickey, T.L. and Guillery, R.W. (1974) An autoradiographic study of retino-geniculate pathways in the cat and the fox. J. Comp. Neurol., 156: 239–254.

Hickey, T.L. and Guillery, R.W. (1979) Variability of laminar patterns in the human lateral geniculate nucleus. J. Comp. Neurol., 183: 221–246.

Huang, K. and Guillery, R.W. (1985) A demonstration of two distinct geniculocortical projection patterns in albino ferrets. Dev. Brain Res., 20: 213–220.

Kaas, J.H., Guillery, R.W. and Allman, J.M. (1972) Some principles of organization in the dorsal lateral geniculate nucleus. Brain Behav. Evol., 6: 253–299.

Kaas, J.H. and Guillery, R.W. (1973) The transfer of abnormal visual field representations from the dorsal lateral geniculate nucleus to the visual cortex in Siamese cats. Brain Res., 59: 61–95.

Kaas, J.H., Harting, J.K. and Guillery, R.W. (1974) Representation of the complete retina in the contralateral superior colliculus of some mammals. Brain Res., 65: 343–346.

Linden, D.C., Guillery, R.W. and Cucchiaro, J. (1981) The dorsal lateral geniculate nucleus of the normal ferret and its postnatal development. J. Comp. Neurol., 203: 189–211.

Mitrofanis, J., Guillery, R.W. (1993). New views of the thalamic reticular nucleus in the adult and the developing brain. TINS Vol.16, No.6: 240–245..

Montero, V.M. and Guillery, R.W. (1968) Degeneration of the dorsal lateral geniculate nucleus of the rat following interruption of the retinal or cortical connections. J. Comp. Neurol., 134: 211–242.

Montero, V.M., Guillery, R.W. and Woolsey, C.N. (1977) Retinotopic organization within the thalamic reticular nucleus demonstrated by the double label autoradiographic technique. Brain Res., 138: 407–421.

Montero, V.M. and Guillery, R.W. (1978) Abnormalities of the cortico-geniculate pathway in Siamese cats. J. Comp. Neurol., 179: 1–12.

Reese, B.E., Guillery, R.W., Marzi, C.A. and Tassinari, G. (1991) Position of axons in the cat's optic tract in relation to their retinal origin and chiasmatic pathway. J. Comp. Neurol., 306: 539–553.

Robson, J.A., Mason, C.A. and Guillery, R.W. (1978) Terminal arbors of axons that have formed abnormal connections. Science, 201: 635–637.

Sanderson, K.J., Guillery, R.W. and Shackelford, R.M. (1974) Congenitally abnormal visual pathways in mink (Mustela vision) with reduced retinal pigment. J. Comp. Neurol., 154: 225–248.

Sherman, S.M. and Guillery, R.W. (1976) Behavioral studies of binocular competition in cats. Vision Res., 16: 1479–1481.

Sherman, S.M., Guillery, R.W., Kaas, J.H and Sanderson, K.J. (1974) Behavioral electrophysiological, and morphological studies of binocular competition in the development of the geniculo-cortical pathways of cats. J. Comp. Neurol., 158: 1–18.

Sherman, S.M. and Guillery, R.W. (1996) Functional organization of thalamocortical relays. J. Neurophysiol, 76: 1367–1395.

Sherman, S.M. and Guillery, R.W. (1998) On the actions that one nerve cell can have on another: distinguishing "drivers" from "modulators". Proc. Natl. Acad. Sci, 95: 7121–7126.

Sherman, S.M. and Guillery, R.W. (2001) Exploring the Thalamus, Academic Press, San Diego, pp. 1–312 (and i–xvii).

Sherman, S.M. and Guillery, R.W. (2003) The role of thalamus in the flow of information to cortex. Phil. Trans. Roy. Soc. B., 357: 1695–1708.

Sherman, S.M., Wilson, J. and Guillery, R.W. (1975) Evidence that binocular competition affects the post-natal development of Y cells in the cat's lateral geniculate nucleus. Brain Res., 100: 441–444.

Taylor, J.S.H. and Guillery, R.W. (1995) Effect of a very early monocular enucleation upon the development of the uncrossed retinofugal pathway in ferrets. J. Comp. Neurol., 357: 331–340.

Torrealba, F., Guillery, R.W., Polley, E.H. and Mason, C.A. (1981) A demonstration of several independent, partially overlapping, retino-topic maps in the optic tract of the cat. Brain Res., 219: 428–432.

Torrealba, F., Guillery, R.W., Eysel, U., Polley, E.H. and Mason, C.A. (1982) Studies of retinal representations within the cat's optic tract. J. Comp. Neurol., 211: 377–396.

Walsh, C. and Guillery, R.W. (1985) Age-related fiber order in the optic tract of the ferret. J. Neurosci., 5: 3061–3070.

Walsh, C., Polley, E.H., Hickey, T.L. and Guillery, R.W. (1983) Generation of cat retinal ganglion cells in relation to central pathways. Nature, 302: 611–614.

Contents

Progress in Brain Research, Vol. 149
ISSN 0079-6123

CHAPTER 1

Pain and the primate thalamus

Henry J. Ralston III*

*Department of Anatomy W. M. Keck Foundation Center for Integrative Neuroscience,
University of California, San Francisco, CA 94143-0452, USA*

Abstract: Noxious stimuli that are perceived as painful, are conveyed to the thalamus by the spinothalamic tract (STT) and the spinotrigeminothalamic tracts (vSTT), arising from the dorsal horn of the spinal cord and medulla, respectively. Most investigators have concluded that the thalamic terminus of these pathways include several nuclei of the somatosensory and intralaminar thalamus. Non-noxious stimuli are carried by the dorsal column/medial lemniscal or the trigeminothalamic pathways which terminate in much more restricted regions of the thalamus than do the STT and vSTT systems. Lesions of components of the somatosensory pathways result in profound changes in the circuitry of the recipient thalamic nuclei. Not only are there the expected losses of the injured axons and their synaptic terminations, but there is also a marked reduction of the intrinsic GABAergic circuitry, even though the GABAergic neurons contributing to the circuitry have not been injured directly by lesions of the afferent pathways. Such changes in the inhibitory circuitry observed in experimental animals may explain the abnormal bursting behavior of thalamic neurons found in patients with central deafferentation pain syndromes.

One potential approach to treating chronic pain would be to selectively remove the neurons of the superficial dorsal horn (lamina I) that specifically respond to noxious stimuli (NS neurons). A toxin has been developed (SSP saporin) that binds to the substance P receptor of NS neurons, is internalized by the neuron and kills the cell. SSP saporin has been shown to be effective in rats, and we have recently demonstrated that it effectively causes lesions in NS neurons of the lumbar spinal cord in the monkey and reduces the animals' response to noxious cutaneous stimuli. The SSP-saporin administration to the lumbar spinal cord destroys a relatively small number of the total neurons that project into the somatosensory thalamus and does not lead to demonstrable changes in the inhibitory circuitry of the thalamus, in contrast to lesions of major pathways that lead to reductions in the thalamic inhibitory circuitry.

Introduction

Organization of the primate somatosensory thalamus

The somatosensory thalamus of the monkey shares an organization that is similar to other sensory relay nuclei (e.g., the lateral geniculate nucleus — LGN) of the primate thalamus. There are two principal

*Tel.: +1-415-476-1861; Fax: +1-415-476-4845;
E-mail: hjr@phy.ucsf.edu

types of neurons: (1) the thalamocortical projection neuron (TCR cell), which constitutes about 75% of the neuronal population; and, (2) the local circuit neuron (LCN), or interneuron, making up about 25% of the population (Ralston, 1984). All LCNs appear to be GABAergic, and possess elaborate dendritic arbors which exhibit numerous varicosities that are presynaptic to TCR dendrites as well as to one another (Ohara et al., 1989). Many LCNs do not appear to have an axon, but respond to peripheral stimulation with action potentials and have receptive fields similar to those of TCR cells (Wilson et al., 1996). The synaptic population

DOI: 10.1016/S0079-6123(05)49001-9

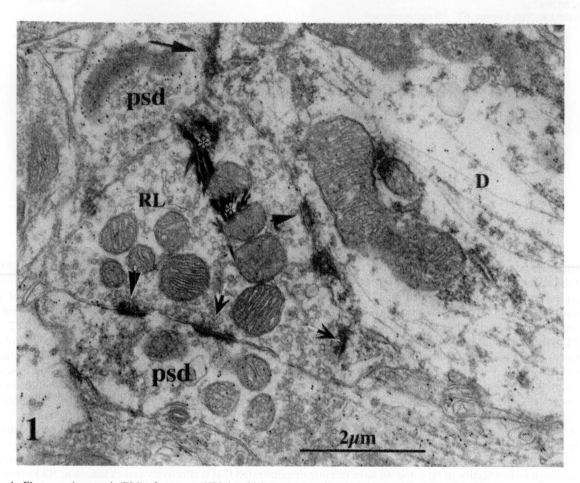

Fig. 1. Electron micrograph (EM) of macaque VPL in which a primary afferent (RL) contacts a dendrite (D) of a projection neuron, which is not GABA immunoreactive (GABA-ir). The RL profile is labeled (asterisks) with crystals of horseradish peroxidase (HRP) following injection of the tracer into the contralateral dorsal column nuclei. Therefore this RL profile is the terminal of a medial lemniscal axon. GABA-ir presynaptic dendrites (PSD) labeled for GABA by the post-embedding immunogold method are also present. Synaptic contacts between the RL, the PSDs and the projection neuron dendrite (D) are indicated by the arrows.

consists of several types of axonal terminals. In the ventroposterolateral nucleus (VPL) the sensory afferent RL profiles (Figs. 1 and 2) are derived either from the dorsal column nuclei of the medial lemniscal system or the spinothalamic tract neurons of the spinal cord dorsal horn. RL profiles are immunoreactive for glutamate, which mediates excitatory synaptic afferent input to VB neurons via both NMDA and non-NMDA receptor subtypes (Dougherty et al., 1996). RS axon terminals (Fig. 2) from the cerebral cortex or brainstem, contain various transmitters. RS terminals of cortical origin are glutamatergic; those from the brainstem may contain serotonin, norepinephrine or

acetylcholine (Westlund et al., 1990). GABA immunoreactive (GABA-ir) axon terminals come from the thalamic reticular nucleus (TRN) or from LCNs, if this latter cell type has axons. These terminals are called F or F-1 (Fig. 3). Finally, there are profiles arising from the dendritic appendages of local circuit neurons (Ralston, 1971), the GABA-ir presynaptic dendrites (PSDs or F-2 terminals: Figs. 1 and 2). The GABAergic circuitry formed by the TRN and LCN cells is believed to play a fundamental role in the complex local information processing (Arcelli et al., 1997) and the synchronous oscillatory activity of thalamic networks (Kim et al., 1997).

3

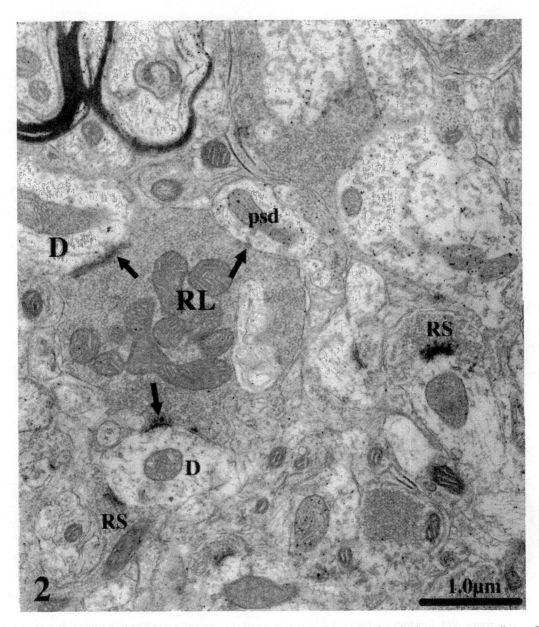

Fig. 2. EM of macaque VPL in which an RL profile contacts (arrows) dendrites (D) of projection neurons as well as a GABA-ir presynaptic dendrite (PSD). RS terminals derived either from corticothalamic axons (of layer 6 neurons) or from the brainstem are also shown.

The RL afferent make synaptic contact with TCR neurons as well as the PSDs of LCNs. However, those RL profiles of the medial lemniscal system are far more likely to contact GABA-ir PSDs than are spinothalamic afferents, indicating greater modulation of the medial lemniscal afferent input than that of the spinothalamic tract (Ralston and Ralston, 1994).

The differences that are described in the synaptic relationships of different classes of somatosensory STT and ML projections have also been described in different classes of projections to the visual thalamus (LGN). The A laminae of the cat LGN receive afferent projections from two functionally distinct classes of retinal ganglion cells, termed

4

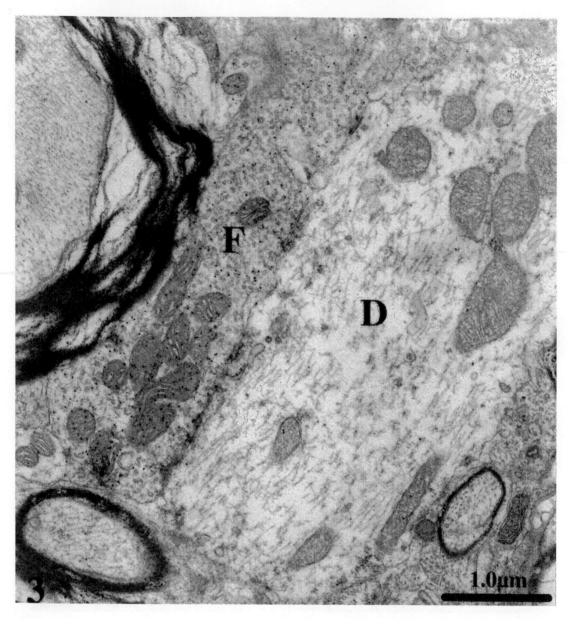

Fig. 3. EM of macaque VPL in which a large GABA-ir axon terminal (F) contacts a dendrite of a projection neuron. Projection neurons are not immunoreactive for GABA.

X- and Y-cells, the axons of which synapse upon X- and Y-cells in the LGN. In an EM study of physiologically identified and intracellularly labeled LGN neurons, Wilson et al. (1984) found that retinal terminals that contacted X-cell dendrites "nearly always formed triadic arrangements" (with the dendrites of projection neurons and the PSDs of interneurons) but those that contacted "Y-cell dendrites" rarely did so. In the primate LGN Wilson (1989) also found differences in the numbers of triadic synaptic arrangements between retinal afferent axons, the dendrites of projection neurons and the dendritic appendages of interneurons in the magnocellular compared to the parvocellular layers of the nucleus. Thus, there is precedent for the conclusion that different functional classes of afferent projections onto thalamic neurons can have different synaptic relationships with projection and local circuit neurons.

RS terminals contact the distal dendrites of both thalamic neuronal cell types, TCR and LCN. F profiles also synapse upon TCR and LCN neurons, the latter type of contact being GABA to GABA, presumably serving a disinhibitory function. The GABA-ir PSDs contact other dendrites, and are postsynaptic to all other types of vesicle-containing axon terminals and GABA-ir PSDs. There is no evidence for axoaxonal contacts in the thalamic sensory relay nuclei.

Most of the detailed studies of thalamic neuronal receptor subtypes have been performed in the LGN. Both NMDA and non-NMDA receptor subunits are present in macaque sensory relay nuclei (Jones et al., 1998), as are GABA$_A$ receptor subunits (Huntsman et al., 1996). GABA$_B$ receptor subunit expression is less prominent in the sensory relay nuclei and may be particularly associated with the GABA-ir F type axon terminals from the thalamic reticular nucleus.

Plasticity of thalamic transmitters and receptors

In the adult macaque LGN, monocular deprivation following injection of tetrodotoxin (TTX) into the eye results in down-regulation of glutamate receptor transcripts as well as calcium–calmodulin-dependent protein kinase isoforms (Tighilet et al., 1998). Intravitreal injection of TTX also results in decreased expression of GABA$_A$ (Hendry and Miller, 1996, Huntsman et al., 1995) and GABA$_B$ (Muñoz et al., 1998) receptor subunits. In cat LGN, retinal lesions have been reported to result in decreased synthesis of GABA (Arckens et al., 1998), while lid suture results in increased GABA levels (Wilson and Forestner, 1995). In macaque VPL, chronic (> 10 years) peripheral nerve lesions have been shown to result in down regulation of GABA$_A$ receptor expression (Rausell et al., 1992). In adult macaques we have shown that acute and chronic lesions of the dorsal column nuclei result in a rapid (2–5 days) and long-lasting (> 6 months) 50% reduction of both types of GABA-ir synapses: F-1 axon terminals and PSDs (F-2) (Ralston et al., 1996). GABA-ir PSDs arising from

inhibitory interneurons (LCN) declined in number to about 25% of their normal population. These trans-synaptic changes were predicted (although the degree of reductions were not anticipated), because PSDs are commonly postsynaptic to ML terminals. The surprising finding was that the GABA-ir axon terminals (F type), most of which presumably arise from thalamic reticular neurons, declined to about 50% of normal. This was unexpected, as F axon terminals are never postsynaptic to ML terminals.

Although it is not surprising that decreased activity or lesions of glutamatergic pathways should result in decreased expression of glutamate receptor subtypes, the reason for reductions in GABA synthesis and GABA receptor subunit expression is not readily apparent. An interesting finding in the rat hippocampus that may shed some light on this issue has been reported (Sepukty et al., 1997). In an experimental epilepsy model in which there is knock-down of the neuronal glutamate transporter, EAAT3, which is localized on both GABAergic and glutamatergic neurons, an abnormal spike activity of thalamic neurons coupled with a 50% reduction in GABA levels was detected. The authors suggested that EAAT3 might regulate GABA metabolism.

Pain pathways to the thalamus

W.R. Mehler's classical studies of the ascending spinothalamic tract (STT) in primate defined its thalamic territory. Mehler (1962) had the extraordinary opportunity to examine human thalamus in specimens from patients who had undergone spinal or medullary tractotomy for pain relief a few weeks before death. Mehler used the Nauta method to stain axonal degeneration and plotted the regions of degeneration in several drawings. In his 1962 paper, Mehler depicted numerous degenerating axons in human posterior-inferior thalamus, the degeneration being shown primarily ventrolateral to VPM. Mehler's work could not distinguish STT projections arising from different laminae of the spinal cord dorsal horn and it is possible that degenerating axons of lamina I fibers had a different thalamic region of termination than those from lamina V.

Boivie (1979), in his seminal paper on the STT projections to macaque thalamus, refined the methods by using the Wiitanen modification of the Fink–Heimer method, which is more sensitive than the older Nauta methods. While describing the STT terminal distribution, he notes: "Cytoarchitectonically, the areas containing the degeneration clusters are indistinguishable from neighboring portions of VPL. The largest cluster area was located ventromedially in the VPL. In its caudal part this region contained the most dense spinothalamic degeneration found anywhere in the thalamus." This region of dense afferent STT degeneration is shown in Boivie's Fig. 2, where it lies directly below VPM. Furthermore, Boivie's statement that the region receiving this dense STT projection was cytoarchitectonically indistinguishable from the neighboring VPL is important because Craig and his colleagues have stated that the STT terminates in a cytoarchitectonically distinct nucleus, VMpo (e.g., Craig et al., 1994 — see below).

This issue was addressed more recently by using axonal transport methods that label most axonal populations. For example, following placement of small crystals of wheat germ agglutinin conjugated to horseradish peroxidase into the spinal cord, the labeled axonal arbors are in a distribution similar to that described in the degeneration studies. Ralston and Ralston (1992) found that most of the axons terminating in this posterior-inferior region traveled in the lateral portion of the STT, where labeled lamina I axons have been found and where stimulation in humans evokes sensations of pain (see The thalamus and human pain syndromes).

Despite the contributions of these and many other studies, the role of particular somatosensory nuclei of the thalamus in transmission of information relating to noxious stimuli that are perceived as painful remains controversial. Most investigators have found that the systems conveying painful stimuli (spinothalamic — STT and spinal trigeminothalamic — sVTT) tract fibers terminate in several domains of the primate ventral posterior lateral (VPL), ventral posterior medial (VPM), and other posterior and intralaminar nuclei (see Graziano and Jones, 2004, for a recent review). Neurons responding to noxious mechanical and thermal stimuli that project to the thalamus via the STT or sVTT are located in the marginal zone and neck of the dorsal horn (laminae I and IV–VI) of the spinal and medullary dorsal horn, respectively. The cells in lamina I are activated specifically by noxious stimuli and are thus termed NS (noxious specific) neurons. Neurons of deeper laminae respond in a graded fashion to innocuous and to painful stimuli and are termed WDR (wide dynamic range) cells. The generally held view is that substantial numbers of lamina I cells as well as neurons of the deeper dorsal horn project to VPM and VPL, as well as to subnuclei located caudal and ventral to VPL and VPM (Ralston and Ralston, 1992). Neurons with pain and temperature-specific stimulus/response properties are described in most nuclei in which STT fibers terminate, including VPM and VPL (Willis et al., 2001, 2002).

However, during the past decade, Craig and his colleagues (e.g., Craig et al., 1994; Blomqvist et al., 2000; Craig and Blomqvist, 2002) have described a region of the macaque and human posterior thalamus in which they describe a cytoarchitectonically distinct nucleus, the ventromedial posterior nucleus (VMpo) that they contend is the main site of termination of lamina I afferents. They have reported that this cell group is characterized by a dense plexus of calbindin–immunoreactive fibers (Craig et al., 1994). Craig and his colleagues have used small injections of anterograde tracers into lamina I of the spinal cord and spinal trigeminal nucleus caudalis and concluded that VMpo was the major recipient of the projections of lamina I neurons, which are believed to play an essential role in pain mechanisms because they respond specifically to noxious stimuli. They have further proposed that the largest nuclei of the somatosensory thalamus, the VPL and VPM nuclei, received few afferent axons from lamina I neurons. Given that lamina I neurons are well known to convey stimuli concerned with both pain and temperature information, Craig has concluded that VMpo is a "specific thalamic nucleus for pain and temperature sensation in both monkey and in human" (Craig et al., 1994). This view is controversial, however, as many other studies of primate VPL and VPM have found evidence of a nociceptive lamina I projection to VPL/VPM (Willis et al., 2002).

A recent study by Graziano and Jones (2004) found no evidence in support of the conclusions by Craig. Graziano and Jones analyzed the terminal arbors of fibers arising from lamina I neurons that project to nuclei in and around the caudal pole of the ventral posterior nuclear complex and especially to a zone of calbindin-dense immunoreactivity (VMpo) identified by Craig and his colleagues as the primary, if not the only, thalamic relay for these fibers and thus for pain. Graziano and Jones concluded that "the densest zone of calbindin immunoreactivity is part of a more extensive, calbindin-immunoreactive region that lies well within the medial tip of the ventral posterior medial nucleus (VPM)." They found widespread fiber terminations of lamina I projections that were not restricted to the calbindin-rich medial tip of VPM and that the lamina I arising fibers are not themselves calbindin immunoreactive. Graziano and Jones stated that their findings "disprove the existence of VMpo as an independent thalamic pain nucleus or as a specific relay in the ascending pain system."

A few months following the publication of the paper by Graziano and Jones, Craig (2004) responded to their conclusions with his own findings that a different calbindin antibody served as a "propitious marker" for the projections of lamina I neurons and did in fact stain sVTT and STT terminations. He further stated that the primary target of these terminations is VMpo and suggested that Graziano and Jones were incorrect in stating that the vSTT terminated in VPM.

It is likely that this argument will continue for some time and it is evident that the subject of the role of particular regions of the thalamus in pain mechanisms is one that can evoke considerable controversy.

The thalamus and human central pain syndromes

Stroke is one of the most common causes of death and disability in western societies, having a prevalence of about 5 per 1000 population, with about 8% of patients having chronic pain as a consequence of the vascular disorder (Andersen et al., 1995). Spinal cord injury also is a frequent cause of chronic pain, which is characterized by dysesthesias and decrease in pain and temperature sensations mediated by pathways in the anterolateral quadrant. Thus, the patient may describe a painful limb as being numb, despite allodynia and hyperalgesia in the same extremity (Boivie et al., 1989). In thalamic recordings from humans with chronic pain following peripheral or

central neural injury, Lenz and his colleagues have found a region in VB from which microstimulation can elicit a report of burning pain (Lenz et al., 1993, 2004) and heightened burst activity of thalamic neurons following innocuous stimulation of the painful body part. These investigators have postulated that these findings in humans may be due to reduced GABA-mediated inhibition of thalamic neurons (Lenz et al., 1994, 1998). These and other studies have led to the hypothesis that central pain following damage of one or more of the somatosensory systems of the CNS is due to reduced GABAergic inhibition at thalamic and cortical levels (Canavero and Bonicalzi, 1998), a hypothesis supported by our findings (Ralston et al., 1996) that lesions of the somatosensory pathways result in decreased GABA expression in somatosensory thalamic nuclei.

In summary, about 50% of neurons of monkey VB have been found to respond to peripheral noxious stimuli (Chung et al., 1986), and the substantial majority are located in the caudal, ventral region of VB (Apkarian and Shi, 1994) to which noxious-specific neurons of lamina I of the dorsal horn project (Ralston and Ralston, 1992). It is precisely this area in which noxious-responding thalamic neurons in humans are found (Lenz et al., 1994), and the area in which we have found major reductions in GABA circuitry following chronic lesions of ascending somatosensory pathways.

Somatosensory deafferentation and pain behavior

In collaboration with colleagues in Gainesville (C.J. Vierck), Houston (P.M. Dougherty), and Nashville (R.G. Wiley), we have used behavioral, physiological and anatomical methods to examine the effects of chronic (> 2 years) lesions of the dorsal column pathway, and/or the STT on pain responses in macaques. In addition, recent studies have used the intrathecal administration of the neurotoxin SSP-saporin, which binds to substance P receptors (neurokinin 1 receptors: NK-1R) receiving primary afferent axons conveying pain stimuli to lamina I STT neurons of the spinal cord. The toxin is internalized by STT cells and specifically destroys them, thus removing the pain transmission link between the spinal cord and the thalamus. Normal animals were evaluated to determine their responses to noxious heat (52–58°C) applied to the lower limbs. Subsequently, the monkeys were anesthetized and had unilateral surgical lesions of somatosensory pathways in the cord, such as the dorsal or the anterolateral spinal cord white matter at midthoracic levels. After recovering from the surgery their pain responses were studied for more than 1 year. In another group of animals, SSP-saporin was administered to the lumbosacral spinal cord. In all cases (surgical lesions of spinal cord pathways or selective SSP-saporin lesions of STT neurons), the animals were found to show a decrease in their responses to noxious heat applied to the lower

limbs. Terminal physiological experiments revealed that the neurons within the lower limb representation of VPL on the side contralateral to the thoracic cord lesion did not have normal receptive fields, and some cells responded to stimulation of both upper and lower limbs. The cells exhibited abnormal bursting properties similar to those found in humans with spinal cord injuries and central pain syndromes. Histological sections of lumbar spinal cord in animals exposed to intrathecal SSP-saporin were stained for NK-1R and showed a significant decrease in lamina I NK-1R positive neurons (Fig. 4). Unlike our earlier studies of VPL following lesions that destroyed

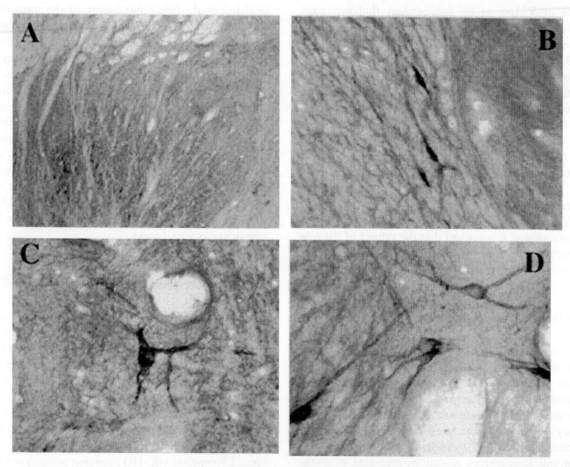

Fig. 4. Light micrographs of the macaque lumbar spinal cord dorsal horn. The lumbar cord of the animal had been exposed to SSP-saporin several months earlier. This toxin destroys neurons that express the substance P receptor (NK-1R). Transverse frozen sections were processed for NK-1 immunoreactivity. A: In this low power view, the superficial dorsal horn is devoid of NK-1R immunoreactive neurons which are normally abundant. B, C and D: Higher power views of deeper layers of the dorsal horn that had not been exposed to the intrathecally-applied SSP-saporin. NK-1R immunoreactive neurons are shown, demonstrating that the antibody labeled the neurons. Original magnifications: A-4x; B-10x; C and D: 25x. Micrographs courtesy of Dr. R. G. Wiley.

a major somatosensory pathway to the thalamus, electron microscopic examination of VPL following SSP-saporin administration did not demonstrate significant reductions in the GABA-ergic circuitry of VPL in these animals with lesions restricted to NK-1R neurons of the superficial dorsal horn of the lumbar cord. We assume that the numbers of somatosensory axons lost following exposure of the cord to SSP-saporin was too small to result in an observable change in the synaptic organization of VPL.

Conclusions

There are several regions of the somatosensory thalamus that receive pain information from noxious stimuli via the STT or the sVTT tracts. Compared to the lemniscal system mediating non-noxious information, the pain transmitting STT terminals in the thalamus have few direct synaptic relationships with GABAergic interneurons. Lesions of afferent pathways result in a substantial reduction in the GABAergic inhibitory thalamic circuitry which may underlie the central deafferentation pain syndromes of humans with spinal cord injury. Finally, the use of neurotoxins that specifically remove pain transmitting neurons in experimental animals has the potential for treating humans with chronic debilitating pain.

Acknowledgments

This work has been supported by NIH grants NS 23347 and NS 21445. I thank Stephanie Hopkins and Sandra Canchola for their excellent technical assistance.

References

Andersen, G., Vestergaard, K., Ingeman-Nielsen, M. and Jensen, T.S. (1995) Incidence of central post-stroke pain. Pain, 61: 187–193.

Apkarian, A.V. and Shi, T. (1994) Squirrel monkey lateral thalamus. I. Somatic nociresponsive neurons and their relation to spinothalamic terminals. J. Neurosci., 14: 6779–6795.

Arcelli, P., Frassoni, C., Regondi, M.C., De Biasi, S. and Spreafico, R. (1997) GABAergic neurons in mammalian thalamus: a marker of thalamic complexity? Brain Res. Bull., 42: 27–37.

Arckens, L., Eysel, U.T., Vanderhaeghen, J.J., Orban, G.A. and Vandesande, F. (1998) Effect of sensory deafferentation on the GABAergic circuitry of the adult cat visual system. Neuroscience, 83: 381–391.

Blomqvist, A., Zhang, E.-T. and Craig, A.D. (2000) Cytoarchtectonic and immunohistochemical characterization of a specific pain and temperature relay, the VMpo nucleus, in the human thalamus. Brain, 123: 601–619.

Boivie, J. (1979) An anatomical reinvestigation of the termination of the spinothalamic tract in the monkey. J. Comp Neurol., 186: 343–370.

Boivie, J., Leijon, G. and Johansson, I. (1989) Central post-stroke pain; a study of the mechanisms through analyses of the sensory abnormalities. Pain, 37: 173–185.

Canavero, S. and Bonicalzi, V. (1998) The neurochemistry of central pain: evidence from clinical studies, hypothesis and therapeutic implications. Pain, 74: 109–114.

Chung, J.M., Lee, K.H., Surmeier, D.J., Sorkin, L.S., Kim, J. and Willis, W.D. (1986) Response characteristics of neurons in the ventral posterior lateral nucleus of the monkey thalamus. J. Neurophysiol., 56: 370–390.

Craig, A.D. (2004) distribution of trigeminothalamic and spinothalamic lamina I terminations in the Macaque monkey. J. Comp. Neurol., 477: 119–148.

Craig, A.D. and Blomqvist, A. (2002) Is there a specific lamina I pathway for pain and temperature sensations in primates? J. Pain, 3: 95–101.

Craig, A.D., Bushnell, M.C., Zhang, E-T. and Blomqvist, A. (1994) A thalamic nucleus specific for pain and temperature sensation. Nature, 372: 770–773.

Dougherty, P.M., Li, Y.J., Lenz, F.A., Rowland, L. and Mittman, S. (1996) Evidence that excitatory amino acids mediate afferent input to the primate somatosensory thalamus. Brain Res., 728: 267–273.

Graziano, A. and Jones, E.G. (2004) Widespread thalamic terminations of fibers arising in the superficial medullary dorsal horn of monkeys and their relation to calbindin immunoreactivity. J. Neurosci., 24: 248–256.

Hendry, S.H. and Miller, K.L. (1996) Selective expression and rapid regulation of GABA$_A$ receptor subunits in geniculo-cortical neurons of macaque dorsal lateral geniculate nucleus. Vis. Neurosci., 13: 223–235.

Huntsman, M.M., Leggio, M.G. and Jones, E.G. (1995) Expression patterns and deprivation effects on GABA$_A$ receptor subunit and GAD mRNAs in monkey lateral geniculate nucleus. J. Comp. Neurol., 352: 235–247.

Huntsman, M.M., Leggio, M.G. and Jones, E.G. (1996) Nucleus-specific expression of GABA$_A$ receptor subunit mRNAs in monkey thalamus. J. Neurosci., 16: 3571–3589.

Jones, E.G., Tighilet, B., Tran, B.V. and Huntsman, M.M. (1998) Nucleus- and cell-specific expression of NMDA and non-NMDA receptor subunits in monkey thalamus. J. Comp. Neurol., 397: 371–393.

Kim, U., Sanchez-Vives, M.V. and McCormick, D.A. (1997) Functional dynamics of GABAergic inhibition in the thalamus. Science, 278: 130–134.

Lenz, F.A., Seike, M., Richardson, R.T., Lin, Y.C., Baker, F.H., Khoja, I., Jaeger, C.J. and Gracely, R.H. (1993) Thermal and pain sensations evoked by microstimulation in the area of human ventrocaudal nucleus. J. Neurophysiol., 70: 200–212.

Lenz, F.A., Kwan, H.C., Martin, R., Tasker, R., Richardson, R.T. and Dostrovsky, J.O. (1994) Characteristics of somatotopic organization and spontaneous neuronal activity in the region of the thalamic principal sensory nucleus in patients with spinal cord transection. J. Neurophysiol., 72: 1570–1587.

Lenz, F.A., Garonzik, I.M., Zirh, T.A. and Dougherty, P.M. (1998) Neuronal activity in the region of the thalamic principal sensory nucleus (ventralis caudalis) in patients with pain following amputations. Neuroscience, 86: 1065–1081.

Lenz, F.A., Ohara, S., Gracely, R.H., Dougherty, P.M. and Patel, S.H. (2004) Pain encoding in the human forebrain: Binary and analogue exteroceptive channels. J. Neurosci., 24: 425–430.

Mehler, W.R. (1962) The anatomy of the so-called "pain tract" in man: an analysis of the course and distribution of the ascending fibers of the fascicularis anterolateralis. In: French, J.D. and Porter, R.W., (Eds.), Basic Research in Paraplegia, Thomas, Springfield, pp. 26–55.

Muñoz, A., Huntsman, M.M. and Jones, E.G. (1998) GABAB receptor gene expression in monkey thalamus. J. Comp. Neurol., 394: 118–126.

Ohara, P.T., Chazal, G. and Ralston, H.J.III. (1989) Ultrastructural analysis of GABA-immunoreactive elements in the monkey thalamic ventrobasal complex. J. Comp. Neurol., 283: 542–558.

Ralston, H.J. III. (1971) Evidence for presynaptic dendrites and a proposal for their mechanism of action. Nature, 230: 585–587.

Ralston, H.J. III. (1984) The fine structure of the ventrobasal thalamus of the monkey and cat. Brain Res., 356: 228–241.

Ralston, H.J. III and Ralston, D.D. (1992) The primate dorsal spinothalamic tract: Evidence for a specific termination in the posterior nuclei (Po/SG) of the thalamus. Pain, 48: 107–118.

Ralston, H.J. III, Ohara, P.T., Meng, X.W., Wells, J. and Ralston, D.D. (1996) Transneuronal changes of the inhibitory circuitry in the macaque somatosensory thalamus following lesions of the dorsal column nuclei. J. Comp. Neurol., 371: 325–335.

Ralston, H.J. III and Ralston, D.D. (1994) Medial lemniscal and spinal projections to the Macaque thalamus: an electron microscopic study of differing GABAergic circuitry serving thalamic somatosensory mechanisms. J. Neurosci., 14: 2485–2502.

Rausell, E., Cusick, C.G., Taub, E. and Jones, E.G. (1992) Chronic deafferentation in monkeys differentially affects nociceptive and nonnociceptive pathways distinguished by specific calcium-binding proteins and down-regulates gamma-aminobutyric acid type A receptors at thalamic levels. Proc. Natl. Acad. Sci. USA, 89: 2571–2575.

Sepukty, J., Eccles, C.U., Lesser, R.P., Dykes-Hoberg, M. and Rothstein, J.D. (1997) Molecular knockdown of neuronal glutamate transporter EAAT3 produces epilepsy and dysregulation of GABA metabolism. Soc. Neurosci. Abstr., 23: 1484.

Tighilet, B., Huntsman, M.M., Hashikawa, T., Murray, K.D., Isackson, P.J. and Jones, E.G. (1998) Cell-specific expression of type II calcium/calmodulin-dependent protein kinase isoforms and glutamate receptors in normal and visually deprived lateral geniculate nucleus of monkeys. J. Comp. Neurol., 390: 278–296.

Westlund, K.N., Sorkin, L.S., Ferrington, D.G., Carlton, S.M., Willcockson, H.H. and Willis, W.D. (1990) Serotoninergic and noradrenergic projections to the ventral posterolateral nucleus of the monkey thalamus. J. Comp. Neurol., 295: 197–207.

Willis, W.D., Zhang, X., Honda, C.N. and Giesler, G.J., Jr. (2001) Projections from the marginal zone and deep dorsal horn to the ventrobasal nuclei of the primate thalamus. Pain, 92: 267–276.

Willis, W.D., Zhang, X., Honda, C.N. and Giesler, G.J., Jr. (2002) A critical review of the role of the proposed VMpo nucleus in pain. J. Pain, 3: 79–94.

Wilson, J.R. (1989) Synaptic organization of individual neurons in the macaque lateral geniculate nucleus. J. Neurosci., 9: 2931–2953.

Wilson, J.R., Friedlander, M.J. and Sherman, S.M. (1984) Fine structural morphology of identified X-and Y-cells in the cat's lateral geniculate nucleus. Proc. R Soc. Lond., 221: 411–436.

Wilson, J.R. and Forestner, D.M. (1995) Synaptic inputs to single neurons in the lateral geniculate nuclei of normal and monocularly deprived squirrel monkeys. J. Comp. Neurol., 362: 468–488.

Wilson, J.R., Forestner, D.M. and Cramer, R.P. (1996) Quantitative analyses of synaptic contacts of interneurons in the dorsal lateral geniculate nucleus of the squirrel monkey. Vis. Neurosci., 13: 1129–1142.

Progress in Brain Research, Vol. 149
ISSN 0079-6123

CHAPTER 2

On the impact of attention and motor planning on the lateral geniculate nucleus

Vivien. A. Casagrande[1,2,3,*], Gyula Sáry[1,7], David Royal[4,5,6] and Octavio Ruiz[1]

[1]*Department of Cell and Developmental Biology,*
[2]*Department of Psychology,*
[3]*Department of Ophthalmology and Visual Sciences,*
[4]*Center for Molecular Neuroscience,*
[5]*Center for Cognitive and Integrative Neuroscience,*
[6]*Vanderbilt Vision Research Center, Vanderbilt University, Nashville, TN, USA*
[7]*Department of Physiology, University of Szeged, Szeged, Hungary*

Abstract: Although the lateral geniculate nucleus (LGN) is one of the most thoroughly characterized thalamic nuclei, its functional role remains controversial. Traditionally, the LGN in primates has been viewed as the lowest level of a set of feedforward parallel visual pathways to cortex. These feedforward pathways are pictured as connected hierarchies of areas designed to construct the visual image gradually — adding more complex features as one marches through successive levels of the hierarchy. In terms of synapse number and circuitry, the anatomy suggests that the LGN can be viewed also as the ultimate terminus in a series of feedback pathways that originate at the highest cortical levels. Since the visual system is dynamic, a more accurate picture of image construction might be one in which information flows bidirectionally, through both the feedforward and feedback pathways constantly and simultaneously. Based upon evidence from anatomy, physiology, and imaging, we argue that the LGN is more than a simple gate for retinal information. Here, we review evidence that suggests that one function of the LGN is to enhance relevant visual signals through circuits related to both motor planning and attention. Specifically, we argue that major extraretinal inputs to the LGN may provide: (1) eye movement information to enhance and bind visual signals related to new saccade targets and (2) top-down and bottom-up information about target relevance to selectively enhance visual signals through spatial attention.

1 Introduction

In this chapter we defend the position that the LGN is involved in the selection of environmental signals by both updating the cortex about anticipated visual and motor events and by highlighting regions of space where relevant visual information is anticipated. The LGN is in an ideal position to carry out these functions because the LGN lies at the interface between the periphery (retina) and the cortex and is potentially informed about levels of arousal, mood, motivation, and intention via a number of non-retinal inputs (Sherman and Guillery, 1996, 2002; Casagrande et al., 2005). Here we focus specifically on the impact of saccadic eye movements and on spatial attention both because more information is available and because evidence suggests that the circuitry involved in attentional selection and target selection for planned eye movements may be shared (Hahnloser et al., 1999; Horwitz and Newsome, 2001).

*Corresponding author. Tel.: +1-615-343-4538; Fax: +1-615-343-4539; E-mail: vivien.casagrande@mcmail.vanderbilt.edu

DOI: 10.1016/S0079-6123(05)49002-0

This chapter is divided into five parts, in addition to this introduction. In Section 2, we introduce the circuitry of the LGN, emphasizing the key elements that constrain the way eye movements and visual attention might impact retinal information passing through the LGN to primary visual cortex (V1). In the next section, we provide a general overview of nonvisual inputs to the LGN and the circuitry of those inputs that are most likely to carry signals related to eye movements and attention. In the fourth section, we discuss evidence that the LGN carries information about motor planning and the circuits that could carry this information. We argue that several nonvisual inputs to the LGN carry oculomotor messages. In the fifth section, we define ways in which visual attention could impact LGN cell responses and the circuits that are most likely to carry this information. The final section provides a summary and outlines the questions that remain to be answered.

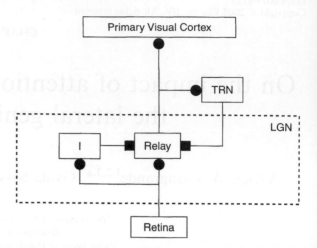

Fig. 1. Diagram of feedforward and feedback inhibitory pathways that influence LGN relay cells. Excitatory inputs are indicated by filled circles. Inhibitory inputs are indicated by filled squares. Abbreviations: TRN: thalamic reticular nucleus, LGN: lateral geniculate nucleus, I: LGN interneuron. See text for details.

2 Basic properties and circuitry of the LGN

To understand how LGN cells are modified by motor planning or attention, it is necessary to review the LGN's organization and circuitry. Rather than reviewing all details of the functional properties and circuitry of the LGN (Casagrande and Norton, 1991; Casagrande, 1994; Sherman and Guillery, 1996, 1998; Hendry and Reid, 2000; Sherman and Guillery, 2002), our goal is to present only a brief review of the ways information flow can be constrained by the LGN's design. Since there is considerable species variation in LGN structure (Kaas et al., 1972), we focus here on the primate LGN. All primate LGNs are layered. Each layer receives input from one hemiretina of one eye and mainly from one of three classes of ganglion cells, koniocellular (K), magnocellular (M), and parvocellular (P). Retinal axons project to only a small number of LGN cells. Therefore, each monocularly innervated LGN layer has a precise map of the opposite hemifield representing either the contralateral nasal retina or the ipsilateral temporal retina. These monocular laminar maps lie in precise retinotopic register. Two cell types are resident within each layer, glutamatergic relay cells (~75–80% of the cells) that send axons to cortex and GABAergic

interneurons (~20–25% of the cells) that maintain connections only within the LGN. LGN relay cells and interneurons relate to each other and to the GABAergic cells of the thalamic reticular nucleus (TRN) in unique feedforward and feedback inhibitory circuits as shown in Fig. 1 (Casagrande and Norton, 1991). Feedforward inhibition is produced by retinal axons and collaterals that synapse simultaneously on both relay cells and nearby interneurons; these interneurons in turn inhibit the same relay cells via dendrodendritic synapses. The LGN relay cells send axons to cortex and collaterals to the TRN, which in turn, feed back inhibition to the relay cells. Since LGN relay cells, interneurons, and TRN cells have many different receptors on their dendrites, including both fast acting ionotropic receptors and slow acting metabotropic receptors, the way signals can be regulated within these LGN circuits via both retinal and nonretinal inputs can be quite complex (Sherman and Guillery, 2001).

The primate LGN receives 30–40% of its synaptic input from the retina (Wilson and Forestner, 1995). Therefore, the majority of synapses in the LGN are from nonretinal sources. In spite of this fact, it has been difficult to identify the functions of the many nonretinal inputs to the LGN primarily because the responses of LGN cells to visual stimuli appear so similar to those of their retinal inputs, at least as defined by average spikes/second over tens of milliseconds (i.e., a standard rate code) in anesthetized preparations (Casagrande and Norton, 1991). The latter definition becomes important because the temporal relationship between spikes can vary between the retina and the LGN. We shall return to this issue shortly. First, it is useful to review the visual receptive field properties defined classically in LGN cells. From the first time responses of primate LGN single units were measured (Wiesel and Hubel, 1966; De Valois et al., 1977; Rodieck and Dreher, 1979), the majority of LGN visual receptive fields were described as organized (same as their retinal ganglion cell inputs) into opposed centers and surrounds (ON center/OFF surround and vice versa). This center/surround organization has been modeled using a difference of Gaussians (DOG) in primate LGN (Irvin et al., 1993; Croner and Kaplan, 1995; White et al., 2001; Xu et al., 2002) and accounts well for the differences in contrast sensitivity between cell classes. This organization, of course, is present already in retinal bipolar cells (Rodieck and Stone, 1965). If the receptive field structure of bipolar cells, retinal ganglion cells, and LGN cells are all so similar, why lengthen the transmission time of visual signals by routing visual information through an intermediary "relay station" like the LGN? It has been argued that center/surround relationships are sharpened in the LGN, reflecting a change in the center/surround relationship. It has also been argued that receptive field surrounds at the level of the LGN are not merely a product of the retina but reflect other contributions from circuits in the LGN itself or other inputs to the LGN given that they do not disappear (as in the retina) under scotopic conditions (for discussion, see Casagrande and Norton, 1991). The latter fact, of course, refutes the idea that the LGN acts as a simple gate to retinal information that passes through it relatively unaltered.

The description above generally assumes a rather static one-way feedforward relationship between inputs and outputs of the visual system. Since the vast majority of information on receptive fields of visual cells has been gathered in anesthetized paralyzed preparations or in slice preparations with a very limited stimulus set, it is natural to build models of this type. The LGN, however, most certainly does not work in isolation from the rest of the brain. In a highly dynamic system retinal signals will always become mixed temporally with signals coming back from cortex and from subcortical sources. Thus, a retinal signal may arrive at an LGN cell at the same time as other signals concerning planned eye movements or the animal's motivational or attentional state. The feedforward LGN signals are also being sent to visual cortical cells at different times given that K, M and P LGN cells respond to the same stimulus with onset latencies that can differ by more than 30 ms (Schmolesky et al., 1998; Ichida et al., 2003, see Fig. 2). The impact of the LGN's message depends ultimately upon how cells in primary visual cortex respond to this input. The fact that each cortical cell in the primary visual cortex receives input from several hundred LGN cells (Davis and Sterling, 1979; Alonso, 2002, for review), not to mention the thousands of local synapses and synapses from many other extrageniculate sources, argues again for the importance of temporal factors in understanding the influence of LGN messages.

Beyond these issues, it is important to appreciate that most LGN cells exhibit spontaneous activity in the absence of visual stimuli that can be modulated by a variety of factors including eye movements and potentially attention (see Section 3). Additionally, the temporal structure of LGN cell firing can adopt modes that do not reflect directly the pattern of their retinal inputs, thus influencing the transfer of visual signals. Sherman and colleagues, as well as others (Guido and Weyand, 1995; Sherman and Guillery, 1996, 1998, 2002; Ramcharan et al., 2000), have shown that LGN and other thalamic relay cells can adopt two basic modes of firing referred to as "burst" and "tonic". During tonic firing, action potentials of LGN relay cells reflect more faithfully the temporal sequence of retinal ganglion cell action potentials. During burst mode, retinal ganglion cell input can trigger a burst of Ca^{2+} spikes after a sufficient period of hyperpolarization. Since burst firing in the thalamus is more effective in causing cortical spikes than tonic firing (Swadlow and Gusev, 2001; Izhikevich et al., 2003) and tonic firing more faithfully represents the retinal input message, Sherman (2001) has suggested that bursts in the

14

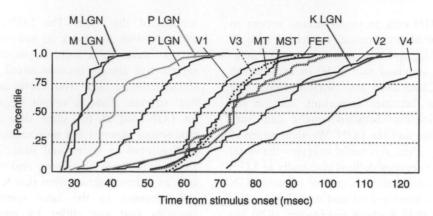

Fig. 2. Cumulative distributions of visually evoked onset response latencies in the LGN, striate and extrastriate visual areas as labeled. Percentile of cells that have begun to respond is plotted as a function of time from stimulus presentation. The V4 curve is truncated to increase resolution of the other curves; the V4 range extends to 159 msec. Abbreviations: M LGN: magnocellular LGN cells, P LGN: parvocellular LGN cells, K LGN: koniocellular LGN cells, V1: primary visual cortex, V2: visual cortical area 2, V3: visual cortical area 3, V4: visual cortical area 4, MT: middle temporal cortical area, MST: medial superior temporal cortical area, FEF: frontal eye field. Modified from Schmolesky et al. (1998) with permission. M LGN (red), P LGN (green), and K LGN (blue) data from Ichida et al. (2003).

LGN of awake animals function as a "wake-up call" for the detection of novel stimuli whereas tonic activity transmits information about stimulus quality (see also below). The timing of bursts and the general synchronization of activity between LGN and cortex may play important roles in coordinating the effectiveness of messages in the visual network (Sillito and Jones, 2002; Wörgötter et al., 2002). Taken together, these facts indicate that both the spatial structure and temporal structure of LGN receptive fields can be modified in a variety of ways depending upon the message. Messages are most likely modified by a combination of extraretinal inputs to the LGN, which are described in the next section.

3 Extraretinal inputs to LGN

Figure 3 shows all of the known connections to the primate LGN with the major connections indicated with bold arrows. A glance at the list can remind the reader of the huge diversity of inputs that can modulate retinogeniculocortical transmission. These sources of input can be classified in various ways. One proposal is to classify these inputs based upon their effect, specific or global (Casagrande and Norton, 1991). Extraretinal inputs from visual sources generally maintain retinotopic fidelity. In

other words, regions representing a common point in visual space are connected. Extraretinal visually related input to the LGN has been documented from the following areas in primates (transmitter type in parentheses): primary visual cortex, V1 (glutamate), some extrastriate areas (possibly glutamate), superior colliculus (glutamate), nucleus of the optic tract, NOT (GABA), parabigeminal nucleus (acetylcholine or ACh), and the visual sector of the thalamic reticular nucleus (GABA) (for review, see Bickford et al., 2000). In primates the majority of the latter inputs to the LGN project to all three LGN cell classes (K, M, and P) but some inputs show a degree of specificity for a particular cell class/layer. Thus, the superior colliculus and extrastriate areas project almost exclusively to K LGN cells, parabigeminal inputs show a preference for K LGN cells, and the input from NOT shows a preference for P LGN cells (Casagrande et al., 2004). Of the latter sources only two, the superior colliculus and NOT, receive direct retinal input. The largest of the visually related sources of input to the LGN comes from V1 and TRN. In addition to these more specific inputs, there are three other main inputs to the LGN. The largest of these is the cholinergic input from the pedunculopontine tegmentum (PPT). This input has been studied in some detail in both cats and monkeys and is known to

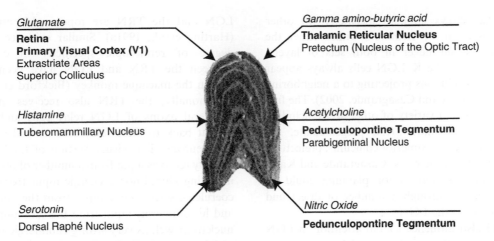

Glutamate

Retina
Primary Visual Cortex (V1)
Extrastriate Areas
Superior Colliculus

Histamine

Tuberomammillary Nucleus

Serotonin

Dorsal Raphé Nucleus

Gamma amino-butyric acid

Thalamic Reticular Nucleus
Pretectum (Nucleus of the Optic Tract)

Acetylcholine

Pedunculopontine Tegmentum
Parabigeminal Nucleus

Nitric Oxide

Pedunculopontine Tegmentum

Fig. 3. Diagram demonstrating the brain areas connected directly with the LGN and their chemical messages. Bold text indicates areas that provide the heaviest input to the LGN in terms of synapse number. Abbreviations: 5-HT: serotonin, GABA: gamma amino-butyric acid, NO: nitric oxide, ACh: acetylcholine. Modified from Casagrande et al. (2005) with permission.

show some evidence of synaptic specificity (Cucchiaro et al., 1988). In addition to ACh, the latter pathway also uses nitric oxide as a transmitter (Bickford et al., 1999). Finally, there are two additional inputs to the LGN that provide for global regulation of information mainly via non-synaptic release of transmitter. These inputs are the histaminergic input from the hypothalamic tubero-mammillary nucleus, which appears to increase activity in the LGN (Hobson and Pace-Schott, 2002; Uhlrich et al., 2002) and the serotonergic input from the dorsal raphé nucleus, which appears to reduce LGN activity in vivo. Here, we consider three examples of major inputs to the LGN that could regulate information concerned with motor planning or spatial attention, although additionally they may contribute to the visual stream by pro-viding information relevant to general states of arousal or motivation (Casagrande et al., 2004 for details).

V1 feedback

V1 provides the largest input in terms of synapse number to the LGN. Almost all of the extraretinal inputs to the LGN could also be sources of signals related to motor planning or attention. V1, for example, receives input not only from the LGN but also from other thalamic nuclei such as the central

lateral (CL) intralaminar nucleus which has been shown to contain cells that respond to various aspects of saccadic eye movements and motor planning (Wyder et al., 2004) and which projects broadly to layer 1 and layer 6 of V1 (Deschenes et al., 1996; Ichinohe et al., 2001). CL also receives input from V1. Additionally, V1 receives a major feedback projection from the middle temporal area (MT, also called V5). MT also has a minor projection directly to the LGN (and also receives direct input from the LGN) but this input appears to involve primarily LGN K cells (Lin and Kaas, 1977; Casagrande and Kaas, 1994; Sincich et al., 2004). Studies by Sillito and Jones (2002) have shown that enhancing the activity of MT feedback cells with a GABAb antagonist and using a moving texture patch to stimulate cells visually changed the activity of topographically matched LGN cells (Jones et al., 2002). Their data show that feedback from MT via V1 can rapidly impact LGN cells which will then dynamically modify the feedforward signal. Given the separation in time of responses of different LGN cell classes (see Fig. 2), this means that the M pathway to MT via V1 (or a direct projection to MT from K cells) and back to the LGN could occur prior to, or simultaneously with, the feedforward inputs from the LGN P and K pathways that travel via V1. The V1 layer 6 cells that project to LGN also receive feedback from many other higher order visual areas including V2, V3, V3a/DM, V4/DL and parts of the temporal cortex. The layer 6 to LGN projection in primates also shows laminar specificity. In other words, axons from V1 terminate within either the M or P layers but never in both sets of layers, although axons to the K LGN cells always appear to be collaterals of axons projecting to a neighboring P or M layer (Ichida and Casagrande, 2002). The fact that V1 projects to a variety of other areas including the claustrum, pulvinar, TRN, pregeniculate, the superficial layers of the superior colliculus, pretectum, and motor nuclei in the pons (Casagrande and Kaas, 1994) also implies that motor planning could be influenced via V1 through a number of direct and indirect circuits to the LGN.

V1 could also influence spatial attention in LGN through many of the top-down and bottom-up circuits outlined above. In a recent study, Przybyszewski et al. (2000) showed that V1 feedback can enhance the contrast gain of both macaque monkey P and M LGN cells significantly. This finding indicates that V1 could be responsible for enhancing its own input. Other studies have provided evidence that feedback to LGN is important for both global integration (or binding) of visual features as well as segmentation (Sillito and Jones, 2002). In the temporal domain, it also has been argued that feedback synchronizes the firing of relay cells (Sillito et al., 1994) as well as changing firing from burst to tonic mode (see section 2).

Regulation by the TRN

TRN has been implicated as an important player in several models of visual attention (Crick, 1984; Guillery et al., 1998). All cells in the TRN contain GABA; however, the pattern and time course of GABA release depends upon which combination of ionotrophic or metabotropic receptors are activated (Sherman and Guillery, 1996, 2002). The major inputs to the TRN are retinotopic connections from the visual cortex and the LGN. Since TRN cells have ON/OFF receptive field centers that are larger than those of their LGN counterparts, they must combine input from more than one LGN cell (Hale et al., 1982). Among primates, the anatomical relationship between the TRN and LGN has been studied most thoroughly in the bush baby where it has been shown that reciprocal connections between all layers of the

LGN and the TRN are topographic and specific (Harting et al., 1991a). Similar evidence of a high degree of retinotopic specificity in connections between the TRN and LGN have been reported also in the macaque monkey (Bickford et al., 2000). Additionally, the TRN also receives input from collateral axons of LGN relay cells and sends its output back to these relay cells as well as to LGN interneurons. This visual portion of the TRN additionally receives input from a number of other sources including global noradrenergic input from the locus coeruleus, serotonergic input from the dorsal raphé, and histaminergic input from the tuberomammillary nucleus as well as very strong cholinergic projections arriving from the PPT and, to a lesser extent, from the basal forebrain (Hobson and Pace-Schott, 2002; Uhlrich et al., 2002). Furthermore, the midbrain reticular formation and several intralaminar thalamic nuclei, including CL, provide input to the TRN.

These circuits allow the TRN to provide not only feedback inhibition to the LGN, but also to regulate LGN cell output in complex ways depending upon other inputs that the TRN receives from both extrastriate visual areas and from the brainstem (Sherman and Guillery, 1996; Guillery et al., 1998, for review; Jones, 2002). For example, inhibitory reticular inputs can modulate the retinogeniculate transfer ratio selectively, pushing the neural circuit toward synchronized oscillation (Le Masson et al., 2002). This process could increase the efficiency of signal transmission between LGN and V1 (Sillito, 2002). Simulations of the LGN-V1-TRN pathway also show that the TRN activity suppresses the background and improves the signal-to-noise ratio (Bickle et al., 1999).

Although seemingly straightforward, the circuitry connecting the TRN and LGN belies the dynamic nature of TRN activation. For example, glutamate, generally considered excitatory, can both excite and inhibit the TRN depending on which group of glutamate receptors is activated (mGluRI and mGluRII respectively) (Cox et al., 1998; Cox and Sherman, 1999). Viewed holistically, this sort of receptor-dependent excitation and inhibition in the TRN allows for greater flexibility in LGN modulation and suggests that the role of the TRN may be quite dynamic depending on the demands of the visual system. Although TRN has been proposed to play specific roles in sleep, arousal, and attention (Crick and Koch, 1990), it seems likely that the TRN is not tied to a specific role relative to LGN activity but is utilized in a variety of ways. Nevertheless, unlike the more global modulatory inputs to the LGN, the visual TRN, like V1 to which it is linked intimately, is in a position to modulate visual activity quite precisely given its retinotopically specific connections with the LGN.

Circuits involving the PPT

It is estimated that as much as 25% of the synapses in the LGN are cholinergic (at least in the cat (Erisir et al., 1997)). Less is known about primate thalamus, however, data show that cholinergic input to the LGN from the midbrain and brainstem forms one of the largest non-retinal brainstem inputs to the primate LGN as well (Bickford et al., 2000). Cholinergic input originates from two sources, the pedunculo-pontine tegmentum (PPT) and the parabigeminal nucleus of the midbrain. Although some differences have been observed in the density of cholinergic input to different LGN layers in different primate species (Fitzpatrick and Diamond, 1980; Graybiel and Ragsdale, 1982; Wilson et al., 1999) this input is found in all LGN layers with the PPT primarily innervating the M and P LGN layers and the parabigeminal nucleus primarily the K LGN layers (Bickford et al., 2000). In addition to acetylcholine, the PPT pathway to the LGN contains the neuro-transmitter nitric oxide and so can regulate activity in a number of ways given that: (1) at least three types of cholinergic receptors are found in the LGN, (2) cholinergic axons project to both interneurons and relay cells, and (3) the PPT provides heavy input to the TRN (Feig and Harting, 1992; Bickford et al., 2000). Added to this complexity is the fact that projections from both the PPT and the parabigeminal nucleus receive input from other sources and project bilaterally to the LGN. In spite of this complexity, the net effect of activation of the PPT pathway in nonprimates has been reported to be excitation of LGN relay cells. Uhlrich et al. (1995) studied the effect of activation of this pathway in cats in some detail and concluded that the main result was response enhancement to visual stimuli but other

changes were also seen including an increase in spontaneous activity as well as more complex effects on the receptive field structure of LGN cells. In primates the PPT pathway to the LGN has been difficult to study in isolation given that the PPT cells that innervate the LGN are scattered among cells that project elsewhere. Nevertheless, many functions have been attributed to this pathway based upon both physiological and clinical data including involvement in rapid eye movement sleep, saccadic eye movements, attention, and arousal (see below and Fitzpatrick et al., 1989 for review).

In contrast to the PPT the parabigeminal nucleus appears to have much more limited connections; primarily with the superior colliculus. Functionally it has not been studied in primates, but in cats data suggest that one likely role of the parabigeminal nucleus is to inform the LGN about target location (Cui and Malpeli, 2003). Why this information would primarily target the LGN K layers in primates remains an open question (Harting et al., 1991b).

4 The LGN and motor planning

In all primates there is a strong specialization for central vision. The visual system is designed to track visual targets closely, recentering the eyes on objects of interest either by smooth pursuit movements, or via ballistic movements, called saccades. Saccades are very rapid and can reach speeds of over 100 degrees per second. These eye movements recenter the eye on objects of interest several times a second reflecting decisions to shift attention. For example, while reading this page you have made thousands of saccades. What is particularly interesting about saccadic eye movements is that saccades sweep the visual field across the retina at remarkable speeds and yet, we are completely unaware of the 'visual blur' that should occur while our eyes are in flight. Furthermore, neither are we aware that we are getting small discrete snapshots of a bigger visual picture instead of a seamless view. The fact that we see a unified picture suggests that visual perception is coordinated with saccadic eye movements at early levels of the system. In fact, as we will see, there is evidence that the LGN is modulated by eye movements and that the circuits that could provide such modulation to the LGN could also receive information relevant to decisions to shift visual attention.

Although there is considerable evidence in both cats and monkeys that LGN cells respond to saccadic eye movements, results have been conflicting. In earlier studies, the focus was on linking the perceptual experience of saccadic suppression with activity in the LGN. In these early studies, the percentages of cells found to exhibit suppression in the LGN varied from almost none (Michael and Ichinose, 1970) to over 50% (Jeannerod and Putkonen, 1971). Some investigators found evidence of saccade related suppression of LGN activity only while animals made saccades to a visual target (Fischer et al., 1998), only a few have reported suppression also associated with spontaneous saccades in total darkness (Buttner and Fuchs, 1973; Bartlett et al., 1976). Presumably, changes in activity in total darkness were simply not detected for technical reasons since it had been shown more than a decade before that rapid eye movement sleep modulates LGN activity (Bizzi, 1966). Also, pulling on the eye muscles of rabbits and cats was shown to modulate LGN activity significantly even when these animals were anesthetized (Molotchnikoff and Casanova, 1985; Lal and Friedlander, 1990a, b). More recently, investigators have focused on not only active suppression of LGN cell responses before or during eye movements, but also upon changes that occur directly after eye movements, changes which might aid in linking relevant images

across eye movements by a postsaccadic facilitation mechanism (Lee and Malpeli, 1998). In fact, Lee and Malpeli (1998) reported that although a percentage of X and Y LGN cells in cats show a modest suppression before and during eye movements, the largest effect was a postsaccadic enhancement of activity. Our results in awake behaving macaque monkeys are in good agreement with those of Lee and Malpeli (1998) in showing that LGN cells of all three classes (K, M and P) exhibit a modest suppression which starts well before saccades are initiated and transitions into a strong post-saccadic enhancement where LGN activity nearly doubles (Royal et al., 2005 (submitted); see also Fig. 4.). Since all of our measurements were performed without direct visual stimulation of receptive fields, it cannot be argued that saccade-related modulations are confounded by transient changes seen when receptive fields sweep visual stimuli during gaze shifts. Although not all studies have found modulation of LGN cell activity with saccades in monkeys (Maunsell et al., 1999), at least two other studies in awake behaving macaque monkeys report that the strongest effect of saccades on visually driven LGN activity is a postsaccadic enhancement (Ramcharan et al., 2001; Reppas et al., 2002).

Most of the above findings were the result of comparing average firing rates during saccades with periods where the animal was fixating. Interestingly, however, Ramcharan et al. (2001) found that both M and P LGN cells in awake behaving macaque monkeys (K cells were not examined) show a

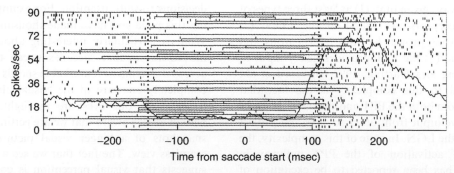

Fig. 4. Effect of spontaneous saccades on LGN cell activity. A peristimulus time histogram for an LGN cell recorded while the monkey produced 53 spontaneous saccades in a completely darkened room. Saccade start was determined by examining eye velocity and segments of the spike train were aligned on saccade start (0 m). The small tick marks represent spikes and the horizontal brackets represent significant increases in interspike interval as determined by a Poisson analysis. The vertical dashed lines represent the modal onset (−144 m) and offset (110 m) of the periods of significant modulation relative to saccade start.

significant suppression of burst firing during saccades, suggesting that the temporal structure of the LGN message is changed during saccades, perhaps increasing the visual threshold in this manner. Our examination of the prevalence of bursts during fixations and saccades in awake behaving monkeys supports the results of Ramcharan et al. (2001), showing that bursts are reduced during saccades (Royal et al., 2003). However, since, on average, less than 6% of spikes met the criteria for being classified as a burst and considering that saccades are generally very short (lasting on average 40 msec), it is not clear if such changes in burst number are behaviorally meaningful (Royal et al., 2003).

Recently, Thilo et al. (2004) addressed the issue of saccade related modulation of the LGN in humans. Although their experimental design prevented them from addressing the issue of postsaccadic enhancement, their data argue that LGN activity is suppressed during saccades. Using a combination of direct retinal stimulation and transcranial visual cortical stimulation to produce phosphenes, they showed that subjects experienced a significant reduction in contrast sensitivity during saccades only when the phosphenes were induced retinally, not cortically, suggesting that the site of saccadic suppression must be the LGN.

Additionally, there are reports suggesting that cells both in the LGN and V1 are sensitive to changes in eye position (Weyand and Malpeli, 1993) and microsaccadic eye movements — local eye movments of less than 2° that presumably refresh the image on the retina (Martinez-Conde et al., 2000). In fact, cells in many extrastriate cortical areas have been reported to be sensitive to changes in eye position (Anderson and Mountcastle, 1983; Andersen et al., 1985; Galletti and Battaglini, 1989). In anesthetized, paralyzed cats, Lal and Friedlander (1989, 1990) demonstrated that modulation of visual responses were eliminated with a retrobulbar block, suggesting that information from eye muscles reaches the LGN. Weyand and Malpeli (1993) reported a monotonic relationship between eye position and excitability in visual cortical cells in cats. It may be then that in addition to providing information about the saccade target of the eye, the LGN extracts information about the absolute external coordinates of visual targets and this information is combined with visual information before reaching V1.

The obvious question then is where do the signals come from that orchestrate the saccade-related and eye position-related changes we see in the LGN. These signals result in changes in gain that are linked in time directly to the saccade. These saccadic modulatory changes in the LGN cannot be driven by motivation since they occur spontaneously in the dark. The timing of saccade related suppression begins so far in advance of the saccade in both cats and monkeys that the signals that arrive at the LGN likely relate more to the decision to shift gaze (i.e., motor planning) than to the actual motor command underlying the gaze shift. The PPT has been implicated both in attentional orienting to a target and to the production of saccades and so may provide both types of information although this input is generally thought to enhance, not suppress, LGN activity (Uhlrich et al., 1995). Nevertheless, the complex circuitry of the PPT and its links to the intermediate layers of the superior colliculus and many other areas suggest that the PPT could function to control the biphasic change in activity seen in the LGN during saccades. It is also possible that several inputs working together provide the signals that modulate LGN activity during eye movements. The simplest explanation for LGN suppression is that the input signals either are directly inhibitory or activate the inhibitory circuits through GABAergic LGN interneurons or GABAergic TRN neurons. One possible source of this inhibitory information is the pretectogeniculate pathway specifically from the NOT (Schmidt, 1996; Schmidt et al., 1996). NOT cells are GABAergic and are excited during saccades (Schmidt, 1996). Schmidt and colleagues (Schmidt, 1996; Schmidt et al., 1996) have argued that NOT cells that project to LGN inhibit LGN interneurons in cats, thus causing excitation of LGN relay cells. The latter circuit again would be more appropriate to explain postsaccadic enhancement than perisaccadic suppression given its effect on relay cells in cats and given that the activation starts after saccades begin. In primates this pathway could contribute to saccade related suppression and enhancement since this pathway projects to both interneurons and relay cells (Feig and Harting, 1994), although it tends to project mainly to P LGN layers. The superior colliculus also is a good candidate to contribute to saccade related modulation given that cells in the intermediate layers show the appropriately timed modulation in relation to saccades (Mohler and Wurtz, 1976). However, the intermediate collicular layers do not project directly to the LGN and the superficial collicular layers that project to the LGN project only to the K layers (Harting et al., 1991a; Lachica and Casagrande, 1993). The colliculus has been proposed to provide saccade related signals indirectly to the LGN in the rabbit (Zhu and Lo, 1996). This circuit involves a projection from the intermediate layers of the superior colliculus to the TRN via the central lateral thalamic nucleus. The central lateral nucleus belongs to the intralaminar nuclear group which has been shown in several studies to contain cells that respond in relationship to saccadic eye movements, motor planning, and shifts in attention (Schlag and Schlag-Rey, 1984, 1985; Wyder et al., 2004). As mentioned earlier, CL projects not only to the basal ganglia but widely to layer I of visual cortex. The beauty of the latter indirect circuit is that the overall time course of activation in the colliculus and suppression in the LGN fit with the time course of saccadic suppression, beginning well before saccade initiation and ending just prior to saccade end.

5 Visual attention in the thalamus and LGN

Attention is defined as the ability to actively select or give priority to relevant internal or external stimuli, cognitive processes, or motor activities (Machinskaia, 2003). As such, attention can refer to a number of processes (Sieb, 1990). Attention should be distinguished from general arousal or the overall sensitivity of a system to events. We know, for example, that LGN activity can be modulated globally by different stages of sleep and arousal (McCormick and Prince, 1986; McCormick and Pape, 1990; Steriade, 1996). Attention is selective. Evidence demonstrates that there are different forms of attention. Selective attention can occur in the form of orienting to stimuli in such a way as to give them priority. Such orienting can either be covert (no movement required) or overt anticipating the necessity for action. Some have argued that orienting may not require higher level processing but be part of a "bottom up" attentional system (Julesz, 1990; Graboi and Lisman, 2003). Other forms of attention clearly require volitional

control involving memory and are generally regarded as part of a "top down" attentional system (Montero, 2000; Freeman et al., 2003; Graboi and Lisman, 2003; Sussman et al., 2003). Posner and Dehaene (1994) proposed that there are three neural networks of attention, a posterior system involved in orienting, an anterior system concerned with directing attention and providing awareness, and a third neural system connecting the two others concerned with vigilance. Vigilance is generally defined as the process of maintaining a particular focus of attention over time. The question we pose here is whether or not the LGN participates in any of these processes defined as attention. The common belief, however, is that the LGN is a low level sensory relay in a feedforward pathway to cortex; attentional effects are thought to mainly involve networks in higher cortical areas especially the frontal and parietal lobes (Corbetta, 1998). Nevertheless, some investigators have argued that shifting attention is the reason the thalamus exists since thalamic nuclei form the major gateway to cortex for all sensory information except olfaction (Crick, 1984; Jones, 2002). In fact, Crick (1984) proposed twenty years ago that the main function of the TRN was to direct the "searchlight" of attention. Given that the TRN lacks a direct connection with cortex, the TRN can communicate with cortex only through an intermediate thalamic nucleus such as the LGN.

Now that the concept of attention is introduced, let us consider whether LGN responses are influenced by attention. In the literature, the pulvinar is most often cited as the thalamic nucleus or nuclei concerned with shifts in visual attention. The extensive connections of the pulvinar with cortex, the fact that the pulvinar receives its main visual drive from V1 in primates and gets input from the superficial superior colliculus (also implicated in visual attention), and is linked to visual attentional deficits following inactivation (Bender and Youakim, 2001) all have argued in favor of the pulvinar as the main thalamic nucleus concerned with visual attention (Petersen et al., 1987). Additionally, several past studies of visual attention at the cortical level did not find evidence that attention impacts responses of V1 cells as would be expected if the LGN paid attention (Wurtz and Mohler, 1976; Robinson et al., 1980); changes with attention were identified in these same studies in higher cortical visual areas. More recent studies, however, have documented significant effects of attention in V1 although not necessarily in the LGN (Bender and Youakim, 2001). For example, Motter (1993) showed that 30% of the cells in V1, V2, and V4 exhibit enhanced responses in an orientation discrimination task where stimuli were presented either inside or outside the receptive fields of neurons. These effects were just as strong in V1 as in the other visual areas examined. Similarly Haenny and Schiller (1988) found that the responses of V1 neurons were enhanced by attention but the magnitude of this effect was much greater for cells in V4 in the latter study. Roelfsema and Spekreijse (2001) also reported that macaque V1 responses show evidence of attention when monkeys must decide whether a line passing across the receptive field is connected to the fixation point or disconnected from it. In both of the latter tasks the neuron's receptive field received identical stimulation but neural responses differed and reflected the monkey's interpretation of the relevance of the stimulus in relation to a planned saccade to receive a reward.

In all the above examples where attention was found to influence V1 cell responses, the effect of attention served to enhance the response to the attended stimulus. In some cases, however, suppression of unattended stimuli has been found. Vanduffel et al. (1997) used a double-labeling 2-deoxyglucose (2-DG) technique in an orientation discrimination task in macaque monkeys to demonstrate that unattended stimuli in V1 produced lower than baseline labeling suggesting that activity in these unattended areas was suppressed. Relevant to this chapter is the fact that they also saw suppression of labeling magnitude in unattended retinotopic zones in the LGN. Interestingly, the effects in LGN and V1 were confined to the M LGN layers (and possibly the surrounding K layers) and the M dominated cortical layers in V1. Until very recently the latter was the only study that demonstrated clear attentional effects in the LGN. Recently, strong attentional effects were reported using fMRI in human LGN under covert orienting conditions where subjects attended or ignored flickering checkerboard stimuli of variable contrast presented in both hemifields (O'Connor et al., 2002). In the latter experiment eye movements were ruled out based upon control experiments conducted outside of the scanner. The effects of attention within V1 and several other visual cortical areas were also compared (Fig. 5). In both LGN and V1, O'Connor et al. (2002) reported that neural responses were enhanced to attended stimuli and attenuated to ignored stimuli. Furthermore, and perhaps most interestingly, activity in LGN increased on the attended side in the absence of any visual stimulation. Surprisingly, the magnitude of attentional effects were much larger in LGN than in V1 (Fig. 5), suggesting that the attentional modulation in LGN comes not from V1 but from other sources of input to the LGN or from a combination of sources given the magnitude of these effects (see later in the chapter). Given the low spatial resolution of fMRI, it could be argued that the authors were actually seeing attentional effects in the pulvinar rather than the LGN especially since the pulvinar is larger and lies directly adjacent to the LGN. In a second study (Kastner et al., 2004), the authors attempted to rule out this possibility by showing that attention related activation of pulvinar is distinct from that observed in the LGN, suggesting that each nucleus may contribute to a different form of attention; Perhaps the LGN-V1 circuit contributes where precise spatial attention is required and the pulvinar-cortical circuits contribute mainly to nonspatial forms of attention.

Recently, we examined if the effect of attention could be demonstrated at the single cell level in the LGN of awake behaving macaque monkeys (Royal et al., 2004, 2005). In these preliminary studies, the receptive field was stimulated with a flashing square using stimuli optimized for each cell. Monkeys were trained to perform several tasks but in all conditions the LGN receptive fields were stimulated identically under attended and ignored conditions, eye movements were controlled, and any changes in activity were measured prior to the initiation of saccadic eye movements. The monkeys were required to saccade to one of the two stimuli and, if it was rewarded, the monkey could expect to be rewarded at the same location for the next 20–30 trials. An error indicated to the monkeys that the other stimulus was now correct for the next block of trials. Under these conditions while baseline activity generally did not change, some cells demonstrated a significant enhancement of the response when the receptive field target was correct and thus located in the

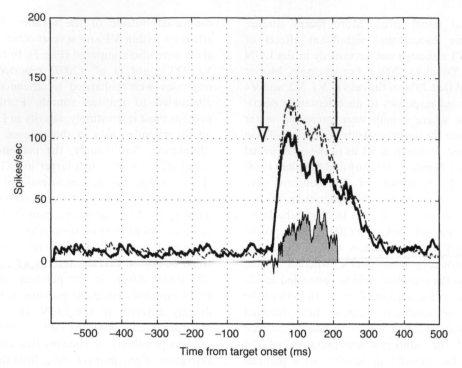

Fig. 5. Attentional modulation of LGN cells in macaque monkey. Peristimulus time histogram showing average firing rates of one LGN unit over 20 trials per condition during a task where the monkey was presented with two stimuli simultaneously. One stimulus was always in the receptive field (RF) of the neuron, the other was placed symmetrically, at the same eccentricity, outside of the RF (nonRF stimulus). The location of the rewarded stimulus alternated in blocks of 20 trials. Arrows indicate target onset and mean latency of the saccades. Dashed curve shows cellular activity in the condition when the rewarded target was in the RF of the neuron, bold line shows the mean response level when the animal had to make a saccade to the nonRF stimulus. Grey area shows the difference of the areas under the curves. The responses differed significantly, i.e., the same pair of stimuli elicited larger responses when the animal had to make a saccade to the RF compared to the condition, when the target of the saccade was the nonRF stimulus. From Royal et al. (2004). (See text for details.)

presumed attended field relative to the response when the non-receptive field target was correct (Fig. 6.). We used the same paradigm to test whether an attentional effect could be demonstrated when both targets were placed in the upper and lower quadrants of the same hemifield. The result was the same, i.e., when the correct target was in the receptive field the response differed from the response when this target was incorrect. The results from the task where targets were presented in the same hemifield suggest that attentional regulation of responses may be spatially quite restricted. These preliminary results support the idea that attention may regulate LGN responses but given that each block of trials was not presented more than once, more comprehensive experiments will be required to confirm these results. This form of restricted spatial attention has also been reported in

V1 but has not been reported for the dorsomedial pulvinar where more global spatial attentional shifts are reported and where the receptive fields of cells are very large (Petersen et al., 1987). Taken together with imaging results in humans, these results support the view that the LGN can pay attention. However, again, further analysis and tests will be required to rule out other explanations.

Given that very few studies have been done to examine the responses of LGN cells in awake primates (see also Sherman and Guillery, 1996, 1998), many questions still remain about the types of attention that can be demonstrated at the level of the LGN and the circuitry involved in these LGN attentional effects. The results summarized above support the idea that LGN and V1 responses to restricted attended targets can be enhanced much as

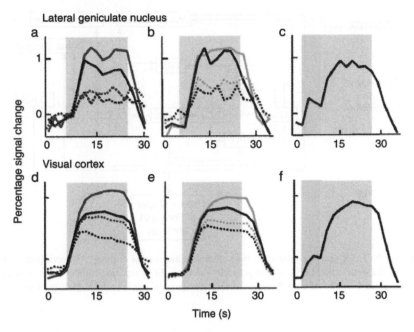

Fig. 6. Time series of fMRI signals in the LGN (a–c) and visual cortex (d–f). Group analysis (*n* = 4). Data from the LGN and visual cortex were combined across left and right hemispheres. Activity in visual cortex was pooled across areas V1, V2, V3/VP, V4, TEO, V3A and MT/MST. (a,d) Attentional enhancement. During directed attention to the stimuli (red curves), responses to both the high-contrast stimulus (100%, solid curves) and low-contrast stimulus (5%, dashed curves) were enhanced relative to an unattended condition (black curves). (b, e) Attentional suppression. During an attentionally demanding fixation task (black curves), responses evoked by both the high-contrast stimulus (10%, dashed curves) were attenuated relative to an easier attention task at fixation (green curves). (c, f) Baseline increases. Baseline activity was elevated during directed attention to the periphery of the visual hemifield in expectation of the stimulus onset (blue). Gray shades indicate periods of checkerboard presentation. From O'Connor et al. (2002) with permission.

would be predicted by Crick's hypothesized "searchlight" of attention. That imaging results show a smaller attentional effect in V1 than in LGN argues against feedback from V1 as the searchlight source, although it is, however, possible that the impact of V1 feedback is enhanced via collateral branches within the TRN (see above), particularly if the TRN also is responsible for suppressing activity in regions that are not retinotopically aligned with the target stimulus.

The superior colliculus is unlikely to provide this input directly to LGN even though very similar attentional effects have been reported in the superficial layers of the colliculus (Goldberg and Wurtz, 1972; Wurtz and Goldberg, 1972; Ignashchenkova et al., 2004). This is because colliculo-geniculate input primarily targets the K LGN layers. As with visual cortex, however, collicular input could impact LGN responses via the TRN given that collicular

projections are retinotopic and the TRN sends a topographically specific projection back to all LGN layers. Since attentional effects in one LGN can be compared between the two hemifields and each LGN only represents one hemifield, this presumably means that relevant information must pass either cortically or subcortically between hemispheres. Visual cortical, TRN, and collicular inputs to LGN remain ipsilateral but cholinergic input to the LGN from the PPT is bilateral. The wide connections of this pontine region with the rest of the brain (Fig. 7) and the fact that stimulation within this region results in enhanced responses in the LGN emphasize that connections from PPT may contribute although they cannot alone account for retinotopic specificity of the spatial attentional effects reported by many. Other inputs to the LGN described above seem less likely to contribute to attentional shifts. Serotonergic input from the dorsal raphé and histaminergic input from

24

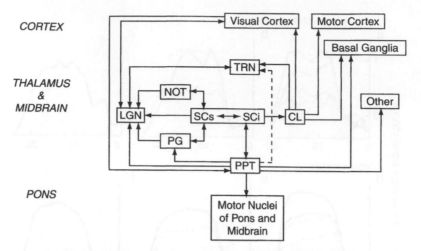

Fig. 7. Circuits involving the LGN that are related to both attention and motor control. Abbreviations: TRN: thalamic reticular nucleus, NOT: nucleus of the optic tract, LGN: lateral geniculate nucleus, SCs: superior colliculus (superficial layers), SCi: superior colliculus (intermediate layers), CL: central lateral nucleus, PG: parabigeminal nucleus, PPT: pedunculopontine tegmentum. See text for details.

the tuberomammillary nucleus have been proposed to provide for either global suppression or global enhancement, respectively, of activity in the LGN without much topographic specificity and so would need to work together with other inputs to contribute to any spatial attention seen in LGN. GABAergic input from the NOT and cholinergic input from the parabigeminal nucleus (Fig. 3) could also contribute when motor planning is involved, but attentional effects have not been described for either of the areas. It seems likely given the dynamic nature of the system that the signals from many of these areas contribute to the final output of each LGN cell.

Experiments of Davidson et al. (1999) support the idea that the cholinergic input from the PPT could contribute to the spatial attentional effects seen in the LGN. Davidson and colleagues (1999) observed a dose-dependent increase in reaction time and decrease in accuracy of eye movements in a task where the target was preceded by a visual cue when the cholinergic muscarinic antagonist scopolamine was administered. The slowing was most prominent when the animal received valid cues in either visual field. Slowing, however did not occur in those trials whose cues lacked spatial information, or in tasks in which attention was directed to events at the fixation point. These results provide additional support for the hypothesis that ACh plays a key role in reflexive

attentional shifting to peripheral visual targets and supports the idea that the PPT pathway to the LGN may contribute to this role.

Conclusions and remaining questions

As we have described above, the LGN receives many non-retinal sources of input that together outnumber the retinal input to the LGN. Given the diversity of connections that each of these input sources has with the rest of the brain, it is clear that LGN cells are probably modulated by many different sensory, motor, and cognitive messages. Closer inspection of the types of circuits that impact the LGN suggest that signals leaving this nucleus are mainly influenced by three types of information. First, LGN cells are clearly influenced by the global state of the animal. Many investigations have documented the differences in LGN responses that occur when animals are awake or asleep (McCormick and Prince, 1986; McCormick and Pape, 1990; Steriade, 1996). Second, many inputs to the LGN appear to be concerned with motor planning — conveying signals concerning saccade targets, eye position, as well as eye movements themselves. Finally, evidence indicates that several inputs to the LGN carry signals that are designed to enhance activity to particular visual targets or to visual stimuli within particular spatial locations via prominent inputs from both brainstem and cortex via shifts in attention. The fact that some of these inputs to the LGN, like the cholinergic input from the PPT, also carry signals concerned with saccadic eye movements supports previous models which have suggested that spatial attention is intimately linked to planned saccadic eye movements (Fig. 7; Hahnloser et al., 1999; Horwitz and Newsome, 2001). Some have argued that this relationship is obligatory, namely, that one cannot make a saccadic eye movement without switching attention to the target of that eye movement (Deubel and Schneider, 1996; Ditterich et al., 2000). Others have argued for very separate circuits (Murthy et al., 2001). We would argue for a partial relationship since some inputs to the LGN do appear to carry eye movement or eye position related signals that have not been directly linked to attention such as the NOT and the parabigeminal nucleus. The latter connections suggest that modulation of LGN by eye movements may not always be linked to attentional modulation in an obligatory way.

Since very few studies have directly examined the impact of motor planning and attention on LGN activity in awake behaving animals, many questions still remain to be answered. Some of these questions are listed below. Improvements in the resolution of imaging techniques and the ability to record from multiple brain sites simultaneously in awake behaving animals open new doors that will allow us to answer some of these questions in future studies.

- Why do collicular, parabigeminal, and extrastriate inputs project mainly to LGN K layers?
- Why does the input from NOT target mainly the P layers?
- Does the PPT contribute to eye movement related modulation of LGN activity?
- Does the visual TRN in primates show saccade or attention related modulation?
- Is cholinergic input from the PPT the essential circuit for the attentional effects seen in LGN?
- Are the attention related effects in V1 and LGN really independent as fMRI data suggest?
- Which high-level processes influence LGN activity and under what conditions is modulation most evident/favorable?

Abbreviations

LGN	lateral geniculate nucleus
TRN	thalamic reticular nucleus
V1	primary visual cortex
V2	visual cortical area 2
V3	visual cortical area 3
V3a	visual cortical area 3a
V4	visual cortical area 4
V5	visual cortical area 5
K	koniocellular
P	parvocellular
M	magnocellular
GABA	gamma-aminobutyric acid
PPT	pedunculopontine tegmentum
fMRI	functional magnetic resonance imaging
2-DG	2-deoxyglucose
NOT	nucleus of the optic tract
DOG	difference of Gaussians
ACh	acetylcholine
CL	central lateral nucleus
MT	middle temporal cortical area
DM	dorsomedial cortical area
DL	dorsolateral cortical area
mGluRI	metabotropic glutamate receptor, type I
mGluRII	metabotropic glutamate receptor, type II

Acknowledgments

We are grateful to Julia Mavity-Hudson for the help with illustrations and comments on the manuscript, and Ilya Khaytis for help proofing the manuscript. Supported by EY01778 (VAC), IBN-0234646 (VAC), 1F31NS44691 (DWR), and core grants EY08126 and HD15052.

References

Alonso, J.M. (2002) Neural connections and receptive field properties in the primary visual cortex. Neuroscientist., 8(5): 443–456.

Andersen, R.A. and Mountcastle, V.B. (1983) The influence of the angle of gaze upon the excitability of the light-sensitive neurons of the posterior parietal cortex. J. Neurosci., 3(3): 532–548.

Andersen, R.A., Essick, G.K. and Siegel, R.M. (1985) Encoding of spatial location by posterior parietal neurons. Science, 230(4724): 456–458.

26

Bartlett, J.R., Doty, R.W., Lee, B.B., Sr. and Sakakura, H. (1976) Influence of saccadic eye movements on geniculostriate excitability in normal monkeys. Exp. Brain Res., 25: 487–509.

Bender, D.B. and Youakim, M. (2001) Effect of attentive fixation in macaque thalamus and cortex. J. Neurophysiol., 85: 219–234.

Bickford, M.E., Carden, W.B. and Patel, N.C. (1999) Two types of interneurons in the cat visual thalamus are distinguished by morphology, synaptic connections, and nitric oxide synthase content. J. Comp. Neurol., 413(1): 83–100.

Bickford, M., Ramcharan, E., Godwin, D., Erisir, A., Gnadt, J. and Sherman, S. (2000) Neurotransmitters contained in the subcortical extraretinal inputs to the monkey lateral geniculate nucleus. J. Comp. Neurol., 424: 701–717.

Bickle, J., Bernstein, M., Heatley, M., Worley, C. and Stiehl, S. (1999) A functional hypothesis for LGN-V1-TRN connectivities suggested by computer simulation. J. Computat. Neurosci., 6: 251–261.

Bizzi, E. (1966) Discharge patterns of single geniculate neurons during the rapid eye movements of sleep. J. Neurophysiol., 29(6): 1087–1095.

Buttner, U. and Fuchs, A. (1973) Influence of saccadic eye movements on unit activity in simian lateral geniculate and perigeniculate nuclei. J. Neurophysiol., 36: 127.

Casagrande, V.A. (1994) A third visual pathway to primate V1. Trends in Neurosci., 17: 305–310.

Casagrande, V.A. and Kaas, J.H. (1994) The afferent, intrinsic, and efferent connections of primary visual cortex in primates, in Cerebral Cortex. In: Peters A. and Rockland, K.S., (Eds.), Primary Visual Cortex of Primates. Vol. 10, Plenum Press, New York, pp. 201–259.

Casagrande, V.A. and Norton, T.T. (1991) The lateral geniculate nucleus: A review of its physiology and function. In: Leventhal, A.G., Ed., The Neural Basis of Visual Function. Vol. 4 of Vision and Visual Disfunction, Ed. Cronley-Dillon, J.R. MacMillan Press, London, pp. 41–84.

Casagrande, V.A., Royal, D.W., Sáry, Gy. (2005) Extraretinal inputs and feedback mechanisms to the lateral geniculate nucleus (LGN). John Wiley and Sons. (In press).

Corbetta, M. (1998) Frontoparietal cortical networks for directing attention and the eye to visual locations: identical, independent, or overlapping neural systems? Proc. Natl. Acad. Sci., 95: 831–838.

Cox, C.L. and Sherman, S.M. (1999) Glutamate inhibits thalamic reticular neurons. J. Neurosci., 19(15): 6694–6699.

Cox, C.L., Zhou, Q. and Sherman, S.M. (1998) Glutamate locally activates dendritic outputs of thalamic interneurons. Nature, 394(6692): 478–482.

Crick, F. (1984) Function of the thalamic reticular complex: the searchlight hypothesis. Neurobiol., 81: 4586–4590.

Crick, F. and Koch, C. (1990) Towardsa Neurobiological Theory Of Consciousness. Sem. Neurosci., 2: 263–275.

Croner, L.J. and Kaplan, E. (1995) Receptive fields of P and M ganglion cells across the primate retina. Vision Res., 35: 7–24.

Cui, H. and Malpeli, J.G. (2003) Activity in the parabigeminal nucleus during eye movements directed at moving and stationary targets. J. Neurophysiol., 89: 3128–3142.

Cucchiaro, J.B., Uhlrich, D.J. and Sherman, S.M. (1988) Parabrachial innervation of the cat's dorsal lateral geniculate nucleus: an electron microscopic study using the tracer Phaseolus vulgaris leucoagglutinin (PHA-L). J. Neurosci., 8(12): 4576–4588.

Davidson, M.C. Cutrell, E.B. and Marrocco, R.T. (1999) Scopolamine slows the orienting of attention in primates to cued visual targets Psychopharmacology, 142(1): 1–8.

Davis, T.L. and Sterling, P. (1979) Microcircuitry of cat visual cortex: classification of neurons in layer IV of area 17, and identification of the patterns of lateral geniculate input. J. Comp. Neurol., 188(4): 599–627.

Deschenes, M., Bourassa, J. and Parent, A. (1996) Striatal and cortical projections of single neurons from the central lateral thalamic nucleus in the rat. Neurosci., 72(3): 679–687.

Deubel, H. and Schneider, W.X. (1996) Saccade target selection and object recognition: evidence for a common attentional mechanism. Vision Res., 36(12): 1827–1837.

De Valois, R.L., Snodderly, D.M. Jr., Yund, E.W. and Hepler, N.K. (1977) Responses of macaque lateral geniculate cells to luminance and color figures. Sensory Processes., 1(3): 244–259.

Ditterich, J., Eggert, T. and Straube, A. (2000) Relation between the metrics of the presaccadic attention shift and of the saccade before and after saccadic adaptation. J. Neurophysiol., 84(4): 1809–1813.

Erisir, A., VanHorn, S.C. and Sherman, S.M. (1997) Relative numbers of cortical and brainstem inputs to the lateral geniculate nucleus. PNAS, 94(4): 1517–1520.

Feig, S. and Harting, J.K. (1992) Ultrastructural Studies of the Primate Parabigeminal Nucleus — Electron-Microscopic Autoradiographic Analysis of the Tectoparabigeminal Projection in Galago-Crassicaudatus. Brain Res., 595(2): 334–338.

Feig, S. and Harting, J.K. (1994) Ultrastructural studies of the primate lateral geniculate nucleus: morphology and spatial relationships of axon terminals arising from the retina, visual cortex (area 17), superior colliculus, parabigeminal nucleus, and pretectum of Galago crassicaudatus. J. Comp. Neurol., 343: 17–34.

Fischer, W.H., Schmidt, M. and Hoffmann, K.P. (1998) Saccade-induced activity of dorsal lateral geniculate nucleus X- and Y-cells during pharmacological inactivation of the cat pretectum. Vis. Neurosci., 15(2): 197–210.

Fitzpatrick, D. and Diamond, I.T. (1980) Distribution of acetylcholinesterase in the geniculo striate system of Galago senegalensis and Aotus trivirgatus: evidence for the origin of the reaction product in the lateral geniculate body. J. Comp. Neurol., 194(4): 703–719.

Fitzpatrick, D., Diamond, I.T. and Raczkowski, D. (1989) Cholinergic and monoaminergic innervation of the cat's thalamus: comparison of the lateral geniculate nucleus with other principal sensory nuclei. J. Comp. Neurol., 288: 647–675.

Freeman, E., Driver, J., Sagi, D. and Zhaoping, L. (2003) Top-down modulation of lateral interactions in early vision: does attention affect integration of the whole or just perception of the parts? Curr. Bio., 13(11): 985–989.

Galletti, C. and Battaglini, P.P. (1989) Gaze-dependent visual neurons in area V3A of monkey prestriate cortex. J. Neurosci., 9(4): 1112–1125.

Goldberg, M.E. and Wurtz, R.H. (1972) Activity of superior colliculus in behaving monkey. II. Effect of attention on neuronal responses. J. Neurophysiol., 35(4): 560–574.

Graboi, D. and Lisman, J. (2003) Recognition by top-down and bottom-up processing in cortex: the control of selective attention. J. Neurophysiol., 90(2): 798–810.

Graybiel, A.M. and Ragsdale, C.W., Jr. (1982) Pseudocholinesterase staining in the primary visual pathway of the macaque monkey. Nature, 299(5882): 439–442.

Guido, W. and Weyand, T. (1995) Burst responses in thalamic relay cells of the awake behaving cat. J. Neurophysiol., 74: 1782–1786.

Guillery, R.W., Feig, S.L. and Lozsádi, D.A. (1998) Paying attention to the thalamic reticular nucleus. Trends Neurosci., 21: 28–32.

Haenny, P.E. and Schiller, P.H. (1988) State dependent activity in monkey visual cortex. I. Single cell activity in V1 and V4 on visual tasks. Exp. Brain Res., 69(2): 225–244.

Hahnloser, R., Douglas, R.J., Mahowald, M. and Hepp, K. (1999) Feedback interactions between neuronal pointers and maps for attentional processing. Nature Neurosci., 2(8): 716–752.

Hale, P.T., Sefton, A.J., Baur, L.A. and Cottee, L.J. (1982) Interrelations of the rat's thalamic reticular and dorsal lateral geniculate nuclei. Exp. Brain Res., 45(1–2): 217–229.

Harting, J.K., Huerta, M.F., Hashikawa, T. and van Lieshout, D.P. (1991a) Projection of the mammalian superior colliculus upon the dorsal lateral geniculate nucleus: organization of tectogeniculate pathways in nineteen species. J. Comp. Neurol., 304(2): 275–306.

Harting, J.K., van Lieshout, D.P., Hashikawa, T. and Weber, J.T. (1991b) The parabigeminogeniculate projection: connectional studies in 8 mammals. J. Comp. Neurol., 305: 559.

Hendry, S.H.C. and Reid, R.C. (2000) The koniocellular pathway in primate vision. Annu. Rev. Neurosci., 23: 127–153.

Hobson, J.A. and Pace-Schott, E.F. (2002) The cognitive neuroscience of sleep: Neuronal systems, consciousness and learning. Nat. Rev. Neurosci., 3: 679–693.

Horwitz, G.D. and Newsome, W.T. (2001) Target selection for saccadic eye movements: Direction-selective visual responses in the superior colliculus. J. Neurophysiol., 86(5): 2527–2542.

Ichida, J.M. and Casagrande, V.A. (2002) Organization of the feedback pathway from striate cortex (V1) to the lateral geniculate nucleus (LGN) in the owl monkey (Aotus trivirgatus). J. Comp. Neurol., 454(3): 272–283.

Ichida, J., Royal, D.W., Sáry, Gy., Schall, J., & Casagrande, V. (2003) Are there significant onset latency differences between LGN cells that carry S cone signals compared to those that carry M or L cone signals? Soc. Neurosci. (abstract).

Ichinohe, N., Iwatsuki, H. and Shoumura, K. (2001) Intrastriatal targets of projection fibers from the central lateral nucleus of the rat thalamus. Neurosci. Let., 302(2–3): 105–108.

Ignashchenkova, A., Dicke, P.W., Haarmeier, T. and Thier, P. (2004) Neuron-specific contribution of the superior colliculus to overt and covert shifts of attention. Nature Neurosci., 7(1): 56–64.

Irvin, G.E., Casagrande, V.A. and Norton, T.T. (1993) Center/surround relationships of magnocellular, parvocellular, and koniocellular relay cells in primate lateral geniculate nucleus. Visual Neurosci., 10: 363–373.

Izhikevich, E.M., Desai, N.S., Walcott, E.C. and Hoppensteadt, F.C. (2003) Bursts as a unit of neural information: selective communication via resonance. Trends Neurosci., 26: 161–167.

Jeannerod, M. and Putkonen, P.T. (1971) Lateral geniculate unit activity and eye movements: saccade-locked changes in dark and in light. Exp. Brain Res., 13(5): 533–546.

Jones, E.G. (2002) Thalamic circuitry and thalamocortical synchrony. Philos. Trans. R. Soc. Lond. B. Biol. Sci., 357(1428): 1659–1673.

Jones, H.E., Wang, W., Andolina, I.M., Salt, T.E. & Sillito, A.M. (2002) MT feedback effects in the primate LGN. Soc. Neurosci. Abstr., 28: 658.17.

Julesz, B. (1990) Early vision is bottom-up, except for focal attention. Cold Spring Harbor Symposia. Quant. Bio., 55: 973–978.

Kaas, J.H., Guillery, R.W. and Allman, J.M. (1972) Some principles of organization in the dorsal lateral geniculate nucleus. Brain, Behavior & Evolution, 6(1): 253–299.

Kastner, S., O'Connor, D.H., Fukui, M.M., Fehd, H.M., Herwig, U. and Pinsk, M.A. (2004) Functional imaging of the human lateral geniculate nucleus and pulvinar. J. Neurophysiol., 91: 438–448.

Lachica, E.A. and Casagrande, V.A. (1993) The morphology of collicular and retinal axons ending on small relay (W-like) cells of the primate lateral geniculate nucleus. Vis. Neurosci., 10(3): 403–418.

Lal, R. and Friedlander, M.J. (1990a) Effect of passive eye position changes on retinogeniculate transmission in the cat. J. Neurophysiol., 63: 502–522.

Lal, R. and Friedlander, M.J. (1990b) Effect of passive eye movement on retinogeniculate transmission in the cat. J. Neurophysiol., 63: 523–538.

Le Masson, G., Le Masson, S., Debay, D. and Bal, T. (2002) Feedback inhibition controls spike transfer in hybrid thalamic circuits. Nature, 417(20): 854–858.

Lee, D. and Malpeli, J.G. (1998) Effects of saccades on the activity of neurons in the cat lateral geniculate nucleus. J. Neurophysiol., 79: 922–936.

Lin, C.S. and Kaas, J.H. (1977) Projections from cortical visual areas 17, 18, and MT onto the dorsal lateral geniculate nucleus in owl monkeys. J. Comp. Neurol., 173(3): 457–474.

Machinskaia, R.I. (2003) Neurophysiological mechanisms of voluntary attention: a review. Zhurnal Vysshei Nervnoi Deiatelnosti Imeni I. P. Pavlova., 53(2): 133–150.

Martinez-Conde, S., Macknik, S.L. and Hubel, D.H. (2000) Microsaccadic eye movements and firing of single cells in the striate cortex of macaque monkeys. Nat. Neurosci., 3(3): 251–258.

Maunsell, J.H.R., Ghose, M., Assad, J.A., McAdams, C.J., Boudre, C.E. and Noerager, B.D. (1999) Visual response latencies of magnocellular and parvocellular LGN neurons in macaque monkeys. Vis. Neurosci., 16: 1.

McCormick, D.A. and Pape, H.C. (1990) Noradrenergic and serotonergic modulation of a hyperpolarization-activated cation current in thalamic relay neurons. J. Physiol., 431: 319–342.

McCormick, D.A. and Prince, D.A. (1986) Acetylcholine induces burst firing in thalamic reticular neurones by activating a potassium conductance. Nature, 319: 402–405.

Michael, J.A. and Ichinose, L.Y. (1970) Influence of oculomotor activity on visual processing. Brain Res., 22(2): 249–253.

Mohler, C.W. and Wurtz, R.H. (1976) Organization of monkey superior colliculus: intermediate layer cells discharging before eye movements. J. Neurophysiol., 39(4): 722–744.

Molotchnikoff, S. and Casanova, S. (1985) Reactions of the geniculate cells to extraocular proprioceptive activation in rabbits. J. Neurosci. Res., 14: 105–115.

Montero, V.M. (2000) Attentional activation of the visual thalamic reticular nucleus depends on "top-down" inputs from the primary visual cortex via corticogeniculate pathways. Brain Res., 864: 95–104.

Motter, B.C. (1993) Focal attention produces spatially selective processing in visual cortical areas V1, V2, and V4 in the presence of competing stimuli. J. Neurophysiol., 70: 909–919.

Murthy, A., Thompson, K.G. and Schall, J.D. (2001) Dynamic dissociation of visual selection from saccade programming in frontal eye field. J. Neurophysiol., 86(5): 2634–2637.

O'Connor, D.H., Fukui, M.M. and Kastner, S. (2002) Attention modulates responses in the human lateral geniculate nucleus. Nature Neurosci., 5: 1203–1209.

Petersen, S.E., Robinson, D.L. and Morris, J.D. (1987) Contributions of the pulvinar to visual spatial attention. Neuropsychologia., 25(1A): 97–105.

Posner, M.I. and Dehaene, S. (1994) Attentional networks. Trends Neurosci., 17: 75–79.

Przybyszewski, A.W., Gaska, J.P., Foote, W. and Pollen, D.A. (2000) Striate cortex increases contrast gain of macaque LGN neurons. Vis. Neurosci., 17(4): 485–494.

Ramcharan, E.J., Gnadt, J.W. and Sherman, S.M. (2000) Burst and tonic firing in thalamic cells of unanesthetized, behaving monkeys. Vis. Neurosci., 17: 55–62.

Ramcharan, E.J., Gnadt, J.W. and Sherman, S.M. (2001) The effects of saccadic eye movements on the activity of geniculate relay neurons in the monkey. Vis. Neurosci., 18: 253–258.

Reppas, J.B., Usrey, W.M. and Reid, R.C. (2002) Saccadic eye movements modulate visual responses in the lateral geniculate nucleus. Neuron, 35(5): 961–974.

Robinson, D.L., Baizer, J.S. and Dow, B.M. (1980) Behavioral enhancement of visual responses of prestriate neurons of the rhesus monkey. Invest. Ophthalmol., 19: 1120–1123.

Rodieck, R.W. and Stone, J. (1965) Analysis of receptive fields of cat retinal ganglion cells. J. Neurophysiol., 28(5): 833–849.

Rodieck, R.W. and Dreher, B. (1979) Visual suppression from nondominant eye in the lateral geniculate nucleus: a comparison of cat and monkey. Exp. Brain Res., 35(3): 465–477.

Roelfsema, P.R. and Spekreijse, H. (2001) The representation of erroneously perceived stimuli in the primary visual cortex. Neuron, 31(5): 853–863.

Royal, D., Sáry, Gy., Schall, J. and Casagrande, V. (2003) Are spike bursts and pseudo-bursts in the lateral geniculate nucleus (LGN) related to behavioral events? Soc. Neurosci., (Abs.).

Royal, D., Sáry, Gy., Schall, J. and Casagrande, V. (2004) Does the lateral geniculate nucleus (LGN) pay attention? Vision Sci. Soc., (Abs.).

Royal, D., Sáry, Gy., Schall, J. and Casagrande, V. (2005) Correlates of motor planning and postsaccadic fixation in the macaque monkey lateral geniculate nucleus (LGN) (submitted).

Schlag, J. and Schlag-Rey, M. (1985) Unit activity related to spontaneous saccades in frontal dorsomedial cortex of monkey. Exp. Brain Res., 58(1): 208–211.

Schlag, J. and Schlag-Rey, M. (1984) Visuomotor functions of central thalamus in monkey. II. Unit activity related to visual events, targeting, and fixation. J. Neurophysiol., 51(6): 1175–1195.

Schmidt, M. (1996) Neurons in the cat pretectum that project to the dorsal lateral geniculate nucleus are activated during saccades. J. Physiol., 76: 2907–2918.

Schmidt, M., Lehnert, G., Baker, R.G. and Hoffmann, K.P. (1996) Dendritic morphology of projection neurons in the cat pretectum. J. Comp. Neurol., 369(4): 520–532.

Schmolesky, M.T., Wang, Y., Hanes, D.P., Thompson, K.G., Leutgeb, S., Schall, J.D. and Leventhal, A.G. (1998) Signal timing across the macaque visual system. J. Neurophysiol., 79: 3272–3278.

Sherman, S.M. and Guillery, R.W. (1996) Functional organization of thalamocortical relays. J. Neurophysiol., 76(3): 1367–1395.

Sherman, S.M. and Guillery, R.W. (1998) On the actions that one nerve cell can have on another: distinguishing "drivers" from "modulators". Proc. Natl. Acad. Sci., 95: 7121–7126.

Sherman, S.M. and Guillery, R.W. (2001) Exploring the thalamus, Academic, San Diego.

Sherman, S.M. and Guillery, R.W. (2002) The role of thalamus in the flow of information to cortex. Philos. Trans. R. Soc. Lond., 357: 1695–1708.

Sieb, R.A. (1990) A brain mechanism for attention. Med. Hypo., 33(3): 145–153.

Sillito, A.M. and Jones, H.E. (2002) Corticothalamic interactions in the transfer of visual information. Philos. Trans. R. Soc. Lond., 357(1428): 1739–1752.

Sillito, A.M., Jones, H.E., Gerstein, G.L. and West, D.C. (1994) Feature-linked synchronization of thalamic relay cell firing induced by feedback from the visual cortex. Nature, 369: 479–482.

Steriade, M. (1996) Arousal: revisiting the reticular activating system. Science, 272(5259): 225–226.

Sussman, E., Winkler, I. and Schroger, E. (2003) Top-down control over involuntary attention switching in the auditory modality. Psychonom. Bull. & Rev., 10(3): 630–637.

Swadlow, H.A. and Gusev, A.G. (2001) The impact of "bursting" thalamic impulses at a neocortical synapse. Nat. Neurosci., 4(4): 402–408.

Thilo, K.V., Santoro, L., Walsh, V. and Blakemore, C. (2004) The site of saccadic suppression. Nat. Neurosci., 7: 13–14.

Uhlrich, D.J., Manning, K.A. and Xue, J.-T. (2002) Effects of activation of the histaminergic tuberomammillary nucleus on visual responses of neurons in the dorsal lateral geniculate nucleus. J. Neurosci., 22: 1098–1107.

Uhlrich, D.J., Tamamaki, N., Murphy, P.C. and Sherman, S.M. (1995) The effects of brain stem parabrachial activation on receptive field properties of cells in the cat's lateral geniculate nucleus. J. Neurophysiol., 73: 2428–2447.

Vanduffel, W., Payne, B.R., Lomber, S.G. and Orban, G.A. (1997) Functional impact of cerebral connections. Proc. Natl. Acad. Sci. USA., 94: 7617–7620.

Weyand, T.G. and Malpeli, J.G. (1993) Responses of neurons in primary visual cortex are modulated by eye position. J. Neurophysiol., 69(6): 2258–2260.

White, A.J., Solomon, S.G. and Martin, P.R. (2001) Spatial properties of koniocellular cells in the lateral geniculate nucleus of the marmoset Callithrix jacchus. J. Physiol., 533: 519–535.

Wiesel, T.N. and Hubel, D.H. (1966) Spatial and chromatic interactions in the lateral geniculate body of the rhesus monkey. J. Neurophysiol., 29: 1115–1156.

Wilson, J.R., Manning, K.A., Forestner, D.M., Counts, S.E. and Uhlrich, D.J. (1999) Comparison of cholinergic and histaminergic axons in the lateral geniculate complex of the macaque monkey. Anat. Record, 255(3): 295–305.

Wilson, J.R. and Forestner, D.M. (1995) Synaptic Inputs to single neurons in the lateral geniculate nuclei of normal and monocularly deprived squirrel monkeys. J. Comp. Neurol., 362: 468–488.

Wörgötter, F., Eyding, D., Macklis, J.D. and Funke, K. (2002) The influence of the corticothalamic projection on responses in thalamus and cortex. Philos. Trans. R. Soc. Lond. B. Biol. Sci., 357(1428): 1823–1834.

Wurtz, R.H. and Goldberg, M.E. (1972) The primate superior colliculus and the shift of visual attention. Investigative Ophthalmol., 11(6): 441–450.

Wurtz, R.H. and Mohler, C.W. (1976) Enhancement of visual responses in monkey striate cortex and frontal eye fields. J. Neurophysiol., 39(4): 766–772.

Wyder, M.T., Massoglia, D.P. and Stanford, T.R. (2004) Contextual modulation of central thalamic delay-period activity: representation of visual and saccadic goals. J. Neurophysiol., 91(6): 2628–2648.

Xu, X., Bonds, A.B. and Casagrande, V.A. (2002) Modeling receptive-field structure of koniocellular, magnocellular, and parvocellular LGN cells in the owl monkey (Aotus trivigatus). Vis. Neurosci., 19: 703–711.

Zhu, J.J. and Lo, F.S. (1996) Time course of inhibition induced by a putative saccadic suppression circuit in the dorsal lateral geniculate nucleus of the rabbit. Brain Res. Bull., 41: 281–291.

Progress in Brain Research, Vol. 149
ISSN 0079-6123

CHAPTER 3

The vibrissal system as a model of thalamic operations

Martin Deschênes*, Elena Timofeeva, Philippe Lavallée and Caroline Dufresne

CRULRG, Université Laval, Quebec, QC, G1J 2G3, Canada

Abstract: The highly segregated organization of the vibrissal system of rodents offers a unique opportunity to address key issues about thalamic operations in primary sensory and second order thalamic nuclei. In this short review, evidence showing that reticular thalamic neurons and relay cells with receptive fields on the same vibrissa form topographically closed loop connections has been summarized. Within whisker-related thalamic modules, termed barreloids, reticular axons synapse onto the cell bodies and dendrites of residing neurons as well as onto the distal dendrites of neurons that are located in adjacent barreloids. This arrangement provides a substrate for a mechanism of lateral inhibition whereby the spread of dendritic trees among surrounding barreloids determines whisker-specific patterns of lateral inhibition. The relay of sensory inputs in the posterior group, a second order nucleus associated with the vibrissal system is also examined. It is shown that in lightly anesthetized rats posterior group cells are tonically inhibited by GABAergic neurons of the ventral division of zona incerta. These observations suggest that a mechanism of disinhibition controls transmission of sensory signals in the posterior group nucleus. We further propose that disinhibition operates in a top-down manner, via motor instructions sent by cortex to brainstem and spinal cord. In this way posterior group nucleus would forward to the cerebral cortex sensory information that is contingent upon its action.

Introduction

On each side of the rat snout there are five horizontal rows of whiskers which form an orderly array of low-threshold mechanoreceptors. Primary afferents innervating these mechanoreceptors respond to only one vibrissa and, centrally, the arrangement of the whisker pad is maintained in arrays of cellular aggregates referred to as barrelettes (brainstem), barreloids (thalamus) and barrels (cortex) (Woolsey and Van der Loos, 1970; Van der Loos, 1976). Because of this morphologically demonstrable, homologous arrangement of each of its major component

parts, the vibrissal system of rodents has become one of the most valuable models for research in neuroscience. Here we shall briefly review key features of this system, and examine how its highly segregated organization provides a unique opportunity to study structure/function relationships at the thalamic level.

Overview of the vibrissal system

The vibrissal system of rodents comprises two main ascending pathways (Waite, 2003; see Fig. 1): (1) a lemniscal pathway which arises from the principal trigeminal nucleus (PrV), transits through the barreloids of the ventral posterior medial nucleus (VPM) of the thalamus and terminates in the granular zone of the cortical barrel field; (2) a paralemniscal pathway

---

*Corresponding author. Tel.: +1-418-663-5747; Fax: +1-418-663-8756; E-mail: martin.deschenes@crulrg.ulaval.ca

DOI: 10.1016/S0079-6123(05)49003-2

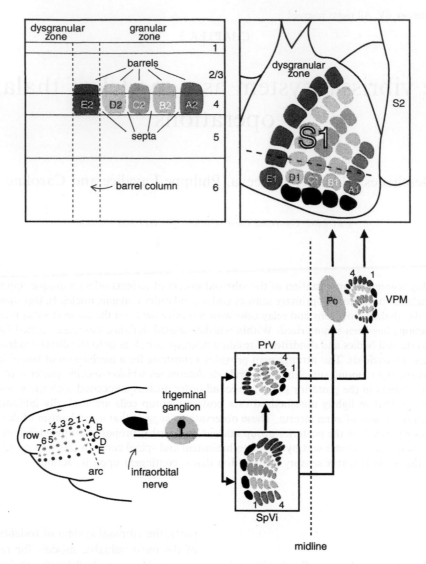

Fig. 1. Schematic organization of the lemniscal and paralemniscal streams of vibrissal information in rodents. The orderly arrangement of whiskers on the rat snout (rows A, B, C, D, E and arcs 1, 2, etc.) is represented centrally by arrays of cellular aggregates in brainstem, thalamus and somatosensory cortex. The upper right hand drawing shows the layout of barrels in a tangential section of the primary somatosensory cortex (S1). In sections cut along the dashed line in this drawing, barrels appear as a series of cytochrome oxidase reactive blobs in layer 4 (upper left hand drawing). See text for a detailed description of pathways. Abbreviation: S2, second somatosensory area.

which arises from the interpolar division of the spinal trigeminal complex (SpVi), transits through the posterior group nucleus (Po), and terminates in the dysgranular zone of the barrel field. In the brainstem, lemniscal and paralemniscal streams of information processing are not totally isolated from each other, in that PrV receives abundant projections from the spinal complex (Jacquin et al., 1990).

Primary vibrissa afferents form ladder-like projection patterns throughout the trigeminal column where they give off several puffs of terminations that are spatially restricted to the homotopic barrelettes (Henderson and Jacquin, 1995). Principalis cells that give rise to the lemniscal pathway have dendrites confined within the limit of their home barrelette, and thus have receptive fields dominated by a single whisker (the principal whisker, PW) (Henderson and Jacquin, 1995; Veinante and Deschênes, 1999). In contrast, interpolaris neurons have dendritic trees that extend across several barrelettes, and they respond vigorously to deflection of several whiskers (Jacquin et al., 1989; Veinante et al., 2000). In lightly anesthetized animals, multiwhisker responses of SpVi neurons are effectively relayed to PrV by internuclear axons, which renders PrV and VPM cells responsive to several adjacent whiskers (Minnery and Simons, 2003; Timofeeva et al., 2004). Lesion studies in which ascending internuclear axons have been severed provided clear evidence that adjacent whisker responses in PrV and VPM rely almost exclusively on projections from the spinal trigeminal complex to PrV (Rhoades et al., 1987; Friedberg et al., 1999; Timofeeva et al., 2004).

The VPM of rodents has a simple organization; it contains a single class of relay neurons with bushy radiating dendrites that are clustered within whisker-related arrays termed barreloids (Barbaresi et al., 1986; Harris, 1986; Ohara and Havton, 1994; Varga et al., 2002). Axons of barreloid cells do not branch locally, but give off collaterals in the reticular thalamic nucleus (RT) as they head towards the barrel cortex (Harris, 1987; Pinault and Deschênes, 1998). Relay cells in barreloids only receive three main types of input: (1) an ascending excitatory input from PrV axons that makes synaptic contacts on thick proximal dendrites (Spacek and Lieberman, 1974; Williams et al., 1994), (2) an excitatory cortico-thalamic input from the barrel field that principally distributes over the distal dendrites (Hoogland et al., 1987; Mineff and Weinberg, 2000), and (3) an inhibitory input from RT cells that distributes throughout the dendritic trees (Ohara and Lieberman, 1993; Varga et al., 2002). At a unitary level these pathways are composed of axons with terminal fields topographically restricted to the barreloid representing the PW of their receptive field (Bourassa et al., 1995; Veinante and Deschênes, 1999; Désîlets-Roy et al., 2002).

The paralemniscal stream of vibrissal information principally arises from large-sized, multiwhisker responsive cells in SpVi (Jacquin et al., 1989; Veinante et al., 2000). These neurons project to Po and several brainstem regions (pontine nuclei, ventral division of zona incerta, perirubral area, superior colliculus, anterior pretectal nucleus) by means of branching axons (Williams et al., 1994; Veinante et al., 2000). The posterior group belongs to the class of second order thalamic nuclei that have reciprocal connections with a number of cortical areas, which include the primary and second somato-sensory areas, the perirhinal and insular regions and the motor cortex (Deschênes et al., 1998). Like most second order thalamic nuclei, Po receives a dual corticothalamic input: one that arises from lamina 6 cells in cortical areas innervated by Po axons, and another one from layer 5 cells that are exclusively located in the granular and dysgranular zones of the barrel field (Veinante et al., 2000). Latter projection consists of collaterals of long-range axons that project to the tectum, zona incerta, and lower brainstem. These collaterals do not supply a branch in RT nor in VPM, but establish large synaptic contacts with the proximal dendrites of Po neurons (Hoogland et al., 1987). The posterior group in rats receives a dual inhibitory input: one from RT neurons, and the other from the ventral division of zona incerta (ZIv). Incertal axons make large terminations with multiple release sites on cell bodies and proximal dendrites (Bartho et al., 2002).

Relay cells in barreloids

In cytochrome oxidase-stained tissue, barreloids appear as darkly reactive, curved, tapering rods that extend through the thickness of the VPM (Land et al., 1995; Haidarliu and Ahissar, 2001). The structure of barreloids can also be revealed by retrograde labeling. Provided that tracer injections are confined within the limit of a single barrel column, the pattern of retrograde labeling in VPM precisely matches the shape and dimension of the barreloids seen in cytochrome oxidase-stained sections (Land et al., 1995; Varga et al., 2002). Figures 2, 3C and 4A show how sharply individual barreloids can be outlined following small iontophoretic injections of Fluoro-Gold in corresponding barrels.

By combining the backfilling of a single barreloid with the juxtacellular labeling of individual VPM neurons it was shown that the dendritic field of relay cells is asymmetric, variously oriented with respect to the geometry of the barreloids, and that all cells

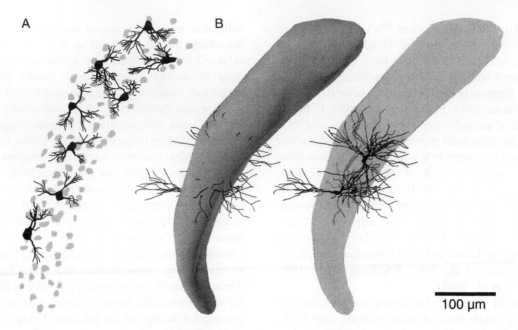

A   B

100 μm

Fig. 2. Relationship between the dendroarchitecture of relay cells and the structure of barreloids. The proximal dendrites of 8 cells responsive to the C1, C2 or D2 whiskers were reconstructed after juxtacellular staining with Neurobiotin. Cells were placed in a "reference" barreloid (here, barreloid C2 outlined in gray tone), according to their actual location and orientation in their respective barreloid. Note that thick dendrites do not cross barreloid boundaries, but that distal dendrites do, as shown in the renderings with and without transparency in B. (Modified from Varga et al., 2002)

extend dendrites outside their home barreloid (Fig. 2). Extrabarreloid dendrites are of small size (< 1.5 μm), and represent up to 54% (range: 11–54%) of the total dendritic length. In contrast, thick proximal dendrites, which receive lemniscal input, remain confined within the home barreloid of the cell being directed towards its center or along its margin (Fig. 2A). Electron microscopic examination of labeled cells showed that extrabarreloid dendrites are exclusively contacted by synaptic terminals of cortical and RT origin, whereas intrabarreloid dendrites also receive contacts from lemniscal terminals (Varga et al., 2002). Thus, for most barreloid cells one can define three functional dendritic domains: (1) a PW afferent domain consisting of proximal and second order intrabarreloid dendrites that receive contacts from PrV axons; (2) a PW recurrent domain made of intrabarreloid dendrites that receive contacts from RT and corticothalamic cells with PW receptive field located on the same vibrissa; and (3) AW recurrent domains consisting of extrabarreloid distal dendrites that receive contacts from RT and corticothalamic cells

with PW receptive field located on adjacent whiskers. These morphofunctional divisions emphasize the whisker-specific ordering of synaptic contacts on VPM relay cells, and provide a framework to study cross-whisker interactions.

Closed and open loop inhibitory circuits in barreloids

Taking advantage of the highly segregated organization of the vibrissal system, it was examined whether RT cells form closed or open loop connections with their thalamic targets (Désîlets-Roy et al., 2002). A thalamic barreloid was retrogradely labeled by injecting Fluoro-Gold in an identified barrel column, and axons of single RT cells with receptive field on the same whisker were anterogradely labeled by juxtacellular application of a biotinylated tracer. These experiments revealed that RT cells exclusively project to the barreloid representing the PW of their receptive field (Fig. 3). Reticular cells either form

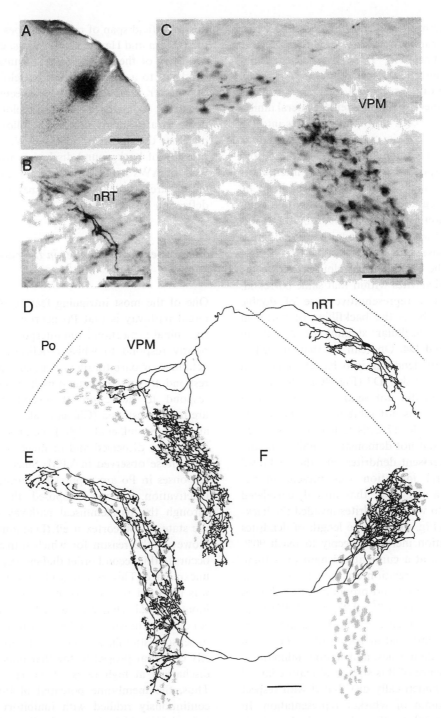

Fig. 3. Terminal fields of RT axons into thalamic barreloids. Relay cells forming the D2 barreloid were backfilled following a Fluoro-Gold injection into the D2 barrel column (A), and a RT cell that responded to deflection of the same vibrissa was juxtacellularly stained with biotinylated dextran (B). Note the precise overlap of axonal terminations with the array of labeled somata (C). Terminal fields either distribute in different segments (D, F) or across the whole extent of a barreloid (E). Scale bars: 500 μm in A; 100 μm in B–D. (Modified from Désilets-Roy et al., 2002).

small compact terminal fields in the dorsalmost part of a barreloid, or more extensive fields filling a large expanse of the barreloid. Thus, from a strict anatomical viewpoint, a RT cell should exert both, recurrent inhibition on cells that relay input from its PW, and simultaneously impose remote lateral inhibition onto the relay cells that send dendrites into the activated barreloid. This proposal was tested in a preparation in which thalamic cells were rendered monowhisker responsive by lesion of the interpolaris nucleus. Again, single barreloids were outlined by retrograde labeling and individual cells within adjacent barreloids were stained with Neurobiotin. It was further examined whether the magnitude of inhibition produced in those cells by deflecting the vibrissa represented in the backfilled barreloid related to the spread of their dendrites within that same barreloid. Figure 4 shows a representative case of double labeling that combines the backfilling of barreloid D3 with the juxtacellular staining of 2 cells in barreloids D2 and D4. One can see that the cell in barreloid D4 sent dendrites into barreloid D3 and was inhibited by whisker D3 (Fig. 4C), whereas the D2-responsive cell did not send any dendrite into barreloid D3 and was not inhibited by whisker D3 (Fig. 4D). Among the 17 cells tested and recovered after staining, 5 did not demonstrate inhibition, and none of the latter sent dendrites into the backfilled barreloid. Lateral inhibition was present in the other cells with a magnitude that strongly correlated with the extent to which dendrites invaded the backfilled barreloid (Fig. 4E). As the length of dendrites increases, inhibition increases steeply to reach 90% spike suppression at a cumulated length of ~ 1 mm. An almost perfect correlation was found between the magnitude of inhibition and proximity of cell bodies to the labeled barreloid ($R^2 = 0.97$; $p < 0.0001$) (Fig. 4F). As distance between cell bodies and the border of the backfilled barreloid increases, dendritic length in that barreloid diminishes, and so does inhibition.

As a consequence of this structural feature lateral inhibition is asymmetrically distributed with respect to row and column of whisker representation. In sections cut normal to their long axis barreloids appear as an array of rectangular blobs with center-to-center spacing of ~ 100 μm along rows, and of ~ 200 μm along arcs of whisker representation (Land et al., 1995; Haidarliu and Ahissar, 2001). Since the

dendritic field span of relay cells does not exceed 250 μm (Ohara and Havton, 1991; Varga et al., 2002), the geometry of the barreloids thus limits the spread of dendrites to a single adjacent barreloid along an arc of whisker representation. In agreement with these geometric constraints most barreloid cells fail to demonstrate lateral inhibition following deflection of either the dorsal or ventral AW. Significant suppression of background discharges was produced by 92% of AWs within rows ($n = 59$), by 48% of AWs within arcs ($n = 58$), and was never observed after deflection of non-AWs ($n = 31$).

Whisker-evoked responses in the paralemniscal pathway

One of the most intriguing feature of the paralemniscal pathway is that Po neurons receive a robust trigeminal projection from interpolaris cells, but they poorly respond to whisker deflection. Under light ketamine or barbiturate anesthesia, they often fail to respond to any somatic stimuli, whereas they best respond to deflection of several whiskers under urethane anesthesia (Chiaia et al., 1991; Diamond et al., 1992; Sosnik et al., 2001). Yet, responses are more temporally dispersed and of much lower magnitude than those observed in VPM. Since whisker-evoked responses in Po are suppressed during barrel cortex inactivation, it was proposed that transmission through the paralemniscal pathway depends upon the state of the cortex itself (Diamond et al., 1992). However, the reason for which transmission failure occurs in this second order thalamic nucleus remained unexplained. This issue was addressed recently after it was reported that Po receives a strong GABAergic input from ZIv (Bartho et al., 2002). Under anesthetic conditions known to render Po neurons unresponsive to sensory stimuli, we found that whisker-responsive ZIv cells that project to the thalamus spontaneously discharged at high rates (20–60 Hz) (Figs. 5B, C). Thus, the membrane potential of Po neurons was continuously riddled with inhibitory post-synaptic potentials, which prevented vibrissal inputs from reaching spike threshold (Fig. 5D). Together these results suggest that a mechanism of disinhibition controls transmission of sensory signals in this second order thalamic nucleus. Inhibitory cells that

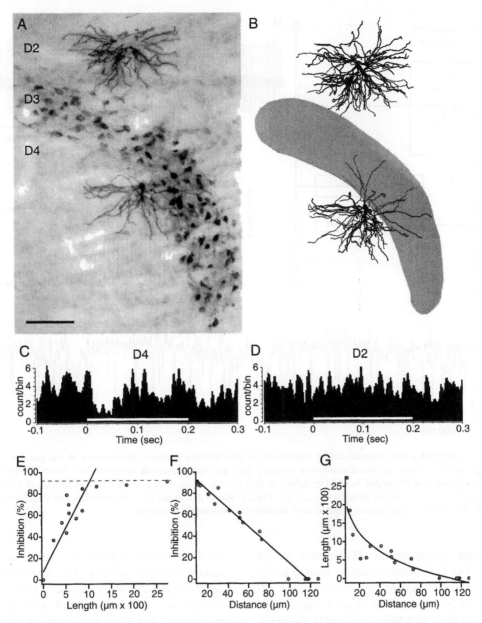

Fig. 4. Relationship between dendroarchitecture and lateral inhibition in the barreloids. In the histological material (A) barreloid D3 was backfilled by Fluoro-Gold injection in barrel D3, and two cells, located in barreloids D2 and D4 respectively, were labeled juxtacellularly after assessing the magnitude of spike suppression produced by whisker D3 deflection. Barreloid and cell reconstructions are shown in B. The D4-responsive cell sent dendrites within barreloid D3 and was inhibited by whisker D3 (peristimulus histogram in C), whereas the D2-responsive cell did not send any dendrite within barreloid D3 and was not inhibited (peristimulus histogram in D). Scale bar in A, 100 μm. Graph E shows how the magnitude of AW-evoked inhibition relates to the total length of dendritic segments in the corresponding barreloid. Data points are best fitted by linear regression with $R^2 = 0.86$; $p < 0.0001$. Note that data point at 0,0 represents 5 cells. The dashed line indicates the average degree of inhibition produced by PW deflection (e.g., 92%). Graph F shows that the magnitude of inhibition produced by an AW is linearly related to the distance that separates cell bodies from the border of the corresponding barreloid ($R^2 = 0.97$; $p < 0.0001$). Graph G shows how the length of extrabarreloid dendrites in an adjacent barreloid decreases with distance that separates cell bodies from the border of that barreloid ($R^2 = 0.82$; $p < 0.0001$). (Modified from Lavallée and Deschênes, 2004).

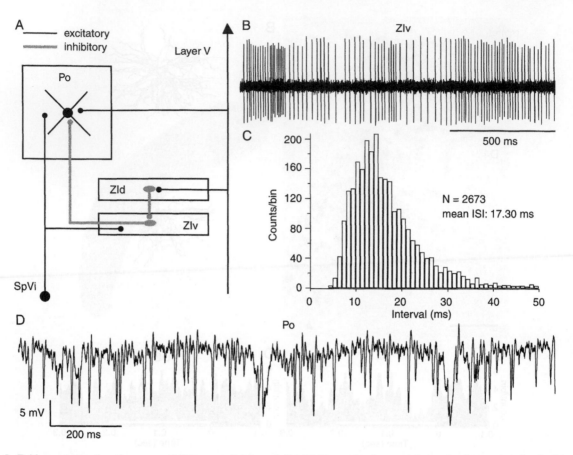

Fig. 5. Evidence supporting the proposal that a mechanism of disinhibition controls transmission in the paralemniscal pathway. Wiring diagram in A summarizes the disinhibitory circuitry (see text for additional information). Trace B shows spontaneous discharges of a ZIv cell that responded to whisker deflection (not shown). Histogram C shows the distribution of interspike intervals (ISI) compiled over a 1-min period of spontaneous activity. Trace D shows that under the same experimental conditions the membrane potential of Po neurons was continuously riddled with inhibitory postsynaptic potentials.

could suppress discharges in ZIv remain as yet unidentified, but GABAergic neurons located in the dorsal division of ZI might be involved. Since ZI receives abundant input from layer 5 corticofugal neurons (Mitrofanis and Mikuletic, 1999), disinhibition might operate in a top-down manner (see schema in Fig. 5A). Top-down disinhibition would allow sensory inputs that are time related to motor control of whisking (but not to whisking per se) to be relayed in a parallel manner to the cerebral cortex. Thus, the disinhibitory hypothesis invites us to consider the role of Po from a central viewpoint, which is in line with the psychophysical and behavioral evidence that perception is an active process intimately linked to the motor activities of the animal. For the moment,

the disinhibitory hypothesis needs additional experimental support, and it is not clear whether it could also be applied to other second order nuclei in rats or in other species. In this regard, however, it is worth mentioning that ZIv was also shown to project to the lateral dorsal and lateral posterior nuclei in rats, two second order nuclei that are associated with the visual system (Power et al., 1999).

Abbreviations

AW	adjacent whisker
Po	posterior group nucleus
PrV	principal trigeminal nucleus

PW	principal whisker
VPM	ventral posterior medial nucleus
RT	reticular thalamic nucleus
SpVi	interpolar division of the spinal trigeminal complex
S1	primary somatosensory area
S2	second somatosensory area
ZI	zona incerta
ZIv	ventral division of zona incerta

Acknowledgments

This work was supported by Canadian Institutes for Health Research Grant MT-5877 to M.D. and a Fonds de la recherche en santé du Québec doctoral fellowship to P.L.

References

Barbaresi, P., Spreafico, R., Frassoni, C. and Rustioni, A. (1986) GABAergic neurons are present in the dorsal column nuclei but not in the ventroposterior complex of rats. Brain Res., 382: 305–326.

Bartho, P., Freund, T.F. and Acsady, L. (2002) Selective GABAergic innervation of thalamic nuclei from zona incerta. Eur. J. Neurosci., 16: 999–1014.

Bourassa, J., Pinault, D. and Deschênes, M. (1995) Cortico-thalamic projections from the cortical barrel field in rats: a single fiber study using biocytin as an anterograde tracer. Eur. J. Neurosci., 7: 19–30.

Chiaia, N.L., Rhoades, R.W., Bennett Clarke, C.A., Fish, S.E. and Killackey, H.P. (1991) Thalamic processing of vibrissal information in the rat I. Afferent input to the medial ventral posterior and posterior nuclei. J. Comp. Neurol., 314: 201–216.

Deschênes, M., Veinante, P. and Zhang, Z-W. (1998) The organization of corticothalamic projections: reciprocity versus parity. Brain Res. Rev., 28: 286–308.

Désîlets-Roy, B., Varga, C., Lavallée, P. and Deschênes, M. (2002) Substrate for cross-talk inhibition between thalamic barreloids. J. Neurosci., 22: RC218.

Diamond, M.E., Armstrong-James, M. and Ebner, F.F. (1992) Somatic sensory responses in the rostral sector of the posterior group (POm) and in the ventral posterior medial nucleus (VPM) of the rat thalamus. J. Comp. Neurol., 318: 462–476.

Friedberg, M.H., Lee, S.M. and Ebner, F.F. (1999) Modulation of receptive field properties of thalamic somatosensory neurons by the depth of anesthesia. J. Neurophysiol., 81: 2243–2252.

Haidarliu, S. and Ahissar, E. (2001) Size gradients of barreloids in the rat thalamus. J. Comp. Neurol., 429: 372–387.

Harris, R.M. (1986) Morphology of physiologically identified thalamocortical relay neurons in the rat ventrobasal thalamus. J. Comp. Neurol., 251: 491–505.

Harris, R.M. (1987) Axon collaterals in the thalamic reticular nucleus from thalamocortical neurons of the rat ventrobasal thalamus. J. Comp. Neurol., 258: 397–406.

Henderson, T.A. and Jacquin, M.F. (1995) What makes subcortical barrels. In: Jones, E.G. and Diamond, I.T., (Eds.), Cerebral Cortex, the Barrel Cortex of Rodents, Vol. 12, Plenum, New York, pp. 123–187.

Hoogland, P.V., Welker, E. and Vander Loos, H. (1987) Organization of the projections from barrel cortex to thalamus in mice studied with Phaseolus vulgaris leuco-agglutinin and HRP. Exp. Brain Res., 68: 73–87.

Jacquin, M.F., Barcia, M. and Rhoades, R.W. (1989) Structure-function relationships in rat brainstem subnucleus interpolaris: IV Projection neurons. J. Comp. Neurol., 282: 45–62.

Jacquin, M.F., Chiaia, N.L., Haring, J.H. and Rhoades, R.W. (1990) Intersubnuclear connections within the rat trigeminal brainstem complex. Somatosens. Mot. Res., 7: 399–420.

Land, P.W., Buffer, S.A. and Yaskosky, J.D. (1995) Barreloids in adult rat thalamus: three-dimensional architecture and relationship to somatosensory cortical barrels. J. Comp. Neurol., 355: 573–588.

Lavallée, P. and Deschênes, M. (2004) Dendroarchitecture and lateral inhibition in thalamic barreloids. J. Neurosci., 24: 6098–6105.

Mineff, E.M. and Weinberg, R.J. (2000) Differential synaptic distribution of AMPA receptor subunits in the ventral posterior and reticular thalamic nuclei of the rat. Neuroscience, 101: 969–982.

Minnery, B.S. and Simons, D.J. (2003) Response properties of whisker-associated trigeminothalamic neurons in rat nucleus principalis. J. Neurophysiol., 89: 40–56.

Mitrofanis, J. and Mikuletic, L. (1999) Organisation of the cortical projection to the zona incerta of the thalamus. J. Comp. Neurol., 412: 173–185.

Ohara, P.T. and Havton, L.A. (1994) Dendritic architecture of rat somatosensory thalamocortical projection neurons. J. Comp. Neurol., 341: 159–171.

Ohara, P.T. and Lieberman, A.R. (1993) Some aspects of the synaptic circuitry underlying inhibition in the ventrobasal thalamus. J. Neurocytol., 9: 815–825.

Pierret, T., Lavallée, P. and Deschênes, M. (2000) Parallel streams for the relay of vibrissal information through thalamic barreloids. J. Neurosci., 20: 7455–7462.

Power, B.D., Kolmac, C.I. and Mitrofanis, J. (1999) Evidence for a large projection from the zona incerta to the dorsal thalamus. J. Comp. Neurol. 404: 554–565.

Pinault, D. and Deschênes, M. (1998) Anatomical evidence for a mechanism of lateral inhibition in the rat thalamus. Eur. J. Neurosci., 10: 3462–3469.

Rhoades, R.W., Belford, G.R. and Killackey, H.P. (1987) Receptive field properties of rat VPM neurons before and after selective kainic acid lesions of the trigeminal brainstem complex. J. Neurophysiol., 57: 1577–1600.

Sosnik, R., Haidarliu, S. and Ahissar, E. (2001) Temporal frequency of whisker movement I. Representations in brain stem and thalamus. J. Neurophysiol., 86: 339–353.

Spacek, J. and Lieberman, A.R. (1974) Ultrastructure and three-dimensional organization of synaptic glomeruli in rat somatosensory thalamus. J. Anat., 117: 487–516.

Timofeeva, E., Lavallée, P., Arsenault, D. and Deschênes, M. (2004) The synthesis of multi-whisker receptive fields in subcortical stations of the vibrissa system. J. Neurophysiol., 91: 1510–1515.

Van der Loos, H. (1976) Barreloids in the mouse somatosensory thalamus. Neurosci. Lett., 2: 1–6.

Varga, C., Sik, A., Lavallée, P. and Deschênes, M. (2002) Dendroarchitecture of relay cells in thalamic barreloids: a substrate for cross-whisker modulation. J. Neurosci., 22: 6186–6194.

Veinante, P. and Deschênes, M. (1999) Single- and multi-whisker channels in the ascending projections from the principal trigeminal nucleus in the rat. J. Neurosci., 19: 5085–5095.

Veinante, P., Jacquin, M.F. and Deschênes, M. (2000) Thalamic projections from the whisker-sensitive regions of the spinal trigeminal complex in the rat. J. Comp. Neurol., 420: 233–243.

Veinante, P., Lavallée, P. and Deschênes, M. (2000) Corticothalamic projections from layer 5 of the vibrissal barrel cortex in the rat. J Comp Neurol., 424: 197–204.

Waite, P.M.E. (2003) Trigeminal sensory system. In: Paxinos, G. (Ed.), The rat nervous system, Elsevier Academic Press, San Diego, pp. 797–851.

Williams, M.N., Zahm, D.S. and Jacquin, M.F. (1994) Differential foci and synaptic organization of the principal and spinal trigeminal projections to the thalamus in the rat. Eur. J. Neurosci., 6: 429–453.

Woolsey, T.A. and Van der Loos, H. (1970) The structural organization of layer IV in the somatosensory region (S1) of mouse cerebral cortex: the description of a cortical field composed of discrete cytoarchitectonic units. Brain Res., 17: 205–242.

Progress in Brain Research, Vol. 149
ISSN 0079-6123

CHAPTER 4

Connexon connexions in the thalamocortical system

Scott J. Cruikshank, Carole E. Landisman, Jaime G. Mancilla
and Barry W. Connors*

*Department of Neuroscience, Division of Biology & Medicine,
Brown University, Providence, RI 02912, USA*

Abstract: Electrical synapses are composed of gap junction channels that interconnect neurons. They occur throughout the mammalian brain, although this has been appreciated only recently. Gap junction channels, which are made of proteins called connexins, allow ionic current and small organic molecules to pass directly between cells, usually with symmetrical ease. Here we review evidence that electrical synapses are a major feature of the inhibitory circuitry in the thalamocortical system.

In the neocortex, pairs of neighboring inhibitory interneurons are often electrically coupled, and these electrical connections are remarkably specific. To date, there is evidence that five distinct subtypes of inhibitory interneurons in the cortex make electrical interconnections selectively with interneurons of the same subtype. Excitatory neurons (i.e., pyramidal and spiny stellate cells) of the mature cortex do not appear to make electrical synapses. Within the thalamus, electrical coupling is observed in the reticular nucleus, which is composed entirely of GABAergic neurons. Some pairs of inhibitory neurons in the cortex and reticular thalamus have mixed synaptic connections: chemical (GABAergic) inhibitory synapses operating in parallel with electrical synapses. Inhibitory neurons of the thalamus and cortex express the gap junction protein connexin36 (C×36), and knocking out its gene abolishes nearly all of their electrical synapses.

The electrical synapses of the thalamocortical system are strong enough to mediate robust interactions between inhibitory neurons. When pairs or groups of electrically coupled cells are excited by synaptic input, receptor agonists, or injected current, they typically display strong synchrony of both subthreshold voltage fluctuations and spikes. For example, activating metabotropic glutamate receptors on coupled pairs of cortical interneurons or on thalamic reticular neurons can induce rhythmic action potentials that are synchronized with millisecond precision.

Electrical synapses offer a uniquely fast, bidirectional mechanism for coordinating local neural activity. Their widespread distribution in the thalamocortical system suggests that they serve myriad functions. We are far from a complete understanding of those functions, but recent experiments suggest that electrical synapses help to coordinate the temporal and spatial features of various forms of neural activity.

Introduction

The most familiar neuronal signaling mechanism is the neurotransmitter-dependent chemical synapse.

*Corresponding author. Tel.: +1-401-863-2982; Fax: +1-401-863-7688; E-mail: BWC@brown.edu

Electrical synapses, which are composed of neuronal gap junctions, offer a very different type of signaling that is faster, bidirectional, and simpler in both structure and function (synonyms for electrical synapses include "electrotonic synapses" and "electrical coupling"; for review see Bennett, 1977, 1997; Connors and Long, 2004). Although there are forms of electrical communication between neurons that do not

DOI: 10.1016/S0079-6123(05)49004-4

42

involve gap junctions, such as "ephaptic" interactions (Jefferys, 1995), they are not included in this study.

The idea that neurons communicate through direct electrical connections (Cowan and Kandel, 2001) predates the discovery of electrical synapses in crayfish and shrimp by almost a century (Furshpan and Potter, 1957; Watanabe, 1958). Vertebrate electrical synapses were observed soon after in the brainstem of fish (Bennett et al., 1959), but they proved much harder to demonstrate in mammalian brains. The most convincing way to detect electrical coupling is to record intracellularly and simultaneously from two connected cells, which is exceptionally difficult to do in the intact mammalian brain. The first mammalian evidence — obtained from certain brainstem nuclei in vivo — was necessarily indirect (e.g., Baker and Llinás, 1971; Korn et al., 1973; Wylie, 1973).

Improved microelectrode methods, in vitro slice preparations, and molecular genetic technologies cracked the practical barriers to the study of mammalian electrical synapses. The presence of electrical synapses is now clearly established in the inferior olivary nucleus, locus coeruleus, striatum, cerebellar cortex, pre-Botzinger complex, hippocampus, retina, suprachiasmatic nucleus, olfactory bulb (Connors and Long, 2004), as well as the thalamocortical system. Judging from the distribution of connexin36 (Cx36), the neuronal protein most responsible for electrical synapses, it seems likely that they occur in every major region of the central nervous system (Condorelli et al., 2000; Degen et al., 2004). Considering their speed, simplicity, and reciprocity, this should probably come as no surprise.

In this review the presence, properties, and potential functions of the electrical synapses that interconnect many inhibitory neurons of the thalamus and the neocortex have been analyzed. Figure 1 shows a basic circuit diagram of the electrical (and chemical) synaptic connections in the thalamocortical system, based on the present study results (see also Amitai et al., 2002; Gibson and Connors, 2003; Beierlein et al., 2003).

Electrical synapses in the neocortex

The neocortex is the largest part of the mammalian brain, and it is essential for normal perception, motor

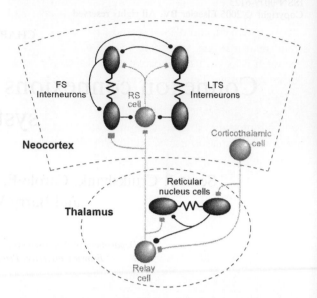

Fig. 1. Electrical synapses in the somatosensory thalamocortical system. Major connections via electrical synapses (zigzags) and chemical synapses (inhibitory: dots, excitatory: squares); the central neuron in the cortex is a spiny stellate, regular-spiking cell (RS cell), which is excitatory, as is the corticothalamic cell; FS and LTS cells are inhibitory interneurons. In thalamus, relay cells are excitatory, whereas cells of the reticular nucleus are inhibitory. Cortical circuit represents layer 4 only.

control, cognition, and many forms of memory. Neocortex carries out some of the most complex neural functions anywhere in nature. Electrical synapses appear to be an important component of its complicated circuitry.

In 1972 John Sloper published a short paper describing electron microscopic observations of gap junctions between neurons of the mature monkey sensorimotor cortex. He followed this in 1978 with a more complete description, coauthored with Thomas Powell, that included many dramatic micrographs of dendrodendritic and dendrosomatic gap junctions interconnecting cells that had the telltale characteristics of inhibitory interneurons. These papers described the first compelling evidence for electrical synapses in the mammalian forebrain, yet they apparently passed with little notice at the time. They accurately predicted much of our current state of understanding about electrical synapses in the neocortex yet, surprisingly, over the ensuing decades each paper has been cited fewer than 100 times.

43

A key conclusion of Sloper and Powell (1978) was that neuronal gap junctions occur predominantly between cells with the morphological characteristics of interneurons. This has recently been substantiated by the work of Fukuda and Kosaka (2003), who observed dendrodendritic gap junctions between parvalbumin-immunolabeled inhibitory interneurons of primary somatosensory, auditory, and visual areas in mature rats.

Gap junctions are morphological entities, and the presence of neuronal gap junctions alone can provide only indirect evidence for functional electrical synapses. Direct electrophysiological recordings are required for a definitive functional demonstration. In recent years, such recording studies have been conducted (Fig. 2), confirming that electrical synapses are localized largely to inhibitory interneurons, and that these synapses are strong enough to influence cortical function. The first of these studies were published by Galarreta and Hestrin (1999) and Gibson et al. (1999). Several general properties of interneuron coupling were immediately apparent, and were subsequently confirmed and extended:

(1) Electrical synapses are very common among closely neighboring pairs of inhibitory

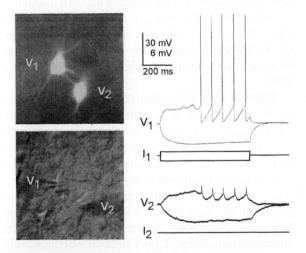

Fig. 2. Electrically coupled FS inhibitory interneurons in neocortex. GFP-expressing interneurons from neocortical slice in vitro viewed under fluorescence (top left) and infrared-differential interference contrast optics (bottom left). Paired whole-cell recordings from the same interneurons showing electrical coupling (right). (Mancilla, Cruikshank, Huang and Connors, unpublished.)

interneurons (from 60% to as high as 90% in some samples). On the other hand, there are very few reports of electrical coupling among cell pairs that include excitatory neurons (Venance et al., 2000; also discussed on pages 44–46).

(2) Electrical synapses are cell-type specific; interneurons of a particular subtype tend to be coupled only to cells of the same subtype, and mixed interneuron types are coupled only about 5% of the time (Gibson et al., 1999, 2004).

(3) Electrical coupling is relatively strong. On average, the "coupling coefficient" for slow events is nearly 0.1, and can reach as high as 0.4 (coupling coefficient defined here as: the voltage deflection in cell B divided by the voltage deflection in cell A, when the two cells are electrically coupled, and the voltage deflection is initiated in A); the mean cell–cell coupling conductance is about 1.6 nS, with a maximum up to 5.5 nS.

(4) The average strength of coupling is more than enough to allow neighboring neurons to synchronize their spiking patterns with high precision (about ±1 ms; see pages 50–51 and Figs 4 and 7), and to deliver signals about as strong as chemical EPSPs.

(5) Some pairs of inhibitory interneurons are connected by both electrical *and* inhibitory (i.e., chemical) synapses.

(6) Electrical coupling has been observed in several areas of neocortex, among interneurons in all cortical layers (Gibson et al., 1999; Blatow et al., 2003; Chu et al., 2003), and in fully mature animals (Galarreta and Hestrin, 2002).

A lot of information about the anatomical/spatial properties of electrical coupling between cortical interneurons is available today (Gibson et al., 1999, 2004; Amitai et al., 2002; Long et al., 2004). Coupling is strongest and most prevalent between cells <50 μm apart, and essentially absent at distances >200 μm. The distance-dependence function and measures of interneuron density imply that each interneuron is directly coupled to about 20–50 other interneurons. This information, combined with average unitary conductances and input resistances, allows us to estimate that the net conductance through all the electrical synapses of an interneuron contribute approximately half of the total resting membrane conductance (Amitai et al., 2002). In other words, networks of interneurons are very densely coupled and this is likely to have a powerful influence on cortical processing.

The neocortex has a variety of distinct types of GABAergic interneurons (Monyer and Markram, 2004). Remarkably, inhibitory interneurons seem to make electrical synapses only with cells of similar type. Our laboratory has studied electrical synapses amongst two interneuron types in particular. The most commonly encountered type is the "fast-spiking" (FS) cell, which generates exceptionally brief action potentials that can fire at unusually high rates without adaptation (McCormick et al., 1985). Most neighboring pairs of FS cells are electrically coupled to each other (Figs. 1–3; Gibson et al., 1999; Galarreta and Hestrin, 1999). Another major type of inhibitory interneuron, characterized in both rats (Gibson et al., 1999) and mice (Deans et al., 2001), expresses the neuroactive peptide somatostatin, generates broader spikes with adapting patterns, and is often called the "low threshold-cspiking" (LTS) cell (Kawaguchi and Kubota, 1997). LTS cells are also usually coupled to each other electrically. Pairs of FS and LTS cells are coupled to one another only very occasionally, and such connections are usually weak (Gibson et al., 1999, 2004). In addition, Blatow et al. (2003) described a type of interneuron they named the "multipolar bursting" (MB) cell, which was coupled to cells of the same type but not to FS cells. Chu et al. (2003) characterized a "late-spiking" (LS) type of inhibitory interneuron in layer I of the neocortex that made electrical synapses to other LS cells 83% of the time, but coupled to non-LS interneurons only 2% of the time. Most recently, Galarreta et al. (2004) showed that a fifth type of interneuron — an irregularly spiking, cannabinoid-expressing cell of the upper cortical layers — is also selectively electrically coupled. Thus, the evidence to date is consistent with the hypothesis that, with rare exceptions, neuronal gap junctions in neocortex interconnect inhibitory interneurons of the same type (Fig. 3).

So far, independent evidence for morphological gap junctions and functional electrical synapses have been discussed. However, the electrical synapses

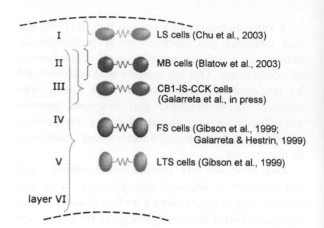

Fig. 3. Five subtypes of inhibitory interneurons in neocortex, each with cell type-specific electrical synapses. Late-spiking cells (LS), multipolar bursting cells (MB), cannabinoid-sensitive, irregularly spiking cells (CB1-IS), fast-spiking (FS), low threshold-spiking cells (LTS).

characterized biophysically in interneurons are almost certainly mediated by gap junctions. Tamás and colleagues have elegantly combined biophysical and ultrastructural methods to definitively demonstrate that electrically coupled FS interneurons (Tamás et al., 2000), as well as electrically coupled non-FS interneurons (so called "regular-spiking non-pyramidal cells" (Szabadics et al., 2001), actually do form dendrodendritic gap junctions. In addition, when the critical neuronal gap junction protein C×36 is knocked out, nearly all electrical synapses between interneurons are abolished (Deans et al., 2001).

There is very little compelling evidence that the excitatory neurons (i.e., pyramidal cells or spiny stellate cells) of the mature neocortex are electrically coupled. Decades of detailed ultrastructural investigations of neocortex have yielded very few convincing micrographs of gap junctions connecting excitatory cells. The only compelling example available was published by Alan Peters in 1980, in a chapter of Advanced Neurology about the mechanisms of anticonvulsant drugs. Direct tests of electrical coupling between pairs of excitatory cells, or pairs of excitatory and inhibitory cells, in neocortex have yielded generally negative results (Thomson and Deuchars, 1997; Galarreta and Hestrin, 1999; Gibson et al., 1999). There is at least one report of C×36 mRNA in pyramidal cells, and very occasional electrical coupling between interneuron–pyramidal cell pairs in immature cortex (Venance et al., 2000; Meyer et al., 2002), but this has not been observed by others (Galarreta and Hestrin, 1999; Gibson et al., 1999). Gutnick and Prince (1981) reported dye-coupling between mature pyramidal neurons, but subsequent studies found that pyramidal cell dye-coupling was prominent during the first post-natal week and very low thereafter (Connors et al., 1983; Peinado et al., 1993; Roerig et al., 1995; Bittman et al., 1997). It is important to note that dye-coupling, particularly when applied to brain slices using sharp microelectrodes, may not be a very reliable measure of gap junctional coupling among some types of neurons (Knowles et al., 1982; Connors et al., 1984; Gutnick et al., 1985).

Electrical synapses in the thalamic reticular nucleus

The thalamic reticular nucleus (TRN) is a sheet of GABAergic neurons that surround the thalamic relay nuclei (Guillery and Harting, 2003). TRN cells receive excitatory input from both thalamocortical and corticothalamic axons, and send their projections, which are entirely inhibitory, to thalamic relay cells (Figs. 1 and 4). Thus, the TRN is in a position to influence, and be influenced by, the entire thalamo-cortical system. Consistent with this, the TRN has been implicated in processes as diverse as sensory transformations, generation of sleep-related EEG rhythms, and behavioral attention (Guillery et al., 1998; Pinault, 2004). It had long been assumed that TRN neurons interact with one another exclusively via inhibitory synapses (Ohara, 1988), but our work shows that this is far from true. Using paired recordings from neighboring TRN cells in rats and mice, we found that electrical coupling is common (Landisman et al., 2002; Long et al., 2004). The prevalence, strength, biophysical properties, and C×36-dependence of electrical connections in TRN are very similar to those in the neocortex.

Electrical coupling in TRN may differ from neocortex in its spatial dimensions; TRN cells apparently form much more compact coupled clusters than cortical interneurons (Long et al., 2004). Electrical coupling in TRN seems to be restricted to cells no more than 40 µm apart. In this sense, coupling in

TRN resembles the spatially localized coupling in the inferior olivary nucleus (Devor and Yarom, 2002). Surprisingly, in paired-cell recordings from TRN in vitro, monosynaptic IPSPs were extremely rare (~1 in 100 pairs for closely juxtaposed neurons; Landisman, unpublished).

As in the cortex, electrical synapses can effectively coordinate both the action potentials and slow sub-threshold rhythms of local groups of TRN neurons (Fig. 4B–D; see pages 50–51).

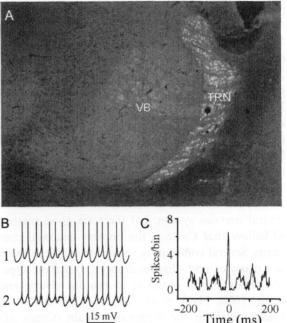

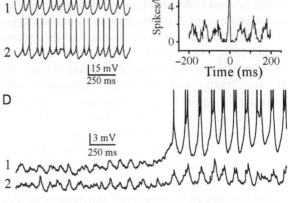

Fig. 4. Electrical synapses in the TRN. A. A fluorescent image of a thalamic slice in which the cresent-shaped TRN is outlined by the presence of GFP-expressing cells (B13 line, Cruikshank, Connors and Huang, unpublished observations). Barreloids in the VB can also be visualized by the clustering of GFP-positive axon terminals (originating from TRN cells). B–D. Activation of mGluRs excites TRN neurons, and induces close synchrony of both action potentials (B–C) and subthreshold membrane fluctuations (D) mediated by electrical synapses. (From Long et al., 2004.)

Electrical synapses in the thalamocortical system require C×36

Gap junctions are structurally distinct, electron-dense, intercellular connections that bridge the narrow gap of extracellular fluid (about 2–3 nm thick) separating the membranes of two cells. Gap junctions are composed of clusters of transcellular channels. Each channel is created by the union of two hemichannels, one from each cell. Each of these hemi-channels, also known as "connexons', is each made of six connexin subunits. Gap junction channels are permeable to all biologically interesting inorganic ions, and also to some small organic molecules. There are about 20 connexin isoforms distributed over nearly all tissues in the body (Willecke et al., 2002). The most common nomenclature uses their predicted molecular weights (e.g., C×36 is about 36 kDa). Most cells can express multiple connexins, and connexons can be homomeric or heteromeric. Only some combinations of connexons can form functional heterotypic channels; current evidence is that C×36 channels only function homotypically (Al-Ubaidi et al., 2000; Teubner et al., 2000).

About half of the connexins are abundant in the central nervous system, but there are good reasons to believe that C×36 is the primary neuronal con-nexin. Several connexin types are strongly expressed in astrocytes and oligodendrocytes, but these types are almost never observed in neurons (Nagy and Rash, 2000; Nagy et al., 2001). C×36 mRNA is found widely in the mammalian brain (Condorelli et al., 2000), and C×36-like immunoreactivity consistently appears in neuron–neuron gap junc-tions but not gap junctions between glia (Rash et al., 2001). Single-cell RT-PCR shows that C×36 message is often present in interneurons of hippo-campus and neocortex (Venance et al., 2000), and a histochemical reporter enzyme driven by the C×36 promoter labeled a variety of intererneurons that included both parvalbumin- and somatostatin-expressing cells (Deans et al., 2001).

The most telling evidence that C×36 forms most electrical synapses comes from work on knockout mice. It has been found that electrical coupling between interneurons of two types in the neocortex (Deans et al., 2001), and between neurons in the

TRN (Landisman et al., 2002), inferior olive (Long et al., 2002), and suprachiasmatic n. (Long et al., 2005) is virtually abolished in C×36 knockout mice. In addition, electrical coupling between MB interneurons of neocortex (Blatow et al., 2003), and neurons in hippocampus (Hormuzdi et al., 2001) and retina (Deans et al., 2002) is also C×36-dependent.

Within the thalamus, several lines of evidence indicate the presence of C×36 mediated electrical coupling in the TRN, but not in relay nuclei. This includes in situ hybridization for C×36 mRNA (Condorelli et al., 2000), expression of C×36 repor-ter gene (Deans et al., 2001), C×36-like immuno-reactivity (Liu and Jones, 2003), and paired-cell recording in C×36 knockout mice (Landisman et al., 2002). However, there is some indirect electrophysiological evidence for electrical coupling in relay cells as well (Hughes et al., 2002, 2004). It remains possible that if electrical synapses occur in relay cells, they depend on a gap junction protein other than C×36. Interestingly, even in the TRN, where there is general agreement about the role of C×36 in electrical synaptic transmission, electron microscopic studies have not revealed neuronal gap junctions per se (Liu and Jones, 2003). It is possible that connexin mediated channels are not clustered together in large gap junctional plaques in the TRN.

As prevalent as C×36 seems to be, it is probably not the only connexin involved in mammalian elec-trical synapses. Neurons thought to be electrically coupled, but which may not express C×36, include those of locus coeruleus (Alvarez et al., 2002), the horizontal cells of the retina (Deans and Paul, 2001), and perhaps some pyramidal cells in the hippocampus (MacVicar and Dudek, 1981; Schmitz et al., 2001). C×45 is apparently expressed in neurons of olfactory epithelium and bulb (Zhang and Restrepo, 2002), in horizontal cells (David Paul, personal communica-tion), and in other brain regions (Maxeiner et al., 2003), and is a candidate neuronal gap junction protein. In addition, a newly described family of invertebrate-like gap junction proteins — the "pan-nexins" — has been discovered in the mammalian genome, and two of them are expressed in the brain (Bruzzone et al., 2003).

Biophysical properties of electrical synapses

Gap junction channels have the unique ability to interconnect the cytoplasmic compartments of two adjacent cells. The number and permeation properties of these channels have profound effects on the characteristics of individual electrical synapses. Most connexin channels have large single-channel conductances (up to 300 pS; Harris, 2001), but $Cx36$, the central nervous system-specific connexin, has the smallest conductance of any connexin tested, about 10–15 pS (Srinivas et al., 1999). It is likely that only a small fraction of the channels in a gap junction is open at any moment (Lin and Faber, 1988; Pereda et al., 2003). A rough estimate can be done so as to understand the state of a prototypical electrical synapse in the neocortex: First, we assume its channels are comprised of $Cx36$ (Deans et al., 2001), with a unitary channel conductance of 14 pS (Teubner et al., 2000). Second, the typical gap junction interconnecting two mature interneurons has about 150–380 connexin channels (Fukuda and Kosaka, 2003). Third, we assume one of these gap junctions per electrical synapse. Fourth, as Galarreta and Hestrin (2002) reported, the mean conductance of electrical junctions between mature interneurons is about 0.2 nS These data imply that only 4–9% of junctional channels are open in a mature electrical synapse at any moment; the fraction would be even lower if there were more than one gap junctional contact per electrical synapse (Fukuda and Kosaka, 2003). Since immature neocortical interneurons tend to be more strongly coupled (mean strengths of 0.7–1.6 nS (Galarreta and Hestrin, 1999; Gibson et al., 1999), the gating properties of their channels or the size of their gap junctions — or both — may be different compared to mature neurons. Nevertheless, if only a small proportion of channels tend to be open, there is an interesting opportunity to modulate the strength of an electrical synapse by either decreasing or increasing the open probability of its channels.

Most connexin channels are moderately permeable to organic molecules (including tracers such as Lucifer yellow and neurobiotin, and endogenous substances such as cAMP, cGMP, IP_3, glucose, and Ca^{2+}), but $Cx36$ channels may be relatively less permeable (Teubner et al., 2000). It is important to point out that, in principle at least, neuronal gap junctions may be more important for conveying chemical signals than electrical signals. There is only the most indirect of evidence for this sort of function in central neurons, but it remains feasible (Hatton, 1998; Roerig and Feller, 2000). The apparently poor permeability of $Cx36$ channels for dyes is unfortunate, because the phenomenon of "dye-coupling" — when it works well — can be exploited to reveal complex spatial patterns of gap junction connections between neurons (e.g., Vaney, 2002). Some dye-coupling between neocortical interneurons has been reported (Connors et al., 1983; Benardo, 1997), but it has generally been difficult to observe in neocortical interneurons and TRN under the same conditions where electrophysiological demonstrations of electrical coupling are undeniable (e.g., Gibson et al., 1999; Landisman et al., 2002). Dye-coupling across $Cx36$-dependent gap junctions is easier to see where neurons are coupled unusually strongly, as the AII amacrine cells of the retina seem to be (Deans et al., 2002). Recently, by using relatively high neurobiotin concentrations and long diffusion times, it has been possible to show dye-coupling between electrical coupled neocortical interneurons (Cruikshank and Connors, unpublished observations).

Connexin channels are slowly gated by their transjunctional voltage (V_j; the potential difference of the cytoplasms of two coupled cells), with maximal conductance centered on $V_j=0$. However, $Cx36$ subunits form the most poorly voltage-dependent of connexin channels. Even when V_j varies by ±100 mV, $Cx36$ channel conductance falls by less than half (Srinivas et al., 1999; Al-Ubaidi et al., 2000). This is consistent with our measurements from neocortical interneurons, where no measurable voltage dependence was apparent over a range of ±40 mV (Gibson et al., 2004). Thus, $Cx36$ channels behave as linear, non-rectifying conductors under physiological conditions.

Electrical signals passing between neurons via electrical synapses are, of course, also a subject to influence the non-junctional membranes of the neurons involved (Bennett, 1977). Gap junctions in the neocortex are typically located at soma-dendritic or dendro-dendritic sites (Sloper and Powell, 1978;

Tamás et al., 2000; Fukuda and Kosaka, 2003). Signals originating in one soma must typically traverse a dendrite, the gap junction itself, and another dendrite before arriving at the soma of the second cell. Because of membrane time constants and dendritic cable effects associated with this arrangement, electrical synapses behave as first-order, low-pass electrical filters. Typically for cell pairs within the thalamocortical system, the corner frequencies are about 10 Hz (Galarreta and Hestrin, 1999; Landisman et al., 2002; Gibson et al., 2004). Thus, relatively small signals that are slow, such as after-hyperpolarizations, burst envelopes, or subthreshold oscillations, are communicated more effectively than action potentials, which are much larger but briefer (Fig. 6; also discussed in pages 50–51).

Despite the lack of transjunctional voltage dependence of C×36 channels, strong voltage-dependent effects of gap junction signals have been observed in TRN (Landisman and Connors, unpublished). Depolarization of the resting post-synaptic membrane can effectively increase the spike-evoked PSP transmitted via gap junctions by as much as three-fold, due to the activation of persistent sodium currents in the post-synaptic membrane. This effect does not depend on transjunctional voltage differences, and the voltage amplification can be completely blocked by the application of low concentrations of tetrodotoxin. Similar voltage-dependent modulation of gap junction signals has been observed in neocortical interneurons (Gibson et al., 2004) and at the Mauthner cell synapse of goldfish (Curti and Pereda, 2004).

Modulation, regulation, and pharmacology of electrical synapses

Chemical synapses are famously plastic, and enormous effort has been spent trying to understand how, when, why, and by what mechanisms they are regulated. Electrical synapses can also be modified, by activity and chemicals, but little is known about these processes in the mammalian brain. Understanding the regulation of electrical synapses in the thalamocortical system is an important line of research, but efforts (and progress) have so far been modest; and hence, this section is short.

The conductances of gap junction channels are often affected by changes in intracellular $[H^+]$ or $[Ca^{2+}]$ (Rose and Rick, 1978; Rozental et al., 2001), and these effects may constitute physiological mechanisms of electrical synapse regulation. Neural activity can induce significant changes of intracellular pH (pH_i) in central mammalian neurons (Chesler, 2003), and channels made from the neuronal connexin, C×36, can be closed by strong acidification in expression systems (Teubner et al., 2000). More direct evidence for activity-dependent regulation of mammalian electrical synapses does not yet exist, but the prospects for finding it are good. Experiments in goldfish show that electrical synapses can either increase or decrease their junctional conductance for hours as a function of prior neural activity (Yang et al., 1990). Enhancement seems to depend on a close interaction between C×35 channels and neighboring glutamatergic receptor channels (Smith and Pereda, 2003; Pereda et al., 2003), and depends on NMDA receptor activation, post-synaptic $[Ca^{2+}]_i$, and Ca^{2+}/calmodulin-dependent protein kinase II (Pereda et al., 1998). (Shades of hippocampal long-term potentiation!) This has very interesting implications for the mammalian case, because fish C×35 and mammalian C×36 are orthologues, and include several shared phosphorylation consensus sites that modulate their conductance (Mitropoulou and Bruzzone, 2003).

As with pH_i and neural activity, little research has been done on the chemical modulation of electrical synapses in the mammalian brain (Roerig and Feller, 2000). The best data come from the studies on retina, where dopamine-induced activation of adenylyl cyclase, increased cAMP concentrations, and activated cyclic AMP-dependent protein kinase (PKA) leads to reduced electrical synapse strength and altered visual receptive fields (McMahon et al., 1989). Preliminary experiments in the thalamocortical system suggest that the strength of electrical synapses between cortical interneurons is reduced during application of serotonin (Cruikshank and Connors, 2002), and coupling between TRN neurons decreases for long periods after transient activation of metabotropic glutamate receptors (Landisman and Connors, 2004). The mechanisms responsible for these effects are under investigation.

Drugs are important tools in biological research, and the study of gap junctions is no exception. A wide variety of chemicals reduce gap junction function, but unfortunately most of them tend to be low in potency, only partially effective, and poorly selective. In the brain, most gap junction blockers affect glial connexins as well as those in neurons, and they are non-specific, affecting non-connexin ion channels, receptors, and enzymes (Rozental et al., 2001). Octanol, halothane, and carbenoxolone in particular have been widely used in neurophysiology, and their positive effects are often the primary evidence for implicating electrical synapses in the phenomena under study. Considering the well documented side effects of these drugs, it becomes obvious that such results should be interpreted with caution.

A few other gap junction blockers have recently shown more promise. All-trans-retinoic acid potently reduces electrical coupling between horizontal cells of fish retina (Zhang and McMahon, 2000), and other gap junction-coupled systems. Quinine, the antimalarial drug, selectively blocks $C \times 36$ and $C \times 50$, and has little effect on other connexins (Srinivas et al., 2001). However, quinine has a variety of non-junctional effects on neural systems. Mefloquine, a quinine derivative, is 100-fold more potent than quinine in blocking $C \times 36$, and seems much more specific (Fig. 5; Cruikshank et al., 2004). Unlike quinine, mefloquine causes little change in action potentials. Furthermore, at concentrations sufficient to block electrical coupling between cortical interneurons, mefloquine has virtually no effect on evoked chemical synaptic transmission or resting membrane potential (Fig. 5B). Mefloquine is not the perfect drug, however, since it induces an increase in miniature chemical synaptic events in interneurons. Like quinine, mefloquine has a high degree of potency for the main neural connexin ($C \times 36$), with only moderate effects on glial connexins (e.g., $C \times 26$, $C \times 32$, $C \times 43$; Fig. 5C), so it should prove useful as an experimental tool.

Functions of electrical synapses in the thalamocortical system

What role do electrical synapses play in thalamocortical function? Perhaps this is an unfair question at this early stage (electrical synapses were discovered in neocortical interneurons five years ago, and in TRN

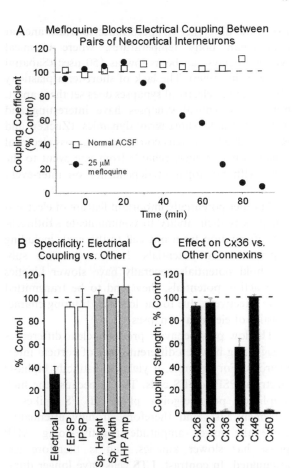

Fig. 5. Specific block of electrical coupling by mefloquine. A. Effect of mefloquine on electrical coupling between a pair of FS interneurons in somatosensory cortex of acute slices. Coupling is nearly eliminated after 90 min of mefloquine perfusion whereas no change occurs for the pair recorded in normal ACSF. B. Group effects of mefloquine on electrical coupling and other properties after approximately 1 h of 25–30 μM mefloquine, in acute slices. The only major effect is a reduction in electrical coupling. C. Effects of 10 μM mefloquine on coupling between N2A cells transfected with selected connexin cDNAs. Each bar represents 4–10 pairs. While pairs expressing the neural gap junction protein ($C \times 36$) are completely uncoupled by mefloquine, those expressing most other connexins are only modestly affected; the exception being $C \times 50$, a lens connexin. (From Cruikshank et al., 2004.)

cells only three years ago). However the classical properties of gap junctions and recent studies of the thalamocortical system offer clues.

Although electrical synapses are faster than chemical synapses (Bennett, 1977, 1997; Jaslove and Brink,

1987), the difference in speed fades to irrelevance at mammalian body temperatures, where chemical synaptic delays can be as low as 150 µsec (Sabatini and Regehr, 1996). The lack of short-term plasticity observed with electrical synapses does set them apart, however. Chemical synapses have interesting and widely variable short-term dynamics (Zucker and Regehr, 2002), whereas conductance across electrical synapses is extremely reliable from one event to the next, with no apparent dependence on inter-event interval.

Another potentially important feature of electrical synapses is their ability to communicate subthreshold information from one cell to the next, including hyperpolarizing potentials. In fact, because subthreshold potentials generally have slower kinetics than action potentials, they tend to be transmitted more effectively, due to the low pass filtering characteristics of electrical synapses.

The low pass behavior produces clear differences in signaling between different types of cortical interneurons. For example, it yields a distinctly biphasic electrical PSP for FS cells. This is because the high amplitude positive-going phase of FS spikes is extremely fast, and therefore strongly attenuated, while the lower amplitude negative-going AHP phase has slower kinetics, and is therefore less attenuated. In contrast, LTS cells have longer duration positive phases and weaker AHPs, which produces fairly monophasic electrical PSPs (Fig. 6A). Low pass filtering also has functional implications in the thalamus, given the classic ability of thalamic neurons to generate state-dependent firing in either tonic or bursting modes (Jahnsen and Llinás, 1984). The depolarizing envelope that underlies a burst in TRN cells is rather slow compared to sodium spikes, and such bursts generate electrical PSPs that are about 5 times the amplitude and 25 times the area of the electrical PSPs evoked by single spikes (Fig. 6B). Furthermore, when coupling is weak, individual spike-evoked electrical PSPs ('spikelets') are imperceptible, but burst-evoked PSPs ('burstlets') are still ~1 mV in amplitude (Long et al., 2004).

Perhaps the most remarkable property of electrical synapses is bidirectionality; the vast majority of chemical synapses are emphatically unidirectional, or at best highly asymmetric. When gap junctions interconnect neurons with similar biophysical

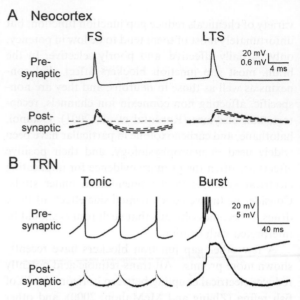

Fig. 6. Electrical post-synaptic potentials (PSPs) differ according to cell type and state. A. recordings from pairs of neocortical interneurons. Average presynaptic action potentials (top) and PSPs with standard error lines (bottom) from FS ($n=9$) and LTS ($n=16$) cell pairs are plotted. The action potentials are from steady state firing during a long (600 ms) current step. The FS-PSP has a biphasic nature, which is lacking in the LTS-PSP. (From Gibson et al., 2004.) B. Recordings from pairs of TRN cells in tonic mode (left) and burst mode (right). Note the difference in electrical PSP size between the two spike modes. (From Long et al., 2004.)

properties, as they very often do, the resulting electrical synapses work equally well in both directions. "Presynaptic" and "post-synaptic" often cease to have meaning. Electrically synapses spread the word, regardless of the message.

One consequence of rapid, reliable, bidirectional signaling tends to be closely coordinated activity. When two or more electrically coupled neurons are active, the most consistent and robust outcome is synchronization. Differences in membrane potential, even small ones, between coupled neurons lead to the flow of small current through their electrical synapses. Thus, an action potential in one neuron causes a small positive deflection in the membrane potential of its coupled neighbors; this tends to bring them more quickly to spike threshold. A hyperpolarizing event (such as an IPSP or afterhyperpolarization) will transiently hyperpolarize coupled neighbors, often phase-delaying their spikes by a small amount.

In electrically coupled neuronal systems of mammals, both action potentials (Galarreta and Hestrin, 1999; Gibson et al., 1999; Mann-Metzer and Yarom, 1999; Landisman et al., 2002) and subthreshold fluctuations (Benardo and Foster, 1986; Christie et al., 1989; Beierlein et al., 2000; Long et al., 2002) can robustly synchronize (Figs. 4 and 7). Computational models of coupled neurons predict that weak coupling can sometimes lead to antiphasic or asynchronous spike firing, and the stability of the synchronous and antisynchronous states may depend strongly on the frequency of firing and the detailed properties of the neurons (e.g., Sherman and Rinzel, 1992; Chow and Kopell, 2000; Lewis and Rinzel, 2003; Pfeuty et al., 2003).

The situation becomes more interesting and complex in neuronal systems with both electrical and chemical synapses operating in parallel. An example is the network of FS interneurons of neocortex, which are densely interconnected by both gap junctions and GABAergic synapses (Gibson et al., 1999). Experiments on pairs of FS cells show that inhibitory synapses alone tend to promote antisynchronous (out-of-phase) spiking, especially at low firing frequencies (Gibson et al., 2004). However, if weak electrical coupling is added to the inhibitory network, synchronous states tend to be more prevalent, and under some conditions the FS pairs are bistable, existing in either synchronous or antisynchronous states (Mancilla et al., 2004). The implications of these complex dynamics are not yet clear, although there is increasing evidence that networks of FS interneurons are important in the generation of certain cortical rhythms of the electroencephalogram (EEG; Whittington and Traub, 2003).

The effects of electrical synapses have been studied in larger groups of neurons by activating them with receptor agonists. When mGluRs or muscarinic cholinergic receptors are activated in neocortex, the LTS class of interneurons fires in irregular patterns that are closely synchronized and driven by well correlated subthreshold membrane fluctuations (Beierlein et al., 2000). Muscarinic receptors also drive synchronous rhythms in MB interneurons, and in this case both electrical and GABAergic inhibitory synapses participate (Blatow et al., 2003). In the thalamus, when mGluRs are activated by endogenous or exogenous agonists, local neighborhoods of

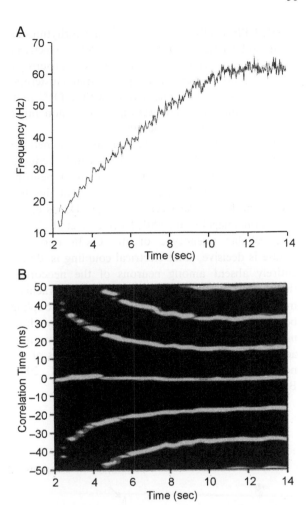

Fig. 7. Electrical coupling between cortical interneurons can induce robust spike synchrony. Recordings are from two coupled FS cells in which linear current ramps (>10 sec duration) are injected into both cells to progressively increase firing rates. The current levels for the ramps were selected to roughly match the spike rates for the two cells. Panel A plots the frequencies for each cell (shown separately in gray and black) throughout the ramps. Notice the high degree of frequency locking, even during the very small fluctuations in rate. Such frequency locking could not be achieved in cells that were uncoupled. Panel B plots data from the same experiment to show the phase relation between the cells during the ramp stimuli. The spike cross-correlation (indicated by gray levels in the z-axis; lighter intensities correspond to higher correlation values) is highest at zero phase lag (y-axis). There are additional smaller peaks 1, 2, and 3 cycles out (cycle width depends on rate, which gets faster throughout the ramp, as shown in panel A). Notice that the peaks are very narrow (<3 msec), indicating a high degree of precision in the synchrony. Also note that the synchrony persists across a wide range of spike rates.

coupled TRN cells generate synchronized rhythms at about 10 Hz (Fig 4B–D; Long et al., 2004). Electrical synapses may serve to coordinate local groups of TRN neurons, given their tight spatial clustering, whereas more distant interactions within TRN may occur via inhibitory connections or common input from cortex and relay thalamus.

A classical way to test the function of something is to eliminate it. Electrical synapses can be reduced or abolished in most central mammalian neurons by knocking out the gene for C×36, and this has been done by several research groups (Deans et al., 2001; Guldenagel et al., 2001; Hormuzdi et al., 2001). The cellular phenotype of the C×36 knockout mouse is decisive, since electrical coupling is almost entirely absent among neurons of the neocortex, thalamus, hippocampus, inferior olive, suprachiasmatic nucleus, and retina. The absence of coupling between interneurons strongly reduces the synchronized activity induced by metabotropic receptor activation in both LTS and MB interneurons of the neocortex (Beierlein et al., 2000; Deans et al., 2001; Blatow et al., 2003).

The role of electrical synapses in systems-level functions of the thalamocortical system has not been well explored. This may prove difficult using the knockout approach, or even systemically applied blockers of gap junctions, given the widespread distribution of connexins throughout the brain. For example, the pathways from rod photoreceptors to ganglion cells are virtually absent in the knockouts due to the loss of critical electrical synapses (Deans et al., 2002), making sensory studies of visual thalamocortical properties complicated. Knockout animals also have deficits in their sleep–wake cycles that may be related to a loss of electrical synapses in the suprachiasmatic nuclei (Long et al., 2005). In addition, these mice have a measurable decrease in the power of their EEG in the gamma frequency range, compared to wild type controls (Buhl et al., 2003), which may, or may not, be due to the loss of thalamocortical gap junctions. Furthermore, some compensatory developmental changes have also been reported in C×36 knockouts (De Zeeuw et al., 2003), and this may be part of the reason why predicted deficits in behavior following C×36 deletion are

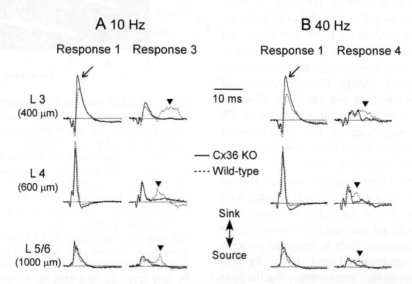

Fig. 8. Effect of knocking out C×36 on cortical responses to thalamic input. A. Current source density (CSD) responses to the 1st and 3d stimuli in a 10 Hz thalamic train. Responses were recorded at 9 cortical depths, separated by 200 μm each, beginning at the pia. However, only three depths are shown, which correspond to the major sinks in layers 3, 4, and 5/6. For the 1st response in the train, the layer 2/3 sink is larger for the knockout (arrow). By the 3d response in the train, the sinks across all the layers are longer lasting for the WT but not for the KO (arrowheads). B. Similar effects were observed for 40 Hz stimulation, but extension of sink durations was most pronounced for the 4th stimulus in 40 Hz trains. Data represent averages across slices from 7 KO and 8 WT mice. Stimulus intensities were 3X threshold.

subtle (Kistler et al., 2002; Long et al., 2002; Placantonakis et al., 2004).

Despite the difficulties, it is obviously important to determine the roles of thalamic and cortical electrical synapses in sensation and other functions mediated by these systems. The prevalence of electrical synapses in cortical interneurons, and the importance of these inhibitory interneurons in controlling cortical responses to thalamic input (Swadlow, 2003), suggests that electrical synapses play a major role in thalamo-cortical transformations. In an attempt to address this, we have examined cortical responses to thalamic stimulation using laminar current source density (CSD) in isolated brain slices from C×36 knock-out and wild-type mice. Preliminary findings are depicted in Fig. 8, where CSD sinks indicate excitatory synaptic events. The initial layer 4 responses are virtually identical for the two genotypes. However, there do appear to be two subtle differences at later time points. First, the sinks in layer 2/3 are larger for the knockout animal. This is consistent with disruption of the inhibitory network in layer 4, allowing greater excitatory throughput to the upper layers. Second, the late sinks in all layers, produced by repetitive stimulation, are reduced in the knockouts. This suggests that electrical coupling between cortical interneurons, or perhaps even TRN cells, may be involved in responding to the sort of rhythmic repetitive input that occurs during active sensory exploration. Obviously these experiments are in their infancy and much work needs to be done. It will be extremely interesting, as more systems-level results come in, to find out whether or not electrical synapses do play the types of functional roles that are indirectly implicated for them by the large array of cellular data reviewed here.

Acknowledgments

We thank our colleagues Yael Amitai, Michael Beierlein, Erika Fanselow, Jay Gibson, Michael Long, David Pinto, Cynthia Rittenhouse, and Saundy Patrick for their contributions to the work described here. This research was supported by NIH grants NS25983, DA125000, and by post-doctoral fellowships from the Helen Hay Whitney Foundation and the Epilepsy Foundation of America.

References

Al-Ubaidi, M.R., White, T.W., Ripps, H., Poras, I., Avner, P., Gomes, D. and Bruzzone, R. (2000) Functional properties, developmental regulation, and chromosomal localization of murine connexin36, a gap-junctional protein expressed preferentially in retina and brain. J. Neurosci. Res., 59: 813–826.

Alvarez, V.A., Chow, C.C., Van Bockstaele, E.J. and Williams, J.T. (2002) Frequency-dependent synchrony in locus ceruleus: role of electrotonic coupling. Proc. Natl. Acad. Sci. USA, 99: 4032–4036.

Amitai, Y., Gibson, J.R., Beierlein, M., Patrick, S.L., Ho, A.M., Connors, B.W. and Golomb, D. (2002) The spatial dimensions of electrically coupled networks of interneurons in the neocortex. J. Neurosci., 22: 4142–4152.

Baker, R. and Llinás, R. (1971) Electrotonic coupling between neurones in the rat mesencephalic nucleus. J. Physiol., 212: 45–63.

Beierlein, M., Gibson, J.R. and Connors, B.W. (2000) A network of electrically coupled interneurons drives synchronized inhibition in neocortex. Nat. Neurosci., 3: 904–910.

Beierlein, M., Gibson, J.R. and Connors, B.W. (2003) Two dynamically distinct inhibitory networks in layer 4 of the neocortex. J. Neurophysiol., 90: 2987–3000.

Benardo, L.S. (1997) Recruitment of GABAergic inhibition and synchronization of inhibitory interneurons in rat neocortex. J. Neurophysiol., 77: 3134–3144.

Benardo, L.S. and Foster, R.E. (1986) Oscillatory behavior in inferior olive neurons: mechanism, modulation, cell aggregates. Brain Res. Bull., 17: 773–784.

Bennett, M.V.L., Crain, S.M. and Grundfest, H. (1959) Electrophysiology of supramedullary neurons in *Spheroides maculates*: I. Orthodromic and antidromic responses. J. Gen. Physiol., 43: 159–188.

Bennett, M.V.L. (1977) Electrical transmission: a functional analysis and comparison with chemical transmission. In: Kandel, E.R. (Ed.), Cellular Biology of Neurons, Handbook of Physiology, The Nervous System. Vol. 1, Williams and Wilkins Co., Baltimore, pp. 357–416.

Bennett, M.V. (1997) Gap junctions as electrical synapses. J. Neurocytol., 26: 349–366.

Bittman, K., Owens, D.F., Kriegstein, A.R. and LoTurco, J.J. (1997) Cell coupling and uncoupling in the ventricular zone of developing neocortex. J. Neurosci., 17: 7037–7044.

Blatow, M., Rozov, A., Katona, I., Hormuzdi, S.G., Meyer, A.H., Whittington, M.A., Caputi, A. and Monyer, H. (2003) A novel network of multipolar bursting interneurons generates theta frequency oscillations in neocortex. Neuron, 38: 805–817.

Bruzzone, R., Hormuzdi, S.G., Barbe, M., Herb, A. and Monyer, H. (2003) Pannexins, a novel family of gap junction proteins expressed in the brain. Proc. Natl. Acad. Sci. USA, 100: 13644–13649.

Buhl, D.L., Harris, K.D., Hormuzdi, S.G., Monyer, H. and Buzsaki, G. (2003) Selective impairment of hippocampal gamma oscillations in connexin-36 knock-out mouse in vivo. J. Neurosci., 23: 1013–1018.

Chesler, M. (2003) Regulation and modulation of pH in the brain. Physiol. Rev., 83: 1183–1221.

Chow, C.C. and Kopell, N. (2000) Dynamics of spiking neurons with electrical coupling. Neural Comput., 12: 1643–1678.

Christie, M.J., Williams, J.T. and North, R.A. (1989) Electrical coupling synchronizes subthreshold activity in locus coeruleus neurons in vitro from neonatal rats. J. Neurosci., 9: 3584–3589.

Chu, Z., Galarreta, M. and Hestrin, S. (2003) Synaptic interactions of late-spiking neocortical neurons in layer 1. J. Neurosci., 23: 96–102.

Condorelli, D.F., Belluardo, N., Trovato-Salinaro, A. and Mudo, G. (2000) Expression of Cx36 in mammalian neurons. Brain Res. Brain Res. Rev., 32: 72–85.

Connors, B.W., Benardo, L.S. and Prince, D.A. (1983) Coupling between neurons of the developing rat neocortex. J. Neurosci., 3: 773–782.

Connors, B.W., Benardo, L.S. and Prince, D.A. (1984) Carbon dioxide sensitivity of dye-coupling among glia and neurons of the neocortex. J. Neurosci., 4: 1324–1330.

Connors, B.W. and Long, M.A. (2004) Electrical synapses in the mammalian brain. Ann. Rev. Neurosci., 27: 393–418.

Cowan, W.M. and Kandel, E.R. (2001) A brief history of synapses and synaptic transmission. In: Cowan, W.M., Südhof, T.C. and Stevens, C.F., (Eds.), Synapses. Johns Hopkins University Press, Baltimore, pp. 1–88.

Cruikshank S.J., Connors, B.W. (2002) Serotonin reduces synaptic inhibition and its short-term depression in identified neurons of barrel cortex. Soci. Neurosci. Abst., 450.6.

Cruikshank, S.J., Hopperstad, M., Younger, M., Connors, B.W., Spray, D.C. and Srinivas, M. (2004) Potent block of Cx36 and Cx50 gap junction channels by mefloquine. Proc Natl. Acad. Sci., USA, 101: 12364–12369.

Curti, S. and Pereda, A.E. (2004) Voltage-dependent enhancement of electrical coupling by a subthreshold sodium current. J. Neurosci., 24: 3999–4010.

Deans, M.R., Gibson, J.R., Sellitto, C., Connors, B.W. and Paul, D.L. (2001) Synchronous activity of inhibitory networks in neocortex requires electrical synapses containing connexin 36. Neuron, 31: 477–485.

Deans, M.R. and Paul, D.L. (2001) Mouse horizontal cells do not express connexin26 or connexin36. Cell. Commun. Adhes., 8: 361–366.

Deans, M.R., Volgyi, B., Goodenough, D.A., Bloomfield, S.A. and Paul, D.L. (2002) Connexin36 is essential for transmission of rod-mediated visual signals in the mammalian retina. Neuron, 36: 703–712.

Degen, J., Meier, C., Van Der Giessen, R.S., Sohl, G., Petrasch-Parwez, E., Urschel, S., Dermietzel, R., Schilling, K., De Zeeuw, C.I. and Willecke, K. (2004) Expression pattern of lacZ reporter gene representing connexin36 in transgenic mice. J. Comp. Neurol., 473: 511–525.

Devor, A. and Yarom, Y. (2002) Electrotonic coupling in the inferior olivary nucleus revealed by simultaneous double patch recordings. J. Neurophysiol., 87: 3048–3058.

De Zeeuw, C.I., Chorev, E., Devor, A., Manor, Y., Van Der Giessen, R.S. (2003) Deformation of network connectivity in the inferior olive of connexin 36-deficient mice is compensated by morphological and electrophysiological changes at the single neuron level. J. Neurosci., 23: 4700–4711.

Fukuda, T. and Kosaka, T. (2003) Ultrastructural study of gap junctions between dendrites of parvalbumin-containing GABAergic neurons in various neocortical areas of the adult rat. Neuroscience, 120: 5–20.

Furshpan, E.J. and Potter, D.D. (1957) Mechanism of nerve-impulse transmission at a crayfish synapse. Nature, 180: 342–343.

Galarreta, M., Erdélyi, F., Szabó, G., Hestrin, S. (2004) Electrical coupling among irregular-spiking GABAergic interneurons expressing cannabinoid receptors. J. Neurosci., 24(44): 9770–9778.

Galarreta, M. and Hestrin, S. (1999) A network of fast-spiking cells in the neocortex connected by electrical synapses. Nature, 402: 72–75.

Galarreta, M. and Hestrin, S. (2001) Electrical synapses between GABA-releasing interneurons. Nat. Rev. Neurosci., 2: 425–433.

Galarreta, M. and Hestrin, S. (2002) Electrical and chemical synapses among parvalbumin fast-spiking GABAergic interneurons in adult mouse neocortex. Proc. Natl. Acad. Sci., 99: 12438–12443.

Gibson, J.R., Beierlein, M. and Connors, B.W. (1999) Two networks of electrically coupled inhibitory neurons in neocortex. Nature, 402: 75–79.

Gibson, J.R., Beierlein, M., Connors, B.W. (2004) Functional properties of electrical synapses between inhibitory interneurons of neocortical layer 4. J. Neurophysiol. In press.

Gibson, J.R. and Connors, B.W. (2003) Chemical and electrical synapses in neocortex. In: Arbib, M.A. (Ed.), 2nd edn, Handbook of Brain Theory and Neural Networks. MIT Press, pp. 725–729.

Guillery, R.W., Feig, S.L. and Lozsadi, D.A. (1998) Paying attention to the thalamic reticular nucleus. Trends Neurosci., 21: 28–32.

Guillery, R.W. and Harting, J.K. (2003) Structure and connections of the thalamic reticular nucleus: Advancing views over half a century. J. Comp. Neurol., 463: 360–371.

Guldenagel, M., Ammermuller, J., Feigenspan, A., Teubner, B., Degen, J., Sohl, G., Willecke, K. and Weiler, R. (2001) Visual transmission deficits in mice with targeted disruption of the gap junction gene connexin36. J. Neurosci., 21: 6036–6044.

Gutnick, M.J., Lobel-Yaakov, R. and Rimon, G. (1985) Incidence of neuronal dye-coupling in neocortical slices depends on the plane of section. Neuroscience, 15: 659–666.

Gutnick, M.J. and Prince, D.A. (1981) Dye coupling and possible electrotonic coupling in the guinea pig neocortical slice. Science, 211: 67–70.

Harris, A.L. (2001) Emerging issues of connexin channels: biophysics fills the gap. Q. Rev. Biophys., 34: 325–472.

Hatton, G.I. (1998) Synaptic modulation of neuronal coupling. Cell Biol. Int., 22: 765–780.

Hormuzdi, S.G., Pais, I., LeBeau, F.E., Towers, S.K., Rozov, A., Buhl, E.H., Whittington, M.A. and Monyer, H. (2001) Impaired electrical signaling disrupts gamma frequency oscillations in connexin 36-deficient mice. Neuron, 31: 487–495.

Hughes, S.W., Lorincz, M., Cope, D.W., Blethyn, K.L., Kekesi, K.A., Parri, H.R., Juhasz, G. and Crunelli, V. (2004) Synchronized oscillations at alpha and theta frequencies in the lateral geniculate nucleus. Neuron, 42: 253–268.

Hughes, S.W., Blethyn, K.L., Cope, D.W. and Crunelli, V. (2002) Properties and origin of spikelets in thalamocortical neurones in vitro. Neuroscience, 110: 395–401.

Jahnsen, H. and Llinás, R. (1984) Electrophysiological properties of guinea-pig thalamic neurones: an in vitro study. J. Physiol., 349: 205–226.

Jaslove, S.W. and Brink, P.R. (1987) Electrotonic coupling in the nervous system. In: De Mello, W.C. (Ed.), Cell-to-Cell Communication. Plenum Publishing, New York, pp. 103–147.

Jefferys, J.G. (1995) Nonsynaptic modulation of neuronal activity in the brain: electric currents and extracellular ions. Physiol. Rev., 75: 689–723.

Kawaguchi, Y. and Kubota, Y. (1997) GABAergic cell subtypes and their synaptic connections in rat frontal cortex. Cereb Cortex, 7: 476–486.

Kistler, W.M., De Jeu, M.T., Elgersma, Y., Van Der Giessen, R.S., Hensbroek, R. (2002) Analysis of Cx36 knockout does not support tenet that olivary gap junctions are required for complex spike synchronization and normal motor performance. Ann. N. Y. Acad. Sci., 978: 391–404.

Knowles, W.D., Funch, P.G. and Schwartzkroin, P.A. (1982) Electrotonic and dye coupling in hippocampal CA1 pyramidal cells in vitro. Neuroscience, 7: 1713–1722.

Korn, H., Sotelo, C. and Crepel, F. (1973) Electronic coupling between neurons in the rat lateral vestibular nucleus. Exp. Brain Res., 16: 255–275.

Landisman CE, Connors BW. (2004) Modulation of electrical synapses in the thalamic reticular nucleus by activation of metabotropic glutamate receptors. Soc. Neurosci. Abstracts, 640.17.

Landisman, C.E., Long, M.A., Beierlein, M., Deans, M.R., Paul, D.L. and Connors, B.W. (2002) Electrical synapses in the thalamic reticular nucleus. J. Neurosci., 22: 1002–1009.

Lewis, T.J. and Rinzel, J. (2003) Dynamics of spiking neurons connected by both inhibitory and electrical coupling. J. Comput. Neurosci., 14: 283–309.

Lin, J.W. and Faber, D.S. (1988) Synaptic transmission mediated by single club endings on the goldfish Mauthner cell. I. Characteristics of electrotonic and chemical postsynaptic potentials. J. Neurosci., 8: 1302–1312.

Liu, X.B. and Jones, E.G. (2003) Fine structural localization of connexin-36 immunoreactivity in mouse cerebral cortex and thalamus. J. Comp. Neurol., 466: 457–467.

Long, M.A., Deans, M.R., Paul, D.L. and Connors, B.W. (2002) Rhythmicity without synchrony in the electrically uncoupled inferior olive. J. Neurosci., 22: 10898–10905.

Long, M.A., Landisman, C.E. and Connors, B.W. (2004) Small clusters of electrically coupled neurons generate synchronous rhythms in the thalamic reticular nucleus. J. Neurosci., 24: 341–349.

Long, M.A., Jutras, M.J., Connors, B.W., Burwell, R.D. (2005) Electrical synapses coordinate activity in the suprachiasmatic nucleus. Nature Neuroscience. 8(1): 61–66.

MacVicar, B.A and Dudek, F.E. (1981) Electrotonic coupling between pyramidal cells: a direct demonstration in rat hippocampal slices. Science, 213: 782–785.

Mancilla, J.G., Lewis, T.J., Pinto, D.J., Rinzel, J., Connors, B.W. (2004) Phase-locking in pairs of neocortical fast-spiking interneurons promoted by inhibitory synapses. Soc. Neurosci. Abst. 977.7.

Mann-Metzer, P. and Yarom, Y. (1999) Electrotonic coupling interacts with intrinsic properties to generate synchronized activity in cerebellar networks of inhibitory interneurons. J. Neurosci., 19: 3298–3306.

Maxeiner, S., Kruger, O., Schilling, K., Traub, O., Urschel, S. and Willecke, K. (2003) Spatiotemporal transcription of connexin45 during brain development results in neuronal expression in adult mice. Neuroscience, 119: 689–700.

McCormick, D.A., Connors, B.W., Lighthall, J.W. and Prince, D.A. (1985) Comparative electrophysiology of pyramidal and sparsely spiny neurons of the neocortex. J. Neurophysiol., 54: 782–806.

McMahon, D.G., Knapp, A.G. and Dowling, J.E. (1989) Horizontal cell gap junctions: single-channel conductance and modulation by dopamine. Proc. Natl. Acad. Sci. USA, 86: 7639–7643.

Meyer, A.H., Katona, I., Blatow, M., Rozov, A. and Monyer, H. (2002) In vivo labeling of parvalbumin-positive interneurons and analysis of electrical coupling in identified neurons. J. Neurosci., 22: 7055–7064.

Mitropoulou, G. and Bruzzone, R. (2003) Modulation of perch connexin35 hemi-channels by cyclic AMP requires a protein kinase A phosphorylation site. J. Neurosci. Res., 72: 147–157.

Monyer, H. and Markram, H. (2004) Molecular and genetic tools to study GABAergic interneuron diversity and function. Trends Neurosci., 27: 90–97.

56

Nagy, J.I. and Rash, J.E. (2000) Connexins and gap junctions of astrocytes and oligodendrocytes in the CNS. Brain Res. Rev., 32: 29–44.

Nagy, J.I., Li, X., Rempel, J., Stelmack, G., Patel, D. (2001) Connexin26 in adult rodent central nervous system: demonstration at astrocytic gap junctions and colocalization with connexin30 and connexin43. J. Comp. Neurol., 441: 302–323.

Ohara, P.T. (1988) Synaptic organization of the thalamic reticular nucleus. J. Electron Microsc. Tech., 10: 283–292.

Peinado, A., Yuste, R. and Katz, L.C. (1993) Extensive dye coupling between rat neocortical neurons during the period of circuit formation. Neuron, 10: 103–114.

Pereda, A.E., Bell, T.D., Chang, B.H., Czernik, A.J., Nairn, A.C. (1998) Ca^{2+}/calmodulin-dependent kinase II mediates simultaneous enhancement of gap-junctional conductance and glutamatergic transmission. Proc. Natl. Acad. Sci. USA, 95: 13272–13277.

Pereda, A., O'Brien, J., Nagy, J.I., Bukauskas, F., Davidson, K.G., Kamasawa, N., Yasumura, T. and Rash, J.E. (2003) Connexin35 mediates electrical transmission at mixed synapses on Mauthner cells. J. Neurosci., 23: 7489–7503.

Peters, A. (1980) Morphological correlates of epilepsy: Cells in the cerebral cortex. Adv. Neurology, 27: 21–48.

Pfeuty, B., Mato, G., Golomb, D. and Hansel, D. (2003) Electrical synapses and synchrony: the role of intrinsic currents. J. Neurosci., 23: 6280–6294.

Pinault, D. (2004) The thalamic reticular nucleus: structure, function and concept. Brain Res Rev. In press.

Placantonakis, D.G., Bukovsky, A.A., Zeng, X.H., Kiem, H.P. and Welsh, J.P. (2004) Fundamental role of inferior olive connexin 36 in muscle coherence during tremor. Proc. Natl. Acad. Sci. USA, 101: 7164–7169.

Rash, J.E., Yasumura, T., Dudek, F.E. and Nagy, J.I. (2001) Cell-specific expression of connexins and evidence of restricted gap junctional coupling between glial cells and between neurons. J. Neurosci., 21: 1983–2000.

Roerig, B. and Feller, M.B. (2000) Neurotransmitters and gap junctions in developing neural circuits. Brain Res. Rev., 32: 86–114.

Roerig, B., Klausa, G. and Sutor, B. (1995) Beta-adrenoreceptor activation reduces dye-coupling between immature rat neocortical neurones. Neuroreport, 6: 1811–1815.

Rose, B. and Rick, R. (1978) Intracellular pH, intracellular free Ca, and junctional cell-cell coupling. J. Membr. Biol., 44: 377–415.

Rozental, R., Srinivas, M. and Spray, D.C. (2001) How to close a gap junction channel: Efficacies and potencies of uncoupling agents. In: Bruzzone, R., Giaume, C. and Totwa, (Eds.), Methods in Molecular Biology, Connexin Methods and Protocols. Vol. 154, Humana Press, New Jersey, pp. 447–476.

Sabatini, B.L. and Regehr, W.G. (1996) Timing of neurotransmission at fast synapses in the mammalian brain. Nature, 384: 170–172.

Schmitz, D., Schuchmann, S., Fisahn, A., Draguhn, A., Buhl, E.H. (2001) Axo-axonal coupling. a novel mechanism for ultrafast neuronal communication. Neuron, 31: 831–840.

Sherman, A. and Rinzel, J. (1992) Rhythmogenic effects of weak electrotonic coupling in neuronal models. Proc. Natl. Acad. Sci. USA, 89: 2471–2474.

Sloper, J.J. (1972) Gap junctions between dendrites in the primate neocortex. Brain Res., 44: 641–646.

Sloper, J.J. and Powell, T.P. (1978) Gap junctions between dendrites and somata of neurons in the primate sensorimotor cortex. Proc. R. Soc. Lond. B. Biol. Sci., 203: 39–47.

Smith, M. and Pereda, A.E. (2003) Chemical synaptic activity modulates nearby electrical synapses. Proc. Natl. Acad. Sci., 100: 4849–4854.

Srinivas, M., Hopperstad, M.G. and Spray, D.C. (2001) Quinine blocks specific gap junction channel subtypes. Proc. Natl. Acad. Sci. USA, 98: 10942–10947.

Srinivas, M., Rozental, R., Kojima, T., Dermietzel, R., Mehler, M., Condorelli, D.F., Kessler, J.A. and Spray, D.C. (1999) Functional properties of channels formed by the neuronal gap junction protein connexin36. J. Neurosci., 19: 9848–9855.

Swadlow, H.A. (2003) Fast-spike interneurons and feedforward inhibition in awake sensory neocortex. Cereb. Cortex., 13: 25–32.

Szabadics, J., Lorincz, A. and Tamás, G. (2001) Beta and gamma frequency synchronization by dendritic gabaergic synapses and gap junctions in a network of cortical interneurons. J. Neurosci., 21: 5824–5831.

Tamás, G., Buhl, E.H., Lorincz, A. and Somogyi, P. (2000) Proximally targeted GABAergic synapses and gap junctions synchronize cortical interneurons. Nat. Neurosci., 3: 366–371.

Teubner, B., Degen, J., Sohl, G., Guldenagel, M., Bukauskas, F.F. (2000) Functional expression of the murine connexin 36 gene coding for a neuron-specific gap junctional protein. J. Membr. Biol., 176: 249–262.

Thomson, A.M. and Deuchars, J. (1997) Synaptic interactions in neocortical local circuits: dual intracellular recordings in vitro. Cereb. Cortex., 7: 510–522.

Vaney, D.I. (2002) Retinal neurons: cell types and coupled networks. Prog. Brain Res., 136: 239–254.

Venance, L., Rozov, A., Blatow, M., Burnashev, N., Feldmeyer, D. and Monyer, H. (2000) Connexin expression in electrically coupled postnatal rat brain neurons. Proc. Natl. Acad. Sci., 97: 10260–10265.

Watanabe, A. (1958) The interaction of electrical activity among neurons of lobster cardiac ganglion. Jpn. J. Physiol., 8: 305–318.

Whittington, M.A. and Traub, R.D. (2003) Interneuron diversity series: inhibitory interneurons and network oscillations in vitro. Trends Neurosci., 26: 676–682.

Willecke, K., Eiberger, J., Degen, J., Eckardt, D., Romualdi, A. (2002) Structural and functional diversity of connexin genes in the mouse and human genome. Biol. Chem., 383: 725–737.

Wylie, R.M. (1973) Evidence of electrotonic transmission in the vestibular nuclei of the rat. Brain Res., 50: 179–183.

Yang, X.D., Korn, H. and Faber, D.S. (1990) Long-term potentiation of electrotonic coupling at mixed synapses. Nature, 348: 542–545.

Zhang, D.Q. and McMahon, D.G. (2000) Direct gating by retinoic acid of retinal electrical synapses. Proc. Natl. Acad. Sci. USA, 97: 14754–14759.

Zhang, C. and Restrepo, D. (2002) Expression of connexin 45 in the olfactory system. Brain Res., 929: 37–47.

Zucker, R.S. and Regehr, W.G. (2002) Short-term synaptic plasticity. Annu. Rev. Physiol., 64: 355–405.

Progress in Brain Research, Vol. 149
ISSN 0079-6123

CHAPTER 5

Neural substrates within primary visual cortex for interactions between parallel visual pathways

Edward M. Callaway

*Systems Neurobiology Laboratories, The Salk Institute for Biological Studies,
10010 North Torrey Pines Road, La Jolla, CA 92037, USA*

Introduction

Parallel processing is a common feature of sensory systems in the mammalian brain. Specialized sensory receptors and neural circuits extract behaviorally relevant information from the environment and the brain integrates this information to generate perception and behavior. At the broadest level, parallel pathways are apparent in the specialized systems that extract information pertaining to each of the individual senses. For example, the receptors and circuits in the retina that are optimized for identifying distant objects based on the emission and reflection of visible light are distinct from those that are specialized for taste. Similarly, within each of these sensory modalities, separate receptors and circuits are specialized for identifying distinct components from within the environmental cues that are accessible to that modality. And just as information across sensory modalities is integrated within the brain to give rise to a coherent percept of the world, separately extracted cues from within each sensory domain must also be integrated to give rise to a coherent percept for the corresponding modality.

The sensation of dark chocolate is not perceived simply as distinct bitter and sweet components, but as a unique taste that is also complemented by texture and smell. A colorful kite soaring across the sky is not perceived separately as a moving object, a diamond-shaped item, and an entity moving up and down. Interestingly, the conscious percepts and categories generated by vision are more distantly related to the specificities of neurons at the periphery than sensation related to taste. For example, we are conscious of distinct bitter or sweet tastes and also have distinct bitter and sweet taste receptors (Chandrashekar et al., 2000; Nelson et al., 2001; Zhang et al., 2003). But the colors which we perceive and categorize are not closely related to the color specificities of retinal neurons; they are instead related to responses of neurons in higher cortical areas (Hanazawa et al., 2000). Ironically, then, despite our distinct impression that vision is our most useful sense and can be understood intuitively, it is in fact more highly derived and our visual percepts are only distantly related to the patterns of light that activate each type of photoreceptor.

In trichromatic primates, daytime visual sensation begins from three types of cone photoreceptors (plus rods for night vision) and retinal circuits extract further information by comparing activity across receptor populations. Parallel retinal subcircuits extract features and these computations are represented and carried in parallel to the central

DOI: 10.1016/S0079-6123(05)49005-6

nervous system by more than a dozen types of retinal ganglion cells (Dacey et al., 2003). This retinal output provides a compact representation of the visual world that can be efficiently carried through the bottleneck of the optic nerve. But these parallel pathways do not bear a one-to-one relationship to unique percepts or even to the separably distinguishable features of visual objects, such as shape, motion, and color, that will be derived from later computations (De Yoe and Van Essen, 1988). The creation of behaviorally relevant feature detectors, as well as the generation of a coherent visual percept, requires integration of information across streams and this integration begins in the primary visual cortex (V1). The parallel visual pathways that originate in the primate (macaque monkey) retina, the functional organization of input from the lateral geniculate nucleus of the thalamus (LGN) to V1, the local circuits within V1 that mediate integration of information across streams, and the relationships between each of V1's separate subcircuits and the extrastriate visual areas to which they project are reviewed in this chapter.

As detailed below, the sites of termination of LGN input within V1 correspond to the zones that stain dark for cytochrome oxidase (Livingstone and Hubel, 1982) and each functionally distinct pathway provides input to a distinct zone within V1. Despite the notion popularized in some textbooks, however, these pathways do not remain segregated as information is further processed within V1. The neurons that project from V1 to higher visual cortical areas carry information that reflects integration across multiple pathways.

One popular scenario has information from the parvocellular visual pathway contributing to blobs and interblobs in V1 and then providing the exclusive V1 input to ventral visual areas. The magnocellular pathway is, in turn, considered to connect to layer 4B of V1 and provide the sole contribution to dorsal visual areas. Since dorsal visual areas are specialized for processing motion and ventral areas for shape and color (Desimone and Ungerleider, 1989), these relationships would leave the magnocellular pathway solely responsible for carrying information used for motion processing and the parvocellular pathway solely responsible for shape and color.

This scenario, however, fails to incorporate the available functional and anatomical data on nearly every count. Anatomical studies, detailed below, show that layer 4B of V1 is not the sole source of input to dorsal visual areas, nor does it receive exclusively magnocellular input. Furthermore, ventral visual areas receive input from layer 4B, as well as from blobs and interblobs, and the blobs and interblobs receive convergent input from multiple visual pathways. Functional studies show that visual activities in both dorsal and ventral visual areas are influenced by both magnocellular and parvocellular pathways (Maunsell et al., 1990; Merigan et al., 1991b; Ferrera et al., 1992; 1994; Nealey and Maunsell, 1994). Also, motion perception and direction discrimination persist following lesions of the magnocellular layers of LGN (Merigan et al., 1991a).

From retina to cortex

Although as many as a dozen distinct types of retinal ganglion cells project in parallel to the LGN (Dacey et al., 2003), based on our present understanding, information conveyed from the retina to more central visual processing centers can be divided into three functionally distinct systems (Dacey, 2000; Hendry and Reid, 2000). Funtionally we can divide the retino-geniculo-cortical pathways into an achromatic pathway, a red–green color opponent pathway, and a blue–yellow opponent pathway. The achromatic, magnocellular (M) pathway originates from parasol retinal ganglion cells, which connect to the two most ventral, M layers of the LGN (Michael, 1988). These LGN neurons in turn project to layer 4Cα of V1 (Blasdel and Lund, 1983; Hendrickson et al., 1978) and convey achromatic input to this layer (Chatterjee and Callaway, 2003). The M pathway is also characterized functionally, by neurons with very good sensitivity to low contrast stimuli, fast conduction velocities, transient responses, and somewhat poor spatial acuity relative to P cells (Levitt et al., 2001).

At the level of the retina, midget ganglion cells are considered to be the origin of the parvocellular (P) visual pathway. Red-green opponent retinal signals are carried by midget ganglion cells (Dacey, 2000) to the four most ventral, P layers of the LGN (Michael, 1988). There is also evidence that some OFF midget ganglion cells receive input from S (blue) cones and carry a blue-OFF/yellow-ON opponent signal to the LGN (Klug et al., 2003). Most LGN neurons in the P layers have red–green color opponency, but cells with blue–yellow opponency can also be found in these layers (Wiesel and Hubel, 1966; Schiller and Malpeli, 1978; Michael, 1988; Hendry and Reid, 2000;). Parvocellular LGN cells project primarily to layer $4C\beta$ of V1 (Hendrickson et al., 1978; Blasdel and Lund, 1983) and convey red–green opponent input (but not blue–yellow) to this layer (Chatterjee and Callaway, 2003). Layer 4A may also receive input from parvocellular LGN (Hendrickson et al., 1978; Blasdel and Lund, 1983; Hendry and Yoshioka, 1994), but functionally the input to this layer is blue-OFF/yellow-ON (Chatterjee and Callaway, 2003), consistent with an origin from the subset of OFF midget ganglion cells that receives S cone-OFF input (Klug et al., 2003). In addition to color-opponency, P cells in the LGN are also characterized funtionally as having poor contrast sensitivity to achromatic stimuli, high spatial acuity, and slow conduction velocities relative to M cells (Levitt et al., 2001).

The koniocellular (K) visual pathway is poorly defined. At the level of the retina, it is sometimes considered to subsume all retinal ganglion cells that are not either parasol (magnocellular) or midget (parvocellular). But it is generally agreed that bistratified retinal ganglion cells compose at least part of the K pathway. Both large and small bistratified retinal ganglion cells have blue-ON/yellow-OFF receptive fields (Dacey and Lee, 1994; Calkins et al., 1998; Chichilnisky and Baylor, 1999; Dacey, 2000; Dacey et al., 2003). The bistratified retinal ganglion cells probably connect to dorsal LGN, where they connect to koniocellular LGN neurons (Dacey, 2000; Hendry and Reid, 2000).

At the level of the LGN, the koniocellular pathway is defined as cells that express αCAM kinase and/or calbindin (Hendry and Yoshioka, 1994; Hendry and Reid, 2000). These cells are found primarily in the intercalated zones, between the main M and P layers, but are also scattered within these layers. Retrograde tracers injected into the superficial layers of V1 (above layer 4A) label only αCAM kinase and/or calbindin-positive K cells (Hendry and Yoshioka, 1994). Thus, the CO blobs and layer 1 of V1 (Livingstone and Hubel, 1982) receive exclusively koniocellular LGN input. It has not been possible to exclusively label K cells with an anterograde tracer or to inject a retrograde tracer into deeper layers of V1 without also involving more superficial layers. Thus, it is unclear whether LGN K cells might contribute input to layers 4A or 4C of V1. It is clear, however, that most of the input to these layers is not koniocellular (Hendry and Yoshioka, 1994). Recordings from LGN afferents at their sites of termination in V1 have shown that cells projecting to layer 3 blobs have blue-ON receptive fields (Chatterjee and Callaway, 2003), further solidifying the continuity of a K pathway originating from bistratified ganglion cells.

Substrates for integration of parallel inputs by V1 local circuits

Mixing within layer 4C of V1

Although achromatic, red–green opponent, blue-ON, and blue-OFF LGN afferents terminate separately in distinct zones within V1 (Chatterjee and Callaway, 2003), they are likely to begin mixing at the first possible stage of V1 processing. Achromatic, magnocellular, and red–green opponent, parvocellular neurons project in parallel to layers $4C\alpha$ and $4C\beta$ of V1, respectively, suggesting that most layer 4C neurons receive input exclusively from one or the other pathway. But many layer 4C neurons have dendritic arbors that span across the middle of layer 4C and thus could receive input from both pathways (Mates and Lund, 1983; Yoshioka et al., 1994; Callaway and Wiser, 1996; Yabuta and Callaway, 1998). In addition, recordings of the visual responses of layer 4C neurons show that their functional properties shift gradually within layer 4C rather than abruptly at the $4C\alpha/4C\beta$ border (Blasdel and Fitzpatrick, 1984), further supporting the likelihood of mixing within layer 4C. Layer 4C neurons with dendrites in both layers $4C\alpha$ and $4C\beta$ project their axons through layer 4B without branching and then arborize in both blobs and interblobs of layer 3 (Yabuta and Callaway, 1998). Thus, these observations alone suggest that both blobs and interblobs also receive inputs from both M and P pathways.

62

Convergent inputs to layer 4B of V1

The notion that layer 4B of V1 receives exclusively M input, via layer 4Cα, was intially posited based on the assumption that neurons receive input only from axons that terminate in the same cortical layer as their cell bodies. Since the axons of layer 4Cα neurons arborize in layer 4B, but those of layer 4Cβ neurons pass through layer 4B without branching, it was thought that the layer 4B neurons would receive no layer 4Cβ input. It is now much more widely appreciated that the extensive dendritic arbors of neurons in zones outside the home layer can receive inputs that are just as strong as more proximal inputs (Magee and Cook, 2000). In the case of layer 4B neurons, about 70% of these cells have a pyramidal morphology and dendritic arbors that extend into layer 3 (Callaway and Wiser, 1996). Within layer 3, the apical dendrites of layer 4B pyramidal cells overlap extensively with the dense axonal arbors of layer 4Cβ neurons (Yabuta and Callaway, 1998). Functional studies have explicit tested whether layer 4Cβ neurons make functional connections to these cells (Sawatari and Callaway, 1996; Yabuta et al., 2001). These experiments show that layer 4B pyramidal neurons receive strong input from layer 4Cβ that is about half the strength of the input from layer 4Cα. Thus, both M and P pathways contribute relatively directly to layer 4B pyramids, with the M input being the strongest. Interestingly, about 20% of layer 4B neurons are spiny stellates and these do not receive detectable layer 4Cβ input (Yabuta et al., 2001). Thus, these cells provide a pathway out of V1 that is unlikely to be strongly influenced by the P pathway. Layer 4B pyramidal neurons might also receive blue-ON and/or blue-OFF inputs from the LGN afferents that overlap with their apical dendrites in layers 4A and 3 (Chatterjee and Callaway, 2003).

CO blobs

It has long been appreciated that the cytochrome oxidase blobs in layer 3 of V1 are a site of convergence of M and P input. Retrograde tracers injected into blobs label both layer 4Cα and layer 4Cβ neurons, as well as layer 4B neurons (Lachica et al., 1992). These connections are also demonstrated by intracellular

labeling of single neurons and anterograde tracer injections (Yoshioka et al., 1994; Yabuta et al., 2001). In addition to integrating M and P input, blobs also receive K inputs (Livingstone and Hubel, 1982; Hendry and Yoshioka, 1994) that are functionally blue-ON (Chatterjee and Callaway, 2003). Basal dendrites of some layer 3 neurons also extend into layer 4A where they could receive blue-OFF LGN input (Chatterjee and Callaway, 2003).

Input to interblobs

Interblobs, like blobs, have been shown to be influenced functionally by both the M and P pathways (Nealey and Maunsell, 1994). However, it was initially unclear what was the source of M input to interblobs. Retrograde label following tracer injections in interblobs labeled neurons in layer 4Cβ, but not the M-recipient neurons in the most superficial part of layer 4Cα (Lachica et al., 1992). More recently, however, neurons were identified in the middle of layer 4C with dendrites confined to an M-recipient zone in the lower part of layer 4Cα (Yabuta and Callaway 1998). These cells project dense axonal arbors specifically to the interblob zones in layer 3. In addition, cells in the upper part of layer 4Cβ have dendrites that extend into layer 4Cα and these M and P recipient cells project dense axons to both blobs and interblobs in layer 3 (Yabuta and Callaway, 1998).

Projections from V1 to V2

Much of the evidence for differential parceling of M and P pathways to dorsal versus ventral visual areas hinges on the organization of connections from V1 to V2. Since layer 4B receives stronger input from layer 4Cα than from layer 4Cβ and this layer provides the direct input to areas V3 and MT, these connections are consistent a strong M contribution to these dorsal areas. But these dorsal visual areas also receive input from thick stripes in V2 (Merigan and Maunsell, 1993). Although experiments in squirrel monkeys initially revealed connections to V2 thick stripes exclusively from layer 4B of V1 (Livingstone and Hubel, 1987), more recent experiments in macaque monkeys have revealed additional connections from layer 3 (Sincich and Horton, 2002). Since layer 3 is dominated by P inputs from layer $4C\beta$ (Yabuta et al., 2001), this observation suggests an additional source of strong P input to dorsal visual areas. Similarly, input to thin and interstripes in V2 was thought to come from only layer 3, not layer 4B (Livingstone and Hubel, 1983). This suggested that the input from these compartments of V2 that connect to ventral visual areas were dominated by the P pathway. But it has now been demonstrated that layer 4B also connects to thin and interstripes (Sincich and Horton, 2002), suggesting a stronger M input to ventral visual areas, via V2, than previously appreciated.

Summary

The surprising persistence of the notion that the magnocellular visual pathway is the sole input to dorsal visual areas and is responsible for detection of motion, while the parvocellular pathway is equated to ventral visual areas and is the sole substrate for object identification, is a tribute to the seduction of simplicity. But this hypothesis has been thoroughly discredited by virtually every experiment which tests it. All evidence points to a mixing of M, P, and K pathways within the primary visual cortex to give rise to a new set of pathways that project in parallel (Sincich and Horton, 2003) to higher visual cortical areas. This evidence includes anatomical and functional studies, as well as common sense (De Yoe and Van Essen, 1988).

References

Blasdel, G.G. and Fitzpatrick, D. (1984) Physiological organization of layer 4 in macaque striate cortex. J. Neurosci., 4: 880–895.

Blasdel, G.G. and Lund, J.S. (1983) Termination of afferent axons in macaque striate cortex. J. Neurosci., 3: 1389–1413.

Calkins, D.J., Tsukamoto, Y. and Sterling, P. (1998) Microcircuitry and mosaic of a blue-yellow ganglion cell in the primate retina. J. Neurosci., 18: 3373–3385.

Callaway, E.M. and Wiser, A.K. (1996) Contributions of individual layer 2-5 spiny neurons to local circuits in macaque primary visual cortex. Vis. Neurosci., 13: 907–922.

Chandrashekar, J., Mueller, K.L., Hoon, M.A., Adler, E., Feng, L., Guo, W., Zuker, C.S. and Ryba, N.J. (2000) T2Rs function as bitter taste receptors. Cell, 100: 703–711.

Chatterjee, S. and Callaway, E.M. (2003) Parallel colour-opponent pathways to primary visual cortex. Nature, 426: 668–671.

Chichilnisky, E.J. and Baylor, D.A. (1999) Receptive-field microstructure of blue-yellow ganglion cells in primate retina. Nat. Neurosci., 2: 889–893.

Dacey, D.M. (2000) Parallel pathways for spectral coding in primate retina. Annu. Rev. Neurosci., 23: 743–775.

Dacey, D.M. and Lee, B.B. (1994) The "blue-on" opponent pathway in primate retina originates from a distinct bistratified ganglion cell type. Nature, 367: 731–735.

Dacey, D.M., Peterson, B.B., Robinson, F.R. and Gamlin, P.D. (2003) Fireworks in the primate retina: in vitro photodynamics reveals diverse LGN-projecting ganglion cell types. Neuron, 37: 15–27.

Desimone, R. and Ungerleider, L. (1989) Neural mechanisms of visual processing in monkeys. In: Boller, F. and Grafman, J. (Eds.), Handbook of Neuropsychology, Vol. 2, Elsevier, Amsterdam, pp. 267–299.

De Yoe, E.A. and Van Essen, D.C. (1988) Concurrent processing streams in monkey visual cortex. Trends Neurosci., 11: 219–226.

Ferrera, V.P., Nealey, T.A. and Maunsell, J.H. (1992) Mixed parvocellular and magnocellular geniculate signals in visual area V4. Nature, 358: 756–761.

Ferrera, V.P., Nealey, T.A. and Maunsell, J.H. (1994) Responses in macaque visual area V4 following inactivation of the parvocellular and magnocellular LGN pathways. J. Neurosci., 14: 2080–2088.

Hanazawa, A., Komatsu, H. and Murakami, I. (2000) Neural selectivity for hue and saturation of colour in the primary visual cortex of the monkey. Eur. J. Neurosci., 12: 1753–1763.

Hendrickson, A.E., Wilson, J.R. and Ogren, M.P. (1978) The neuroanatomical organization of pathways between the dorsal lateral geniculate nucleus and visual cortex in Old World and New World primates. J. Comp. Neurol., 182: 123–136.

Hendry, S.H. and Reid, R.C. (2000) The koniocellular pathway in primate vision. Annu. Rev. Neurosci., 23: 127–153.

Hendry, S.H. and Yoshioka, T. (1994) A neurochemically distinct third channel in the macaque dorsal lateral geniculate nucleus. Science, 264: 575–577.

Klug, K., Herr, S., Ngo, I.T., Sterling, P. and Schein, S. (2003) Macaque retina contains an S-cone OFF midget pathway. J. Neurosci., 23: 9881–9887.

Lachica, E.A., Beck, P.D. and Casagrande, V.A. (1992) Parallel pathways in macaque monkey striate cortex: anatomically defined columns in layer III. Proc. Natl. Acad. Sci. USA, 89: 3566–3570.

Levitt, J.B., Schumer, R.A., Sherman, S.M., Spear, P.D. and Movshon, J.A. (2001) Visual response properties of neurons in the LGN of normally reared and visually deprived macaque monkeys. J. Neurophysiol., 85: 2111–2129.

64

Livingstone, M.S. and Hubel, D.H. (1982) Thalamic inputs to cytochrome oxidase-rich regions in monkey visual cortex. Proc. Natl. Acad. Sci. USA, 79: 6098–6101.

Livingstone, M.S. and Hubel, D.H. (1983) Specificity of cortico-cortical connections in monkey visual system. Nature, 304: 531–534.

Livingstone, M.S. and Hubel, D.H. (1987) Connections between layer 4B of area 17 and the thick cytochrome oxidase stripes of area 18 in the squirrel monkey. J. Neurosci., 7: 3371–3377.

Magee, J.C. and Cook, E.P. (2000) Somatic EPSP amplitude is independent of synapse location in hippocampal pyramidal neurons. Nat. Neurosci., 3: 895–903.

Mates, S.L. and Lund, J.S. (1983) Neuronal composition and development in lamina 4C of monkey striate cortex. J. Comp. Neurol., 221: 60–90.

Maunsell, J.H., Nealey, T.A. and De Priest, D.D. (1990) Magnocellular and parvocellular contributions to responses in the middle temporal visual area (MT) of the macaque monkey. J. Neurosci., 10: 3323–3334.

Merigan, W.H., Byrne, C.E. and Maunsell, J.H. (1991a) Does primate motion perception depend on the magnocellular pathway? J. Neurosci., 11: 3422–3429.

Merigan, W.H., Katz, L.M. and Maunsell, J.H. (1991b) The effects of parvocellular lateral geniculate lesions on the acuity and contrast sensitivity of macaque monkeys. J. Neurosci., 11: 994–1001.

Merigan, W.H. and Maunsell, J.H. (1993) How parallel are the primate visual pathways? Annu. Rev. Neurosci., 16: 369–402.

Michael, C.R. (1988) Retinal afferent arborization patterns, dendritic field orientations and the segregation of function in the lateral geniculate nucleus of the monkey. Proc. Natl. Acad. Sci. USA, 85: 4914–4918.

Nealey, T.A. and Maunsell, J.H. (1994) Magnocellular and parvocellular contributions to the responses of neurons in macaque striate cortex. J. Neurosci., 14: 2069–2079.

Nelson, G., Hoon, M.A., Chandrashekar, J., Zhang, Y., Ryba, N.J. and Zuker, C.S. (2001) Mammalian sweet taste receptors. Cell, 106: 381–390.

Sawatari, A. and Callaway, E.M. (1996) Convergence of magno- and parvocellular pathways in layer 4B of macaque primary visual cortex. Nature, 380: 442–446.

Schiller, P.H. and Malpeli, J.G. (1978) Functional specificity of lateral geniculate nucleus laminae of the rhesus monkey. J. Neurophysiol., 41: 788–797.

Sincich, L.C. and Horton, J.C. (2002) Divided by cytochrome oxidase: a map of the projections from V1 to V2 in macaques. Science, 295: 1734–1737.

Sincich, L.C. and Horton, J.C. (2003) Independent projection streams from macaque striate cortex to the second visual area and middle temporal area. J. Neurosci., 23: 5684–5692.

Wiesel, T.N. and Hubel, D.H. (1966) Spatial and chromatic interactions in the lateral geniculate body of the rhesus monkey. J. Neurophysiol., 29: 1115–1156.

Yabuta, N.H. and Callaway, E.M. (1998) Functional streams and local connections of layer 4C neurons in primary visual cortex of the macaque monkey. J. Neurosci., 18: 9489–9499.

Yabuta, N.H., Sawatari, A. and Callaway, E.M. (2001) Two functional channels from primary visual cortex to dorsal visual cortical areas. Science, 292: 297–300.

Yoshioka, T., Levitt, J.B. and Lund, J.S. (1994) Independence and merger of thalamocortical channels within macaque monkey primary visual cortex: anatomy of interlaminar projections. Vis. Neurosci., 11: 467–489.

Zhang, Y., Hoon, M.A., Chandrashekar, J., Mueller, K.L., Cook, B., Wu, D., Zuker, C.S. and Ryba, N.J. (2003) Coding of sweet, bitter, and umami tastes: different receptor cells sharing similar signaling pathways. Cell, 112: 293–301.

Progress in Brain Research, Vol. 149
ISSN 0079-6123

CHAPTER 6

Bottom-up and top-down dynamics in visual cortex

James Schummers, Jitendra Sharma and Mriganka Sur*

*Department of Brain and Cognitive Sciences, Massachusetts Institute of Technology,
Cambridge, MA 02139, USA*

Abstract: A key emergent property of the primary visual cortex (V1) is the orientation selectivity of its neurons. Recent experiments demonstrate remarkable bottom-up and top-down plasticity in orientation networks of the adult cortex. The basis for such dynamics is the mechanism by which orientation tuning is created and maintained, by integration of thalamocortical and intracortical inputs. Intracellular measurements of excitatory and inhibitory synaptic conductances reveal that excitation and inhibition balance each other at all locations in the cortex. This balance is particularly critical at pinwheel centers of the orientation map, where neurons receive intracortical input from a wide diversity of local orientations. The orientation tuning of neurons in adult V1 changes systematically after short-term exposure to one stimulus orientation. Such reversible physiological shifts in tuning parallel the orientation tilt aftereffect observed psychophysically. Neurons at or near pinwheel centers show pronounced changes in orientation preference after adaptation with an oriented stimulus, while neurons in iso-orientation domains show minimal changes. Neurons in V1 of alert, behaving monkeys also exhibit short-term orientation plasticity after very brief adaptation with an oriented stimulus, on the time scale of visual fixation. Adaptation with stimuli that are orthogonal to a neuron's preferred orientation does not alter the preferred orientation but sharpens orientation tuning. Thus, successive fixation on dissimilar image patches, as happens during natural vision, combined with mechanisms of rapid cortical plasticity, actually improves orientation discrimination. Finally, natural vision involves judgements about where to look next, based on an internal model of the visual world. Experiments in behaving monkeys in which information about future stimulus locations can be acquired in one set of trials but not in another demonstrate that V1 neurons signal the acquisition of internal representations. Such Bayesian updating of responses based on statistical learning is fundamental for higher level vision, for deriving inferences about the structure of the visual world, and for the regulation of eye movements.

Introduction

The primary visual cortex (V1) has long been studied as a model of the general principles of cortical functioning. In particular, the emergent property of orientation tuning in V1 provides an interesting test case for the role of different classes of inputs in

shaping the functional response properties of cortical neurons. Much work has attempted to distinguish whether orientation selectivity is derived from "feedforward" inputs from the thalamus, or "recurrent" inputs within the cortical circuit. There is substantial evidence for an important role of both types of inputs in shaping the tuning properties of V1 neurons, with a growing consensus that the dynamics and plasticity of tuning involves both inputs. Beyond the limited scope of orientation tuning, the issue has broad implications for the mode in which cortical

*Corresponding author. Tel.: +1-671-253-8784; Fax: +1-617-253-9829; E-mail: msur@mit.edu

DOI: 10.1016/S0079-6123(05)49006-8

circuits operate. Do cortical neurons inherit their properties from the specific configuration of feedforward
inputs, or does the cortical circuitry itself generate
new properties based on features of the recurrent
circuitry and top-down inputs?

The feedforward model of orientation tuning was
the first proposed (see Static linear feedforward
models), and many conceptual models of cortical
function are based on the principle of strong feedforward determination of response properties. However,
there is increasing evidence that the local circuitry can
dramatically influence the responses of V1 neurons.
As a consequence of the orderly mapping of orientation onto the 2D cortical sheet, the local cortical
networks are diverse, and this diversity has implications for both intracortical computations and the
stability of response properties. Several lines of
evidence suggest that the local cortical circuit may be
a meaningful functional unit of cortical computations.
Thus, the response properties of individual neurons
cannot be fully understood except in the context of
these circuits. We have shown that a careful balance of
inhibition and excitation can elegantly generate, and
maintain, sharp orientation tuning across a diversity
of local circuit layouts. This balance may be more or
less delicate at different locations in the orientation
map, and thus render tuning more or less susceptible
to perturbations of excitation or inhibition.

In order for V1, and other "lower" cortical areas,
to perform useful computations for vision, action,
and behavior, they need to have access to information
from "higher" cortical areas that monitor the behavioral and cognitive contingencies of the task at hand.
Recent evidence from several studies, including those
from our laboratory, has bolstered the view that
even in V1, which may not explicitly code for task
dependent features, the responses are strongly dependent on a number of influences that reflect behavioral
contingencies in alert animals. This suggests that
"top-down" inputs from higher cortical areas can
modulate the response properties of V1 neurons. In
some cases, the changes in V1 responses are fairly
complex, beyond simple up or down scaling of response magnitude.

Models of V1 function based on feedforward
principles tend to portray V1 neurons as static
linear spatio-temporal filters. Such models have
difficulty accounting for complex top-down response

modulation. However, a view of V1 with balanced
excitation and inhibition in the local circuitry can
accommodate changes in tuning properties by top-
down inputs. Interestingly, neurons at specific cortical
locations, for example near pinwheel centers of the V1
orientation map, should be more modifiable within
this framework. Given that top-down influences
are variable from cell to cell, we tentatively propose
that these differences may relate to position in the
orientation map. Confirmation of this hypothesis will
require technical advances that enable recording from
neurons at specific sites in the orientation map in
awake, behaving animals.

The orientation map and local circuits

Orientation tuning is a prominent feature of the
receptive fields of neurons in V1. Since the original
description of this response property over four
decades ago (Hubel and Wiesel, 1962), tremendous
effort, both experimental and theoretical, has been
devoted to describing the synaptic mechanisms
responsible for generating this tuning (Vidyasagar
et al., 1996; Sompolinsky and Shapley, 1997; Ferster
and Miller, 2000). To a large extent this debate can be
simplified to a question of whether orientation tuning
is created by the feedforward inputs from the LGN,
or recurrent connections within the cortical circuit. In
this context, it is important to note that the cortical
circuit is not uniform with respect to the layout of
orientation; orientation is represented in a map of
orientation preference, with a pinwheel configuration.
Pinwheel centers are tiled regularly across the cortical
surface, and orientation preference is represented
radially on the spokes around the pinwheel center.
Figure 1A shows an example of such an orientation
map, measured by optical imaging of intrinsic signal
responses to drifting gratings. The preferred orientation at each point on the cortical surface is represented by the color code indicated at the upper right
corner of the map. Pinwheel centers are the points at
which all of the orientations converge. Orientation
domains are the regions of relatively constant orientation preference interspersed between the pinwheel
centers. This structure of the orientation map needs to
be taken into account in order to understand the role
of intracortical circuits in orientation tuning.

67

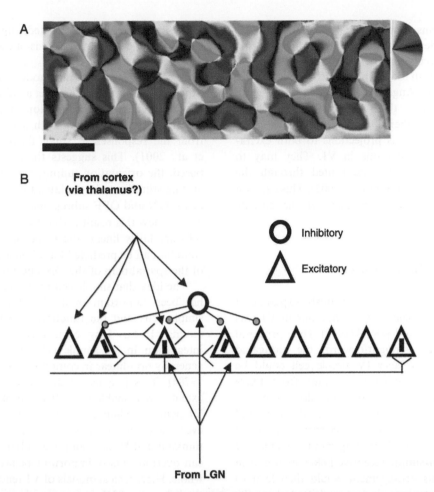

Fig. 1. Schematic depiction of cortical circuitry relevant for orientation tuning and dynamics. A. Orientation preference map obtained with optical imaging of intrinsic signals in cat area V1. Each pixel represents the preferred orientation, computed as the vector average of responses to eight orientations of drifting grating. The orientation value is continuously color coded as indicated in the hemisphere at the upper right corner of the map. The scale bar represents 1 mm of cortical distance. B. Cartoon representation of the components of the cortical circuit involved in creating or modifying orientation tuning. Excitatory neurons are depicted as triangles, and inhibitory neurons as circles. Interareal excitatory connections are depicted by arrow heads; intra-areal excitatory connections by viper-tongues; intra-areal inhibitory connections by gray circles. The feedforward inputs from the LGN synapse on excitatory and inhibitory neurons within one hypercolumn. Intracortical excitatory connections impinge on both local and long range excitatory neurons. Excitatory to inhibitory connections are not shown for the sake of clarity. Inhibitory connections are local within one hypercolumn. Feedback connections from higher visual cortical and eye movement areas contact excitatory and inhibitory neurons.

Another issue that has been heavily debated is the role of inhibition in shaping the orientation tuning of V1 neurons. Most current models of orientation tuning incorporate inhibition to some extent, but its particular role is not fully resolved. Figure 1B shows a schematic representation of the different classes of inputs to, and within, V1 that are likely to play some role in generating or shaping orientation tuning.

The feedforward inputs from the LGN contact both excitatory and inhibitory neurons over a limited cortical extent. They play an important role in the initial generation of tuning, though the degree to which they bias, or determine, tuning remains debated. With a limited extent of less than one hypercolumn, local cortical projections densely interconnect local excitatory (and inhibitory — not shown for clarity) neurons. Long-range projections between separated iso-orientation columns may play a role in modulating receptive field properties, but will not be discussed in detail here (see Gilbert, 1992; Somers et al., 2001; Angelucci et al., 2002; Lund et al., 2003 for a review of these projections). Top-down projections from higher cortical areas in the visual pathway send numerous projections to both excitatory and inhibitory neurons in V1. They may to some considerable extent, be routed through the thalamus (Sherman and Guillery, 2002). This cartoon demonstrates the key components of the circuits discussed below.

Static linear feedforward models

The first model to propose a mechanistic explanation for the orientation selectivity of neurons in V1 was proposed by Hubel and Wiesel (1962). Their proposal was intuitive and straightforward; the elongated receptive field of a layer IV simple cell could be created by the convergence of inputs from LGN neurons with receptive fields lying along the axis of elongation of the cortical cell. If the ON and OFF subfields of the input LGN receptive fields lined up, this would create alternating bands of ON and OFF response in simple receptive fields, as found in cat neurons. This arrangement would then lead to greater response to bars flashed or drifted along the extended axis of the receptive field than to bars presented along the narrow axis. This model has come to be called the feedforward model, because it relies solely on the arrangement of the afferent projections to V1, and not on the interactions or circuitry within V1.

This model has received substantial experimental support of several types. The proposal that the elongated ON and OFF subfields in simple receptive fields are inherited from direct projections of LGN neurons is strongly suggested by cross-correlation studies. Reid and Alonso found that pairs of LGN-V1 neurons were much more likely to exhibit cross-correlation histograms indicative of a direct synaptic connection if the subfield sign (ON or OFF), size and position of both matched closely (Reid and Alonso, 1995; Alonso et al., 2001). Cell pairs with overlapping location, but with mismatched subfield sign were

generally not strongly connected, suggesting a strong specificity of connectivity consistent with the feedforward model.

A second aspect of the model has also received experimental support. Lampl et al. (2001) were able to predict the degree of orientation tuning of responses to drifting grating stimuli with a simple model built from the responses to small flashed spots (Lampl et al., 2001). This suggests that, as originally proposed, the orientation tuning, measured with bar or grating stimuli can be explained by the spatial profile of the ON and OFF subregions of the field. Another way to view this result is that the responses of simple cells are fairly linear: the response to any arbitrary stimulus can be predicted based on a characterization of the spatial map of the ON and OFF regions.

The idea that simple cell receptive fields are linear has been important in driving the thinking about simple cells and the function of V1 in visual processing. It has long been recognized that spatial integration in V1 simple cells is fairly linear, and generally non-linear in complex cells (Movshon et al., 1978a). This is a useful distinction, and to a large extent, a reasonable simplification of the behavior of V1 neurons. Simplification can be dangerous, however, and extensions of the linearity of simple cells to a thinking that V1 acts simply as a bank of linear filters can overlook many important behaviors of V1 as a whole. Hierarchical models of V1 tend to oversimplify the behavior of V1 neurons, and may bias us to miss some of the interesting and important aspects of V1 (reviewed in Riesenhuber and Poggio, 2000). We will highlight several features of orientation tuning in V1 that suggest a more dynamic processing of bottom-up and top-down inputs.

Mechanisms that balance excitation and inhibition

Feedforward models of orientation tuning generally disregard the influence of recurrent cortical circuitry. However, the local cortical inputs to cortical neurons are numerically the majority (Ahmed et al., 1994), and physiological estimates suggest that they provide roughly 60–70% of the excitatory drive to layer IV neurons (Reid and Alonso, 1995; Ferster et al., 1996; Chung and Ferster, 1998; Ferster and Miller, 2000; Alonso et al., 2001). Outside of layer IV, the recurrent local projections likely provide almost all of the excitatory drive. Thus, even if feedforward inputs to layer IV are the major determinant of tuning width, the intracortical inputs can have a strong influence on tuning.

This influence has been demonstrated by a series of experiments that reversibly blocked a subset of the inputs by iontophoresis (Crook and Eysel, 1992; Crook et al., 1997; Crook et al., 1998). When the blocked inputs are orthogonally oriented, the tuning width broadens substantially, but when they are iso-oriented, the effect on tuning is minimal. This finding strongly suggests the existence of strong orthogonal inputs, which are presumably inhibited during normal circuit functioning. A number of other results have also implied a role of inhibition in regulating the sharpness of tuning. Local blockade of inhibition surrounding the recording site can lead to a dramatic decrease in orientation selectivity (Sillito, 1975; Sillito et al., 1980; Sato et al., 1996; Crook et al., 1998; Eysel et al., 1998). Responses of a test grating are suppressed by a second superimposed grating, and the suppression is often maximal with orthogonally orientated mask gratings (Bonds, 1989). These results led to an alternate model of orientation tuning, the cross-inhibition model. In this scheme, non-selective inputs from the LGN are sculpted by orthogonally oriented cortical inhibition to generate sharp tuning. However, two of the main predictions of this model have not been borne out. Blockade of inhibition, intracellularly, in a single neuron, had no demonstrable effect on the sharpness of tuning of that neuron (Nelson et al., 1994). Furthermore, measurements of inhibitory synaptic inputs to V1 neurons have shown that inhibition tends to be strongest at the preferred orientation, rather than at the orthogonal orientation (Ferster, 1986; Anderson et al., 2000; Martinez et al., 2002; Monier et al., 2003). Intriguingly, it is clear that this is not the situation for every cell, suggesting that multiple mechanisms may act to create orientation tuning (Volgushev et al., 1993; Vidyasagar et al., 1996; Martinez et al., 2002; Schummers et al., 2002; Monier et al., 2003). Some of the possible factors responsible for this diversity are discussed below.

None of these results can clearly elucidate a circuit mechanism by which inhibition in the local cortical circuit generates orientation tuning. Taken together, however, they strongly suggest that inhibitory circuitry plays some role in orientation tuning. In fact, the feedforward model requires strong cortical inhibition to account for the contrast invariance of tuning in V1 (Troyer et al., 1998, 2002). While the specific role of inhibition remains to be clarified, the inhibitory regulation of tuning in two respects is examined. First, the importance of inhibition may be more crucial near pinwheel centers in the orientation map. Second, the balance of inhibition and excitation may be a target for modulation by bottom-up and top-down modulation, and the outcome of this interaction with local circuits may be richer than a simple increase or decrease of gain.

To investigate the influence of local cortical circuits on the computation of orientation tuning, we have combined optical imaging of orientation maps and whole cell recording of synaptic integration in individual neurons in V1. Figure 2 illustrates the main results of the measurements of membrane potential (Vm) as a function of orientation map location. Neurons were recorded at sites near pinwheel centers, or far from pinwheel centers, in orientation domains. For each cell, tuning curves were generated for the subthreshold Vm response amplitude as well as the average suprathreshold firing rate. The Vm amplitude was taken as an estimate of the amount of synaptic input to the cell for that stimulus orientation. Figure 2A shows a schematic representation of the average tuning curves for neurons near pinwheel centers (left column), and in orientation domains (right column). As seen in the bottom panel, the tuning curves for firing rate are nearly identical, as has also been reported with extracellular measurements (Maldonado et al., 1997; Dragoi et al., 2001). However, the tuning curves of subthreshold input are different. Near pinwheel centers, the tuning curve is flatter, with much less difference in response amplitude between preferred and orthogonal orientations. By comparison, the tuning curve of orientation domain neurons is more peaked, suggesting a much larger differential in the synaptic input between preferred and orthogonal. The spike threshold is positioned such that the portion of the Vm tuning curve above threshold (the "tip of the iceberg') is equally narrow for the two tuning curves. This suggests that, to some extent, the tuning of synaptic inputs reflect the tuning of the local network.

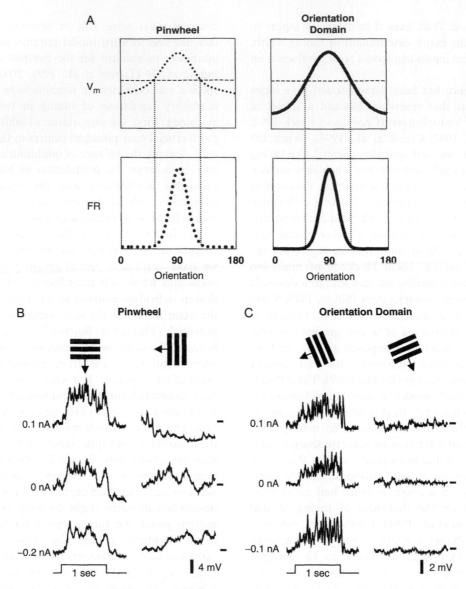

Fig. 2. Subthreshold excitation and inhibition to neurons near pinwheel centers are broader than to orientation domains. A. Schematic depiction of the tuning curves measured near pinwheel centers (left column) and in orientation domains (right column). Mean membrane depolarization (Vm) tuning curves are shown in the top row, and firing rate (FR) tuning curves are shown in the bottom row. Pinwheel neurons have broad subthreshold depolarization, as shown by the Vm curve, with a pedestal (response amplitude at the orthogonal orientation) approximately half the amplitude of the tuning curve peak. The spike threshold is demarcated by the horizontal dashed line. The entire subthreshold portion of the tuning curve is relatively close to the threshold compared with orientation domain neurons. Vertical dashed lines demonstrate the correspondence between the crossing of threshold in the Vm tuning curves, and the firing rate tuning curves. Tuning curves are based on measurements reported in Schummers et al. (2002). B. Demonstration of inhibitory inputs during orthogonal stimulus presentation in a pinwheel center neuron (left column), and the lack thereof in an orientation domain neuron (right column). Each row plots the visually evoked membrane potential for the preferred and orthogonal orientations in the presence of one of three levels of constant current injection. Positive 0.1 nA depolarizes the cells and reveals inhibition as hyperpolarization of Vm. Negative 0.2 nA hyperpolarizes the cells and amplifies the excitatory depolarization of Vm. These examples suggest that the response to orthogonal orientations in pinwheel neurons is composed of both inhibition and excitation, whereas in orientation domain neurons, it is composed of neither. Adapted from Schummers et al. (2002).

As depicted in Fig. 2A, the synaptic inputs on the flanks of the tuning curves of pinwheel center cells push the Vm close to, but not over, the spike threshold. This seems like a precarious balancing act, considering that the spiking response is sharply tuned. How are the synaptic inputs regulated to keep the flank of the tuning curve subthreshold? A likely explanation is that inhibition actively prevents depolarization from leading to spiking. There is qualitative evidence to suggest this is a reasonable explanation. Figure 2B demonstrates an example of Vm responses in a cell near a pinwheel center that suggest inhibition during the orthogonal stimulus (left), and a cell in an orientation domain that does not (right). The responses of the cell were measured under three conditions for each stimulus: resting potential, hyperpolarizing current, and depolarizing current. When the pinwheel cell was hyperpolarized, there was a large stimulus-evoked depolarization that was roughly half the amplitude of the depolarization in response to the preferred orientation. However, when the cell was depolarized, the response to the orthogonal was not hyperpolarizing, suggesting that there was strong inhibitory synaptic input. This was not the case for the orientation domain cell shown on the right. Under all current injection conditions, there was almost no change in Vm in response to the orthogonal grating, suggesting that there was no synaptic input, excitatory, or inhibitory. These examples suggest two conclusions: (1) pinwheel neurons receive strong inputs at all orientations, whereas orientation domain cells only receive inputs near the preferred orientation, commensurate with orientation representation in the orientation map surrounding these sites, and (2) the response at the orthogonal orientation (and at other non-preferred orientations) in pinwheel cells is composed of both excitation and inhibition, which balance each other and help to clamp the Vm below spike threshold and elicit sharp spike tuning (Marino et al., 2003).

These results highlight the important idea that there is a large diversity in the orientation tuning properties in V1. Several recent studies have explicitly examined the diversity in the shapes of tuning curves, and the synaptic mechanisms that might be responsible for these differences (Martinez et al., 2002; Ringach et al., 2002; Schummers et al., 2002; Monier et al., 2003). This diversity is by no means newly discovered (see, for instance Gilbert, 1977; Volgushev et al., 1993; Vidyasagar et al., 1996), but the importance of it has largely been ignored. In particular, models of orientation tuning have generally assumed a prototypical tuning curve for all V1 neurons (Ben-Yishai et al., 1995; Douglas et al., 1995; Somers et al., 1995; Carandini and Ringach, 1997). Naturally, as early attempts to understand network level interactions capable of generating tuning, these simplifying assumptions were necessary. More recent computational models have begun to incorporate features of the orientation map, including pinwheel center organization, into network models of orientation tuning (McLaughlin et al., 2000; Pugh et al., 2000; Kang et al., 2003). Not surprisingly, adding this extra level of complexity has revealed several new insights into the network organization of orientation tuning, including the possible dependence of tuning features on location in the orientation map (Schwabe et al., 2003). As the field moves towards more complete, and therefore sophisticated models of the V1 network, the diversity of response features in individual neurons may be more closely related to features of the network architecture.

Adaptation-induced orientation shifts

The results of the intracellular experiments described in the previous section demonstrate that the synaptic inputs underlying orientation tuning are not the same at all locations in the orientation preference map. Near pinwheel centers, the visually evoked depolarization at orthogonal orientations is strong, yet does not lead to spiking. These inputs are kept below threshold by strong inhibition, which is necessary to balance the excitation, and keep tuning sharp. It is therefore likely that the tuning of neurons near pinwheels is likely to be a more careful balance of excitation and inhibition. It might follow then, that pinwheel neurons are more sensitive to changes in the intracortical inputs. We speculate that manipulation of the local intracortical circuit would have a larger effect on tuning curves in neurons near pinwheel centers. Experiments described above, in which inputs are blocked in adjacent columns, would presumably have a greater effect on neurons near pinwheel centers (Crook et al., 1997, 1998). Indeed, in the experiments of Crook and colleagues, tuning curves were most affected when sites 500 μm away with orthogonal tuning were blocked. It is likely, based on the structure of the orientation preference map, that neurons with orthogonal representation 500 μm from one another are located near pinwheel centers. We suggest, therefore that the effects of such manipulation of the balance of intracortical inputs would be strongest in neurons near pinwheel centers.

This issue has been addressed by experiments that subject neurons to visual pattern adaptation. Pattern adaptation is induced by prolonged visual stimulation by a stimulus with constant features, such as orientation, contrast and/or spatial frequency. In sensory pathways, as in many other brain areas, prolonged synaptic activation leads to a decrease in the strength of cortical activation. There is good evidence in both the visual and somatosensory pathways that sensory adaptation has strong effects at an earlier level than primary cortex (Chung et al., 2002; Solomon et al., 2004). There is also evidence for an intrinsic cellular component to adaptation in V1 neurons (Anderson et al., 2000; Carandini, 2000; Sanchez-Vives et al., 2000a, 2000b). It is likely that both mechanisms contribute to some degree to pattern adaptation in V1.

When the receptive fields of V1 neurons are subjected to adaptation with oriented gratings, the tuning curves of many neurons are altered (Dragoi et al., 2000; Dragoi and Sur, 2003). In particular, the response at the adapting orientation is decreased, the tuning curve broadens, and the preferred orientation of the neuron shifts away from the orientation of the adapting stimulus, i.e., the adaptation leads to a repulsive shift in tuning (all three features are required to explain the population shift in activity consistent with the psychophysical tilt after effect: Sur et al., 2002). What can the response changes after adaptation tell us about the role of different circuits in producing orientation tuning in V1 neurons? An important result that helps answer this question is that the effect of adaptation depends on the location of a neuron in the orientation preference map. Figure 3 demonstrates this effect. Figure 3A–C depicts the effect of adaptation on a neuron in an orientation domain. The location of the cell in the orientation map is shown in Fig. 3A. The pool of intracortical inputs likely to be integrated at the

recording site is located within the dashed white circle. The orientation tuning of this pool is depicted by the histogram in Fig. 3B. The tuning of this histogram is fairly sharp, with most of the inputs coming from a narrow range of orientation, close to the preferred orientation of the recorded cell. This suggests that for this neuron, the influence of the cortical circuit is likely to be constrained to orientations similar to its tuning curve peak. Figure 3C shows the effect of adaptation on the tuning curve of this cell. There is no substantial change in tuning following adaptation with an orientation on one flank of the tuning curve (depicted by the vertical dashed arrow). In sharp contrast, the neuron depicted in Fig. 3D–F shows a dramatic effect of adaptation, with a reduction in response at orientations at and near the adapting orientation, a broadening of the tuning curve, and a shift in the preferred orientation away from the adapting orientation, created by an increase in the response to orientations on the flank of the tuning curve away from the adapting orientation (Fig. 3F). This neuron is located at a pinwheel center (Fig. 3D), and the distribution of orientations in the local circuit is therefore broad (Fig. 3E).

The contrasting effects of adaptation on these two cells suggest that the orientation representation in the local network is a critical factor in determining the effect of pattern adaptation. Indeed, there is a relationship between the orientation selectivity of the local representation, and the magnitude of the effects of adaptation. Figure 4 shows that both the magnitude of tuning shift (Fig. 4A), and the magnitude of change in response magnitude on the near flank of the tuning curve (Fig. 4B) are strongly related to the selectivity of the local orientation representation. Interestingly, the selectivity of the subthreshold Vm tuning is also linearly related to the selectivity in the local orientation map (Fig. 4C). This suggests that the broad subthreshold inputs from the local circuit may provide the synaptic substrate for orientation shifts induced by adaptation. Neurons in orientation domains only receive inputs from a narrow range of orientations, and cannot therefore be modified by adapting stimuli outside that range. Neurons near pinwheel centers, on the other hand, receive substantial subthreshold inputs over a broad range of orientations, and the spike tuning can be shifted by alterations of the excitatory and/or

73

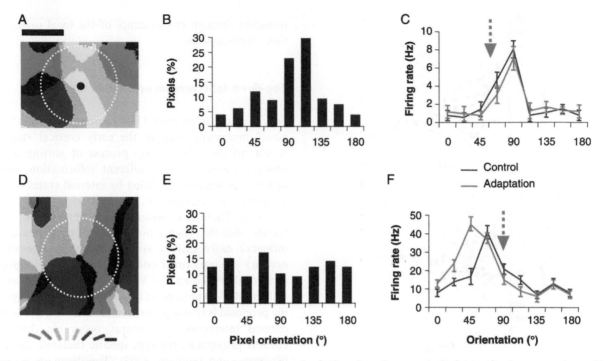

Fig. 3. Adaptation-induced tuning curve changes depend on location in the orientation map. A–C. Adaptation in a neuron located in an orientation domain. A. Orientation map surrounding the location of the recorded cell. Scale bar represent 500 μm. Dashed white line represents a radius of 500 μm centered on the recording site. Orientation color code is as depicted by the color scale in D. B. Histogram of the distribution of preferred orientation values within the white circle in the orientation map in A. Bars are normalized to yield a percentage of total area. C. Firing rate tuning curves obtained pre-adaptation and post-adaptation, color coded as in the legend below the graph. The orientation of the adapting stimulus is indicated by the vertical dashed arrow. D–F. Adaptation in a neuron located in a pinwheel center. All conventions as in A–C. Adapted from Dragoi et al. (2001).

inhibitory synaptic weights across a broad range of orientations. The relationship between the selectivity of the local circuit and the behavior of individual neurons highlights an important point. Pinwheel centers and orientation domains represent the extremes of a continuum of local orientation representation within the map of orientation preference. The inputs to any neuron are in part determined by the representation in the local network. These inputs provide a balance of excitation and inhibition, which regulates the responses and produces invariant output (spike) tuning. The balance can be more critical at some points (pinwheel centers) than others (orientation domains), and thus perturbations of inputs results in larger shifts near pinwheel centers.

In other words, the effects of changes in feedforward inputs can be better understood as influencing

the local network as a whole than by influencing individual neurons in isolation. A similar view has previously been put forward in the context of the influence of stimuli in the receptive field surround on responses to stimuli in the receptive field center (Somers et al., 1998). In a network model of long-range connections in V1, Somers et al. (1998) showed that the contrast-dependent effects of long-range inputs, while counter-intuitive from the perspective of their effect on a single cell, arise naturally through excitatory/inhibitory balance in the local cortical circuit. The same principle may apply to the orientation-dependent effects of specific adaptation of feedforward inputs. In light of the diversity of local networks inherent from the orientation map structure, we can further propose that the influence of changes in inputs on single neurons (be they feedforward, long-range intracortical, or top-down), will be

74

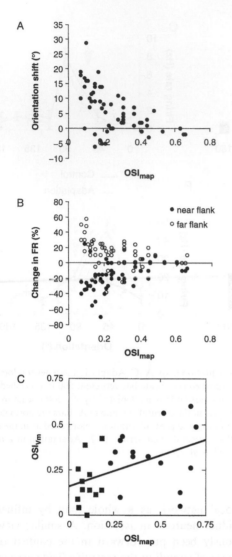

Fig. 4. Adaptation effects vary systematically with position in the orientation map. A. Scatter plot of the magnitude of adaptation-induced orientation shift, as a function of the OSI of the local patch of cortex surrounding the recording site (OSI_{map}). B. Scatter plot of the adaptation-induced changes in response amplitude as a function of OSI_{map} for the same population of cells as in B. Blue points represent changes in firing rate (FR) on the near flank of the tuning curve — orientations intermediate between the preferred orientation and the adapting orientation. Red points indicate changes in firing rate on the far flank — orientations on the opposite side of the preferred orientation, relative to the adapting orientation. C. Scatter plot of the OSI of the membrane depolarization (Vm) tuning curves as a function of OSI_{map}. Squares represent neurons classified as pinwheel center neurons, and circles those designated as orientation domain neurons. Adapted from Dragoi et al. (2000) and Schummers et al. (2002).

refracted through the structure of the local orientation representation.

Top-down influences on orientation tuning

New evidence from several laboratories indicates that visual processing even in the early cortical stages is not merely a bottom-up process of sorting and onward transmission of afferent information, but rather is powerfully modified by internal states such as attention, expectation, or past history of the stimulus. There is considerable anatomical support for the idea that higher order cortical processes can influence early sensory areas through an extensive network of intra-areal connections that are highly reciprocal (Felleman and Van Essen, 1991; Salin and Bullier, 1995; Angelucci et al., 2002). A more intriguing proposal is that top-down influences, and cortico-cortical interactions in general, occur via driving cortical projections through specific thalamic nuclei (Sherman and Guillery, 2002). Top-down or state-dependent inputs can have diverse effects; they can influence perception by increasing stimulus selectivity (by enhancing relevant and/or suppressing irrelevant information), or aid in decision making or guide sensory-motor systems according to behavioral contingencies. In sum, the new findings indicate that early visual cortical areas (or even subcortical structures) are part of a distributed rather than simply a hierarchical network for vision, and that bottom-up and top-down processes interact dynamically so as to continuously recalibrate neuronal responses to behaviorally relevant stimuli.

A recent report used an interesting variation of adaptation to study object based attention in human lateral occipital cortex (LOC), considered to be homologous to inferotemporal (IT) cortex in monkeys (Murray and Wojciulik, 2004). It is generally believed that attention increases neuronal responses to the attended location or stimulus, via either a multiplicative or an additive process. An alternative possibility is that attention causes an increase in selectivity of a specific subpopulation of neurons that responds to the attended stimulus. The authors repeatedly presented the same stimulus in pairs of either the same orientation or different orientations. The subjects' task was to either perform color matching or orientation matching between successive pairs. It was found that the fMRI signal was sharply enhanced when subjects performed orientation matching, and therefore attended to the stimulus orientation. A likely explanation for this finding is that attention increased sensitivity to orientation differences or narrowed the tuning of the sub-population of neurons, thereby increasing the selectivity of these neurons.

One direct consequence of an adaptive process in early visual cortex that enhances sensitivity to changes relates to saccadic behavior during natural vision. Natural viewing involves rapid saccadic eye movements (3–4 saccades per second) interspersed by periods of brief fixation (Yarbus, 1967). During these fixation epochs, neurons encounter image patches that are well correlated in local image features, such as orientation (Dragoi et al., 2002). Brief exposure to such spatially correlated image patches induces short term adaptation that results in reduction in response of neurons at their preferred orientation, thereby possibly reducing the correlation among neuronal responses (Attneave, 1954; Yarbus, 1967; Barlow, 1990). A close examination of saccadic behavior of humans and monkeys during viewing of natural scenes reveals that a substantial percentage of saccades are made to image locations that are uncorrelated in their local attributes. Therefore a brief fixation is typically followed by a saccade to an entirely different part of the scene where the change in local statistics (e.g., orientation) is maximal. In a recent study the role of brief adaptation on orientation discrimination in humans and monkeys was explored (Dragoi et al., 2002). It was found that short-term adaptation by oriented gratings, on the time scale of visual fixation during natural viewing, markedly improves orientation discrimination for orthogonal orientations. We further explored the effect of rapid adaptation on single neuron responses in V1. Specifically, we were interested in the temporal dynamics of orientation tuning under simulated conditions of brief fixational adaptation. By employing a reverse correlation procedure, the dynamics of orientation tuning were captured on a millisecond time scale and allowed us to uncover effects of brief adaptation on the development of orientation tuning. Single neurons exhibited distinct behaviors with and without brief adaptation: adapting orientations near

the preferred orientation of the cells delayed the development of orientation tuned response; conversely response tuning was accelerated after adapting to an orthogonal orientation. Importantly, adaptation near the preferred orientation suppressed responses on the near flank of the tuning curve, broadened the tuning width, and shifting the preferred orientation away from the adapting stimulus. On the other hand, orthogonal adaptation maintained the optimal orientation but sharpened the orientation tuning of the neurons.

These findings are in contrast with the prevalent notion that the role of visual attention is to create a saliency map of the visual scene, which the system arrives at through a "guesswork" based on the relative strength of stimulus features, and which guides decision processes and visuomotor behavior (Treue, 2003). At least one aspect of the visual saccade system seems to be an adaptive process that accentuates differences in image statistics, by a dynamic interaction between top-down and bottom-up influences. Short-term adaptation sharpens neuronal selectivity and continuously updates processing of the visual scene.

Extra-retinal influences on bottom-up processes

Vision, and the response of cortical neurons, is influenced not only by spatial statistics but also by the temporal statistics of visual stimuli. For example, a central aspect of visual processing is the acquisition of an internal representation of stimulus location derived from the temporal order or history of stimulus appearance. Most investigations of the control of visually guided movements have focused on how parietal and frontal cortex, in conjunction with brain stem circuits, are involved in target selection and eye movement control (Platt and Glimcher, 1999; Schall and Thompson, 1999; Corbetta and Shulman, 2002; Glimcher, 2002). However, recent work has claimed a role for early visual cortex in saccade planning and decision making (Schiller and Tehovnik, 2001; Nakamura and Colby, 2002). Recently, the influence of the temporal order of stimuli presented at specific locations on performance in a gaze direction task was examined. The behavioral data point to acquisition of an internal representation of stimulus location based on prior presentations, and the physiological data show a surprising and substantial involvement of V1. The results are consistent with early visual cortex being a key part of a distributed network of cortical areas that is involved in acquiring the internal representation (Sharma et al., 2003).

A gaze direction task was devised in which subjects could acquire information about future stimulus locations in one task condition but not in another. The task consisted of the appearance of a fixation spot at one of three locations on a computer screen placed in front of a subject. In one condition, the location of the fixation spot varied randomly from trial to trial (termed "randomized" trials), while in the other, the spot appeared repeatedly at the same location for a succession of trials (termed "grouped" trials). Subjects did not receive any prior cue as to which sequence was in effect. Human subjects were asked to indicate where the target would appear next as trials progressed in either the randomized or the grouped sequence. While the probability of successful prediction in the randomized trials was independent of trial number, the prediction probability in the grouped trials tracked the Bayesian target probability as the trials progressed. That is, a significant reduction was noticed in prediction uncertainty when the grouped trials were presented compared to randomized trials. Thus, the manner of stimulus presentation, and the order of stimulus appearance at a given location, provided information about future stimulus locations, which observers could assimilate.

Next, alert monkeys were trained in a similar task. Once the fixation spot appeared in one of the three locations, animals made a saccade and achieved stable fixation. Their latency to achieve fixation in the randomized and grouped task conditions was measured. It has been shown previously that the saccade latency to a visual target is a sensitive indicator of the likelihood of the target's appearance (Luce, 1986; Kowler, 1990; Carpenter and Williams, 1995). Similar to human performance in the two task conditions, it was reasoned that fixation latency would shorten as monkeys attained knowledge of target location, but not otherwise. As expected, fixation latency was approximately constant from trial to trial in the randomized condition but shortened significantly as trials progressed in the grouped condition.

Importantly, the performance of humans and monkeys was consistent with the Bayesian probability of target appearance. These findings indicate the acquisition of an internal representation of stimulus location with successive trials in the grouped condition of the task, in both humans and monkeys.

While the monkeys performed the fixation task in the two trial conditions, the single neuron responses in V1 to oriented sinusoidal gratings presented in the receptive field of neurons within 3–5 degrees from the fixation spot were also recorded. It is known that integration of retinal and extra-retinal inputs to the brain is essential for localization of stimuli in space, allocation of attention, or dynamic stabilization of receptive fields (Andersen et al., 1985; Downing, 1988; Motter and Poggio, 1990). A number of studies have reported that responses of a subset of V1 neurons are modulated by the direction of gaze (Weyand and Malpeli, 1993; Guo and Li, 1997; Trotter and Celebrini, 1999; Rosenbluth and Allman, 2002). It is however unclear if the modulation in V1 response is purely gaze related or other top-down processes play a role in this response modification. Our findings demonstrate that V1 responses are modulated by gaze direction in a task dependent manner. Figure 5A depicts orientation tuning curves of a V1 neuron in randomized and grouped trials in three gaze directions. The response of the neuron was significantly modulated when stimuli appeared at a particular gaze direction in a particular sequence: stimuli appearing in a grouped sequence at one location caused neurons to respond significantly more (or, in other neurons, less) than when stimuli appeared randomly. In other words, responses to the same visual stimulus (a grating of optimal orientation for a neuron), presented at the same location (and hence subtending the same angle of gaze), are altered when stimuli are presented in one sequence of trials (the grouped sequence) than in another (the random sequence). It is important to note that each recorded neuron had its own preference for modulation in a particular gaze direction and there was no systematic bias in the neuronal population for a particular orientation or gaze direction. On a population basis, more than 40% of the recorded neurons responded in a manner similar to the neuron of Fig. 5A. An internal representation index (IRI) that signifies response difference in the two trial conditions regardless of

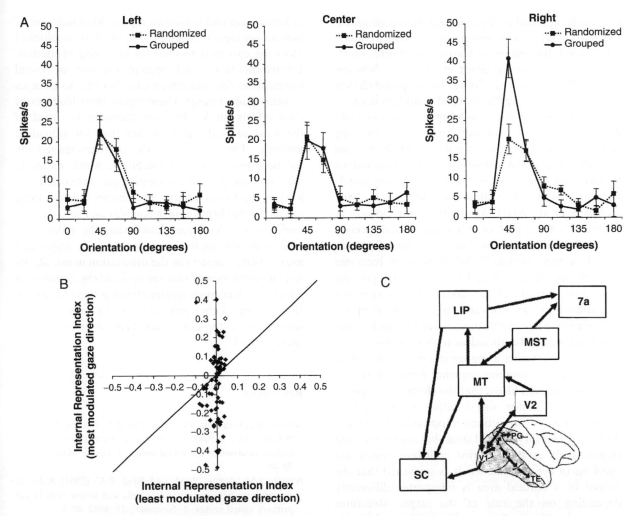

Fig. 5. Modulation of orientation selective responses of V1 neurons in alert monkeys by an internal representation of stimulus location. A. Orientation tuning curves of a V1 neuron when a fixation spot was presented in left, center and right locations on a screen in front of the animal. The darker curves are derived from 'grouped' trials while the lighter ones are from 'randomized' trials. There was a significant increase in response in the grouped condition when the monkey's gaze was directed to the right. B. Scatterplot of the response index of the population data (*n* = 67 cells) in the least modulated gaze direction compared to most modulated gaze direction. The cell of panel A is shown as a red dot. C. Schematic diagram showing interconnectivity among visual cortical areas (of both dorsal and ventral streams) and motor outputs to the superior colliculus (SC). V1 is an integral part of this distributed network that is involved in processing bottom-up and top-down interactions. Abbreviations, primary visual cortex (V1); secondary visual cortex (V2); middle temporal area (MT); lateral intraparietal cortex (LIP); medial superior temporal area (MST). Adapted from Sharma et al. (2003).

gaze direction was calculated. Figure 5B shows the population IRI data calculated for the best modulated gaze direction of individual neurons versus the least modulated gaze direction. Positive IRI values indicate a response increase in grouped trials. These data demonstrate that a substantial proportion of V1 neurons represent in their responses the probability of

target appearance derived from the temporal sequence of stimuli.

How might V1 neurons dynamically alter their responses to signal such an internal representation? The modulation of V1 responses constitutes an active shaping of the orientation tuning curve, for responses to the preferred orientation are specifically and selectively modified as the representation is acquired. Orientation selective responses are similarly modified after visual discrimination learning or during short-term visual memory (Gilbert et al., 2001; Schoups et al., 2001; Super et al., 2001). The response change in V1 neurons during the grouped condition involves the integration of top-down inputs carrying task-dependent signals with bottom-up ones carrying visual signals. Top-down signals are likely to arise from the parietal and frontal cortex, which are known to play a key role in saccade decisions and commands (Andersen et al., 1997; Glimcher, 2001; Schall, 2001; Goldberg et al., 2002). As shown in the cartoon in Figure 5C, V1 is part of this network and receives feedback projections from these areas. Such feedback would in turn modulate the strength of recurrent connections between local V1 neurons (Dragoi and Sur, 2000; Somers et al., 2001), that modify the amplification of feedforward inputs to V1 neurons, and constitute a plausible mechanism by which orientation tuning can be altered as trials progress.

Finally, what does a change in orientation tuning as a function of stimulus sequence imply for vision? It is possible, even likely, that the change in response constitutes a motor signal rather than a purely sensory one. V1 projections importantly target not only higher sensory cortical areas, but also subcortical targets such as the superior colliculus which are involved in eye movements. It is suggested that the output of a cortical area is interpreted differently depending on the role of the target: structures concerned with visual processing would read the V1 output as providing information about the image, whereas structures concerned with eye movements would utilize the output for modulating gaze. On this view, no area of the cortex, not even the primary visual cortex, is only a sensory area — rather, every area potentially contributes to movement as well. Indeed, it has been cogently argued that mechanisms of perception necessarily include action, with the thalamus involved critically in receiving copies of the efferent output (Guillery and Sherman, 2002).

Conclusions

This chapter has analyzed evidence that orientation tuning in V1 can be dynamically modified by changes in bottom-up and top-down inputs. Manipulation of bottom-up inputs by adaptation or pharmacological blockade can lead to changes in tuning properties. Behavioral tasks that require the use of visual information for completion can also lead to changes in orientation tuning. These inputs most likely exert their effects on V1 by interactions at the level of the local cortical circuit, rather than on individual neurons. The local network is characterized by balanced excitation and inhibition, which naturally regulate tuning. Thus, by tapping into network at the level of the local circuitry, bottom-up and top-down inputs can modify tuning in complex and behaviorally useful ways. We have shown that the balance of inhibition and excitation is particularly important near pinwheel centers in the orientation maps. Short-term modification of bottom-up inputs by orientation adaptation has much greater effects at these locations. It is suspected that pinwheel centers may be more susceptible to top-down modification in orientation space as well.

References

Ahmed, B., Anderson, J.C., Douglas, R.J., Martin, K.A. and Nelson, J.C. (1994) Polyneuronal innervation of spiny stellate neurons in cat visual cortex. J. Comp. Neurol., 341: 39–49.

Alonso, J.M., Usrey, W.M. and Reid, R.C. (2001) Rules of connectivity between geniculate cells and simple cells in cat primary visual cortex. J. Neurosci., 21: 4002–4015.

Andersen, R.A., Essick, G.K. and Siegel, R.M. (1985) Encoding of spatial location by posterior parietal neurons. Science, 230: 456–458.

Andersen, R.A., Snyder, L.H., Bradley, D.C. and Xing, J. (1997) Multimodal representation of space in the posterior parietal cortex and its use in planning movements. Annu. Rev. Neurosci., 20: 303–330.

Anderson, J.S., Carandini, M. and Ferster, D. (2000) Orientation tuning of input conductance, excitation, and inhibition in cat primary visual cortex. J. Neurophysiol., 84: 909–926.

Angelucci, A., Levitt, J.B., Walton, E.J., Hupe, J.M., Bullier, J. and Lund, J.S. (2002) Circuits for local and global signal integration in primary visual cortex. J. Neurosci., 22: 8633–8646.

Attneave, F. (1954) Some informational aspects of visual perception. Psychol. Rev., 61: 183–193.

Barlow, H.B. (1990) A theory about the functional role and synaptic mechanism of after-effects. In: Blakemore, C. (Ed.),

Vision: Coding and Efficiency, Cambridge Univeristy Press, Cambridge, UK, pp. 363–375.

Ben-Yishai, R., Bar-Or, R.L. and Sompolinsky, H. (1995) Theory of orientation tuning in visual cortex. Proc. Natl. Acad. Sci. USA, 92: 3844–3848.

Bonds, A.B. (1989) Role of inhibition in the specification of orientation selectivity of cells in the cat striate cortex. Vis. Neurosci., 2: 41–55.

Carandini, M. (2000) Visual cortex: Fatigue and adaptation. Curr Biol., 10: R605–607.

Carandini, M. and Ringach, D.L. (1997) Predictions of a recurrent model of orientation selectivity. Vision Res., 37: 3061–3071.

Carpenter, R.H. and Williams, M.L. (1995) Neural computation of log likelihood in control of saccadic eye movements. Nature, 377: 59–62.

Chung, S. and Ferster, D. (1998) Strength and orientation tuning of the thalamic input to simple cells revealed by electrically evoked cortical suppression. Neuron, 20: 1177–1189.

Chung, S., Li, X. and Nelson, S.B. (2002) Short-term depression at thalamocortical synapses contributes to rapid adaptation of cortical sensory responses in vivo. Neuron, 34: 437–446.

Corbetta, M. and Shulman, G.L. (2002) Control of goal-directed and stimulus-driven attention in the brain. Nat. Rev. Neurosci., 3: 201–215.

Crook, J.M. and Eysel, U.T. (1992) GABA-induced inactivation of functionally characterized sites in cat visual cortex (area 18): effects on orientation tuning. J. Neurosci., 12: 1816–1825.

Crook, J.M., Kisvarday, Z.F. and Eysel, U.T. (1997) GABA-induced inactivation of functionally characterized sites in cat striate cortex: Effects on orientation tuning and direction selectivity. Vis. Neurosci., 14: 141–158.

Crook, J.M., Kisvarday, Z.F. and Eysel, U.T. (1998) Evidence for a contribution of lateral inhibition to orientation tuning and direction selectivity in cat visual cortex: Reversible inactivation of functionally characterized sites combined with neuroanatomical tracing techniques. Eur. J. Neurosci., 10: 2056–2075.

Douglas, R.J., Koch, C., Mahowald, M., Martin, K.A. and Suarez, H.H. (1995) Recurrent excitation in neocortical circuits. Science, 269: 981–985.

Downing, C.J. (1988) Expectancy and visual-spatial attention: effects on perceptual quality. J. Exp. Psychol. Hum. Percept Perform, 14: 188–202.

Dragoi, V. and Sur, M. (2000) Dynamic properties of recurrent inhibition in primary visual cortex: contrast and orientation dependence of contextual effects. J. Neurophysiol., 83: 1019–1030.

Dragoi, V. and Sur, M. (2003) Plasticity of orientation processing in adult visual cortex. In: Chalupa, L.M. and Werner, J.S., (Eds.), The Visual Neurosciences, MIT Press, Cambridge, pp. 1654–1664.

Dragoi, V., Sharma, J. and Sur, M. (2000) Adaptation-induced plasticity of orientation tuning in adult visual cortex. Neuron, 28: 287–298.

Dragoi, V., Rivadulla, C. and Sur, M. (2001) Foci of orientation plasticity in visual cortex. Nature, 411: 80–86.

Dragoi, V., Sharma, J., Miller, E.K. and Sur, M. (2002) Dynamics of neuronal sensitivity in visual cortex and local feature discrimination. Nat. Neurosci., 5: 883–891.

Eysel, U.T., Shevelev, I.A., Lazareva, N.A. and Sharaev, G.A. (1998) Orientation tuning and receptive field structure in cat striate neurons during local blockade of intracortical inhibition. Neuroscience, 84: 25–36.

Felleman, D.J. and Van Essen, D.C. (1991) Distributed hierarchical processing in the primate cerebral cortex. Cereb Cortex, 1: 1–47.

Ferster, D. (1986) Orientation selectivity of synaptic potentials in neurons of cat primary visual cortex. J. Neurosci., 6: 1284–1301.

Ferster, D. and Miller, K.D. (2000) Neural mechanisms of orientation selectivity in the visual cortex. Annu. Rev. Neurosci., 23: 441–471.

Ferster, D., Chung, S. and Wheat, H. (1996) Orientation selectivity of thalamic input to simple cells of cat visual cortex. Nature, 380: 249–252.

Gilbert, C.D. (1977) Laminar differences in receptive field properties of cells in cat primary visual cortex. J. Physiol., 268: 391–421.

Gilbert, C.D. (1992) Horizontal integration and cortical dynamics. Neuron, 9: 1–13.

Gilbert, C.D., Sigman, M. and Crist, R.E. (2001) The neural basis of perceptual learning. Neuron, 31: 681–697.

Glimcher, P. (2002) Decisions, decisions, decisions: choosing a biological science of choice. Neuron, 36: 323–332.

Glimcher, P.W. (2001) Making choices: the neurophysiology of visual-saccadic decision making. Trends Neurosci., 24: 654–659.

Goldberg, M.E., Bisley, J., Powell, K.D., Gottlieb, J. and Kusunoki, M. (2002) The role of the lateral intraparietal area of the monkey in the generation of saccades and visuospatial attention. Ann. N Y Acad. Sci., 956: 205–215.

Guillery, R.W. and Sherman, S.M. (2002) The thalamus as a monitor of motor outputs. Philos. Trans. R Soc. Lond. B Biol. Sci., 357: 1809–1821.

Guo, K. and Li, C.Y. (1997) Eye position-dependent activation of neurones in striate cortex of macaque. Neuroreport, 8: 1405–1409.

Hubel, D.H. and Wiesel, T.H. (1962) Receptive fields, binocular interaction and functional architecture of the cat's visual cortex. J. Physiol., 160: 106–154.

Kang, K., Shelley, M. and Sompolinsky, H. (2003) Mexican hats and pinwheels in visual cortex. Proc. Natl. Acad. Sci. USA, 100: 2848–2853.

Kowler, E. (1990) The role of visual and cognitive processes in the control of eye movement. Rev. Oculomot. Res., 4: 1–70.

Lampl, I., Anderson, J.S., Gillespie, D.C. and Ferster, D. (2001) Prediction of orientation selectivity from receptive field architecture in simple cells of cat visual cortex. Neuron, 30: 263–274.

Luce, R.D. (1986) Response Times: Their Role in Inferring Elementary Mental Organization, Oxford Press, New York.

Lund, J.S., Angelucci, A. and Bressloff, P.C. (2003) Anatomical substrates for functional columns in macaque monkey primary visual cortex. Cereb Cortex, 13: 15–24.

Maldonado, P.E., Godecke, I., Gray, C.M. and Bonhoeffer, T. (1997) Orientation selectivity in pinwheel centers in cat striate cortex. Science, 276: 1551–1555.

Marino, J., Schummers, J. and Sur, M. (2003) Input conductance at different locations within V1 orientation map. Soc. Neurosci. Abst., 29.

Martinez, L.M., Alonso, J.M., Reid, R.C. and Hirsch, J.A. (2002) Laminar processing of stimulus orientation in cat visual cortex. J. Physiol., 540: 321–333.

McLaughlin, D., Shapley, R., Shelley, M. and Wielaard, D.J. (2000) A neuronal network model of macaque primary visual cortex (V1): orientation selectivity and dynamics in the input layer 4Calpha. Proc. Natl. Acad. Sci. USA, 97: 8087–8092.

Monier, C., Chavane, F., Baudot, P., Graham, L.J. and Fregnac, Y. (2003) Orientation and direction selectivity of synaptic inputs in visual cortical neurons: a diversity of combinations produces spike tuning. Neuron, 37: 663–680.

Motter, B.C. and Poggio, G.F. (1990) Dynamic stabilization of receptive fields of cortical neurons (VI) during fixation of gaze in the macaque. Exp. Brain. Res., 83: 37–43.

Movshon, J.A., Thompson, I.D. and Tolhurst, D.J. (1978a) Receptive field organization of complex cells in the cat's striate cortex. J. Physiol., 283: 79–99.

Movshon, J.A., Thompson, I.D. and Tolhurst, D.J. (1978b) Spatial summation in the receptive fields of simple cells in the cat's striate cortex. J. Physiol., 283: 53–77.

Murray, S.O. and Wojciulik, E. (2004) Attention increases neural selectivity in the human lateral occipital complex. Nat. Neurosci., 7: 70–74.

Nakamura, K. and Colby, C.L. (2002) Updating of the visual representation in monkey striate and extrastriate cortex during saccades. Proc. Natl. Acad. Sci. USA, 99: 4026–4031.

Nelson, S., Toth, L., Sheth, B. and Sur, M. (1994) Orientation selectivity of cortical neurons during intracellular blockade of inhibition. Science, 265: 774–777.

Platt, M.L. and Glimcher, P.W. (1999) Neural correlates of decision variables in parietal cortex. Nature, 400: 233–238.

Pugh, M.C., Ringach, D.L., Shapley, R. and Shelley, M.J. (2000) Computational modeling of orientation tuning dynamics in monkey primary visual cortex. J. Comput. Neurosci., 8: 143–159.

Reid, R.C. and Alonso, J.M. (1995) Specificity of monosynaptic connections from thalamus to visual cortex. Nature, 378: 281–284.

Riesenhuber, M. and Poggio, T. (2000) Models of object recognition. Nat. Neurosci., 3 Suppl: 1199–1204.

Ringach, D.L., Shapley, R.M. and Hawken, M.J. (2002) Orientation selectivity in macaque V1: diversity and laminar dependence. J. Neurosci., 22: 5639–5651.

Rosenbluth, D. and Allman, J.M. (2002) The effect of gaze angle and fixation distance on the responses of neurons in V1, V2, and V4. Neuron, 33: 143–149.

Salin, P.A. and Bullier, J. (1995) Corticocortical connections in the visual system: structure and function. Physiol. Rev., 75: 107–154.

Sanchez-Vives, M.V., Nowak, L.G. and McCormick, D.A. (2000a) Membrane mechanisms underlying contrast adaptation in cat area 17 in vivo. J. Neurosci., 20: 4267–4285.

Sanchez-Vives, M.V., Nowak, L.G. and McCormick, D.A. (2000b) Cellular mechanisms of long-lasting adaptation in visual cortical neurons in vitro. J. Neurosci., 20: 4286–4299.

Sato, H., Katsuyama, N., Tamura, H., Hata, Y. and Tsumoto, T. (1996) Mechanisms underlying orientation selectivity of neurons in the primary visual cortex of the macaque. J. Physiol., 494(Pt 3): 757–771.

Schall, J.D. (2001) Neural basis of deciding, choosing and acting. Nat. Rev. Neurosci., 2: 33–42.

Schall, J.D. and Thompson, K.G. (1999) Neural selection and control of visually guided eye movements. Annu. Rev. Neurosci., 22: 241–259.

Schiller, P.H. and Tehovnik, E.J. (2001) Look and see: how the brain moves your eyes about. Prog. Brain. Res., 134: 127–142.

Schoups, A., Vogels, R., Qian, N. and Orban, G. (2001) Practising orientation identification improves orientation coding in V1 neurons. Nature, 412: 549–553.

Schummers, J., Marino, J. and Sur, M. (2002) Synaptic integration by V1 neurons depends on location within the orientation map. Neuron, 36: 969–978.

Sharma, J., Dragoi, V., Tenenbaum, J.B., Miller, E.K. and Sur, M. (2003) V1 neurons signal acquisition of an internal representation of stimulus location. Science, 300: 1758–1763.

Sherman, S.M. and Guillery, R.W. (2002) The role of the thalamus in the flow of information to the cortex. Philos. Trans. R Soc. Lond. B Biol. Sci., 357: 1695–1708.

Sillito, A.M. (1975) The contribution of inhibitory mechanisms to the receptive field properties of neurones in the striate cortex of the cat. J. Physiol., 250: 305–329.

Sillito, A.M., Kemp, J.A., Milson, J.A. and Berardi, N. (1980) A re-evaluation of the mechanisms underlying simple cell orientation selectivity. Brain Res., 194: 517–520.

Solomon, S.G., Peirce, J.W., Dhruv, N.T. and Lennie, P. (2004) Profound contrast adaptation early in the visual pathway. Neuron, 42: 155–162.

Somers, D., Dragoi, V. and Sur, M. (2001) Orientation selectivity and its modulation by local and long-range connections in visual cortex. In: Payne, B.R. and Peters, A., (Eds.), The Cat Primary Visual Cortex, Academic Press, Boston, pp. 471–520.

Somers, D.C., Nelson, S.B. and Sur, M. (1995) An emergent model of orientation selectivity in cat visual cortical simple cells. J. Neurosci., 15: 5448–5465.

Somers, D.C., Todorov, E.V., Siapas, A.G., Toth, L.J., Kim, D.S. and Sur, M. (1998) A local circuit approach to understanding integration of long-range inputs in primary visual cortex. Cereb Cortex, 8: 204–217.

Sompolinsky, H. and Shapley, R. (1997) New perspectives on the mechanisms for orientation selectivity. Curr. Opin. Neurobiol., 7: 514–522.

Super, H., Spekreijse, H. and Lamme, V.A. (2001) A neural correlate of working memory in the monkey primary visual cortex. Science, 293: 120–124.

Sur, M., Schummers, J. and Dragoi, V. (2002) Cortical plasticity: time for a change. Curr. Biol., 12: R168–70.

Treue, S. (2003) Visual attention: the where, what, how and why of saliency. Curr. Opin. Neurobiol., 13: 428–432.

Trotter, Y. and Celebrini, S. (1999) Gaze direction controls response gain in primary visual-cortex neurons. Nature, 398: 239–242.

Troyer, T.W., Krukowski, A.E. and Miller, K.D. (2002) LGN input to simple cells and contrast-invariant orientation tuning: an analysis. J. Neurophysiol., 87: 2741–2752.

Troyer, T.W., Krukowski, A.E., Priebe, N.J. and Miller, K.D. (1998) Contrast-invariant orientation tuning in cat visual cortex: thalamocortical input tuning and correlation-based intracortical connectivity. J. Neurosci., 18: 5908–5927.

Vidyasagar, T.R., Pei, X. and Volgushev, M. (1996) Multiple mechanisms underlying the orientation selectivity of visual cortical neurones. Trends Neurosci., 19: 272–277.

Volgushev, M., Pei, X., Vidyasagar, T.R. and Creutzfeldt, O.D. (1993) Excitation and inhibition in orientation selectivity of cat visual cortex neurons revealed by whole-cell recordings in vivo. Vis. Neurosci., 10: 1151–1155.

Weyand, T.G. and Malpeli, J.G. (1993) Responses of neurons in primary visual cortex are modulated by eye position. J. Neurophysiol., 69: 2258–2260.

Yarbus, A.L. (1967) Eye Movement and Vision., Plenum Press, New York.

Progress in Brain Research, Vol. 149
ISSN 0079-6123

CHAPTER 7

Dynamic properties of thalamic neurons for vision

Henry J. Alitto and W. Martin Usrey*

Center for Neuroscience, University of California at Davis, Davis, CA 95616, USA

Abstract: A striking property of neurons in the lateral geniculate nucleus (LGN) of the thalamus is the ability to dynamically filter and transform the temporal structure of their retinal spike input. In particular, LGN neurons respond to visual stimuli with either burst spike responses or tonic spike responses. While much is known from in vitro studies about the cellular mechanisms that underlie burst and tonic spikes, relatively little is known about the sensory stimuli that evoke these two categories of spikes. This review examines recent progress that has been made towards understanding the spatiotemporal properties of visual stimuli that evoke burst and tonic spikes. Using white-noise stimuli and reverse-correlation analysis, results show that burst and tonic spikes carry similar, but distinct, information to cortex. Compared to tonic spikes, burst spikes (1) occur with a shorter latency between stimulus and response, (2) have a greater dependence on stimuli with transitions from suppressive to preferred states, and (3) prefer stimuli that provide increased drive to the receptive field center and even greater increased drive to the receptive field surround. These results are discussed with an emphasis placed on relating the cellular constraints for burst and tonic activity with the functional properties of the early visual pathway during sensory processing.

Introduction

The lateral geniculate nucleus (LGN) of the thalamus is a major bottleneck for visual information traveling from retina to cortex. As a result, LGN neurons are in a strategic position to influence visual processing. Although once viewed as a simple relay in the visual pathway, several studies now show that the LGN is able to dynamically filter and transform visual input arriving from the retina (Usrey, 2002). A striking example of this property is the ability of LGN neurons to respond to excitatory input with spikes that belong to either burst responses or tonic responses (Jahnsen and Llinás, 1984a,b; Guido et al., 1992; Lu et al., 1992; Sherman, 1996, 2001, 2005).

Whether or not an LGN neuron produces burst or tonic spikes depends critically on the membrane potential history of individual neurons and the activation state of their low-threshold, T-type Ca^{2+} channels (Jahnsen and Llinás, 1984a,b; Huguenard and McCormick, 1992; McCormick and Huguenard, 1992; Zhou et al., 1997; Destexhe et al., 1998). T-type Ca^{2+} channels have the special property that they cannot be opened unless they have been sufficiently hyperpolarized for an appropriate amount of time (typically more than 50 msec). As a result, if the resting potential of a neuron is not hyperpolarized to a level that dc-inactivates T-type channels, then LGN neurons will respond to afferent excitation with a train of tonic Na^+ spikes whose frequency is proportional to the strength of the afferent stimulus. In contrast, if the resting potential of a neuron is hyperpolarized to a greater extent and for a sufficient

*Corresponding author. Tel.: +1-530-754-5468; Fax: +1-530-757-8827; E-mail: wmusrey@ucdavis.edu

DOI 10.1016/S0079-6123(05)49007-X

amount of time to de-inactivate T-type Ca^{2+} channels, then LGN neurons will respond to afferent excitation with a suprathreshold Ca^{2+} current that evokes a burst of Na^+ spikes whose frequency is not related to the strength of the stimulus (Sherman, 1996, 2001, 2005).

Before discussing a possible role for burst and tonic spikes during sensory processing, it is important to acknowledge first the well-documented involvement of thalamic bursts during periods of low arousal and slow-wave sleep when information processing along the thalamocortical pathway is at a minimum (Steriade and Llinas, 1988; McCormick and Feeser, 1990; Steriade et al., 1990; McCormick and Bal, 1994; Steriade, 2001). During slow-wave sleep, excitatory inputs from the brainstem to the thalamus are withdrawn and thalamocortical neurons hyperpolarize. Feedback loops between neurons in relay nuclei (e.g., the LGN) and the reticular nucleus then serve to synchronize large numbers of thalamocortical neurons causing them to oscillate together at low frequencies and produce bursts of spikes en masse. Because bursts occur simultaneously among large numbers of thalamic neurons projecting to the cortex and do not reflect sensory input, information transmission along the thalamocortical pathway is severely disrupted.

An important distinction between bursts that occur during slow-wave sleep and bursts that occur during sensory processing lies in their timing. While bursts are synchronized across large numbers of neurons during sleep, bursts are presumed to be unique to individual neurons or small ensembles of neurons during sensory processing. Nevertheless, it is important to keep in mind that both categories of bursts (those that occur during slow-wave sleep and those that occur during sensory processing) are believed to rely heavily on the same cellular mechanism: a hyperpolarization-dependent, de-inactivation of T-type Ca^{2+} channels.

A number of excellent reviews are available that address the role of burst and tonic spikes during sensory processing (Sherman, 1996, 2001, 2005; Sherman and Guillery, 2002). In general, these reviews regard burst and tonic spikes as representing two distinct activity modes, where mode is determined by non-retinal, modulatory, inputs to the LGN. In the present study, the main focus is on considering what

role the visual stimulus plays in directly driving burst and tonic spikes. It is important to emphasize that these two views concerning burst activity during sensory processing are not exclusive of each other. Rather, retinal and non-retinal inputs almost certainly interact with each other in a dynamic fashion to determine whether or not LGN neurons produce burst or tonic spikes. With that in mind, the temporal and spatial properties of visual stimuli that evoke burst and tonic spikes as well as the dynamic relationship between retinal drive and the low-threshold currents that underlie bursts are examined in the following sections. Finally, the functional consequences of burst and tonic activity for thalamocortical communication during sensory processing are discussed in the concluding section.

Temporal properties of visual stimuli that evoke burst and tonic spikes

Several studies have investigated the spatiotemporal organization of LGN receptive fields (Citron et al., 1981; Cai et al., 1997; Reid et al., 1997; Wolfe and Palmer, 1998; Usrey et al., 1999). Very few, however, have explicitly examined the temporal properties of visual stimuli that evoke burst and tonic spikes in LGN neurons. Using an m-sequence modulated, contrast reversing, sine-wave stimulus to excite LGN neurons, Alitto et al. (2005) identified spikes as either burst or tonic (same section), and performed reverse-correlation analysis on each category of spikes to generate spike-triggered averages. Results of this analysis show that the average stimulus to drive burst spikes is similar to, but significantly different from, the average stimulus to drive tonic spikes.

In the temporal domain, both burst and tonic spikes prefer visual stimuli that undergo transition from a suppressive to a preferred state (Fig. 1). Because suppressive stimuli can hyperpolarize LGN neurons (Singer et al., 1972; Martinez et al., 2003), it seems reasonable to suggest that these stimuli might also be capable of de-inactivating the T-type Ca^{2+} channels necessary for bursts. If so, then one would predict that the suppressive phase of the spike-triggered average preceding burst spikes should be greater than that for tonic spikes. As shown in Figs. 1 and 2, the magnitude (integral) of the suppressive

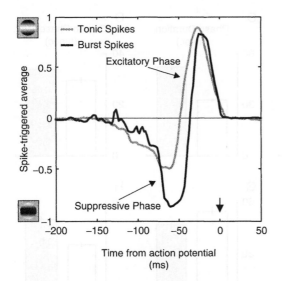

Fig. 1. Spike-triggered averages are similar, but distinct, for burst and tonic spikes. Using reverse-correlation analysis, spike-triggered averages were made from LGN responses ($n = 35$ neurons) to an m-sequence modulated, contrast reversing, sine-wave stimulus. The spike-triggered average shows the temporal sequence of the average stimulus to precede either a burst or tonic spike. Both burst spike (black trace) and tonic spike (gray trace) spike-triggered averages are composed of two phases: an initial suppressive phase followed by an excitatory phase. The suppressive phase is notably larger for burst spikes compared to tonic spikes.

phase of the spike-triggered average is indeed greater for burst spikes than for tonic spikes (0.056 ± 0.003 vs. 0.016 ± 0.001, respectively; $p < 0.00001$). This increase is due to an increase in both the suppressive phase maximum (Fig. 2; burst spikes $= 0.97 \pm 0.02$; tonic spikes $= 0.41 \pm 0.03$; $p < 0.00001$) and the suppressive phase duration (Fig. 2; burst spikes $= 81.9 \pm 2.4$ msec; tonic spikes $= 70.5 \pm 2.4$ msec; $p < 0.01$). These results are consistent with the view that bursts are triggered from a more hyperpolarized state than tonic spikes (see Spatial properties of visual stimuli that evoke burst and tonic spikes).

Alitto et al. (2005) used two criteria to identify the cardinal spikes of bursts: (1) a preceding interspike interval (ISI) greater than 50 msec, and (2) a subsequent ISI less than 4 msec. When these criteria are applied to spike trains in vivo, Sherman and colleagues have shown that they are highly effective at identifying bursts that rely on low threshold Ca^{2+} currents (Lu et al., 1992; Guido et al., 1992). With this in mind, one could nevertheless argue that the

measured differences between the suppressive phases preceding burst and tonic spikes simply reflect differences between spikes that are preceded, on average, by long and short interspike intervals. If so, then one would expect the suppressive phase for tonic spikes to be statistically indistinguishable from that of burst spikes when the two categories of spikes are matched for preceding interspike interval (i.e., a subset of tonic spikes are examined that meet the first criterion for a burst). On the other hand, if a visually induced hyperpolarization is the variable that determines whether or not an LGN neuron will produce a burst, then one would expect the suppressive phase of the spike-triggered average to be greater for burst spikes than for tonic spikes matched for preceding interspike interval. Alitto et al. (2005) tested these possibilities and found that all of the reported differences between the suppressive phases that precede burst and tonic spikes are similarly significantly different for the suppressive phases that precede burst spikes and tonic spikes matched for initial interspike interval (data not shown, see Alitto et al., 2005). These results are consistent with the idea that suppressive stimuli are capable of hyperpolarizing LGN neurons and de-inactivating T-type Ca^{2+} channels that underlie bursts.

The excitatory phase of the spike-triggered average also differs significantly for burst and tonic spikes (Figs. 1 and 2). In particular, the latency between stimulus and response is significantly less for burst spikes than for tonic spikes (Fig. 2; 29.6 ± 1.0 ms vs. 33.8 ± 1.1 ms, respectively; $p < 0.01$). In addition, the magnitude (integral) of the excitatory phase is significantly less for burst spikes than for tonic spikes (0.024 ± 0.001 vs. 0.030 ± 0.001, respectively; $p < 0.00001$); an effect that reflects a decrease in the duration of the excitatory phase (burst spikes $= 32.7 \pm 0.5$ ms; tonic spikes $= 52.3 \pm 1.1$ ms; $p < 0.00001$; Fig. 2), but not a decrease in the maximum of the excitatory phase (burst spikes $= 0.95 \pm 0.02$; tonic spikes $= 0.95 \pm 0.02$; $p < 0.8$; Fig. 2). The finding that both the latency and duration of the excitatory phase are decreased for burst spikes compared to tonic spikes is consistent with results from a previous study examining latency and timing variability of burst and tonic spikes using drifting sine-wave gratings to drive LGN responses (Guido and Sherman, 1998).

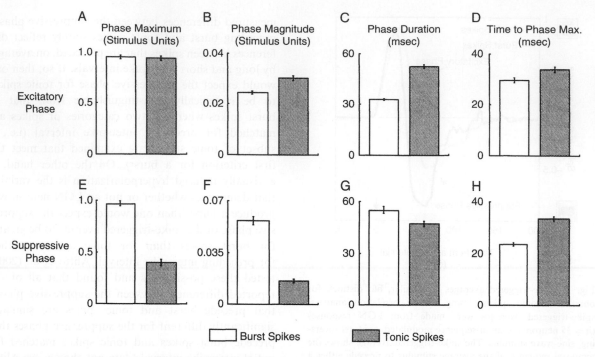

Fig. 2. Comparison of spike-triggered averages made from burst and tonic spikes. A–E, histograms comparing several features of the spike-triggered average excitatory phase (phase maximum, phase magnitude, phase duration, and time to phase maximum). E–H, histograms comparing the same features of the spike-triggered average suppressive phase.

Spatial properties of visual stimuli that evoke bursts and tonic spikes

Using an m-sequence modulated, white-noise stimulus (Reid et al., 1997) to evoke responses from LGN neurons, Alitto et al. (2005) used reverse-correlation analysis to examine the spatial properties of visual stimuli that drive burst and tonic spikes in LGN neurons. Similar to results from their temporal analysis, the average stimulus to drive burst spikes is similar to, but significantly different from, the average stimulus to drive tonic spikes (Rivadulla et al., 2003).

In the spatial domain, burst and tonic receptive fields are always centered at the same spatial location and always share the same center/surround organization (on/off or off/on) (Fig. 3A and B). Closer examination of the center and surround subregions, however, reveals several significant differences between burst and tonic receptive fields that can be quantified by fitting receptive fields to difference

of Gaussians (DOG) equations. A particularly notable difference between burst and tonic receptive fields is a greater surround to center ratio for burst spikes compared to tonic spikes (Fig. 3C; burst spikes: mean ratio $= 0.27 \pm 0.02$, tonic spikes: mean ratio $= 0.23 \pm 0.01$; $p < 0.05$; $n = 32$). The larger surround to center ratio for burst spike receptive fields is not due to changes in the spatial extent of the surround and center subregions (Fig. 3D; mean Δ surround $\sigma_{(burst\,vs.\,tonic)} = -0.025 \pm 0.037$, $p = 0.49$; mean Δ center $\sigma_{(burst\,vs.\,tonic)} = 0.013 \pm 0.014$, $p = 0.36$), but rather, is due to a disproportionate increase in the amplitude of the surround subregion compared to the center subregion (Fig. 3D; mean Δ surround amplitude$_{(burst\,vs.\,tonic)} = 0.155 \pm 0.044$, $p = 0.01$; mean Δ center amplitude$_{(burst\,vs.\,tonic)} = 0.053 \pm 0.016$, $p = 0.01$).

The finding that burst spikes, compared to tonic spikes, require a disproportionate increase in stimulation to the surround and center subregions of the receptive field may reflect an increase in the spike

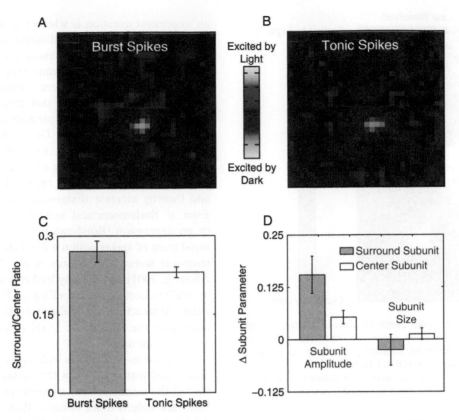

Fig. 3. Spatial properties of burst and tonic receptive fields. Using reverse-correlation analysis, receptive field maps were made from LGN responses to an m-sequence modulated, 16 × 16 checkerboard pattern of pixels. A and B, receptive field maps showing the average spatial stimulus to evoke burst and tonic spikes from a representative neuron. C, histogram comparing the surround to center ratio calculated from the receptive fields (burst and tonic) of 32 LGN neurons. D, histogram showing that the increase in surround to center ratio for burst spikes is due to a disproportionate increase in the strength of surround subregion in the burst receptive field and not due to a change in the spatial extent of subregions.

threshold of burst spikes compared to tonic spikes. This possibility can be illustrated by convolving a model LGN receptive field with the same white-noise stimulus used to map receptive fields. By performing the convolution twice (Fig. 4), once using a low spike threshold and again using a high spike threshold, one can qualitatively mimic the increase in the surround to center ratio of burst spikes (high threshold) compared to tonic spikes (low threshold).

While it may seem reasonable that LGN neurons should require more excitation to reach spike threshold when they are more hyperpolarized (i.e., prior to a burst event), in vitro studies have shown that an otherwise subthreshold current injection can evoke a burst from LGN neurons when T-type Ca^{2+} channels are de-inactivated (Lo et al., 1991). Based on this finding, one might expect bursts to require *less* excitatory drive from a visual stimulus than tonic spikes and certainly not *more* excitatory drive, as reported by Alitto et al. (2005). One possible explanation for this paradoxical set of findings rests on considering the dynamic relationship between low threshold currents in the LGN and retinal drive during visual stimulation. Because LGN neurons receive input from retinal ganglion cells with very similar receptive fields (Levick et al., 1972; Mastronarde, 1987; Usrey et al., 1999), suppressive stimuli that hyperpolarize LGN neurons (via a withdrawal of excitation and/or polysynaptic inhibition) should also hyperpolarize the retinal ganglion cells that provide their

A

Low Threshold

Excited by Light

B

High Threshold

Excited by Dark

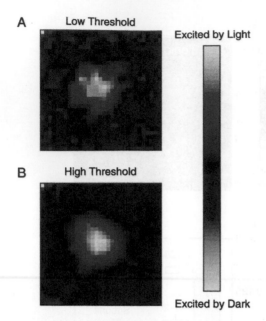

Fig. 4. A variable spike threshold predicts a change in the surround to center ratio under low and high thresholds. A, under low threshold conditions, a linear model of a difference of Gaussians (DOG) receptive field yields a low surround to center ratio. B, under high threshold conditions, the surround to center ratio is increased.

input. However, if LGN neurons hyperpolarize to a greater extent than the retinal ganglion cells that provide their input, then it may be possible for a visual stimulus to de-inactivate T-type Ca^{2+} channels in the LGN, but not T-type Ca^{2+} channels in the retina. As a result, retinal ganglion cells would not have access to low threshold Ca^{2+} currents and would require a stronger visual stimulus to reach spike threshold. In other words, a visual stimulus that decreases spike threshold in an LGN neuron would also decrease the retinal drive necessary for the LGN neuron to reach spike threshold. As a result, a stronger visual stimulus would be needed to drive the retina to a level sufficient for the LGN to reach threshold.

Bursts and thalamocortical processing

While the experiments described above demonstrate that burst and tonic spikes carry distinct spatiotemporal information to the cortex (Reinagel et al., 1999),

an important question is whether or not there exists a cortical mechanism for distinguishing these two categories of spikes. A potential readout for burst spikes is based on the dynamic properties of thalamocortical synapses. Several studies examining synaptic transmission at the thalamocortical synapse report that these synapses experience synaptic depression (Stratford et al., 1996; Gil et al., 1999; Chung et al., 2002). If so, then the long interspike interval preceding the cardinal spike of a burst would allow thalamocortical synapses to recover from depression and thereby increase thalamocortical burst efficacy. Even if thalamocortical synapses experience little or no depression (Boudreau and Ferster, 2003), the rapid train of spikes within a burst should experience temporal summation (Usrey et al., 2000; Roy and Alloway, 2001) and thereby lead to a similar increase in thalamocortical burst efficacy. Either way, the temporal structure of a thalamic burst seems ideal for increasing the efficacy of LGN neurons in driving cortical responses.

Using cross-correlation techniques to study thalamocortical transmission in the somatosensory pathway of the awake rabbit, a recent study reports that burst are indeed more effective than tonic spikes at driving cortical responses (Swadlow and Gusev, 2001). Consistent with the notion that thalamocortical synapses experience synaptic depression, this study also reports that the cardinal spike of a burst is always the most effective spike. Following the cardinal spike, subsequent burst spikes are similar to tonic spikes in their ability to drive cortical responses. Although a direct study of burst efficacy has yet to be performed for neurons in the visual pathway, if one assumes that LGN bursts are similarly more effective than tonic spikes at driving cortical responses, then LGN bursts would seem to have all of the necessary ingredients to represent a distinct mode for processing and conveying visual information to the cortex.

Conclusions and future directions

LGN neurons, like all thalamic neurons, produce two distinct categories of spikes — burst spikes and tonic spikes. While most efforts at understanding burst and tonic activity at a systems level have emphasized a role for extra-retinal inputs and their influence on the membrane properties of thalamic neurons (Steriade and Llinas, 1988; Steriade et al., 1990; Sherman, 1996, 2001), this review has examined recent progress made toward understanding what role the visual stimulus (and presumably the retinogeniculate pathway) plays in directly evoking burst and tonic activity. Compared to tonic spikes, results show that burst spikes (1) occur with a shorter latency between stimulus and response, (2) have a greater dependence on stimuli with transitions from suppressive to preferred states, and (3) prefer stimuli that provide increased drive to the receptive field center and even greater increased drive to the receptive field surround.

While results indicate that burst and tonic spikes follow distinct spatiotemporal patterns of visual stimuli, a number of important questions concerning the influence of sensory stimuli on burst and tonic activity remain unanswered. Perhaps most important, more data needs to be obtained from awake animals. Indeed, all of the data presented in this review come from the anesthetized cat. Given the justified concern that burst activity is diminished in awake animals (Guido and Weyand, 1995; Ramcharan et al., 2000; Weyand et al., 2001; Royal et al., 2003) and therefore may not contribute significantly to sensory processing outside of the anesthetized state, more experiments need to be performed in awake animals to determine the extent to which burst activity contributes to sensory processing. Along these lines, we know little or nothing about what effects do behavioral state, attention, statistics of the visual stimulus, or eye-movement history have on burst and tonic activity. Similarly, we know very little about what effect do cortical feedback and other sources of nonretinal input have on burst activity in awake animals. Given the evidence that bursts are more effective than tonic spikes at driving cortical responses (Swadlow and Gusev, 2001), these are important questions to be answered and the answers will likely change the way we perceive sensory processing and the retinogeniculcortical pathway.

Acknowledgments

This work was supported by NIH grants EY13588, EY12576, EY15387, the McKnight Foundation, the Esther A. and Joseph Klingenstein Fund, and the Alfred P. Sloan Foundation.

References

Alitto, H.J., Weyand, T.G. and Usrey, W.M. (2005) Distinct properties of visually evoked bursts in the lateral geniculate nucleus. J. Neurosci., 25: 514–523.

Boudreau, D.E. and Ferster, D. (2003) Synaptic depression in thalamocortical synapses of the cat visual cortex. Program No. 484.11. Abstract Viewer/Itinerary Planner. Society for Neuroscience, Washington, DC.

Cai, D., DeAngelis, G.C. and Freeman, R.D. (1997) Spatiotemporal receptive field organization in the lateral geniculate nucleus of cats and kittens. J. Neurophysiol., 78: 1045–1061.

Chung, S., Li, X. and Nelson, S.B. (2002) Short-term depression at thalamocortical synapses contributes to rapid adaptation of cortical sensory responses in vivo. Neuron, 34: 437–446.

Citron, M.C., Emerson, R.C. and Ide, L.S. (1981) Spatial and temporal receptive-field analysis of the cat's geniculocortical pathway. Vision Res., 21: 385–396.

Destexhe, A., Neubig, M., Ulrich, D. and Huguenard, J. (1998) Dendritic low-threshold calcium currents in thalamic relay cells. J. Neurosci., 18: 3574–3588.

Gil, Z., Connors, B.W. and Amitai, Y. (1999) Efficacy of thalamocortical and intracortical synaptic connections: quanta, innervation, and reliability. Neuron, 23: 385–397.

Guido, W., Lu, S.M. and Sherman, S.M. (1992) Relative contributions of burst and tonic responses to the receptive field properties of lateral geniculate neurons in the cat. J. Neurophysiol., 68: 2199–2211.

Guido, W. and Sherman, S.M. (1998) Response latencies of cells in the cat's lateral geniculate nucleus are less variable during burst than tonic firing. Visual Neurosci., 15: 231–237.

Guido, W. and Weyand, T. (1995) Burst responses in thalamic relay cells of the awake behaving cat. J. Neurophysiol., 74: 1782–1786.

Huguenard, J.R. and McCormick, D.A. (1992) Simulation of the currents involved in rhythmic oscillations in thalamic relay neurons. J. Neurophysiol., 68: 1373–1383.

Jahnsen, H. and Llinás, R. (1984a) Electrophysiological properties of guinea-pig thalamic neurones: an in vitro study. J. Physiol., 349: 205–226.

Jahnsen, H. and Llinás, R. (1984b) Ionic basis for the electroresponsiveness and oscillatory properties of guineqpig thalamic neurones in vitro. J. Physiol., 349: 227–247.

Levick, W.R., Cleland, B.G. and Dubin, M.W. (1972) Lateral geniculate neurons of cat: retinal inputs and physiology. Inv. Opthalm., 11: 302–311.

Lo, F.S., Lu, S.M. and Sherman, S.M. (1991) Intracellular and extracellular in vivo recordings of different response modes for relay cells of the cat's lateral geniculate nucleus. Exp. Brain Res., 83: 317–328.

Lu, S.M., Guido, W. and Sherman, S.M. (1992) Effects of membrane voltage on receptive field properties of lateral geniculate neurons in the cat: contributions of the low-threshold Ca^{2+} conductance. J. Neurophysiol., 68: 1285–1298.

Martinez, L.M., Alonso, J.M. and Hirsch, J.A. (2003) Synaptic structure of receptive fields in the cat's early visual pathway. Program No. 910.19. Abstract Viewer/Itinerary Planner. Society for Neuroscience, Washington, DC.

Mastronarde, D.N. (1987) Two classes of single-input X-cells in cat lateral geniculate nucleus. II. Retinal inputs and the generation of receptive-field properties. J. Neurophysiol., 57: 381–413.

McCormick, D.A. and Bal, T. (1994) Sensory gating mechanisms of the thalamus. Curr. Opin. Neurobiol., 4: 550–556.

McCormick, D.A. and Feeser, H.R. (1990) Functional implications of burst firing and single spike activity in lateral geniculate relay neurons. Neuroscience, 39: 103–113.

McCormick, D.A. and Huguenard, J.R. (1992) A model of the electrophysiological properties of thalamocortical relay neurons. J. Neurophysiol., 68: 1384–1400.

Ramcharan, E.J., Gnadt, J.W. and Sherman, S.M. (2000) Burst and tonic firing in thalamic cells of unanesthetized, behaving monkeys. Vis. Neurosci., 17: 55–62.

Reid, R.C., Victor, J.D. and Shapley, R.M. (1997) The use of m-sequences in the analysis of visual neurons: Linear receptive field properties. Visual Neurosci., 16: 1015–1027.

Reinagel, P., Godwin, D., Sherman, S.M. and Koch, C. (1999) Encoding of visual information by LGN bursts. J. Neurophysiol., 81: 2558–2569.

Rivadulla, C., Martinez, L., Grieve, K.L. and Cudeiro, J. (2003) Receptive field structure of burst and tonic firing in feline lateral geniculate nucleus. J. Physiol., 553: 601–610.

Roy, S.A. and Alloway, K.D. (2001) Coincidence detection or temporal integration? What the neurons in somatosensory cortex are doing. J. Neurosci., 21: 2462–2473.

Royal, D.W., Sary, G., Schall, J. and Casagrande, V. (2003) Are spike bursts and pseudo-bursts in the lateral geniculate nucleus (LGN) related to behavioral events? Program No. 699.16. Abstract Viewer/Itinerary Planner. Society for Neuroscience, Washington, DC.

Sherman, S.M. (1996) Dual response modes in lateral geniculate neurons: mechanisms and functions. Vis. Neurosci., 13: 205–213.

Sherman, S.M. (2001) Tonic and burst firing: dual modes of thalamocortical relay. Trends Neurosci., 24: 122–126.

Sherman, S.M. (2005) Thalamic relays and cortical functioning. In: Cortial Function: A view from the thalamus (ed: V.A. Casagrande, R.W. Guillery, S.M. Sherman) Prog. in Brain Res., 107–126.

Sherman, S.M. and Guillery, R.W. (2002) The role of the thalamus in the flow of information to the cortex. Philos. Trans. R. Soc. Lond. B Biol. Sci. B., 357: 1695–1708.

Singer, W., Poppel, E. and Creutzfeldt, O. (1972) Inhibitory interaction in the cat's lateral geniculate nucleus. Exp. Brain Res., 14: 210–226.

Steriade, M. (2001) Corticothalamic resonance, states of vigilance and mentation. Neuroscience, 101: 243–276.

Steriade, M., Jones, E.G. and Llinas, R.R. (1990) Thalamic oscillations and signaling. John Wiley and Sons, Inc., New York.

Steriade, M. and Llinas, R.R. (1988) The functional states of the thalamus and the associated neuronal interplay. Physiol. Rev., 68: 649–742.

Stratford, K.J., Tarczy-Hornoch, K., Martin, K.A., Bannister, N.J. and Jack, J.J. (1996) Excitatory synaptic inputs to spiny stellate cells in cat visual cortex. Nature, 382: 258–261.

Swadlow, H.A. and Gusev, A.G. (2001) The impact of "bursting" thalamic impulses at a neocortical synapse. Nat. Neurosci., 4: 402–408.

Usrey, W.M. (2002) Spike timing and visual processing in the retinogeniculocortical pathway. Philos. Trans. R. Soc. Lond. B Biol. Sci., 357: 1729–1737.

Usrey, W.M., Alonso, J.-M. and Reid, R.C. (2000) Synaptic interactions between thalamic inputs to simple cells in cat visual cortex. J. Neurosci., 20: 5461–5467.

Usrey, W.M., Reppas, J.B. and Reid, R.C. (1999) Specificity and strength of retinogeniculate connections. J. Neurophysiol., 82: 3527–3540.

Weyand, T.G., Boudreaux, M. and Guido, W. (2001) Burst and tonic response modes in thalamic neurons during sleep and wakefulness. J. Neurophysiol., 85: 1107–1118.

Wolfe, J. and Palmer, L.A. (1998) Temporal diversity in the lateral geniculate nucleus of cat. Visual Neurosci., 15: 653–675.

Zhou, Q., Godwin, D.W., O'Malley, D.M. and Adams, P.R. (1997) Visualization of calcium influx through channels that shape the burst and tonic firing modes of thalamic relay cells. J. Neurophysiol., 77: 2816–2825.

Progress in Brain Research, Vol. 149
ISSN 0079-6123

CHAPTER 8

Spike timing and synaptic dynamics at the awake thalamocortical synapse

Harvey A. Swadlow[1,*], Tatiana Bezdudnaya[1] and Alexander G. Gusev[1,2]

[1]*Department of Psychology, The University of Connecticut, Storrs, CT 06269, USA*
[2]*Institute of Higher Nervous Activity and Neurophysiology, Russian Academy of Medical Sciences, Moscow 117865, Russia*

Abstract: Thalamocortical (TC) neurons form only a small percentage of the synapses onto neurons of cortical layer 4, but the response properties of these cortical neurons are arguably dominated by thalamic input. This discrepancy is explained, in part, by studies showing that TC synapses are of high efficacy. However, TC synapses display activity-dependent depression. Because of this, in vitro measures of synaptic efficacy will not reflect the situation in vivo, where different neuronal populations have widely varying levels of "spontaneous" activity. Indeed, TC neurons of awake subjects generate high rates of spontaneous activity that would be expected, in a depressing synapse, to result in a *chronic state* of synaptic depression. Here, we review recent work in the somatosensory thalamocortical system of awake rabbits in which the relationship between TC spike timing and TC synaptic efficacy was examined during both thalamic "relay mode" (alert state) and "burst mode" (drowsy state). Two largely independent methodological approaches were used. First, we employed cross-correlation methods to examine the synaptic impact of single TC "barreloid" neurons on a single neuronal subtype in the topographically aligned layer 4 "barrel" — putative fast-spike inhibitory interneurons. We found that the initial spike of a TC burst, as well as isolated TC spikes with long preceding interspike intervals (ISIs) elicited postsynaptic action potentials far more effectively than did TC impulses with short ISIs. Our second approach took a broader view of the postsynaptic impact of TC impulses. In these experiments we examined spike-triggered extracellular field potentials and synaptic currents (using current source-density analysis) generated through the depths of a cortical barrel column by the impulses of single topographically aligned TC neurons. We found that (a) closely neighboring TC neurons may elicit very different patterns of monosynaptic activation within layers 4 and 6 of the aligned column, (b) synaptic currents elicited by TC impulses with long preceding ISIs were greatly enhanced in both of these layers, and (c) the degree of this enhancement differed reliably among neighboring TC neurons but, for a given neuron, was very similar in layers 4 and 6. Thus, results generated by both methodological approaches are consistent with the presence of a chronic depression at the awake TC synapse that is relieved by long ISIs. Since long ISIs necessarily precede TC "bursts", our results are consistent with the notion that these events powerfully activate cortical circuits.

Introduction

Thalamocortical (TC) neurons form only a small percentage of the synaptic contacts onto neurons

within cortical layer 4 (LeVay and Gilbert, 1976; Benshalom and White, 1986; White, 1989; Peters and Payne, 1993), but the response properties of these cortical neurons are arguably dominated by thalamic input (Chung and Ferster, 1998; Alonso et al., 2001). This discrepancy suggests that TC synapses may be especially effective in driving postsynaptic targets in

---

*Corresponding author. Tel.: +1-860-486-2252; Fax: +1-860-486-2760; E-mail: Swadlow@psych.psy.uconn.edu

DOI: 10.1016/S0079-6123(05)49008-1

layer 4, and this has been shown to be the case at both visual (Stratford et al., 1996) and somatosensory TC synapses (Gil et al., 1999). However, TC synapses, in vitro, exhibit a long lasting paired-pulse depression (Stratford et al., 1996; Gil et al., 1997), and similar effects have been observed in vivo (Castro-Alamancos and Connors, 1996; Swadlow and Gusev, 2001; Castro-Alamancos and Oldford, 2002, Chung et al., 2002; Swadlow et al., 2002). Because of this, baseline levels of synaptic efficacy, as measured in vitro cannot be expected to reflect the situation in vivo, where different neuronal populations have varying levels of spontaneous activity. Indeed, in the awake state, TC neurons display high rates of "spontaneous" activity (Ramcharan et al., 2000b; Swadlow and Gusev, 2001; Weyand et al., 2001) that, in a depressing synapse, would be expected to generate a *chronic state* of synaptic depression. If so, then the long interspike intervals (ISIs), such as those that precede TC "bursts", would allow recovery from this depression and subsequent impulses should have an enhanced efficacy in eliciting post-synaptic action potentials (because of enhanced EPSP amplitude, Ramcharan et al., 2000a).

This chapter reviews recent in vivo studies (Swadlow and Gusev, 2001; Swadlow et al., 2002) in awake rabbits that vacillate between states of EEG arousal (associated with thalamic "relay mode") and drowsiness (associated with thalamic "burst mode"). Under these conditions, we examine TC synaptic dynamics using two largely independent approaches. First, we take a *local view* of the impact of single TC neurons on a single neuronal subtype in cortical layer 4: putative fast-spike inhibitory interneurons (suspected inhibitory interneurons, SINs). To do this, we apply methods of cross correlation to the spike trains of topographically aligned TC-SIN pairs to examine the dynamics of the responses of these cortical neurons to the impulses generated by single TC neurons. Our strategy was to compare the efficacy values (Levick et al., 1972) generated by initial spikes of TC "bursts" and by single spikes with differing preceding interspike intervals (ISIs), with the values generated from the entire spike train of the TC neuron (the control efficacy). We found that the initial spike of a TC burst, as well as isolated spikes with long preceding interspike intervals (ISIs), were far more effective in generating postsynaptic action potentials

than were impulses with short ISIs. TC bursts were especially effective in driving cortical targets because later spikes in the burst also contributed to the postsynaptic response. Next we take a *more global view* of the impact of TC impulses by examining the extracellular synaptic currents generated by the impulses of single TC neurons through the depths of the topographically aligned cortical column. To do this, we apply methods of current source-density analysis (e.g., Haberly and Shepherd, 1973; Freeman and Nicholson, 1975) to the spike-triggered average field potentials elicited through the depths of the cortex by the impulses of single TC neurons. We found that (a) closely neighboring TC neurons generated widely differing patterns of monosynaptic activation within layers 4 and 6 of their aligned column, (b) synaptic currents generated by TC impulses with long preceding interspike intervals were greatly enhanced in both of these layers, and (c) the degree of this enhancement differs reliably among neighboring TC neurons but, for a given neuron, is very similar in layers 4 and 6. Thus, results generated by both methodological approaches are consistent with the presence, in the awake state, of a chronic depression at the TC synapse that is relieved by a period of inactivity. Since such periods of inactivity necessarily precede TC "bursts" (Steriade and Llinas, 1988), the results are consistent with the notion that these events powerfully activate cortical circuits (Sherman and Guillery, 1996).

TC synaptic impact on single SINs of layer 4

Methodological considerations

We studied TC connectivity between VB thalamic barreloids (Van Der Loos, 1976) and topographically aligned S1 cortical barrels (Woolsey and Van Der Loos, 1970). Extracellular recordings were obtained from S1 cortical barrel columns and from ventrobasal thalamic barreloids of awake, adult, Dutch-belted rabbits (for details, see Swadlow, 1989, 1995; Swadlow and Gusev, 2001, 2002). A concentric array of seven fine-diameter microelectrodes (interelectrode spacing of 160 microns) was chronically implanted above VB thalamus, with each electrode independently controlled by one of seven miniature microdrives that were permanently fixed to the skull. Microelectrodes were constructed of fine-diameter (40 microns O.D.) quartz–platinum filaments (Reitboeck, 1983), pulled under high temperature to a taper and sharpened to a fine tip. Cortical recordings were obtained from topographically aligned S1 barrels, following mapping procedures. Cortical recordings were obtained acutely, using a similar electrode array within aligned S1 barrels. TC neurons were identified by spike-triggered averages of field potentials elicited in the aligned S1 barrel by TC impulses (Swadlow and Gusev, 2000).

Cortical SINs in rabbit S1 were identified by a high-frequency (>600 Hz) burst of three or more spikes elicited by electrical stimulation of ventrobasal thalamus and by their short-duration action potential (Swadlow, 2003). A small number of SINs (5 to date, see Swadlow et al., 1998, Fig. 13) have been recorded intracellularly after the above identification procedure, and all responded to a depolarizing current pulse with a high-frequency, non-adapting train of action potentials (McCormick et al., 1985; Amitai and Connors, 1995). Topographic alignment of thalamic and cortical recording sites was achieved using receptive field mapping procedures and was confirmed by generating spike-triggered averages of the cortical field potentials elicited by impulses of the thalamic neurons under study (Swadlow and Gusev, 2000).

All data concerning TC-SIN efficacy were collected in the absence of peripheral stimulation, under conditions of "spontaneous" activity. Most SINs of an S1 barrel respond to spikes generated by a topographically aligned TC neuron with a very brief (usually ~ 1 ms) period of enhanced spike probability (Swadlow, 1995; Swadlow and Gusev, 2001). We limited our analysis to strongly connected TC-SIN pairs from which tens of thousands of TC and SIN spikes were generated. This was necessary in order to ensure statistical reliability for many of these analyses that were based on only a small subset of the TC spikes (e.g., Figs. 3C, D). Figure 1 shows the

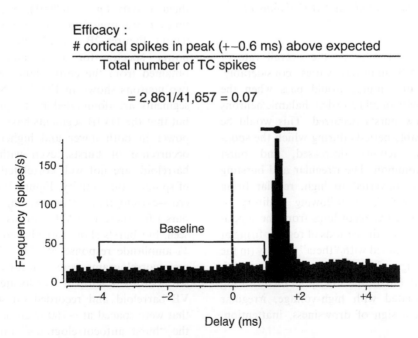

Fig. 1. Cross-correlogram generated by a well-connected TC–SIN pairs and the method for calculating TC efficacy. The dashed vertical line (0 delay) represents the time of the TC spike and histogram values represent SIN spikes. We selected a brief window (±0.6 ms on each side of the peak of the cross-correlogram) for calculation of efficacy values. Efficacy values were calculated by counting the number of action potentials that occurred in the SIN during this brief temporal window, subtracting a baseline number of SIN spikes expected by chance during this period, and dividing this value by the number of triggering TC spikes. We calculated the "chance" spike values only from the period between −4 ms and +1 ms of the TC spike time.

cross-correlogram generated by one such well-connected TC-SIN pair and the method for calculating TC efficacy. We selected a brief window (±0.6 ms on each side of the peak of the cross-correlogram) for calculation of efficacy values because (a) peaks in the thalamocortical cross-correlogram in this system are comparably short and (b) we wanted to limit the analysis to the effects of a single presynaptic impulse. Efficacy values were calculated by counting the number of action potentials that occurred in the SIN during this brief temporal window, subtracting a baseline number of spikes expected by chance during this period, and dividing this value by the number of triggering VB spikes. Thalamocortical "bursts" were identified according to the criteria of Lu et al. (1992), where the initial impulse in a burst is required to have a preceding ISI of at least 100 ms and a subsequent ISI < 4 ms. Subsequent impulses that occurred at intervals of < 4 ms were identified as being part of the burst.

Relay mode and burst mode in VB thalamus of awake rabbits

In awake, restrained subjects, the overall rate of "spontaneous" VB impulses varies considerably. A few seconds or minutes would pass when the spontaneous activity of all recorded thalamic neurons was high and few bursts occurred. This would be followed by variable periods during which the spontaneous impulse activity decreased, and burst responses were common. The irregular and bursting responses readily converted to high, regular firing either "spontaneously", or following auditory or tactile stimulation. EEG recordings from the hippocampus confirmed that the periods of regular firing at high rates were associated with "theta" activity (in the 4–8 Hz range, a sign of arousal, Green and Arduini, 1954). In contrast, bursts and low spontaneous firing rates were associated with high-voltage, irregular activity (HVIR), a sign of drowsiness, inattention, and sleep).

Figure 2A shows a brief segment from a typical recording session, in which two TC neurons (VB1 and VB2) were recorded simultaneously from the same VB barreloid via two microelectrodes separated by ~160 microns. Hippocampal EEG activity

is shown in the lower trace. Note that the initial several seconds of this record are dominated by theta activity. During this period, spontaneous VB activity was high in both neurons, and a single burst response occurred (indicated by dark circles above vertical lines, individual spikes within the bursts cannot be resolved at this time-scale). Within a period of about 1 s, however, the EEG converted to HVIR activity, when spontaneous activity of VB neurons was much lower, and bursts were common. We quantified this relationship, by segmenting data files into periods dominated by either hippocampal theta activity or by HVIR activity. Files were segmented by visual inspection (without knowledge of VB neuronal activity), aided by fast Fourier transforms (FFT) of each segment. In this manner, 20–55% of each data file was classified as "theta", and 30–40% was classified as "HVIR", and the remaining portions could not be classified. For each of six VB neurons studied in this manner, baseline "spontaneous" firing rate was approximately two times higher during the periods of theta activity ($p = <0.0001$), but bursts were 8–20 times more prevalent during HVIR activity ($p = 0.001$). Figures 2B and 2C show the summed FFT power spectra for theta and HVIR segments obtained from the entire data file that yielded the two neurons shown in Fig. 2A. Note that the theta segments are dominated by frequencies of 4–7 Hz, but that the HVIR segments have considerably more power in both lower and higher frequencies. The occurrence of bursts, even within the same VB barreloid, are not well correlated under conditions of spontaneous activity. Figure 2D shows the "burst cross-correlogram" (for the initial spike in each burst) for these two VB neurons. No sharp peak is seen, but bursts show some broad synchrony, with a ½ amplitude response of < 1 s. Very similar burst cross-correlograms were seen for each of 14 pairs of VB neurons. Each pair was located within the same VB barreloid and recorded on separate electrodes that were spaced at ~160 microns. Figure 2E shows the "burst autocorrelograms" (autocorrelogram of the initial spike in each burst) for the two VB neurons shown in Fig. 1A. No clear rhythmicity is apparent in these or in 15 other such burst auto-correlograms, other than a preferred inter-burst interval of 150–300 ms.

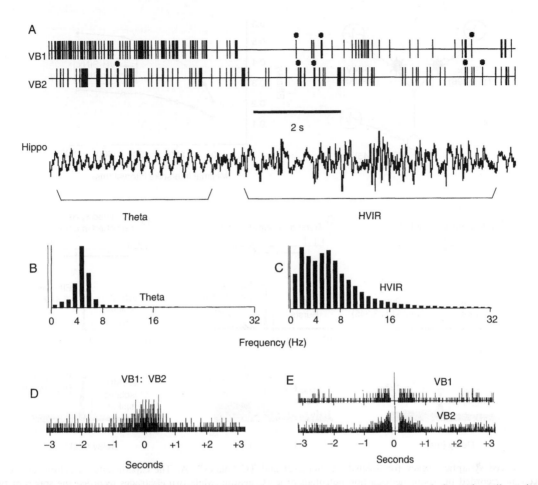

Fig. 2. Transition from "relay" mode to "burst" mode. The upper two traces show ~ 10 s of records from the spike trains of two ventrobasal thalamocortical neurons (VB1 and VB2) recorded via two microelectrodes separated by ~ 160 microns. Individual action potentials are indicated by vertical lines; bursts of 2–5 action potentials are indicated by a vertical line with a filled circle above (the separate action potentials within the bursts cannot be resolved at this time scale). The left side of the figure shows the neurons in "relay mode", showing high rates of firing and only a single burst of action potentials. After about 4 s, however, the firing rate decreases and the number of bursts increases. The lower trace of 1A shows that hippocampal EEG activity is correlated with these different firing patterns. During relay mode, theta activity is seen in the hippocampal EEG. This changes to high voltage, irregular activity (HVIR) during burst mode. Summed FFT power spectra (946 ms samples) of all hippocampal EEG segments classified as being dominated by "theta" (B) and HVIR (C), respectively. The maximal value in each distribution was normalized to a value of 1. D: "Burst cross-correlogram", the correlation between the initial spike in each burst of neuron VB1 and VB2 (shown in Fig 1A). E: "Burst autocorrelograms" of the initial spikes in a burst for the spike trains of neurons VB1 and VB2 . (From: Swadlow and Gusev, 2001.)

Dynamics of the TC synapse onto SINs: enhanced impact of bursts and isolated spikes

Figure 3 shows results from a recording session, where a single TC neuron was studied simultaneously with two SINs (SINx and SINy) that were located in the topographically aligned barrel. The initial cross-correlation analyses (Fig. 3B) were calculated using

the entire spike trains of the VB neuron ($>68{,}000$ spikes) and the SINs ($>120{,}000$ spikes each). This analysis revealed a potent functional connectivity between the VB neuron and both of the SINs. In these correlograms, the VB spike occurs at "0" delay and the cortical spike follows after a brief delay. Note the very brief (~1 ms) and potent increase in spike rate that occurs at intervals of 1.1–2 ms following the

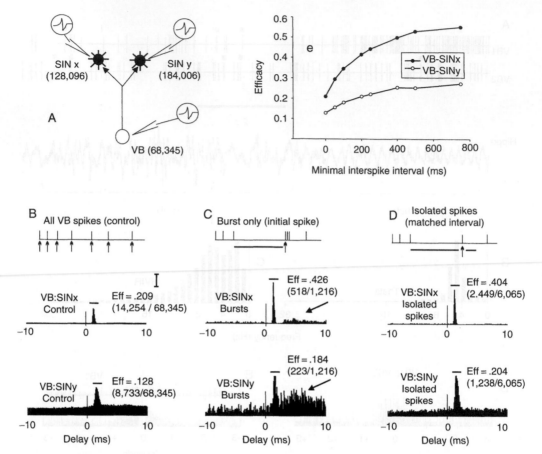

Fig. 3. Enhanced synaptic efficacy for isolated TC impulses and TC "bursts". A: The experimental situation: an extracellular microelectrode recorded the spontaneous action potentials of a TC neuron, while two electrodes recorded the spikes of two SINs (x and y). Data from this triad of neurons is also presented in Fig. 2 (B and C) and in Fig. 5. All correlograms were constructed using a bin width of 0.1 ms and were calculated in the absence of peripheral stimulation. B: Cross-correlograms were initially calculated using the entire spike trains of the TC neuron (vertical arrows, 68,345 spikes), SIN x (128,096 spikes) and SIN y (184,006 spikes). The "efficacy" of the connections was computed for a period of 1.2 ms that was centered on the peak in the cross-correlogram (indicated by horizontal lines above the peaks in the cross-correlograms). The computed efficacies of 0.209 and 0.128 indicate extremely potent synaptic contacts with these two SINs. The ratio of the numbers of SIN spikes in the peak of each correlogram (minus the baseline) and the number of TC spikes used in the calculations is given besides each peak. C: Method for selecting only initial spikes in a thalamocortical burst and computing the cross-correlograms based on these spikes. Only the first spike in each burst was selected (vertical arrow) and the cross-correlogram with each SIN was computed. This resulted in an enhanced efficacy for these selected TC spikes. D: Method for selecting only isolated TC spikes and the computed cross-correlograms based on these spikes. The duration of the interval preceding such spikes was chosen to match those seen in the burst condition. These isolated TC spikes were highly potent in activating the cortical SINs. E: For these same neurons, the duration of the required silent interval that preceding a TC spike was varied from 0 to 750 ms. Efficacy values were clearly related to the duration of this interval. The vertical cal bar in "B" applies to all of the correlograms and represents 500 and 100 spikes per second in the TC-SIN x and TC-SIN y correlograms, respectively. (From Swadlow and Gusev, 2001.)

VB action potential. Computed efficacies were 0.209 and 0.128, between the VB neuron and SINs x and y, respectively, which indicates an extremely potent synaptic contact between the VB neuron and these two SINs. Next (Fig. 3C) we identified 1216 "bursts"

of action potentials that occurred within the spike train of the VB neuron during the two hours of this recording session. We then selected the first spike in each of these bursts (vertical arrow) and computed the cross-correlogram of these selected spikes with the spike trains of each SIN. The efficacy to the initial VB spike in each burst was calculated in a manner identical to that of the control efficacy, around the peak in the cross-correlogram ±0.6 ms. Burst efficacy increased to 0.426 and 0.184 for SINx and SINy, respectively. Similar increases in the efficacy for the initial spike in the thalamocortical burst were seen in each of the seven VB–SIN pairs studied, with mean efficacy values more than doubling (mean=221% of the control value, $p=.005$, paired t test).

It is important to know whether the initial spike in a TC burst had some special property that generates enhanced TC efficacies, or whether long preceding ISIs are sufficient to generate this effect. Figure 3D shows that isolated spikes are, indeed, sufficient and illustrates how such isolated spikes (vertical arrow) were selected. The 1216 bursts recorded in this VB neuron followed the preceding spike at a median interval of 278 ms. Therefore, isolated VB spikes were selected that occurred at a similar interval following the preceding spike (median value = 280 ms). Figure 3D shows that these isolated VB spikes were highly potent in activating the cortical neurons, showing efficacies of 0.404 and 0.204 in SINs x and y, respectively. These values are very similar to those seen under the burst condition (Fig. 3C). Figure 3E shows that the magnitude of the enhanced thalamocortical efficacy for these neurons was clearly related to the duration of the "silent" period that preceded the VB spike. Similar increases in the efficacy for such isolated VB spikes (with matched preceding interval) were seen in each of the seven VB–SIN pairs studied, with mean efficacy values nearly doubling (mean= 174% of the control value, $p = .013$, paired t test).

To further examine the role of the interval that precedes each burst, we compared the thalamocortical efficacy of bursts with those of "pseudo-bursts". Like normal bursts, pseudo-bursts were required to consist of at least two spikes, at interspike intervals of <4 ms. Unlike normal bursts, however, pseudo-bursts had no lengthy preceding interval, and were required to have at least one spike in the interval of 10–80 ms preceding the initial spike in the pseudo-burst. Our analysis compared the thalamocortical efficacy of the initial two spikes of regular bursts with those of such pseudo-bursts. No evidence for enhanced TC efficacy was seen to initial spikes of pseudo-bursts.

We also examined the efficacy of the second and third impulses of TC bursts and found them to be very near the average efficacy value, and to further raise the overall probability of successfully eliciting neocortical spikes. Moreover, in some strongly connected VB–SIN pairs, multiple cortical spikes are elicited by the consecutive impulses of a single burst.

Bursts were relatively rare during hippocampal theta, and pseudo-bursts were rare during HVIR. Because of this, we could not compare thalamocortical efficacy of these events between the two EEG states. However, we could compare, across EEG states, the thalamocortical efficacy of "isolated" VB spikes with long preceding interspike intervals (described above). These spikes are of special interest because they may be generated by the same underlying mechanism (low-threshold calcium spike) that generates thalamic burst responses (Steriade and Llinas, 1988). In each of the five VB–SIN pairs that were adequately studied under both states, thalamocortical efficacy of such isolated spikes was similarly enhanced over control values [(mean = 183% of control values during theta activity (S.D. = 21%), 177% of control values during HVIR activity (S.D. = 27%)].

TC synaptic impact through the depths of the column

Methodological considerations

Methods of spike-triggered averaging have been predominantly used to examine low-amplitude intracellular postsynaptic potentials elicited by single presynaptic elements (e.g., Mendell and Henneman, 1971; Munson and Sypert, 1979; Kirkwood and Sears, 1982a). Spike-triggered averaging can also be used to examine extracellular fields elicited by single presynaptic elements. This method has been predominantly used with large-diameter axons entering the spinal cord, to trace the influence of sensory afferent fibers (Munson and Sypert, 1979), descending central axons (Taylor et al., 1977; Kirkwood, 1995), or spinal interneurons (Kirkwood et al., 1993; Schmidt et al., 1993). Since TC impulses can generate potent responses in the aligned cortical column (e.g., above section, Alonso et al., 2001), we applied this method to awake sensory neocortex, to trace spatial and temporal synaptic influences of individual ventrobasal thalamocortical axons on topographically aligned barrel columns (Swadlow and Gusev, 2000). Notably, impulses of these neurons generate presynaptic (axonal) and postsynaptic field potentials that can be easily detected within the topographically aligned barrel.

Figure 4 shows the spike-triggered average obtained from an S1 recording site following spontaneous impulse activity in a topographically aligned VB neuron. In nearly all the cases studied, the response profile reached a peak within or near layer 4, and could be readily divided into three distinct components: (1) an initially positive, biphasic or triphasic response thought to represent the invasion of the presynaptic impulse into the axon terminal arborization within layer 4 (the axon terminal potential, AxTP), (2) a longer latency, negative-going potential believed to reflect a local, focal synaptic depolarization (the focal synaptic negative potential, FSN), and (3) a subsequent long-lasting positive potential, believed to reflect disynaptic hyperpolarization (the focal synaptic positive potential, FSP). Whereas the AxTP had a mean latency of 0.71 ms following the VB spike and was not affected by infusion of AMPA/kainate antagonists within the barrel, the FSN (mean latency = 1.67 ms) and FSP were virtually eliminated by AMPA/kainate antagonists, confirming the postsynaptic origin of these latter field potentials.

Subsequently we used cortical probes with recording sites separated at vertical distances of 100 microns[1] and applied current source-density analysis to the field potentials generated by TC impulses (Swadlow et al., 2002). The one-dimensional CSD was calculated from the second spatial derivative of the field potential profile using the general methods of Freeman and Nicholson (1975). The probes remained within the cortex for 2–3 days, so as to study the impact, on the same barrel column, of several neighboring neurons from the same VB thalamic barreloid. Two types of topographic alignment were required for these experiments and special care was

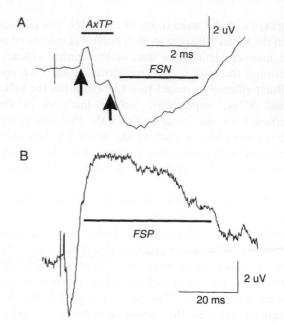

Fig. 4. Spike-triggered average waveform elicited in a cortical barrel by spontaneous action potentials of a TC neuron located in the topographically aligned ventrobasal thalamic barreloid. The left and right arrows indicate the onset of the axon terminal potential (AxTP) and the focal synaptic negativity (FSN, reflecting monosynaptic excitatory events), respectively. B: The same spike-triggered average, taken at a slower sweep speed, showing the time course of the focal synaptic positive potential (FSP). This potential reverses in upper cortical layers and is thought to reflect disynaptic (feed-forward) inhibition. (From Swadlow and Gusev, 2000.)

taken to achieve this: (1) alignment between unit electrodes within the VB barreloid and the 16-channel probe within the S1 cortical barrel and (2) alignment of the 16-channel probe within the barrel column, among the sites within superficial and deep layers. For the CSD analyses, we focused on axonal and monosynaptic excitatory effects occurring within the first few milliseconds following a TC impulse.

The extracellular fields and currents generated in layers 4 and 6 by a TC impulse

In each of six barrel columns, we examined the vertical distribution of field potentials and currents that were generated by the spontaneous spikes of 2–6 aligned TC neurons. Figure 5A illustrates a case in which two microelectrodes (separated by

---

[1]Probes were supplied by the University of Michigan Center for Neural Communication Technology.

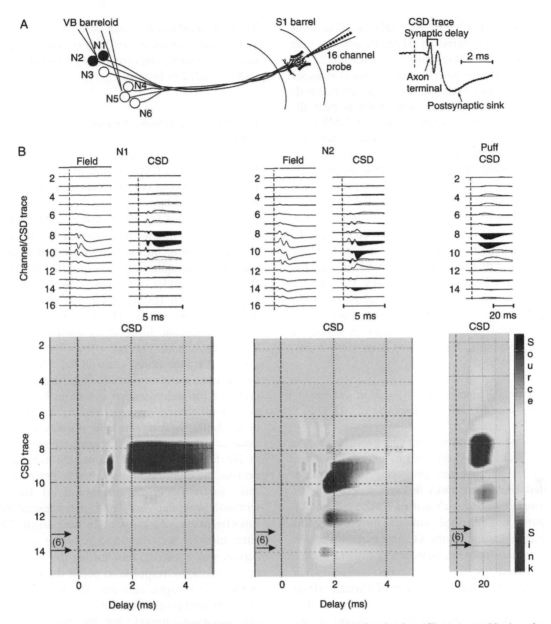

Fig. 5. A: Methods for generating single TC axon CSDs and an illustrative case showing depth profiles generated by impulses of two neighboring TC neurons (N1 and N2), recorded simultaneously, via a single thalamic microelectrode. Two independent microelectrodes were in a single thalamic barreloid. During the course of two recording sessions, three TC neurons were studied via each electrode (N1–N6). The cortical probe is near the center of the aligned barrel, with deeper sites within layer 6. On the right, an example of CSD traces showing the axon terminal potential and the postsynaptic current sink (arrows), and the synaptic delay (time between the onset of these two potentials). The vertical dashed line denotes the time of the TC spike. B: N1 and N2 show spike-triggered field and CSD profiles generated by two TC neurons (N1 and N2 in A) recorded simultaneously via one of the microelectrodes. The vertical dashed lines denote the time of the TC spike. Colorized CSDs are shown below (color intensities reflect source and sink amplitudes). Lower right: CSD profile generated by an air-puff (200 presentations, note the long time base). Horizontal arrows in colorized CSDs here denote sites known to be within layer 6 (because of the presence of corticothalamic neurons of layer 6, antidromically activated at long latencies via microstimulation via VB microelectrodes (Swadlow, 1989). Gains for N1 and N2 are identical, and are 20 × higher than that used for the air-puff stimulus. (From: Swadlow et al., 2002.)

100

~160 microns) recorded from a total of 6 TC neurons of a single thalamic barreloid. Three TC neurons were studied either simultaneously or sequentially on each microelectrode and the total vertical distance between recordings made on each thalamic electrode was <80 microns. The cortical probe is near the center of the aligned barrel column. A CSD trace from layer 4 is shown at the right (trace #8 from N1, below). Figure 5B (left side, N1) shows responses generated within the aligned column by one TC neuron ("N1" in Fig. 1A). Spike-triggered field potentials and CSD analysis of these field potentials are also shown. Responses during the first few milliseconds following the TC spike consist of the two components that were described in Fig. 4: (1) the initial biphasic or triphasic "axon terminal" component and (2) a longer latency (usually 1.2–1.8 ms), negative-going potential. For this neuron, the axon terminal potential had a latency of 0.81 ms and was clearly isolated from the dominant postsynaptic effect, a current sink, with an onset latency of 1.58 ms.

The laminar distribution of postsynaptic current sinks generated by TC impulses

The major postsynaptic current sink generated by the above TC neuron was centered in layer 4. However, three of six TC neurons projecting to this barrel generated significant sinks in layer 6. N2 (Fig. 5) shows profiles of one such neuron ("N2" in Fig. 5A). This neuron was recorded simultaneously, and on the same microelectrode, as the TC neuron shown in N1. Thus, these two TC neurons were very close neighbors and projected to the same barrel column, but generated very different patterns of current within the column under identical recording conditions. The major postsynaptic response extends deeper in N2 (~100 microns) than in N1. Moreover, there is a substantial sink deep within the cortex, in layer 6. Figure 5B (right) shows the CSD profile generated to stimulation of the principle vibrissa (gain is 1/20 that used in N1 and N2). Note the strong sink in the middle of the cortex, which we assume to be centered within layer 4. A weaker current sink is seen in layer 6 (arrows). Of the 24 TC neurons that we studied, 14 generated postsynaptic current sinks that were limited to layer 4 (as in N1, in Fig. 5). Nine of the remaining

TC neurons showed strong current sinks in layer 4, and weaker (7 cases) or similarly strong (2 cases) sinks in layer 6. In only one case was a postsynaptic current sink restricted to layer 6.

Dynamics of postsynaptic currents generated by a TC impulse

Figure 6A shows CSD profiles of a TC neuron that generated powerful current sinks in both layers 4 and 6 of the aligned barrel column. The "control" profile is shown on the left. The center CSD profile was generated by impulses from the same spike train of this TC neuron, but was limited to impulses with preceding interspike intervals of 250–500 ms. Note that the amplitudes of the *postsynaptic* sinks in both layers 4 and 6 (traces magnified in insets) have increased substantially. The amplitude of the *axon terminal* potential, however, is unchanged (arrows). The right side of Fig. 6A shows the CSD profile generated by the initial spike of TC "bursts". Note the clear enhanced current sink in both cortical layers, and that this enhancement is seen in both the early postsynaptic response (generated by the initial spike in the burst) and in the later portion of the postsynaptic response (probably generated by later spikes in the burst). Figure 6B shows, for this same TC neuron, the relationship between the preceding interspike interval and the magnitude of the axonal terminal potential (left) and postsynaptic current sinks (right) as a function of cortical depth. For this latter measure we considered only the value of the current sink occurring only during the initial 1 ms of the postsynaptic response to avoid the possibility of including disynaptic currents. The amplitude of the axon terminal potential is not affected by the preceding interspike interval, but the magnitude of the postsynaptic responses in both layers increases with increasing interspike intervals.

Similar results were obtained in each of 10 additional cases, but the degree of enhancement related to long preceding intervals varied considerably among different TC neurons. Figure 7A shows, for each of these 11 TC neurons, the magnitude of the postsynaptic sink generated in layer 4 by impulses with various preceding interspike intervals. For each TC neuron, the values generated are normalized against

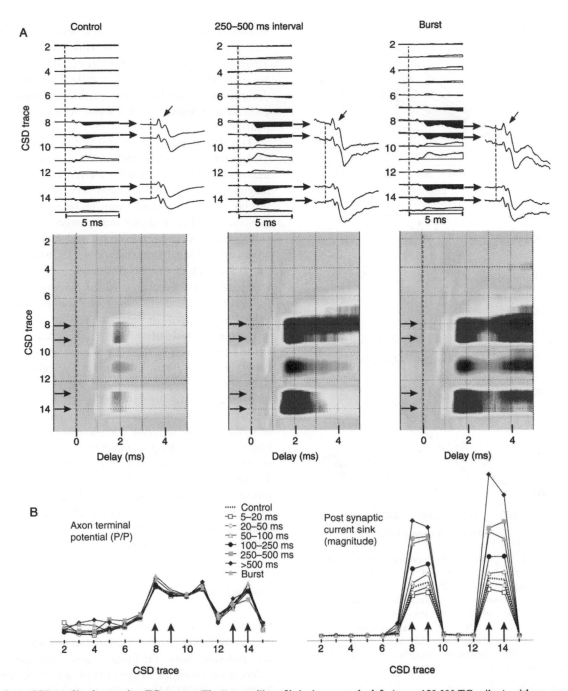

Fig. 6. A: CSD profiles for another TC neuron. The "control" profile is shown on the left. (n = ~ 120,000 TC spikes), with an amplified view (gain is 3.5 × greater) of the responses in layer 4 (upper horizontal arrows) and layer 6 (lower horizontal arrows). Oblique arrows denote axon terminal responses. The colorized CSD profile is shown below. Middle profiles were generated by TC spikes with preceding interspike intervals of 250–500 ms (n = 2290). Profiles on the right were generated by initial spikes of a TC bursts (n = 2427). Gain settings and color intensities for all CSDs are identical. B: The amplitude (peak-to-peak) of the axon terminal response (left) and the magnitude of the initial one ms of the postsynaptic current sink (right) plotted at different CSD sites as a function of preceding interspike interval. Control response, and the response to the initial spike in a TC burst are also plotted. (From: Swadlow et al., 2002.)

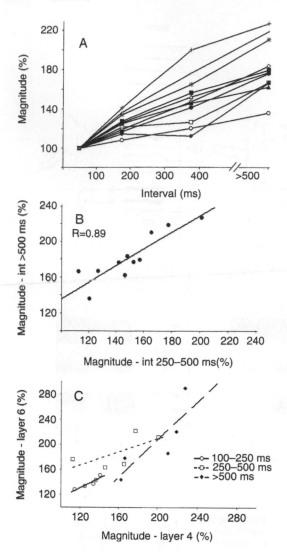

Fig. 7. For 11 TC neurons, the magnitude of postsynaptic current sinks, generated in layer 4 by spikes with various preceding interspike intervals. B: For these same 11 neurons, the correlation between the response to TC spikes with preceding intervals of 250–500 ms, and with preceding interspike intervals of >500 ms. C: Relationship, for 5 TC neurons, between the magnitude of the response in layer 4 and in layer 6, at three preceding interspike intervals. (From: Swadlow et al., 2002.)

showed much less enhancement, and there was a strong correlation between the enhancements generated at the two longest intervals (Fig. 7B, 250–500 ms, vs. $ = $ >500 ms, $r = +. 89$, $p = $ <.001). This shows that differences among TC neurons in the amplitude of the enhanced response reflect a stable feature of the TC neuron.

The above results show stable differences among TC neurons in the dynamics of TC transmission. The next question was whether for a given TC neuron, the magnitude of the enhancement seen in layer 4 was similar to the magnitude seen in layer 6. The case illustrated in Fig. 6 shows that postsynaptic current sinks generated in both layers 4 and 6 are similarly enhanced at longer interspike intervals, and this was found for each of the five TC neurons that we could adequately test. Figure 7C (filled diamonds) shows, for each of these TC neurons, the postsynaptic enhancement seen in layer 4 and in layer 6 at interspike intervals of >500 ms. The strength of the enhancement seen in these two layers was positively correlated ($r = 0.80$). Similar positive relationships were obtained for each of these five TC neurons at interspike intervals of 250–500 ms ($r = .66$) and at intervals of 100–250 ms ($r = .83$). The results of meta analysis of these separate correlations (Johnson and Eagly, 2000) are highly significant ($p = $ <.004). These results show that the individual differences among TC neurons seen in the temporal dynamics of TC transmission apply equally to layers 4 and 6. Moreover, the slope of ~1 in the above correlations indicates that the magnitude of the enhanced responses in these two layers is very similar.

Conclusions

Synaptic dynamics of central neurons display varying degrees of depression/facilitation and a single neuron can generate both facilitation and depression at different postsynaptic targets (Markram et al., 1998; Reyes et al., 1998). Most studies of synaptic dynamics are in vitro, where "spontaneous" activity is either minimal or absent. In the intact brains, however, levels of spontaneous activity in different neuronal systems vary over 100-fold. Some cortical populations are virtually silent in the awake state (e.g., slowly conducting thalamocortical neurons of layer 6, firing

the value for impulses with short interspike intervals (<100 ms). For some TC neurons, current sinks generated by spikes with the longest preceding intervals (>500 ms) were >2 times greater than those generated at the shortest intervals. Other TC neurons at mean rates of $< 1/10$ s, Swadlow, 1988, 1989). In contrast, both the TC neurons studied here (Swadlow and Gusev, 2001), as well as SINs of somatosensory and visual cortices (Swadlow, 1988, 1989) fire spontaneously in the awake state at rates in excess of 10/s. Thus, neurons that display in vitro facilitation would, if spontaneous activity rates were high, be expected to display a chronic state of facilitation. Conversely, neurons that display in vitro depression would, if activity rates were high, be expected to be chronically depressed. This latter condition reflects the state of the awake thalamocortical synapse.

The studies of TC–SIN connectivity suggest that the interval preceding the initial spike in the burst is the key factor in generating the enhanced synaptic efficacy to this spike. Thus, it was found that: (1) there exists a clear relationship between the duration of this preceding interval and thalamocortical synaptic efficacy, (2) a similar enhanced thalamocortical efficacy is generated by single isolated spikes (with matched preceding intervals) that are not part of a burst, (3) the enhanced thalamocortical efficacy generated by such isolated VB spikes is independent of the EEG state (hippocampal theta or HVIR) during which they occur, and (4) the initial spike of "pseudo-bursts" (which have no preceding spike-free interval) does not show an enhanced thalamocortical efficacy. Nevertheless, it is certainly possible that hidden postsynaptic factors are correlated with long interspike intervals in VB neurons, and that these contribute to the enhanced thalamocortical efficacy of VB bursts and isolated spikes.

Our CSD analysis of TC impulses extends the above mentioned finding in two significant ways: (1) These results are not limited to TC synapses onto inhibitory interneurons. TC impulses with long preceding intervals generated current sinks that were much stronger than those with short preceding intervals. These sinks reflect the summed activity of all the synapses made within the column by a given TC neuron. Since the great majority of these synapses are onto dendritic spines (e.g., 83% in rat visual cortex, Peters and Feldman, 1976), we conclude that much of the enhanced current flow is due to activation (largely subthreshold) of excitatory cortical neurons. (2) Enhanced cortical activation occurs in layer 6 as well as in layer 4 and the magnitude of the effect within these layers is similar. This is significant because TC impulses with long preceding interspike intervals are more likely to activate corticothalamic "feedback" neurons of layer 6, which receive substantial synaptic input from TC terminals (White and Hersch, 1982).

Different TC axons studied here showed enhancements of 35% to $> 100\%$ in the magnitude of the postsynaptic response seen at long interspike intervals. The extent of this variability is consistent with findings in vitro, where similar variability is seen in the magnitude of paired-pulse depression seen at different TC synapses onto excitatory cortical neurons (Gil et al., 1997). The results suggest that much of this variability may be globally related to the particular TC neuron under study. Some TC neurons form synapses that are, on average, more depressing than those of other TC neurons, and these differences are maintained over a range of preceding interspike intervals (Fig. 7A–B). Moreover, for a given TC neuron, the dynamics seen in layers 4 and 6 are very similar, but differ consistently from that seen in other TC neurons. This result could be due to intrinsic differences among neighboring TC neurons or, alternatively, could reflect a different composition of postsynaptic elements targeted by the neighboring TC neurons (Markram et al., 1998; Reyes et al., 1998).

Finally, these results show that TC synapses in layers 4 and 6 may serve as significant filters of sensory information. Sensory information carried by impulses with long preceding interspike intervals, including the initial spikes of a thalamic "burst", have a special status: they generate stronger postsynaptic responses than impulses with short preceding intervals. Because of this potent cortical response in layers 4 and 6, these findings are consistent with suggestions that thalamic bursts could serve as a "wake-up" call to the cortex (Sherman and Guillery, 1996; Sherman, 2001). They are also consistent with suggestions that a sensory "interval code" may be decoded through mechanisms of synaptic depression or facilitation (Gerstner et al., 1997; Goldman et al., 1999; Reich et al., 2000; Fuhrmann et al., 2001). The results show that sensory information encoded within the interval distribution of TC impulses may be decoded by the amplitude of the postsynaptic currents generated by those impulses. Thus, at the TC synapse, an "interval code" may be transformed into an "amplitude code", and the nature of this transform may differ considerably among neighboring TC neurons.

Acknowledgments

Supported by grants from NIMH (MH-64024) and NSF (IBN-0077694).

References

Alonso, J.M., Usrey, W.M. and Reid, R.C. (2001) Rules of connectivity between geniculate cells and simple cells in cat primary visual cortex. J. Neurosci., 21: 4002–4015.

Amitai, Y. and Connors, B.W. (1995) Intrinsic physiology and morphology of single neurons in neocortex. In: Jones, E.G. and Diamond, I.T., (Eds.), Cerebral Cortex, Vol. 11, Plenum Press, New York, pp. 299–331.

Benshalom, G. and White, E.L. (1986) Quantification of thalamocortical synapses with spiny stellate neurons in layer 1V of mouse somatosensory cortex. J. Comp. Neurol., 253: 303–314.

Castro-Alamancos, M.A. and Connors, B.W. (1996) Spatiotemporal properties of short-term plasticity in sensorimotor thalamocortical pathways of the rat. J. Neurosci., 16: 2767–2779.

Castro-Alamancos, M.A. and Oldford, E. (2002) Cortical sensory suppression during arousal is due to the activity-dependent depression of thalamocortical synapses. J. Physiol. (London), 541: 319–331.

Chung, S., Lin, X. and Nelson, S.B. (2002) Short-term depression at thalamocortical synapses contributes to rapid adaptation of cortical sensory responses in vivo. Neuron, 34: 437–446.

Chung, S. and Ferster, D. (1998) Strength and orientation tuning of the thalamic input to simple cells revealed by electrically evoked cortical suppression. Neuron, 20: 1177–1189.

Freeman, J.A. and Nicholson, C. (1975) Experimental optimization of current source-density technique for anuran cerebellum. J. Neurophysiol., 38: 369–382.

Fuhrmann, G., Segev, I., Markram, H. and Tsodyds, M. (2001) Coding of temporal information by activity-dependent synapses. J. Neurophyiol., 87: 140–148.

Gerstner, W., Kreiter, A.K., Markram, H. and Herz, A.V.M. (1997) Neural codes: firing rates and beyond. Proc. Natl. Acad. Sci. USA, 94: 12740–12741.

Gil, Z., Connors, B.W. and Amitai, Y. (1997) Differential regulation of neocortical synapses by neuromodulators and activity. Neuron, 19: 679–686.

Gil, Z., Connors, B.W. and Amitai, Y. (1999) Efficacy of thalamocortical and intracortical synaptic connections: quanta, innervation, and reliability. Neuron, 23: 385–397.

Goldman, M.S., Nelson, S.B. and Abbot, L.F. (1999) Decorrelation of spike trains by synaptic depression. Neurocomputing, 26–27: 147–153.

Green, J.D. and Arduini, A.A. (1954) Hippocampal electrical activity and arousal. J. Neurophysiol., 57: 533–557.

Haberly, L.B. and Shepherd, G.M. (1973) Current-density analysis of summed evoked potentials in opossum prepyriform cortex. J. Neurophysiol., 36: 789–803.

Johnson, B.T. and Eagly, A.H. (2000) Quantitative synthesis of social psychological research. In: Reis, H.T. and Judd, C.M., (Eds.), Handbook of Research Methods in Social and Personality Psychology, Cambridge University Press, London, pp. 496–528.

Kirkwood, P.A. (1995) Synaptic excitation in the thoracic spinal cord from expiratory bulbospinal neurones in the cat. J. Physiol. (Lond.), 484: 201–225.

Kirkwood, P.A., Schmidt, K. and Sears, T.A. (1993) Functional identities of thoracic respiratory interneurones in the cat. J. Physiol. (Lond.), 461: 667–687.

Kirkwood, P.A. and Sears, T.A. (1982) Excitatory postsynaptic potentials from single muscle spindle afferents in external intercostal motoneurones of the cat. J. Physiol. (Lond.), 322: 287–314.

LeVay, S. and Gilbert, C.D. (1976) Laminar patterns of geniculocortical projection in the cat. Brain Res, 113: 1–19.

Levick, W.R., Cleland, G.G. and Dubin, M.W. (1972) Lateral geniculate neurons of cat: retinal inputs and physiology. Invest. Opththalmol., 11: 302–311.

Lu, S.-M., Guido, W. and Sherman, S.M. (1992) Effects of membrane voltage on receptive field properties of lateral geniculate neurons in the cat contributions of the low threshold $Ca2+$ conductance. J. Neurophysiol., 68: 2185–2198.

Markram, H., Wang, Y. and Tsodyks, M. (1998) Differential signaling via the same axon of neocortical pyramidal neurons. Proc. Natl. Acad. Sci. USA, 95: 5323–5328.

McCormick, D.A., Connors, B.W., Lighthall, J.W. and Prince, D.A. (1985) Comparative electrophysiology of pyramidal and sparsely spiny stellate neurons of the neocortex. J. Neurophysiol., 54: 782–806.

Mendell, L.M. and Henneman, E. (1971) Terminals of single 1a fibres: location, density and distribution within a pool of 300 homonymous motoneurons. J. Neurophysiol., 34: 171–187.

Munson, J.B. and Sypert, G.W. (1979) Properties of single-fibre excitatory postsynaptic potentials in triceps and surae motoneurones. J. Physiol. (Lond.), 296: 329–342.

Peters, A. and Feldman, M.L. (1976) The projection of the lateral geniculate nucleus to area 17 of the rat cerebral cortex. I. General description. J. Neurocytol., 5: 63–84.

Peters, A. and Payne, B.R. (1993) Numerical relationships between geniculocortical afferents and pyramidal cell modules in cat primary visual cortex. Cereb. Cortex, 3: 69–78.

Ramcharan, E.J., Cox, C.L., Zhan, X.J., Sherman, S.M. and Gnadt, J.W. (2000a) Cellular mechanisms underlying activity patterns in the monkey thalamus during visual behavior. J. Neurophysiol., 84: 1982–1987.

Ramcharan, E.J., Gnadt, J.W. and Sherman, S.M. (2000b) Burst and tonic firing in thalamic cells of unanesthetized, behaving monkeys. Vis. Neurosci., 17: 55–62.

Reich, D.S., Mechler, F., Purpura, K.P. and Victor, J.D. (2000) Interspike intervals, receptive fields, and information encoding in primary visual cortex. J. Neurosci, 20: 1964–1974.

Reyes, A., Lujan, R., Rozov, A., Burnashev, N. and Sakmann, B. (1998) Target-cell specific facilitation and depression in neocortical circuits. Nature Neurosci., 1: 279–285.

Reitboeck, H.J. (1983) Fiber microelectrodes for electrophysiological recordings. J. Neurosci. Methods, 8: 249–262.

Schmidt, K., Kirkwood, P.A., Munson, J.B., Shen, E. and Sears, T.A. (1993) Contralateral projections of thoracic respiratory interneurones in the cat. J. Physiol. (Lond.), 461: 647–665.

Sherman, S.M. (2001) A wake-up call from the thalamus. Nat. Neurosci., 4: 344–346.

Sherman, S.M. and Guillery, R.W. (1996) Functional organization of thalamocortical relays. J. Neurophysiol., 76: 1367–1395.

Stratford, K.J., Tarczy-Hornoch, K., Martin, K.A., Bannister, N.J. and Jack, J.J. (1996) Excitatory synaptic inputs to spiny stellate cells in cat visual cortex. Nature, 382: 258–261.

Steriade, M. and Llinas, R.R. (1988) The functional states of the thalamus and the associated neuronal interplay. Physiol. Rev., 68: 649–742.

Swadlow, H.A. (1988) Efferent neurons and suspected interneurons in binocular visual cortex of the awake rabbit: Receptive fields and binocular properties. J. Neurophysiol., 59: 1162–1187.

Swadlow, H.A. (1989) Efferent neurons and suspected interneurons in S-1 vibrissa cortex of the awake rabbit: receptive fields and axonal properties. J. Neurophysiol., 62: 288–308.

Swadlow, H.A. (1995) The Influence of VPM afferents on putative inhibitory interneurons in S1 of the awake rabbit: evidence from cross-correlation, microstimulation, and latencies to peripheral sensory stimulation. J. Neurophysiol., 73: 1584–1599.

Swadlow, H.A. (2003) Fast-spike interneurons and feed-forward inhibition in sensory neocortex. Cerebral Cortex, 13: 25–32.

Swadlow, H.A., Beloozerova, I. and Sirota, M. (1998) Sharp, local synchrony among putative feed-forward inhibitory interneurons of rabbit somatosensory cortex. J. Neurophysiol., 79: 567–582.

Swadlow, H.A. and Gusev, A.G. (2000) The influence of single VB thalamocortical impulses on barrel columns of rabbit somatosensory cortex. J. Neurophysiol., 83: 2803–2813.

Swadlow, H.A. and Gusev, A.G. (2001) The impact of "bursting" thalamic impulses at a neocortical synapse. Nat. Neurosci., 4: 402–408.

Swadlow, H.A. and Gusev, A.G. (2002) Receptive field construction in cortical inhibitory interneurons. Nat. Neurosci., 5: 403–404.

Swadlow, H.A., Gusev, A.G. and Bezdudnaya, T. (2002) Activation of a cortical column by a thalamocortical impulse. J. Neuroscience, 22: 7766–7773.

Taylor, A., Stephens, J.A., Somjen, G., Appenting, K. and O'Donovan, J.J. (1977) Extracellular spike-triggered averaging for plotting synaptic projections. Brain Res., 140: 344–348.

Van Der Loos, H. (1976) Barreloids in the mouse somatosensory thalamus. Neurosci. Lett., 2: 1–6.

Weyand, T.G., Boudreaux, M. and Guido, W. (2001) Burst and tonic modes in thalamic neurons during sleep and wakefulness. J. Neurophysiol., 85: 1107–1118.

White, E.L. (1989) Cortical Circuits, Birkhauser Press, Boston, MA.

White, E.L. and Hersch, S.M. (1982) A quantitative study of thalamocortical and other synapses involving the apical dendrites of corticothalamic projection cells in mouse SmI cortex. J. Neurocytol., 11: 137–157.

Woolsey, T.A. and Van Der Loos, H. (1970) The description of a cortical field composed of discrete cytoarchitectonic units. Brain Res., 17: 205–242.

Progress in Brain Research, Vol. 149
ISSN 0079-6123

CHAPTER 9

Thalamic relays and cortical functioning

S. Murray Sherman*

*Department of Neurobiology, Pharmacology & Physiology,
University of Chicago, Chicago, IL 60637, USA*

Abstract: Studies on the visual thalamic relays, the lateral geniculate nucleus and pulvinar, provide three key properties that have dramatically changed the view that the thalamus serves as a simple relay to get information from subcortical sites to cortex. First, the retinal input, although a small minority (7%) in terms of numbers of synapses onto geniculate relay cells, dominates receptive field properties of these relay cells and strongly drives them; 93% of input thus is nonretinal and modulates the relay in dynamic and important ways related to behavioral state, including attention. We call the retinal input the *driver* input and the nonretinal, *modulator* input, and their unique morphological and functional differences allow us to recognize driver and modulator input to many other thalamic relays. Second, much of the modulation is related to control of a voltage-gated, low threshold Ca^{2+} conductance that determines response properties of relay cells — *burst* or *tonic* — and this, among other things, affects the salience of information relayed. Third, the lateral geniculate nucleus and pulvinar (a massive but generally mysterious and ignored thalamic relay), are examples of two different types of relay: the LGN is a *first order* relay, transmitting information from a subcortical driver source (retina), while the pulvinar is mostly a *higher order* relay, transmitting information from a driver source emanating from layer 5 of one cortical area to another area. Higher order relays seem especially important to general corticocortical communication, and this view challenges the conventional dogma that such communication is based on direct corticocortical connections. In this sense, any new information reaching a cortical area, whether from a subcortical source or another cortical area, benefits from a thalamic relay. Other examples of first and higher order relays also exist, and generally higher order relays represent the majority of thalamus. A final property of interest emphasized in chapter 17 by Guillery (2005) is that most or all driver inputs to thalamus, whether from a subcortical source or from layer 5 of cortex, are axons that branch, with the extrathalamic branch innervating a motor or premotor region in the brainstem, or in some cases, spinal cord. This suggests that actual information relayed by thalamus to cortex is actually a copy of motor instructions (Guillery, 2005). Overall, these features of thalamic relays indicate that the thalamus not only provides a behaviorally relevant, dynamic control over the nature of information relayed, it also plays a key role in basic corticocortical communication.

Introduction

Virtually all information reaching cortex, and thus conscious perception, must first pass through thalamus. It thus follows that the thalamus sits in a strategically vital position for brain functioning. One would think this enough to ensure that the thalamus was

constantly a major focus of neuroscience research, but that has not been so. Indeed, we have recently emerged from the dark ages of thinking about thalamus: the prevalent idea being that its main purpose during normal waking behavior was simply to relay information from the periphery to cortex, a relay function that was machine-like, unvarying, and rather boring. According to this view, the thalamus only behaved in an interesting fashion during sleep or certain pathological conditions, such as epilepsy

*Tel.: +1-773-834-2900; Fax: +1-773-702-3774;
E-mail: msherman@bsd.uchicago.edu

(Steriade and Llinaás, 1988; Steriade et al., 1993; McCormick and Bal, 1997), but this aspect of thalamic functioning, while interesting and still viable, is beyond the scope of the present study. Rather, the focus here is on the more recent finding that the thalamus plays an interesting and dynamic role during normal, waking behavior of the animal, and there are three aspects to this. First, it is considered that the thalamus provides a changeable relay of information to cortex, the purpose of which is to adjust the nature of relayed information to varying behavioral demands. Second, the thalamus serves not only to relay peripheral information to cortex, but it continues to play a vital role in further cortical processing of this information by acting as a central link in various corticothalamocortical routes of information processing. Third, most or all inputs to thalamus that are relayed to cortex carry information about ongoing motor instructions, so that the main role of thalamic relays is to provide a copy to cortex of these instructions. This last point has enormous implications for cortical functioning, and has been discussed in detail in Chapter 17 of this book (Guillery, 2005).

The vast majority of detailed information we have about the cell and circuit properties of the thalamus comes from studies of the lateral geniculate nucleus, which is the thalamic relay of retinal input to cortex. Studies of the lateral geniculate nucleus derive mostly from carnivores, rodents, and primates. Fortunately, this nucleus has served as an excellent model for thalamus, and all of the major concepts learned from study of this relay that are described below apply widely to thalamus.

Relay functions of the thalamus

One question that remains relevant and profound is: Why does information destined for cortex need to pass through a thalamic relay? Why, for instance, does retinal information pass through the lateral geniculate nucleus instead of projecting directly to cortex? If one looks at information processing in the visual system, it is clear that as one progresses up the hierarchical ladder across the various synaptic zones in retina, the receptive fields of cells become richer and more complex, and this also occurs as one ascends the various hierarchical steps within visual

cortex (reviewed in Dowling, 1970, 1987; Hubel and Wiesel, 1977; van Essen, 1979, 1985; van Essen and Maunsell, 1983; van Essen et al., 1992). These increasingly elaborate receptive fields represent the processing of visual information, and especially elaborate receptive fields in cortex are thought to underlie specific perceptual processes. For instance, the complex receptive fields in the middle temporal cortical area in monkeys are thought to be a key neural substrate for the processing of visual motion (Britten et al., 1993; O'Keefe and Movshon, 1998; Grunewald et al., 2002; Kohn and Movshon, 2003; Osborne et al., 2004).

The one synapse across which there is virtually no receptive field elaboration is the retinogeniculate synapse (Hubel and Wiesel, 1961; Sherman, 1985; Sherman and Guillery, 1996). A similar pattern holds for the other main sensory systems involving a thalamic relay[1]: somatosensory information involves little or no receptive field elaboration across the synapse from the medial lemniscus to the ventral posterior nucleus, and likewise there is essentially no such elaboration across the synapse from the inferior colliculus to the medial geniculate nucleus, although in both systems there is significant receptive field elaboration across synapses peripheral to thalamus and within the cortex (Purves et al., 1997; Kandel et al., 2000).

These observations used to be viewed as evidence that not much was happening in thalamus during normal information processing, leading to the above-mentioned "dark ages" for thalamic enquiry. In fact, this pattern is now interpreted to mean that the thalamus has an absolutely unique role to play in information processing. That is, while other subcortical and cortical stages involved have a function that is related to receptive field elaboration, the thalamus does something completely different. It controls the flow of information to cortex. Indeed, the complex cell and circuit properties controlling

---

[1]The olfactory system is unusual in that information passes from a subcortical to a cortical level without a thalamic relay, although the cortex in this case is paleocortex rather than neocortex. There is a higher level olfactory input to the medial dorsal nucleus of the thalamus which may be relayed to frontal neocortex, but it is not clear whether this is the only entry of olfactory information to cortex or whether a nonthalamic route from paleocortex to neocortex exists.

relay cell responses contradict the notion that the thalamus behaves as a simple relay.

Thalamic relay cell properties

Like all other brain neurons, thalamic relay cells possess many membrane conductances controlled by membrane voltage or specific ion concentrations, in addition to synaptic activity. This supplies the cell with a highly variable, dynamic range of responses that thereby varies the nature of information relayed to cortex. A detailed discussion of all these properties is beyond the scope of the present account and can be found elsewhere (McCormick and Huguenard, 1992; Sherman and Guillery, 1996, 2001). The focus here is a voltage gated Ca^{2+} conductance involving a T type Ca^{2+} channel found in the cell body and dendrites that, when activated, leads to an inward current, I_T.

Tonic and burst firing modes

Figure 1 shows the basic voltage dependence of I_T (Jahnsen and Llinaás, 1984a,b; McCormick and Huguenard, 1992; Sherman and Guillery, 1996, 2001; Smith et al., 1998; Zhan et al., 1999; Gutierrez et al., 2001). Anyone who understands the basic properties of the Na^+/K^+ action potential, will appreciate that the properties of IT are qualitatively identical to those of the Na^+ channel involved with the action potential, albeit with important quantitative differences. Like the Na^+ channel, the T type Ca^{2+} channel has two voltage sensitive gates, activation and inactivation gates, and both must be open for Ca^{2+} to flow into the cell. The sequence of events is shown in Fig. 1 starting at the lower left panel and moving clockwise:

(1) At a relatively hyperpolarized membrane potential (V_m), more than about 5 mV below rest, the inactivation gate is open, but the activation gate is closed, and there is no I_T. In this condition, I_T is said to have its inactivation removed, or it is "deinactivated", but because the activation gate is closed, it is also deactivated.

(2) Depolarization above threshold (roughly −65 mV to −60 mV) then rapidly opens the activation gate, and Ca^{2+} flows into the cell in the form of I_T. This creates a depolarizing, all-or-none Ca^{2+} spike that propagates through the dendritic tree and cell body, but not the axon, which lacks a sufficient concentration of these channels. I_T is thus activated.

(3) After a period of sustained depolarization lasting for ~100 ms[2], the inactivation gate closes, and thus I_T is now inactivated. A variety of slower, non-inactivating K^+ conductances also come into play, and this plus I_T inactivation serves to repolarize the cell.

(4) Even though it is back at the starting membrane potential, I_T remains inactivated for ~100 ms. After this time, the inactivation of I_T is removed (i.e., it becomes deinactivated). The cycle is then reset as the initial starting conditions as in panel 1 are re-established.

There are several implications to the above. First, while activation of I_T is very fast, both inactivation and deinactivation take time, on the order of 100 ms. For inactivation, this means that a typical, fast excitatory post-synaptic potential (EPSP) or even an action potential will not much inactivate I_T. Likewise, for deinactivation, a fast inhibitory post-synaptic potential (IPSP) will not do. For either process, it is necessary to sustain a change in V_m. Second, the all-or-none Ca^{2+} spike created when I_T is activated propagates through the dendrites and soma, but not up the axon, because there are virtually no T channels there. Nonetheless, as shown in more detail below, this spike does affect the pattern of conventional action potentials generated and thus will affect the signal sent up the axon to cortex. This Ca^{2+} spike is commonly called the "low threshold spike", because its activation threshold is hyperpolarized with respect to that of the action potential. This means that, with some exceptions (Gutierrez et al., 2001), if I_T is deinactivated, a ensuing depolarization will activate I_T and the low threshold spike before activating a conventional action potential. Third, as noted, the T channel behaves qualitatively just like the Na^+ channel involved in the action potential — both

---

[2]Actually, inactivation and deinactivation are complex functions of voltage and time so that the more the cell is depolarized, the faster I_T inactivates, and the more the cell is hyperpolarized, the faster I_T deinactivates.

The Low Threshold Ca²⁺ Spike

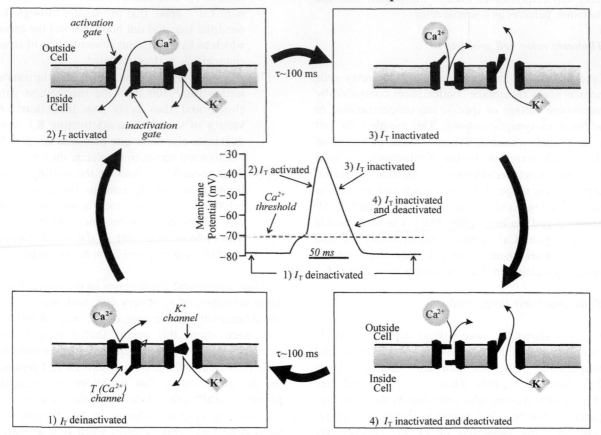

Fig. 1. Schematic view of actions of voltage dependent T (Ca²⁺) and K⁺ channels underlying low threshold Ca²⁺ spike. The 4 numbered panels show the sequence of channel events in a clockwise fashion, and the central graph shows the effects on membrane potential. The T channel has 2 voltage dependent gates: an *activation* gate that opens with depolarization and closes at hyperpolarized levels; and an *inactivation* gate that shows the opposite voltage dependency. Both of these gates must be open for Ca²⁺ to enter the cell, and this flow of Ca²⁺ is an inward current known as I_T. The K⁺ channel shown is really a heterogenous conglomeration of different K⁺ channels with only a single gate that opens during depolarization; thus, these channels do not inactivate. (1). At a relatively hyperpolarized resting membrane potential (∼70 mV), the inactivation gate of the T channel is open, and so the T channel is deinactivated, but the activation gate is closed. The single gate for the K⁺ channel is closed. (2) With sufficient depolarization to reach its threshold, the activation gate of the T channel opens, and Ca²⁺ flows into the cell, producing I_T. The T channel is now activated. This further depolarizes the cell, providing the rise of the low threshold spike, which is all-or-none. (3) The inactivation gate of the T channel closes after ∼100 ms of depolarization, and so the channel is now inactivated. The K⁺ channel also opens. These actions repolarize the cell. (4) Even though the initial resting potential is reached, the T channel remains inactivated, because it takes ∼100 ms of hyperpolarization to deinactivate it. Eventually, the T channel deinactivates, and the conditions of panel 1 are restored. Note that the behavior of the T channel qualitatively matches that of the Na⁺ channel involved with the action potential, but with several quantitative differences: the T channel is slower to inactivate and deinactivate, and it operates in a more hyperpolarized regime.

channels inactivate with a similar voltage dependency and the time required for deinactivation establishes a refractory period — but there are important quantitative differences. Thus the T channel has a much slower time course for inactivation and deinactivation, a longer duration spike, a more hyperpolarized regime (by about 10 mV), and little or no distribution in the axon.

Figure 2 shows some of the functional implications of I_T. When the cell has been sufficiently depolarized, I_T is inactivated and plays no role in the cell's response. Now, a suprathreshold excitatory input

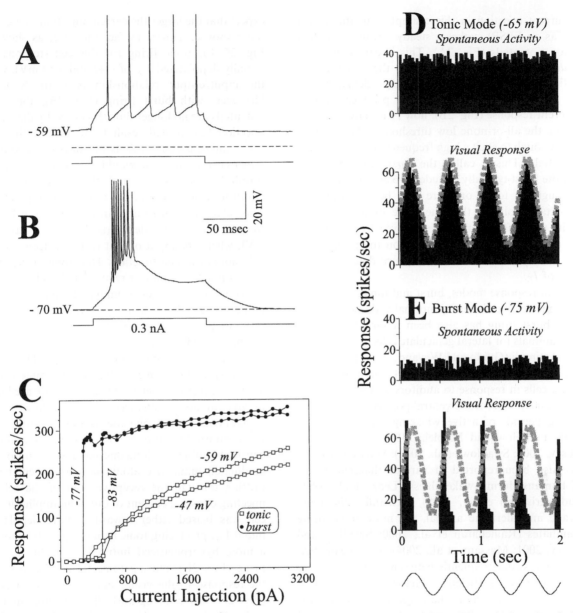

Fig. 2. Various properties of the low threshold Ca^{2+} spike. A, B: Intracellular recording of a relay cell from the lateral geniculate nucleus of a cat in vitro. At an initial V_m of −59 mV, I_T is inactivated and thus the cell responds in tonic mode (A). Thus, the response to a depolarizing 3 nA current injection is a steady stream of unitary action potentials. At an initial V_m of −70 mV, I_T is deinactivated and thus the cell responds in burst mode (B). Now, the very same current injection activates the low threshold Ca^{2+} spike, which in turn activates, in this case, a burst of 8 conventional action potentials. C: Initial response of cell in A, B to various levels of current injection from different initial V_ms. At levels that inactivate I_T and produce tonic firing (−47 mV and −59 mV), a fairly linear relationship ensues. At levels that deinactivate I_T and produce burst firing (−77 mV and −83 mV), a very nonlinear relationship in the form of a step function is seen. D,E: Effect of firing mode on response to drifting sinusoidal grating from a relay cell in the lateral geniculate nucleus of an anesthetized cat recorded intracellularly in vivo. The sinusoidal contrast changes in the visual stimulus are shown below the histograms and is also shown as a gray dashed line for the lower histograms of D,E. At an initial V_m (−65 mV) that promotes tonic firing (D), the spontaneous activity is relatively high, and the response to the grating has a sinusoidal profile. At an initial V_m (−75 mV) that promotes burst firing (E), the spontaneous activity is relatively low, and the response to the grating no longer has a sinusoidal profile.

(a current injection in this example, but think of it also as an EPSP) evokes a steady stream of unitary action potentials (Fig. 2A). This is called the *tonic mode* of firing. However, when the same cell is sufficiently hyperpolarized so that I_T is deinactivated, the exact same excitatory input produces a very different response (Fig. 2B): now I_T is activated, producing the all-or-none low threshold spike, which is large enough to elicit a high frequency volley of action potentials. This is called the *burst mode* of firing, and the burst typically includes 2–6 action potentials, although up to 10 or more may be involved. The important point is that the same excitatory input elicits two different messages relayed to cortex (i.e., the action potentials) depending on the recent voltage history of the cell, which in turn determines the state of I_T.

Both response modes, burst and tonic, are seen in thalamic relay cells during normal waking behavior. Thus burst firing has also been reported in awake, alert animals for lateral geniculate cells in response to visual stimuli (Guido and Weyand, 1995; Ramcharan et al., 2000; Weyand et al., 2001); for medial geniculate cells in response to auditory stimuli (Massaux et al., 2004); and for the ventral posterior medial cells during periods of active whisking (Nicolelis et al., 1995; Fanselow and Nicolelis, 1999; Swadlow and Gusev, 2001; Swadlow et al., 2002). Such burst firing has also been reported in various thalamic nuclei of humans during wakefulness (Lenz et al., 1998; Radhakrishnan et al., 1999). Generally, the more awake and alert the animal, the more tonic firing dominates (Ramcharan et al., 2000; Swadlow and Gusev, 2001; Massaux et al., 2004). This means that relay cells switch frequently between modes, reflecting a change in V_m sufficient to change the inactivation state of I_T. A major challenge is to define the conditions and mechanisms for this switching, and some preliminary insights into this are presented below. Another challenge is to understand the significance for information processing of the response mode, and part of this is introduced in Figs. 2C–E.

Implications of firing mode for thalamic relays

Note that, in the case of tonic firing (Fig. 2A), the action potentials are evoked directly from the depolarizing current injection. Thus one would

expect that the larger the current injection, the greater the response. This is in fact the case, as shown in Fig. 2C for tonic firing for this cell (responses at initially depolarized V_m of −47 and −59 mV), where the input/output relationship is relatively linear. However, with burst firing (Fig. 2B), the action potentials are no longer directly caused by the current injection but instead result from the low threshold Ca^{2+} spike; because this is an all-or-none spike, a larger current injection would not evoke a larger low threshold Ca^{2+} spike, and thus a larger current injection would not evoke more action potentials. This relationship for burst firing is shown in Fig. 2C (responses at initially depolarized V_m of −77 and −83 mV), where the input/output relationship is a decidedly nonlinear step function. Thus tonic firing represents a much more linear relay than does burst firing.

Another way of determining the effect of firing mode on the thalamic relay is to see its effect on response properties of the relay cell as determined by receptive field analysis: this reflects how incoming information is relayed to the cortex. Figs 2D, E shows a prototypical example of this. The example is from a lateral geniculate relay cell recorded intracellularly in vivo in an anesthetized cat, and shown is the spontaneous activity plus the visual responses evoked by a sinusoidal grating (i.e., a visual stimulus of constant luminance along one axis and of sinusoidally modulated luminance along the perpendicular axis) drifting through the receptive field of the cell. By injecting constant current of different amplitudes, the cell was biased either toward a more depolarized initial V_m, producing tonic firing (Fig. 2D) or toward a more hyperpolarized initial V_m, producing burst firing (Fig. 2E). During tonic firing, the profile of the response to the visual stimulus looks sinusoidal (Fig. 2D, lower histogram), like the stimulus itself, and thus there is a close correlation between firing rate and stimulus contrast (compare the firing with the superimposed stimulus contrast represented by the dashed, gray curve). This is another way of saying that the response is very linear. The visual response to the same stimulus during burst firing is quite different, because it no longer is sinusoidal in shape (Fig. 2E, lower histogram). This nonlinearity during burst firing is predicted from the nonlinear input/output relationship of burst firing depicted in Fig. 2C.

The advantage of tonic firing and its more linear relay is self-evident, because the type of nonlinear distortion imposed on the relay by burst firing limits the extent to which visual cortex can faithfully reconstruct the visual scene. Any advantage of burst firing is harder to discern, but one such advantage is tied to spontaneous activity (i.e., background firing or responsiveness when there is no visual stimulus present). As shown in the upper histograms of Figs. 2D, E, this is considerably lower during burst firing. Because spontaneous activity represents responsiveness that, by definition, bears no relationship to a visual stimulus, it actually represents noise in the relay to cortex. The response to the visual stimulus (Figs. 2D, E, lower histograms) is the signal, which is quite large in both firing modes. What is of interest here is the signal-to-noise ratio, which, chiefly because of the lower noise during burst firing, is higher during burst firing. A higher signal-to-noise ratio is often associated with stimulus detectability. This suggestion of improved detectability during burst firing has been supported experimentally (Guido et al., 1995).

However, not only does burst firing improve stimulus detectability, it also provides for a more powerful activation of cortex. To understand the reason for this, it helps to look at the special pattern of firing seen in burst mode, a pattern revealed by plotting a two-dimensional interspike interval distribution on logarithmic axes (Fig. 3). This plot shows that groups of action potentials are clustered and not spread evenly in time. In particular, the cluster at the lower right (in the shaded area) represents the first action potentials of bursts due to low threshold Ca^{2+} spikes. The second to penultimate action potentials in a burst are indicated by the cluster at the lower left of each histogram, and the last action potentials in a burst are found at the left side of each histogram. All other action potentials are during tonic firing. The criteria developed for the first action potentials in a burst are represented by the shaded area: the action potential must follow a silent period of ≥ 100 ms and be followed by the next action potential within 2ms (Lu et al., 1992), and minor variants of these criteria exist (e.g., Lenz et al., 1998; Zirh et al., 1998). The reason for this is as follows. In order for a burst to occur, I_T must be activated to produce the underlying low threshold spike. For this to happen, I_T must

first be deinactivated, and that requires ≥ 100 ms or so of sustained hyperpolarization. The sustained hyperpolarization means that, by definition, there can be no evoked action potentials, and so this requirement to deinactivate I_T leads to a silent period of ≥ 100 ms before the first spike in a burst. In contrast to the clusters related to burst firing, the action potentials evoked during tonic firing tend to occupy one cloud of points with interspike intervals relatively evenly distributed, mostly between 5 and 30 ms.

One significance of this distribution of action potentials during the two firing modes has to do with properties of the thalamocortical synapse, which shows paired-pulse depression (Stratford et al., 1996;

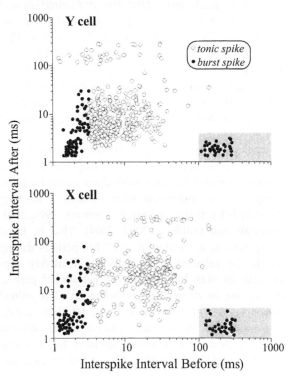

Fig. 3. Two-dimensional interspike interval plots for two representative relay cells in the lateral geniculate nucleus of an anesthetized cat recorded extracellularly in vivo. For each action potential recorded during a given period of time, the interval to the previous spike is shown on the abscissa, and the interval to the next spike is shown on the ordinate. Tonic and burst spikes are shown separately. Note the cluster of burst spikes on the lower right of each histogram. These follow a silent period of ≥ 100 ms and are followed by another spike within ~ 2 ms. These are known to be the first spike in a burst (Lu et al., 1992). For further details see text.

Beierlein and Connors, 2002; Castro-Alamancos and Oldford, 2002; Chung et al., 2002; Nicolelis, 2002). This means that for a period of time following an evoked EPSP from this synapse, EPSP amplitudes will be substantially depressed. However, for most of these synapses, a silent period of ≥ 100 ms as occurs before the first action potential in a burst would relieve the depression and lead to a maximum EPSP. In contrast, tonic firing has interspike intervals that are generally too brief to permit much relief of the depression, so the synapse will be considerably depressed throughout tonic firing. Recent work studying efficacy of the thalamocortical synapse in the somatosensory system of the awake rabbit has shown that, on average, the first action potential in a burst is much more effective at driving cortical circuitry than is a tonic action potential (Swadlow and Gusev, 2001; Swadlow et al., 2002, 2005). This does not even take into account that the following action potentials in a burst will produce extra EPSPs, that, while depressed, would temporally sum and enhance the response. The result is that a burst punches through to cortex very effectively compared to tonic action potentials.[3]

These different features related to firing mode — a more linear relay for tonic firing versus better stimulus detectability and cortical activation for burst firing — have suggested what remains a working hypothesis for further research (Sherman, 1996, 2001; Sherman and Guillery, 2002, 2004). That is, burst firing acts as a "wake-up call" for periods during which the relevant relay cells are relatively suppressed, as may happen during periods of general inattention or drowsiness or when an alert animal directs its attention elsewhere. Under these conditions, the idea is that any change in the afferent input, such as a new visual stimulus for a lateral geniculate relay cell, evokes a burst that "wakes up"

cortex with a signal that something has changed out there. This could then lead to a switch in the relay to tonic firing so that information about the changed environment can be relayed more linearly and thus more faithfully.

There is some very limited, indirect evidence consistent with this view (for details, see Sherman, 1996, 2001; Sherman and Guillery, 2002, 2004). One is that, as noted above, thalamic relay cells in a variety of nuclei and species (including rats, rabbits, cats, monkeys, and humans) show both tonic and burst firing during the animal's waking behavior, although in the alert animal bursting occurs much less frequently than does tonic firing (Guido and Weyand, 1995; Nicolelis et al., 1995; Lenz et al., 1998; Fanselow and Nicolelis, 1999; Radhakrishnan et al., 1999; Ramcharan et al., 2000; Swadlow and Gusev, 2001; Weyand et al., 2001; Swadlow et al., 2002; Massaux et al., 2004). Also, the amount of bursting increases as the animal becomes drowsy or inattentive, which is consistent with the hypothesis that bursting serves as suggested as a "wake-up call" (Ramcharan et al., 2000; Swadlow and Gusev, 2001; Massaux et al., 2004). It follows that such "wake-up calls" are especially important when the animal is drowsy or otherwise inattentive for the information being relayed through thalamus. Finally, recordings from lateral geniculate relay cells in the awake cat suggest a tendency for bursting to the first presentation of a novel stimulus with a switch to tonic firing as the stimulus remains (Guido and Weyand, 1995), and this, too, is consistent with the hypothesis.

For this to make sense, there must be thalamic circuitry available to control response mode efficiently, and this indeed is the case.

Thalamic circuit properties

Pattern of inputs to relay cells

Figure 4A schematically shows the various afferents that synapse onto relay cells; again the lateral geniculate nucleus is the example, but with relatively minor variations in the equivalent of the nonretinal afferents, the circuitry is similar for other thalamic relays, with the major change being the nature of the

---

[3]This scenario assumes that thalamocortical synapses show paired-pulse depression. However, the beauty of burst firing is that one would expect bursts to activate cortex more powerfully than tonic firing even if the thalamocortical synapse shows paired-pulse facilitation. This is because facilitation works well for short interspike intervals, and the short interspike intervals in a burst ensure considerable facilitation. Just as the interspike intervals during tonic firing are too short to relieve a depressed synapse, they are generally too long to produce facilitation for a facilitating synapse.

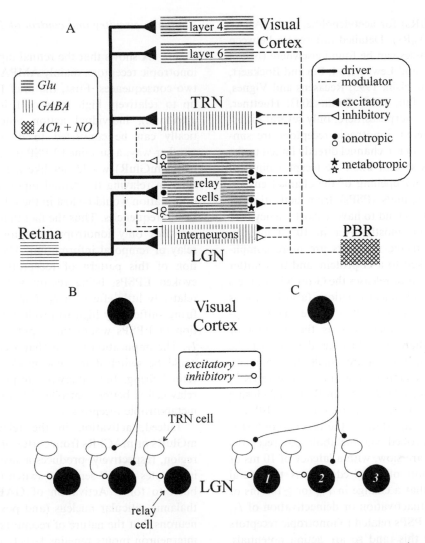

Fig. 4. Innervation patterns for the lateral geniculate nucleus. A: Inputs to relay cells, showing transmitters and post-synaptic receptors (ionotropic and metabotropic) involved. B, C: Two patterns among others possible for corticothalamic projection from layer 6 to reticular and relay cells. Simple excitation and feedforward inhibition is shown in B, and C shows a more complicated pattern in which activation of a cortical axon can excite some relay cells directly and inhibit others through activation of reticular cells. (*ACh*, acetylcholine; *GABA*, γ-aminobutyric acid; *Glu*, glutamate; *LGN*, lateral geniculate nucleus; *NO*, nitric oxide; *PBR*, parabrachial region; *TRN*, thalamic reticular nucleus.) For further details see text.

input to be relayed (e.g., instead of retinal input for the lateral geniculate nucleus, there would be medial lemniscal or inferior collicular input for the ventral posterior nucleus or medial geniculate nucleus, respectively, or, as noted below, cortical input from layer 5 for higher order relays).

Figure 4A, in addition to showing the inputs, also indicates the transmitters and post-synaptic receptors involved. There are two general classes of receptor: ionotropic and metabotropic. Ionotropic receptors relevant to Fig. 4A include AMPA and NMDA receptors (AMPARs and NMDARs) for glutamate, nicotinic receptors (nAChRs) for acetylcholine, and GABA$_A$ receptors (GABA$_A$Rs); metabotropic receptors include various metabotropic glutamate receptors (mGluRs), various muscarinic receptors (mAChRs) for acetylcholine, and $GABA_B$ receptors ($GABA_B$Rs). Detailed differences between these receptor classes can be found elsewhere (Nicoll et al., 1990; Mott and Lewis, 1994; Pin and Bockaert, 1995; Pin and Duvoisin, 1995; Recasens and Vignes, 1995; Conn and Pin, 1997; Conn, 2003; Huettner, 2003), but for the purposes here, only several differences are considered: ionotropic receptors are simpler, usually with an ion channel directly linked to the receptor complex so that when the receptor binds to a transmitter, rapid opening of the channel ensues. Post-synaptic potentials (PSPs) from activation of ionotropic receptors tend to have a short latency (~ 1 ms) and duration (mostly over in 10–20 ms). In contrast, metabotropic receptors are more complicated: each is linked to a G-protein, and transmitter binding to the receptor releases the G-protein and sets off a chain of biochemical reactions (also known as second messenger actions) that create many intracellular changes. Among them is the opening or closing of ion channels, which in the case of the receptors shown in Fig. 4A are usually K^+ channels. Opening the K^+ channel allows more positive (K^+) ions to leave the cell, leading to an IPSP, and closing the channel does the opposite, producing an EPSP.

What is more important in the present context is that the PSPs evoked via metabotropic receptors in the relay cells are slow, with a latency of 10 ms or so and a duration of hundreds of ms to several seconds. Recall that a change in V_m for ≥ 100 ms or so is needed for inactivation or deinactivation of I_T, and thus the fast PSPs related to ionotropic receptors are ill-suited for this (and so are action potentials, which are over in a ms or so). In contrast, the sustained PSPs of the metabotropic receptors are ideal for control of I_T. That is, the sustained EPSP related to the mGluR or the mAChR serves well to inactivate I_T and convert burst firing to tonic; similarly, the sustained IPSP of the $GABA_B$R will deinactivate I_T and convert tonic firing to burst. These actions of metabotropic receptors are not limited to control of I_T: the sustained PSPs will also serve to control other slower voltage gated conductances that exist, such as I_h and I_A (for details of these other conductances, see McCormick and Huguenard, 1992; Sherman and Guillery, 1996, 2001), and the sustained alterations in V_m will also affect the overall excitability of the relay cell.

Thalamic circuitry and control of I_T

Figure 4A shows that the retinal input activates only ionotropic receptors, mainly AMPARs[4], and this has two consequences. First, the brief EPSP means that up to relatively high rates of firing in the retinal afferent(s), individual action potentials presynaptically can be converted to discrete EPSPs. Put another way, a sustained EPSP (e.g., from activation of an mGluR) would act like a low-pass temporal filter in relaying the retinal input, so that temporal information would be lost in the relay at higher input firing frequencies. Thus the fact that the retinal input activates only ionotropic receptors maximizes the relay of temporal information. The second implication of this pattern of receptors is that retinally evoked EPSPs, being relatively brief, would have relatively little effect on I_T. Only at rates of retinal firing sufficiently high to produce temporal summation of EPSPs would this input serve to inactivate I_T. The implication here is that a cell in burst mode could be switched to tonic mode by high rates of retinal firing, but otherwise, response mode of the relay cell is better controlled by inputs that activate metabotropic receptors.

Indeed, activation in the relay cell of either mGluRs or mAChRs from cortex or the parabrachial region, respectively, produces a sustained EPSP that inactivates I_T and serves to switch firing mode from burst to tonic. Activation of $GABA_B$Rs from the thalamic reticular nucleus (and possibly from interneurons, but the nature of receptors post-synaptic to interneuron inputs remains largely unexplored) does the opposite by producing a sustained EPSP that deinactivates I_T and switches firing mode from tonic to burst. Thus the two major extrathalamic, non-retinal inputs to the lateral geniculate nucleus — from cortex and the parabrachial region — control firing mode fairly effectively: the direct inputs to relay cells from both can promote tonic firing, and indirect

---

[4]Any role of NMDARs here is complicated by their voltage dependency, so that they will not contribute to an EPSP unless the cell is already fairly depolarized (Mayer and Westbrook, 1987; Nakanishi et al., 1998; Ozawa et al., 1998; Qian and Johnson, 2002). The role of NMDARs in control of I_T remains unclear.

inputs involving the thalamic reticular nucleus (and, perhaps, interneurons) can promote burst firing.

However, there are important differences in these inputs. As noted in Fig. 4A, parabrachial axons branch to innervate relay cells and both types of local GABAergic inhibitory cell (reticular cells and interneurons). The main effect on relay cells is excitatory while the simultaneous effect on the local inhibitory cells is inhibitory. This neat trick is effected by different post-synaptic receptors: mainly nAChRs and the M1 type of mAChR on relay cells to produce EPSPs and the M2 type of mAChRs on the GABAergic cells to produce IPSPs. This means that activity in these inputs has a straightforward depolarizing effect on relay cells due to direct excitation and indirect disinibition (i.e., inhibition of the GABAergic inputs), and this in turn implies that the more active these inputs, the more likely the relay cells fire in tonic mode.

The effect of cortical inputs is less obvious, because, according to Fig. 4A, it can produce direct excitation and indirect inhibition. Here, much depends on the details of circuitry, details of which are very little known, and this point is illustrated in Figs. 4B, C. If the corticothalamic circuitry is organized in a simple feedforward inhibitory circuit (Fig. 4B), then the net result of cortical activation will be relatively balanced increases in EPSPs and IPSPs. This would likely have little overall effect on V_m and thus on I_T. However, recent evidence (Chance et al., 2002; Abbott, 2005) suggests that such a balanced increase in EPSPs and IPSPs, while slightly affecting V_m, will increase synaptic conductance; this in turn reduces neuronal input resistance, making the relay cell less responsive to other (e.g., retinal) inputs. In this way, the circuitry of Fig. 4B can serve as a gain control mechanism. Fig. 4C shows another possible arrangement, and here the result of corticothalamic activation is quite different. For any specific cortical axon (or, perhaps, a small related group), activation will directly depolarize some relay cells (represented by *cell* 2), inactivating I_T to promote tonic firing, and indirectly hyperpolarize others (represented by *cells* 1 and 3), deinactivating I_T to promote burst firing. While there is some evidence for the arrangement shown in Fig. 4C (Tsumoto et al., 1978), it is plausible that heterogeneity exists in the corticothalamic circuits, so that those shown in Fig. 4B,C, as well as others not shown, exist.

Role of thalamus in corticocortical communication

The discussion in the previous section offers some functions for the thalamus to perform in relaying information to cortex, and other functions will doubtless be added as we learn more about this topic. This section examines the case that thalamus does more than just relay peripheral information to cortex; instead, it continues to play a role in how cortex processes such information. The logic underlying these arguments begins with a consideration of inputs to thalamic relay cells.

Drivers and modulators

Functional differences

A glance back at Fig. 4A shows that there are multiple inputs to lateral geniculate relay cells, yet only one of these, the retinal input, represents the information actually relayed. What are all the nonretinal inputs doing? A consideration of numbers only adds to the mystery, because the presumably dominant retinal input contributes only 7% of the synaptic inputs to relay cells; the rest are contributed roughly equally, about 30% each, from local GABAergic sources, from layer 6 of cortex, and from the parabrachial region (van Horn et al., 2000). Small numbers of serotonergic, noradrenergic, and histaminergic inputs are also present (reviewed in Sherman and Guillery, 1996, 2001) but are not considered further here. The point is that not all physical inputs are equal, as if they participate in some sort of anatomical and functional democracy. Indeed, the retinal inputs, despite the number, produce disproportionately large EPSPs in relay cells.

In terms of the lateral geniculate nucleus, there are a number of criteria that distinguish the retinal input from the nonretinal (Sherman and Guillery, 1996, 1998, 2001):

- Retinal inputs to relay cells provide the main receptive field properties and are necessary for the existence of the receptive fields, whereas nonretinal inputs produce only subtle changes in receptive field properties.

- Retinal inputs end in very large terminals, indeed by far the largest in the thalamus, and contribute up to 10 or more distinct synaptic contact zones. The smaller nonretinal terminals rarely have more than one synaptic contact zone each.
- Retinal terminals are limited to proximal dendrites, often in complex synaptic arrangements known as triads found within elaborate synaptic glomeruli, whereas modulator terminals can be found anywhere on the dendritic arbor.
- As noted, despite the small number of synapses, retinal EPSPs are large, suggesting powerful synapses, whereas individual nonretinal inputs are weak.
- Again as noted, retinal inputs activate only ionotropic glutamate receptors, whereas nonretinal inputs typically activate metabotropic receptors as well.
- There is relatively little convergence of retinal inputs onto relay cells, whereas many or most nonretinal inputs show considerable convergence.
- Retinal inputs do not innervate the thalamic reticular nucleus, whereas nonretinal inputs do.
- Retinal synapses show paired-pulse depression (following an evoked retinal EPSP, further EPSPs from retina are reduced in amplitude for 50–100 ms or so), whereas corticogeniculate synapses, the only nonretinal input so far tested for this effect, show paired-pulse facilitation (the opposite of depression, so that evoked EPSPs for 50–100 ms or so are enhanced in amplitude).

These systematic differences between retinal and nonretinal inputs led to the concept that these thalamic afferents could be divided into *drivers* and *modulators*, the former being the retinal inputs, so named because they strongly drive relay cells and transmit the message that is processed by cortex, and the latter being all other inputs, so named because their role is to modulate retinogeniculate transmission. One example of this modulation, among many others, is the abovementioned control of I_T by cortical and parabrachial input, both designated as modulators here. This division of afferents to relay cells into drivers and modulators works well in other thalamic

relays for which sufficient information exists: for instance the driver inputs to the ventral portion of the medial geniculate nucleus or to the ventral posterior nucleus are, respectively, from the inferior colliculus or the medial lemniscus. As with the retinal input to the lateral geniculate nucleus, these other drivers bring the information to be relayed and thus confer the basic receptive field properties onto their target relay cells.

This concept that not all anatomical pathways are the same, and that some are important to the transmission of basic information (e.g., retinal inputs), while others play a subtler role in modulating how that information is transformed or relayed (e.g., nonretinal inputs), has a number of other implications considered below. A particularly interesting possibility is that this distinction between drivers and modulators can be extended beyond thalamus, for instance, into cortex. There are reasons for thinking this: there is now considerable evidence that the input that confers the basic receptive field properties onto layer 4 cells of primary visual cortex are the corticogeniculate axons (Hubel and Wiesel, 1962, 1977; Ferster et al., 1996; Ferster and Miller, 2000; Usrey et al., 2000; Alonso et al., 2001; Kara et al., 2002; Ferster, 2004); these synapses have many of the features of a driver from the bulleted list above, including large EPSPs with paired-pulse depression (Stratford et al., 1996), large terminals on proximal dendrites; and these contribute only about 6% of the synapses onto these layer 4 cells (Ahmed et al., 1994, 1997). As noted above, only 7% of input to geniculate relay cells derives from retina, and thus the 6% contribution made by geniculocortical inputs is remarkably close to this value, suggesting either an extraordinary coincidence or a common functional feature of driver inputs. Below, we consider further the possibility that other pathways in cortex can also be divided into drivers and modulators.

Drivers and the labeled line

Given that retinal input to geniculate relay cells is the defined driver and yet represents a minority of inputs, we can ask: What is the consequence in cortex of a change in geniculate firing produced by a modulator input? This could happen, for instance, if a highly active period of corticogeniculate input were to elevate geniculate firing, although evidence cited below suggests this happens only rarely. The suggested answer follows from the concept that a driver input represents a "labeled line". This means that altered firing of the geniculate relay cell must always be interpreted by its cortical targets as due to altered firing of the retinal inputs. This concept is very much like the concept of labeled lines in sensory pathways. For instance, if one applies pressure to the side of the eyeball, the perception is of spots appearing in the visual field. That is, the resultant increased intraocular pressure changes retinal firing, and this is perceived not as a pressure change in the eye but rather as a visual signal.

The same principle is suggested to apply to the drivers throughout thalamus. If large numbers of relay cell action potentials were due to modulator inputs rather than drivers, this could create difficulties in information processing. However, evidence from the lateral geniculate nucleus suggests that this is rare: that is, simultaneous recording from a geniculate relay cell and its retinal input indicates that nearly every action potential in a relay cell result from one in its retinal afferent (Cleland et al., 1971; Usrey et al., 1999), but the caution here is that these data derive from anesthetized preparations.

Modulation via ionotropic receptors

The point made above is that an important feature of modulator inputs to relay cells is that, as a group, they activate metabotropic receptors, and the long PSPs that result are key to controlling the state of many slow acting, voltage-dependent conductances, such as that involving I_T. However, as shown in Fig. 4A, most pathways activate ionotropic receptors as well, and it is not clear if certain pathways, such as the corticothalamic, reticulothalamic, or those from the brainstem, include single axons that activate purely one or the other type of receptor.

As noted in the context of Fig. 4B, Abbot and colleagues have provided a clear modulatory role for inputs that activate ionotropic receptors, whether or not metabotropic receptors might also be involved (Chance et al., 2002; Abbott, 2005). That is, combined input from modulatory inhibitory and excitatory sources balanced to have little net effect on V_m can nonetheless affect neuronal input resistance and thus affect the gain of any driver input. A different modulatory role can also be imagined if the combined input is unbalanced, leading to a change in V_m. This would then lead to a change in spontaneous activity, another key modulatory function that affects how driver inputs will be processed. For instance, higher spontaneous activity could subserve more linear processing (i.e., reducing rectification in the processed signal), a lower signal-to-noise ratio, and could also have effects on the state of the synaptic efficacy of the post-synaptic cell as regards its status as a depressing or facilitating synapse.

One further point is important to consider in the case that a group of excitatory inputs becomes relatively more (or less) active, resulting in increased firing in the target cell. One possible interpretation is that the enhanced input that was once a modulator now becomes a driver, implying a dynamic shifting in the function of inputs between driver and modulator. While this cannot be ruled out, it would require more complex processing if the above idea of a labeled line is valid, because this would also require dynamic shifting in how targets of the cell in question preform computations on these messages. It seems more parsimonious to regard such changes in relative strength of excitatory versus inhibitory inputs as a means to control spontaneous activity, a purely modulatory function.

First and higher order thalamic relays

One of the problems in understanding the functional role of a thalamic relay is to identify the information it relays to cortex, and essentially this boils down to identifying the driver input. This is fairly straightforward for the primary visual, somatosensory, and auditory relays. However, in this regard, much of thalamus has, until recently, remained *terra incognita*. As a road map exploring thalamus more generally, one can start with the bulleted list above, identifying which inputs to such relays as the pulvinar, medial dorsal, or intralaminar nuclei are likely to be drivers. Doing so leads to the conclusion that thalamic relays can be divided into two groups — *first* and *higher order* — depending on the origin of the driver input

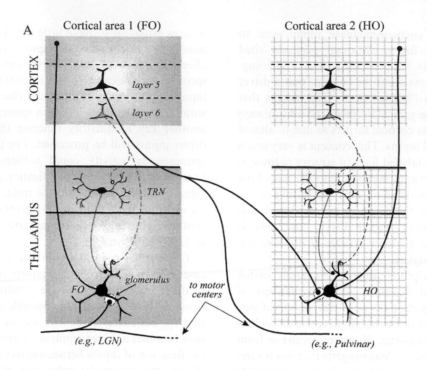

A Cortical area 1 (FO)   Cortical area 2 (HO)

CORTEX

layer 5

layer 6

THALAMUS

TRN

glomerulus

FO

to motor centers

HO

(e.g., LGN)   *(e.g., Pulvinar)*

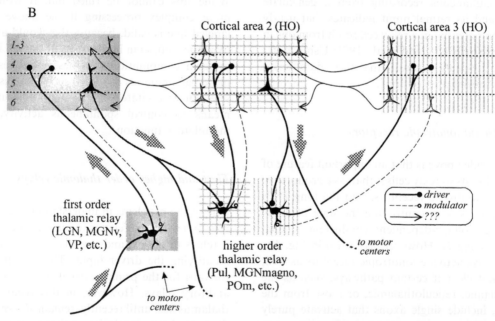

B

Cortical area 2 (HO)   Cortical area 3 (HO)

1-3

4

5

6

first order
thalamic relay
(LGN, MGNv,
VP, etc.)

higher order
thalamic relay
(Pul, MGNmagno,
POm, etc.)

to motor centers

to motor centers

driver
modulator
???

Fig. 5. Schematic diagrams showing first order and higher order relays. A: Distinction between first order and higher order relays. A first order thalamic relay (*left*) represents the first relay of peripheral or subcortical information of a particular type to a first order or primary cortical area. A higher order relay (*right*) relays information from layer 5 of one cortical area to another cortical area; this can be between first order and higher order cortical area (as shown) or between two higher order cortical areas (not shown). The difference is the driver input, which is subcortical (*left*) for a first order relay and from layer 5 of cortex (*right*) for a higher order relay. A feature of driver inputs to thalamus is a thick axon with a large terminal innervating a proximal dendritic site, often in complex synaptic zones known as glomeruli. Other distinguishing features are described in the text. Thus all thalamic relays receive an input from layer 6 of

(Guillery, 1995; Sherman and Guillery, 1996, 2001, 2002; Guillery and Sherman, 2002a). This is summarized in Fig. 5A.

First order relays receive their driver input from a subcortical site and relay that information for the first time to cortex. Examples of drivers and first order relays are retinal input to the lateral geniculate nucleus, medial lemniscal input to the ventral posterior nucleus, inferior collicular input to the ventral portion of the medial geniculate nucleus, and cerebellar input to the ventral anterior and lateral nuclei. Higher order relays, in contrast, receive their driver input from layer 5 of a cortical area and relay this input to another cortical area. Examples of higher order relays are most or all of pulvinar and of the medial dorsal nucleus. Overall, there appears to be considerably more thalamus devoted to higher order than to first order relays (Sherman and Guillery, 2001).

An implication that immediately springs from the appreciation of higher order thalamic relays is illustrated in Fig. 5B. That is, these relays serve as a critical link in a corticothalamocortical route for information transfer. Thus a great deal of corticocortical communication involves these routes with higher order thalamic relays.

An important challenge to this concept derives from a consideration of neuron numbers. Van Essen (2005) points out that numbers of neurons in pulvinar are orders of magnitude fewer than those in any cortical area, and that even for area V1 outputs to other cortical areas, this poses a severe bottleneck on information transfer. Nonetheless, given that a very small percentage of V1 neurons are represented by the layer 5 efferents that could provide the afferent link in the corticothalamocortical pathway (Callaway and Wiser, 1996), these numbers do not seem to pose a limitation on the role of the pulvinar as a central relay structure for these layer 5 inputs. Thus a related question raised is whether or not the limited number of layer 5 efferents is sufficient to project all of the information processed by a cortical area, such as V1. The answer is the nature of this information that is passed on is not known, and the ignorance here is such that the possibility that the small subset of layer 5 efferent cells is up to the task cannot be ruled out. Nonetheless, it is also possible that the full range of information processed in a cortical region requires an additional route, presumably involving direct corticocortical pathways.

What, then, of these direct corticocortical projections, of which there are many? The answer to this question may depend on the nature of these connections. For instance, if these, like thalamic inputs, can be divided into drivers and modulators, then the answer will depend on the subset of these direct pathways that are drivers, and thus it becomes important to characterize these connections functionally; to date virtually all have been defined strictly on light microscopic connectional bases with emphasis on their laminar origin and termination, and these criteria are insufficient to characterize their function. One should not be dazzled by sheer numbers here. That is, the fact that there are many more direct corticocortical inputs to a cortical area than there are thalamocortical does not mean that these are functionally dominant. Recall that only 7% of inputs to lateral geniculate relay cells are retinal while nearly a third derive from the brainstem parabrachial region: if this logic of numbers dictating function were applied to the lateral geniculate nucleus, one would be misled to the conclusion that this nucleus relays parabrachial information, with the small retinal input playing some minor, ethereal role.

Even if these direct corticocortical connections contain many drivers and thus subserve corticocortical communication, there is at least one important difference between this information route and that involving higher order thalamic relays. This has to do with the nature of driver afferents to thalamus.

cortex, which is mostly feedback, but higher order relays in addition receive a layer 5 input from cortex, which is feedforward. B: Role of higher order thalamic relays in corticocortical communication. The suggested route of much of this communication involves a projection from layer 5 of cortex to a higher order thalamic relay to another cortical area. In question is the function, driver or modulator, of the direct corticocortical projections. Note in both A and B that the driver inputs, both subcortical and from layer 5, are typically from branching axons, the significance of which is elaborated in the text. (*FO*, first order; *HO*, higher order; *LGN*, lateral geniculate nucleus; *MGNmagno*, magnocellular portion of the medial geniculate nucleus; *MGNv*, ventral portion of the medial geniculate nucleus; *POm*, posterior medial nucleus; *Pul*, pulvinar; *TRN*, thalamic reticular nucleus; *VP*, ventral posterior nucleus.)

For both first order and higher order relays (Figs. 5A, B), most and perhaps all of these afferents are axons that branch, with one branch innervating thalamus and other(s) innervating apparent motor subcortical centers (Guillery and Sherman, 2002b; Guillery, 2003, 2005). As examples, most or all retinal axons innervating the lateral geniculate nucleus branch to innervate the midbrain as well, and these midbrain structures are involved in various oculomotor tasks; likewise, most or all layer 5 axons innervating pulvinar branch to innervate other subcortical structures, such as the pons and midbrain, that are involved in motor control. This pattern has led to the notion that the actual information being relayed to cortex via both first order and higher order relays are actually copies of motor commands. This notion and its implications for cognitive processing have been explored elsewhere (Guillery and Sherman, 2002b; Guillery, 2003) and are more fully developed by Guillery in Chapter 17. The main issue here, however, is that any messages sent by way of direct corticocortical drivers are messages that stay within cortex, whereas those sent by way of higher order thalamic relays are shared with various subcortical structures, implying that the very nature of the messages is likely to be quite different.

There is another point made by Fig. 5B, which is that most or all information reaching a cortical area, whether originating in the periphery or another cortical area, benefits from a thalamic relay. That is, just as retinal information passes through thalamus and does not directly innervate cortex, so does most or all information directed from one cortical area to another. The same benefits conferred to the relay of retinal information through the lateral geniculate nucleus — whatever they may be — apply as well to corticocortical information flow when a higher order thalamic relay is involved. As just one example, consider burst and tonic firing of thalamic relay cells. It has been suggested that the burst mode may be present in the lateral geniculate nucleus when attention is either reduced during drowsiness or directed elsewhere, so that the relay cells are generally inactive and presumably hyperpolarized. This results in a burst response to a novel visual stimulus, a response that is better detected and more strongly activates cortex, producing a sort of "wake up call"; tonic mode is then initiated to ensure a more faithful

relay of information about the new stimulus. This same process may occur for inputs carried by cortical layer 5 axons to higher order thalamic relays. Thus if such a layer 5 cell has been inactive for a time due to drowsiness or other factors related to inattention, the target thalamic relay cells may be in burst mode, and now new activity from the layer 5 cell will activate a burst in the thalamic relay cell that "wakes up" the transthalamic cortical target area; tonic firing then commences for continued information processing along this route. Firing mode in the higher order thalamic relays would be controlled as in the first order relays like the lateral geniculate nucleus, with modulatory brainstem and layer 6 cortical inputs and their influence on the thalamic reticular nucleus providing this control.

Conclusions

It should now be clear that the thalamus actually plays a central and dynamic role in cortical functioning. Thalamus controls the flow of virtually all information to cortex, and does so in interesting ways that we are just beginning to resolve; it not only relays peripheral information to cortex in the first place but also plays a continuing role in further corticocortical processing; and the nature of the information relayed to cortex in many and perhaps all cases seems to be a copy of motor commands, allowing the target cortical areas to be updated about these commands. The complex cell and circuit properties of thalamus belie any sort of trivial, machine-like relay that was thought to be its only function until recently. One dynamic relay function that we are just beginning to understand is the control of response mode — burst or tonic — although we are clearly still far from a complete understanding of its control and behavioral significance. Yet this is probably just the tip of the iceberg: there are undoubtedly many more dynamic relay functions that remain to be identified.

The other two features of thalamic functioning — a continued role in corticocortical communication and the information relayed being motor commands — are summarized schematically in Fig. 6. This places the ideas presented here (Fig. 6B) in bold relief by comparing them to the conventional view of thalamic functioning (Fig. 6A). In the conventional view

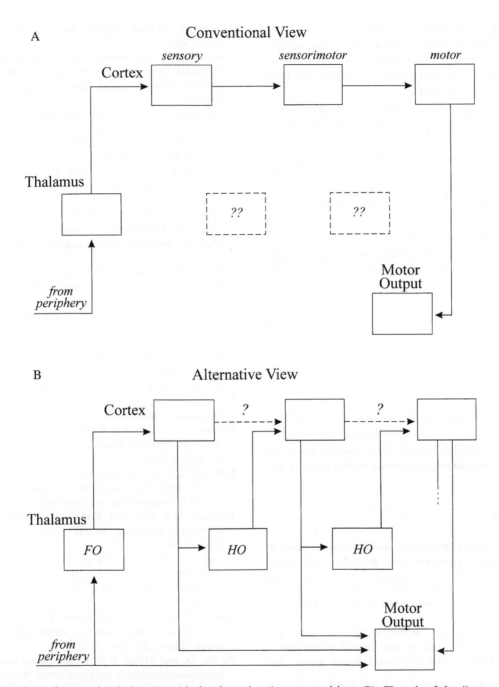

Fig. 6. Comparison of conventional view (A) with the alternative view proposed here (B). The role of the direct corticocortical connections in B (*dashed lines*) is questioned (see text for details). (*FO*, first order; *HO*, higher order.)

(Felleman and Van Essen, 1991; van Essen et al., 1992; Purves et al., 1997; Kandel et al., 2000), peripheral information, which is largely sensory, is relayed through appropriate thalamic relays to primary sensory cortex. This information then stays entirely within cortex, passing through sensorimotor and motor hierarchical levels, and finally a motor command is computed to be transmitted to subcortical motor centers. All corticocortical communication is handled by direct connections wholly within cortex. One problem with this view is that it provides no role for the majority of thalamic relays, which we have designated as higher order.

The view presented here (Alternative View, Fig. 6B) clearly places the higher order relays in the thick of things by having them serve as essential links in a corticothalamocortical route for cortical processing. This view also shows that most or all of the information actually passed on to thalamus for relay, both through first order and higher order relays, is carried by branching axons that also innervate motor centers. In this view, cortical processing can be thought of as a continuing elaboration and fine tuning of these motor commands. One final point stands out: if the scheme shown in Fig. 6B has any truth to it, it is obvious that one can no longer think about cortical functioning without considering thalamus.

Acknowledgments

This research has been supported by funding from the National Eye Institute of the National Institutes of Health. I would like to thank R.W.Guillery for many helpful discussions and comments on this manuscript.

References

Abbott, L.F. (2005) Drivers and modulators from push-pull and balanced synaptic input. *Prog. Brain Res.*, this volume.

Ahmed, B., Anderson, J.C., Douglas, R.J., Martin, K.A.C. and Nelson, J.C. (1994) Polyneuronal innervation of spiny stellate neurons in cat visual cortex. J. Comp. Neurol., 341: 39–49.

Ahmed, B., Anderson, J.C., Martin, K.A.C. and Nelson, J.C. (1997) Map of the synapses onto layer 4 basket cells of the primary visual cortex of the cat. J. Comp. Neurol., 380: 230–242.

Alonso, J.M., Usrey, W.M. and Reid, R.C. (2001) Rules of connectivity between geniculate cells and simple cells in cat primary visual cortex. J. Neurosci., 21: 4002–4015.

Beierlein, M. and Connors, B.W. (2002) Short-term dynamics of thalamocortical and intracortical synapses onto layer 6 neurons in neocortex. J. Neurophysiol., 88: 1924–1932.

Britten, K.H., Shadlen, M.N., Newsome, W.T. and Movshon, J.A. (1993) Responses of neurons in macaque MT to stochastic motion signals. Visual Neuroscience, 10: 1157–1169.

Callaway, E.M. and Wiser, A.K. (1996) Contributions of individual layer 2–5 spiny neurons to local circuits in macaque primary visual cortex. Visual Neurosci, 13: 907–922.

Castro-Alamancos, M.A. and Oldford, E. (2002) Cortical sensory suppression during arousal is due to the activity-dependent depression of thalamocortical synapses. Journal of Physiology, 541: 319–331.

Chance, F.S., Abbott, L.F. and Reyes, A. (2002) Gain modulation from background synaptic input. Neuron, 35: 773–782.

Chung, S., Li, X. and Nelson, S.B. (2002) Short-term depression at thalamocortical synapses contributes to rapid adaptation of cortical sensory responses in vivo. Neuron, 34: 437–446.

Cleland, B.G., Dubin, M.W. and Levick, W.R. (1971) Sustained and transient neurones in the cat's retina and lateral geniculate nucleus. J. Physiol. (Lond.), 217: 473–496.

Conn, P.J. (2003) Physiological roles and therapeutic potential of metabotropic glutamate receptors. Prog. Neurobiol., 1003: 12–21.

Conn, P.J. and Pin, J.P. (1997) Pharmacology and functions of metabotropic glutamate receptors. Annual Review of Pharmacology & Toxicology, 37: 205–237.

Dowling, J.E. (1970) Organization of vertebrate retinas. Investigative Ophthalmology, 9: 655–680.

Dowling, J.E. (1987) The Retina: An Approachable Part of the Brain. Belknap Press of Harvard University Press, Cambridge, MA.

Fanselow, E.E. and Nicolelis, M.A. (1999) Behavioral modulation of tactile responses in the rat somatosensory system. Journal of Neuroscience, 19: 7603–7616.

Felleman, D.J. and Van Essen, D.C. (1991) Distributed hierarchical processing in the primate cerebral cortex. Cerebral Cortex, 1: 1–47.

Ferster, D. (2004) Assembly of receptive fields in primary visual cortex. In: Chalupa, L.M. and Werner, J.S. (Eds.), The Visual Neurosciences. MIT Press, Cambridge, MA., pp. 695–703.

Ferster, D., Chung, S. and Wheat, H. (1996) Orientation selectivity of thalamic input to simple cells of cat visual cortex. Nature, 380: 249–252.

Ferster, D. and Miller, K.D. (2000) Neural mechanisms of orientation selectivity in the visual cortex. Annual Review of Neuroscience, 23: 441–471.

Grunewald, A., Bradley, D.C. and Andersen, R.A. (2002) Neural correlates of structure-from-motion perception in macaque V1 and MT. Journal of Neuroscience, 22: 6195–6207.

Guido, W., Lu, S.-M., Vaughan, J.W., Godwin, D.W. and Sherman, S.M. (1995) Receiver operating characteristic (ROC) analysis of neurons in the cat's lateral geniculate nucleus during tonic and burst response mode. Visual Neuroscience, 12: 723–741.

Guido, W. and Weyand, T. (1995) Burst responses in thalamic relay cells of the awake behaving cat. Journal of Neurophysiology, 74: 1782–1786.

Guillery, R.W. (1995) Anatomical evidence concerning the role of the thalamus in corticocortical communication: A brief review. Journal of Anatomy, 187: 583–592.

Guillery, R.W. (2003) Branching thalamic afferents link action and perception. J. Neurophysiol., 90: 539–548.

Guillery, R. W. (2005) Anatomical pathways that link action to perception. Progress in Brain Research, this volume.

Guillery, R.W. and Sherman, S.M. (2002a) Thalamic relay functions and their role in corticocortical communication: Generalizations from the visual system. Neuron, 33: 1–20.

Guillery, R.W. and Sherman, S.M. (2002b) The thalamus as a monitor of motor outputs. Philosophical Transactions of the Royal Society of London.B: Biological Sciences, 357: 1809–1821.

Gutierrez, C., Cox, C.L., Rinzel, J. and Sherman, S.M. (2001) Dynamics of low-threshold spike activation in relay neurons of the cat lateral geniculate nucleus. Journal of Neuroscience, 21: 1022–1032.

Hubel, D.H. and Wiesel, T.N. (1961) Integrative action in the cat's lateral geniculate body. Journal of Physiology (London), 155: 385–398.

Hubel, D.H. and Wiesel, T.N. (1962) Receptive fields, binocular interaction and functional architecture in the cat's visual cortex. J. Physiol., 160: 106–154.

Hubel, D.H. and Wiesel, T.N. (1977) Functional architecture of macaque monkey visual cortex. Proceedings of the Royal Society of London [Biology], 198: 1–59.

Huettner, J.E. (2003) Kainate receptors and synaptic transmission. Progress in Neurobiology, 70: 387–407.

Jahnsen, H. and Llinaás, R. (1984a) Electrophysiological properties of guinea-pig thalamic neurones: an in vitro study. Journal of Physiology (London), 349: 205–226.

Jahnsen, H. and Llinaás, R. (1984b) Ionic basis for the electroresponsiveness and oscillatory properties of guinea-pig thalamic neurones in vitro. Journal of Physiology (London), 349: 227–247.

Kandel, E.R., Schwartz, J.H. and Jessell, T.M. (2000) Principles of Neural Science. McGraw Hill, New York.

Kara, P., Pezaris, J.S., Yurgenson, S. and Reid, R.C. (2002) The spatial receptive field of thalamic inputs to single cortical simple cells revealed by the interaction of visual and electrical stimulation. Proceedings of the National Academy of Sciences of the United States of America, 99: 16261–16266.

Kohn, A. and Movshon, J.A. (2003) Neuronal adaptation to visual motion in area MT of the macaque. Neuron, 39: 681–691.

Lenz, F.A., Garonzik, I.M., Zirh, T.A. and Dougherty, P.M. (1998) Neuronal activity in the region of the thalamic principal sensory nucleus (ventralis caudalis) in patients with pain following amputations. Neuroscience, 86: 1065–1081.

Lu, S.-M., Guido, W. and Sherman, S.M. (1992) Effects of membrane voltage on receptive field properties of lateral geniculate neurons in the cat: contributions of the low threshold Ca^{++} conductance. Journal of Neurophysiology, 68: 2185–2198.

Massaux, A., Dutrieux, G., Cotillon-Williams, N., Manunta, Y. and Edeline, J.M. (2004) Auditory thalamus bursts in anesthetized and non-anesthetized states: contribution to functional properties. J. Neurophysiol., 91: 2117–2134.

Mayer, M.L. and Westbrook, G.L. (1987) The physiology of excitatory amino acids in the vertebrate central nervous system. Progress in Neurobiology, 28: 197–276.

McCormick, D.A. and Bal, T. (1997) Sleep and arousal: Thalamocortical mechanisms. Annual Review of Neuroscience, 20: 185–215.

McCormick, D.A. and Huguenard, J.R. (1992) A model of the electrophysiological properties of thalamocortical relay neurons. Journal of Neurophysiology, 68: 1384–1400.

Mott, D.D. and Lewis, D.V. (1994) The pharmacology and function of central GABAB receptors. International Review of Neurobiology, 36: 97–223.

Nakanishi, S., Nakajima, Y., Masu, M., Ueda, Y., Nakahara, K., Watanabe, D., Yamaguchi, S., Kawabata, S. and Okada, M. (1998) Glutamate receptors: brain function and signal transduction. Brain Research Reviews, 26: 230–235.

Nicolelis, M.A., Baccala, L.A., Lin, R.C. and Chapin, J.K. (1995) Sensorimotor encoding by synchronous neural ensemble activity at multiple levels of the somatosensory system. Science, 268: 1353–1358.

Nicolelis, M.A.L. (2002) Depression at thalamocortical synapses: The key for cortical neuronal adaptation? Neuron, 34: 331–332.

Nicoll, R.A., Malenka, R.C. and Kauer, J.A. (1990) Functional comparison of neurotransmitter receptor subtypes in mammalian central nervous system. Physiological Reviews, 70: 513–565.

O'Keefe, L.P. and Movshon, J.A. (1998) Processing of first- and second-order motion signals by neurons in area MT of the macaque monkey. Visual Neuroscience, 15: 305–317.

Osborne, L.C., Bialek, W. and Lisberger, S.G. (2004) Time course of information about motion direction in visual area MT of macaque monkeys. Journal of Neuroscience, 24: 3210–3222.

Ozawa, S., Kamiya, H. and Tsuzuki, K. (1998) Glutamate receptors in the mammalian central nervous system. Progress in Neurobiology, 54: 581–618.

Pin, J.P. and Bockaert, J. (1995) Get receptive to metabotropic glutamate receptors. Current Opinion in Neurobiology, 5: 342–349.

Pin, J.P. and Duvoisin, R. (1995) The metabotropic glutamate receptors: structure and functions. Neuropharmacology, 34: 1–26.

126

Purves, D., Augustine, G.J., Fitzpatrick, D., Katz, L.C., Lamantia, A.-S. and McNamara, J.O. (1997) Neuroscience. Sinauer, Sunderland, MA.

Qian, A. and Johnson, J.W. (2002) Channel gating of NMDA receptors. Physiol. Behav., 77: 577–582.

Radhakrishnan, V., Tsoukatos, J., Davis, K.D., Tasker, R.R., Lozano, A.M. and Dostrovsky, J.O. (1999) A comparison of the burst activity of lateral thalamic neurons in chronic pain and non-pain patients. Pain, 80: 567–575.

Ramcharan, E.J., Gnadt, J.W. and Sherman, S.M. (2000) Burst and tonic firing in thalamic cells of unanesthetized, behaving monkeys. Visual Neuroscience, 17: 55–62.

Recasens, M. and Vignes, M. (1995) Excitatory amino acid metabotropic receptor subtypes and calcium regulation. Annals of the New York Academy of Sciences, 757: 418–429.

Sherman, S.M. (1985) Functional organization of the W-,X-, and Y-cell pathways in the cat: a review and hypothesis. In: Sprague, J.M. and Epstein, A.N. (Eds.), Progress in Psychobiology and Physiological Psychology. Vol. 11, Academic Press, Orlando, pp. 233–314.

Sherman, S.M. (1996) Dual response modes in lateral geniculate neurons: mechanisms and functions. Visual Neuroscience, 13: 205–213.

Sherman, S.M. (2001) Tonic and burst firing: dual modes of thalamocortical relay. Trends in Neurosciences, 24: 122–126.

Sherman, S.M. and Guillery, R.W. (1996) The functional organization of thalamocortical relays. Journal of Neurophysiology, 76: 1367–1395.

Sherman, S.M. and Guillery, R.W. (1998) On the actions that one nerve cell can have on another: Distinguishing "drivers" from "modulators". Proceedings of the National Academy of Sciences USA, 95: 7121–7126.

Sherman, S.M. and Guillery, R.W. (2001) Exploring the Thalamus. Academic Press, San Diego.

Sherman, S.M. and Guillery, R.W. (2002) The role of thalamus in the flow of information to cortex. Philosophical Transactions of the Royal Society of London.B: Biological Sciences, 357: 1695–1708.

Sherman, S.M. and Guillery, R.W. (2004) Thalamus. In: Shepherd, G.M. (Ed.), Synaptic Organization of the Brain. Oxford University Press., pp. 311–359.

Smith, G. D., Cox, C. L., Sherman, S. M., & Rinzel, J. (1998) Fourier analysis of sinusoidally driven thalamocortical relay neurons from cat thalamic slice and a minimal integrate-and-fire-or-burst model. Society for Neuroscience, 24, 139.

Steriade, M. and Llinaás, R. (1988) The functional states of the thalamus and the associated neuronal interplay. Physiological Reviews, 68: 649–742.

Steriade, M., McCormick, D.A. and Sejnowski, T.J. (1993) Thalamocortical oscillations in the sleeping and aroused brain. Science, 262: 679–685.

Stratford, K.J., Tarczy-Hornoch, K., Martin, K.A.C., Bannister, N.J. and Jack, J.J.B. (1996) Excitatory synaptic inputs to spiny stellate cells in cat visual cortex. Nature, 382: 258–261.

Swadlow, H. A. Bezdudnaya T, & Gusev, A. G. (2005). Spike timing and synaptic dynamics at the awake thalamocortical synapse. Progress in Brain Research, this volume.

Swadlow, H.A. and Gusev, A.G. (2001) The impact of "bursting" thalamic impulses at a neocortical synapse. Nature Neuroscience, 4: 402–408.

Swadlow, H.A., Gusev, A.G. and Bezdudnaya, T. (2002) Activation of a cortical column by a thalamocortical impulse. Journal of Neuroscience, 22: 7766–7773.

Tsumoto, T., Creutzfeldt, O.D. and Legendy, C.R. (1978) Functional organization of the cortifugal system from visual cortex to lateral geniculate nucleus in the cat. Experimental Brain Research, 32: 345–364.

Usrey, W.M., Alonso, J.M. and Reid, R.C. (2000) Synaptic interactions between thalamic inputs to simple cells in cat visual cortex. Journal of Neuroscience, 20: 5461–5467.

Usrey, W.M., Reppas, J.B. and Reid, R.C. (1999) Specificity and strength of retinogeniculate connections. J. Neurophysiol., 82: 3527–3540.

Van Essen, D. C. (2005) [to be determined]. Progress in Brain Research, this volume.

van Essen, D.C. (1979) Visual areas of the mammalian cerebral cortex. Annual Reviews in Neuroscience, 2: 227–263.

van Essen, D.C. (1985) Functional organization of primate visual cortex. In: Peters, A. and Jones, E.G. (Eds.), Cerebral Cortex. Vol. 3, Plenum., pp. 259–329.

van Essen, D.C., Anderson, C.H. and Felleman, D.J. (1992) Information processing in the primate visual system: an integrated systems perspective. Science, 255: 419–423.

van Essen, D.C. and Maunsell, J.H.R. (1983) Hierarchical organization and functional streams in the visual cortex. Trends in Neurosciences, 6: 370–375.

van Horn, S.C., Erişir, A. and Sherman, S.M. (2000) The relative distribution of synapses in the A-laminae of the lateral geniculate nucleus of the cat. Journal of Comparative Neurology, 416: 509–520.

Weyand, T.G., Boudreaux, M. and Guido, W. (2001) Burst and tonic response modes in thalamic neurons during sleep and wakefulness. Journal of Neurophysiology, 85: 1107–1118.

Zhan, X.J., Cox, C.L., Rinzel, J. and Sherman, S.M. (1999) Current clamp and modeling studies of low threshold calcium spikes in cells of the cat's lateral geniculate nucleus. Journal of Neurophysiology, 81: 2360–2373.

Zirh, T.A., Lenz, F.A., Reich, S.G. and Dougherty, P.M. (1998) Patterns of bursting occurring in thalamic cells during parkinsonian tremor. Neuroscience, 83: 107–121.

Progress in Brain Research, Vol. 149
ISSN 0079-6123

CHAPTER 10

Functional cell classes and functional architecture in the early visual system of a highly visual rodent

Stephen D. Van Hooser[1,*], J. Alexander Heimel[1,2] and Sacha B. Nelson[1]

[1]*Brandeis University, 415 South St., Waltham, MA 02454, USA*
[2]*The Netherlands Ophthalmic Research Institute, Meibergdreef 47, 1105 BA Amsterdam ZO, The Netherlands*

Abstract: Over the last 50 years, studies of receptive field properties in mammalian visual brain structures such as lateral geniculate nucleus (LGN) and primary visual cortex (V1) have suggested the existence of cell classes with unique functional response properties, and in visual cortex of many mammals these functional response properties show considerable spatial organization termed functional architecture. In recent years, there has been considerable interest in understanding the cellular mechanisms that underlie visual responses and plasticity in intact animals, and studies of individual neurons in brain slices have identified distinct cell classes on the basis of anatomical features, synaptic connectivity, or gene expression. However, the relationships between cell classes identified in studies of brain slices and those in the intact animal remain largely unclear. Rodents offer many advantages for investigating these relationships, as they are appropriate for a wide variety of experimental techniques and genetically modified mice are relatively easy to obtain or produce. Unfortunately, a barrier to using these animals in vision research is a lack of understanding of the relationship of rodent visual systems to the visual systems in more commonly studied mammals such as carnivores and non-human primates. Here we review recent comparative studies of functional response properties in LGN and V1 of a highly visual diurnal rodent, the gray squirrel. In the LGN, our data are consistent with the idea that all mammals have a class of LGN neurons that is sustained, another class that is transient, and a third class of more heterogeneous cells, but some response properties such as linearity of spatial summation, contrast gain, and dependence of receptive field size on eccentricity vary from species to species. In V1, the squirrel has many orientation-selective neurons, and these orientation-selective cells can be further subdivided into simple and complex cells. Despite the fact that squirrel has greater visual acuity and a physically larger V1 than some mammals that have orientation maps in V1, we do not find orientation maps in V1 of squirrel, which is similar to results in other less visual rodents. We suggest that orientation maps are not necessary for high acuity vision or orientation selectivity and that cortical functional architecture can vary greatly from species to species.

Introduction

To understand the function of the mammalian visual system, neuroscientists have, over the last 50 years, characterized numerous functional and anatomical properties of neurons in visual brain areas such as the

retina, lateral geniculate nucleus (LGN) and primary visual cortex (V1). Physiological and anatomical studies, mainly using carnivores and nonhuman primates, have suggested the existence of cell classes in these structures with unique functional response properties (Hubel and Wiesel, 1962; Stone, 1983). In addition, studies of V1 in several mammals have revealed considerable spatial organization, termed functional architecture (Hubel and Wiesel, 1962;

---

*Corresponding author. Tel.: +1-781-736-2319, Fax: +1-781-736-3107; vanhoosr@brandeis.edu

DOI: 10.1016/S0079-6123(05)49010-X

Mountcastle, 1997). Neurons with similar functional properties are grouped together vertically in a columnar fashion, and these functional properties tend to change smoothly as one moves across the cortical surface.

In recent years there has been considerable interest in understanding the cellular mechanisms that underlie functional responses, functional architecture, development, and plasticity in the early visual system, and this interest has led to detailed studies of intrinsic properties, anatomical morphology, synaptic connections, and protein markers or gene expression at the level of individual neurons in brain slices (Feng et al., 2000; Gupta et al., 2000; Kozloski et al., 2001; Callaway, 2002). These studies, like the studies in whole animals described above, have revealed neuron classes that are anatomically, functionally, or genetically distinct. The relationship between the cell classes that have been identified by cellular properties and those identified by physiological responses in the intact animal remains a mystery.

Rodents offer many advantages for these studies because they are appropriate for a wide variety of experimental techniques, including whole animal studies and brain slice studies, and because, at least in the case of mice, genetically modified animals are relatively easy to obtain or produce. Unfortunately, a major barrier to using rodents in this type of research is a lack of understanding of the visual systems of rodents. There is considerable variation in structure and function across mammalian species, and relatively little is known about physiological responses and functional architecture in visual brain areas of rodents.

Comparative studies across different mammals can identify which properties are common to all or most mammals and which are unique or peculiar to particular species (Kaas et al., 1972; Casagrande and Kaas, 1994; Kahn et al., 2000). To better understand the relationship between the visual system of rodents and the visual systems of other mammals, we have recently examined receptive field properties and functional organization in LGN and V1 of a highly visual rodent, the gray squirrel (*Sciurus carolinensis*). Squirrels may be an excellent preparation for studying cellular mechanisms underlying function and disease in the human visual system. Many tree- and ground squirrels are diurnal, have good blue–green color vision, and have cone-dominated retinas, similar to the primate fovea. Squirrels have relatively good acuity and high contrast sensitivity (Jacobs et al., 1982) that is slightly superior to tree shrews (Petry et al., 1984), and possess a highly elaborated visual system, including large eyes with good optics (McCourt and Jacobs, 1984), a large and well-laminated lateral geniculate nucleus and V1 with robust visual responses (Hall et al., 1972; Kaas et al., 1972; Van Hooser et al., 2003; Heimel et al., 2005), and a large superior colliculus and pulvinar.

Cell types in lateral geniculate nucleus

In the early mammalian visual system, ganglion cells in the retina project to relay cells in the LGN, which in turn project to the V1. Visual neuroscientists have characterized many properties of retinal ganglion cells (RGCs) and LGN neurons and have classified these cells into discrete groups using many criteria, including anatomical features, laminar location in the LGN, physiological response properties, physiological conduction velocities, and protein markers (Kaplan and Shapley, 1986; Diamond et al., 1993; Hendry and Reid, 2000). However, neurons in different animals have different anatomical and physiological features, and the criteria used to distinguish cell groups vary by species. Are there fundamental LGN cell classes that share features and are homologous across mammals or does each animal possess a unique set of LGN cells that is unrelated to cells in other mammals?

Neurons in carnivores and nonhuman primates have received the most attention from investigators, and in both orders, LGN cells have been divided into three classes, called X, Y, and W cells in carnivores and parvocellular (P), magnocellular (M), and koniocellular (K) cells in primates. Each of these groups has unique anatomical and physiological properties, and there are two principal ideas about the homological relationships among these neurons. X and P cells both show sustained firing in response to constant visual stimulation, and have smaller receptive field properties at a given eccentricity than Y or M cells (Enroth-Cugell and Robson, 1966; Dreher et al., 1976). Y and M cells respond transiently to constant stimulation and have shorter response latencies than X or P cells, respectively (Enroth-Cugell and Robson, 1966; Fukada, 1971; Dreher et al., 1976; Kaplan and Shapley, 1982). On the basis of these and other similarities, some investigators have suggested that X and P cells are instantiations of a single cell class that is homologous across most mammals and that Y and M cells are similarly related (Rodieck and Brening, 1983; Norton et al., 1988; Casagrande and Norton, 1991; Levitt et al., 2001). However, P cells differ from M, X, and Y cells in that they show relatively small increases in firing rate with increasing contrast, i.e., they have low contrast gains, whereas M, X, and Y cells have contrast gains that are similar to one another and are about 10 times larger than P cells (Kaplan and Shapley, 1982; Benardete et al., 1992). In addition, M cells can show either linear or nonlinear spatial summation across their receptive fields while all X cells show linear spatial summation and all Y cells show non-linear spatial summation (Hochstein and Shapley, 1976a; Kaplan and Shapley, 1982). Finally, P cells are color-selective in trichromatic monkey species, whereas M, X, and Y cells are never color selective in any animal (Wiesel and Hubel, 1966; Pearlman and Daw, 1970). These and other differences have led other investigators to the view that linear and non-linear M cells are homologous to X cells and Y cells, respectively, and that P cells are a fundamentally different cell type found only in primates (Shapley and Perry, 1986). The W and K cells are heterogeneous groups, consisting of cells with long latencies, cells with sluggish or variable responses, blue-ON cells, and other cells that have not been well characterized (Martin et al., 1997; Stone, 1983; Hendry and Reid, 2000).

Comparative studies across mammals can identify which properties are common across all mammals and which vary from species to species or from order to order. To identify functionally distinct neuron classes and to compare these classes across different animals, it is important to measure many different receptive field properties for each cell (Rodieck and Brening, 1983; Stone, 1983) because properties that distinguish LGN neurons in one species may not distinguish LGN neurons in another species and because homologous neuron groups could differ in a few properties and nonhomologous neuron

groups could have a few properties in common. Measurements of many LGN cell receptive field properties have been made in opossum, rabbit, and tree shrew, but the properties of LGN cell groups in these animals do not strongly implicate either of the hypotheses above regarding the relationship between X, Y, and W cells and P, M, and K cells. In opossum, cell groups closely resemble the X, Y, and W cells of the cat (Kirby and Wilson, 1986). The rabbit has sustained and transient center–surround cells and other cells resembling W or K cells, but, unlike carnivores or primates, all or most of these sustained and transient neurons show nonlinear spatial summation (Swadlow and Weyand, 1985). Although studies in the diurnal tree shrew have shown this mammal has a class of small-celled neurons resembling the W or K group of carnivores and primates (Diamond et al., 1993; Holdefer and Norton, 1995), studies of the larger LGN cells are equivocal. One early study reported X-like and Y-like cells (Sherman et al., 1975), but a later study that measured more receptive field properties did not find properties that identified groups among the larger cells besides ON and OFF cells (Holdefer and Norton, 1995). Thus it seemed important to characterize many receptive field properties of LGN neurons in another diurnal species.

We examined several response properties in 165 LGN neurons (Van Hooser et al., 2003). The LGN in squirrel is well laminated and consists of five layers, labeled 1, 2, 3a, 3b, and 3c. Layers 1, 3a, and 3c receive input from the contralateral eye and layers 2 and 3b receive input from the ipsilateral eye. In our recordings, we noticed dramatic differences in responses across some of the layers, with layer 1 and 2 cells generally showing sustained responses to a spot of light and layer 3abc cells generally showing transient responses (Fig. 1). Visual responses in layers 1 and 2 were relatively homogenous and cells in the two layers appeared very similar to one another, as evident in the histogram of response latencies shown in Fig. 2. Almost all layer 1 and 2 cells showed center–surround organization, low peak firing rate variability, and response latencies around 25 ms. Responses in layer 3abc, however, were more complicated. Layer 3a, 3b, and 3c appeared to be comprised of similar mixtures of neurons but also appeared to contain more than one class of neuron. Figure 2 shows response latencies for all layer 3abc cells; while some

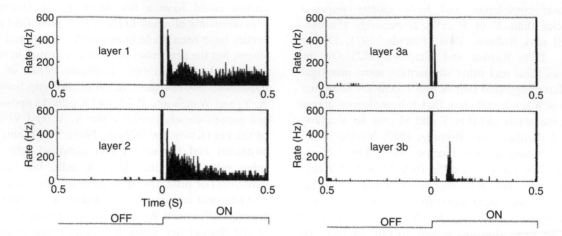

Fig. 1. Average responses of four LGN cells to sign-appropriate spots of light in the center of their receptive fields. The stimulus alternated from off to on each 500 ms. Cells in layers 1 and 2 generally showed very sustained responses whereas cells in layers 3abc generally showed transient responses. Reprinted from Van Hooser et al. (2003).

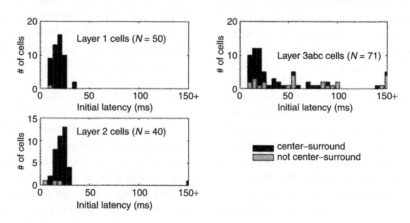

Fig. 2. Histogram of response latencies to the same spot stimulus as in Fig. 1. Layer 1 and 2 cell latencies cluster around a mean of about 25 ms. Across 14 receptive field properties studied, layer 1 and 2 cell responses were rather homogenous and similar to one another, leading us to believe they corresponded to a single cell class that receives projections from the contralateral and ipsilateral eye, respectively. Layer 3abc latency responses were more complicated, with some cell latencies clustering around 20 ms but with other cells showing widely scattered latencies. Across 14 receptive field properties, layer 3abc cells seemed to include more than one cell type. Reprinted from Van Hooser et al. (2003).

cells appear to cluster around 20 ms, other latencies were widely scattered. Most of the short latency cells in layer 3abc also tended to show center–surround organization and low peak firing rate variability, while the longer-latency cells were quite heterogeneous in their response properties.

On the basis of these responses, we divided cells in squirrel LGN into three groups. Cells in layers 1 and 2

with center–surround organization, response latencies less than 50 ms, and peak response coefficients of variation (CV) less than 0.9 were grouped together and called X-like cells because they share some properties with cells in carnivores, rodents, and tree shrews called X cells. Cells in layers 3abc with center–surround organization, response latencies less than 40 ms, and peak response CVs less than 0.9 were

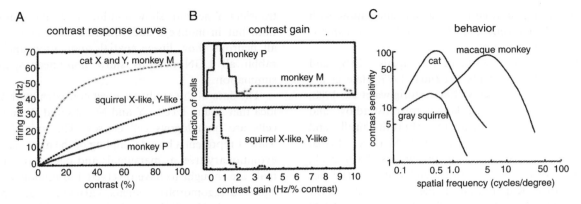

Fig. 3. Squirrel LGN neurons show shallow, linear contrast response functions more comparable to monkey P cells than cat X, Y, or monkey M cells. (A) Average contrast response functions for cat X and Y cells, monkey P and M cells, and squirrel X-like and Y-like cells (Shapley and Perry, 1986; Van Hooser et al., 2003). (B) Histograms of contrast gain for monkey P, M cells, and squirrel X-like, Y-like cells (Croner and Kaplan, 1995; Van Hooser et al., 2003). (C) Behavioral contrast sensitivity curves for macaque monkey (DeValois et al., 1974), cat (Blake et al., 1974), and gray squirrel (Jacobs et al., 1982). The high contrast gain of cat X, Y, and monkey M cells correlates with the high behavioral contrast sensitivity of these animals, while the squirrel's lower contrast gain correlates with its lower behavioral contrast sensitivity. From Van Hooser et al. (2003).

grouped together and called Y-like cells because they have some properties in common with Y cells in other species. All other cells were lumped together and called W-like cells. The W-like group certainly contains more than one class of neuron, but we grouped these neurons together because they remind us of the heterogeneous W cell group in the cat and koniocellular cell group in the monkey (Stone, 1983; Hendry and Reid, 2000).

We examined several characteristics of squirrel X-like, Y-like, and W-like cells to see if response properties in the squirrel supported either of the hypotheses above about homological relationships among cat and monkey neurons. X-like cells generally showed sustained responses to spots of light while Y-like cells were generally transient. Y-like cells had shorter response latencies than X-like cells, and this is true even if one controls for the latency parameters used to divide the cells into groups. Interestingly, receptive field center sizes of X-like and Y-like cells were not significantly different from one another (1.5 ± 0.1° and 1.9 ± 0.3°, respectively), and there was little or no relationship between eccentricity and receptive field center size for either cell type. The lack of a relationship between eccentricity and receptive field size mirrors the fact that the density of photoreceptors on the squirrel retina remains very high

across a large region as one moves away from the center (Long and Fisher, 1983). We examined contrast response curves of these cells by stimulating with sinusoidal gratings of different contrast, and fit the responses with Naka–Rushton functions (Naka and Rushton, 1966). Representative contrast response curves and contrast gain for monkey, cat, and squirrel neurons are shown in Fig. 3. Squirrel neurons show a much shallower and linear contrast response curve than monkey M cells or cat X and Y cells, and are most similar to monkey P cells.

Finally, the linearity of spatial summation was analyzed by examining responses to counterphase gratings at multiple spatial frequencies. Some neurons have a purely linear center–surround organization, being excited by sign-appropriate light in the center of their receptive fields and inhibited by light in the surround, but other neurons like cat Y neurons have receptive fields that are comprised of additional small subunits (Hochstein and Shapley, 1976b). Within these subunits, these cells respond to both increases and decreases in contrast and are thus spatially non-linear. Linear and non-linear cells can be distinguished by their responses to sinusoidal gratings: linear cells will respond at one phase of the grating whereas cells with subunits of mixed signs will respond at two phases. The vast majority of all cells in the squirrel showed linear spatial summation, with 92% of X-like cells and 76% of Y-like cells exhibiting a linear signature.

Physiological studies of marsupials (Kirby and Wilson, 1986), rodents (Fukuda, 1977; Hale et al., 1979; Lennie and Perry, 1981; Morigiwa et al., 1988; Gabriel et al., 1996), lagomorphs (Swadlow and Weyand, 1985), carnivores (Enroth-Cugell and Robson, 1966; Hochstein and Shapley, 1976a; Bullier and Norton, 1979), prosimians (Irvin et al., 1986; Norton et al., 1988), and primates (Dreher et al., 1976; Kaplan and Shapley, 1982, 1986; Levitt et al., 2001) have now identified three classes of LGN cells based on receptive field properties and latency to optic tract stimulation. Receptive field properties of cells in several mammalian species resembling X and Y cells of cats or parvocellular (P) and magnocellular (M) cells of macaque monkey are compared in Table 1. It is interesting to examine what properties are common across these mammals and what properties vary from species to species. Only three properties are common across the two principal cell groups in these species: (1) each animal has one class of neurons that shows sustained responses to constant stimulation and another that shows transient responses; (2) these cells have center–surround organization; and (3) the transient neurons have shorter response latencies than the sustained neurons.

All other parameters examined vary from species to species. Whereas sustained cells have smaller receptive fields at a given eccentricity than transient cells in macaque monkey, cat, rabbit, and opossum, there are no significant differences between these two cell groups in gray squirrel or rat, and recent reports indicate the same is true in the mouse (Carcieri SM et al., 2003; Grubb and Thompson, 2003). In addition, although macaque monkey, cat, and rabbit show a strong relationship between eccentricity and receptive field size, gray squirrel and rat show only a weak relationship and recent data from the mouse suggests mice are similar to squirrels and rats in this regard (Grubb and Thompson, 2003). Monkey M and cat X and Y cells all show steep, saturating contrast response curves and high contrast gain while monkey P cells have a more shallow, linear curve, but both squirrel X-like and Y-like neurons have fairly shallow, linear contrast responses that are more similar to P cells than M, X, or Y cells. In the cat the more

transient Y neurons show non-linear spatial summation, but in monkeys and squirrels the majority of all neurons show linear spatial summation and in rabbit all LGN neurons show non-linear spatial summation.

The data of this study are most consistent with the idea that X and P cells, Y and M cells and W and K cells are homologous cell classes. The animals in Table 1 represent a broad sampling of the mammalian evolutionary tree, as marsupials and placental mammals are thought to have diverged 150 million years ago and lagomorphs, rodents, carnivores, and primates probably all diverged about 65 million years ago. All of these mammals have a class of LGN cells that is center–surround and sustained, another class that is center–surround and transient, and a third class of more heterogeneous cells.

In addition to similarities in receptive field properties, X and P, Y and M, and W and K cells share anatomical features and synaptic connections consistent with the idea that these groups are homologous. Macaque monkey, cat, and gray squirrel all have well laminated LGNs, and in these animals sustained neurons similar to the X/P groups are located exclusively in the laminae furthest from the optic tract (Dreher et al., 1976; Illing and Wassle, 1981), dorsally in the case of monkey and cat, and rostromedially in the case of squirrel. The locations of cells similar to the Y/M groups are more variable. In the cat, Y cells are mixed with X cells in the A laminae and W cells in the C laminae (Illing and Wassle, 1981), while Y-like cells in squirrel exist among W-like cells in LGN layers 3a, 3b, and 3c. In most prosimians and monkeys, magnocellular cells exist in distinct laminae in the ventral portion of the nucleus (Dreher et al., 1976; Sherman et al., 1976). In every species studied, including cat (Stone, 1983), several primates and prosimians (Kaas et al., 1978; Irvin et al., 1986), squirrel (Robson and Hall, 1976), tree shrew (Diamond et al., 1993; Holdefer et al., 1995), rat (Hale et al., 1979), rabbit (Swadlow and Weyand, 1985), and opossum (Kirby and Wilson, 1986), cells similar to W/K cells are located just adjacent to the optic tract. The degree to which these cells exist in other LGN laminae appears to vary from animal to animal, and in many prosimians (Irvin et al., 1986), primates (Kaas et al., 1978), and tree shrew (Diamond et al., 1993; Holdefer et al., 1995) there are bands of

TABLE 1 Selected relative and absolute properties of LGN neurons for several mammals

Animal	Cat (Felis Domesticus)		Rhesus monkey (Macaca mulatta)		Owl monkey (Aotus trivirgatus)		Gray squirrel (Sciurus carolinensis)		Rat (Rattus norvegicus)		Rabbit (Oryctolagus cuniculus)		Opossum (Didelphis virginiana)	
Order	Carnivora		Primate		Primate		Rodentia		Rodentia		Lagomorpha		Didelphimorphia	
Cell type	X	Y	P	M	P	M	X-like	Y-like	X	Y	concentric sustained	concentric transient	X	Y
Selected Relative Properties														
Relative receptive field center size	smaller	larger	smaller	larger	smaller	larger	no sig. diff.	no sig. diff.	no sig. diff.	no sig. diff.	smaller	larger	smaller	larger
Relative latency (to visual or elec. stimulation)	slower	faster	slower	faster	slower	faster	slower	faster	slower	faster	slower	faster	slower	faster
Relative transience	more sustained	more transient	more sustained	more transient	more sustained	more transient	more sustained	more transient	more sustained	more transient	more sustained	more transient	more sustained	more transient
Selected Absolute Properties														
Non-linear spatial summation (%)	0	100	1	25	0	0–4[3,4]	8	24	0	100	100	100	0	100
Peak latency (to visual stimulation)	85ms[1]	60 ms[1]	38 ms[2]	25 ms[2]	48.8 ms	40.4 ms	32.9 ms	28.6 ms						
Color opponency	No	No	Yes	No	No	No								
Central receptive field size	0.1°	0.3°	0.01°	0.06°	0.2°	1.0°	1.6°	2.0°	3.9°	4.6°	2.02°	2.58°	2.9°	2.8°
Contrast gain	High	High	Low	High	Low	High	Low	Low						
Center size dependence on eccentricity	Strong	Strong	Weak	Strong	Strong	Strong	Weak	Weak	Weak	Weak	Strong	Strong		
Center-surround organization	Yes	Yes	Yes	Yes	Yes	Yes	Yes	Yes	Yes	Yes	Yes	Yes	Yes	Yes

All mammals have a class of LGN cells that is sustained, another that is transient, and the transient class has a shorter response latency than the sustained class. Other properties such as linearity of spatial summation, contrast gain, and dependence of receptive field size on eccentricity vary from species to species.

References: cat (Shapley and Perry, 1986); rhesus monkey (Shapley and Perry, 1986); owl monkey (Usrey and Reid, 2000); gray squirrel (Van Hooser et al., 2003); rat (Hale et al., 1979; Gabriel et al., 1996); rabbit (Swadlow and Weyand, 1985); opossum (Kirby and Wilson, 1986).

[1]Sestokas and Lehmkuhle (1986).
[2]Maunsell et al. (1999).
[3]Usrey and Reid (2000).
[4]Xu et al. (2001). From Van Hooser et al. (2003).

W/K cells intercalated among layers of X/P and Y/M cells. In many species, including cats, many prosimians and primates, tree shrew, squirrels, and rabbit, K/W/W-like cells receive input from the superior colliculus (Robson and Hall, 1976; Harting et al., 1991a) and in cat, opossum, rat, squirrel, galago, and macaque these cells have also been shown to receive input from the parabigeminal nucleus (Harting et al., 1991b). The connections of W/K neurons to primary visual cortex have been well studied in macaque monkey, cat, and tree shrew, and in all of these animals W/K cells project to the supragranular layers (Leventhal, 1979; Fitzpatrick et al., 1983; Conley et al., 1984; Usrey et al., 1992).

The ultimate proof of homology among mammalian LGN neurons may lie in genetic analyses. Natural selection creates functional and genetic changes in homologous neurons that benefit each species, but it is possible that homologous neurons retain some genetic similarities if one examines many genes. There is already some preliminary evidence for common gene expression in X and P, Y and M, and W and K cells. The antibodies Cat-301 and SMI-32 selectively stain Y cells in the cat LGN and darkly stain magnocellular neurons in the macaque while staining few parvocellular neurons (Hendry et al., 1984; Hockfield and Sur, 1990). In addition, some W and K cells share common gene expression, as antibodies to calbindin-28k label W/K cells in primates and tree shrews, whereas antibodies to parvalbumin do not (Jones and Hendry, 1989; Diamond et al., 1993). However, these antibodies label interneurons in cat and rat LGN (Celio, 1990; Demeulemeester et al., 1991), and it is presently unclear whether these antibodies label proteins directly related to visual function or some indirect property such as cell size (Jones, 1998). Future gene expression studies of these LGN cell classes will be required to test ideas about homology more rigorously.

Cell types in primary visual cortex

In primary visual cortex, many cells respond preferentially to bars or edges at a particular orientation. Orientation selective neurons have been further divided into several (overlapping) subgroups, including simple cells, complex cells, and direction-selective cells. To see if these cell types are found universally across mammals, 221 single neurons were characterized in primary visual cortex of isoflurane-anesthetized squirrels.

Many neurons in the visual cortex of squirrel showed orientation selectivity. Two thirds of squirrel V1 neurons responded more than twice as vigorously to a sinusoidal grating of a preferred orientation as compared to an orthogonal grating. The median tuning width of these oriented neurons (Fig. 4), assessed as half the tuning width at half the maximum response, was 28°, which is very comparable to median tuning widths reported in other species: 29° in mink (LeVay et al., 1987), 27° in owl monkey (O'Keefe et al., 1998), or over 24° in macaque (Ringach et al., 2002). The fraction of unoriented neurons in squirrel was larger than the 10–16% reported in some other highly visual mammals, such as cats, owl monkeys, or macaque monkeys (Schiller et al., 1976; Maldonado et al., 1997; O'Keefe et al., 1998), but oriented neurons were much more common than the 30–45% reported in some less visual rodents and marsupials such as mouse, hamster, opossum, and brush tailed opossum (Dräger, 1975; Rocha-Miranda et al., 1976; Tiao and Blakemore, 1976; Mangini and Pearlman, 1980; Crewther et al., 1984; Métin et al., 1988).

We also found evidence for simple and complex cell classes in squirrel V1. Simple cell receptive fields have distinct excitatory and inhibitory subdivisions, while complex cells have spatially overlapping subregions (Hubel and Wiesel, 1962), and these cells can be distinguished by examining responses to sinusoidal gratings (Schiller et al., 1976; Movshon et al., 1978). Responses of simple cells are primarily modulated at the stimulus frequency (F1 response), while complex cells give a more constant response (F0 response). A histogram of the F1/F0 ratio for squirrel V1 neurons is shown in Fig. 4D. The distribution appears bimodal, suggesting the existence of simple and complex cell classes. The laminar distribution of the F1/F0 ratio is shown in Fig. 5B. As in many species, such as rat, cat, and macaque monkey (Hubel and Wiesel, 1962; Schiller et al., 1976; Gilbert, 1977, Henry et al., 1979; Parnavelas et al., 1983), the major cortical layers receiving input from the LGN,

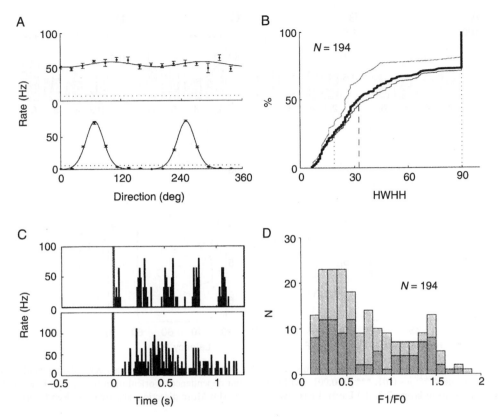

Fig. 4. Examples of orientation tuning and simple and complex responses in squirrel V1. (A) Example orientation tuning curves for an unselective cell and a particularly selective cell. (B) Cumulative histogram of tuning width (HWHH). Thick black line shows all cells. Dark gray thin line shows complex cells. Light gray shows simple cells. Dotted vertical lines indicate tuning width of example cells in A. (C) Example responses of a simple cell (top) and complex cell (bottom) to drifting grating at 4Hz. (D) Histogram of F1/F0 ratio. Light gray includes all cells, dark gray are only oriented cells. The oriented cells have a bimodal distribution, suggesting the squirrel has simple and complex cells. From Van Hooser et al. (2005).

layers 4 and 6 (Harting and Huerta, 1983), tend to have more simple cells than the other layers.

One major difference noted between squirrel and other animals was that the squirrel's relatively low fraction of direction-selective neurons. Only 10% of the cells in the sample had directionality index larger than 2/3. This is fewer than in other rodents (mouse: 24%, Métin et al., 1988; rat: 37%, Girman et al., 1999) and other animals (rabbit: 19%, Chow et al., 1971; macaque: 27%, Orban et al., 1986; owl monkey: 34%, O'Keefe et al., 1998). In squirrel, the processing of motion may bypass V1 more than is the case in other species, as it is thought that most direction selective cells in the ground squirrel project exclusively to the superior colliculus (Michael, 1970) as opposed to LGN. We found a significantly higher proportion of directionally selective cells in layer 6 (see Fig. 5).

Finally, neurons in squirrel V1 tended to respond at higher temporal frequencies than some other mammals. Reported median optimal temporal frequencies in different mammals range from around 2 Hz in mouse and rat to 10 Hz in macaque, as shown in Table 2. The squirrel and macaque monkey show the largest median optimal temporal frequencies, suggesting that diurnal animals in general may have higher temporal frequency preferences than nocturnal animals.

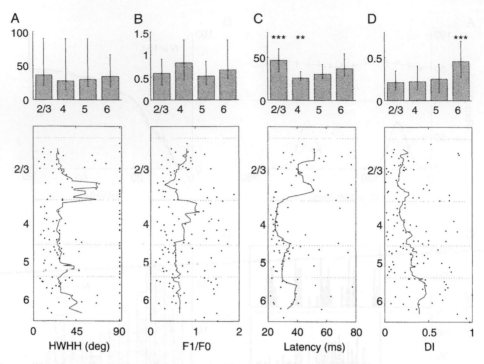

Fig. 5. Laminar profiles of receptive field properties in squirrel V1. Line represents median value over a sliding window with length of 12% of cortical thickness. **: $p < 0.01$; ***: $p < 0.001$. (A) Little laminar dependence of orientation tuning. (B) Fewer complex cells in layer 4. Few simple cells in layers 2/3. (C) Layer 4 has lowest latency. (D) More direction selectivity in deep layers.

TABLE 2 Relationship among waking rhythm, acuity, and temporal frequency for several mammals

Animal	Rhythm	Acuity (cpd)	Median or mean optimal temporal frequency (Hz)
Gray squirrel	diurnal	3	5.3
Macaque	diurnal	50	3.7–10[1]
Cat	crepuscular	6	2.4–4.5[2]
Wallaby	crepuscular	4	3–5
Rat	nocturnal	1.2	2.5
Mouse	nocturnal	0.6	2–4 (from VEPs)
Bush baby	nocturnal	2	2.7
Owl monkey	nocturnal	10	3.0

Diurnal animals have higher mean temporal frequency responses in V1.

[1]Forster and colleagues measured 3.7 Hz under N2O plus pentobarbitone anesthesia. Hawken et al. measured 10 Hz under a higher contrast using sufentanil citrate.

[2]Median is 2.4 Hz in area 17 and 4.5 Hz in area 18. References: squirrel (Heimel et al., in preparation), macaque (Foster et al., 1985; Hawken et al., 1996), cat (Bierer and Freeman, 2003), wallaby (Ibbotson and Mark, 2003), rat (Girman et al., 1999), mouse (Porciatti et al., 1999), bush baby (DeBruyn et al., 1993), owl monkey (O'Keefe et al., 1998).

Functional architecture of primary visual cortex

A central feature of many areas within the mammalian neocortex is the orderly arrangement of columns of neurons, termed functional architecture (Hubel and Wiesel, 1962). Neurons below a single position on the cortical surface have remarkably similar receptive field properties, and these properties generally change smoothly as one travels along the surface. This organization has been described in many cortical areas (Mountcastle, 1997) and is thought to be important for information processing by facilitating connections among neurons with similar properties (Ben-Yishai et al., 1995; Somers et al., 1995). In visual cortex, many neurons respond preferentially to bars or edges at a particular orientation, and in the visual cortex of primates, carnivores, and tree shrews, orientation-selective cells are arranged in a smooth map across the cortical surface (Hubel and Wiesel, 1963; Hubel et al., 1978; Bosking et al., 1997). Curiously, orientation maps have not been found in many rodent species including rats (Girman et al., 1999), mice (Métin et al., 1988; Schuett et al., 2002), and hamsters (Tiao and Blakemore, 1976), and a lagomorph, the rabbit (Murphy and Berman, 1979), despite the fact that individual V1 neurons in these animals are orientation selective.

One could imagine several explanations for the lack of orientation maps in previously examined rodents. First, these rodents do not rely heavily on vision, and therefore might not have faced the evolutionary pressure to develop a highly derived and structured visual system. These animals not only lack orientation maps but they do not have the acuity and contrast sensitivity of primates, carnivores, and tree shrews, and have poorly laminated visual brain structures such as lateral geniculate nucleus and primary visual cortex. Perhaps good acuity, clear lamination, and orientation maps are hallmarks of a highly derived mammalian visual system that go hand in hand. Second, it could be that all mammals possess all the necessary mechanisms to develop orientation maps, but orientation maps do not form in animals with small absolute V1 size such as rats and mice. Anatomical studies (Ts'o et al., 1986; Gilbert and Wiesel, 1989; Malach et al., 1993; Bosking et al., 1997) have suggested that cells with similar orientation preferences tend to make synaptic connections with one another, so perhaps orientation maps in large animals facilitate such connections but are not necessary in small animals because these connections can be made easily without local grouping. Finally, rodents and lagomorphs may simply have a different system of organization in area V1 that does not involve orientation maps.

To examine these ideas, we studied the organization of orientation selectivity in primary visual cortex of the gray squirrel (Van Hooser et al., 2005). Squirrels have highly elaborated visual brain areas and good visual acuity. Importantly, contrast sensitivity and acuity in squirrel is slightly better than in tree shrew and mink, both animals in which orientation maps are present. In addition, V1 in squirrel is much larger than in other studied rodents, being nearly ten times as large as in rat, larger than V1 in tree shrew, and of comparable size to V1 in mink and ferret. Thus, the squirrel is a particularly suitable animal model for testing the hypotheses above about the presence or absence of orientation modules in mammals.

Using optical imaging of intrinsic signals, we assessed the spatial organization of orientation selectivity in primary visual cortex of six squirrels. We initially obtained a retinotopic map by showing sinusoidal gratings of variable orientation in rectangular patches at six locations. The existence of a well-defined map and good response timecourse were taken to indicate a healthy visual cortex with good hemodynamic responses. After obtaining a retinotopic map, we showed sinusoidal gratings at four different orientations on the whole screen. Finally, we obtained another retinotopic map to ensure the brain was healthy and showed good hemodynamic responses during the orientation stimulation.

Responses to one such experiment are shown in Fig. 6. Figure 6A shows a retinotopic map in response to the initial retinotopy stimuli. The map is evident in both the average responses to individual stimuli and a false-color image that indicates which stimulus was maximal for each pixel that showed significantly different activity across stimuli (Kruskal–Wallis test, $\alpha = 0.05$). Another false-color map and average responses to individual orientation stimuli are shown in Fig. 6B. There is a large response to each of the individual orientation stimuli, but the responses are all very similar to one another and in

138

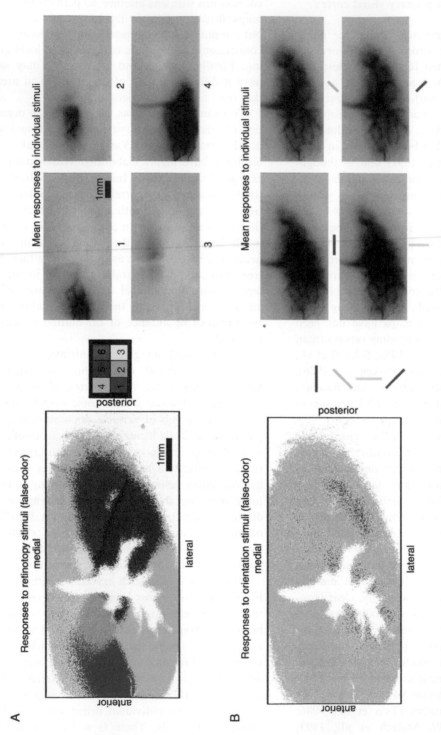

Fig. 6. Optical imaging of intrinsic signals reveals robust retinotopic maps but no orientation map. (A) Responses to retinotopic stimuli (center). The monitor was divided into six regions, and gratings that randomly changed orientation were shown in each region. Left: False-color image of responses to retinotopic stimuli. Pixels are colored if they showed significant differences across stimuli, and pixels are gray if they show no significant differences across stimuli. Some pixels showed artifactually high or low standard deviations across stimuli and were excluded and colored white. Right: Individual responses to four stimuli. (B) Responses to full screen gratings of different orientations. Few pixels show significant differences across stimuli, and across four animals the fraction of significant pixels across stimuli was at chance levels. From Van Hooser et al. (2005).

the false-color image there are only a few scattered pixels that show significant differences across stimuli. No orientation map similar to those observed in tree shrews (Bosking et al., 1997; Humphrey et al., 1980), monkeys (Hubel et al., 1978; Blasdel and Salama, 1986), and cats (Hubel and Wiesel, 1963; Grinvald et al., 1986) is apparent in either the false-color map or the individual responses. In four squirrels tested in this way, the average fraction of pixels that showed very significant differences ($p < 0.001$) across the retinotopy stimuli was 37.2%, but on average only 1.4% of pixels were significantly different for the orientation stimuli.

We also studied the organization of orientation selectivity in many single neuron recordings made in vertical microelectrode penetrations. In the previous section we described that the squirrel has many orientation-selective neurons in V1 and that the orientation tuning width in these cells is similar to what is observed in many other mammals. The progression of orientation-selectivity in a typical vertical electrode penetration is shown in Fig. 7A. Unlike the highly ordered progression of preferred orientation angles observed in monkeys, cats, and tree shrews (Hubel and Wiesel, 1963; Humphrey and Norton, 1980), the orientation preference appears to

change randomly throughout the electrode penetration in squirrel. To examine this quantitatively, we plotted the change in preferred orientation angle as a function of the distance between pairs of neurons recorded in the same penetration as shown in Fig. 7B. There is some weak clustering of cells with similar orientation preferences closer than 100 μm, but if two cells are 100 μm or farther apart, knowing the orientation preference of one cell gives no information about the orientation preference of the other cell. The single unit results are thus in good agreement with the results from intrinsic imaging and suggest that squirrels do not have an orientation map that resembles those of monkeys, carnivores, and tree shrews.

The fact that squirrels lack orientation maps despite possessing highly elaborated visual brain areas, higher visual acuity, and a physically larger V1 than some animals that have orientation maps suggests that the functional architecture of V1 in squirrels is of a different character than that found in primates, carnivores, and tree shrews. Because many mammals including squirrels, mice, rats, hamsters, and rabbits have orientation-selective neurons without having orientation maps, it is likely that orientation maps are not necessary for the computation of

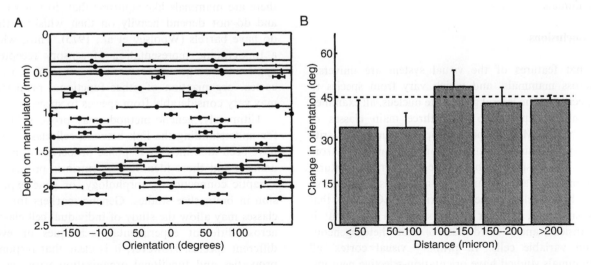

Fig. 7. There is little spatial organization of orientation selectivity in vertical electrode penetrations. (A) Orientation selectivity along a typical electrode penetration. Each cell's orientation angle preference is plotted twice (modulo 180°) to aid visibility, and horizontal bars indicate orientation tuning width. (B) Change in orientation angle as a function of distance for pairs of cells recorded in the same penetration. Cells closer than 100 μm show a slight tendency towards having similar orientation angles but there is no relationship among angle preferences for cells separated by 100 μm or more. From Van Hooser et al. (2005).

orientation selectivity. In addition, the results suggest that orientation maps are not required for achieving the relatively high behavioral acuity found in squirrels.

These results also have implications for models of the development of orientation maps. Many developmental models of orientation maps posit a fixed, Mexican hat type of intracortical connections with local excitation and longer-range inhibition (Erwin et al., 1995; Miller et al., 1999). Combined with Hebbian plasticity, such schemes create a smooth map. In addition, some investigators have suggested that 1–2 mm long-range connections, which are present before orientation maps developmentally, could be a framework underlying the creation of orientation maps (Katz and Callaway, 1991; Ruthazer and Stryker, 1996; Shouval et al., 2000). However, adult squirrels also have 1–2 mm horizontal connections in V1 (Kaas et al., 1989), and cytoarchitecture and anatomically defined cell types in rodent V1 are coarsely similar to those in primates and carnivores. Therefore, these models would also predict orientation maps in squirrels, and the developmental mechanisms underlying orientation map formation remain unclear. It is possible that comparative studies of development will reveal subtle differences that are responsible for orientation map formation in some mammals.

Conclusions

What features of the visual system are universal across mammals, and which vary from species to species? In the lateral geniculate nucleus, all examined mammals appear to have three main classes of LGN cells. Many response properties such as linearity of spatial summation and contrast gain vary from species to species, but there are certain features common to all mammals. All mammals examined so far have a class of center–surround LGN cells that is sustained, another center–surround class that is transient, and a third class of more heterogeneous and variable cells. In primary visual cortex, all mammals studied have orientation-selective neurons, although the fraction of orientation-selective cells and their laminar organization vary from species to species. In addition, the vast majority of mammals have simple cells and complex cells, with tree shrews

being the only known mammal to lack simple cells in V1 (Mooser et al., 2004). Squirrels seem to have a lower proportion of direction selective cells in V1 compared to other mammals.

While all mammalian primary cortical sensory areas examined to date have a topographic representation of the sensory receptors (Kaas, 1997), several other features of functional architecture vary across mammals. In visual cortex, only some mammals appear to have additional spatial organization in the form of orientation maps, ocular dominance bands, or cytochrome oxydase blobs. Mice, squirrels, and rabbits lack all of these (Dräger, 1974; Tiao and Blakemore, 1976; Murphy and Berman, 1979; Hollander and Halbig, 1980; Harting and Huerta, 1983; Métin et al., 1988; Schuett et al., 2002), sheep and many New World monkeys lack ocular dominance bands (Livingstone, 1986; LeVay and Nelson, 1991; Adams and Horton, 2003), and tree shrews lack cytochrome oxidase blobs (Wong-Riley and Norton, 1988). This variation in cortical organization is not limited to visual cortex. Some rodents and marsupials show specialized rings of high or low cell density and thalamic input called barrels in regions mediating responses from the mystacial vibrissae, but there are some mammals like the opossum that whisk and use their whiskers heavily that do not have barrels and there are mammals like squirrels that do not whisk and do not depend heavily on their whiskers that do have barrels (Woolsey et al., 1975). Thus, while a topographic representation of sensory receptors appears to be a general feature of mammalian sensory cortex, organization of other functional properties may vary considerably from species to species.

Ultimately, genetic methods may prove valuable for understanding the link between cell classes that have been identified by response properties in intact animals and those identified by intrinsic properties, synaptic connections, morphology, or gene expression in brain slice studies. Genetic markers for cell classes may allow the study of individual cell classes across different experimental techniques or even different species. However, it is clear that response properties and functional organization vary across mammalian species, so great care must be taken when inferring general principles from studies of neurons using different techniques or different species, such as when applying conclusions from brain slice studies in rodents to neurons recorded in intact cats or monkeys. Comparative studies of response properties, functional organization, and gene expression across mammals may identify general genetic markers for several homologous cell classes across mammals. Studies of such identified cell types using many experimental techniques, such as developmental manipulations, brain slice physiology, and whole animal physiology, may allow fundamental principles of the cellular mechanisms underlying development, function, and disease in the visual system to be uncovered.

Abbreviations

LGN	lateral geniculate nucleus
V1	primary visual cortex
P cell	Parvocellular cell
M cell	Magnocellular cell
K cell	Koniocellular

Acknowledgments

The authors would like to thank Dr. Sooyoung Chung, who participated in many of these experiments, and Dr. Louis Toth, who participated in the intrinsic imaging experiments. The authors also thank Justine Barry and Keow Essig for histological processing.

References

Adams, D.L. and Horton, J.C. (2003) Capricious expression of cortical columns in the primate brain. Nat. Neurosci., 6: 113–114.

Benardete, E.A., Kaplan, E. and Knight, B.W. (1992) Contrast gain control in the primate retina: P cells are not X-like, some M cells are. Vis. Neurosci., 8: 483–486.

Blake, R., Cool, S.J. and Crawford, M.L. (1974) Visual resolution in the cat. Vision Res., 14: 1211–1217.

Ben-Yishai, R., Bar-Or, R.L. and Sompolinsky, H. (1995) Theory of orientation tuning in visual cortex. Proc. Natl. Acad. Sci. USA, 92: 3844–3848.

Blasdel, G.G. and Salama, G. (1986) Voltage-sensitive dyes reveal a modular organization in monkey striate cortex. Nature, 321: 579–585.

Bierer, S. and Freeman, R.D. (2003) A comparison of response properties of cells in striate and extrastriate cortex. Program No. 229.2. Abstract Viewer/Itinery Planner. Washington, DC: Soc. for Neurosci.

Bosking, W.H., Zhang, Y., Schofield, B. and Fitzpatrick, D. (1997) Orientation selectivity and the arrangement of horizontal connections in tree shrew striate cortex. J. Neurosci., 15: 2112–2127.

Bousfield, J.D. (1977) Columnar organisation and the visual cortex of the rabbit. Brain Res., 136: 154–158.

Bullier, J. and Henry, G.H. (1980) Ordinal position and afferent input of neurons in monkey striate cortex. J. Comp. Neurol., 193: 913–935.

Bullier, J. and Norton, T.T. (1979) X and Y relay cells in cat lateral geniculate nucleus: quantitative analysis of receptive-field properties and classification. J. Neurophysiol., 42: 244–273.

Callaway, E.M. (2002) Cell type specificity of local cortical connections. J. Neurocytol., 31: 231–237.

Carcieri, S.M., Jacobs, A.L. and Nirenberg, S. (2003) Classification of retinal ganglion cells: a statistical approach. J Neurophysiol., 90: 1704–1713.

Casagrande, V.A. and Kaas, J.H. (1994) The afferent, intrinsic, and efferent connections of primary visual cortex in primates. In: Peters, A. and Rockland, K.S. (Eds.), Cerebral Cortex. Primary Visual Cortex in Primates, Vol. 10. Plenum Press, New York.

Casagrande, V.A. and Norton, T.T. (1991) Lateral geniculate nucleus: a review of its physiology and function. In: Leventhal, A.G. (Ed.), The Neural Basis of Visual function, Macmillan Press, London.

Celio, M.R. (1990) Calbindin D-28k and parvalbumin in the rat nervous system. Neuroscience, 35: 375–475.

Chow, K.L., Masland, R.H. and Stewart, D.L. (1971) Receptive field characteristics of striate cortical neurons in the rabbit. Brain Res., 33: 337–352.

Conley, M., Fitzpatrick, D. and Diamond, I.T. (1984) The laminar organization of the lateral geniculate body and the striate cortex in the tree shrew (Tupaia glis). J. Neurosci., 4: 171–197.

Crewther, D.P., Crewther, S.G. and Sanderson, K.J. (1984) Primary visual cortex in the brushtailed possum: receptive field properties and corticocortical connections. Brain Behav. Evol., 24: 184–197.

Croner, L. and Kaplan, E. (1995) Receptive fields of P and M ganglion cells across the primate retina. Vision Res., 35: 7–24.

Demeulemeester, H., Arckens, L., Vandesande, F., Orban, G.A., Heizmann, C.W. and Pochet, R. (1991) Calcium binding proteins and neuropeptides as molecular markers of GABAergic interneurons in the cat visual cortex. Exp. Brain Res., 84: 538–544.

DeBruyn, E.J., Casagrande, V.A., Beck, P.D. and Bonds, A.B. (1993) Visual resolution and sensitivity of single cells in the primary visual cortex (V1) of a nocturnal primate (bushbaby): correlations with cortical layers and cytochrome oxidase patterns. J Neurophysiol 69: 3–18.

DeValois, R.L., Morgan, H. and Snodderly, D.M. (1974) Psychophysical studies of monkey vision. III. Spatial luminance contrast sensitivity tests of macaque and human observers. Vision Res., 14: 75–81.

Diamond, I.T., Fitzpatrick, D. and Schmechel, D. (1993) Calcium binding proteins distinguish large and small cells of the ventral posterior and lateral geniculate nuclei of the prosimian galago and the tree shrew (Tupaia belangeri). Proc. Natl. Acad. Sci. USA, 90: 1425–1429.

Dräger, U.C. (1974) Autoradiography of tritiated proline and fucose transported transneuronally from the eye to the visual cortex in pigmented and albino mice. Brain Res., 82: 284–292.

Dräger, U.C. (1975) Receptive fields of single cells and topography in mouse visual cortex. J. Comp. Neurol., 160: 269–290.

Dreher, B., Fukada, Y. and Rodieck, R.W. (1976) Identification, classification and anatomical segregation of cells with X-like and Y-like properties in the lateral geniculate nucleus of old-world monkeys. J. Physiol., 258: 433–452.

Enroth-Cugell, C. and Robson, J.G. (1966) The contrast sensitivity of retinal ganglion cells of the cat. J. Physiol., 187: 517–552.

Erwin, E., Obermayer, K. and Schulten, K. (1995) Models of orientation and ocular dominance columns in the visual cortex: a critical comparison. Neural. Comput., 7: 425–468.

Feng, G., Mellor, R.H., Bernstein, M., Keller-Peck, C., Nguyen, Q.T., Wallace, M., Nerbonne, J.M., Lichtman, J.W. and Sanes, J.R. (2000) Imaging neuronal subsets in transgenic mice expressing multiple spectral variants of GFP. Neuron, 28: 41–51.

Fitzpatrick, D., Itoh, K. and Diamond, I.T. (1983) The laminar organization of the lateral geniculate body and the striate cortex in the squirrel monkey (Saimiri sciureus). J. Neurosci., 3: 673–702.

Foster, K.H., Gaska, J.P., Nagler, M. and Pollen, D.A. (1985) Spatial and temporal frequency selectivity of neurones in visual cortical areas V1 and V2 of the macaque monkey. J Physiol., Aug; 365: 331–363.

Fukada, Y. (1971) Receptive field organization of cat optic nerve fibers with special reference to conduction velocity. Vision Res., 11: 209–226.

Fukuda, Y. (1977) A three-group classification of rat retinal ganglion cells: histological and physiological studies. Brain Res., 119: 327–334.

Gabriel, S., Gabriel, H.J., Grutzmann, R., Berlin, K. and Davidowa, H. (1996) Effects of cholecystokinin on Y, X, and W cells in the dorsal lateral geniculate nucleus of rats. Exp. Brain Res., 109: 43–55.

Gilbert, C.D. (1977) Laminar differences in receptive field properties of cells in cat primary visual cortex. J. Physiol., 268: 391–421.

Gilbert, C.D. and Wiesel, T.N. (1989) Columnar specificity of intrinsic horizontal and corticocortical connections in cat visual cortex. J. Neurosci., 9: 2432–2442.

Girman, S.V., Sauve, Y. and Lund, R.D. (1999) Receptive field properties of single neurons in rat primary visual cortex. J. Neurophysiol., 82: 301–311.

Grinvald, A., Lieke, E., Frostig, R.D., Gilbert, C.D. and Wiesel, T.N. (1986) Functional architecture of cortex revealed by optical imaging of intrinsic signals. Nature, 324: 361–364.

Grubb, M.S. and Thompson, I.D. (2003) Quantitative characterization of visual response properties in the mouse dorsal lateral geniculate nucleus. J. Neurophysiol., 90: 3594–3607.

Gupta, A., Wang, Y. and Markram, H. (2000) Organizing principles for a diversity of GABAergic interneurons and synapses in the neocortex. Science, 287: 273–278.

Hale, P.T., Sefton, A.J. and Dreher, B. (1979) A correlation of receptive field properties with conduction velocity of cells in the rat's retino-geniculo-cortical pathway. Exp. Brain Res., 35: 425–442.

Hall, W.C., Kaas, J.H., Killackey, H. and Diamond, I.T. (1971) Cortical visual areas in the grey squirrel (Sciurus carolinensis): a correlation between cortical evoked potential maps and architectonic subdivisions. J. Neurophysiol., 34: 437–452.

Harting, J.K. and Huerta, M.F. (1983) The geniculostriate projection in the grey squirrel: preliminary autoradiographic data. Brain Res., 272: 341–349.

Harting, J.K., Huerta, M.F., Hashikawa, T. and van Lieshout, D.P. (1991a) Projection of the mammalian superior colliculus upon the dorsal lateral geniculate nucleus: organization of tectogeniculate pathways in nineteen species. J. Comp. Neurol., 304: 275–306.

Harting, J.K., Van Lieshout, D.P., Hashikawa, T. and Weber, J.T. (1991b) The parabigeminogeniculate projection: connectional studies in eight mammals. J. Comp. Neurol., 305: 559–581.

Hawken, M.J., Shapley, R.M. and Grosof, D.H. (1996) Temporal-frequency selectivity in monkey visual cortex. Vis Neurosci., May–Jun;13(3): 477–492.

Heimel, J.A.F., Van Hooser, S.D., Nelson, S.B. Laminar Organization of Response Properties in Primary Visual Cortex of the Gray squirrel (Sciurus carolinensis). In preparation.

Hendry, S.H. and Reid, R.C. (2000) The koniocellular pathway in primate vision. Annu. Rev. Neurosci., 23: 127–153.

Hendry, S.H.C., Hockfield, S., Jones, E.G. and McKay, R. (1984) Monoclonal antibody that identifies subset of neurons in the central visual system of monkey and cat. Nature, 307: 267–269.

Henry, G.H., Harvey, A.R. and Lund, J.S. (1979) The afferent connections and laminar distribution of cells in the cat striate cortex. J. Comp. Neurol., 187: 725–744.

Hockfield, S. and Sur, M. (1990) Monoclonal antibody Cat-301 identifies Y-cells in the dorsal lateral geniculate nucleus of the cat. J. Comp. Neurol., 300: 320–330.

Hochstein, S. and Shapley, R.M. (1976a) Quantitative analysis of retinal ganglion cell classifications. J. Physiol., 262: 237–264.

Hochstein, S. and Shapley, R.M. (1976b) Linear and nonlinear subunits in Y cat retinal ganglion cells. J. Physiol., 262: 265–284.

Holdefer, R.N. and Norton, T.T. (1995) Laminar organization of receptive field properties in the dorsal lateral geniculate nucleus of the tree shrew (Tupaiaglis belangeri). J. Comp. Neurol., 358: 401–413.

Hollander, H. and Halbig, W. (1980) Topography of retinal representation in the rabbit cortex: an experimental study using transneuronal and retrograde tracing techniques. J. Comp. Neurol., 193(3): 701–710.

Hubel, D.H. and Wiesel, T.N. (1959) Receptive fields of single neurones in the cat's striate cortex. J. Physiol., 148: 574–591.

Hubel, D.H. and Wiesel, T.N. (1962) Receptive fields, binocular interaction and functional architecture in the cat's visual cortex. J. Physiol., 160: 106–154.

Hubel, D.H. and Wiesel, T.N. (1963) Shape and arrangement of columns in cat's striate cortex. J. Physiol., 165: 559–568.

Hubel, D.H., Wiesel, T.N. and Stryker, M.P. (1978) Anatomical demonstration of orientation columns in macaque monkey. J. Comp. Neurol., 177: 361–380.

Humphrey, A.L. and Norton, T.T. (1980) Topographic organization of the orientation column system in the striate cortex of the tree shrew (Tupaia glis). I. Microelectrode recording. J. Comp. Neurol., 192: 531–547.

Illing, R.B and Wassle, H. (1981) The retinal projection to the thalamus in the cat: a quantitative investigation and a comparison with the retinotectal pathway. J. Comp. Neurol., 202: 265–285.

Ibbotson, M.R. and Mark, R.F. (2003) Orientation and spatiotemporal tuning of cells in the primary visual cortex of an Australian marsupial, the wallaby Macropus eugenii. J Comp Physiol A Neuroethol Sens Neural Behav Physiol. Feb;189(2): 115–123.

Irvin, G.E., Norton, T.T., Sesma, M.A. and Casagrande, V.A. (1986) W-like response properties of interlaminar zone cells in the lateral geniculate nucleus of a primate (Galago crassicaudatus). Brain Res., 362: 254–270.

Jacobs, G.H., Birch, D.G. and Blakeslee, B. (1982) Visual acuity and spatial contrast sensitivity in tree squirrels. Behav. Process, 7: 367–375.

Jones, E.G. (1998) Viewpoint: the core and matrix of thalamic organization. Neuroscience, 85: 331–345.

Jones, E.G. and Hendry, S.H. (1989) Differential calcium binding protein immunoreactivity distinguishes classes of relay neurons in monkey thalamic nuclei. Eur. J. Neurosci., 1: 222–246.

Kaas, J.H., Hall, W.C. and Diamond, I.T. (1972) Visual cortex of the grey squirrel (Sciurus carolinensis): architectonic subdivisions and connections from the visual thalamus. J. Comp. Neurol., 145: 273–305.

Kaas, J.H., Huerta, M.F., Weber, J.T. and Harting, J.K. (1978) Patterns of retinal terminations and laminar organization of the lateral geniculate nucleus of primates. J. Comp. Neurol., 182: 517–554.

Kaas, J.H., Krubitzer, L.A. and Johanson, K.L. (1989) Cortical connections of areas 17 (V-I) and 18 (VII) of squirrels. J. Comp. Neurol., 281: 426–446.

Kahn, D.M., Huffman, K.J. and Krubitzer, L. (2000) Organization and connections of V1 in Monodelphis domestica. J. Comp. Neurol., 428: 337–354.

Kaas, J.H. (1997) Topographic Maps are Fundamental to Sensory Processing. Brain Res. Bull., 44: 107–112.

Kaplan, E. and Shapley, R.M. (1982) X and Y cells in the lateral geniculate nucleus of macaque monkeys. J. Physiol., 330: 125–143.

Kaplan, E. and Shapley, R.M. (1986) The primate retina contains two types of ganglion cells, with high and low contrast sensitivity. Proc. Natl. Acad. Sci. USA, 83: 2755–2757.

Katz, L.C. and Callaway, E.M. (1991) Emergence and refinement of local circuits in cat striate cortex. In: Lam, D.M.-K., and Shatz, C.J. (Eds.), Development of the Visual System, MIT Press, Cambridge, MA, pp. 197–216.

Kirby, M.A. and Wilson, P.D. (1986) Receptive field properties and latencies of cells in the lateral geniculate nucleus of the North American opossum (Didelphis virginiana). J. Neurophysiol., 56: 907–933.

Kozloski, J., Hamzei-Sichani, F. and Yuste, R. (2001) Stereotyped position of local synaptic targets in neocortex. Science, 293: 868–872.

Lennie, P. and Perry, V.H. (1981) Spatial contrast sensitivity of cells in the lateral geniculate nucleus of the rat. J. Physiol., 315: 69–79.

Leventhal, A.G. (1979) Evidence that the different classes of relay cells of the cat's lateral geniculate nucleus terminate in different layers of the striate cortex. Exp. Brain. Res., 37: 349–372.

Levitt, J.B., Schumer, R.A., Sherman, S.M., Spear, P.D. and Movshon, J.A. (2001) Visual response properties of neurons in the LGN of normally reared and visually deprived macaque monkeys. J. Neurophysiol., 85: 2111–2129.

LeVay, S., McConnell, S.K. and Luskin, M.B. (1987) Functional organization of primary visual cortex in the mink (Mustela vison), and a comparison with the cat. J. Comp. Neurol., 257: 422–441.

LeVay, S., and Nelson, S.B. (1991). Columnar organization of the visual cortex. In: Leventhal, A.G. (Ed.), The Neural Basis of Visual Function. pp. 266–315.

144

Leventhal, A.G. and Hirsch, H.V. (1978) Receptive-field properties of neurons in different laminae of visual cortex of the cat. J. Neurophysiol., 41: 948–962.

Livingstone, M.S. (1986) Ocular dominance columns in New World monkeys. J. Neurosci., 16: 2086–2096.

Long, K.O. and Fisher, S.K. (1983) The distributions of photoreceptors and ganglion cells in the California ground squirrel Spermophilus beecheyi. J. Comp. Neurol., 221: 329–340.

Malach, R., Amir, Y., Harel, M. and Grinvald, A. (1993) Relationship between intrinsic connections and functional architecture revealed by optical imaging and in vivo targeted biocytin injections in primate striate cortex. Proc. Natl. Acad. Sci. USA, 90: 10469–10473.

Maldonado, P.E., Godecke, I., Gray, C.M. and Bonhoeffer, T. (1997) Orientation selectivity in pinwheel centers in cat striate cortex. Science, 276: 1551–1555.

Mangini, N.J. and Pearlman, A.L. (1980) Laminar distribution of receptive field properties in the primary visual cortex of the mouse. J. Comp. Neurol., 193: 203–222.

Martin, P.R., White, A.J., Goodchild, A.K., Wilder, H.D. and Sefton, A.E. (1997) Evidence that blue-on cells are part of the third geniculocortical pathway in primates. Eur. J. Neurosci., 9: 1536–1541.

Maunsell, J.H., Ghose, G.M., Assad, J.A., McAdams, C.J., Boudreau, C.E. and Noerager, B.D. (1999) Visual response latencies of magnocellular and parvocellular LGN neurons in macaque monkeys. Vis. Neurosci., 16: 1–14.

McCourt, M.E. and Jacobs, G.H. (1984) Refractive state, depth of focus and accommodation of the eye of the California ground squirrel (Spermophilus beecheyi). Vision Res., 24: 1261–1266.

Métin, C., Godement, P. and Imbert, M. (1988) The primary visual cortex in the mouse: receptive field properties and functional organization. Exp. Brain Res., 69: 594–612.

Michael, C.R. (1970) Integration of retinal and cortical information in the superior colliculus of the ground squirrel. Brain Behav. Evol., 3: 205–209.

Miller, K.D., Erwin, E. and Kayser, A. (1999) Is the development of orientation selectivity instructed by activity? J. Neurobiology, 41: 44–57.

Mooser, F., Bosking, W.H. and Fitzpatrick, D. (2004) A morphological basis for orientation tuning in primary visual cortex. Nat. Neurosci., 7: 872–879.

Morigiwa, K., Sawai, H., Wakakuwa, K., Mitani-Yamanishi, Y. and Fukuda, Y. (1988) Retinal inputs and laminar distributions of the dorsal lateral geniculate nucleus relay cells in the eastern chipmunk (Tamias sibiricus asiaticus). Exp. Brain Res., 71: 527–540.

Mountcastle, V.B. (1997) The columnar organization of the neocortex. Brain, 120: 701–722.

Movshon, J.A., Thompson, I.D. and Tolhurst, D.J. (1978) Spatial summation in the receptive fields of simple cells in the cat's striate cortex. J. Physiol., 283: 53–77.

Murphy, E.H. and Berman, N. (1979) The rabbit and the cat: a comparison of some features of response properties of single cells in the primary visual cortex. J. Comp. Neurol., 188(3): 401–427.

Naka, K.I. and Rushton, W.A. (1966) S-potentials from colour units in the retina of fish (Cyprinidae). J. Physiol., 185: 536–555.

Norton, T.T., Casagrande, V.A., Irvin, G.E., Sesma, M.A. and Petry, H.M. (1988) Contrast-sensitivity functions of W-, X-, and Y-like relay cells in the lateral geniculate nucleus of bush baby, Galago crassicaudatus. J. Neurophysiol., 59: 1639–1656.

O'Keefe, L.P., Levitt, J.B., Kiper, D.C., Shapley, R.M. and Movshon, J.A. (1998) Functional organization of owl monkey lateral geniculate nucleus and visual cortex. J. Neurophysiol., 80: 594–609.

Orban, G.A., Kennedy, H. and Bullier, J. (1986) Velocity sensitivity and direction selectivity of neurons in areas V1 and V2 of the monkey: influence of eccentricity. J. Neurophysiol., Aug;56(2): 462–480.

Parnavelas, J.G., Burne, R.A. and Lin, C.S. (1983) Distribution and morphology of functionally identified neurons in the visual cortex of the rat. Brain Res., 261: 21–29.

Pearlman, A.L. and Daw, N.W. (1970) Opponent color cells in the cat lateral geniculate nucleus. Science, 167: 84–86.

Petry, H.M., Fox, R. and Casagrande, V.A. (1984) Spatial contrast sensitivity of the tree shrew. Vision Res., 24: 1037–1042.

Polkoshnikov, E. and Supin, A. (1988) Receptive field properties of neurons in the squirrel striate cortex.48: 49–69.

Polkoshnikov, E.V. and Revishchin, A.V. (1998) Functional characteristics of the binocular sector neurones of the squirrel Sciurus vulgaris striate cortex. Zh. Evol. Biokhim. Fiziol., 34: 598–610.

Porciatti, V, Pizzorusso, T. and Maffei, L. (1999) The visual physiology of the wild type mouse determined with pattern VEPs. Vision Res. Sep;39(18): 3071–3081.

Pribram, K.H., Lassonde, M.C. and Ptito, M. (1981) Classification of receptive field properties in cat visual cortex. Exp. Brain Res., 43: 119–130.

Ringach, D.L., Shapley, R.M. and Hawken, M.J. (2002) Orientation selectivity in macaque V1: diversity and laminar dependence. J. Neurosci., 22: 5639–5651.

Robson, J.A. and Hall, W.C. (1976) Projections from the superior colliculus to the dorsal lateral geniculate nucleus of the grey squirrel (Sciurus carolinensis). Brain Res., 113: 379–385.

Rocha-Miranda, C.E., Linden, R., Volchan, E., Lent, R. and Bombar Dieri, R.A. Jr. (1976) Receptive field properties of single units in the opossum striate cortex. Brain Res., 104: 197–219.

Rodieck, R.W. and Brening, R.K. (1983) Retinal ganglion cells: properties, types, genera, pathways, and trans-species comparisons. Brain Behav. Evol., 23: 121–164.

Ruthazer, E.S. and Stryker, M.P. (1996) The role of activity in the development of long-range horizontal connections in area 17 of the ferret. J. Neurosci., 16: 7253–7269.

Schiller, P.H., Finlay, B.L. and Volman, S.F. (1976) Quantitative studies of single-cell properties in monkey striate cortex. I. Spatiotemporal organization of receptive fields. J. Neurophysiol., 39: 1288–1319.

Schuett, S., Bonhoeffer, T. and Hubener, M. (2002) Mapping retinotopic structure in mouse visual cortex with optical imaging. J. Neurosci., 22: 6549–6559.

Sestokas, A.K. and Lehmkuhle, S. (1986) Visual response latency of X- and Y-cells in the dorsal lateral geniculate nucleus of the cat. Vision Res., 26: 1041–1054.

Shapley, R.M. and Perry, V.H. (1986) Cat and monkey retinal ganglion cells and their visual functional roles. Trends Neurosci., 9: 229–235.

Sherman, S.M., Norton, T.T. and Casagrande, V.A. (1975) X- and Y-cells in the dorsal lateral geniculate nucleus of the tree shrew (Tupaia glis). Brain Res., 93: 152–157.

Sherman, S.M., Wilson, J.R., Kaas, J.H. and Webb, S.V. (1976) X and Y cells in the dorsal lateral geniculate nucleus of the owl monkey (Aotus trivirgatus). Science, 192: 475–477.

Shouval, H.Z., Goldberg, D.H., Jones, J.P., Beckerman, M. and Cooper, L.N. (2000) Structured long range connections can provide a scaffold for orientation maps. J. Neurosci., 20: 1119–1128.

Somers, D.C., Nelson, S.B. and Sur, M. (1995) An emergent model of orientation selectivity in cat visual cortical simple cells. J. Neurosci., 15: 5448–5465.

Stone, J. (1983) Parallel Processing in the Visual System: The Classification of Retinal Ganglion Cells and Its Impact on the Neurobiology of Vision. Plenum Press, New York.

Swadlow, H.A. and Weyand, T.G. (1985) Receptive-field and axonal properties of neurons in the dorsal lateral geniculate nucleus of awake unparalyzed rabbits. J. Neurophysiol., 54: 168–183.

Tiao, Y.C. and Blakemore, C. (1976) Functional organization in the visual cortex of the golden hamster. J. Comp. Neurol., 168: 459–481.

Ts'o, D.Y., Gilbert, C.D. and Wiesel, T.N. (1986) Relationships between horizontal interactions and functional architecture in cat striate cortex as revealed by cross-correlation analysis. J. Neurosci., 6: 1160–1170.

Usrey, W.M., Muly, E.C. and Fitzpatrick, D. (1992) Lateral geniculate projections to the superficial layers of visual cortex in the tree shrew. J. Comp. Neurol., 319: 159–171.

Usrey, W.M. and Reid, R.C. (2000) Visual physiology of the lateral geniculate nucleus in two species of New World monkey: Saimiri sciureus and Aotus trivirgatis. J. Physiol., 523: 755–769.

Van Hooser, S.D., Heimel, J.A. and Nelson, S.B. (2003) Receptive field properties and laminar organization of lateral geniculate nucleus in the gray squirrel (Sciurus carolinensis). J. Neurophysiol., 90: 3398–3418.

Van Hooser, S.D., Heimel, J.A., Chung, S., Nelson, S.B. and Toth, L.J. (2005) Orientation selectivity without orientation maps in visual cortex of a highly visual mammal. J. Neurosci., 25: 19–28.

Wiesel, T.N. and Hubel, D.H. (1966) Spatial and chromatic interactions in the lateral geniculate body of the rhesus monkey. J. Neurophysiol., 29: 1115–1156.

Woolsey, T.A., Welker, C. and Schwartz, R.H. (1975) Comparative anatomical studies of the SmL face cortex with special reference to the occurrence of "barrels" in layer IV. J. Comp. Neurol., 164: 79–94.

Wong-Riley, M.T. and Norton, T.T. (1988) Histochemical localization of cytochrome oxidase activity in the visual system of the tree shrew: normal patterns and the effect of retinal impulse blockage. J. Comp. Neurol., 272: 562–578.

Xu, X., Ichida, J.M., Allison, J.D., Boyd, J.D., Bonds, A.B. and Casagrande, V.A. (2001) A comparison of koniocellular, magnocellular, and parvocellular receptive field properties in the lateral geniculate nucleus of the owl monkey (Aotus trivirgatus). J. Physiol., 531: 203–218.

Progress in Brain Research, Vol. 149
ISSN 0079-6123

CHAPTER 11

Drivers and modulators from push-pull and balanced synaptic input

L.F. Abbott[1],* and Frances S. Chance[2]

[1]*Volen Center and Department of Biology, Brandeis University, Waltham, MA 02454-9110, USA*
[2]*Department of Neurobiology and Behavior, University of California at Irvine,
Irvine, CA 92697-4550, USA*

Abstract: In 1998, Sherman and Guillery proposed that there are two types of inputs to cortical neurons; drivers and modulators. These two forms of input are required to explain how, for example, sensory driven responses are controlled and modified by attention and other internally generated gating signals. One might imagine that driver signals are carried by fast ionotropic receptors, whereas modulators correspond to slower metabotropic receptors. Instead, we have proposed a novel mechanism by which both driver and modulator inputs could be carried by transmission through the same types of ionotropic receptors. In this scheme, the distinction between driver and modulator inputs is functional and changeable rather than anatomical and fixed. Driver inputs are carried by excitation and inhibition acting in a push-pull manner. This means that increases in excitation are accompanied by decreases in inhibition and vice versa. Modulators correspond to excitation and inhibition that covary so that they increase or decrease together. Theoretical and experimental work has shown that such an arrangement modulates the gain of a neuron, rather than driving it to respond. Constructing drivers and modulators in this manner allows individual excitatory synaptic inputs to play either role, and indeed to switch between roles, depending on how they are linked with inhibition.

Introduction

Cognitive processing often relies on one region of the brain controlling and modulating the actions of another. One mechanism for such control is gain modulation, a prominent feature of neural activity recorded in behaving animals (Salinas and Thier, 2000). Gain modulation is a multiplicative (or divisive) scaling effect on neuronal responses, equivalent to a change in slope of the firing rate versus current (f-I) curve, that is distinct from the additive (or subtractive) shifts in the firing rate produced by

pure excitation or inhibition acting as a driving input (Gabbiani et al., 1994; Holt and Koch, 1997).

The distinction between driver and modulator inputs (Sherman and Guillery, 1998), is illustrated in Fig. 1. Figure 1A shows the well-known effect of increasing either the excitatory or inhibitory component of the total synaptic input to a model neuron, which is a left- or rightward shift of the f-I curve. This additive or subtractive effect of excitation or inhibition corresponds to a driving input. In contrast, Fig. 1B illustrates a multiplicative alteration in the f-I curve (the curves are approximate multiples of each other), the signature characteristic of gain modulation. It is important to appreciate that gain modulation is a change in the sensitivity of a neuron, similar to adjusting the volume control on an amplifier, not simply an additive enhancement or subtractive

*Corresponding author. Tel.: +1-781-736-2876; Fax: +1-781-736-3142; E-mail: abbott@brandeis.edu

DOI: 10.1016/S0079-6123(05)49011-1

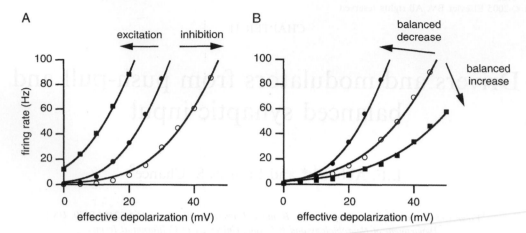

Fig. 1. Effects of excitatory and inhibitory input on the firing rate versus input current (f-I) curve of an integrate and fire model neuron. Input current is plotted in terms of the equivalent amount of depolarization produced in the resting neuron with spiking blocked, a convenient measure. (A) The effect of increased excitation is a leftward shift of the f-I curve, while increased inhibition produces a rightward shift. (B) Modifying levels of both excitation and inhibition in a balanced manner produces a multiplicative enhancement (reduced excitation and inhibition) or a divisive reduction (increased excitation and inhibition) in the firing rate. In both figures, dots are simulation results and solid curves are a fit using Eq. 3.

diminution of its response. This change of sensitivity is the key to its usefulness as a mechanism for switching and modifying neural circuits.

Gain modulation appears to be a primary mechanism by which cortical neurons non-linearly combine input signals. It shows up in a wide range of contexts including the gaze-direction dependence of visual neurons in posterior parietal cortex (Andersen and Mountcastle, 1983; Andersen et al., 1985, Murphy and Miller, 2003), the effects of attention on visually responsive neurons (Connor et al., 1996, 1997; McAdams and Maunsell, 1999a,b; Treue and Martínez-Trujillo, 1999), auditory processing in birds (Peña and Konishi, 2001), and visual escape responses in locusts (Gabbiani et al., 1999). Gain modulation is seen in early visual processing (Weyland and Malpeli, 1993; Pouget and Sejnowski, 1994, 1997; Trotter and Celebrini, 1999), and it has been proposed as a mechanism for generating a variety of non-classical receptive field effects for neurons in primary visual cortex (Heeger, 1992, 1993; Carandini and Heeger, 1994; Carrandini et al., 1997; Tolhurst and Heeger, 1997) and for the decorrelation of natural images (Simoncelli and Schwartz, 1999; Schwartz and Simoncelli, 2001a,b). The neural computations required for coordinate

transformations during reaching tasks (Zipser and Andersen, 1988; Salinas and Abbott, 1995; Pouget and Sejnowski, 1997) and for object recognition (Salinas and Abbott, 1997) also appear to involve gain modulation.

Although the importance of gain modulation (and multiplicative interactions in general) in neurons has been appreciated for many years (Mel and Koch, 1990; Koch and Poggio, 1992; Pouget et al., 1993, Pouget and Sejnowski, 1994, 1997; Salinas and Abbott, 1995, 1997), it has proven difficult to uncover a realistic biophysical mechanism by which it can occur. (It is important to note that, despite comments in the literature to the contrary, divisive inhibition of neuronal responses cannot arise from so called shunting inhibition. As has been shown both theoretically (Gabbiani et al., 1994; Holt and Koch, 1997) and experimentally (Chance et al., 2002), inhibition has the same subtractive effect on firing rates whether it is of the shunting or hyperpolarizing variety. Thus, shunting inhibition does not provide a plausible mechanism for neuronal gain modulation.) In particular, it has not been known how restrictive gain modulation might be; for example, whether it requires relatively non-specific neuromodulatory systems (Marder and Calabrese, 1996), relies on slow metabotropic receptors (Sherman and Guillery, 1998), or requires blocks of neurons to be modulated together (Salinas and Abbott, 1996; Hahnloser et al., 2000). Despite a number of attempts (Srinivasan and Bernard, 1976; Koch and Ullman, 1985; Koch and Poggio, 1992; Mel, 1993; Salinas and Abbott, 1996; Koch, 1998; Hahnloser et al., 2000), no really satisfactory proposal existed until recently (Doiron et al., 2001; Chance et al., 2002; Prescott and De Koninck, 2003; Mitchell and Silver, 2003).

Gain modulation from balanced synaptic input

Neurons typically receive a massive barrage of excitatory and inhibitory synaptic input. The functional role of this noisy background activity has been a long-standing puzzle in neuroscience. Background activity dramatically affects neuronal response properties (Bernander et al., 1991; Douglass et al., 1993; Collins et al., 1996; Levin and Miller, 1996; Nozaki et al., 1999; Destexhe and Paré, 1999; Hô and Destexhe, 2000; Anderson et al., 2000a; Tiesinga et al., 2001; Destexhe et al., 2001) in part by increasing overall conductance (Rapp et al., 1992; Borg-Graham, 1998; Hirsch et al., 1998; Destexhe and Paré, 1999; Shelley et al., 2002).

Cortical neurons exhibit a remarkably high level of response variability (Burns and Webb, 1976; Dean, 1981; Softky and Koch, 1992, 1994; Holt et al., 1996; Anderson et al., 2000a). This led to the suggestion that, in addition to the push-pull excitation and inhibition (Anderson et al., 2000b) that drives or suppresses their responses, cortical neurons receive a high degree of parallel excitation and inhibition (Shadlen and Newsome, 1994, 1998; Tsodyks and Sejnowski, 1995; van Vreeswijk and Sompolinsky, 1996; Troyer and Miller, 1997, Stevens and Zador, 1998). Although this so-called balanced synaptic input generates little mean overall current, due to the cancellation of excitatory and inhibitory components, it produces a highly fluctuating input that contributes to response variability.

Previous work has treated the balanced component of synaptic input as a constant source of noise that continuously underlies the stimulus-evoked increases in excitation that drive neuronal responses. However, when the overall level of background activity is varied, an interesting thing happens. The example of gain modulation shown in Fig. 1B was obtained from an integrate-and-fire model neuron receiving large amounts of excitation and inhibition in a balanced configuration. The responsiveness of the model neuron was investigated by plotting the firing rate evoked by various levels of injected current (the f-I curve). The difference between the three curves lies in the different levels of balanced excitation and inhibition that the neuron received.

The gain modulating effect of balanced synaptic input has also been seen in neurons in layer 5 of rat somatosensory cortex (Chance et al., 2002). In these experiments, the dynamic clamp was used to simulate, within in the normally quiescent slice preparation, the high conductance changes and fluctuations in membrane potential that are characteristic of in vivo cortex. For the parameters that achieved realistic conductance changes and levels of noise, the synaptic inputs were in a configuration in which excitation approximately balanced inhibition. In particular, to simulate typical in vivo conditions, excitatory inputs were generated at a rate of 7000 Hz and inhibitory inputs at a rate of 3000 Hz, representing the summed effects of many simulated afferents. The arrival times of these synaptic inputs were randomly generated with Poisson statistics. The unitary synaptic conductance for each synaptic input was calculated as a difference of exponentials, with time constants of 0.1 ms for the rising phase and either 5 ms (excitatory) or 10 ms (inhibitory) for the falling phase. The peak unitary synaptic conductances were set to 2% (excitatory) or 6% (inhibitory) of the measured resting membrane conductance.

The balanced background synaptic activity introduced with the dynamic clamp was not very effective at driving the recorded neuron. Instead, the dominant effect of this background activity was to introduce noise into the neuronal response, as illustrated in Fig. 2. The level of variability matched quite well with levels seen in vivo (Fig. 2).

Varying the level of background activity had a significant effect on the gain of the neuron as measured by driving it with different levels of constant injected current (the driving current) in addition to the simulated background synaptic activity. In other words, the firing rate was measured as a function of driving current for different levels of

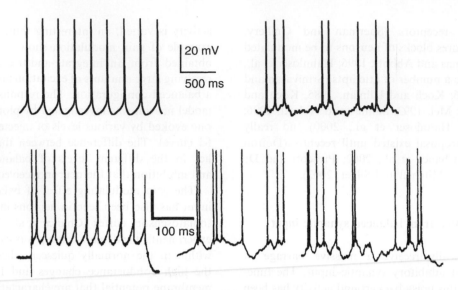

Fig. 2. Top panels: (adapted from Chance et al., 2002) Intracellular recordings from a layer 5 pyramidal neuron in a slice of rat somatosensory cortex. Constant current was injected to drive the neuron at approximately 5 Hz. The two traces represent the firing of the neuron with (right) and without (left) simulated background activity. For comparison, the bottom traces (adapted from Holt et al., 1996) are intracellular recordings from pyramidal neurons of cat visual cortex driven with constant current in slice (left) or in vivo (middle), and when driven by visual activity in vivo (right).

background activity. The dominant effect of changing the level of background activity was to multiplicatively scale the curve of firing-rate versus input current for the neuron (Fig. 3). This effect is equivalent to changing the gain of the neuron, where gain is defined as the slope of the firing rate curve.

Through this mechanism, gain modulation occurs without a corresponding change in firing rate variability (measured as the coefficient of variation of the interspike intervals). The multiplicative effect is not simply a result of the increased conductance induced by the dynamic clamp simulated input (see Chance et al., 2002 for more details). Briefly, two fundamental components of synaptic input increase when background synaptic activity is increased: the overall conductance and the variance of the synaptic current entering the neuron. The increase in conductance has a subtractive effect on the firing rate curve of the neuron (Gabbiani et al., 1994; Holt and Koch, 1997, Chance et al., 2002) while the increase in synaptic current variance leads to a decrease in gain, along with an additive effect (Chance et al., 2002). When the rate of background synaptic input is increased, these effects combine. For a certain parameter range, the

subtractive effect of the conductance increase cancels the additive effect of the current variance increase, leaving the divisive gain change.

Of relevance for the connection with the idea of driver and modulator inputs (Sherman and Guillery, 1998) is the fact that mixed multiplicative/divisive and additive/subtractive effects are obtained if the levels of excitation and inhibition in the background synaptic activity is not completely balanced. For example, in the right panel of Fig. 3, inhibition was slightly stronger than excitation. As background synaptic activity was increased, this produced a subtractive effect (shifting of the curve to the right along the input axis) as well as a divisive effect. Therefore, mixed multiplicative and additive effects can arise from this mechanism through non-balanced synaptic input.

A firing-rate description of gain modulation

Many network models in neuroscience are constructed by using firing rates to characterize neuronal activity. The use of firing-rate descriptions (Wilson and Cowan, 1972; Dayan and Abbott, 2001) is

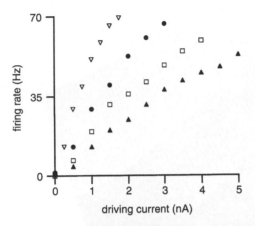
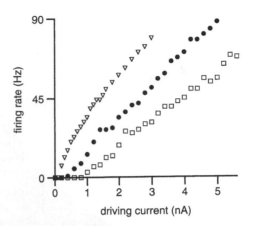

Fig. 3. Gain modulation by background synaptic activity for two different neurons (adapted from Chance et al., 2002). Firing rate plotted against driving current for different levels of background activity. Open inverted triangles represent the responses of the neuron in the absence of any background synaptic activity. The filled circles represent the responses recorded in the standard condition (see text and Chance et al., 2002). To produce the open squares and filled triangles, the input rates of the background excitatory and inhibitory synaptic inputs were doubled and tripled, respectively.

standard practice in network modeling because it greatly accelerates the construction of networks and facilitates our understanding of what they are doing. By having an accurate expression for the firing rate of a spiking neuron, it is possible to build network models rapidly, analyze their behavior and then, if the network seems interesting, build the corresponding spiking network model. The latter is obviously more realistic and more interesting from a biological standpoint, but more difficult to construct from scratch. A commonly used form for the f-I curve in such models is the threshold-linear function. It is actually easier for what follows to express the firing rate r in terms of the steady-state membrane potential, V_{ss}, that the neuron would obtain in response to the given input current if it was held constant and the spiking mechanisms of the neuron was inactivated. In terms of this steady-state voltage, which is typically related in a linear manner to the input current, and a threshold potential V_{th},

$$r = \frac{(V_{ss} - V_{th})\Theta(V_{ss} - V_{th})}{\tau(V_{th} - V_{reset})}, \qquad (1)$$

where τ is an arbitrary constant, although in many models it corresponds to the membrane time

constant, and $\Theta(x)$ is a step function that takes the value 1 if $x > 0$ and zero otherwise.

Equation 1 gives the firing rate in terms of an input current, or equivalently the effective steady-state potential it produces. This formula is valid in the absence of "noise", which means non-variable synaptic input. This result should be extended to the case where this variable input causes fluctuations in the membrane potential. The magnitude of these fluctuations is characterized by their standard deviation denoted by σ_V. It is well-known that such fluctuations "soften" the threshold present in Eq. 1. In other words, when its membrane potential fluctuates, a neuron can fire even when the steady-state potential V_{ss} is less than the threshold potential V_{th}. To account for this effect, the Θ function should be "softened" in Eq. 1. The function required for this purpose must satisfy a number of conditions. First, it should go to 0 when $(V_{ss} - V_{th})/\sigma_V \ll 0$ because in this limit the noise level is insufficient to make the neuron fire. Second, it should go to 1 when $(V_{ss} - V_{th})/\sigma_V \gg 0$ because over this range the noise is irrelevant. Third, if the neuron is to fire when $V_{ss} = V_{th}$, the factor that replaces the Θ function in Eq. 1 must grow without bound proportional to $1/(V_{ss} - V_{th})$ near the point where $V_{ss} = V_{th}$. Finally, this function should approach a Θ function in the limit of no noise, $\sigma_V \to 0$.

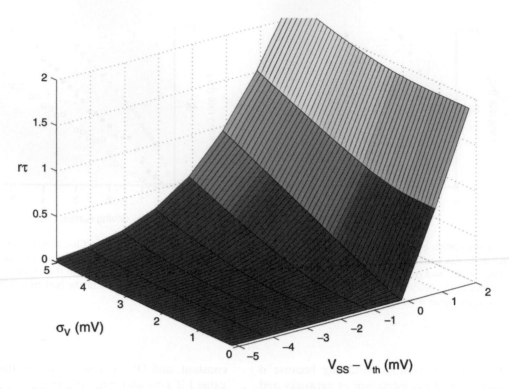

Fig. 4. The firing of Eq. 3 times the constant τ plotted as a function of the steady-state voltage minus the threshold voltage and the standard deviation of the membrane potential fluctuations.

If one sticks to using standard functions, it is clear that the replacement one wants to make in order to satisfy these conditions is

$$\Theta(V_{ss} - V_{th}) \rightarrow \frac{1}{1 - \exp\left(-a(V_{ss} - V_{th})/\sigma_V\right)},$$

$$(2)$$

where a is a constant parameter. Making this replacement in Eq. 1 leads to the functional form proposed for describing how the firing rate in the presence of variable input depends on both the mean steady-state potential and the standard deviation of the membrane potential,

$$r = \frac{(V_{ss} - V_{th})}{\tau(V_{th} - V_{reset})\left(1 - \exp(-a(V_{ss} - V_{th})/\sigma_V)\right)}.$$

$$(3)$$

This formula, suggested as a simpler alternative for an exact expression for the firing rate of an integrate-and-fire model neuron receiving a white noise input (Ricciardi, 1977; Tuckwell, 1988), works quite well in all the cases where it has been tried. For example, the solid lines in Fig. 1 were generated using Eq. 3. Figure 4, displays how the firing rate given by this formula depends on the steady-state membrane potential and membrane potential variance over a range of values.

Discussion

High levels of highly variable synaptic input are a distinctive and puzzling feature of cortical circuitry. Previous work has treated this input purely as a source of noise and response variance. The results reported show that, in real cortical neurons, high levels of synaptic input can produce a more interesting effect, modulating the gain of neuronal responses.

Given the high levels of synaptic activity in cortical circuitry, modulatory effects are inevitable, so it is important to characterize them fully and to understand their roles in cortical processing. We suggest Eq. 3 as one such compact and useful description.

We propose that the driving and modulatory inputs that Sherman and Guillery (1998) suggested neurons in cortical circuits receive are not distinguished anatomically, they are distinguished functionally. In the present study both classes of inputs operate through ordinary AMPA- and GABA-mediated fast, ionotropic conductances, which allows modulatory inputs to be as specific and rapid as driving inputs. Driving inputs to the neuron are carried along excitatory and inhibitory afferents that operate in an opposing, push–pull manner (Anderson et al., 2000b). Modulatory inputs consist of excitatory and inhibitory afferents in a balanced configuration (Shadlen and Newsome, 1994, 1998; Troyer and Miller, 1997) that produces little net drive to the neuron. If the balance between the excitatory and inhibitory components is modified, this produces an additive or subtractive shift in the responsiveness of the neuron, corresponding to conventional excitation and inhibition. If the excitatory and inhibitory components are varied in parallel, maintaining the balance between excitation and inhibition, this produces a multiplicative or divisive modulation in the gain or sensitivity of the neuronal response. Together, these two forms of response modulation provide a powerful mechanism for modifying and switching network function. Furthermore, specific excitatory afferents can rapidly switch from one type to the other by changing their correlation with associated inhibitory inputs.

Acknowledgments

This research was supported by National Science Foundation Grant IBN-0235463.

References

Andersen, R.A. and Mountcastle, V.B. (1983) The influence of the angle of gaze upon the excitability of light-sensitive neurons of the posterior parietal cortex. J. Neurosci., 3: 532–548.

Andersen, R.A., Essick, G.K. and Siegel, R.M. (1985) Encoding of spatial location by posterior parietal neurons. Science, 230: 450–458.

Anderson, J.S., Lampl, I., Gillespie, D.C. and Ferster, D. (2000a) The contribution of noise to contrast invariance of orientation tuning in cat visual cortex. Science, 290: 1968–1972.

Anderson, J.S., Carandini, M. and Ferster, D. (2000b) Orientation tuning of input conductance, excitation, and inhibition in cat primary visual cortex. J. Neurophysiol., 84: 909–926.

Bernander, O., Douglas, R.J., Martin, K.A.C. and Koch, C. (1991) Synaptic background activity influences spatiotemporal integration in single pyramidal cells. Proc. Natl. Acad. Sci. USA, 88: 11569–11573.

Borg-Graham, L.J., Monier, C. and Fregnac, Y. (1998) Visual input evoles transient and strong shunting inhibition in visual cortical neurons. Nature, 393: 369–372.

Burns, B.D. and Webb, A.C. (1976) The spontaneous activity of neurones in the cat's visual cortex. Proc. R. Soc. Lond. B. Biol. Sci., 194: 211–223.

Carandini, M. and Heeger, D. (1994) Summation and division by neurons in primate visual cortex. Science, 264: 1333–1336.

Carrandini, M., Heeger, D.J. and Movshon, J.A. (1997) Linearity and normalization in simple cells of the macaque primary visual cortex. J. Neurosci., 17: 8621–8644.

Chance, F.S., Abbott, L.F. and Reyes, A.D. (2002) Gain modulation from background synaptic input. Neuron, 35: 773–782.

Collins, J.J., Imhoff, T.T. and Grigg, P. (1996) Noise-enhanced information transmission in rat SA1 cutaneous mechanoreceptors via aperiodic stochastic resonance. J. Neurophysiol., 76: 642–645.

Connor, C.E., Gallant, J.L., Preddie, D.C. and Van Essen, D.C. (1996) Responses in area V4 depend on the spatial relationship between stimulus and attention. J. Neurophysiol., 75: 1306–1308.

Connor, C.E., Gallant, J.L., Preddie, D.D. and Van Essen, D.C. (1997) Spacial attention effects in macaque area V4. J. Neurosci., 17: 3201–3214.

Dayan, P. and Abbott, L.F. (2001) Theoretical Neuroscience, MIT Press, Cambridge MA.

Dean, A.F. (1981) The variability of discharge of simple cells in the cat striat cortex. Exp. Brain. Res., 44: 437–440.

Destexhe, A. and Pare, D. (1999) Impact of network activity on the integrative properties of neocortical pyramidal neurons in vivo. J. Neurophysiol., 81: 1531–1547.

Destexhe, A., Rudolph, M., Fellous, J.-M. and Sejnowski, T.J. (2001) Fluctuating synaptic conductances recreate in vivo-like activity in neocortical neurons. Neurosci., 107: 13–24.

Doiron, B., Longtin, A., Berman, N. and Maler, L. (2001) Subtractive and divisive inhibition: effect of voltage-dependent inhibitory conductances and noise. Neural. Comp., 13: 227–248.

154

Douglass, J.K., Wilkens, L., Pantazelou, E. and Moss, F. (1993) Noise enhancement of information transfer in crayfish mechanoreceptors by stochastic resonance. Nature, 365: 337–340.

Gabbiani, F., Krapp, H.G. and Laurent, G. (1999) Computation of object approach by a wide-field, motion-sensitive neuron. J. Neurosci., 19: 1122–1141.

Gabbiani, F., Midtgaard, J. and Knopfel, T. (1994) Synaptic integration in a model of cerebellar granule cells. J. Neurophysiol., 72: 999–1009.

Hahnloser, R.H., Sarpeshkar, R., Mahowald, M.A., Douglas, R.J. and Seung, H.S. (2000) Digital selection and analogue amplification coexist in a cortex-inspired silicon circuit. Nature, 405: 947–951.

Heeger, D.J. (1992) Normalization of cell responses in cat striate cortex. Vis. Neurosci., 9: 181–198.

Heeger, D.J. (1993) Modeling simple-cell direction selectivity with normalized, half-squared, linear operators. J. Neurophysiol., 70: 1885–1898.

Hirsch, J.A., Alonso, J.-M., Reid, R.C. and Martinez, L.M. (1998) Synaptic integration in striate cortical simple cells. J. Neurosci., 18: 9517–9528.

Ho, N. and Destexhe, A. (2000) Synaptic background activity enhances the responsiveness of neocortical pyramidal neurons. J. Neurophysiol., 84: 1488–1496.

Holt, G.R. and Koch, C. (1997) Shunting inhibition does not have a divisive effect on firing rates. Neural. Comp., 9: 1001–1013.

Holt, G.R., Softky, W.R., Koch, C. and Douglas, R.J. (1996) Comparison of discharge variability in vitro and in vivo in cat visual cortex neurons. J. Neurophysiol., 75: 1806–1814.

Koch, C. (1998) Biophysics of Computation: Information Processing in Single Neurons, Oxford University Press, New York.

Koch, C. and Poggio, T. (1992) Multiplying with synapses and neurons. In: McKeena, T., Davis, J. and Zornetzer, S. (Eds.), Single Neuron Computation, Academic Press, Orlando Fl.

Koch, C. and Ullman, S. (1985) Shifts in selective visual attention: towards the underlying neural circuitry. Hum. Neurobiol., 4: 219–227.

Levin, J.E. and Miller, J.P. (1996) Broadband neural encoding in the cricket cercal sensory system enhanced by stochastic resonance. Nature, 380: 165–168.

Marder, E. and Calabrese, R.L. (1996) Principles of rhythmic motor pattern generation. Physiol. Rev., 76: 687–717.

McAdams, C.J. and Maunsell, J.H.R. (1999a) Effects of attention on orientation-tuning functions of single neurons in macaque cortical area V4. J. Neurosci., 19: 431–441.

McAdams, C.J. and Maunsell, J.H.R. (1999b) Effects of attention on the reliability of individual neurons in monkey visual cortex. Neuron, 23: 765–773.

Mel, B.W. (1993) Synaptic integration in an excitable dendritic tree. J. Neurophysiol., 70: 1086–1101.

Mel, B.W. and Koch, C. (1990) Sigma-pi learning: on radial basis functions and cortical associative learning. In: Touretzsky, D.S. (Ed.), Advances in Neural Information Processing Systems. Vol 2, Morgan Kaufmann, San Mateo CA.

Mitchell, S.J. and Silver, R.A. (2003) Shunting inhibition modulates neuronal gain during synaptic excitation. Neuron, 38: 433–443.

Murphy, B.K. and Miller, K.D. (2003) Multiplicative gain changes are induced by excitation or inhibition alone. J. Neurosci., 23: 10040–10051.

Nozaki, D., Collins, J.J. and Yamamoto, Y. (1999) Mechanism of stochastic resonance enhancement in neuronal models driven by 1/f noise. Phys. Rev., E60: 4637–4644.

Peña, J.L. and Konishi, M. (2001) Auditory spatial receptive fields created by multiplication. Science, 292: 249–252.

Pouget, A., Fisher, S.A. and Sejnowski, T.J. (1993) Egocentric spatial representation in early vision. J. Cogn. Neurosci., 5: 151–161.

Pouget, A. and Sejnowski, T.J. (1994) A neural model of the cortical representation of egocentric distance. Cereb. Cortex, 4: 314–329.

Pouget, A. and Sejnowski, T.J. (1997) Spatial transformations in the parietal cortex using basis functions. J. Cogn. Neurosci., 9: 222–237.

Prescott, S.A. and De Koninck, Y. (2003) Gain control of firing rate by shunting inhibition: roles of synaptic noise and dendritic saturation. Proc. Natl. Acad. Sci. USA, 100: 2076–2081.

Rapp, M., Yarom, Y. and Segev, I. (1992) The impact of parallel fiber background activity on the cable properties of cerebellar Purkinje cells. Neural. Comp., 4: 518–532.

Ricciardi, L.M. (1977) Diffusion Processes and Related Topics in Biology, Springer-Verlag, Berlin.

Salinas, E. and Abbott, L.F. (1995) Transfer of Coded Information from Sensory to Motor Networks. J. Neurosci., 15: 6461–6474.

Salinas, E. and Abbott, L.F. (1996) A model of multiplicative neural responses in parietal cortex. Proc. Natl. Acad. Sci. USA, 93: 11956–11961.

Salinas, E. and Abbott, L.F. (1997) Invariant visual responses from attentional gain fields. J. Neurophysiol., 77: 3267–3272.

Salinas, E. and Thier, P. (2000) Gain modulation: a major computation principle of the central nervous system. Neuron, 27: 15–21.

Schwartz, O. and Simoncelli, E.P. (2001a) Natural signal statistics and sensory gain control. Nat. Neurosci., 4: 819–825.

Schwartz, O. and Simoncelli, E.P. (2001b) Natural sound statisics and divisive normalization in the auditory system. In: Lean, T.K., Dietterich, T.G. and Tresp, V. (Eds.), Advances in Neural Information Processing Systems Vol. 13, MIT Press, Cambridge MA.

Shadlen, M.N. and Newsome, W.T. (1994) Noise, neural codes and cortical organization. Curr. Op. Neurobiol., 4: 569–579.

Shadlen, M.N. and Newsome, W.T. (1998) The variable discharge of cortical neurons: implications for connectivity, computation, and information coding. J. Neurosci., 18: 3870–3896.

Shelley, M., McLaughlin, D., Shapley, R. and Wielaard, J. (2002) States of high conductance in a large-scale model of the visual cortex. J. Computational Neurosci., 13: 93–109.

Sherman, S.M. and Guillery, R.W. (1998) On the actions that one nerve cell can have on another: distinguishing "drivers" from "modulators". Proc. Natl. Acad. Sci. USA, 95: 7121–7126.

Simoncelli, E.P. and Schwartz, O. (1999) Modeling surround suppression in V! neurons with a statistically-derived normalization model. In: Kearns, M.S., Solla, S.A. and Cohn, D.A. (Eds.), Advances in Neural Information Processing Systems Vol. 11, MIT Press, Cambridge MA.

Softky, W.R. and Koch, C. (1992) Cortical cells should spike regularly but do not. Neural. Comp., 4: 643–646.

Softky, W.R. and Koch, C. (1994) The highly irregular firing of cortical cells is inconsistent with temporal integration of random EPSPs. J. Neurosci., 13: 334–350.

Srinivasan, M.V. and Bernard, G.D. (1976) A proposed mechanism for the multiplication of neural signals. Biol. Cybern., 21: 227–236.

Stevens, C.F. and Zador, A.M. (1998) Input synchrony and the irregular firing of cortical neurons. Nat. Neurosci., 3: 210–217.

Tiesinga, P.H.E., Jose, J.V. and Sejnowski, T.J. (2001) Comparison of current-driven and conductance-driven neocortical model neurons with Hodgkin-Huxley voltage-gated channels. Phys. Rev., E62: 8413–8419.

Tolhurst, D.J. and Heeger, D.J. (1997) Contrast normalization and a linear model for the directional selectivity of simple cells in cat striate cortex. Vis. Neurosci., 14: 19–25.

Treue, S. and Martínez-Trujillo, J.C. (1999) Feature-based attention influences motion processing gain in macaque visual cortex. Nature, 399: 575–579.

Trotter, Y. and Celebrini, S. (1999) Gaze direction contrls response gain in primary visual-cortex neurons. Nature, 398: 239–242.

Troyer, T.W. and Miller, K.D. (1997) Physiological gain leads to high ISI variability in a simple model of a cortical regular spiking cell. Neural. Comput., 9: 971–983.

Tsodyks, M. and Sejnowski, T.J. (1995) Rapid switching in balanced cortical network models. Network, 6: 1–14.

Tuckwell, H.C. (1988) Introduction to Theoretical Neurobiology, Cambridge University Press, Cambridge, UK.

van Vreeswijk, C. and Sompolinsky, H. (1996) Chaos in neuronal networks with balanced excitatory and inhibitory activity. Science, 274: 1724–1726.

Weyland, T.G. and Malpeli, J.G. (1993) Responses of neurons in primary visual cortex are modulated by eye position. J. Neurophysiol., 69: 2258–2260.

Wilson, H.R. and Cowan, J.D. (1972) Excitatory and inhibitory interactions in localized poulations of model neurons. Biophys. J., 12: 1–24.

Zipser, D. and Andersen, R.A. (1988) A back-propagation programmed network that simulates response properties of a subset of posterior parietal neurons. Nature, 331: 679–684.

Progress in Brain Research, Vol. 149
ISSN 0079-6123

CHAPTER 12

Neural mechanisms underlying target selection with saccadic eye movements

Peter H. Schiller* and Edward J. Tehovnik

*Department of Brain and Cognitive Sciences, Massachusetts Institute of Technology,
77 Massachusetts Avenue, E25-634, Cambridge, MA 02139, USA*

Abstract: In exploring the visual scene we make about three saccadic eye movements per second. During each fixation, in addition to analyzing the object at which we are looking, a decision has to be made as to where to look next. Although we perform this task with the greatest of ease, the computations to perform the task are complex and involve numerous brain structures. We have applied several investigative tools that include single-cell recordings, microstimulation, pharmacological manipulations and lesions to learn more about the neural control of visually guided eye saccadic movements. Electrical stimulation of the superior colliculus (SC), areas V1 and V2, the lateral intraparietal sulcus (LIP), the frontal eye fields (FEF) and the medial eye fields (MEF) produces saccadic eye movements at low current levels. After ablation of the SC, electrical microstimulation of V1, V2, and LIP no longer elicits saccadic eye movements whereas stimulation of the FEF and MEF continues to be effective. Ablation of the SC but not of the FEF eliminates short-latency saccadic eye movements to visual targets called "express saccades," whereas lesions of the FEF selectively interfere with target selection. Bilateral removal of both the SC and the FEF causes major, long lasting deficits: all visually elicited saccadic eye movements are eliminated. In intact monkeys, subthreshold electrical microstimulation of the FEF and MEF as well as the lower layers of V1 and V2 and of some subregions of LIP greatly facilitates the choice of targets presented in the receptive fields of the stimulated neurons. By contrast, stimulation of the upper layers of V1 and V2 and other sub-regions of LIP produces a dramatic interference in target selection. Examination of the role of inhibitory circuits in eye-movement generation reveals that local infusion of muscimol, a GABA (gamma-aminobutyric acid) agonist, or bicuculline, a GABA antagonist, interferes with target selection in V1. On the other hand, infusion of bicuculline into the FEF produces facilitation in target choice and irrepressible saccades. It appears therefore that inhibitory circuits play a central role in visual analysis in V1 and in the generation of saccadic eye movements in the FEF. It is proposed that two major streams can be discerned in visually guided eye-movement control, the posterior from occipital and parietal cortex that reaches the brainstem via the SC and the anterior from the FEF and MEF that has direct access to the brainstem oculomotor centers.

Introduction

We make about three saccadic eye movements per second, more than 170,000 a day and about five billion in an average lifetime. During the 200–500 ms duration fixations that intervene between successive saccades, the eyes are stationary in the orbit only when neither the head nor the object viewed is in motion. If there is motion, the object remains on the fovea by virtue of smooth-pursuit tracking. The neural systems involved in the control of visually guided saccadic eye movements are numerous and

*Corresponding author. Tel.: +1-617-253-5754; Fax: +1-617-253-8943; E-mail: phschill@mit.edu

DOI: 10.1016/S0079-6123(05)49012-3

complex yet tremendously robust. Seldom does one hear about individuals complaining at the end of the day of having become exhausted making eye movements.

Each eye is moved around in the orbit with six extraocular muscles (see Schiller, 1998). Four of these are the recti muscles, the medial, lateral, superior and inferior. Each opponent pair may be thought of as moving the eyes along two prime axes, the horizontal and the vertical. Diagonal eye movements are brought about by the combined action of the four recti muscles. The remaining two muscles, the superior and inferior obliques, participate mostly in inducing rotatory motion, the kind of motion that comes into play when the head is tilted.

Three sets of cranial nuclei contain the neurons that innervate the six extraocular muscles of each eye through the third, fourth and sixth cranial nerves: the oculomotor nuclei whose neurons innervate all the muscles except for the lateral rectus and the superior oblique, the trochlear nucleus whose neurons innervate the superior oblique, and

the abducens nucleus whose neurons innervate the lateral rectus.

The generation of visually guided saccadic eye movements involves numerous brain areas from which signals are sent down to the oculomotor complex in the brainstem. One of the methods used to determine the relevance of various brain structures in eye-movement control is electrical microstimulation. It has now been established that saccadic eye movements can be elicited at low current levels from quite a number of brain sites (Schiller, 1984; Tehovnik et al., 2000; Schiller and Tehovnik, 2001); these include, in addition to the oculomotor complex, the superior colliculus (SC) of the midbrain, and the cortical areas V1, V2, the lateral intraparietal sulcus (LIP), the frontal eye fields (FEF), and the medial eye fields (MEF). Electrical stimulation has also contributed to understanding the coding operations of these areas. Stimulation of a specific site within the SC, V1, V2, LIP, and the FEF produces constant vector saccades in which the direction and amplitude of the

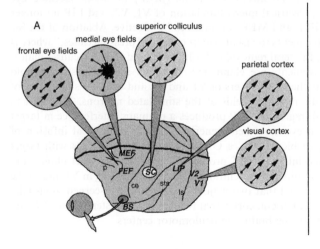 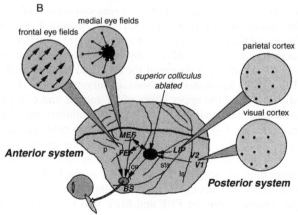

Electrical stimulation in intact monkey   Electrical stimulation after SC ablation

Fig. 1. A: Eye movements elicited from five brain areas in the rhesus monkey, the superior colliculus (SC), area V1, the lateral intraparietal sulcus in parietal cortex (LIP), the frontal eye fields (FEF), and the medial eye fields (MEF). Within all areas but the MEF electrical stimulation produces constant vector saccades. The vector produced depends on the subregion stimulated in these areas. In the MEF electrical stimulation elicits saccades that move the eyes to a terminal zone defined as an invariant orbital position. Different regions represent different orbital positions. B: The effects of cortical electrical stimulation after ablation of the SC. Stimulation of the FEF and MEF is still effective, but stimulation of the parietal and visual cortices no longer elicits saccadic eye movements. The findings have lead to the hypothesis that there are two major systems for visually guided saccadic eye movement generation, the anterior and the posterior. The posterior system reaches the brainstem oculomotor complex through the SC whereas the anterior system has direct access to the brainstem.

saccade produced is the same irrespective of the initial position of the eye in orbit. This state of affairs is depicted in Fig. 1A. The vector produced depends on where within each of these structures one stimulates. In the left hemisphere these structures code rightward vectors and in the right hemisphere leftward vectors. Figure 1 furthermore illustrates, that the MEF carries a different kind of code. Stimulation of this area produces saccades that take the eyes to a particular orbital location (Schlag and Schlag-Rey, 1987; Tehovnik and Lee, 1993). Different subregions of the MEF code different orbital positions. Thus this area carries a "place code."

How do the signals generated in these cortical areas reach the brainstem oculomotor centers? There is still a debate about this. One possibility is that all these signals reach the brainstem through the SC (Hanes and Wurtz, 2001). In other words, according to this hypothesis the SC is the gateway to the brainstem for visually triggered saccadic eye movements. An alternative hypothesis is that some of these areas bypass the SC and make direct connections to the brainstem oculomotor complex. Anatomical studies show that the FEF and MEF do make such direct connections (Leichnetz, 1981; Huerta and Kaas, 1990). In previous studies, it was shown that when the SC is ablated, as depicted in Fig. 1B, electrical stimulation of the FEF and MEF can still elicit saccadic eye movements whereas electrical stimulation of the posterior cortex no longer does so (Schiller, 1977; Keating et al., 1983; Tehovnik et al., 1994).

On the basis of these observations it is suggested that the control of visually guided eye movements involves two major systems, the anterior and the posterior (Schiller, 1998). The posterior system reaches the brainstem oculomotor complex through the SC, whereas the anterior system has direct access to the brainstem. The two systems interconnect, of course, enabling the organism to make proper, coordinated saccadic eye movements.

In this study further evidence supporting the two streams hypothesis is presented and inferences are made about how different cortical areas mediate eye-movement control. To do so evidence from three kinds of studies is presented: the effects of selective ablations, the effects of electrical microstimulation, and the effects of infusing various pharmacological agents into some of these areas.

Ablation studies

This section describes the effects of lesions made to the SC, the FEF, and the MEF. When any one of these areas is ablated either unilaterally or bilaterally only relatively subtle deficits are observed after a few weeks of recovery. Examination of the behavior of such animals fails to reveal obvious deficits. One needs to turn to more careful assessments that necessitate the recording of eye movements and psychophysical measurements. After SC lesions it has been reported that monkeys make fewer spontaneous eye movements and make hypometric saccades with decreased saccadic velocities (Schiller, 1998). A few weeks after FEF or MEF lesions, and even after paired FEF and MEF lesions there are no obvious effects on saccadic frequencies and velocities.

It has been established that one of the more dramatic effects that occurs after unilateral SC lesions is a long-term deficit in the generation of express saccades in monkeys (Schiller et al., 1987). Fischer and Boch (1983) had discovered that the latency distribution of saccades made to single targets becomes bimodal after a period of training. They termed the first mode "express saccades." The frequency with which express saccades are generated is increased when a gap is placed between the dousing of the fixation spot and the appearance of the single target. An example of such a bimodal distribution of saccadic latencies obtained in a monkey is shown in the top panel of Fig. 2A. After unilateral ablation of the SC, as shown in the second set of panels in Fig. 2B, express saccades are no longer made for the ablated representation but continue to be evident for the intact side. Not only are express saccades absent for the ablated representation, there is also an increased latency for regular saccades. The data shown were collected 70 days after the lesion. When tested even a year later, no express saccades were generated. By contrast, as shown in the bottom set of panels of Fig. 2C, after unilateral FEF lesions express saccades were still generated. Not shown is the fact that the bimodal distribution of saccades is unaffected

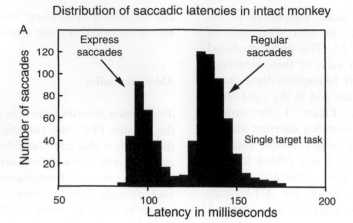

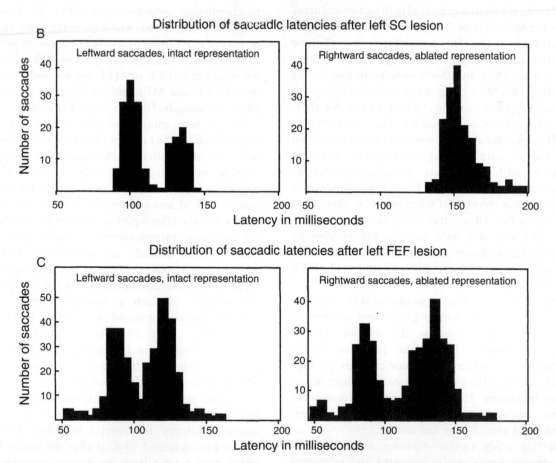

Fig. 2. The distribution of saccadic latencies made to single visual targets. A: Intact monkey. B: The distribution of leftward and rightward saccadic latencies 70 days after left SC ablation. Express saccades are no longer made into the ablated representation and regular saccadic latencies are also longer than to the intact representation. C: The distribution of saccadic latencies after left FEF lesion. Express saccades are generated toward both the intact and ablated representations.

by MEF lesions as well as paired FEF and MEF lesions (Schiller et al., 1987; Schiller, 1998).

These findings suggest therefore that the *posterior system* that has access to the brainstem through the SC plays an important role in the generation of rapid, short-latency saccadic eye movements.

Several studies have shown that the frontal cortex, in particular the FEF, plays a significant role in target selection (Schiller and Chou, 1998; Schall and Thompson, 1999; Schiller and Tehovnik, 2001). Every time we move our eyes to a new target location in a natural setting, numerous stimuli impinge on the retina. The ensuing eye movement can of course be made to only one of these targets. One of the central tasks in eye-movement control is to select that target and to then generate an accurate saccade to it. This is not a trivial task. This fact is highlighted by the observation that when two or more sites in the SC or the FEF are electrically stimulated simultaneously, the saccade generated is a vector average of the individually triggered sites (Robinson, 1972; Schiller et al., 1979b). Yet when visual targets are placed at the receptive field of cells at these same sites, the organism will select one target and make an accurate eye movement to it. Accurate execution of the saccade to one target fails only when the visual targets in the scene are placed very close to each other (Chou et al., 1999). It appears therefore that a selection process occurs that "accepts" some sites and "rejects" others for the generation of an accurate saccadic eye movement that probably occurs as a result of the interplay between excitatory and inhibitory circuits which are not activated in an integrated fashion with electrical stimulation. The neural systems involved in this are described in more detail in the last section of this review.

To examine target selection processes we used a paradigm in which we present two targets after monkeys fixate a central fixation spot as depicted in Fig. 3A. The two targets are presented with varied temporal asynchronies. When one does this with the targets placed with a 90° angular separation, two results are noteworthy, as shown by the eye-movement records in this top panel. The first is that this monkey made fairly accurate saccades to one or the other target. Only a few vector averaged saccades are evident. The second is that when the two targets were presented simultaneously, the monkey chose one or the other of the targets with roughly equal probability. On the other hand, when there was a temporal asynchrony between the targets (shown are 34 ms asynchronies) the monkey made most of his eye movements to the target that had appeared first.

We can now proceed to analyse how unilateral FEF lesions alter the target selection process. Two sets of data are shown in Fig. 3. In Fig. 3B eye movement records are shown once again, but in this case using targets that have a smaller angular separation of 40°. The upper set of eye-movement records in Fig. 3B shows the eye movements made in the intact monkey. When the two targets are simultaneous, in addition to selecting one or the other of the targets accurately, several vector averaged saccades are also evident. The lower panel shows what happens after unilateral left FEF lesions. Equal probability choice of the two targets now occurs when there is a 100 ms temporal offset between them, with the first target in the affected hemifield. This is also the point at which there is the highest incidence of vector averaged saccades. One may say, therefore, that the information necessary to generate eye movements arrives in the brainstem from the two hemsipheres with a 100 ms delay.

This inference is supported further by examining how targets are selected as a function of the temporal asynchrony between them after unilateral FEF and MEF lesions, when the targets are presented with an angular separation of 90° that minimizes vector averaging. These data appear in Fig. 3C. These data show that after left FEF lesions there is a dramatic shift in the equal probability point. Two weeks after the lesions the target in the affected hemifield has to be presented 116 ms before the target appearing in the intact field to obtain equal probability choice. This then recovers gradually over time, but even four years later there is a sizable deficit.

By contrast, when the same experiment is performed after a MEF lesion, there is only a small deficit that recovers within four months. The curves to the right of Fig. 3C demonstrate this.

The last question being addressed regarding lesion studies is this: what happens when instead of single lesions to the SC or the FEF both of these areas are removed bilaterally? What happens is dramatic — after such paired lesions monkeys no longer make

162

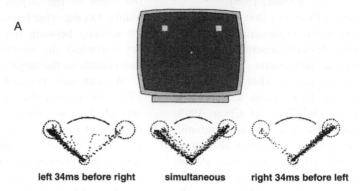

Eye movements of intact monkey made to paired targets presented
with varied asynchronies using 90 degree angular separation

A

left 34ms before right   **simultaneous**   **right 34ms before left**

Eye movements made to paired targets in intact and FEF ablated monkey
presented with varied asynchronies using 40 degree angular separation

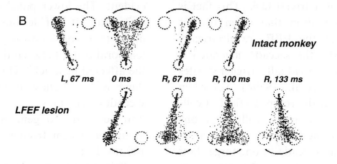

B

Intact monkey

L, 67 ms   *0 ms*   *R, 67 ms*   *R, 100 ms*   *R, 133 ms*

LFEF lesion

C

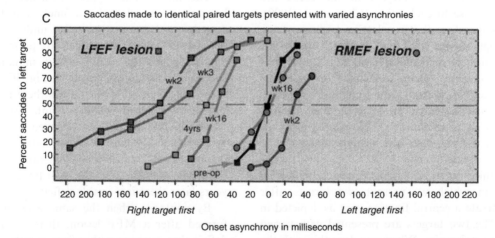

Saccades made to identical paired targets presented with varied asynchronies

Percent saccades to left target

LFEF lesion ■   RMEF lesion ○

wk2   wk3
wk16   wk16
4yrs   wk2
pre-op

Right target first   Left target first

Onset asynchrony in milliseconds

Fig. 3. The two-target task and eye movement records for three temporal asynchronies, left target onset 34 ms before right target onset, simultaneous appearance, right target onset 34 ms before left target onset. B: Records of saccadic eye movements made to targets separated by 40 angular degrees. In intact monkey, vector averaged saccades occur most frequently when the two targets are simultaneous. After left FEF lesion vector averaged saccades are most frequent when the target in the representation of the ablated FEF appears 100 ms prior to the target in the intact representation. C: Performance on the two-target task various times after left FEF and right MEF lesions. Targets were presented with a 90° angular separation. Deficits after the FEF lesion were long lasting whereas deficits after the MEF lesion recovered in four months.

any visually guided saccadic eye movements (Schiller et al., 1980).

These observations made on the basis of stimulation and lesion studies support our contention that there are two major systems involved in visually guided saccadic eye movement control — the anterior and the posterior. The *posterior system* seems to play an important role in the generation of rapid, short latency saccadic eye movements whereas the *anterior system* plays an important role in target selection. A great deal of additional work is required to more clearly specify what aspects of eye movements these two systems control and how these two systems interact.

The influence of electrical microstimulation on visual target selection

In the quest to learn more about the role various brain areas play in visually guided saccadic eye movements, we have recently initiated a series of studies in which we examine how visual target selection can be influenced by electrical microstimulation. So far we have studied six areas: V1, V2, V4, LIP, FEF, MEF.

The experimental procedures we used in these studies are described in Fig. 4. The top left panel shows the brain structures into which microelectrodes have been placed through which first single-cell activity is recoded followed by the administration of electrical stimulation. Panels 1–5 describe the procedure of the experiments. While recording in areas where single cells have visual receptive fields, first their location is mapped out. Monkeys have been trained to maintain fixation when the fixation spot is red in color. While fixating, the receptive field is mapped by drifting a bar of light across the visual field whose size, orientation and distance of travel can be controlled. This is depicted in panel 1. The next step is to electrically stimulate the neurons at the tip of the electrode. This elicits a saccade that shifts the center of gaze into the receptive field of the stimulated neurons. By varying current levels, the thresholds for triggering a saccade are established. Next, a visual stimulus is placed into the receptive field of the stimulated neurons, as shown in panel 3 of Fig. 4, that elicits the same vector saccade as does the electrical stimulation. This assures that everything is lined up correctly for the experiment.

The next step, as shown in panel 4 of Fig. 4, is to present two targets in the visual field with one of them in the receptive field of the neurons at the tip of the electrode. The two targets are presented with various temporal asynchronies. On some trials electrical stimulation is delivered concurrently with the visual stimulus in the receptive field. Electrical stimulation is delivered 30 ms after visual stimulus onset as it takes approximately this time for the signal impinging on the receptors to arrive in the cortex. Stimulations parameters have most commonly been set at 200 Hz for 80 ms.

The procedure shown in panel 5 is described in the next section.

Figure 5 shows representative data obtained in V1, LIP, MEF, and FEF on the two-target task. Plotted are curves showing the percent choice for the target appearing in the receptive field of the stimulated neurons as a function of the temporal asynchrony between the two targets. Separate curves are shown for the no stimulation condition and for stimulation at various current levels.

Panel A in Fig. 5 shows the effects of delivering electrical stimulation in the upper layers of V1 concurrently with visual target presentation using three current levels, 15, 20, and 25 μA. The stimulation produced major *interference* — the visual target appearing in the receptive fields of the stimulated neurons was chosen less frequently than the other target. Increasing current levels increased the level of interference. The percent values shown in the figure after the current level indicate that electrical stimulation in the absence of any visual target did not elicit a saccade under any of the conditions.

Panel B in Fig. 5 shows what happens when the lower layers of V1 are stimulated. Here stimulation produced *facilitation* — the target in the receptive field of the stimulated neurons was chosen with a higher probability when paired with electrical stimulation. In layer five of V1 a significant portion of the neurons project to the SC. The facilitation observed by stimulating this region may be due to the activation of the colliculus via the corticotectal cells (Finlay et al., 1976).

Electrical stimulation in V2 produced results quite similar to those of V1. In the upper layers *interference* was obtained and in the lower layers, *facilitation*. In contrast with the results obtained in V1 and

Experimental procedures

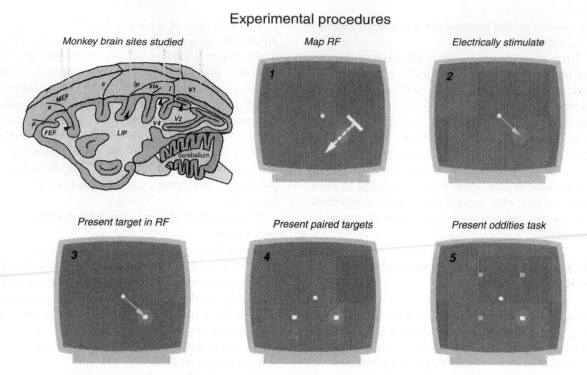

Monkey brain sites studied *Map RF* *Electrically stimulate*

Present target in RF *Present paired targets* *Present oddities task*

Fig. 4. Experimental methods: Top left figure shows monkey brain and the six areas studied. Areas V1, V2, V4, the lateral intraparietal sulcus (LIP) the frontal eye fields (FEF) and the medial eye fields (MEF). ce, central sulcus; p, principal sulcus; ip, intraparietal sulcus; sts, superior temporal sulcus; ls, lunate sulcus. The steps taken in experimental sessions were: 1. The receptive field (RF) of the neurons recorded from was mapped. 2. The motor field (MF) was established by eliciting saccadic eye movements with electrical stimulation. 3. One target was then placed into the RF/MF that elicited saccades with the same vector. 4. Two targets were presented with varied temporal asynchronies with one of them placed into the RF/MF. 5. Four targets were presented one of which was different from the others in luminance. The luminance, size, wavelength and shape of the three identical distracters could be systematically varied. Data were collected pairing electrical stimulation with target presentation and examining the effects of infusing pharmacological agents.

V2, electrical stimulation of area V4 was ineffective. Even at high current levels (150 μA) the stimulation did not produce an effect.

Panels C and D in Fig. 5 show results obtained when two sites in LIP were stimulated. At one of these sites the stimulation produced *facilitation* whereas at the other site it produced *interference*. It is not certain whether these effects are laminar or columnar, but the idea that it is columnar is favored. One reason for this is that in LIP yet another effect has been found, which occurred when neurons were stimulated that discharge vigorously while the animal maintains fixation. Such neurons, which are found in batches, have been reported previously by Motter and Mountcastle (1981). They discharge during fixation irrespective of gaze angle. Electrical stimulation in

LIP at these sites prolongs fixation time as made evident by the increased latencies with which saccades are initiated.

Panels E and F show the effects of stimulation the MEF and FEF. In both areas stimulation consistently produced *facilitation*.

Previous work in the MEF (Tehovnik and Lee, 1993) resulted in the observation of an additional effect — when the fixation spot was placed into the terminal zone of the stimulated neurons, electrical stimulation delayed saccade generation. Thus both in the MEF and in the fixation cell regions of LIP stimulation prolonged fixation time. This suggests that these areas may play a role in the decision process involved in how long to look at a stimulus before initiating the next saccade. The difference between the

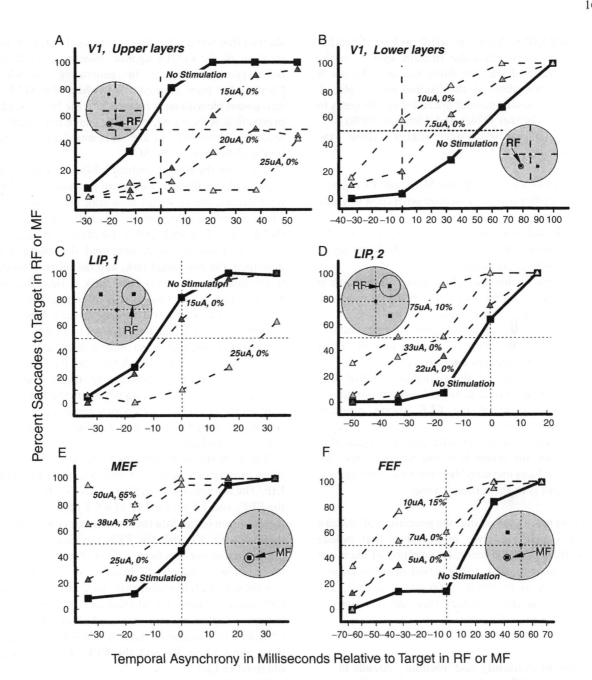

Fig. 5. The effects of electrical stimulation of area V1, the lateral intraparietal sulcus (LIP), the medial eye fields (MEF) and the frontal eye fields (FEF) on target selection using the two-target task. Plotted are curves showing the probability with which targets presented in the receptive field are chosen as a function of the temporal asynchrony of the two targets and the current of electrical stimulation used. The current levels used are indicated for each curve. The percent values that follow indicate the percent of saccades generated to electrical stimulation when it was administered in the absence of any target. The insets show the location of the receptive fields and the layout of the targets (RF, receptive field; MF, motor field). A: Stimulation of the upper layers of V1 produces interference. B: Stimulation of the lower layers of V1 produces facilitation. C: In some regions of LIP stimulation produces interference. D: In other regions of LIP facilitation is produced by electrical stimulation. E: In the MEF stimulation produces facilitation. F: In the FEF stimulation produces facilitation.

MEF and LIP is that in the MEF prolonged fixation time arises only when the fixation spot is in the terminal zone of the stimulated neurons whereas in LIP it occurs wherever the fixation spot is placed. Whether termination zones are coded in LIP needs to be explored further (Thier and Andersen, 1998)

These microstimulation studies show the following:

(1) Areas V1, V2, LIP, the MEF, and FEF play a significant role in saccade generation to visual targets.

(2) Stimulation of the upper of V1 and V2 produces *interference* and of the lower layers produces *facilitation*.

(3) Area V4 does not seem to play a direct role in saccade initiation or in target selection with saccadic eye movements.

(4) Stimulation of some regions of LIP produces *facilitation* whereas stimulation of other regions produces *interference*.

(5) Stimulation of those regions of LIP that contain fixation cells prolongs fixation time.

(6) Stimulation of the FEF always produces *facilitation*.

(7) Stimulation of the MEF produces facilitation when the target is in the terminal zone and produces increased fixation time when fixation spot is in the terminal zone.

These result suggest that the generation of saccadic eye movements involves several steps that include (a) analysis of visual scene, (b) selection of the target to be looked at next, (c) rejection of other targets, (d) decision as to when to initiate a saccade, and (e) computing the trajectory (size and direction) of an accurate saccadic vector.

The role of excitatory and inhibitory circuits in saccade generation

The fact that electrical stimulation can produce not only facilitation but also interference in some brain regions suggests saccade generation involves an interplay between excitatory and inhibitory neural circuits. This has already been shown to be the case in an elegant study by Hikosaka and Wurtz (1985). They showed that when inhibition is increased in the SC by infusion of the GABA agonist muscimol, monkeys have great difficulties in generating saccades. Conversely, they showed that when the GABA antagonist bicuculline is infused into the SC, saccade production is increased; monkeys make irrepressible saccades whose vectors are represented by the disinhibited neurons in the SC.

To study the role of cortical inhibitory circuits in vision and saccadic eye-movement generation, studies were carried out in which muscimol and bicuculline were infused into three areas: V1, LIP, and the FEF (Schiller and Tehovnik, 2003). To examine the effects of such infusions two tasks were used: the one already described, the two-target task, and the other, a visual discrimination task. This latter task is described in Fig. 4, panel 5. The task used is often referred to as the oddities task. Several targets (usually four) are presented — one of which is different from the others. The monkeys are trained to make a direct saccade to the odd target to be rewarded. One can then vary the degree of difference between the target and the distracters thereby generating psychometric functions that establish the animal's visual capacity along a number of tested parameters that include contrast, size, color, and shape.

Figure 6 shows performance on these two tasks when muscimol was infused into V1, the FEF, and LIP. The dosages used were 0.8 μL for V1, 0.5 μL for the FEF, and 1.5 μL for LIP of a 0.5 μg/μL solution. Examination of the data for the two-target task shows that in both V1 and the FEF muscimol infusion produced a major *interference* effect (Panels A and C): the target in the receptive fields of the infused neurons was chosen much less frequently after the infusion. In LIP, however, only a mild effect was obtained even though a higher volume was used (Panel E). With infusion levels similar to those at which major effects were obtained in V1 and the FEF, no effect was obtained in LIP.

Performance on the discrimination task was devastated when muscimol was infused into V1 (Panel B), but had only a small effect with FEF infusion (Panel D) and no significant effect in LIP (Panel F).

Figure 7 shows what happens when these same areas are infused with the GABA antagonist bicuculline. In V1 this agent, just like muscimol, produced major *interference* in target selection and disrupted

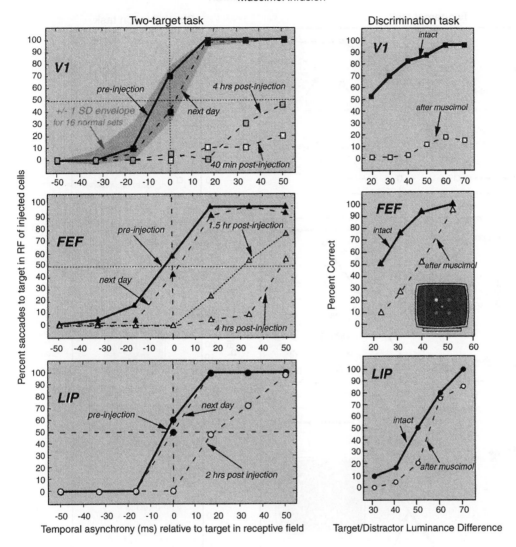

Fig. 6. The effects of infusing muscimol into areas V1, LIP and FEF on the two-target task and the discrimination task. Plotted on the left (Two-target task, A, C, and E) is the percent of time the target presented in the receptive and/or motor fields of the neurons was chosen as a function of the temporal asynchrony between the two targets. Muscimol injections in V1 were 0.8 μL, in the FEF 0.5 μL, and in LIP 1.5 μL of 0.5 μg/μL solution. Each data point shown in the graphs is based on a minimum of 20 and a maximum of 100 trials. The gray regions shown in the top two panels denote the ±1 standard deviation (SD) envelope collected for 16 normal sets of data (20 blocks each). Each block had 15 conditions consisting of 8 single targets presented at 4 target locations and 7 paired targets presented with various temporal asynchronies. On the right (Discrimination task, B, D, and F) the effects of muscimol infusion on the concurrently collected brightness discrimination task are shown. Inset in center panel shows the brightness discrimination task. The percent contrast difference between the target (bright stimulus) and the distracters was presented in a randomized order. The luminance of the background and the target was kept constant. In area V1 the muscimol infusion produced a significant loss in the ability to discriminate brightness differences. In the FEF and LIP the infusion produced only a mild deficit.

168

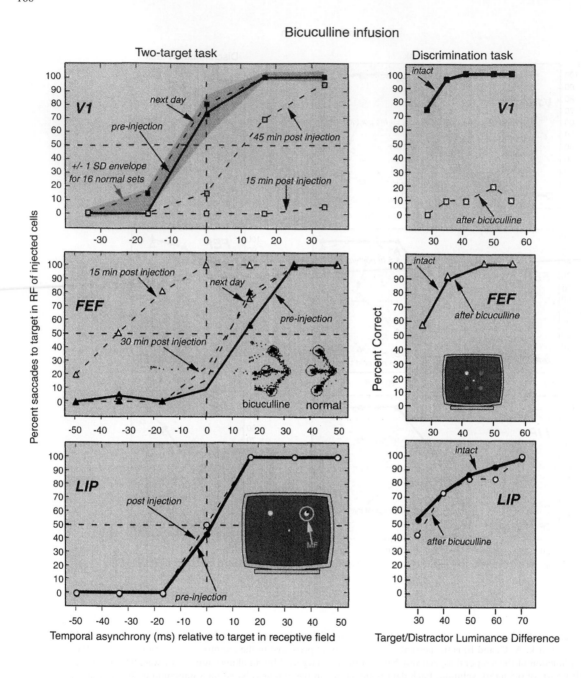

Fig. 7. The effects of infusing bicuculline into areas V1, LIP, and FEF on the two-target task and the discrimination task. On the left (Two-target task, A, C, and E) plotted is the percent of time the target presented in the receptive and/or motor fields of the neurons is chosen as a function of the temporal asynchrony between the two targets. Bicuculline injections in V1 were 0.5 μL, in the FEF 0.3 μL, and in LIP 0.4 μL of 1 μg/μL solution. In V1 the bicuculline infusion produced a major deficit. In the FEF the infusion produced facilitation and irrepressible saccades. In LIP the infusion was ineffective. On the right (Discrimination task, B, D, and F) the effects of bicuculline infusion on the concurrently collected brightness discrimination task are shown. In V1 the infusion caused a major deficit in visual discrimination whereas in the FEF and LIP the infusion had no effect on this task. Each data point is based on 20 to 100 trials.

visual discrimination (Panels A and B). By contrast, infusion of bicuculline into the FEF had a major *facilitatory* effect on the two-target task (Panel C). The inset showing the eye movements demonstrates that after the infusion the monkey made many irrepressible saccades. On the discrimination task performance was unaffected indicating that the monkey's ability to process visual information was not affected (Panel D). Lastly, infusion of bicuculline into LIP had no significant effect on either the two-target task or the discrimination task (Panel F).

These results suggest the following:

(1) In V1 inhibitory circuits play a central role in processing visual information such that activation or inactivation of this circuit disrupts target selection and visual analysis.
(2) In the FEF, inhibitory circuits play a central role in saccadic eye-movement generation. Increasing inhibition reduces saccade production, decreasing inhibition produces *facilitation* and irrepressible saccades. It appears therefore that the FEF and the SC, based on the work of Hikosaka and Wurtz (1985), use similar inhibitory mechanisms for the execution of saccadic eye movements. This reinforces the idea that two systems are used by the cerebral cortex to gain access to the saccade generator, one by way of the SC and the other by way of the frontal lobe.
(3) GABAergic inhibitory circuits do not play a direct role in saccadic eye movement generation in the LIP.

Discussion

The generation of visually guided saccadic eye movements involves a great many neural structures and is far more complex than has been realized. The production of each saccade necessitates the identification of objects in the visual scene during each fixation. This is followed by a selection process that picks out one object from many. Once picked, a coordinate system is utilized to produce an accurate saccadic eye movement to the intended target.

Our contention is that the networks controlling visually guided saccadic eye movements form two major systems: the anterior and the posterior. The posterior system is comprised of the visual pathways originating in the retina that pass through the lateral geniculate nucleus on the way to the visual cortex from where outputs stream to the superior colliculus and then to the brainstem oculomotor complex. This posterior system utilizes a vector code which computes predominantly a retinal error signal.

The anterior system of visually guided saccadic eye movements receives input from the occipital, parietal, and temporal cortices and is comprised of two subdivisions, one of which passes through the frontal eye fields and the other through the dorsomedial frontal cortex. The subdivision of which the frontal eye fields are a part also carries a vector code. In contrast, the subdivision that passes through the dorsomedial frontal cortex carries a place code. The posterior system, whose prime conduit to the brainstem is through the superior colliculus, plays an important role in the generation of rapid, reflex-like eye movements that enable the organism to respond quickly to suddenly appearing visual stimuli. In line with this view is the fact that express saccades are eliminated by lesions of the superior colliculus. The portion of the anterior subsystem that involves the frontal eye fields is believed to contribute to higher level eye-movement generation important for object selection and for planning sequences of eye movements. The portion of the anterior subsystem that includes the dorsomedial frontal cortex is believed to integrate information about the location of objects in space and also to play a role in hand–eye coordination as well as visuo-motor learning.

The essential structures and pathways involved in eliciting saccadic eye movements are laid out in Fig. 8. The visual information originating in the retina for eye-movement generation is processed through three major systems in the primate: the *midget*, the *parasol*, and the *w*. The *w* system is actually a grab-bag of several separate systems yet to be clarified. Some portions of the *w* system project directly to the SC; other portions project into the lateral geniculate nucleus of the thalamus (LGN) where they terminate predominantly in the intralaminar layers (Hendry and Yoshioka, 1994). In the monkey the midget system projects to the parvocellular layers and the parasol

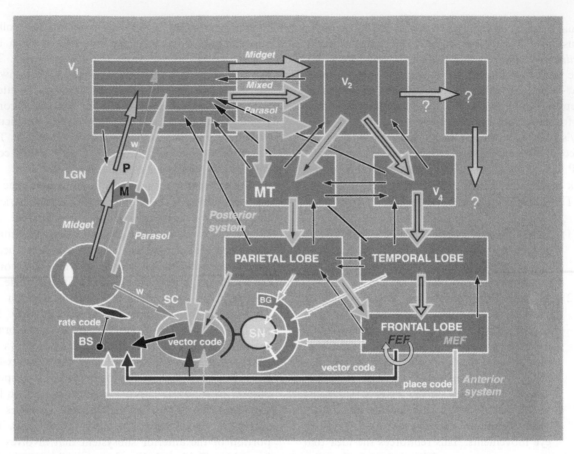

Fig. 8. The neural structures and circuitry involved in the generation of visually guided saccadic eye movements.

system to the magnocellular layers of the LGN. Ray Guillery has made major contributions elucidating the laminar organization of the LGN in the cat (Guillery, 1966, 1969).

In V1 the visual input from the LGN undergoes major reorganization. Here orientation and direction specificities become established. There is convergence of input from the two eyes, convergence of the ON and OFF systems, and partial convergence from the midget and parasol systems (Hubel and Wiesel, 1962; Schiller et al., 1976a,b,c; Schiller, 1982, 1995). The input from layer five of V1 to the superior colliculus is driven predominantly, if not exclusively, by the parasol system (Finlay et al., 1976). The inputs to MT appear to be dominated by the parasol system, whereas inputs to V4 are mixed (Maunsell, 1983). The inputs from posterior cortex to the SC form the posterior system for visually guided saccadic eye-

movement control. The anterior system, comprised predominantly of the FEF and MEF, that receives a mixed input from the midget and parasol channels, has direct access to the brain stem. So far two sets of inhibitory circuts have been identified that play a significant role in target selection and the execution of accurate saccadic eye movements. One of these involves the substantia nigra that makes inhibitory GABAergic connections with the superior colliculus (Hikosaka and Wurtz, 1985) and the other intrinsic inhibitory circuits in the frontal eye fields (Schiller and Tehovnik, 2003). These circuits make it evident that the generation of a saccade requires both excitatory and disinhibitory activity in these neural circuits. Further control of the cohesive and accurate generation of saccadic eye movements is accomplished by virtue of extensive feedback circuits that are indicated by the black arrows in Fig. 8.

Abbreviations

FEF	frontal eye fields
GABA	gamma-aminobutyric acid
LIP	lateral intraparietal sulcus
MEF	medial eye fields
SC	superior colliculus
V1	visual area 1 (striate cortex)
V2	visual area 2

Acknowledgments

This work was supported by the NIH, NEI EY08502 and EY00676. The authors thank Warren Slocum for his help.

References

Chou, I., Sommer, M.A. and Schiller, P.H. (1999) Vision Res., 39: 4200–4216.

Conway, J.L. and Schiller, P.H. (1983) J. Neurophysiol., 50: 1330–1342.

Ferrsra, V.P., Nealey, T.A. and Maunsell, J.H. (1992) Nature, 358: 756–761.

Finlay, B.L., Schiller, P.H. and Volman, S.F. (1976) J Neurophysiol., 39: 1352–1361.

Fischer, B. and Boch, R. (1983) Brain Res., 260: 21–26.

Guillery, R.W. (1966) J. Comp. Neurol., 128: 21–50.

Guillery, R.W. (1969) Z. Zellforsch. Mikrosk Anat., 96: 1–38.

Hanes, D.P. and Wurtz, R.H. (2001) J. Neurophysiol., 85: 804–815.

Hendry, S.H. and Yoshioka, T. (1994) Science, 264: 575–577.

Hikosaka, O. and Wurtz, R.H. (1985) J. Neurophysiol., 53: 266–291.

Hubel, D.H. and Wiesel, T.N. (1962) J. Physiol., 160: 106–154.

Huerta, M.F. and Kaas, J.H. (1990) J. Comp. Neurol., 293: 299–330.

Keating, E.G., Gooley, S.G., Pratt, S.E. and Kelsey, J.E. (1983) Brain. Res., 269: 145–148.

Leichnetz, G.R. (1981) J. Neurol. Sci., 49: 387–396.

Maunsell, J.H, Nealey, T.A. and Depreist (1990) J. Neuro Sci., 10: 3323–3334.

Motter, B.C. and Mountcastle, V.B. (1981) J. Neurosci., 1: 3–26.

Perkel, D.J., Bullier, J. and Kennedy, H. (1986) J. Comp. Neurol., 253: 374–402.

Robinson, D.A. (1972) Vision Res., 12: 1795–1808.

Schall, J.D. and Thompson, K.G. (1999) Annu. Rev. Neurosci., 22: 241–259.

Schiller, P.H. (1977) Brain Res., 122: 154–156.

Schiller, P.H. (1982) Nature, 297: 580–583.

Schiller, P.H. (1984) Handbook of Physiology, Section 1: The Nervous System. Sensory Processes. In: Darien-Smith, I. (Ed.), Vol. 111, American Physiological Society, Bethesda, MD, pp. 457–505.

Schiller, P.H. (1993) Vis Neurosci., 10: 717–746.

Schiller, P.H. (1996) Progress in Retinal and Eye Research. In: Osborne, N.N. and Chader, G.J., (Eds.), Vol. 15, Pergamon Press, Oxford, England, pp. 173–195.

Schiller, P.H. (1998). Cognitive neuroscience of attention: a developmental perspective. In: Richards, J.E. (Ed.), Erlbaum, Mahwah, N.J., pp. 3–50.

Schiller, P.H. and Chou, I.H. (1998) Nat. Neurosci., 1: 248–253.

Schiller, P.H., Finlay, B.L. and Volman, S.F. (1976a) J. Neurophysiol., 39: 1288–1319.

Schiller, P.H., Finlay, B.L. and Volman, S.F. (1976b) J. Neurophysiol., 39: 1320–1333.

Schiller, P.H., Finlay, B.L. and Volman, S.F. (1976c) J. Neurophysiol., 39: 1334–1351.

Schiller, P.H. and Malpeli, J.G. (1977) J. Neurophysiol., 40: 428–445.

Schiller, P.H., Malpeli, J.G. and Schein, S.J. (1979) J. Neurophysiol., 42: 1124–1133.

Schiller, P.H., Sandell, J.H. and Maunsell, J.H. (1987) J. Neurophysiol., 57: 1033–1049.

Schiller, P.H. and Tehovnik, E.J. (2001) Prog. Brain Res., 134: 127–142.

Schiller, P.H. and Tehovnik, E.J. (2003) Eur. J. Neurosci., 18: 3127–3133.

Schiller, P.H., True, S.D. and Conway, J.L. (1979b) Brain Res., 179: 162–164.

Schiller, P.H., True, S.D. and Conway, J.L. (1980) J. Neurophysiol., 44: 1175–1189.

Schlag, J. and Schlag-Rey, M. (1987) J. Neurophysiol., 57: 179–200.

Tehovnik, E.J. and Lee, K. (1993) Exp. Brain Res., 96: 430–442.

Tehovnik, E.J., Lee, K. and Schiller, P.H. (1994) Exp. Brain Res., 98: 179–190.

Tehovnik, E.J., Slocum, W.M. and Schiller, P.H. (2002) Eur. J. Neurosci., 16: 751–760.

Tehovnik, E.J., Sommer, M.A., Chou, I.H., Slocum, W.M. and Schiller, P.H. (2000) Brain Res. Brain Res. Rev., 32: 413–448.

Thier, P. and Andersen, R.A. (1998) J. Neurophysiol., 80: 1713–1735.

Progress in Brain Research, Vol. 149
ISSN 0079-6123

Corticocortical and thalamocortical information flow in the primate visual system

David C. Van Essen*

Washington University School of Medicine, Department of Anatomy & Neurobiology, 660 South Euclid Avenue, St. Louis, MO 63110, USA

Abstract: Visual cortex in primates contains a mosaic of several dozen visual areas that collectively occupy a large fraction of cerebral cortex ($\sim 50\%$ in the macaque; $\sim 25\%$ in humans). These areas are richly interconnected by hundreds of reciprocal corticocortical pathways that underlie an anatomically based hierarchy containing multiple processing streams. In addition, there is a complex pattern of reciprocal connections with the pulvinar, which itself contains about 10 architectonically distinct subdivisions. Information flow through these corticocortical and corticothalamic circuits is regulated very dynamically by top-down as well as bottom-up processes, including directed visual attention. This chapter evaluates current hypotheses and evidence relating to the interaction between thalamocortical and corticocortical circuitry in the dynamic regulation of information flow.

Introduction

Numerous anatomical and neurophysiological studies of primate visual cortex during the 1980s and early 1990s led to several broad hypotheses about cortical organization and function. (1) *Multiplicity of areas.* Cerebral cortex includes a complex mosaic of several dozen visual areas that differ from one another in cortical architecture, connectivity, visual topography, and/or functional characteristics (Maunsell and Van Essen, 1983; Van Essen, 1985; Desimone and Ungerleider, 1989; Kaas, 1997). (2) *Distributed hierarchical organization.* Visual areas can be arranged into an anatomically defined hierarchy (Maunsell and Van Essen, 1983) that includes 10 levels of cortical processing (Felleman and Van Essen, 1991). This hierarchical scheme is based on feedforward,

feedback, and lateral directions of information flow suggested by the laminar patterns of connectivity among several hundred identified corticocortical pathways. However, not all anatomical data fit perfectly with this scheme (Felleman and Van Essen, 1991), and there are alternate schemes involving different numbers of hierarchical levels (Hilgetag et al., 2000). Hence, it may be more appropriate to consider the cortex as "quasi-hierarchical" in its organization. (3) *Multiple processing streams.* At each hierarchical level there are multiple processing streams, manifested by anatomically distinct yet intertwined compartments at early cortical levels (areas V1 and V2) and by physically separate dorsal and ventral streams at higher levels (DeYoe and Van Essen, 1988; Desimone and Ungerleider, 1989; Goodale and Milner, 1992; Van Essen and Gallant, 1994). More recent studies have highlighted that cross-talk between streams is extensive at multiple levels (Yabuta et al., 2001; Sincich and Horton, 2002). (4) *Dynamic routing of information.* The control of

*Tel.: 7 +1-314-362-7043; Fax: 7 +1-314-747-3436;
E-mail: vanessen@brainvis.wustl.edu

DOI: 10.1016/S0079-6123(05)49013-5

information flow is highly dynamic within the anatomically defined hierarchy and is powerfully regulated by visual attention. Directed visual attention constitutes an information bottleneck that allows only a tiny fraction (<1%) of the information passing through the optic nerve to reach conscious perception (Van Essen et al., 1992; Olshausen et al., 1993; Anderson et al., 2005). The attentional system requires circuitry for deciding where to attend and at what spatial scale. In addition, there must be circuitry that implements these decisions rapidly, perhaps by way of pulvinarcortical circuits that selectively gate corticocortical information flow (Olshausen et al., 1993). While this model provides an attractive framework that accounts for many aspects of attention, many other models of attention have been proposed that differ in a variety of ways (Itti and Koch, 2001; Itti et al., 2005).

With this background in mind, the present chapter addresses several general issues relating to the flow of information within the primate visual system. The overaraching objective is to compare the nature of information flow through corticopulvinarcortical (CPC) circuits versus that through corticocortical (CC) pathways. Sherman and Guillery (1998, 2005 (this volume)) have suggested that in general (i) cortico-thalamo-cortical circuits may be a major if not the dominant route for "driving" ascending sensory information and that (ii) direct cortico-cortical circuits may be largely modulatory rather than driving in their function. This hypothesis is essentially the opposite of the hypothesis that CPC pathways modulate the flow of visual information carried by direct CC pathways (Olshausen et al., 1993; Anderson et al., 2005). As argued in Corticocortical vs. corticopulvinarcortical information flow, consideration of the numbers of neurons available to represent the results of successive stages of cortical processing make the extreme form of the CPC driver hypothesis very unlikely. Nonetheless, the fundamental issue of whether the pulvinar and CPC circuits have a driving or a modulatory role is a central but unresolved issue.

The number of neurons present in any given structure or pathway places strong constraints on the amount of information that can be communicated and in the options available for representing this information. Individual neurons are fundamentally "noisy" devices, generally capable of conveying only a few (3–10) bits of information per second (Eliasmith and Anderson, 2002). For this reason, the 10^6 axons in each optic nerve constitute a fundamental early bottleneck, restricting information flow to $3–10\times10^6$ bits/sec rather than the far greater information rate encoded by retinal photoreceptors. This information is packaged into three major retinal ganglion cell classes, each acting as a distinct "channel" that efficiently conveys information associated with a restricted portion of spatio-temporo-chromatic space (Van Essen and Anderson, 1995). The encoding at this stage is compact, or "dense", in the sense that retinal ganglion cells and LGN (lateral geniculate nucleus) neurons have relatively high spontaneous firing rates and have stereotyped center–surround receptive fields that are modulated by a broad range of stimuli encroaching on the classical receptive field.

Beyond the optic nerve bottleneck, the amount of information encoded about a visual scene cannot increase, even though the number of neurons in visual cortex is vastly greater. Instead, the increased neuronal numbers allow for extensive reformatting of the visual representation, in order to make it more useful for subsequent computations. This is at the heart of cortical information processing strategies (Van Essen and Anderson, 1995). The next two sections summarize key aspects of the functional organization of visual cortex and pulvinar in the macaque monkey. The section on visual cortex considers the arrangement and size of different visual areas, patterns of corticocortical connectivity and receptive field characteristics. The section on the pulvinar considers the arrangement of its subdivisions, the pattern of pulvinarcortical connectivity, and the total number of pulvinar neurons.

Cortical areas and surface-based atlases

Primate cortex contains dozens of distinct areas that are largely or entirely visual in function. A combination of obstacles has made it very difficult to chart the arrangement of these areas and to establish their identities unequivocally. (i) *Subtle transitions*: Except for a few areas (e.g., areas V1 and the middle temporal area, MT), the boundaries between visual areas are difficult to discern over most of cortex, because the transitions are often subtle by any of the anatomical and physiological methods available and because there is internal heterogeneity within each area. (ii) *Cortical convolutions*: The extensive convolutions of macaque cortex (and even more so in humans) have been a major impediment to many aspects of analyzing and making comparisons across individuals. (iii) *Individual variability*: Well defined areas such as V1 and MT vary by two- or three-fold in surface area across individual hemispheres (Van Essen et al., 1984; Maunsell and Van Essen, 1987; Sincich et al., 2003). The variability in location of each area relative to gyral and sulcal boundaries, while far less in the macaque than in humans, is nonetheless on the order of 2–3 mm and thus a major fraction of the dimensions of most areas. Moreover, the precise pattern of convolutions is variable from one individual to the next.

Dozens of partitioning schemes for part or all of cerebral cortex have been described over the past century, starting with Brodmann and other classical neuroanatomists. For visual cortex alone in the macaque, a dozen schemes remain in current use, and numerous schemes exist for other regions in frontal, parietal, and temporal cortex. Comparisons between these schemes have been impeded by the fact that the various schemes have generally been presented on different atlases or individual brains using a variety of display formats (e.g., brain slices, hemisphere views, views of schematically inflated hemispheres, and flat maps generated manually or by computerized methods).

In order to facilitate comparisons and help resolve discrepancies, this "tower of Babel" of partitioning schemes needs to be brought into a common spatial framework that provides flexible visualization options. To this end, a surface-based atlas of macaque cortex and associated visualization and analysis software has been developed. To illustrate the general approach, Fig. 1 shows fiducial, inflated, and flat map

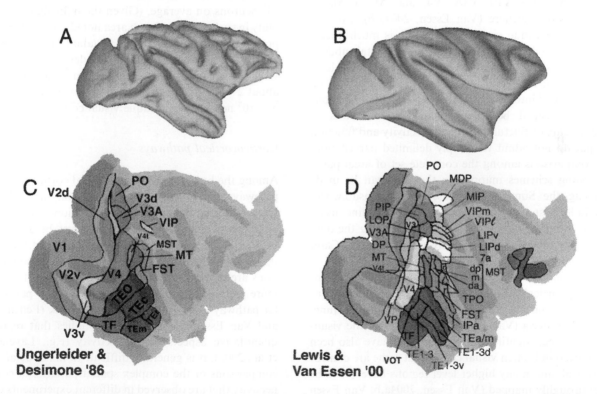

Fig. 1. A surface-based atlas of macaque cortex right hemisphere. A. Lateral view of fiducial surface. B. Lateral view of the inflated atlas surface. C. Ungerleider and Desimone (1986) partitioning scheme on the atlas flat map: D. Lewis and Van Essen (2000a) partitioning scheme. Data sets can be visualized online or downloaded for offline visualization using Caret by accessing http://sumsdb.wustl.edu:8081/sums/archivelist.do?archivid=685946.

representations of the right hemisphere of a macaque atlas (the "F99UA1" atlas, based on high resolution structural MRI). Fourteen different partitioning schemes have been mapped to this atlas, in most cases using surface based registration in which geographical landmarks (sulci and gyri) are used to constrain the registration (Van Essen et al., 2001; 2004; Van Essen, 2004a). In the two examples shown in Fig. 1, there are numerous differences between the Desimone and Ungerleider (1986) scheme (Fig. 1C) and the Lewis and Van Essen (2000a) scheme (Fig. 1D). These differences reflect a combination of factors, including the criteria used to identify boundaries, experimental errors in changing areal boundaries, individual variability across monkeys, and distortions introduced in the registration process.

More generally, there is concordance across many studies regarding the existence, location, and approximate extent of seven visual areas: V1, V2, V3d (or V3), V3v (or VP), V3A, V4, and MT (V5), as discussed elsewhere (Van Essen, 2004a,b). For the rest of macaque visual cortex, there is much uncertainty and debate regarding the fundamental subdivisions. Indeed, it is conceivable that some high-level regions in temporal and parietal cortex may not be subdivided into genuinely distinct areas. Such regions might instead be heterogeneous on the basis of gradients or fluctuations in connectivity and function that do not admit to sharply delimited parcellation. Comparisons among the complete set of areal partitioning schemes mapped to the atlas can be made using the SumsDB database (http://sumsdb.wustl.edu:8081/sums) by visualizing results online using the WebCaret interface or by downloading the data sets for offline analysis and visualization using Caret software (http://brainvis.wustl.edu/caret).

Human visual cortex occupies about 20–30% of total cortical surface area and contains numerous subdivisions, based mainly on topographic and functional criteria (Van Essen, 2004). Most of the visuotopic areas identified in the macaque have also been charted in human visual cortex, but some are controversial, and many higher level regions have yet to be thoroughly mapped (Van Essen, 2004a,b; Van Essen et al., 2004).

Altogether, the current status of cortical cartography is arguably similar in important respects to that of 17th century earth cartographers, who were forced to choose among many competing versions of the basic arrangement of earth's geographic and political subdivisions. Progress in resolving these issues will require extensive additional data that can be analyzed at high spatial resolution and in a way that allows accurate registration across individuals.

Cortical numbers

Cortical areas in the macaque range widely in size and thus in the number of constituent neurons. Area V1 occupies ~ 1000–1300 mm^2 of surface area (Van Essen et al., 1984; Sincich et al., 2003) and has an estimated 1.6×10^8 neurons in each hemisphere (O'Kusky and Colonnier, 1982). Area V2 is about 1000 mm^2 in surface area (Sincich et al., 2003) but is like the rest of neocortex in having a lower neuronal density than in V1. Assuming 10^5 neurons per mm^2 surface area (Rockel et al., 1980), V2 contains about 10^8 neurons on average. (Given the individual variability in surface area of each area noted above, there is presumably twofold or more variability in neuronal numbers for each area.) The remainder of extrastriate visual cortex occupies about 2400 mm^2 and contains about 2.4×10^8 neurons, for an approximate total of 5×10^8 neurons in macaque visual cortex.

Corticocortical pathways

Among the hundreds of known visual corticocortical pathways, most have been described only in qualitative or at best semiquantitative fashion. Typically, estimates of connection strengths must be assessed by viewing selected histological sections (or drawings thereof) on which retrograde or anterograde connections are displayed. In such cases it is difficult to be more precise than simply characterizing any particular pathway as strong, moderate, or weak (Felleman and Van Essen, 1991). Even in studies that report quantitative aspects of connectivity (e.g., Lavenex et al., 2002), it is generally difficult to make detailed comparisons of the complex spatial patterns of connectivity that are observed in different experiments on different hemispheres.

Surface-based atlases provide a valuable approach for bringing connectivity data, both quantitative

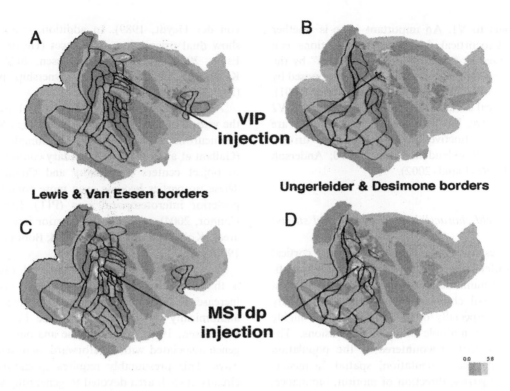

A. **Lewis & Van Essen borders**

B. **Ungerleider & Desimone borders**

VIP injection

MSTdp injection

00   58

Fig. 2. Connectivity patterns in relation to partitioning schemes. A. VIP injection, with Lewis and Van Essen (2000a,b) areas overlaid. B. Same VIP injection, but with Ungerleider and Desimone (1986) areal boundaries. C. MSTdp injection with Lewis and Van Essen areas. D. Same MSTdp injection with Ungerleider and Desimone areas. Cell densities are indicated as $\log(\text{cells/mm}^2)$.

and qualitative, into a common spatial framework. Figure 2 illustrates results from two experiments involving injections of retrograde tracers into different cortical locations (areas VIP and MSTdp) in different monkeys (Lewis and Van Essen, 2000b). The pattern of retrogradely labeled cells was charted quantitatively (as labeled cells/mm^2) in the individual experimental hemispheres, and the data were then registered to the macaque surface-based atlas using geographical landmarks to constrain the registration (Van Essen et al., 2004). Once in the atlas framework, the injection patterns can be compared with one another and also with any of the partitioning schemes available on the atlas. This is illustrated by overlaying the Lewis and Van Essen (2000a) scheme on the connectivity for injections of VIP (ventral intraparietal area) and MSTdp (medial superior temporal area, dorso-posterior subdivision) in Fig. 2A and 2C, respectively, and by overlaying the Ungerleider and Desimone (1986) scheme over these same injections in

Fig. 2B, D. In this way, one can assign connection strengths (as percent of total labeled neurons) to each area for each partitioning scheme of interest. In addition, the same data can be described/analyzed more objectively by expressing connection strengths for cortical locations encoded by surface-based coordinates (e.g., polar coordinates on the atlas spherical map), thereby circumventing the need to use areal assignments that may not stand the test of time.

The most powerful single pathway, and one of the best studied to date, is the reciprocal link between V1 and V2, the two largest areas. The projection to V2 arises from layers 2, 3, and 4B of V1, which collectively contain about 6×10^7 neurons per hemisphere (O'Kusky and Colonnier, 1982). About 80% of these (5×10^7) are pyramidal cells, but only about half of them (2.5×10^7) have extrinsic projections (Callaway and Wiser, 1996), the great majority of which target V2. Thus, the direct projection from V1 to V2 is about 20–25-fold greater numerically than the

LGN inputs to V1. An important issue is whether direct corticocortical feedforward projections can be categorized as "drivers" or "modulators" by the morphological and physiological criteria proposed by Sherman and Guillery (1998) and Sherman (2001). Morphological studies of V1 axons projecting to V2 are inconclusive, but the axons from V1 to MT are anatomically distinctive and suggestive of a "driver" morphology (Rockland and Virga 1990; Anderson et al., 1998; Rockland, 2002).

Receptive field characteristics in the ventral stream

Neuronal response characteristics of visual cortical neurons differ from their LGN precursors dramatically and in numerous ways. For area V1, the most striking general characteristic is that the majority of neurons (especially outside layer 4C) are highly selective along multiple stimulus dimensions. The types of selectivity encountered in the population include tuning for orientation, spatial frequency, binocular disparity, direction of motion, luminance, color, and orientation contrast (Van Essen and Gallant, 1994). In general, the neuronal representation in V1 is far "sparser" than in the LGN, insofar as most neurons are responsive over a much smaller portion of the overall stimulus space than for LGN neurons (Olshausen and Field, 2004). This obviously demands a large number of neurons if all featural dimensions and all of visual space are to be represented at high resolution. Another important consideration is that significant neuronal redundancy is necessary in order to provide a good signal-to-noise ratio for information carried at spatial frequencies coarser than the maximum visual acuity associated with any given retinal location (Anderson and DeAngelis, 2004). Viewed from this perspective, the 20–25-fold greater numbers of V2-projecting neurons compared to LGN inputs hardly seems excessive.

Neurons in V2 preserve (or regenerate) selectivity along the many stimulus dimensions explicitly encoded in V1. In addition, many V2 cells show complex spatial properties that are absent or rare in V1. This includes tuning for stereoscopic depth edges (von der Heydt et al., 2000), relative rather than absolute binocular disparity (Thomas et al., 2002), and subjective contour responsiveness (Peterhans and von der Heydt, 1989). In addition, many neurons show dual orientation preferences (Hegde and Van Essen, 2000; Anzai and Van Essen, 2002; Ito and Komatsu, 2004) or border ownership properties (Zhou et al., 2000).

Among the many intermediate visual areas along the ventral stream, the best studied is area V4. Many V4 neurons show selectivity for complex gratings (Gallant et al., 1993) and boundary contours relative to object centers (Pasupathy and Connor, 2001). These properties become even more complex in the posterior inferotemporal area (PIT), (Brincat and Connor, 2004), and in more anterior inferotemporal areas (Kobatake and Tanaka, 1994; Booth and Rolls, 1998).

In extrastriate cortex, one general observation is that receptive field sizes at a given eccentricity increase progressively at successive stages of the anatomically defined hierarchy (see Felleman and Van Essen, 1991), reflecting the anatomical convergence associated with feedforward anatomical pathways. This presumably requires specialized neural circuits in each area devoted to generating selectivity to low level dimensions (e.g., orientation) at a coarser spatial scale than at lower hierarchical levels. A more striking set of characteristics relates to the emergence of progressively stronger scale invariance and position invariance at higher cortical levels. In parallel, the degree of attentional modulation increases at progressively higher cortical levels (Maunsell and Cook, 2002). The issue of how attentional scale and position are controlled is discussed further in Attentional control and the pulvinar.

The latency of visual responses varies widely within the neuronal population in each visual area but shows systematic differences across areas. For V1 and V2 the earliest latencies ($\sim$40 ms and $\sim$50 ms, respectively) and the median latencies correlate with their position in the anatomical hierarchy, but for higher areas the correlation is poor (Bullier, 2001). This presumably reflects the fact that many pathways jump across multiple hierarchical levels and some are also notably fast conducting (e.g., the V1 to MT projection). While of major importance for understanding temporal aspects of information processing, these findings do not constitute strong evidence against the notion of hierarchical processing per se.

Functional organization of the pulvinar

The primate pulvinar is much larger than the neighboring LGN yet is far less well understood. Progress in elucidating the functional organization of the pulvinar has been impeded by a combination of technical obstacles that differ from those facing investigators of cerebral cortex. (1) *Non-coextensive subdivisions*: The pulvinar contains many architectonic subdivisions revealed most clearly using a combination of immunocytochemical and histochemical methods, though the number is not nearly as great as for cerebral cortex. However, while architectonic transitions in the pulvinar are generally more robust than the subtle transitions between most cortical areas, the relationship of pulvinar architectonic subdivisions to those defined by connectivity and visual topography is more complex. (2) *Lack of layers*: The pulvinar lacks well defined internal layers or other anatomical features that are suitable for making 2-dimensional maps of the type that have been extremely useful for cortical studies and have also been successfully applied to the LGN (Connolly and Van Essen, 1984). (3) *Lack of a high resolution electronic atlas*: Comparisons across studies would be greatly facilitated if a high resolution electronic atlas of the pulvinar were available and if methods were available for registering data from individuals to the atlas. Progress towards this goal has been impeded by the fact that the pulvinar and its constituent subdivisions are difficult to visualize using conventional structural MRI. In the meantime, an image based online database, XANAT (Press et al., 2001) and 3-dimensional computerized reconstructions of the pulvinar (Shipp, 2001) represent useful steps forward.

Architectonic subdivisions

As with cerebral cortex, many different architectonic partitioning schemes have been proposed for the macaque pulvinar. The classical scheme of inferior, lateral, medial, and anterior subdivisions (Jones, 1985) has been superseded by schemes based heavily on calbindin and parvalbumin immunochytochemistry and on acetylcholinesterase staining (Gutierrez et al., 1995, 2000; Stepnowski and Kaas, 1997; Adams et al., 2000; Shipp, 2001). This includes four subdivisions of the inferior pulvinar (PI_P, PI_M, PI_{CM}, and PI_{CL}) (Stepnowski and Kaas, 1997), two subdivisions of the lateral pulvinar (PL_{VM} and PL_{VL}) (Adams et al., 2000), and four subdivisions of the dorsal (medial/oral) pulvinar complex (PLd, PMl, PMm, and PMm-c) (Gutierrez et al., 2000). Although some discrepancies remain to be resolved, this suggests that the pulvinar contains approximately 10 architectonic subdivisions.

Topography, connections, and physiology of ventral pulvinar

The classical physiological mapping study by Bender (1981) revealed two topographically organized areas within ventral and lateral pulvinar, now identified as the P1 and P2 fields by Adams et al. (2000) and the VP1 and VP2 fields by Shipp (2003). Bender (1981) suggested that the P1 field included all of the inferior pulvinar plus part of the lateral pulvinar, but Adams et al. (2000) consider P1 to include only PI_{CL} and PL_{VM}. The P2 field corresponds to PL_{VL}. The P3 field includes PI_P, PI_M, and PI_{CM} within the inferior pulvinar, but its visuotopic organization remains unclear.

Numerous retrograde and anterograde labeling studies indicate that each pulvinar subdivision has a distinctive pattern of reciprocal projections with multiple cortical visual areas (Baizer et al., 1993; Adams et al., 2000; Shipp, 2001; Weller et al., 2002 and references therein). In general, the inferior and lateral pulvinar are extensively connected with V1, V2, and ventral stream areas (including V4 and inferotemporal cortex). The dorsal pulvinar complex is extensively connected with dorsal stream areas and with non-visual areas; and overlap between dorsal and ventral streams is strongest in PMl.

For the inferior and lateral pulvinar, Adams et al. (2000) report that PL_P projects into V4 and MT, but not into V1 or V2; PI_M projects into V2 and more heavily to MT, but not into V1 or V4; PI_{CM} projects into V2, V4, and MT, but not into V1; and PI_{CL}, PL_{VM}, and PL_{VL} project into all four areas, but most heavily into V4. Shipp (2001, 2003) reports little overlap between the MT-projecting and V4-projecting portions of these subdivisions (PI_{CM}, PI_{CL}, PL_{VM}, and PL_{VL}).

The various subdivisions of dorsal pulvinar (PLd, PMl, PMm, and PMm-c) have a differential pattern of connections with frontal, parietal, and temporal regions, including non-visual (superior temporal gyrus) as well as visual (V4; intraparietal sulcus and inferior parietal lobule, dorso-lateral prefrontal cortex, and inferotemporal) regions (Bayleydier and Morel, 1992; Baizer et al., 1993; Adams et al., 2000; Gutierrez et al., 2000). Most relevant to the current focus is that PMl is strongly connected with area V4 and with posterior parietal, and inferotemporal regions; within this region there is some segregation but also some direct convergence of dorsal and ventral streams.

Two other important aspects of pulvinar circuitry are its inputs from other subcortical structures and its intrinsic circuitry. The superior colliculus provides a major source of visual inputs to the pulvinar (Jones, 1985), though it apparently is not a driving input (Bender, 1983). As in other thalamic nuclei, intrinsic connections within pulvinar are sparse and local (Ogren and Hendrickson, 1977, 1979). While intrinsic circuits offer relatively little opportunity for integration within or across pulvinar subdivisions, the adjacent reticular nucleus provides an important substrate for such interactions (Guillery and Harting, 2003).

Pulvinar receptive field characteristics

In the inferior and lateral pulvinar, neurons in P1 and P2 have small receptive fields that are comparable to those in V1 and V2 at any given eccentricity (Bender, 1981; 1982). This suggests a driving role for V1 (Bender, 1983) and perhaps V2 inputs and a modulatory role for other corticopulvinar inputs. Many pulvinar neurons are selective for orientation and/or direction of motion, but the tuning for these dimensions is considerably broader on average than in V1 or V2. Response latencies for neurons in the P1 map range from 44 to 70 ms (Bender, 1982), well within the ranges reported for V1 and V2 neurons. In the dorsal pulvinar, visually responsive neurons tend to be more difficult to drive, even in the alert monkey, and are often modulated by visual attention (Petersen et al., 1985; Bender and Youakim, 2001).

Pulvinar size and neuronal numbers

Surprisingly, estimates of the size of the macaque pulvinar (its volume and neuronal number) have not been reported in the literature. There are even major discrepancies in the overall extent of the pulvinar (and other thalamic nuclei, including the medial dorsal nucleus) in different macaque atlases (e.g., Paxinos et al., 2000; Kusama and Mabuchi, 1970). Nonetheless, rough approximations can be made indirectly by combining data for other structures (the medial dorsal nucleus of the thalamus, MD) and other species (human). Such estimates are important because they provide strong constraints on hypotheses about pulvinar function.

The macaque MD nucleus contains an estimated 1.2×10^6 neurons in a volume of 75 mm^3 (Dorph-Petersen et al., 2004; volume not corrected for within-plane section shrinkage). This implies a neuronal density of 1.6×10^4/mm^3, much lower than the cell density in primate neocortex. In humans, the pulvinar is about twice the size of MD (680 to 990 mm^3 for MD and 840–1640 mm^3 for pulvinar (Byne et al., 2001; Danos et al., 2003; Kemether et al., 2003)). If the ratio of pulvinar to MD volume is the same in macaque and humans, and if neuronal density is comparable in the pulvinar and MD (as appears to be the case from inspection of the Paxinos et al., 2000 atlas) then the macaque pulvinar contains about 2.4×10^6 neurons. The percentage of these that are projection neurons is 60–75% (Arcelli et al., 1997; Dorph-Petersen et al., 2004), so the total number of macaque pulvinar projection neurons is unlikely to exceed 2 million in each hemisphere. Of these, only a subset are the parvalbumin-positive type that are putative "driver" projection neurons (Jones, 2002).

Corticocortical vs. corticopulvinarcortical information flow

It is instructive to consider two extremes on a spectrum: (i) *The CPC driver hypothesis*: the pulvinar is the sole source of driving influences on extrastriate visual areas, with corticocortical pathways playing a purely modulatory role. (ii) *The CC driver hypothesis*: corticocortical pathways are the sole source of driving influences on extrastriate visual areas; the pulvinar plays a purely modulatory role. These extreme hypotheses can be evaluated by considering V1 and V2, which are the largest visual areas and where many key data are available.

The projection from V1 to the pulvinar arises exclusively from layer 5 and includes only about 20% of the 2×10^7 neurons in this layer, for a total of about 4×10^6 neurons (Callaway and Wiser, 1996; O'Kusky and Colonnier, 1982). This projection terminates in the main visuotopic fields P1 and P2, though not in their most posterior portions (Ungerleider et al., 1983; Shipp, 2001). Fields P1 and P2 constitute perhaps half of total pulvinar volume and hence only about 1 million pulvinar projection neurons in total. Given these numbers, it is not possible for the V1-recipient portions of the pulvinar to preserve an explicit representation of many stimulus dimensions with the same fine-grained spatial resolution encountered in V1. Rather, it is evident from the neurophysiological characteristics described above that the pulvinar has opted to retain a fine-grained spatial representation in its P1 and P2 fields and in exchange to represent orientation and other dimensions much more coarsely.

By the CPC driver hypothesis, the sharp tuning for orientation and other dimensions that occurs commonly in V2 would need to be regenerated essentially de novo from a set of pulvinar inputs that are concentrated in the P2 field (PL_{VL}) but also include some inputs from the P1 and P3 fields. Since each of these fields has stronger projections into other visual areas, the total number of pulvinar neurons projecting into V2 is not known but is probably well under 1 million; the number of candidate "driver" neurons (parvalbumin-containing) must be even smaller. Moreover, these pulvinar inputs are generally not very orientation selective or direction selective. The sharply tuned CC inputs from V1 would by the CPC driver hypothesis only be available as modulatory rather than driving inputs. It would be particularly challenging to generate V2 receptive fields having subfields with different (and sharply tuned) orientation preferences. In contrast, it is relatively straightforward to account for the multiorientation tuning characteristics of V2 cells (at least qualitatively) if one assumes such cells receive driving inputs from V1

neurons that differ in orientation and receptive field location. Altogether, the CC driver hypothesis provides an attractive (albeit unproven) framework to account for many important V2 properties. In contrast, the CPC driver hypothesis places severe computational burdens on a relatively small population of pulvinar neurons whose characteristics appear to be poorly suited for such tasks. Note that this argument regarding neuronal numbers is based on a fundamentally different logic than the synaptic numbers argument raised by Sherman and Guillery (1998, 2004), who note very appropriately that the driving inputs to a structure (e.g., the LGN or V1) can be successfully mediated by a rather small percentage of its total synaptic inputs.

If one accepts the argument that pulvinar neurons are unlikely to be the sole, or even the primary source of driving inputs to extrastriate visual cortex, what alternatives should receive prime consideration? Pulvinar inputs might nonetheless still be drivers, while remaining relegated to a backseat by virtue of their small numbers relative to CC projections. The alternative that they play a strong modulatory role is more attractive in several respects, especially in relation to hypotheses about visual attention.

Attentional control and the pulvinar

Lesion studies provide some support for the hypothesis that the pulvinar plays a role in visual attention (Petersen et al., 1985, 1987; Desimone and Ungerleider, 1989; Danziger et al., 2004). However, the remarkable complexity of corticocortical and corticopulvinar circuitry reviewed above poses interesting challenges for thinking about the precise functional role of the pulvinar. In an earlier hypothesis for a role of the pulvinar in visual attention (Olshausen et al., 1993), it was formulated in the overall context of a tripartite division of labor conceptualized for the attentional system. For the first stage of this process, it was hypothesized that bottom-up cues (e.g., salient stimuli) and top-down influences (e.g., verbal instructions) combine to form a single "saliency map', in which a winner-take-all mechanism (e.g., Koch and Ullman, 1985) determines

182

the location and spatial scale for the next attentional shift. In the second stage, the output from the saliency map (putatively located in parietal cortex) is transmitted to the pulvinar and converted into control signals. In the third stage, these pulvinar control signals are used to regulate information flow into inferotemporal cortex, thereby providing the inputs needed to perceive objects within the attended location.

As originally noted, there are two problems with this hypothesis that suggest an alternative formulation. First, as noted above, the anatomical interactions between dorsal (parietal) streams and ventral streams is mainly restricted to a limited portion of the dorsal pulvinar. For this reason, the outputs of a parietal saliency map would not have access to the entire pulvinar, and would instead need to operate mainly through a single dorsal pulvinar subnucleus (PMl). Another issue is that when visual stimuli are presented as isolated objects without the normal background clutter of natural visual scenes, "involuntary" attentional shifts driven by highly salient stimuli appear to occur very rapidly (Nakayama and Meckeben, 1989) — probably more rapidly than could be mediated by a system that required obligatory activation of a parietal saliency map.

An alternative speculation proposed here is that the ventral pulvinar mediates involuntary attentional shifts and the dorsal pulvinar mediates voluntary attentional shifts. In theory, this division of labor offers the advantage of speed for the involuntary process and flexibility for the voluntary process. On the other hand, it poses significant implementation challenges for how attentional shifts would be controlled under the frequent conditions where voluntary and involuntary cues interact.

Conclusion

Progress in solving major questions of systems neuroscience is increasingly dependent on a combined neurobiological, computational, and behavioral cognitive approach. Nowhere is this more evident than in the fascinating phenomena of visual perception and visual attention. It is vital that hypotheses about perception and attention be based on sound neurobiological principles and closely grounded in hard neuroanatomical and neurophysiological facts. Access to these facts will be greatly facilitated by further advances in atlases and databases that provide efficient access to information in formats that are most informative. It is equally critical that these hypotheses be formulated in a way that reflect good engineering principles at the level of single neurons, small circuits, and system-wide organization (Eliasmith and Anderson, 2002) and that they respect the overall system performance revealed by psychophysical studies. A compelling resolution to the question of what role the pulvinar plays in vision is still unattained. Prospects for deeper insights will benefit from consistent application of the strategies outlined in this chapter.

Abbreviations

V1–V4	visual areas 1-4
CC	corticocortical
CPC	corticopulvinar cortical
LGN	lateral geniculate nucleus
MT	middle temporal area
MRI	magnetic resonance imaging
MSTd	medial superior temporal area, dorsal
VIP	ventral intraparietal area
MSTdp	medial superior temporal area, dorsal, posterior
PI_{CL}	inferior pulvinar, central-lateral subdivision
PI_P	inferior pulvinar, posterior subdivision
PI_M	inferior pulvinar, medial subdivision
PI_{cM}	inferior pulvinar, central-medial subdivision
PL_{VM}	lateral pulvinar, ventro-medial subdivision
PLd	lateral pulvinar, dorsal subdivision
PMl	medial pulvinar, lateral subdivision
PMm	medial pulvinar, medial subdivision
PMm-c	medial pulvinar, medial-central subdivision
MD	medial dorsal nucleus

Acknowledgments

Work from the author's laboratory was supported by grants from NEI (EY02091), joint funding from the

National Institutes of Mental Health, National Institute of Biomedical Imaging and Bioengineering, and the National Science Foundation (MH60974) and the Mathers Foundation. The author would also like to thank Susan Danker for help in manuscript preparation.

References

Adams, M.M., Hof, P.R., Gattas, R., Webster, M.J. and Ungerleider, L.G. (2000) Visual cortical projections and chemoarchitectue of macaque monkey pulvinar. J. Comp. Neurol., 419: 377–393.

Anderson, J.C., Binzegger, T., Martin, K.A.C. and Rockland, K.S. (1998) The connection from cortical area V1–V5: a light and electron microscopic study. J. Neurosci., 18: 10525–10540.

Anderson, C.H. and DeAngelis, G.C. (2004) Poulation codes and signal to noise ratios in primary visual cortex. Soc. Neurosci. Abstr. #822.3. Online.

Anderson, C.H., Van Essen, D.C., and Olshausen, B.A. (2005) Directed visual attention and the dynamic control of information flow. In: Itti, L., Rees, G. and Tsotsos, J. (Eds.), Neurobiology of Attention. Elsevier, San Diego.

Anzai, A. and Van Essen, DC (2002) Receptive field structure of orientation selective cells in monkeyV2. Soc. Neurosci. Abstr. #720.12. Online (www.sfn.org).

Arcelli, P., Frassoni, C., Regondi, M.C., Debiasi, S. and Spreafico, R. (1997) GABAergic neurons in mammalian thalamus: A marker of thalamic complexity? Brain Res. Bull, 42: 27–37.

Baizer, J.S., Ungerleider, L.G. and Desimone, R. (1991) Organization of visual inputs to the inferior temporal and posterior parietal cortex in macaques. J. Neurosci., 11(1): 168–190.

Baizer, J.S., Ungerleider, L.G. and Desimone, R. (1993) Comparison of subcortical connections of inferior temporal and posterior parietal cortex in monkeys. Visual Neurosci., 10: 59–72.

Bayleydier, C. and Morel, A. (1992) Segregated thalamocrotical pathways to inferior parietal and inferotemporal cortex in macaque monkey. Vis. Neurosci., 8: 391–405.

Bender, D.B. (1981) Retinotopic organization of macaque pulvinar. J. Neuorphysiol., 46: 672–693.

Bender, D.B. (1982) Receptive field properties of neurons in the macaque inferior pulvinar. J. Neurophysiol., 48: 1–17.

Bender, D.B. (1983) Visual activation of neurons in the primate pulvinar depends on cortex but not colliculus. Brain Res., 279(1–2): 258–261.

Bender, D.B. and Youakim, M. (2001) Effect of attentive fixation in macaque thalamus and cortex. J. Neurophysiol., 85: 219–234.

Booth, M.C. and Rolls, E.T. (1998) view-invariant representations of familiar objects by neurons in the inferior temporal visual cortex. Cereb. Cortex, 8: 510–523.

Brincat, S.L. and Connor, C.E. (2004) Underlying principles of visual shape selectivity in posterior inferotemporal cortex. Nat. Neurosci., 7: 880–886.

Bullier, J. (2001) Integrated model of visual processing. Brain Res. Rev., 36: 96–107.

Byne, W., Buchsbaum, M.S., Kemether, E., Hazlett, E.A., Shinwari, A., Mitropoulou, V. and Siever, L.J. (2001) Magnetic resonance imaging of the thalamic mediodorsal nucleus and pulvinar in schizophrenia and schizotypal personality disorder. Arch. Gen. Psychiatry, 2001 Feb, 58(2): 133–140.

Callaway, E.M. and Wiser, A.K. (1996) Contributions of individual layer 2–5 spiny neurons to local circuits in macaque primary visual cortex. Vis. Neurosci., 13: 907–922.

Connolly, M.P. and Van Essen, D.C. (1984) The representation of the visual field in parvicellular and magnocellular laminae of the lateral geniculate nucleus of the macaque monkey. J. Comp. Neurol., 226: 544–564.

Danos, P., Baumann, B., Kramer, A., Bernstein, H.G., Stauch, R., Krell, D., Falkai, P. and Bogerts, B. (2003) Volumes of association thalamic nuclei in schizophrenia: A postmortem study. Schizophr. Res., 60: 141–155.

Danziger, S., Ward, R., Owen, V. and Rafal, R. (2004) Contributions of the human pulvinar to linking vision and action. Cognitve, Affective & Behavioral Neuroscience, 4: 89–99.

Desimone, R. and Ungerleider, L.G. (1989) Neural mechanisms of visual processing in monkeys. In: Boller, F. and Graman, J. (Eds.), Handbook of Neuropsychology. Elsevier, Amsterdam, pp. 267–299.

DeYoe, E.A. and Van Essen, D.C. (1988) Concurrent processing streams in monkey visual cortex. Trends in Neurosci., 11: 219–226.

Dorph-Petersen, K.A., Pierri, J.N., Sun, Z., Sampson, A.R. and Lewis, D.A. (2004) Stereological analysis of the mediodorsal thalamic nucleus in schizophrenia: volume, neuron number, and cell types. J. Comp. Neurol., 472: 449–462.

Eliasmith, C.E. and Anderson, C.H. (2002) Neural Engineering. Computation, Representation, and Dynamics in Neurobiological Systems. MIT Press, 384 p.

Felleman, D.J. and Van Essen, D.C. (1991) Distributed hierarchical processing in primate cerebral cortex. Cerebral Cortex, 1: 1–47.

Gallant, J.L., Braun, J. and Van Essen, D.C. (1993) Selectivity for polar, hyperbolic, and Cartesian gratings in macaque visual cortex. Science, 259: 100–103.

Goodale, M.A. and Milner, A.D. (1992) Separate visual pathways for perception and action. Trends Neurosci., 15: 20–25.

184

Guillery, R.W. and Harting, J.K. (2003) Structure and connections of the thalamic reticular nucleus: Advancing views over half a century. J. Comp. Neurol., 463: 360–371.

Gutierrez, C., Cola, M.G., Seltzer, B. and Cusick, C. (2000) Neurochemical and connectional organization of the dorsal pulvinar complex in monkeys. J. Comp. Neurol., 419: 61–86.

Gutierrez, C., Yaun, A. and Cusick, C.G. (1995) neurochemical subdivisions of the inferior pulvinar in macaque monkeys. J. Comp. Neurol., 363: 545–562.

Hegde, J. and Van Essen, D.C. (2000) Selectivity for complex shapes in primate visual area V2. J. Neurosci., 20: RC61–66.

Hilgetag, C.C., O'Neill, M.A. and Young, M.P. (2000) Hierarchical organization of macaque and cat cortical sensory systems explored with a novel network processor. Philos. Trans. R Soc. Lond. B Biol. Sci., 355(1393): 71–89.

Itti, L. and Koch, C. (2001) Computational modelling of visual attention. Nat. Rev. Neurosci., 2(3): 194–203.

Itti, L., Rees, G. and Tsotsos, J. eds. (2005). Neurobiology of Attention (eds. Ilti, L., Rees, G. and Tsotsos, J.K.) Academic Press/Elsevier, San Diego.

Ito, M. and Komatsu, H. (2004) Representation of angles embedded within contour stimuli in area V2 of macaque monkeys. J. Neurosci., 24(13): 3313–3324.

Jones, EG. (2002) Thalamic circuitry and thalamocortical synchrony. Philos. Trans. R Soc. Lond. B Biol. Sci., 357: 1659–1673.

Jones, E.G. (1985) The Thalamus. Plenum Press, New York.

Kaas, J.H. (1997) Theories of visual cortex organization in primates. In: Rockland, K.S., Kaas, J.H. and Peters, A. (Eds.), Cerebral Cortex, Extrastriate Cortex in Primates, Vol. 12. Plenum Press, New York, pp. 91–125.

Kemether, E.M., Buchsbaum, M.S., Byne, W., Hazlett, E.A., Haznedar, M., Brickman, A.M., Platholi, J. and Bloom, R. (2003) Magnetic resonance imaging of mediodorsal, pulvinar, and centromedian nuclei of the thalamus in patients with schizophrenia. Arch. Gen. Psychiatry, 60: 983–991.

Kobatake, E. and Tanaka, K. (1994) Neuronal selectivities to complex object features in the ventral visual pathway of the macaque cerebral cortex. J. Neurophysiol., 71: 856–867.

Koch, C. and Ullman, S. (1985) Shifts in selective visual attention: Towards the underlying neural circuitry. Hum Neurobiol., 4: 219–227.

Kusama, T. and Mabuchi, M. (1970) Stereotaxic Atlas of the Brain of Macaca Fuscata. Univeristy of Tokyo Press, Tokyo.

Lavenex, P., Suzuki, W.A. and Amaral, D.G. (2002) Perirhinal and parahippocampal cortices of the macaque monkey: projections to the neocortex. J. Comp. Neurol., 447: 394–420.

Lewis, J.W. and Van Essen, D.C. (2000a) Mapping of architectonic subdivisions in the macaque monkey, with emphasis on parieto-occipital cortex. J. Comp. Neurol., 428: 79–111.

Lewis, J.W. and Van Essen, D.C. (2000b) Cortico-cortical connections of visual, sensorimotor, and multimodal processing areas in the parietal lobe of the Macaque monkey. J. Comp. Neurol., 428: 112–137.

Maunsell, J.H. and Cook, E.P. (2002) The role of attention in visual processing. Philos. Trans. R Soc. Lond. B Biol. Sci., 357: 1063.

Maunsell, J.H.R. and Van Essen, D.C. (1983) The connections of the middle temporal visual area (MT) and their relationship to a cortical hierarchy in the macaque monkey. J. Neurosci., 3: 2563–2586.

Maunsell, J.H.R. and Van Essen, D.C. (1987) The topographic organization of the middle temporal visual area in the macaque monkey: representational biases and the relationship to callosal connections and myeloarchitectonic boundaries. J. Comp. Neurol., 266: 535–555.

Nakayama, K. and Meckeben, M. (1989) Sustained and transient compounds of focal attention. Vision Res., 29: 1631–1647.

Ogren, M.P. and Hendrickson, A.E. (1977) The distribution of pulvinar terminals in visual areas 17 and 18 of the monkey. Brain Res., 137: 343–350.

Ogren, M.P. and Hendrickson, A.E. (1979) The morphology and distribution of striate cortex terminals in the inferior and lateral subdivisions of the Macaca monkey pulvinar. J. Comp. Neurol., 188: 179–199.

O'Kusky, J. and Colonnier, M. (1982) A laminar analysis of the number of neurons, glia, and synapses in the adult cortex (area 17) of adult macaque monkeys. J. Comp. Neurol., 210(3): 278–290.

Olshausen, B.A. and Field, D.J. (2004) Sparse coding of sensory inputs. Curr. Opin. Neurobiol., 14: 481–487.

Olshausen, B.A., Anderson, C.H. and Van Essen, D.C. (1993) A neurobiological model of visual attention and invariant pattern recognition based on dynamic routing of information. J. Neurosci., 13: 4700–4719.

Pasupathy, A. and Connor, C.E. (2001) Shape representation in Area V4: Position-specific tuning for boundary conformation. J. Neurophysiol., 86: 2505–2519.

Paxinos, G., Huant, X-F and Toga, A.W. (2000) The Rhesus Monkey Brain in Stereotaxic Coordinates. Academic Press.

Perkel, D.J., Bullier, J. and Kennedy, H. (1986) Topography of the afferent connectivity of area 17 in the macaque monkey: A double-labelling study. J. Comp. Neurol., 253: 374–402.

Peterhans, E. and von der Heydt, R. (1989) Mechanisms of contour perception in monkey visual cortex II. Contour bridging gaps. J. Neurosci., 9: 1749–1763.

Petersen, S.E., Robinson, D.L. and Keys, W. (1985) Pulvinar nuclei of the behaving rhesus monkey: Visual responses and their modulation. J. Neurophysiol., 54: 867–886.

Petersen, S.E. Robinson, D.L. and Morris, J.D. (1987) Contributions of the pulvinar to visual spatial attention. Neuropsychologia. 25: 97–105.

Press, W.A., Olshausen, B.A. and Van Essen, D.C. (2001) A graphical anatomical database of neural connectivity. Phil. Trans. Royal Soc., Ser B, 356: 1131–1146.

Rockel, A.J., Hiorns, R.W. and Powell, T.P. (1980) The basic uniformity in structure of the neocortex. Brain, 103: 221–244.

Rockland, K.S., Kaas, J.H. and Peters, A. (1997) Cerebral Cortex. Extrastriate Cortex in Primates, Vol. 12. Plenum Press, New York.

Rockland, K.S. and Virga, A. (1990) Organization of individual cortical axons projecting from area V1 (area 17) to V2 (area 18) in the macaque monkey. Vis. Neurosci., 4: 11–28.

Rockland, K.S. (2002) Visual cortical organization at the single axon level: a beginning. Neurosci. Res., 42: 155–166.

Sherman and Guillery 2004 – this volume.

Sherman, S.M. (2001) Thalamic relay functions. Prog. Brain Res., 134: 51–69.

Sherman, S.M. and Guillery, R.W. (1998) On the actions that one neve cell can have on another: distinguishing "drivers" from "modulators". Proc. Natl. Acad. Sci. USA, 95: 7121–7126.

Shipp, S. (2001) Corticopulvinar connections of areas V5, V4, and V3 in the macaque monkey: a dual model of retinal and cortical topographies. J. Comp. Neurol., 439(4): 469–490.

Shipp, S. (2003) The functional logic of cortico-pulvinar connections. Philos. Trans. R Soc. Lond. B Biol. Sci., 358(1438): 1605–1624.

Sincich, LC., Adams, D.L. and Horton, J.C. (2003) Complete flatmounting of the macaque cerebral cortex. Vis. Neurosci., 20(6): 663–686.

Sincich, L.C. and Horton, J.C. (2002) Divided by cytochrome oxidase: a map of the projections from V1 to V2 in macaques. Science, 295(5560): 1734.

Stepniewska, I. and Kaas, J.H. (1997) Architectonic subdivisions of the inferior pulvinar in New World and Old World monkeys. Vis. Neurosci., 14: 1043–11060.

Thomas, O.M., Cumming, B.G. and Parker, A.J. (2002) A specialization for relative disparity in V2. Nature Neuroscinece, 5: 472–478.

Ungerleider, L.G., Galkin, T.W. and Mishkin, M. (1983) Visuotopic organization of projections from striate cortex to inferior and lateral pulvinar in rhesus monkey. J. Comp. Neurol., 217(2): 137–157.

Ungerleider, L.G. and Desimone, R. (1986) Cortical connections of visual area MT in the macaque. J. Comp. Neurol., 248: 190–222.

Van Essen, D.C. (1985) Functional organization of primate visual cortex. In: Jones, E.G. and Peters, A. (Eds.), Cerebral Cortex, Vol. 3. Plenum Press, New York, pp. 259–329.

Van Essen, D.C. (2004) Organization of visual areas in Macaque and human cerebral cortex. In: Chalupa, L. and Werner, J.S. (Eds.), The Visual Neurosciences. MIT Press, Cambridge, MA, pp. 507–521.

Van Essen, D.C. and Anderson, C.H. (1995) Information processing strategies and pathways in the primate visual system. In: Zornetzer, S., Davis, J.L., Lau, C. and McKenna, T. (Eds.), 2nd edn., An Introduction to Neural and Electronic Networks. Academic Press, FL, pp. 45–76.

Van Essen, D.C. and Gallant, J.L. (1994) Neural mechanisms of form and motion processing in the primate visual system. Neuron, 13: 1–10.

Van Essen, D.C., Lewis, J.W., Drury, H.A., Hadjikhani, N., Tootell, R.B., Bakircioglu, M. and Miller, M.I. (2001) Mapping visual cortex in monkeys and humans using surface-based atlases. Vision Research, 41: 1359–1378.

Van Essen, D.C., Anderson, C.H. and Felleman, D.J. (1992) Information processing in the primate visual system: An integrated systems perspective. Science, 255: 419–423.

Van Essen, D.C., Harwell, J., Hanlon, D. and Dickson, J. (2004a) Surface-Based Atlases and a Database of Cortical Structure and Function. In: Koslow, S.H. and Subramaniam, S. (Eds.), Databasing the Brain: From Data to Knowledge (Neuroinformatics). John Wiley & Sons, NJ.

Van Essen, D.C. (2004b) Surface-based comparisons of macaque and cortical organization. In: Dehaene, S. (Ed.), From Monkey to Brain: Proceedings of a Fyssen Foundation Colloquium, June, 2003. MIT Press, Cambridge, MA.

Van Essen, D.C., Newsome, W.T. and Maunsell, J.H.R. (1984) The visual field representation in striate cortex of the macaque monkey: Asymmetries, anisotropies and individual variability. Vision Res., 24: 429–448.

von der Heydt, R., Zhou, H. and Friedman, H.S. (2000) Representation of stereoscopic edges in monkey visual cortex. Vision Res., 40: 1955–1967.

Weller, R.E., Steele, G.E. and Kaas, J.H. (2002) Pulvinar and other subcortical connections of dorsolateral visual cortex in monkeys. J. Comp. Neurol., 450: 215–240.

Yabuta, N.H., Sawatari, A. and Callaway, E.M. (2001) Two functional channels from primary visual cortex to dorsal visual cortical areas. Science, 292(5515): 297–300.

Zhou, H., Friedman, H.S. and von der Heydt, R. (2000) Coding of border ownership in monkey visual cortex. J. Neurosci., 20: 6594–6611.

Progress in Brain Research, Vol. 149
ISSN 0079-6123

CHAPTER 14

Corollary discharge and spatial updating: when the brain is split, is space still unified?

Carol L. Colby[1],*, Rebecca A. Berman[1], Laura M. Heiser[1] and Richard C. Saunders[2]

[1]*Department of Neuroscience, University of Pittsburgh, Center for the Neural Basis of Cognition,
Mellon Institute, Room 115, 4400 Fifth Ave., Pittsburgh, PA 15213-2683, USA*
[2]*Laboratory of Neuropsychology, National Institute of Mental Health, Room 1B80, Building 49,
49 Convent Drive, MSC 4415, Bethesda, MD 20892-4415, USA*

Abstract: How does the brain keep track of salient locations in the visual world when the eyes move? In parietal, frontal and extrastriate cortex, and in the superior colliculus, neurons update or 'remap' stimulus representations in conjunction with eye movements. This updating reflects a transfer of visual information, from neurons that encode a salient location before the saccade, to neurons that encode the location after the saccade. Copies of the oculomotor command — corollary discharge signals — must initiate this transfer.

We investigated the circuitry that supports spacial updating in the primate brain. Our central hypothesis was that the forebrain commissures provide the primary route for remapping spatial locations across visual hemifields, from one cortical hemisphere to the other. Further, we hypothesized that these commissures provide the primary route for communicating corollary discharge signals from one hemisphere to the other. We tested these hypotheses using the double-step task and subsequent physiological recording in two split-brain monkeys. In the double-step task, monkeys made sequential saccades to two briefly presented targets, T1 and T2. In the visual version of the task, the representation of T2 was updated either within the same hemifield ("visual-within"), or across hemifields ("visual-across"). In the motor version, updating of the visual stimulus was always within-hemifield. The corollary discharge signal that *initiated* the updating, however, was generated either within the same hemisphere ("motor-within") or in the opposite hemisphere ("motor-across"). We expected that, in the absence of the forebrain commissures, both visual-across and motor-across conditions would be impaired relative to their "within" controls.

In behavioral experiments, we observed striking initial impairments in the monkeys' ability to update stimuli across visual hemifields. Surprisingly, however, both animals were ultimately capable of performing the visual-across sequences of the double-step task. In subsequent physiological experiments, we found that neurons in lateral intraparietal cortex (LIP) can remap stimuli across visual hemifields, albeit with a reduction in the strength of remapping activity. These behavioral and neural findings indicate that the transfer of visual information is compromised, but by no means abolished, in the absence of the forebrain commissures. We found minimal evidence of impairment of the motor-across condition. Both monkeys readily performed the motor-across sequences of the double-step task, and LIP neurons were robustly active when within-hemifield updating was initiated by a saccade into the opposite hemifield. These results indicate that corollary discharge signals are available bilaterally. Altogether, our findings show that both visual and corollary discharge signals from opposite hemispheres can converge to update spatial representations in the absence of the forebrain commissures. These investigations provide new evidence that a unified and stable representation of visual space is supported by a redundant circuit, comprised of cortical as well as subcortical pathways, with a remarkable capacity for reorganization.

---

*Corresponding author. E-mail: ccolby@cnbc.cmu.edu

DOI: 10.1016/S0079-6123(05)49014-7
187

Introduction

We perceive a visual world that is richly detailed, stable, and continuous. This perception allows us to perform a range of spatial behaviors, from reaching for a cup of coffee to navigating through a busy street. The ease with which we perform these actions gives the impression that our sensory experience is a direct — and passive — reflection of the world around us. Our perception, however, is by no means a transparent read-out of incoming sensory inputs. The active nature of perception is readily appreciated when we consider the nature of the visual signals that arrive at the periphery. We explore and analyze the world using the high-acuity center of the retina, the fovea. In order to direct the fovea toward objects of interest we make rapid eye movements, called saccades, about three times each second. About every 300 milliseconds, the brain receives a new image, yet we are oblivious to these nearly continuous displacements of the retinal scene. What we perceive is an internal representation of the visual world, which seamlessly compensates for our own movements.

How does the mind construct this stable representation of visual space from such constantly changing input? In 1866, Helmholtz observed that when he passively displaced his eye by gently pressing it, the image of the world was also displaced (Helmholtz, 1866). In contrast, when he displaced his eye by generating a voluntary eye movement, the image of the world remained still. Helmholtz proposed that our perception of the visual world is kept stable by the "effort of will" associated with making an eye movement. This "effort of will," placed in the context of contemporary physiological studies, is a copy of the motor command that generates the saccadic eye movement. This *corollary discharge* can support the computations needed to anticipate what the visual world will look like once the eyes reach their new location. By using corollary discharge signals, the brain can update the internal representation of space, keeping it in register with the incoming retinal signals. In this way, the brain compensates for the retinal displacements caused by eye movements, producing a stable representation of objects in the visual world. This dynamic process, known as spatial updating, is the focus of the present study.

Updating involves a transfer of visual and motor signals

In the past two decades, neurophysiological studies have provided considerable insight into neural mechanisms that contribute to the phenomenon of spatial constancy. Single-unit recording studies in awake, behaving monkeys indicate that several brain areas participate in updating spatial representations when the eyes move. In parietal, frontal, and extrastriate cortex, and in the superior colliculus, neurons exhibit a surprising kind of activity, which exemplifies the important influence of action upon perception. Neurons in these areas have classical visual responses, firing when stimuli appear within the receptive field. These neurons also fire, however, when a saccade brings the receptive field onto a previously stimulated location — even though no physical stimulus ever appears within the field (Mays and Sparks, 1980; Goldberg and Bruce, 1990; Duhamel et al., 1992a; Walker et al., 1995; Umeno and Goldberg, 1997, 2001; Nakamura and Colby, 2002). This firing, called *remapping*, is a response to a memory trace of the stimulated location, which has been updated in conjunction with an eye movement. Remapping provides a dynamic internal representation of the visual world that takes our eye movements into account.

Remapping requires the communication of visual as well as motor signals. When the eyes move, the *visual* representation must be transferred from neurons that encode the stimulus location before the eye movement, to neurons that will encode the location after the eye movement (Colby and Goldberg, 1999). This transfer must be initiated by a copy of the *motor* command, the corollary discharge signal. Recent studies emphasize that these motor signals contribute vitally to visual processing and spatial behavior (Guillery and Sherman, 2002a,b; Guillery, 2003; Sommer and Wurtz, 2004b). Spatial updating is one such instance in which corollary discharge information must play a role. For example, if the eyes are going to move 10° to the right, information about the impending saccade must be available to visual areas, initiating a transient 10° shift in receptive field locations. The current experiments investigate the circuitry supporting the communication of these visual and oculomotor signals. In the following sections, we describe the rationale for these experiments and our specific hypotheses. We then present behavioral and physiological evidence that reveals an intriguing dissociation between pathways that mediate the communication of visual as compared to corollary discharge signals are also presented.

Both visual and motor signals must be communicated between hemispheres

One of the most noteworthy aspects of remapping is that, at the time of the eye movement, neurons are responsive to locations outside their classical receptive fields. Accordingly, neurons must have access to information from throughout the visual field, even from the opposite visual hemifield. In the original experiments on remapping in the lateral intraparietal cortex (LIP), stimulus representations were updated from one visual hemifield to another (Duhamel et al., 1992a). This neural activity has a behavioral complement: both humans and monkeys are capable of performing spatial tasks that require across-hemifield remapping (Goldberg et al., 1990; Duhamel et al., 1992b; Li and Andersen, 2001; Jeffries et al., 2003; Zivotofsky et al., 2003). Successful across-hemifield updating must require a transfer of information between neurons in opposite hemispheres, as the representation of visual stimuli is highly lateralized (Trevarthen, 1990; Medendorp et al., 2003; Merriam et al., 2003). Similarly, physiological and behavioral studies indicate that corollary discharge signals must also be transferred between hemispheres. Oculomotor signals, like visual signals, are highly lateralized. Yet neurons in area LIP exhibit updating activity regardless of saccade direction (Heiser and Colby, 2003), and updating behavior is accurate when a saccade into one hemifield initiates updating within the opposite hemisphere (Heide et al., 1995). What pathways provide the substrate for these signals to travel between hemispheres?

Hypothesis: Forebrain commissures are necessary for communication between hemispheres during spatial updating

The forebrain commissures — the corpus callosum and anterior commissure — provide the most obvious path for the interhemispheric transfer of both visual and oculomotor signals during spatial updating. The corpus callosum, with roughly half a billion fibers, constitutes the most prominent route for interhemispheric communication (Lamantia and Rakic, 1990; Houzel et al., 2002), and the anterior commissure provides an immediate link between virtually all visual areas in the temporal lobes (Jouandet and Gazzaniga, 1979; Demeter et al., 1990). Of particular interest for spatial updating are the extensive callosal connections between parietal cortices in each hemisphere, and between parietal cortex and areas in the frontal lobe (Pandya and Vignolo, 1969; Hedreen and Yin, 1981; Seltzer and Pandya, 1983; Petrides and Pandya, 1984; Schwartz and Goldman-Rakic, 1984). These direct corticocortical connections could support the rapid relay of visual and oculomotor signals required to influence receptive field properties in conjunction with saccades. The importance of the forebrain commissures is further suggested by neuropsychological evidence of their functional role. Studies of split-brain humans and monkeys have demonstrated the necessity of the corpus callosum and anterior commissure for the across-hemisphere integration of visual and visuomotor processes (Gross et al., 1977; Holtzman, 1984; Gazzaniga, 1987; Eacott and Gaffan, 1989; Trevarthen, 1990; Desimone et al., 1993; Corballis, 1995). In light of this anatomical and behavioral evidence, we reasoned that the forebrain commissures are critical for interhemispheric transfer of the signals involved in spatial updating.

We hypothesized that the forebrain commissures are necessary for communicating both visual and corollary discharge signals from one hemisphere to the other. In Part I, we asked whether the forebrain commissures are required when visual representations must be updated from one hemifield to the other. In Part II, we asked whether these commissures are required when spatial updating within a single hemifield is initiated by a saccade into the opposite hemifield.

Approach

We tested these hypotheses by measuring the behavioral and neural correlates of spatial updating in two rhesus macaques whose forebrain commissures were surgically transected. We measured spatial behavior using the double-step task, a classic method for assessing subjects' ability to localize targets after an intervening saccade (Hallett and Lightstone, 1976; Mays and Sparks, 1980; Goldberg and Bruce, 1990). The subject must make eye movements to two successively flashed targets, T1 and T2 (Fig. 1A). The critical feature of this task is that the second target (T2) disappears before the eyes leave the initial fixation point. If the subject generates the sequence based only on the retinal location of the T2, the second saccade will be incorrect (Fig. 1B). For accurate performance of the sequence, the location of T2 must be updated in conjunction with the saccade to T1 (Fig. 1C). Subsequent to behavioral testing, we asked whether neurons in parietal cortex are active when remapping requires the communication of either visual or corollary discharge signals between hemispheres.

We evaluated the integrity of spatial updating in three conditions of the double-step task, illustrated in Fig. 2. (1) In the within condition (Fig. 2A), both visual and corollary discharge signals are communicated within the same hemisphere. The second target (T2) must be updated from one location to another within the same visual hemifield. This condition therefore requires a transfer of visual information between neurons in the same cortical hemisphere. Furthermore, the initiating saccade (the saccade to the first target, T1) is directed into the same visual field in which T2 is updated. As a result, the corollary discharge signal is generated by the same hemisphere in which the transfer of visual information occurs. We compared updating in the within-condition to updating in two interhemispheric conditions. (2) In the across-hemifield condition (Fig. 2B), T2 is updated from one visual hemifield to the other. This condition is also referred to as the *visual-across* condition, to emphasize that the visual representation of T2 must be updated across hemifields. (3) In the motor-across condition (Fig. 2C), like the within condition, the representation of T2 is updated within the same visual hemifield. The critical difference is the direction of the saccade that initiates spatial updating. In the motor-across condition, the initiating saccade to T1 is directed into the opposite hemifield. The corollary discharge signal therefore must be communicated interhemispherically, from the hemisphere generating

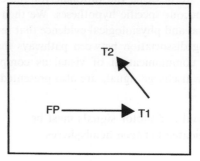

A. Double-step sequence

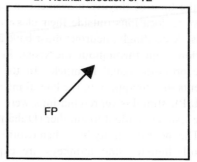

B. Retinal direction of T2

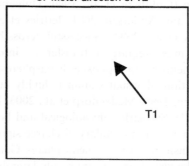

C. Motor direction of T2

Fig. 1. Performance of the double-step saccade task requires spatial updating. (A) The double-step sequence. Subjects make two consecutive saccades, to the first target (T1) and then to the second target (T2). The second target appears very briefly, and so is visible only when the eyes are at initial fixation (FP). When the eyes are at fixation, the retinal location of T2 is up and to the right (B). If the subject generates this retinal saccade from T1, however, it will be inaccurate. For accurate completion of the sequence (C), the representation of T2 must be updated to take the saccade to T1 into account.

the saccade command, to the hemisphere in which the T2 representation is updated. This condition is referred to as *motor-across* to emphasize that spatial updating requires an interhemispheric transfer of

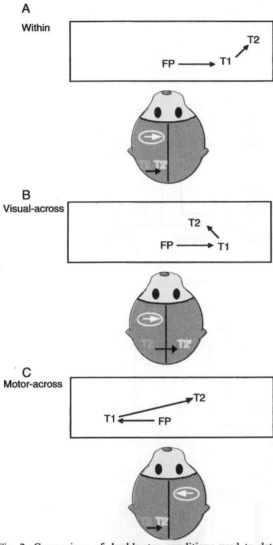

A
Within

B
Visual-across

C
Motor-across

Fig. 2. Comparison of double-step conditions used to determine whether the forebrain commissures are required for
interhemispheric transfer of visual and corollary discharge
signals. In each condition, the monkey's task is to make a
visually-guided saccade to T1, followed by a memory-guided
saccade to T2. (A) In the within condition, T2 appears in the
right visual field when the eyes are at FP. Its retinal location is
represented by neurons in the left hemisphere (orange T2).
When the eyes reach T1, T2 itself is gone, but a memory trace
of T2 is still in the right visual field, encoded by neurons within
the left hemisphere (yellow T2'). Updating therefore involves a
transfer of visual signals between sets of neurons located within
the same cortical hemisphere. The saccade that initiates this
transfer — a rightward saccade — is also generated by the left
hemisphere (white arrow). (B) In the visual-across condition,
T2 appears in the right visual field when the eyes are at FP, but
its memory trace is located in the left visual field once the eyes

oculomotor signals. We predicted that spatial updating in the split-brain monkey would be severely
disrupted if not abolished in the visual-across and
motor-across conditions, but not in the within-
condition.

We designed the behavioral paradigms to incorporate controls for sensory, motor, and cognitive
factors, as all training and testing were necessarily
conducted after the commissurotomy to prevent
infection. Once healing was complete, the animals
were trained to perform the double-step task. In the
first stage of training, we used vertical sequences, in
which the first saccade was either straight up or
straight down. Updating was therefore always within-
hemifield. The monkeys were trained to perform
interleaved vertical sequences at a minimum criterion
of 75% correct, demonstrating a generalized understanding of the task. In the second stage of training,
monkeys learned to perform a central condition in
which the first saccade was horizontal (Fig. 3A, black
lines). In the central sequences, T2 appeared directly
above T1, so that the updated representation of T2
was available bilaterally and performance did not
require interhemispheric transfer. Once the monkeys
reached criterion on these sequences, we simultaneously introduced two novel test conditions: either
within and visual-across (Part I) or within and motor-
across (Part II). In each case, the conditions were
matched in saccade amplitude and novelty, and
counterbalanced for direction of the second saccade
(e.g., Fig. 3A). Further, the sequences were randomly
interleaved, so that the monkeys had to rely on an
updated visual representation to complete each trial.
This design isolated the difference of interest: accurate

reach T1. Consequently, updating in this condition involves a
transfer of visual information between sets of neurons in
opposite cortical hemispheres. (C) In the motor-across condition, T2 is updated within the same hemisphere, just as in panel
A. The motor-across condition is distinguished by the direction
of the initiating saccade. This leftward movement to T1 is
generated by the opposite hemisphere (white arrow).
Consequently, the corollary discharge signal from the right
hemisphere must be relayed to visual areas in the left
hemisphere. It was expected that performance of the visual-
across and motor-across conditions, but not the within
condition, would be impaired in the absence of the forebrain
commissures.

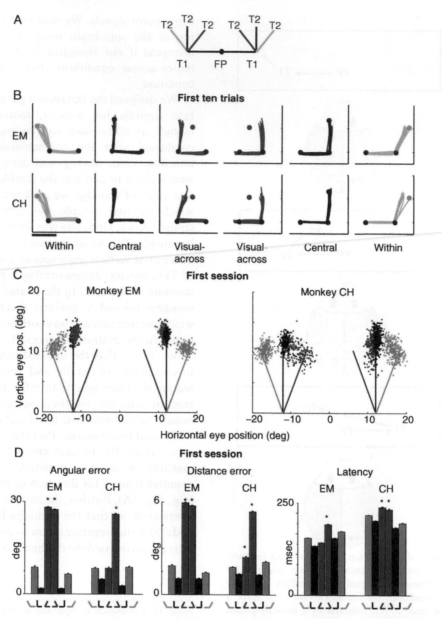

Fig. 3. Initial impairment of visual-across sequences. (A) The six randomly interleaved sequences of the double-step task: trained central sequences (black), novel within-hemifield (green) and visual-across (red) sequences. (B) Eye traces show double-step performance in the first ten trials of the first testing session, for monkey EM (top row) and monkey CH (bottom). Individual panels show the eye path for each sequence, in degrees of visual angle; scale bar represents 10°. Dots indicate the locations of the central fixation point, T1 and T2. The monkeys accurately performed the central and within conditions but demonstrated substantial impairment on the visual-across condition. (C) Second-saccade (S2) endpoints from the entire first testing session. For monkey EM (left), impairment on the visual-across condition persisted in both visual fields, throughout the first session. For monkey CH (right), performance of the visual-across sequence improved during the first session in the left but not the right visual field. (D) Quantitative measures of double-step performance in initial testing sessions. Each bar represents the mean value (±SE) of error or latency for one of the six sequences of the double-step task. In each panel, the first six bars are from monkey EM, second six from monkey CH. Bars are arranged according to the sequence locations (icons below). Black, central; green, within; red, across. Asterisks indicate significantly greater error or longer latency for the visual-across sequence as compared to matched central and within sequences.

double-step performance required a transfer of information either within or across hemispheres. We first asked whether spatial behavior was impaired when updating involved an interhemispheric transfer of visual information. Could these split-brain monkeys perform double-step sequences that required updating from one visual hemifield to the other?

Part I: The forebrain commissures are the primary path, though not the only path, for interhemispheric transfer of visual signals during spatial updating

Behavioral correlates of visual-across updating

We found that both monkeys exhibited a striking and selective deficit when performance of the double-step task required across-hemifield updating of the visual representation. This impairment is evident in the first ten trials of the first testing session (Fig. 3B). The monkeys were very accurate on the trained central sequences, as expected. Performance of the within condition was also accurate, even though the sequences were novel. In contrast, both monkeys made inaccurate eye movements on every trial of the first ten visual-across sequences. Saccade endpoints from the entire first session of testing demonstrate the visual-across impairment (Fig. 3C). For the central (black) and within sequences (green), endpoints are clustered near the correct T2 locations. For the visual-across sequences (red), however, most endpoints are clustered inaccurately near the central target location. These endpoint data also reveal an unanticipated finding: the beginning of recovery is already evident in the left hemifield of monkey CH.

We assessed the monkeys' initial double-step performance by analyzing the accuracy and latency of the second saccade for the entire first session of testing (~ 200 trials per condition, per monkey). We quantified accuracy using two measures: (1) angular error, the angular offset between the actual and target trajectory, and (2) distance error, the distance between the saccade endpoint and T2. Saccadic latency was computed as the time between the end of the first saccade and the beginning of the second saccade. We conducted two-way ANOVAs, separately for each monkey, to determine whether accuracy and latency measures depended significantly

on updating condition (central, within, or visual-across) or direction of the first saccade (right or left). Of greatest interest was the prospect that individual sequences of the visual-across condition were significantly impaired. Accordingly, we used post hoc analyses to compare performance of each visual-across sequence to that of three matched control sequences: the central sequence in the same visual field (matched for the first saccade), the within sequence in the same visual field (matched for novelty and the first saccade), and the within sequence in the opposite visual field (matched for novelty and the second saccade). If performance of the visual-across sequence was significantly worse than each of the matched controls, we concluded that the impairment reflected a deficit in spatial updating. We found significant impairment for each of the individual visual-across sequences, manifest in increased error, increased reaction time, or both (Fig. 3D; Tukey's HSD, $p < 0.05$). These data indicate a deficit in the split-brain monkeys' ability to update spatial locations across visual hemifields.

Three supporting lines of evidence demonstrate that this visual-across impairment is specific to disrupted updating in the absence of the forebrain commissures. First, humans and monkeys with the commissures intact can perform these sequences accurately (Li and Andersen, 2001; Jeffries et al., 2003; Zivotofsky et al., 2003). Second, we found that the split-brain monkeys were not selectively impaired on single memory-guided saccades to the visual-across T2 locations. Thus, the visual-across impairment could not be attributed to any sensory, mnemonic, or motor deficits. Third, we determined that the monkeys could readily perform comparable double-step sequences when T2 was placed directly on the midline, and therefore was represented bilaterally. The monkeys' success in this midline paradigm demonstrates that the initial visual-across deficit did not reflect a general difficulty in reversing the direction of the second eye movement. These data support the conclusion that across-hemifield spatial updating is disrupted in the absence of the forebrain commissures.

Despite this initial deficit, both monkeys were able to learn to perform the visual-across sequences. Improvement occurred quite rapidly in some cases, as demonstrated by the first-session endpoints of

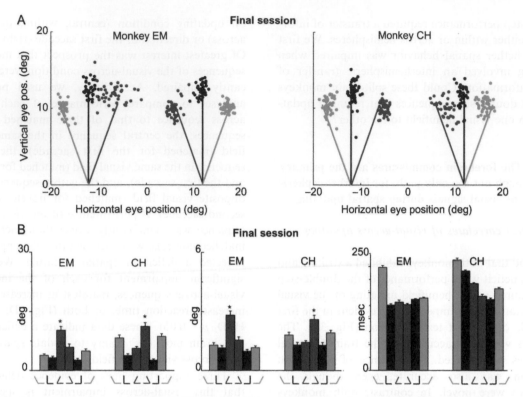

Fig. 4. Visual-across sequences can be learned. S2 endpoints (A) and quantitative data (B) show improved performance for visual-across sequences following multiple testing sessions (64 sessions for monkey EM, 27 sessions for monkey CH).

monkey CH (Fig. 4A). In the left visual field, many endpoints are clustered near the correct T2 location. These reflect the monkey's accurate performance, which emerged during the first 75 trials of this sequence. After multiple sessions of testing, performance of both visual-across sequences was relatively accurate for both monkeys (Fig. 4B). These findings indicate that, although the forebrain commissures serve as the primary route for interhemispheric updating, they are not the sole route.

Physiology of visual-across updating

The monkeys' ultimate success in performing the visual-across sequences implies the existence of neurons that update visual representations across hemispheres, even in the absence of the forebrain commissures. In the second stage of the experiment, we used single-unit recording to ask whether such

neurons are found in the lateral intraparietal area (LIP). We considered two possibilities. One is that across-hemifield updating in the split-brain animal is accomplished using circuitry entirely outside of parietal cortex. If this were the case, we would expect to observe no remapping activity in area LIP. Alternatively, neurons in parietal cortex might still be an integral component of the circuitry for the interhemispheric transfer of visual signals. In this case, we would expect LIP neurons to exhibit remapping activity for visual-across conditions. This second possibility seemed more probable in the light of evidence that parietal cortex is necessary for accurate spatial behavior in the double-step task (Duhamel et al., 1992b; Heide et al., 1995; Li and Andersen, 2001).

We tested these possibilities by recording from area LIP in these same monkeys during the single-step task. This task reveals the neural activity associated with updating a visual location when the eyes move

(Duhamel et al., 1992a). In each trial, the monkey makes a single saccade, bringing the neuron's receptive field onto a location where a stimulus has recently appeared (Fig. 5A). Critically, no physical stimulus ever appears in the receptive field. Rather, the neuron can be driven only by a memory trace of the stimulus, which has been updated in conjunction with the eye movement. We recorded from single neurons in LIP during two conditions of the single-step task, within and visual-across.

We found robust neural activity in area LIP for within-hemifield updating. The neuron shown in Fig. 5 exhibited a strong burst of activity even before the onset of the eye movement and continued to fire after completion of the saccade. Remarkably, this same neuron also fired for visual-across updating, though this activity began later and was less robust than within-hemifield activity. This neuron did not respond in any of corresponding control conditions. It did not fire when the stimulus was presented alone while the animal fixated centrally (Figs. 5G, H), nor when the animal generated the saccade alone, with no stimulus presented (Figs. 5J, K). The activity observed during the single-step task can be attributed only to remapping the memory trace of the flashed stimulus. These data demonstrate that neurons in area LIP can still participate in across-hemifield updating, despite the absence of the primary link between the cortical hemispheres.

At the population level, as in the single-unit example, remapping signals were present but reduced for the visual-across condition. We assessed the updating activity of 223 visually-responsive LIP neurons during a standard epoch (0–200 ms, beginning at saccade onset). None of the neurons responded in the stimulus-alone task, though some neurons exhibited a response in the saccade-alone task, likely due to remapping of the central fixation point. We adjusted for this activity by computing the average firing rate in the identical epoch of the saccade-alone control, and subtracting it from the average activity in the single-step task. This adjusted firing rate was computed identically for all conditions and represents the activity attributed to updating of the memory trace. We used this adjusted firing rate to ask two questions. First, is updating activity equally strong for visual-across and within conditions? We found that the magnitude of remapping was

significantly greater for the within as compared to the visual-across condition (Fig. 6A). Second, do the two conditions differ in the timecourse of neural activity? The latency of remapping was significantly delayed for visual-across as compared to within-conditions (Fig. 6B). These data show that visual representations can be updated from one hemisphere to the other in the absence of direct cortico-cortical links. The forebrain commissures, then, are not the sole mediators of across-hemifield updating. Nevertheless, the diminished strength and delayed latency of visual-across remapping provide clear evidence that the forebrain commissures are the predominant pathway for updating visual representations across hemispheres.

Part II: The forebrain commissures are not the primary path for interhemispheric transfer of motor signals

Behavioral correlates of motor-across updating

Our findings indicate that the forebrain commissures indeed serve as the primary route for transferring visual signals between the cortical hemispheres at the time of an eye movement. Are these same commissures also the primary route for relaying information about the impending eye movement, in order to initiate visuospatial updating? We addressed this question by testing the monkeys on a configuration that allowed us to compare performance of the within condition to the motor-across condition (Fig. 7A). In the motor-across condition, the representation of T2 is updated in the same hemifield, and thus the transfer of visual information is within-hemisphere. The corollary discharge signal that initiates the updating, however, is thought to arise in the opposite hemisphere. The conditions of interest, motor-across and within, were introduced after the monkey reached criterion of 75% correct on the central training sequences. We asked whether the monkeys were impaired selectively on the motor-across sequences.

We found that performance of the motor-across sequences was relatively unimpaired, as shown by the eye traces from the first ten trials (Fig. 7B). Both monkeys performed this sequence effortlessly, with one exception. Monkey EM made large errors in the

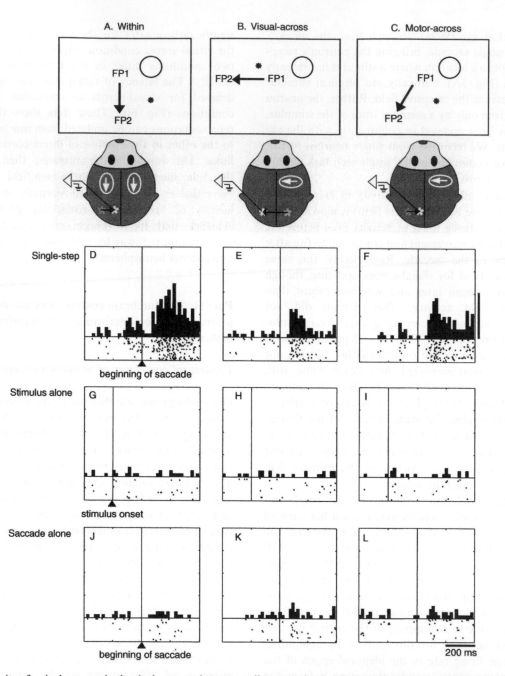

Fig. 5. Activity of a single neuron in the single-step and corresponding control tasks. Top panels show the spatial configurations for the within (A), visual-across (B), and motor-across (C) conditions. Spatial configurations are determined by the neuron's receptive field, located in the upper right quadrant; the neuron under study was located in the left hemisphere. Cartoons illustrate the presumed communication of signals required for spatial updating in each condition. The neuron fired briskly for all three conditions of the single-step task (D–F). The corresponding control conditions show that activity was minimal when the stimulus appeared alone (G–I) and when the saccade was generated in the absence of the stimulus (J–L). In each panel, the histogram shows summed activity in 18 ms bins. Rasters represent individual trials; each tic mark is a single action potential. The vertical bar to the right of F indicates a firing rate of 40 spikes per second.

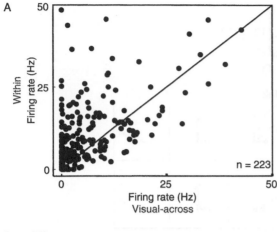

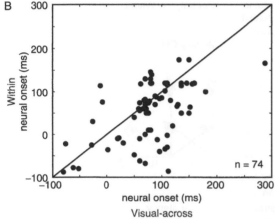

Fig. 6. Firing rate and neural latency for visual-across as compared to the within condition. Each point represents a single cell. (A) LIP neurons fire more strongly for updating within-hemifields as compared to across-hemifields. For each neuron, mean firing rate in the visual-across condition (x-axis) is plotted against mean firing rate in the within condition (y-axis). Firing rate was computed for each neuron using a 200 ms epoch, which began at saccade onset; mean firing rate during the single-step task was adjusted by subtracting mean firing rate during the same saccade-aligned epoch of the saccade-alone control task. Points falling along the unity line indicate that both single-step conditions elicited the same magnitude of remapping activity. Most points fall above the line, indicating that neurons fired more strongly for within-hemifield as compared to visual-across updating. (B) LIP neurons exhibit earlier remapping for the within as compared to the visual-across condition. For this analysis, we included only those neurons that met the following two criteria: first, the latency was definable for both the within and visual-across conditions; second, there was no significant activity in either control condition. Most points fall below the line, indicating that the onset of remapping activity occurred later for the visual-across condition.

first few motor-across trials in the right visual field. The monkey nevertheless learned this sequence rapidly, as is evident in the saccade endpoints from the entire session (Fig. 7C). Endpoints for the motor-across condition are clustered near the correct T2 location for all sequences, indicating that both animals were readily capable of performing the motor-across sequences as well as the within sequences.

The monkeys' overall success in performing the motor-across condition is evident in the measures of saccadic accuracy and latency (Fig. 7D). ANOVAs revealed a significant effect of updating condition for both monkeys, for both measures of accuracy (all $p < 0.001$). The pattern of conditional differences, however, did not reflect an overall impairment of the motor-across sequence. Rather, overall error values were increased for the within condition relative to both the central and motor-across conditions. We conducted post hoc analyses as for the visual-across experiments, asking whether the accuracy of each motor-across sequence was significantly worse than the accuracy of the matched central and within sequences. There was significant impairment for only one of the motor-across sequences (Fig. 7D). This was the sequence in the right field, which monkey EM had initially performed incorrectly (Fig. 7B). The remaining motor-across sequences were not significantly less accurate than their matched counterparts.

We considered the possibility that, despite the monkeys' accurate performance, the reaction times for the second saccade might still be slowed for the motor-across condition as compared to the within condition. It was found that latencies for the motor-across sequences were either equivalent to, or faster than, those of the controls; none were significantly prolonged relative to matched central and within sequences ($p > 0.05$, Tukey's HSD). This finding, in concert with the accuracy data, indicates that performance of the motor-across double-step task is only minimally disrupted in the absence of the forebrain commissures.

Why was overall performance better for the motor-across sequences than the visual-across sequences? The most parsimonious explanation is that the transfer of motor signals, unlike that of visual signals, is not typically accomplished via the

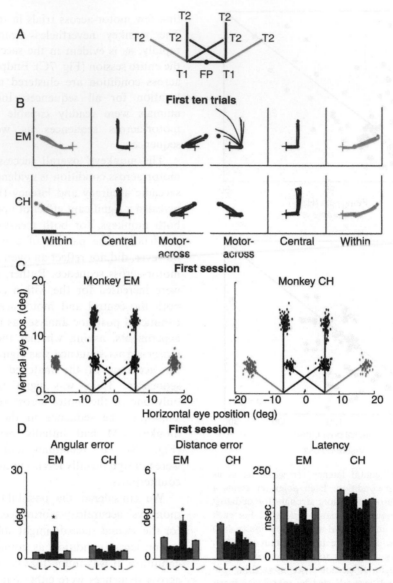

Fig. 7. Initial performance of visual-across sequences. (A) The six randomly interleaved sequences of the double-step task: trained central sequences (black), novel within (green) and motor-across (blue) sequences. (B) Eye traces show that performance of motor-across sequences was relatively unimpaired as compared to within sequences. Individual panels show the eye path, in degrees of visual angle, for the first ten trials of each sequence; conventions as in Fig. 3. Monkey EM made initial errors in the motor-across condition in the right visual field, but began to adjust the trajectory toward the target as the trials progressed. (C) Second-saccade endpoints from the entire first testing session for the motor-across condition. (D) Quantitative measures of double-step performance in the initial motor-across testing session. Each bar represents the mean value (±SE) of error or latency for one of the six sequences of the double-step task. In each panel, the first six bars are from monkey EM, second six from monkey CH. Bars are arranged according to the sequence locations (icons below). Black, central; green, within; blue, motor-across. Asterisks indicate significantly greater error or longer latency for the motor-across sequence as compared to matched central and within sequences.

forebrain commissures. Before reaching this conclusion, however, we needed to rule out an alternative explanation, which emerged from the use of different configurations for the motor-across and visual-across testing. The motor-across sequence may have been easier due to the different spatial location of T2 or the metrics of the first saccade. We addressed this possibility by employing a new spatial configuration, in which the motor-across and visual-across sequences were directed to the identical T2 location. The sequences were also matched for the amplitude of the first saccade, and were interleaved randomly with the central sequences in the same session (Fig. 8A). We conducted this experiment in monkey EM,

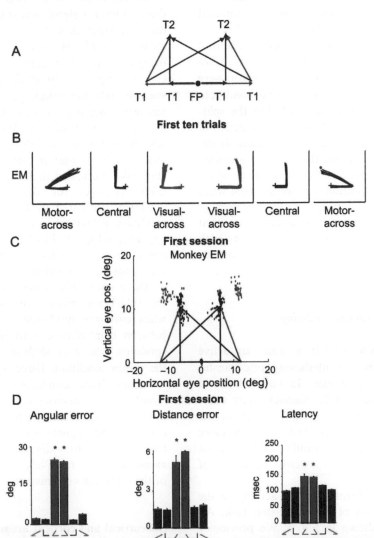

Fig. 8. Performance of visual-across sequences is impaired when tested directly against motor-across sequences. (A) The six randomly interleaved sequences of the double-step task: trained central sequences (black), novel visual-across (red) and motor-across (blue) sequences. (B) Eye traces show that performance of motor-across sequences was unimpaired as compared to visual-across sequences. Individual panels show the eye path, in degrees of visual angle, for the first ten trials of each sequence; conventions as in Fig. 3. (C) Second-saccade endpoints from the entire testing session that directly compared visual-across and motor-across conditions. (D) Quantitative measures of double-step performance. Asterisks indicate significantly greater error or longer latency for the visual-across sequence as compared to matched central and motor-across sequences.

who continued to exhibit visual-across impairment in the standard paradigm prior to testing the new configuration.

The monkey was able to perform the double-step task accurately for the motor-across but not the visual-across sequences. This dissociation is evident in the first ten trials, in the saccade endpoint data from the entire testing session (Fig. 8B), and in the measures of accuracy and latency (Fig. 8D). We compared the accuracy of individual sequences using the standard post hoc procedure, except that each visual-across sequence was now compared to its matched central and *motor-across* (rather than within) sequences. We found that both angular and distance error were significantly greater for the visual-across condition, for both visual fields. This indicates that the split-brain monkey could accurately reach the location of the second target when updating was within-hemifield, even though the saccade that initiated updating was directed into the opposite hemifield. By contrast, the very same target location was not attained when updating was across-hemifield. The relative lack of impairment for motor-across sequences suggests that the forebrain commissures are not the primary path for relaying information about an upcoming saccade to cortical areas representing visual locations.

Physiology of motor-across updating

Finally, we asked whether LIP neurons are active when updating requires the interhemispheric transfer of corollary discharge signals. In our behavioral experiments, we found that the monkeys were effectively unimpaired when performing the motor-across condition of the double-step task. We therefore expected that LIP neurons would exhibit robust updating activity in the motor-across condition of the single-step task.

We observed significant updating activity in the motor-across condition of the single-step task. An example neuron is shown in Fig. 5. We previously described this neuron's activity in the within (Fig. 5D) and visual-across conditions (Fig. 5E), noting that it exhibited remapping in both conditions, though activity was reduced in the visual-across condition. This same neuron had strong and significant activity in the motor-across condition (Fig. 5F).

We assessed the strength of remapping in the motor-across condition in a population of 116 LIP neurons (Fig. 9). We first compared the within and motor-across conditions wered compared (Fig. 9A), plotting the average firing rates against one another and asking whether activity was greater for the within condition (y-axis) than the motor-across condition (x-axis). Most points fall near the unity line, representing equivalent firing for the two conditions. We nevertheless found a significant diminution of activity in the motor-across condition (average of 12.3 Hz, compared to 13.8 Hz in the within condition, adjusted firing rates, $p < 0.05$, paired t-test). The small difference in firing rate between these conditions (1.5 Hz on average) indicates a slight yet systematic reduction in remapping activity for the motor-across as compared to the within condition. We next asked whether activity in the motor-across condition differed significantly from that in the visual-across condition (Fig. 9B). We found that neural activity was significantly stronger for the motor-across condition (12.3 Hz, compared to 8.4 Hz in the visual-across condition; $p < 0.0001$, paired t-test). This difference is apparent in Fig. 9B, in which a majority of points fall above the unity line, indicating stronger remapping in the motor-across condition.

These observations indicate that LIP neurons in the split-brain monkey exhibit robust remapping when corollary discharge signals must be relayed between hemispheres: activity in the motor-across condition was only slightly diminished relative to the within condition. Direct comparison of the two interhemispheric conditions — motor-across and visual-across — demonstrated that remapping signals in LIP were significantly stronger in the motor-across condition. We concluded that the interhemispheric transfer of corollary discharge signals, unlike that of visual signals, is relatively unaffected by the absence of the forebrain commissures.

Subcortical and cortical areas contribute to remapping

Transfer of visual signals

Our behavioral and physiological findings indicate that the across-hemispheric updating of visual

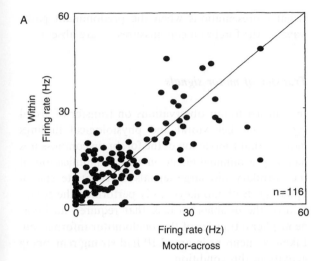

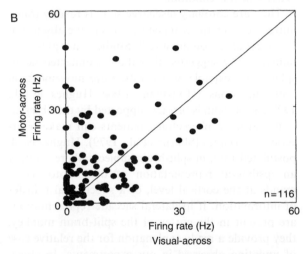

Fig. 9. Remapping activity in the single-step task, for the motor-across condition as compared to the within condition (A) and visual-across condition (B). When average remapping activity in the motor-across condition (x-axis) is plotted against activity in the within condition (y-axis), the distribution of points is primarily centered on the unity line. More points fall above the line, indicating slightly higher firing rates for the within condition (mean = 13.8 Hz for within, 12.3 Hz for motor-across, $p < 0.05$). In B, when remapping activity in the motor-across condition (y-axis) is compared to that of the visual-across condition (x-axis) most points fall above the unity line (mean = 12.3 Hz for motor-across, 8.4 Hz for visual-across, $p < 0.0001$). These data show that, on average, the motor-across condition elicited remapping activity that was slightly diminished in magnitude compared to that of the within condition, and substantially greater than that of the visual-across condition.

representations is compromised in the absence of the forebrain commissures. In behavioral experiments, we found that split-brain monkeys exhibited an initial impairment in performance of double-step sequences that required updating across visual hemifields. In physiological experiments, we found that remapping activity in LIP was less robust when visual information had to be transferred across hemifields as compared to within. These deficits indicate that the forebrain commissures provide a principle, direct route for visual information to be updated from one hemisphere to the other. Despite these clear deficits, however, remapping was not abolished as was expected. Instead, we observed an ultimate recovery of function in spatial behavior, as measured by the double-step task. This behavioral success was paralleled by our discovery in subsequent recording studies that parietal neurons exhibited significant remapping when across-hemisphere transfer of visual information was required. Additional pathways must be recruited to transmit information from one hemisphere to the other.

What brain structures participate in across-hemifield updating in the absence of the forebrain commissures? The superior colliculus (SC) likely plays an important role. Neurons in the intermediate layer of the SC demonstrate remapping activity (Walker et al., 1995). In the normal monkey, this activity is thought to be a reflection of signals generated in parietal cortex, which is considered to be critical for spatial updating (Duhamel et al., 1992b; Heide et al., 1995; Quaia et al., 1998; Li and Andersen, 2001). In the split-brain monkey, the updated visual representation may still be constructed in LIP, by use of a more circuitous route, and imposed on the SC. Alternatively, remapping activity in LIP may reflect processes that originate in the SC.

The SC, via the intertectal commissures, is an obvious candidate for supporting interhemispheric visual transfer in the absence of the forebrain commissures (Moschovakis et al., 1988; Munoz and Istvan, 1998, Olivier et al., 1998). Yet it is one among many structures that may participate in across-hemifield remapping. The pulvinar nucleus of the thalamus is another such structure. The pulvinar is thought to contribute to visual, oculomotor, and attentional functions (Robinson, 1993), and has been implicated as a conduit for interhemispheric transfer in the absence of the forebrain commissures (Corballis, 1995). Remapping has not yet been investigated in the pulvinar, but it is interconnected with areas that exhibit remapping (Hardy and Lynch, 1992; Lynch et al., 1994). Furthermore, its visual responses can be modulated by extraretinal signals — possibly corollary discharge signals — related to saccades (Robinson and Petersen, 1985). These findings demonstrate that the functional properties of the pulvinar are consistent with contributing to spatial updating.

The connectivity of the pulvinar suggests two main ways in which it could transmit information for remapping. First, the pulvinar may act as an ascending link between superior colliculus and cortex (Benevento and Fallon, 1975; Hardy and Lynch, 1992; Clower et al., 2001; Stepniewska et al., 2000). This ascending route has long been considered as a second visual pathway for visual sensory signals to reach the cortex (Diamond and Hall, 1969), and physiological studies have emphasized the notion that it conveys cognitive signals, particularly those related to visual attention (Robinson, 1993; Bender and Youakim, 2001; Wurtz et al., this volume). Second, the pulvinar may provide a transthalamic link between cortical areas involved in remapping. This compelling possibility emerges from studies indicating that much of the pulvinar receives its driving input from cortical rather than subcortical structures (Bender, 1983; Feig and Harting, 1998; Guillery et al., 2001; Van Horn and Sherman, 2004). This connectivity has led to the proposal that the pulvinar is a higher-order thalamic nucleus: it does not simply relay information from subthalamic regions to the cortex, but rather, is primarily involved in transmitting and modifying complex signals between cortical areas (Guillery, 1995; Guillery and Sherman, 2002a). It is intriguing to consider how these cortico-thalamocortical paths may contribute to spatial updating, both in the normal and in the split brain.

Our discussion of the circuitry for transferring visual signals in the split-brain monkey has focused on the superior colliculus and pulvinar, but this is by no means an exhaustive consideration of possible pathways. In all likelihood, a broad network of regions, both cortical and subcortical, must work together to carry out interhemispheric remapping of visual representations when the predominant pathways — the forebrain commissures — are absent.

Transfer of motor signals

In contrast to our observations on transfer of visual signals, our behavioral and physiological findings indicate that transection of the forebrain commissures has only a minimal effect on the communication of the corollary discharge signals that initiate spatial updating. Both monkeys easily performed the condition of the double-step task that required an interhemispheric transfer of this oculomotor information. Likewise, neurons in area LIP had strong remapping activity in this condition.

How are corollary discharge signals readily transmitted between the two hemispheres in the absence of the forebrain commissures? Studies in split-brain humans have suggested that the disconnected hemispheres are capable of generating eye movements in both directions (Holtzman, 1984; Hughes et al., 1992). This claim is further supported by the observation that hemispherectomy patients can make bidirectional saccades (Sharpe et al., 1979). Hughes et al. postulated that, in split-brain subjects, there is either an ipsilateral representation of oculomotor commands at the cortical level, or a subcortical transfer of information. If ipsilateral saccade representations are present in the cortex of the split-brain monkey, they provide a ready explanation for the relative ease of updating observed in our experiments. In effect, updating in this condition would be accomplished easily because the transfer of corollary discharge signals is intrahemispheric. Physiological studies provide scant evidence, however, that the cortical eye fields represent ipsiversive saccades.

A growing body of evidence favors a role for subcortical pathways in relaying the corollary discharge signals required for spatial updating. One of the most promising is the ascending path from the superior colliculus to the frontal eye field (FEF). Anatomical and microstimulation studies have shown that neurons in the intermediate layer of the SC project to the FEF via the mediodorsal thalamus (Lynch et al., 1994; Sommer and Wurtz, 1998). These projections are predominantly ipsilateral. In other words, information about a rightward saccade is represented in the left hemisphere, at the level of SC and at the level of cortex.

Of direct relevance to our results, stimulation studies have recently identified a *crossed* pathway from the SC to the FEF. In a population of FEF neurons receiving input from the SC, roughly 20% of the cells received projections from the contralateral SC (M. Sommer, personal communication). This crossed ascending path could serve to transmit a corollary discharge signal interhemispherically, in both the normal and the split-brain monkey. In other words, a copy of the command to make a rightward saccade — generated in the left SC — could be sent to the right FEF. This corollary discharge command could then act upon visual representations in the right cortical hemisphere, potentially in area LIP. An alternate possibility is that the corollary discharge signal generated in one SC could cross at the level of the intertectal commissures, then travel via the uncrossed ascending tectocortical pathway. Either route could support the accurate updating observed in the present study. The anatomical basis of corollary discharge signals is an active area of research (Guillery and Sherman, 2002b; Guillery, 2003; Sommer and Wurtz, 2002, 2004a,b). These signals may arise from many brain structures, both cortical and subcortical. Our findings indicate that information about our impending eye movements is readily available to modify visual representations in each of the cortical hemispheres.

Conclusion

The phenomenon of remapping, in which visual representations are updated in conjunction with saccades, demonstrates the influence of motor signals on perceptual processing. When a command is issued to move the eyes, a corollary discharge of this command is sent to visual areas, inducing a transfer of visual information from neurons that represent a salient location before the saccade, to those that will represent the location after the saccade. We have used behavioral and physiological methods to investigate the circuitry underlying the transfer of these visual and motor signals between hemispheres.

The central implication of our findings is that direct cortico-cortical paths — the forebrain commissures — are differentially involved in the communication of visual as compared to motor signals in spatial updating. These commissures are likely the primary conduit for the transfer of visual signals from one hemisphere to the other. They are not, however, strictly necessary. Our findings indicate that subcortical pathways play an important role in the recovery of function, and are sufficient to support across-hemifield updating when the direct cortico-cortical paths have been removed. In contrast, the forebrain commissures do not appear to be the primary route for the transfer of motor signals in spatial updating. It appears that subcortico-cortical circuits can readily communicate corollary discharge signals to visual areas in both cortical hemispheres. Together, these conclusions emphasize the idea that spatial updating is subserved by a network of cortical and subcortical structures, in which motor signals can act upon visual information to create a stable representation of the external world.

References

Bender, D.B. (1983) Visual activation of neurons in the primate pulvinar depends on cortex but not colliculus. Brain Res., 279: 258–261.

Bender, D.B. and Youakim, M. (2001) Effect of attentive fixation in macaque thalamus and cortex. J. Neurophysiol., 85: 219–234.

Clower, D.M., West, R.A., Lynch, J.C. and Strick, P.L. (2001) The inferior parietal lobule is the target of output from the superior colliculus, hippocampus, and cerebellum. J. Neurosci., 21: 6283–6291.

Colby and Goldberg (1999) Space and attention in parietal cortex. Annu. Rev. Neurosci., 22: 319–349.

Corballis, M.C. (1995) Visual integration in the split brain. Neuropsychologia., 33: 937–959.

Demeter, S., Rosene, D.L. and Van Hoesen, G.W. (1990) Field of origin and pathways of the interhemispheric commissures in the temporal lobe of macaques. J. Comp. Neurol., 302: 29–53.

Desimone, R., Moran, J., Schein, S.J. and Mishkin, M. (1993) A role for the corpus callosum in visual area V4 of the macaque. Vis. Neurosci., 10: 159–171.

Diamond, I.T. and Hall, W.C. (1969) Evolution of neocortex. Science, 164: 251–262.

Duhamel, J.R., Colby, C.L. and Goldberg, M.E. (1992a) The updating of the representation of visual space in parietal cortex by intended eye movements. Science, 255: 90–92.

204

Duhamel, J.R., Goldberg, M.E., Fitzgibbon, E.J., Sirigu, A. and Grafman, J. (1992b) Saccadic dysmetria in a patient with a right frontoparietal lesion. The importance of corollary discharge for accurate spatial behaviour. Brain, 115: 1387–1402.

Eacott, M.J. and Gaffan, D. (1989) Interhemispheric transfer of visual learning in monkeys with intact optic chiasm. Exp. Brain Res., 74: 348–352.

Feig, S. and Harting, J.K. (1998) Corticocortical communication via the thalamus: ultrastructural studies of corticothalamic projections from area 17 to the lateral posterior nucleus of the cat and inferior pulvinar nucleus of the owl monkey. J. Comp. Neurol., 395: 281–295.

Gazzaniga, M.S. (1987) Perceptual and attentional processes following callosal section in humans. Neuropsychologia, 25: 119–133.

Goldberg, M.E., Colby, C.L. and Duhamel, J.R. (1990) Representation of visuomotor space in the parietal lobe of the monkey. Cold Spring Harb. Symp. Quant. Biol., 55: 729–739.

Goldberg, M.E. and Bruce, C.J. (1990) Primate frontal eye fields. III. Maintenance of a spatially accurate saccade signal. J. Neurophysiol., 64: 489–508.

Gross, C.G., Bender, D.B. and Mishkin, M. (1977) Contributions of the corpus callosum and the anterior commissure to visual activation of inferior temporal neurons. Brain Res., 131: 227–239.

Guillery, R.W. (1995) Anatomical evidence concerning the role of the thalamus in corticcortical communication: a brief review. J. Anat., 187: 583–592.

Guillery, R.W. (2003) Branching thalamic afferents link action and perception. J. Neurophysiol., 90: 539–548.

Guillery, R.W., Feig, S.L. and Van Lieshout, D.P. (2001) Connections of higher order visual relays in the thalamus: a study of corticothalamic pathways in cat. J. Comp. Neurol., 438: 66–85.

Guillery, R.W. and Sherman, S.M. (2002a) Thalamic relay functions and their role in corticocortical communication: generalizations from the visual system. Neuron., 33: 163–175.

Guillery, R.W. and Sherman, S.M. (2002b) The thalamus as a monitor of motor outputs. Philos. Trans. R. Sco. Lond. B Biol. Sci., 358: 1809–1821.

Hallett, P.E. and Lightstone, A.D. (1976) Saccadic eye movements to flashed targets. Vision Res., 16: 107–114.

Hardy, S.G. and Lynch, J.C. (1992) The spatial distribution of pulvinar neurons that project to two subregions of the inferior parietal lobule in the macaque. Cereb. Cortex., 2: 217–230.

Hedreen, J.C. and Yin, T.C. (1981) Homotopic and heterotopic callosal afferents of caudal inferior parietal lobule in Macaca mulatta. J. Comp. Neurol., 197: 605–621.

Heide, W., Blankenburg, M., Zimmermann, E. and Kompf, D. (1995) Cortical control of double-step saccades: implications for spatial orientation. Ann. Neurol., 38: 739–748.

Heiser, L.M. and Colby, C.L. (2003). Is remapping universal?. Soc. Neurosci. Abstr., 29: 386.14.

Helmholtz, H. (1866). Treatise on Physiological Optics. Dover, New York.

Holtzman, J.D. (1984) Interactions between cortical and subcortical visual areas: evidence from human commissurotomy patients. Vision Res., 24: 801–813.

Houzel, J.C., Carvalho, M.L. and Lent, R. (2002) Interhemispheric connections between primary visual areas: beyond the midline rule. Braz. J. Med. Biol. Res., 35: 1441–1453.

Hughes, H.C., Reuter-Lorenz, P.A., Fendrich, R. and Gazzaniga, M.S. (1992) Bidirectional control of saccadic eye movements by the disconnected cerebral hemispheres. Exp. Brain Res., 91: 335–339.

Jeffries, S.M., Kusunoki, M., Cohen, I.S. and Goldberg, M.E. (2003). Localization error in a double-step saccade task are qualitatively explained by peri-saccadic response patterns in LIP. Soc. Neurosci. Abstracts, 386.13..

Jouandet, M.L. and Gazzaniga, M.S. (1979) Cortical field of origin of the anterior commissure of the rhesus monkey. Exp. Neurol., 66: 381–397.

Lamantia, A.S. and Rakic, P. (1990) Cytological and quantitative characteristics of four cerebral commissures in the rhesus monkey. J. Comp. Neurol., 291: 520–537.

Li, C.S. and Andersen, R.A. (2001) Inactivation of macaque lateral intraparietal area delays initiation of the second saccade predominantly from contralesional eye positions in a double-saccade task. Exp. Brain. Res., 137: 45–57.

Lynch, J.C., Hoover, J.E. and Strick, P.L. (1994) Input to the primate frontal eye field from the substantia nigra, superior colliculus, and dentate nucleus demonstrated by transneuronal transport. Exp. Brain Res., 100: 181–186.

Mays, L.E. and Sparks, D.L. (1980) Dissociation of visual and saccade-related responses in superior colliculus neurons. J. Neurophysiol., 43: 207–232.

Medendorp, W.P., Goltz, H.C., Vilis, T. and Crawford, J.D. (2003) Gaze-centered updating of visual space in human parietal cortex. J. Neurosci., 23: 6209–6214.

Merriam, E.P., Genovese, C.R. and Colby, C.L. (2003) Spatial updating in human parietal cortex. Neuron, 39: 361–373.

Moschovakis, A.K., Karabelas, A.B. and Highstein, S.M. (1988) Structure-function relationship in the primate superior colliculus. I. Morphological classification of efferent neurons. J. Neurophysiol., 60: 232–262.

Munoz, D.P. and Istvan, P.J. (1998) Lateral inhibitory interactions in the intermediate layers of the monkey superior colliculus. J. Neurophysiol., 79: 1193–1209.

Nakamura, K. and Colby, C.L. (2002) Updating of the visual representation in monkey striate and extrastriate cortex during saccades. Proc. Natl. Acad. Sci., 99: 4026–4031.

Olivier, E., Porter, J.D. and May, P.J. (1998) Comparison of the distribution and somatodendritic morphology of tectotectal neurons in the cat and monkey. Vis. Neurosci., 15: 903–922.

Pandya, D.N. and Vignolo, L.A. (1969) Interhemispheric projections of the parietal lobe in the rhesus monkey. Brain Res., 15: 49–65.

Petrides, M. and Pandya, D.N. (1984) Projections to the frontal cortex from the posterior parietal region in the rhesus monkey. J. Comp. Neurol., 228: 105–116.

Quaia, C., Optican, L.M. and Goldberg, M.E. (1998) The maintenance of spatial accuracy by the perisaccadic remapping of visual receptive fields. Neural. Netw., 11: 1229–1240.

Robinson, D.L. (1993) Functional contributions of the primate pulvinar. Prog. Brain Res., 95: 371–380.

Robinson, D.L. and Petersen, S.E. (1985) Responses of pulvinar neutrons to real and self-induced stimulus movement. Brain. Res., 338: 392–394.

Schwartz, M.L. and Goldman-Rakic, P.S. (1984) Callosal and intrahemispheric connectivity of the prefrontal association cortex in rhesus monkey: relation between intraparietal and principal sulcal cortex. J. Comp. Neurol., 226: 403–420.

Seltzer, B. and Pandya, D.N. (1983) The distribution of posterior parietal fibers in the corpus callosum of the rhesus monkey. Exp. Brain Res., 49: 147–150.

Sharpe, J.A., Lo, A.W., and Rabinovitch, H.E. (1979) Control of the saccadic and smooth pursuit systems after cerebral hemidecortication. Brain, 102: 387–403.

Sommer, M.A. and Wurtz, R.H. (1998) Frontal eye field neurons orthodromically activated from the superior colliculus. J. Neurophysiol., 80: 3331–3335.

Sommer, M.A. and Wurtz, R.H. (2002) A pathway in primate brain for internal monitoring of movements. Science, 296: 1480–1482.

Sommer, M.A. and Wurtz, R.H. (2004a) What the brain stem tells the frontal cortex. I. Oculomotor signals sent from superior colliculus to frontal eye field via mediodorsal thalamus. J. Neurophysiol., 91: 1381–1402.

Sommer, M.A. and Wurtz, R.H. (2004b) What the brain stem tells the frontal cortex. II. Role of the SC-MD-FEF pathway in corollary discharge. J. Neurophysiol., 91: 1403–1423.

Stepniewska, I., Qi, H.-X., Kaas, J.H. (2000) Projections of the superior colliculus to subdivisions of the inferior pulvinar in New World and Old World monkeys, Vis. Neurosci., 17: 529–549.

Trevarthen, C. (1990) Integrative functions of the cerebral commissures. In: Boller, F.G.J. (Ed.), Handbook of Neuropsychology, Elsevier Science Publishers, B.V. (Biomedical Division), pp. 49–83.

Umeno, M.M. and Goldberg, M.E. (1997) Spatial processing in the monkey frontal eye field. I. Predictive visual responses. J. Neurophysiol., 78: 1373–1383.

Umeno, M.M. and Goldberg, M.E. (2001) Spatial processing in the monkey frontal eye field. II. Memory responses. J. Neurophysiol., 86: 2344–2352.

Van Horn, S.C. and Sherman, S.M. (2004) Differences in projection patterns between large and small corticothalamic terminals. J. Comp. Neurol., 475: 406–415.

Walker, A.V., Fitzgibbon, E.J. and Goldberg, M.E. (1995) Neurons in the monkey superior colliculus predict the visual result of impending saccadic eye movements. J. Neurophysiol., 73: 1988–2003.

Zivotofsky, A.Z., Tzur, R., Caspi, A. and Gordon, C.R. (2003). Evidence for co-processing of orthogonal compared to co-linear saccades. Soc. Neurosci. Abstracts, 441.6.

Progress in Brain Research, Vol. 149
ISSN 0079-6123

CHAPTER 15

Drivers from the deep: the contribution of collicular input to thalamocortical processing

Robert H. Wurtz*, Marc A. Sommer and James Cavanaugh

Laboratory of Sensorimotor Research, National Eye Institute, National Institutes of Health, Bethesda, MD 20892-4435, USA

Abstract: A traditional view of the thalamus is that it is a relay station which receives sensory input and conveys this information to cortex. This sensory input determines most of the properties of first order thalamic neurons, and so is said to drive, rather than modulate, these neurons. This holds as a rule for first order thalamic nuclei, but in contrast, higher order thalamic nuclei receive much of their driver input back from cerebral cortex. In addition, higher order thalamic neurons receive inputs from subcortical movement-related centers. In the terminology popularized from studies of the sensory system, can we consider these ascending motor inputs to thalamus from subcortical structures to be *modulators*, subtly influencing the activity of their target neurons, or *drivers*, dictating the activity of their target neurons? This chapter summarizes relevant evidence from neuronal recording, inactivation, and stimulation of pathways projecting from the superior colliculus through thalamus to cerebral cortex. The study concludes that many inputs to the higher order nuclei of the thalamus from subcortical oculomotor areas — from the superior colliculus and probably other midbrain and pontine regions — should be regarded as motor drivers analogous to the sensory drivers at the first order thalamic nuclei. These motor drivers at the thalamus are viewed as being at the top of a series of feedback loops that provide information on impending actions, just as sensory drivers provide information about the external environment.

Introduction

The thalamus has long been recognized as a gateway to the cerebral cortex for sensory information flowing into the brain from the periphery (Sherman and Guillery, 2001; Jones, 2002). Everything we know about the world necessarily results from the inflow of such sensory information. The same may be true about movement information; it seems likely that much, perhaps all, of the precise information our brain receives regarding our actions comes from

*Corresponding author. Tel.: +1-301-496-7170; Fax: +1-301-402-0511; E-mail: bob@lsr.nei.nih.gov

feedback to the cerebral cortex through the thalamus (Guillery and Sherman, 2002a). But although a great deal of information has accumulated about the function of thalamic neurons conveying the qualities and receptive fields of sensory input, little is known about the characteristics and movement fields of thalamic neurons that monitor our actions. This chapter aims to draw on the recent experimental observations of ascending motor pathways passing through the thalamus in the hope of bringing the emerging understanding of these motor pathways closer to the extensive understanding of the sensory pathways.

The study begins with reviewing the concepts that have been developed for the ascending sensory

DOI: 10.1016/S0079-6123(05)49015-9

208

pathways by Guillery and Sherman (Sherman and Guillery, 2001, 2002; Guillery and Sherman, 2002a,b; Guillery, 2003). Next it is investigated how the ascending motor information fits with their view of thalamocortical organization, particularly their concepts of drivers and modulators. Since these experiments explore the nature of *signals* at different levels in the ascending motor systems, the analysis concentrates on this functional level rather than on anatomical structure — on signals rather than synapses. In addition, the experimental observations pertain to the guidance of saccadic eye movements, so the discussion of the nature of ascending signals concentrates on visual and oculomotor functions.

To begin with the sensory side, Fig. 1, which is based on the review by Guillery and Sherman (Guillery and Sherman, 2002b), gives an outline of these ideas. Sensory information from the periphery passes through thalamic nuclei devoted to the sensory pathway: first order thalamic relays (Fig. 1, left). In addition to these first order nuclei, other thalamic nuclei that do not transmit such unmistakably ascending information have been referred to as higher order nuclei (Fig. 1, right). Instead of passing sensory

information up to cortex, these higher order nuclei are thought to convey information between cortical areas by transmitting signals from cortex to thalamus and then back to the cortex, providing a route for information flow between cortical areas that is independent of the direct corticocortical connections. In the visual system (on which the study concentrates), the lateral geniculate nucleus (LGN) is the first order nucleus, and other nuclei, particularly the medial dorsal nucleus (MD) and the pulvinar nuclei, are examples of higher order nuclei.

In addition to the source and destination of projections, what Sherman and Guillery established is that inputs to the thalamus can be distinguished on the basis of their anatomical and physiological characteristics. Inputs referred to as *drivers* are those that determine the receptive field properties of the relay neurons on which they impinge. More generally, these inputs carry the basic information on which the neuronal computations are based (Guillery and Sherman, 2002b). At an anatomical level the drivers frequently form a tight glomerular synaptic structure on the thalamic relay neuron. In the case of the visual system, the driver is the retinal input conveyed by the optic tract to the lateral geniculate nucleus, since the receptive fields of LGN neurons are dominated by signals from the retina, and the glomerular structure is striking in the LGN (drivers are the solid lines in Fig. 1). In the case of higher order nuclei, receptive field structure and synaptic organization led Guillery and Sherman to conclude that the input from cortical layer 5 is a driver input in such higher order thalamic nuclei as has recently been demonstrated in the pulvinar (Van Horn and Sherman, 2004).

In contrast to drivers, *modulator* inputs are those that modify but do not dominate the information content of the signals relayed by the thalamus. This modulation is present in both first and higher order nuclei; both the LGN and pulvinar, for example, receive such modulatory input from layer 6 of cortex (modulators are the dashed lines in Fig. 1). The study does not specifically consider modulators further although their interactions, particularly from the thalamic reticular nucleus (Montero, 1997, 2000; McAlonan et al., 2000; McAlonan and Wurtz, 2004), clearly influence the visual pathways.

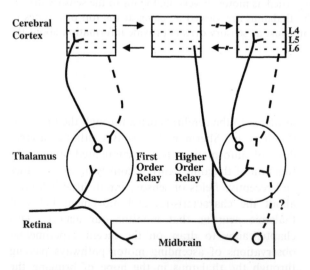

Fig. 1. Schematic representation of drivers and modulators and the problem of subcortical input. Solid lines represent drivers, dashed lines modulators, and the dotted line with the question mark represents the input considered in this article. See text of Introduction for description. Diagram after Guillery and Sherman (2002a).

The organization shown in Fig. 1 represents an established view of the thalamic organization of sensory signals, including the outputs from layers 5 and 6 of cortex to the higher order nuclei. But inputs to higher order nuclei are not limited to the descending cortical inputs demonstrated by Sherman and Guillery; there are prominent inputs to these nuclei from subcortical areas as well. In the case of a first order nucleus, the LGN modulation of visual activity by eye movements has been recognized for many years and the effect on visual responses has recently been quantified (Ramcharan et al., 2001; Reppas et al., 2002). This modulation appears to arise from the brainstem (see discussion by Reppas et al., 2002). Since these subcortical inputs seem to alter the gain of the transmission through the LGN but not the fundamental organization of the thalamic neuronal receptive fields, these inputs have been regarded as modulators.

For higher order nuclei, such subcortical inputs have been equally well documented. Inputs from the superior colliculus (SC) to MD and the pulvinar (Benevento and Fallon, 1975; Harting et al., 1980; Stepniewska et al., 1999) are prominent examples considered in detail in this chapter. These subcortical inputs are represented by the line ascending from the midbrain to the higher order nucleus in Fig. 1 (dotted line, lower right). The unresolved question is, what is the nature of this subcortical input to the higher order nuclei? In the parlance of Guillery and Sherman, are these inputs drivers or modulators? Since it is known that the subcortical inputs to the first order thalamic relays that have been studied (such as the LGN) are modulators, there is reason to believe that this might be the case in general for first order nuclei, and that this may hold for higher order nuclei as well. There is no reason to doubt the modulatory role of subcortical input on first order relays, but there are a number of functional reasons to believe it might not be prudent to assign these inputs an exclusively modulatory role on higher order relays. The present thesis is that the projections from superior colliculus to thalamus are drivers too.

In this chapter a few observations on the pathway from the SC through the MD thalamus to the frontal eye field (FEF) region of prefrontal cortex are reviewed first. The observations on this pathway will be relevant to evaluating the functional role of subcortical inputs to a higher order thalamic nucleus. Both the characteristics of neuronal activity along the pathway and the finding that the signals conveyed by this pathway play a role in providing a corollary discharge are taken into consideration. The main arguments are listed next as to why these SC–MD projections are considered as drivers. Finally the study considers whether the shift of visual attention that is seen as a result of electrical stimulation of the SC, the results of which most likely reach cortex through the pulvinar, is more consistent with a driver or modulator function. Taking these observations together, it is concluded that all of these ascending projections from the SC should be considered drivers rather than modulators of higher order thalamic nuclei. The point is that these inputs to the thalamus convey driving signals that encode imminent movements, used as corollary discharge, just as the driving inputs from the periphery encode recent sensory events.

Signals conveyed by the SC–MD–FEF pathway

The first step in determining the signal conveyed to a higher order nucleus from a subcortical area and then to the cerebral cortex is to specifically identify the neurons that relay the information. MD conveys information from multiple subcortical areas, including the superior colliculus, the cerebellar nuclei, and the basal ganglia, to wide regions of the frontal cortex. The seemingly impossible problem of determining which neurons in MD receive a given input and project to a given region of cortex can be solved by supplementing single neuron recordings with the classic physiological techniques of antidromic and orthodromic stimulation (Sommer and Wurtz, 2004a). From previous work, it is known that one of the visuomotor areas in frontal cortex, the FEF, is a main target of the SC–MD pathway (Lynch et al., 1994). MD neurons projecting into FEF could be identified by antidromically activating them from FEF (Fig. 2A). MD neurons receiving inputs from SC could be identified by orthodromically activating them from the SC (see Sommer and Wurtz, 2004a for limitations to the orthodromic method). Neurons that met *both* of these criteria were considered to be MD relay neurons, and the characteristics of the

210

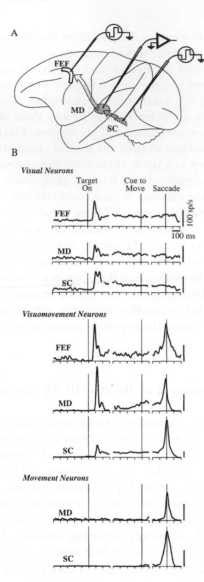

Fig. 2. Visual, delay, and movement activity of neurons in the SC–MD–FEF pathway. A. All MD neurons were identified as relay neurons by being antidromically activated from the FEF and orthodromically activated from the SC. B. Signals conveyed in the ascending pathway as determined using the delayed-saccade tasks. The monkey looked at a fixation spot and then a peripheral target appeared (Target On). The target remained on during an extended delay period, and disappearance of the fixation spot was the cue to make a saccade to the target location (Cue to Move). The records for Visual, Visuomovement, and Movement neurons are spike density functions (Gaussian width 10 ms) showing the average firing rates of example FEF recipient, MD relay, and SC source neurons during the task. Data are aligned to target onset at left, to fixation spot offset (Cue to Move) in the middle, and to saccade onset at right. From Sommer and Wurtz (2004a).

information conveyed through MD that is described is based on these identified relay neurons. In addition, neurons were identified in the SC that were the source of the input to MD by identifying SC neurons that were antidromically activated from MD, and neurons were identified in FEF that were the recipients of input from SC through MD by orthodromically activating them from SC. A sample of neurons was thus obtained at each of the steps from SC to MD to FEF, with each neuron in each sample shown to be a part of this pathway.

What signals do the neurons along this pathway convey? A delayed saccade task was used to determine whether the neurons responded to visual stimuli, whether they were active with saccades, and whether they had continuing delay activity between the visual and saccade related activity. The sequence of events in this delayed saccade task is indicated by labels at the top of Fig. 2B, and each section of Fig. 2B shows comparative examples of individual MD relay neurons, FEF recipient neurons, and SC source neurons. It was found that 87% of the MD neurons fell into three categories: some had only a phasic or tonic visual response but no presaccadic activity (Visual Neurons, Fig. 2B top), some had presaccadic activity but no visual response (Movement Neurons, Fig. 2B bottom), and others had both visual and presaccadic activity (Visuomovement Neurons, Fig. 2B middle). These same categories could be identified equally well in both FEF and SC (except for Movement Neurons, which were never found in the FEF recipient neuron sample). Figure 3A shows the frequencies of these categories at each step of the pathway. A number of salient observations emerge from comparing the activity at different levels of the pathway:

(1) Nearly every neuron in the pathway was active in the oculomotor task, with only a small proportion at each stage showing no significant change in activity during the task (the "other" neurons). This indicates that many of the signals are seen in the pathway and thus one can draw conclusions with some confidence on the information the pathways conveys.

(2) The distributions of neuron types along the pathway may be compared. From SC to MD there was no significant change in the distribution of neuron types, consistent with the

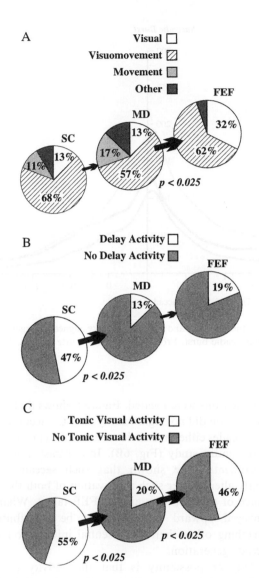

Fig. 3. Frequency of types of neurons at each stage in the ascending SC–MD–FEF pathway. A. Percentages of Visual, Visuomovement, and Movement neurons, B. Percentage of neurons having delay activity. C. Percentage of neurons having tonic visual activity. Bold arrows indicate significantly different distributions. The charts represent 47 SC neurons, 46 MD neurons, and 37 FEF neurons. From Sommer and Wurtz (2004a).

possibility that the controlling input to MD was from the superior colliculus. From MD to FEF the distribution changed significantly: the FEF distribution had much more visual activity than would be expected from its MD

input. In addition, when this visual response occurred, it was found that it was nearly simultaneous in MD and the SC but about 15 ms earlier in the FEF (Fig. 4). Thus it seems likely that the visual input from MD is added on to an existing visual response in FEF that presumably results from extrastriate input.

(3) As is evident in Fig. 2B, many of the neurons also had delay activity, a signal occurring after target disappearance and before saccade initiation, which may be involved in higher level cognitive functions such as target selection or working memory (Goldman-Rakic, 1995; Fuster, 1997). Delay activity was present in all of the visuomovement neurons in Fig. 2B, for example. Figure 3B shows that from SC to MD, the proportion of neurons with delay activity dropped significantly, while from MD to FEF it did not change. Thus the connection from SC to MD seemed to act like a high-pass filter; the connection seemed to let *bursts* of activity through more readily than *sustained* activity. Consistent with this possibility, it was also found that the proportion of neurons carrying another sustained signal, tonic visual activity, decreased from SC to MD (Fig. 3C). In contrast, the proportion of tonic visual signals *increased* from MD to FEF, which also provides added evidence that the FEF recipient neurons are generally more visual than expected from their MD input, consistent with the suggestion that the FEF recipient neurons receive additional visual signals from elsewhere such as from extrastriate cortex. But the main point is that delay activity is largely suppressed at the SC–MD synapse.

Figure 5 summarizes the signals conveyed in the SC–MD–FEF pathway. Diverse signals, from visual to delay to motor, are sent up to thalamus from the SC and most of them continue on to the FEF except for highly damped delay activity (Fig. 5A). The signals that enter the FEF from the SC via MD must have different influences (Fig. 5B): the visual activity arrives too late to directly cause visual responses in FEF and the delay activity seems too little in quantity to be of any substantial import, but

212

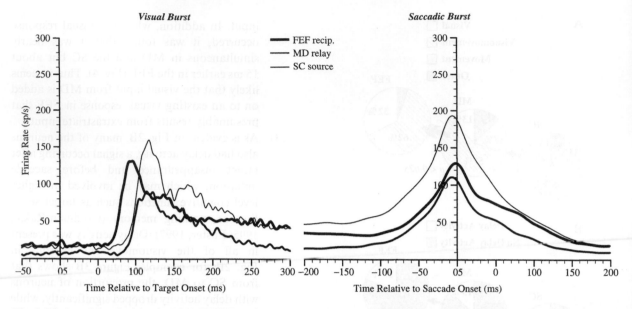

Fig. 4. Timing of signals along the SC–MD–FEF pathway. Mean activity in the SC, MD, and FEF samples are aligned to target onset (*left*) to show the visual burst and to saccade onset (*right*) to show the presaccadic burst. From Sommer and Wurtz (2004a).

the motor-related activity seems just right to exert an important impact, as it is very common, strong in magnitude, and arrives just prior to a saccade.

A corollary discharge function for the SC–MD–FEF pathway

Activity in the SC–MD–FEF pathway could provide a variety of types of information and probably does so not only for the visual tasks that have been investigated but for other tasks as well. The next task after determining the types of signals conveyed through MD was to explore what the function of these signals might be (Sommer and Wurtz, 2004b). The obvious possibility given the visual responses and the presaccadic activity is that these neurons are providing a signal for the guidance of saccades. This was tested in the same way that this question has been investigated previously in the SC and the FEF, by inactivating the neurons and then testing the effect on the monkey's ability to make saccades to visual targets. MD neurons were inactivated using musci-mol, a GABA agonist, injected at sites where the MD

relay neurons were located. Figure 6 shows that such inactivation did not significantly alter the accuracy of the saccades either in individual examples (Fig. 6A) or in the entire study (Fig. 6B). In contrast, previous experiments have shown that such saccades are clearly altered after such inactivation of both the SC source of this pathway and its FEF target. What is conveyed upward by MD must be contributing something other than the essential information for saccade generation.

Another possibility is that the activity is not conveying information for generating the movement but for keeping track of it, that is, it is carrying a corollary discharge (efference copy) of the intended movement. This could also be tested by inactivating MD while using a task designed to reveal a change in behavior if the corollary discharge for saccadic eye movement were impaired. In this double saccade task the monkey fixated a spot, the spot disappeared, and two targets briefly appeared in sequence (Fig. 7A). To receive a reward the monkey had to make two sequential saccades to the locations of the targets. The targets were brief flashes so that both had disappeared before the first saccade began, and the monkey was in the dark with no other visual cues present.

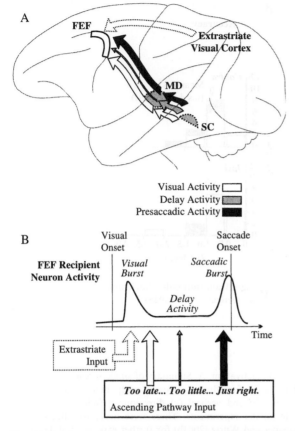

Fig. 5. Summary of the signal content in the SC–MD–FEF pathway. A. Visual, delay, and pre-saccadic activity are all sent from SC to MD, and all three continue to FEF except that the amount of delay activity is severely reduced. At the FEF, neurons receiving this ascending input also seem to receive extra visual input, presumably from extrastriate cortex. B. The relative contribution of SC input to the FEF. MD to FEF visual signals from the ascending pathway arrive too late to cause the FEF visual burst, which is probably initiated by extrastriate input. It appears that too little delay activity survives through the pathway to be of major importance. However, the presaccadic activity seems just right; it travels unhindered through the pathway and arrives precisely at the appropriate time to contribute to saccadic bursts in the FEF neurons. From Sommer and Wurtz (2004a).

The location of the target pairs was randomized so that the monkey could not predict which pattern of targets would occur on any given trial. The point of the task is this: in order to make the second saccade straight up, the monkey has to know that its eye moved and where it moved to during the first saccade. If it did not know this, it should make a diagonal

saccade up and to the right as if the eye were still looking at the original target point. The constant internal monitoring of saccadic behavior needed for this task must result from an extraretinal signal which is hypothesized as from the corollary discharge information conveyed by the SC–MD–FEF. The reason for this is that proprioception is unlikely to provide the eye position information; this has been discussed previously (Sommer and Wurtz, 2004b). Note that the fact that neurons in the pathway increase activity *before* the saccade (Fig. 4, right) indicates that activity cannot be proprioceptive since the eye has not yet begun to move.

Figure 7B shows saccades during an MD inactivation in the double step task. The monkey had to make a rightward saccade and then an upward saccade in response to two flashed targets. Figure 7B, top shows all the saccades made *before* MD was inactivated. Most second saccades were made appropriately upward. *During* MD inactivation (Fig. 7B, bottom), the monkey's behavior was nearly the same except that the second, upward saccades seemed to be tilted toward the upper right, in the direction expected if the monkey did not know the first saccade had been made. In Fig. 7C all the trials in this session are summarized by showing the means and SDs of the initial fixations, first saccade endpoints, and second saccade endpoints before and during inactivation. The most obvious effect of the inactivation seemed to be a roughly horizontal shift in second saccade endpoints, and this shift was significant. In contrast, neither the initial fixations nor the first saccade endpoints shifted in either the horizontal or vertical direction. This result was confirmed across multiple injections in two monkeys (Sommer and Wurtz, 2004b).

If the corollary discharge occurs with each saccade, it would also be expected to see deficits on a trial-by-trial basis when the corollary discharge is impaired, and this did happen. That is, not only the mean accuracy was affected but also the precision, trial-by-trial, was impaired. Figure 8A, left, shows the trial-by-trial variation in second saccade vectors that resulted from the fact that the first rightward horizontal saccade had slight variability in amplitude from trial to trial for which the second saccade compensated. In Fig. 8A, the second saccades have been ordered according to the end of the first horizontal saccade

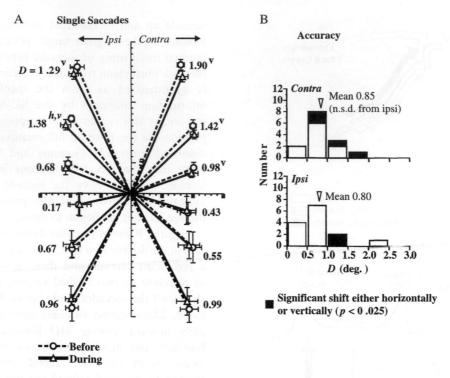

Fig. 6. Lack of impairment for saccades made to single targets during MD inactivation. A. Summary of single saccades made before and during one example inactivation. The panels represent 12 pairs of before–during saccadic endpoints in each direction (contraversive and ipsiversive), and the difference (D) in the horizontal (h) and vertical (v) directions is indicated in degrees. B. Histograms showing how accuracy was affected by inactivation in all the experiments. There were negligible effects and no significant difference in contraversive vs. ipsiversive directions. See Sommer and Wurtz (2004b) for further experimental details.

(the shortest first saccade at the top, the longest at the bottom). Before the injection (Fig. 8A, left) the second saccade compensated for the variation in first saccade amplitude: shorter first saccades (top) tended to be followed by a saccade that went further to the right to compensate for the first saccade falling short; longer saccades (bottom) tended to be followed by a saccade that was actually directed backward to the left to compensate for the first saccade being too long. Thus the monkey was quite deft at precisely adjusting the second saccade direction, from which it is inferred that it had information about where the first saccade ended with each saccade made.

In contrast, during the inactivation of MD (Fig. 8A, right) there was much less compensation: all of the second saccades were directed toward the right regardless of whether the first saccade was relatively short or long on a particular trial. Figure 8B shows

this result quantitatively by comparing the directions (θ) of ideal second saccades that would be expected from perfect compensation (Sommer and Wurtz, 2004b) with those of the actual second saccades that were observed. Before inactivation, when corollary discharge was present (bold circles and line), a correlation was noticed between the ideal and observed data, and the linear regression slope was near one. During the inactivation (thin triangles and line) the relationship was reduced: the correlation became insignificant. This result was representative of all the inactivations. In sum, monkeys normally adjusted their second saccade directions from trial to trial to compensate for slight fluctuations in first saccades, and this was disrupted by inactivation. It is concluded, therefore, that corollary discharge is normally precise and that MD inactivation impairs this precision.

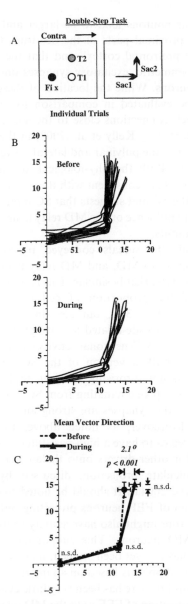

Fig. 7. Loss of corollary discharge during MD inactivation. A. Spatial aspects of the double step task. Monkeys initially looked at a fixation spot (Fix) and then two targets (T1 and T2) appeared sequentially in the periphery. The task was to make two saccades (Sac1 and Sac2) to the locations of the extinguished targets. B. Example data from the double-step task before and during MD inactivation. Superimposed are saccades from correct trials. C. Summary of the correct trials before and during inactivation, showing the means and SDs of initial fixation locations, first saccade endpoints, and second saccade endpoints. The only significant change during inactivation was a contraversive shift in second saccade endpoints, indicating a loss of corollary discharge accuracy. n.s.d., not significantly different. From Sommer and Wurtz (2004b).

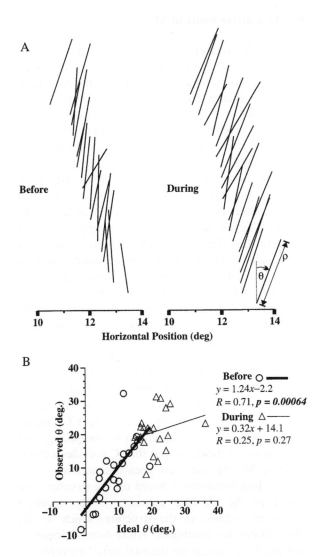

Fig. 8. Loss of corollary discharge precision during MD inactivation: a trial-by-trial analysis. A. Individual second saccades from an experiment with targets positioned as shown in Fig. 7A. Second saccades before inactivation are shown at *left* and during inactivation at *right*. Each saccade is represented by a vector connecting its initial and final position with a line, and the vectors are ordered by the starting position of the second saccade *which indicates the ending position of the first saccade*. B. How well the monkey adjusted its second saccade directions to account for trial-by-trial fluctuations in its first saccades. The observed θ for each second saccade (from the vectors in A) is plotted against the ideal θ (if corollary discharge was perfect). Before inactivation there was a direct correlation between observed θ and ideal θ with a linear regression slope near unity (1.24), but during inactivation the correlation was not significant and the slope was only 0.32. From Sommer and Wurtz (2004b).

SC As a driver input to MD

Thus far recent work on the signals that are conveyed through the SC–MD–FEF pathway were reviewed. Inspired by anatomical evidence for such a disynaptic route (Benevento and Fallon, 1975; Harting et al., 1980; Lynch et al., 1994) neurons were physiologically identified throughout the pathway and inactivated at the thalamic level. It was concluded that the pathway carries corollary discharge information. These conclusions presuppose that the SC drives MD relay neurons, but what direct evidence is there for this presumption? Is the SC really a driver of MD relay neurons, as the functional evidence suggests, or is it a modulator? The present observations, taken as a whole, make a strong case for the SC input as being a driver onto MD, but we readily concede that no one piece of evidence is conclusive. For example, perhaps inactivating MD caused corollary discharge deficits because the MD relay neurons carry corollary discharge as supplied not by SC ascending input, but by collaterals of FEF layer 5 descending projections as depicted in Fig. 1. Fundamentally, therefore, skeptics could still protest that it remains ambiguous as to whether MD relay neuron activity is driven by ascending SC input or by descending FEF input. In this section the seemingly most compelling four arguments for the thesis that the SC provides a driver input to MD neurons have been summarized.

The first argument is based on the structure and speed of the SC–MD connection. The speed is necessarily related to the structure, which is why these points are combined. While direct evidence is not available concerning the anatomical arrangement of synapses on MD neurons comparable to that in other thalamic regions (e.g., the pulvinar, Guillery, 1995; Reichova and Sherman, 2004), there are a few observations that suggest that the SC to MD synapses are strong and secure, which make them reasonable candidates for drivers. First of all, it was found that single pulse stimulation in the SC activated MD neurons with short latency (median 1.4 ms, including a presumed synaptic delay of only 0.57 ms) and required normal current thresholds for this type of study (mean 264 μA). While ultrastructural anatomy of MD is not yet available in the monkey, the anatomy of synapses in the rat have been studied by Kuroda and Price (1991). They found that the

"collicular boutons tend to be larger and distribute to more proximal parts of the dendrites than those from the prefrontal cortex" and that the SC inputs made asymmetric, excitatory synapses onto the thalamic neurons. While the location of these synapses has to be evaluated in comparison to other structures, such connections close to the soma have also been reported by Kelly et al. (2003) in the collicular projection to the pulvinar and lateral posterior nuclei of the cat. Both the physiological and anatomical observations are consistent with the strong driving of MD by the SC and suggests that SC inputs probably have more influence on the MD relay neurons than do cortical inputs.

Second, the signals conveyed by SC neurons projecting up to MD, and MD relay neurons themselves, are remarkably similar. This is true not only in terms of the proportion of cell classes in each population (Fig. 3A), but also in terms of their visual- and saccade-related activity profiles (Fig. 4). In essence, the MD neuronal activity simply looks like a slightly muffled version of the SC activity; this damping is not surprising and just implies that not every single spike emanating from SC causes a spike in MD — the synapses are strong and fast but not perfect. Moreover, as noted above, the SC–MD synapse seems to have a high-pass filter characteristic as seen for other drivers onto thalamus (e.g., in the retinogeniculate projection, discussed by Sommer and Wurtz, 2004a). It should be noted that the subpopulation of FEF neurons projecting onto the MD relay neurons might also have activity profiles similar to the MD neurons. This subpopulation of FEF neurons has not yet been studied, however.

The third point is based on an interesting negative result: thus far there has been very little evidence for a strong projection of FEF onto the MD relay neurons. Present observations on this matter are limited but seem to suggest that the FEF influence on MD relay neurons is very weak. Figure 9 shows one example. Recording was done from an MD neuron while applying a brief pulse of stimulation in the FEF. The purpose was to see if the neuron could be activated antidromically the neuron which would demonstrate that it projected into the FEF (Fig. 9A, "Anti"). But the stimulation could also orthodromically activate the MD neuron if it were receiving input from the FEF (Fig. 9A, "Ortho"), and indeed this

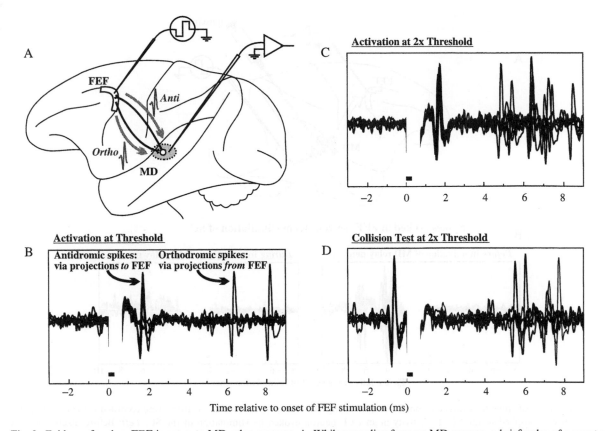

Fig. 9. Evidence for slow FEF input onto MD relay neurons. A. While recording from an MD neuron, a brief pulse of current was applied to the FEF. This evoked an action potential (depicted in gray) that could travel either backwards in the ascending axon of the MD neuron (i.e., antidromically, *Anti*), or forwards in the descending axons of FEF neurons (i.e., orthodromically, *Ortho*). B. Action potentials from an example MD relay neuron while stimulating at threshold. Results of several trials are superimposed; stimulation in FEF started at time 0 and its duration is indicated by the short bar above the abscissa. Because stimulation was at threshold, it evokes spikes in the neuron on about half of trials. As labeled, antidromic spikes occur early (about 1.2 ms latency) and orthodromic spikes late (about 6–8 ms latency). C. Same experiment but using twice threshold current, and the early antidromic and late orthodromic spikes are clearly seen to be caused by the stimulation. D. Collision test at twice threshold. Stimulation is synchronized to occur just after the initiation of a spontaneous action potential of the neuron (occurring at about −1 ms). This caused the annihilation of the early cluster of spikes (compare the waveforms in the range 1–2 ms between this panel and panel C), showing that they were antidromically activated, but it did not annihilate the later spikes, showing that they were orthodromically activated. For review of the collision test, see Lemon (1984).

occasionally happened (in about 10% of MD relay neurons). Figure 9B shows antidromic and orthodromic activation on a single MD neuron at the threshold current for antidromic activation (55 µA). An antidromic spike occurred in half of the trials, and a few later spikes also occurred. By increasing the current (Fig. 9C) it became obvious that the later spikes were being caused by the FEF stimulation. Application of the collision test (Fig. 9D) proved that the early, highly stable spikes were antidromic (they

disappeared) while the later ones were orthodromic (they remained). This neuron, therefore, both projected to the FEF and received projections from it. The long and variable latencies of the orthodromic activation (~4.5–8 ms) indicated that the influence of the FEF on the MD thalamic neuron was rather weak and inconsistent. Moreover, attributing this activation to a monosynaptic projection from the FEF has been generous, as it easily could have been due to polysynaptic pathways. In sum, the influence of FEF

A

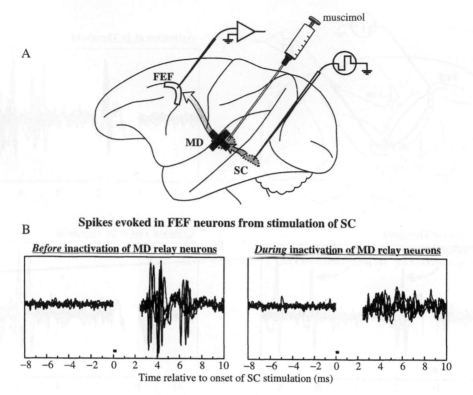

B **Spikes evoked in FEF neurons from stimulation of SC**

Before inactivation of MD relay neurons

During inactivation of MD relay neurons

Time relative to onset of SC stimulation (ms)

Fig. 10. Blockade of spike transmission from SC to FEF using MD inactivation. A. FEF neurons were recorded while brief pulses of stimulation were applied to the SC. B. Activity in an FEF neuron evoked by stimulation of the SC. *Left*: Before inactivation, SC stimulation (starting at time 0 for the duration indicated by the bar) caused a volley of spikes in the FEF. *Right*: During inactivation, the volley was severely reduced, indicating that the driving input of SC onto FEF was dependent on MD relay neurons.

on MD relay neurons would appear to be very limited and presumably modulatory according to these data. In contrast, as noted above, identical stimulation in the SC causes strong, short-latency (median 1.4 ms) orthodromic activation of MD relay neurons, consistent with its being a driver input.

One caveat, however, is that the layer 5 projections from other cortical areas could also provide a driver input onto the MD relay neurons, but evaluating this from the present experiments is not possible because areas beyond the FEF were not stimulated. There has been no reason to reject the possibility of multiple driver inputs to the MD relay neurons.

The fourth and final point indicating a driving influence of SC onto MD is derived from the recent experiments (yet unpublished) using recording, inactivation, and stimulation simultaneously to determine the contribution of SC input through MD on FEF

activity (Fig. 10A). We recorded from FEF neurons and attempted to drive each one with SC stimulation. When an FEF neuron that was orthodromically activated from the SC and thus presumably was driven through the SC–MD–FEF pathway was found, this presumption was tested explicitly by reversibly inactivating the MD relay neurons with muscimol. A typical result is shown in Fig. 10B. Before inactivation (Fig. 10B, left) stimulation in the SC caused a strong volley of action potentials in the FEF neuron (consisting of a shorter latency, larger amplitude spike and a second, later, smaller spike). Other orthodromic spikes were present in the background activity but are obscured by the large spikes. During inactivation of the MD relay neurons (Fig. 10B, right), using 0.9 μL of 5 μg/μL muscimol, the SC stimulation failed to activate the two (larger and smaller) FEF neurons. Some background orthodromic activity was still present, but it seems likely that with a larger injection in MD this would have disappeared too. The point made by this experiment is that SC activation drives FEF neurons, and this driving is critically dependent on the activity of MD relay neurons; hence, activity in the SC must be driving MD relay neurons.

SC and visual spatial attention

In other recent experiments, another likely SC input onto the cerebral cortex has been identified, one related to the enhancement of visual processing through shifts of attention. The goal was to test the idea that common subcortical mechanisms underlie both the generation of saccades to one part of the visual field and shifts of attention to that same part of the visual field — a motor theory of attention (Rizzolatti, 1983; Sheliga et al., 1994; Moore et al., 2003). It was hypothesized that these two functions do not diverge until a point in the neuronal circuitry close to the actual motor neurons. Consequently, the well-known visuomotor map in the intermediate layers of the SC was targeted (Robinson, 1972), assuming that the point of divergence occurs after the SC. In addition to the increase in activity just preceding a saccade that was emphasized with respect to the SC–MD–FEF pathway, many of the neurons in the intermediate layers of the SC also have delay activity related to gradual selection of the saccade to be made (Glimcher and Sparks, 1992; Dorris and Munoz, 1995; Basso and Wurtz, 1998; Bell et al., 2004). Such selection-related activity occurs at the same time that neuronal activity in visual areas of the cortex is enhanced during attentional tasks (Reynolds and Desimone, 1999; Ghose and Maunsell, 2002). This SC selection-related activity is modulated when the monkey attends to a region of the visual field (Kustov and Robinson, 1996), and this modulation occurs only with a spatial cue for that region (Ignashchenkova et al., 2004). The logic then is that the delay activity of these SC neurons might be directed not only to preparing for a saccade to one part of the visual field but also to providing a spatial attention signal to cortex that modulates the activity of visual cortical neurons related to the same part of the visual field.

Since it was vital to the experiment to effectively manipulate the allocation of visual attention, we wanted to use a visual task that is strongly affected by visual attention. The task we chose was change blindness. Change blindness is the failure to see large changes in a visual scene that occur at the same time as global visual transients, such as the naturally occurring blurring caused by rapid or saccadic eye movements between fixations, or by brief blanks interposed between successive visual scenes presented during continued fixation. Attention shifts to the site of the change counter this "blindness" by improving both detection of the change and reaction time to the change. We developed a change blindness paradigm for visual motion and then showed that presenting an attentional cue diminished the blindness in monkeys as well as in humans. In this change blindness task (Fig. 11A), the subjects began each trial by fixating on a spot in the center of the screen in front of them and then three patches of random dot motion appeared: one target and two distractors (for details see Cavanaugh and Wurtz, 2005). On 65% of the trials, the direction of motion in the target patch changed, and the subject indicated such a change by making a saccade to the target if it changed, and continued fixating if the direction did not change. The direction of motion in the distractor patches never changed, and the location of the target patch was randomized among trials. On half the trials, before the patches appeared, a visual cue indicated which patch was the target while on the other half of the trials there was no such cue. To induce change blindness on cued and non-cued trials, a visual transient was initiated just when the direction of dot motion in the target might change. To measure the attentional cue's influence on change blindness the subject's performance on trials without a cue was compared with performance on trials with a cue. As expected, it was found that introducing the blank made the change in the direction of motion hard to see, thus demonstrating for the first time change blindness in monkeys as well as humans. It was also found that shifting attention by providing a visual cue increased the detection of the change in the target and decreased the reaction time for indicating the location of change — the two classic measures of visual spatial attention.

220

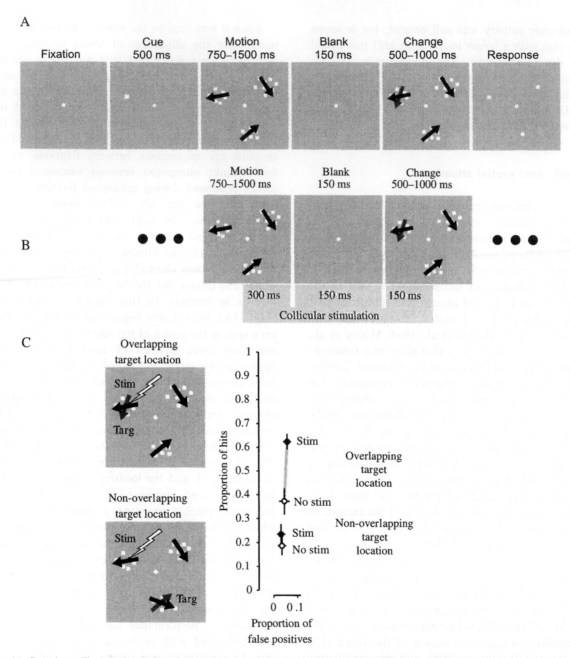

Fig. 11. Superior colliculus stimulation alters attention in a change blindness task. A. Sequence of stimuli presented in the behavioral change blindness task for those trials in which a cue was given. B. Time course of sub-threshold collicular stimulation. Stimulation began 300 ms before the blank period, and continued for 600 ms, ending 150 ms after the patches reappeared. C. Sample results from an SC stimulation experiment showing the difference when stimulation was given (closed symbols) and not given (open symbols). The graph shows sample results from a single stimulation site, with the ordinate and abscissa indicating proportions of hits and false positives, respectively. In overlapping experiments, stimulation occurred when the target patch spatially overlapped the visual field location of the collicular stimulation site. In non-overlapping experiments, stimulation occurred when one of the distractors spatially overlapped the collicular stimulation site. When the target overlapped the site of collicular stimulation, the proportion of hits increased greatly, while there was little change in the occurrence of false positives to this location. In the non-overlapping experiment, neither hits nor false positives changed significantly. From Cavanaugh and Wurtz (2005).

The experiment was then changed for the monkeys. Instead of providing a visual cue to indicate target location, the SC was electrically stimulated during the period when the change in direction might be occurring (Fig. 11B). After first identifying the part of the visual field to which the SC was related by evoking saccades with electrical stimulation, the stimulation frequency was reduced until it was too weak to elicit an eye movement. This low level stimulation was found to produce results compatible with a shift of attention — increased detection of the change and a faster reaction time. In the example shown in Fig. 11C, SC stimulation significantly increased the proportion of hits ($p = 0.0001$) when the target patch spatially overlapped the stimulation site. SC stimulation also reduced the reaction time for correct responses on these trials.

A separate set of trials was run to determine whether the increase in hits from stimulation resulted from some general effect of stimulation, such as arousal. In this set of trials, the SC was stimulated only when the target was in the opposite visual hemifield and did not overlap the stimulation site. In the example experiment (Fig. 11C) for this non-overlapping case, no significant increase in hit rate was observed ($p = 0.44$).

Note that for this example stimulation site, in neither the overlapping nor the non-overlapping case did the false positive rate change significantly ($p > 0.34$). If SC stimulation simply caused more saccades, there would be more false positives to the target (incorrect saccades) as well as hits (correct saccades). The increase in just the correct saccadic responses suggests that stimulating the SC countered change blindness in a spatially selective manner, akin to shifting covert attention with a visual cue.

This effect was repeated over a number of SC stimulation sites and a modulation of performance was found to varying degrees. The mean increase in hit rate across overlapping experiments was significant (9.2%, $p < 0.0001$) as was the reduction in mean reaction time (-14.9 ms, $p = 0.0001$). Thus the observed change in the animal's performance met both criteria used to determine a shift of visual attention: a spatially selective increase in hits, and a reduction in reaction time. These results provide support for the motor theory of attention, specifically the hypothesis that the SC activity preceding the generation of saccadic eye movements to one part of the visual field also contributes a spatially selective attentional input for the enhanced visual processing seen in visual cortical areas.

What is the relevance of this for the present consideration of the nature of subcortical inputs to the thalamus? Unlike the pathway which has been identified from SC to MD to FEF, the pathway mediating the attention effect is a matter of speculation. Assuming that the shift of attention was due to direct activation of the SC (and not, for example, due to antidromic activation of the FEF by way of its projections down to the SC), the signals underlying the shift of attention must pass through the thalamus. One possibility is that the SC delay activity, which is thought to be related to directing visual attention, passes through MD, the same pathway that has been considered with respect to the corollary discharge. However, recall that in this SC–MD–FEF pathway the delay activity preceding a saccade *decreased* in MD compared to the same activity in the SC (Fig. 3B), making this pathway an unlikely conduit for delay activity. A more likely pathway is through the pulvinar. So although one particular pathway has been suspected as conveying this attentional signal, it is acknowledged that there is little physiological evidence for this so far.

This SC stimulation experiment thus provides another example of subcortical motor information modifying cortical activity. It is inferred that the SC stimulation affects visual processing in the cortex since the determination of direction of visual motion (the basis of the change blindness task) depends on identified areas of visual cortex, specifically extrastriate area MT (Newsome et al., 1985; Newsome and Pare, 1988). A recent report by Müller et al. (2005) appeared to confirm this.

Conclusion: Motor drivers and sensory drivers

Not only do higher order thalamic neurons receive collateral inputs from the output of the cerebral cortex, they also receive inputs from subcortical movement related areas as well. This study has considered whether these motor inputs are best regarded as modulatory inputs acting on the sensory based activity derived from the cortex or whether they

222

are best regarded as driver inputs comparable in significance to the drivers studied so far in the sensory system. While much less is known about the ascending motor related activity than the activity ascending in the sensory pathways, the experimental evidence that has been considered in the SC to MD to FEF pathway provides some clues as to the nature of the input. The evidence from the visual-oculomotor activity seen in MD can be regarded as largely the result of driver input from SC. Another input from the SC to visual cortex has been shown to contribute to visual spatial attention, and this input via an as yet unidentified thalamic relay also is best viewed as a driver of thalamic activity rather than a modulator. Thus in Fig. 1 the dotted line representing ascending motor information from the midbrain should be a solid line indicative of a driver input. We conclude that the inputs to the higher order nuclei of the thalamus from the subcortical oculomotor areas should be regarded as motor drivers in parallel to the sensory drivers at the first order thalamic nuclei.

One consequence of this identification of a motor driver input to some higher order thalamic nuclei is the recognition of the potentially different information conveyed directly from one cortical region to another compared to the information conveyed indirectly from one cortical region to another through a higher order thalamic nucleus (Fig. 12). The higher order thalamic nucleus can convey information to a cortical area both from another cortical area via the descending pathway from layer 5 of cortex and from the ascending motor pathway. The pathway through the higher order nucleus offers the possibility of combining current information from cortex with new information on the impending movement. In contrast the direct cortical–cortical connections convey only information from the other cortical area. Thus these probably should not be regarded as alternate routes between successive cortical areas but rather as routes that contribute different information.

The drivers considered here are both essentially corollary discharges — they are copies of information in the motor pathway that are sent to the cerebral cortex — even though only the MD signal has been primarily referred to as a corollary discharge. There are other signals arriving at higher order thalamic nuclei, however, that could be driver inputs but not corollaries. For example, inputs to MD other than

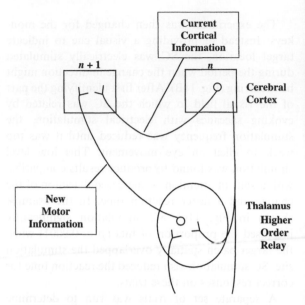

Fig. 12. Difference between the information conveyed to a cortical area from another cortical area and from a higher order thalamic nucleus. The higher order thalamic nucleus can convey *both* current information from another cortical area and new motor information from the ascending motor pathway. In contrast the direct cortical—cortical connections convey only the current information from the other cortical area.

those from the superior colliculus come from the cerebellum and the basal ganglia, and these may contribute to the control of movement rather than producing a corollary signal of that movement; thus far there is not enough evidence to decide (Sommer, 2003).

These motor drivers to the thalamus can be envisioned as the top of a series of loops in the primate brain that provide information to upper levels at the same time as they provide instructions to lower levels, usually, but not necessarily, for the control of movement (Fig. 13). Just as layer 5 of cortex can project into a subcortical area such as the SC and have a collateral to higher order thalamic nuclei, the SC can project to pontine areas and have a driving collateral that projects back to the thalamus. Note that at each step there is both a descending instruction and a collateral projection with a corollary of the instruction, with the exception that the thalamic nuclei project up to the cerebral cortex but do not themselves provide descending outputs. But this study considers the corollary conveyed by the

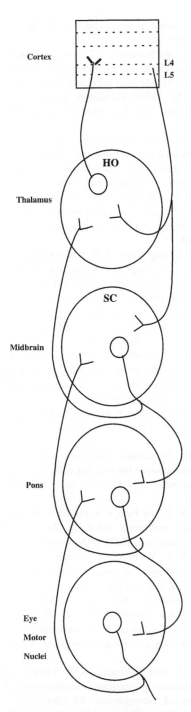

Fig. 13. Comparison of driver input and corollary discharge. The ascending collateral to the higher order nucleus of the thalamus from the SC conveys a corollary of the movement information sent downstream from the SC. It is suggested that this is one example of a pattern recurring repeatedly along the axis from cerebral processing to motor nuclei.

thalamus as no different conceptually from the other corollaries below it on the path.

One ambiguous aspect of this discussion on drivers and modulators relates to the behavioral evidence that has been presented, specifically that the input from SC through thalamus modifies behavior once it reaches the cerebral cortex. If it ends up modifying behavior, in a rather subtle and covert way — e.g., through a shift of attention — why is the input at the cortex not considered a modulator? The hidden assumption in this question is that cortical processing is based primarily on sensory input, and that movement-related input simply impinges on and modifies this processing. If this were true, the input received by the cortex from the SC via thalamus would appropriately be regarded as modulatory. But a great deal of evidence on the activity of neurons in the extrastriate visual areas, along with the parietal and frontal cortex, has shown that inputs other than the sensory make an equal if not larger contribution to neuronal activity. For example, in comparing activity in V1 and V4 in the extrastriate visual pathway, Haenny et al. (1988) found that neuronal activity became more determined by the monkey's set related to a search stimulus than to the stimulus itself. Therefore the assumption is made that cortical activity beyond the primary sensory areas is driven as much by processing and inputs that are distinct from the sensory input as by the sensory input itself. One of the major inputs is likely to be the input back to cortex from the higher order nuclei of the thalamus, as Guillery and Sherman have emphasized, and if the motor input to these thalamic nuclei is regarded as drivers, there is every reason to regard their contribution to cortical processing as much a driver as is the sensory input. In this sense the modification discussed here is a result of altering this mix of sensory and motor drivers, not just a modulation of the driver sensory input. Cortical processing should be regarded as resulting from inputs reporting the results of movement and/or prior processing as much as it results from current sensory input.

References

Basso, M.A. and Wurtz, R.H. (1998) Modulation of neuronal activity in superior colliculus by changes in target probability. J. Neurosci., 18: 7519–7534.

224

Bell, A.H., Fecteau, J.H. and Munoz, D.P. (2004) Using auditory and visual stimuli to investigate the behavioral and neuronal consequences of reflexive covert orienting. J. Neurophysiol., 91: 2172–2184.

Benevento, L.A. and Fallon, J.H. (1975) The ascending projections of the superior colliculus in the rhesus monkey (Macaca mulatta). J. Comp. Neurol., 160: 339–361.

Cavanaugh, J. and Wurtz R. H. (2004) Subcortical modulation of attention counters change blindness. J. Neurosci., 24: 11236–11243.

Dorris, M.C. and Munoz, D.P. (1995) A neural correlate for the gap effect on saccadic reaction times in monkey. J. Neurophysiol., 73: 2558–2562.

Fuster, J.M. (1997) The prefrontal cortex. Anatomy, Physiology, and Neuropsychology of the Frontal Lobe, 3rd edition, Lippincott-Raven, Philadelphia.

Ghose, G.M. and Maunsell, J.H.R. (2002) Attentional modulation in visual cortex depends on task timing. Nature, 419: 616–620.

Glimcher, P.W. and Sparks, D.L. (1992) Movement selection in advance of action in the superior colliculus. Nature, 355: 542–545.

Goldman-Rakic, P.S. (1995) Cellular basis of working memory. Neuron, 14: 477–485.

Guillery, R.W. (1995) Anatomical evidence concerning the role of the thalamus in corticocortical communication: A brief review. J. Anat., 187(3): 583–592.

Guillery, R.W. (2003) Branching thalamic afferents link action and perception. J. Neurophysiol., 90: 539–548.

Guillery, R.W. and Sherman, S.M. (2002a) The thalamus as a monitor of motor outputs. Philos. Trans. R Soc. Lond. B Biol. Sci., 357: 1809–1821.

Guillery, R.W. and Sherman, S.M. (2002b) Thalamic relay functions and their role in corticocortical communication: Generalizations from the visual system. Neuron, 33: 163–175.

Haenny, P.E., Maunsell, J.H.R. and Schiller, P.H. (1988) State dependent activity in monkey visual cortex II. Retinal and extraretinal factors in V4. Exp. Brain Res., 69: 245–259.

Harting, J.K., Huerta, M.F., Frankfurter, A.J., Strominger, N.L. and Royce, G.J. (1980) Ascending pathways from the monkey superior colliculus: An autoradiographic analysis. J. Comp. Neurol., 192: 853–882.

Ignashchenkova, A., Dicke, P.W., Haarmeier, T. and Their, P. (2004) Neuron-specific contribution of the superior colliculus to overt and covert shifts of attention. Nat. Neurosci., 7: 56–64.

Jones, E.G. (2002) Thalamic organization and function after Cajal. Prog. Brain Res., 136: 333–357.

Kelly, L.R., Li, J., Carden, W.B. and Bickford, M.E. (2003) Ultrastructure and synaptic targets of thectothalamic terminals in the cat lateral posterior nucleus. J. Comp. Neurol., 464: 472–486.

Kuroda, M. and Price, J.L. (1991) Ultrastructure and synaptic organization of axon terminals from brainstem structures to the mediodorsal thalamic nucleus of the rat. J. Comp. Neurol., 313: 539–552.

Kustov, A.A. and Robinson, D.L. (1996) Shared neural control of attentional shifts and eye movements. Nature, 384: 74–77.

Lemon, R. (1984) Methods for neuronal recording in conscious animals. In: IBRO Handbook Series. Methods in the Neurosciences, Vol. 4. J. Wiley & Sons, New York, pp. 95–102.

Lynch, J.C., Hoover, J.E. and Strick, P.L. (1994) Input to the primate frontal eye field from the substantia nigra, superior colliculus, and dentate nucleus demonstrated by transneuronal transport. Exp. Brain Res., 100: 181–186.

McAlonan, K., Brown, V.J. and Bowman, E.M. (2000) Thalamic reticular nucleus activation reflects attentional gating during classical conditioning. J. Neurosci., 20: 8897–8901.

McAlonan, K. and Wurtz, R.H. (2004) Cross modal attention modulation of thalamic reticular neurons in the macaque monkey. Soc. Neuroscience Abst. 175.8.

Montero, V.M. (1997) c-fos induction in sensory pathways of rats exploring a novel complex environment: Shifts of active thalamic reticular sectors by predominant sensory cues. Neuroscience, 76: 1069–1081.

Montero, V.M. (2000) Attentional activation of the visual thalamic reticular nucleus depends on "top-down" inputs from the primary visual cortex via corticogeniculate pathways. Brain Res., 864: 95–104.

Moore, T., Armstrong, K.M. and Fallah, M. (2003) Visuomotor origins of covert spatial attention. Neuron, 40: 671–683.

Müller, J.R., Philiastides, M.G. and Newsome, W.T. (2005) Microstimulation of the superior colliculus focuses attention without moving the eyes. Proc. Natl. Acad. Sci. USA, 102: 525–529.

Newsome, W.T. and Pare, E.B. (1988) A selective impairment of motion perception following lesions of the middle temporal visual area (MT). J. Neurosci., 8: 2201–2211.

Newsome, W.T., Wurtz, R.H., Dursteler, M.R. and Mikami, A. (1985) Deficits in visual motion processing following ibotenic acid lesions of the middle temporal visual area of the macaque monkey. J. Neurosci., 5: 825–840.

Ramcharan, E.J., Gnadt, J.W. and Sherman, S.M. (2001) The effects of saccadic eye movements on the activity of geniculate relay neurons in the monkey. Vis. Neurosci., 18: 253–258.

Reichova, I. and Sherman, S.M. (2004) Somatosensory corticothalamic projections: Distinguishing drivers from modulators. J. Neurophysiol., 92: 2185–2197.

Reppas, J.B., Usrey, W.M. and Reid, R.C. (2002) Saccadic eye movements modulate visual responses in the lateral geniculate nucleus. Neuron, 35: 961–974.

Reynolds, J.H. and Desimone, R. (1999) The role of neural mechanisms of attention in solving the binding problem. Neuron, 24:19–29, 111–125.

Rizzolatti, G. (1983) Mechanisms of selective attention in mammals. In: Ewert, J.-P., Capranica, R. and Ingle, D.J. (Eds.), Advances in Vertebrate Neuroethology. London, Plenum Publishing Corp.

Robinson, D.A. (1972) Eye movements evoked by collicular stimulation in the alert monkey. Vision Res., 12: 1795–1808.

Sheliga, B.M., Riggio, L. and Rizzolatti, G. (1994) Orienting of attention and eye movements. Exp. Brain Res., 98: 507–522.

Sherman, S.M. and Guillery, R.W. (2001) Exploring the Thalamus. Academic Press, San Diego, CA.

Sherman, S.M. and Guillery, R.W. (2002) The role of the thalamus in the flow of information to the cortex. Philos. Trans. R Soc. Lond. B Biol. Sci., 357: 1695–1708.

Sommer, M.A. (2003) The role of the thalamus in motor control. Curr. Opin. Neurobiol., 13: 663–670.

Sommer, M.A. and Wurtz, R.H. (2004a) What the brain stem tells the frontal cortex. I. Oculomotor signals sent from superior colliculus to frontal eye field via mediodorsal thalamus. J. Neurophysiol., 91: 1381–1402.

Sommer, M.A. and Wurtz, R.H. (2004b) What the Brain Stem Tells the Frontal Cortex. II. Role of the SC–MD–FEF Pathway in Corollary Discharge. J. Neurophysiol., 91: 1403–1423.

Stepniewska, I., Qi, H.X. and Kaas, J.H. (1999) Do superior colliculus projection zones in the inferior pulvinar project to MT in primates? Eur. J. Neurosci., 11: 469–480.

Van Horn, S.C. and Sherman, S.M. (2004) Differences in projection patterns between large and small corticothalamic terminals. J. Comp. Neurol., 475: 406–415.

Progress in Brain Research, Vol. 149
ISSN 0079-6123

CHAPTER 16

Interacting competitive selection in attention and binocular rivalry

Gene R. Stoner, Jude F. Mitchell, Mazyar Fallah and John H. Reynolds*

Systems Neurobiology Laboratory, The Salk Institute for Biological Studies, 10010 North Torrey Pines Road, La Jolla, CA 92037-1099, USA

Abstract: Visuomotor processing is selective — only a small subset of stimuli that impinge on the retinae reach perceptual awareness and/or elicit behavioral responses. Both binocular rivalry and attention involve visual selection, but affect perception quite differently. During rivalry, awareness alternates between different stimuli presented to the two eyes. In contrast, attending to one of the two stimuli impairs discrimination of the ignored stimulus, but without causing it to perceptually disappear. We review experiments demonstrating that, despite their phenomenological differences, attention and rivalry depend upon shared competitive selection mechanisms. These experiments, moreover, reveal stimulus selection that is surface-based and requires coordination between the different neuronal populations that respond as a surface changes its attributes (type of motion) over time. This surface-based selection, in turn biases interocular competition, favoring the eye whose image is consistent with the selected surface. The review ends with speculation about the role of the thalamus in mediating this dynamic coordination, as well as thoughts about what underlies the differences in the phenomenology of selective attention and rivalry.

Introduction

Lesion studies in monkeys have found evidence that extrastriate cortex plays a key role in visual selection. Lesions of MT (the medial temporal area) or V4 cause only relatively mild impairments in basic sensory processing such as contrast sensitivity, wavelength and brightness discrimination, form vision, orientation discrimination, motion, flicker perception, and stereopsis. In contrast, these lesions cause a profound deficit in the ability to discriminate features of a target stimulus when it is presented among salient distractors (Schiller, 1993; De Weerd et al., 1999). Lesions of Area TEO likewise cause only minor impairments in orientation discrimination, except when the discriminandum is presented with more salient distractors (De Weerd et al., 1999).

Single unit recording studies in the monkey have provided important mechanistic insights into the role of extrastriate cortex in selecting targets from among distractors. Neuronal recordings made in Areas MT and V4 have found that the response evoked by a preferred stimulus placed within the classical receptive field (CRF) is typically suppressed by the addition of a second poor stimulus within the CRF (Snowden et al., 1991; Recanzone and Wurtz, 1997). These pair responses typically correspond to an average of the responses to the preferred and poor stimuli presented individually and are consistent with competitive neuronal interactions (Reynolds and Chelazzi, 2004). Studies in V4 (Reynolds et al., 1999; Reynolds and Desimone, 2003) and MT (Recanzone and Wurtz, 1999) suggested a relationship between these competitive interactions and

*Corresponding author. Tel.: +1-858-453-4100;
Fax: +1-858-552-8285; E-mail: reynolds@salk.edu

DOI: 10.1016/S0079-6123(05)49016-0

227

selective attention. These studies looked at the consequence of placing both a poor and a preferred stimulus within the CRF when attention was directed away from the CRF. Consistent with earlier studies, responses evoked by the preferred stimulus were suppressed by the addition of the poor stimulus even when the latter was excitatory when presented alone. The magnitude of this suppression was found to be determined by the neuron's selectivity for the two stimuli, such that a very poor stimulus is typically more suppressive than a stimulus that elicits an intermediate response. The relationship between the changes in firing rate associated with selective attention and these competitive interactions was studied next. It was found that directing attention to the poor stimulus magnified its suppressive effect, whereas directing attention to the preferred stimulus reduced the suppressive effect of the ignored poor stimulus. These pair responses approximate a weighted average of the responses to the stimuli presented individually. These patterns of neuronal responses are consistent with a model of selective attention in which feedback signals from areas such as the frontal eye fields (Moore and Fallah, 2001; Moore and Armstrong, 2003) bias competitive circuitry intrinsic to the visual cortex.

If different stimuli are presented to the two eyes, *binocular rivalry* usually results — only one of the two stimuli is perceived at any given time. Binocular rivalry involves visual selection of a qualitatively different sort than that observed during selective attention in which attending to one of the two stimuli does not render the unattended stimulus invisible. Despite this important phenomenological difference, there is reason to think that attention and rivalry may depend on common stimulus selection mechanisms (Lumer et al., 1998; Leopold and Logothetis, 1999), an idea that has been debated as far back as the late 19th century (James, 1890; Helmholtz, 1909). There are neurophysiological data supporting this view. Single-unit recording studies of binocular rivalry suggest that neuronal suppression becomes more strongly correlated with perceptual suppression as one moves from V1 to IT (Sheinberg and Logothetis, 1997; Logothetis, 1998). A similar trend can be seen in attention, where attended stimuli gain increased influence over neuronal responses as one moves from early to later stages of processing

(Motter, 1993; Chelazzi et al., 1993; Reynolds et al., 1999; Sheinberg and Logothetis, 2001). Thus, selection during attention, as well as during rivalry, appears to depend on competitive interactions occurring at multiple stages with progressively greater accumulated effect as one ascends the cortical hierarchy. This neurophysiological commonality suggests a potential relationship between selective attention and binocular rivalry.

What is selected: features, locations, eyes, or surfaces?

Another connection between binocular rivalry and selective attention is that the question of exactly what is selected has been the subject of debate in both domains. The attention studies discussed above used spatially separated stimuli that were defined by different features (e.g., upward vs. downward motion). Therefore, it is not possible to say whether the competitive mechanisms examined mediate selection of a spatial location, a specific feature, or the object that occupies the attended location. However, while it is well established in the attention literature that spatial locations (Posner, 1980; Treisman and Gelade, 1980) and single features (Saenz et al., 2002) can be selected for preferential processing, it is now recognized that an object or surface can also be selected (Duncan, 1984; He and Nakayama, 1995). For example, Blaser et al. (2000) found that observers were able to track the color, orientation or spatial frequency of one grating when another grating was spatially superimposed. They found that tracking two features of one grating was no more difficult than tracking one feature, suggesting that attention selects the whole stimulus. Tracking two similar features of different gratings was markedly more difficult, suggesting that selecting one stimulus impaired selection of the other stimulus. In the rivalry literature, the debate over what is selected has centered on whether rivalry reflects competition between stimulus representations (stimulus-based rivalry), interocular competition (eye-based rivalry), or some combination of the two (Blake and Logothetis, 2002). The latter view, consistent with the neurophysiological findings discussed above, implies that interocular competition within area V1 and feature-based competition within extrastriate cortex both contribute to binocular rivalry. This view remains controversial, however, as functional imaging studies suggest that inter-ocular competition within area V1 may be sufficient to account for the perceptual suppression occurring during binocular rivalry (Tong and Engel, 2001, Polonsky et al., 2000).

Recent psychophysical studies have shown that attention can select surfaces or objects (Valdes-Sosa et al., 2000; Pinilla et al., 2001; Mitchell et al., 2003; Reynolds et al., 2003). These studies have ruled out spatial selection by using spatially superimposed dot fields and have ruled out attention to a single feature by having the dot fields abruptly change from rotation to translation in a random direction. This approach has been adapted to determine whether binocular rivalry and attention shared a surface-based selection mechanism (Mitchell et al., 2004). This paradigm is illustrated in Fig. 1. Observers viewed rigid patterns of dots presented to both eyes at the start of each trial. The dot patterns rotated in opposite directions around the fixation point, yielding a percept of two superimposed transparent surfaces. After a period of dual rotation, one of the surfaces underwent a brief translation in one of eight directions, and the observer discriminated its direction of motion. This brief translation has previously been found to have a cueing effect such that the translated surface has a temporary perceptual advantage (Valdes-Sosa et al., 2000; Pinilla et al., 2001; Mitchell et al., 2003; Reynolds et al., 2003). Accordingly, the surface that underwent translation is referred to as the *cued surface*. Following this translation, the cued surface was removed from one eye and the uncued surface was removed from the other eye. This dichoptic condition yielded a rivalrous percept. To determine whether the cued surface was dominant during rivalry, observers were asked to report whether one surface was clearly dominant at the end of dichoptic presentation, and if so, which surface. By varying the duration of dichoptic presentation from trial to trial, the time course of dominance from 0–1850 ms was traced.

As illustrated in Fig. 2A, for a brief time after the switch to dichoptic presentation, neither surface clearly dominated, consistent with previous measures of the time for perceptual dominance to develop during rivalry (Wolfe, 1986; de Belsunce

and Sireteanu, 1991; Leonards and Sireteanu, 1993). However, after 300 ms of dichoptic viewing, rivalry was perceived on 70% of the trials, and the cued surface was usually dominant. The translation that cued attention was presented equally to both eyes. Nonetheless, the translating surface was dominant, irrespective of whether it appeared in the right or left eye during subsequent dichoptic viewing. Thus, the dominance of the cued surface did not result directly from a bias of interocular competition.

Rather, it appears as though the visual system selected the translating surface and suppressed the other surface. If so, observers should be impaired in making judgments of the suppressed surface. Observers had to perform a double translation task, in which they reported the direction of a second translation that occurred during rivalry. As before, 150 ms after the first translation, one surface from each eye was deleted, but instead of asking observers to report which surface was then dominant, they were asked to report the direction of the second translation. As illustrated in Fig. 2B, observers were impaired in judging the uncued surface during rivalry. This impairment was weak but significant (two-tailed t-test, $p < 0.05$) immediately after the onset of dichoptic viewing, agreeing with the relatively weak perceptual dominance found following the shortest period of dichoptic viewing (Fig. 2A). Observers were strongly impaired at judging translations of the uncued surface at longer dichoptic presentation times, when they had reported that the cued surface was dominant. Note that this impairment was surface- and not merely feature-dependent: the identical translation (e.g., an upward translation) was either reported accurately or not, depending only on which surface had previously translated. Thus, a surface-based cue during binocular viewing determined which surface would be judged accurately during subsequent rivalry, and this cueing effect had a timecourse that matched that of perceptual dominance.

A simple modification of the stimulus enabled the study to directly compare the impairments observed during attention and rivalry. In the double translation task, trials in which the stimuli were perceived as superimposed transparent surfaces were interleaved throughout the trial. On half of these transparency trials, both surfaces were presented to both eyes

230

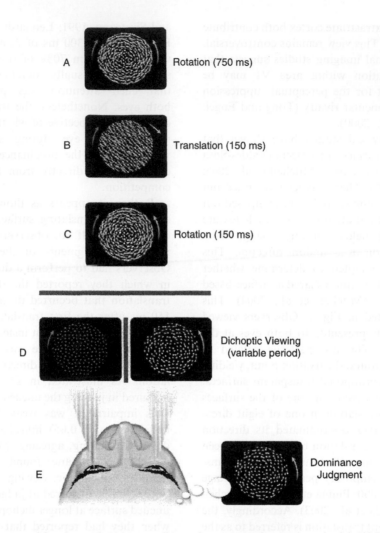

Fig. 1. Task. Panels are arranged from top to bottom according to the sequence of events in each trial. (A) Two sets of dots rotated in opposite directions around a common point, yielding a percept of superimposed transparent surfaces viewed through an aperture. Both sets of dots were identical in color. They differ here in gray level for purposes of illustration. (B) One of the surfaces translated for 150 ms in one of eight directions, while the other surface continued to rotate. Subjects reported the direction of translation. (C) Both surfaces resumed rotating for 150 ms. (D) One surface was removed from each eye, resulting in rivalry. Subjects judged which surface was dominant at the end of this variable-length period of rivalrous viewing. (E) Observers usually perceived the previously translated surface as dominant. (Reproduced courtesy of Nature.)

throughout the trial, a condition that would be referred to as *binocular transparency*. On the other half of the transparency trials, both surfaces were deleted from one eye 150 ms after the first translation. This *monocular transparency* condition controlled for the momentary disruption caused by deleting surfaces in the switch from normal binocular viewing to rivalrous viewing, but without actually inducing rivalry, as there was no competing stimulus in the

other eye. Despite this transient event, when switching to monocular transparency there were no significant differences in observers' performance on monocular and binocular transparency trials. Therefore, we focus on monocular transparency, as it provides a more direct comparison to rivalry.

As illustrated in Fig. 2C observers were impaired in judging the uncued surface during monocular transparency, but with a different timecourse than

231

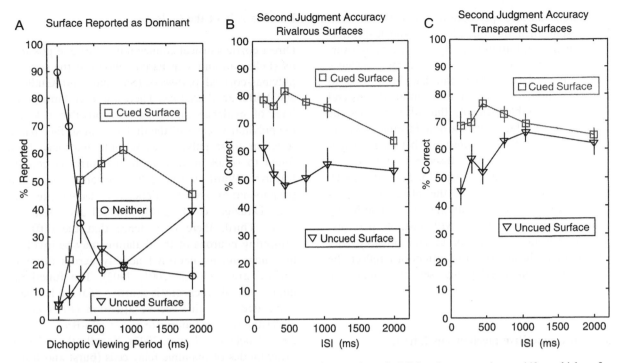

Fig. 2. (A) Seven observers reported whether either surface was dominant at the end of dichoptic presentation, and if so, which surface had been dominant. The mean percentage of trials on which the cued or uncued surface was reported to be dominant is indicated by the square symbols and triangle symbols, respectively. The percentage of trials on which neither surface was clearly dominant is indicated by circle symbols. (B) Mean accuracy in reporting the direction of the second translation averaged across trials in which the surfaces were presented dichoptically. (C) Mean accuracy in reporting the direction of the second translation when both surfaces were presented to one eye, and thus appeared as transparent. Lines in B and C indicate whether the cued (square symbols) or uncued surface (triangles) translated second. The interstimulus interval (ISI) is the delay between the end of the first translation and start of the second translation (ISI = dichoptic viewing period +150 ms). Error bars indicate standard errors of the mean (SEM) across subjects. (Reproduced courtesy of Nature.)

in rivalry. The impairment was strongest 150 ms after the first translation and disappeared within 1000 ms. In contrast, the peak impairment in rivalry was delayed until 450 ms after the first translation, and the impairment persisted even for the longest period tested. This difference in the size of the impairment and its timecourse was highly statistically significant.

Discussion

These experiments provide the first evidence that surface-based attention influences selection during binocular rivalry. Presenting the first translation binocularly ensures that dominance could not result directly from biasing interocular competition. Rather,

the translation during transparency caused a surface to be selected and to emerge as dominant during subsequent dichoptic viewing. This selection was not feature based — the translation cue impaired direction-of-motion judgments of the non-dominant surface during rivalry but not of the dominant surface. This surface-specific impairment during rivalry followed the same timecourse as that seen for the dominance judgments. These results thus extend the notion of stimulus-based rivalry (Diaz-Caneja, 1928; Whittle et al., 1968; Kulikowski, 1992; Kovacs et al., 1996; Logothetis et al., 1996; Alais and Blake, 1998; Alais and Blake, 1999; Lee and Blake, 1999) to include surface-based rivalry.

The fact that a surface-based cue presented during binocular viewing determines the surface that will be judged accurately during both rivalry and transparent surface perception supports the view that, despite their obvious phenomenological differences, rivalry and attention rely on a partially overlapping set of competitive mechanisms. Evidence for stimulus-based competition has been used to argue that binocular rivalry falls within the general class of multistable percepts that also includes the Necker cube, the face–vase illusion, bistable cylinders and other stimuli that alternate between competing interpretations in the absence of inter-ocular differences (Logothetis, 1998; Dodd et al., 2001). The present results thus raise the intriguing possibility that the selection of ambiguous or conflicting stimulus interpretations (as with bistable percepts) and the selection of one of several possibly relevant stimuli (during selective attention) reflect the operation of an overlapping set of competitive mechanisms.

How do competitive mechanisms interact?

Neurons selective for rotation, translation, and eye-of-origin reside, for the most part, in different cortical areas. Thus, although neurons selective for direction of translation are found in various cortical areas, there are several lines of evidence that demonstrate the importance of area MT in the recovery of direction of object motion especially, as reviewed above, in the presence of multiple stimuli. Neurons selective for direction of rotation conversely are found in MST but rarely in MT (e.g., Lagae et al., 1994). Neurons with strong ocular biases are found exclusively in area V1. Given these cortical specializations, the continued dominance of a surface as it sequentially activates rotation-selective neurons and translation-selective neurons would seem to require that different neuronal populations in areas MT and MST communicate the identity of the dominant surface to one another as first one and then another become selectively activated. Likewise, the continued dominance of the cued surface after the transition to rivalrous viewing suggests that the motions encoded in areas MST and MT are somehow linked, in a surface-specific manner, with V1 neurons selective for eye-of-origin. Neither the mechanisms nor the neuronal pathways that subserve this linkage are known.

Possible role of the thalamus

Direct corticocortical connections offer one possibility (Felleman and Van Essen, 1991) but the cortico-pulvinar-cortical pathways (Sherman and Guillery, 2003) offer an alternative. There are several intriguing lines of evidence that suggest a possible role for the pulvinar nucleus of the thalamus in surface based selection. First, pulvinar lesions in humans have been found to result in an inability to correctly conjoin features (Ward et al., 2002). Second, lesions of the pulvinar also result in deficits in selective attention (e.g., Danziger et al., 2004; Michael and Desmedt, 2004). Third, there is evidence that the diffusely projecting neurons of the thalamus may be involved in synchronizing neuronal activity across different cortical areas (Jones, 2001, 2002). The functional importance of synchrony is controversial but has been implicated in both selective attention (Fries et al., 2001) and feature binding (e.g., Castelo-Branco et al., 2000, Thiele and Stoner, 2003). Fourth, the different firing modes of thalamic relay cells (burst and tonic) may underlie selective processing of stimuli, with bursting associated with shifts of attention and tonic firing associated with continued scrutiny (Sherman and Guillery, 2003). These various lines of evidence, taken together, suggest the (admittedly highly speculative) idea that the thalamus may play a critical role in surface-based selection.

What accounts for differing phenomenology of attention and rivalry?

The double translation experiments isolated the contribution of neurons that mediate inter-ocular competition. Transparency and dichoptic viewing trials began identically, with one of the two surfaces cued by a sudden translation. Stimulus conditions were identical during cueing, so the same neurons logically must have been engaged, regardless of whether transparent or rivalrous viewing ensued. From this, it is surmised that the same object-based mechanisms initiated selection for both transparency and rivalry trials. However, after the cueing phase, the sole difference between the rivalry and monocular transparency conditions was that the two deleted stimuli were removed from different eyes in one condition and from a single eye in the other. Thus, whereas dominance during rivalry and transparency must have been triggered by the same object-based mechanisms, the differences in the timecourses of selection and phenomenology can only be due to neurons with eye-of-origin information.

As neurons with strong selectivity for eye-of-origin are found in V1, these differences plausibly are due to the involvement of V1. One way of reconciling the evidence that binocular rivalry depends upon interocular competition with the evidence implying competition at multiple interacting stages is to assume that interocular competition within V1 underlies the complete perceptual suppression associated with binocular rivalry, but that which eye's input is dominant can be influenced by input from competitive mechanisms within extrastriate areas. If area V1 does indeed play a special role in perceptual suppression during rivalry, it may be because of its unique placement in the cortical hierarchy or perhaps because interocular competition is stronger than feature- and surface-based competition and hence leads to a winner-take-all selection.

Acknowledgments

The authors acknowledge funding provided by NEI grant 5 R01 EY012872-06 (GRS), PHS/33201A/T32MH2002 (JFM), NEI grant 1R01EY13802 (MF), and a grant from The McKnight Endowment Fund for Neuroscience (JHR).

References

Alais, D. and Blake, R.R. (1998) Interactions between global motion and local binocular rivalry. Vision Res., 38: 637–644.

Alais, D. and Blake, R.R. (1999) Grouping visual features during binocular rivalry. Vision Res., 39: 4341–4353.

Blake, R.R. and Logothetis, N.K. (2002) Visual competition. Nature Reviews Neuroscience, 3: 13–23.

Blaser, E., Pylyshyn, Z.W. and Holcombe, A.O. (2000) Tracking an object through feature space. Nature, 408: 196–199.

Castelo-Branco, M., Goebel, R., Neuenschwander, S. and Singer, W. (2000) Neural synchrony correlates with surface segregation rules. Nature, 405: 685–689.

Chelazzi, L., Miller, E.K., Duncan, J. and Desimone, R. (1993) A neural basis for visual search in inferior temporal cortex. Nature, 363: 345–347.

Danziger, S., Ward, R., Owen, V. and Rafal, R. (2004) Contributions of the human pulvinar to linking vision and action. Cogn. Affect Behav. Neurosci., 4: 89–99.

De Weerd, P., Peralta, M.R.3rd, Desimone, R. and Ungerleider, L.G. (1999) Loss of attentional stimulus selection after extrastriate cortical lesions in macaques. Nat. Neurosci., 2: 753–758.

de Belsunce, S. and Sireteanu, R. (1991) The time course of interocular suppression in normal and amblyopic subjects. Invest. Ophthalmol. Vis. Sci., 32(9): 2645–2652.

Diaz-Caneja E. (1928). Sur l'alternance binoculaire. Ann. Oculist October, 721–731.

Dodd, J.F., Krug, K., Cumming, B.G. and Parker, A.J. (2001) Perceptually bistable three-dimensional figures evoke high choice probabilities in cortical area MT. J. Neurosci., 21: 4809–4821.

Duncan, J. (1984) Selective attention and the organization of visual information. J. Exp. Psychol. Gen., 113: 501–517.

Felleman, D.J. and Van Essen, D.C. (1991) Distributed hierarchical processing in the primate cerebral cortex. Cereb. Cortex, 1: 1–47.

Fries, P., Reynolds, J.H., Rorie, A.E. and Desimone, R. (2001) Modulation of oscillatory neuronal synchronization by selective visual attention. Science, 291: 1560–1563.

He, Z.J. and Nakayama, K. (1995) Visual attention to surfaces in three-dimensional space. Proc. Natn. Acad. Sci. USA, 92: 11155–11159.

Helmholtz, H. von (1909) Handbuch der physiologischen Optik, 3rd edition, Hamburg, Voss.

James, W. (1890) The Principles of Psychology, Vol. 1. Henry Holt and Company, New York.

Jones, E.G. (2001) The thalamic matrix and thalamocortical synchrony. Trends Neurosci., 24: 595–601.

Jones, E.G. (2002) Thalamic circuitry and thalamocortical synchrony. Philos. Trans. R Soc. Lond. B Biol. Sci., 357: 1659–1673.

Kovacs, I., Papathomas, T.V., Yand, M. and Feher, A. (1996) When the brain changes its mind: interocular grouping during binocular rivalry. Proc. Natn. Acad. Sci. USA, 93: 15508–15511.

Kulikowski, J.J. (1992) Binocular chromatic rivalry and single vision. Ophthalmol. Physiol. Opt., 12: 168–170.

Lagae, L., Maes, H., Raiguel, S., Xiao, D.K. and Orban, G.A. (1994) Responses of macaque STS neurons to optic flow components: a comparison of areas MT and MST. J. Neurophysiol., 71: 1597–1626.

234

Lee, S.H. and Blake, R. (1999) Rival ideas about binocular rivalry. Vision Res., 39: 1447–1454.

Leonards, U. and Sireteanu, R. (1993) Interocular suppression in normal and amblyopic subjects: the effect of unilateral attenuation with neutral density filters. Percept. Psychophys., 54: 65–74.

Leopold, D.A. and Logothetis, N.K. (1999) Multistable phenomena: changing views in perception. Trends Cogn. Sci., 3: 254–264.

Logothetis, N.K. (1998) Single units and conscious vision. Philos. Trans. R Soc. Lond. B Biol. Sci., 353: 1801–1818.

Logothetis, N.K., Leopold, D.A. and Sheinberg, D.L. (1996) What is rivaling during binocular rivalry? Nature, 380: 621–624.

Lumer, E.D., Friston, K.J. and Rees, G. (1998) Neural correlates of perceptual rivalry in the human brain. Science, 280: 1930–1934.

Michael, G.A. and Desmedt, S (2004) The human pulvinar and attentional processing of visual distractors. Neurosci. Lett., 362: 176–181.

Mitchell, J.F., Stoner, G.R., Fallah, M. and Reynolds, J.H. (2003) Attentional selection of superimposed surfaces cannot be explained by modulation of the gain of color channels. Vision Res., 43: 1323–1328.

Mitchell, J.F., Stoner, G.R. and Reynolds, J.H. (2004) Object-based attention determines dominance in binocular rivalry. Nature, 429: 410–413.

Moore, T. and Fallah, M. (2001) Control of eye movements and spatial attention. Proc. Natn. Acad. Sci., 98: 1273–1276.

Moore, T. and Armstrong, K.M. (2003) Selective gating of visual signals by microstimulation of frontal cortex. Nature, 421: 370–373.

Motter, B.C. (1993) Focal attention produces spatially selective processing in visual cortical areas V1, V2, and V4 in the presence of competing stimuli. J. Neurophysiol., 70: 909–919.

Pinilla, T., Cobo, A., Torres, K. and Valdes-Sosa, M. (2001) Attentional shifts between surfaces: effects on detection and early brain potentials. Vision Res., 41: 1619–1630.

Polonsky, A., Blake, R., Braun, J. and Heeger, D.J. (2000) Neuronal activity in human primary visual cortex correlates with perception during binocular rivalry. Nat. Neurosci., 3: 1153–1159.

Posner, M.I. (1980) Orienting of attention. Q. J. Exp. Psychol., 32: 3–25.

Recanzone, G.H., Wurtz, R.H. and Schwarz, U. (1997) Responses of MT and MST neurons to one and two moving objects in the receptive field. J. Neurophys., 78: 2904–2915.

Recanzone, G.H. and Wurtz, R.H. (1999) Shift in smooth pursuit initiation and MT and MST neuronal activity under different stimulus conditions. J. Neurophys., 82: 1710–1727.

Reynolds, J.H., Chelazzi, L. and Desimone, R. (1999) Competitive mechanisms subserve attention in macaque areas V2 and V4. J. Neurosci., 19: 1736–1753.

Reynolds, J.H., Alborzian, S. and Stoner, G.R. (2003) Surface-based exogenous cueing triggers automatic competitive selection. Vision Res., 43: 59–66.

Reynolds, J.H. and Desimone, R. (2003) Interacting roles of attention and visual salience in V4. Neuron, 37: 853–867.

Reynolds, J.H. and Chelazzi, L. (2004) Attentional modulation of visual processing. Annu. Rev. Neurosci., 27: 611–647.

Saenz, M., Buracas, G.T. and Boynton, G.M. (2002) Global feature-based attention for motion and color. Vision Res., 43: 629–637.

Schiller, P.H. (1993) The effects of V4 and middle temporal (MT) area lesions on visual performance in the rhesus monkey. Vis. Neurosci., 10: 717–746.

Sheinberg, D.L. and Logothetis, N.K. (1997) The role of temporal cortical areas in perceptual organization. Proc. Natn. Acad. Sci. USA, 94: 3408–3418.

Sheinberg, D.L. and Logothetis, N.K. (2001) Noticing familiar objects in real world scenes: The role of temporal cortical neurons in natural vision. J. Neurosci., 21: 1340–1350.

Sherman, S.M. and Guillery, R.W. (2003) The role of the thalamus in the flow of information to the cortex. Philos. Trans. R Soc. Lond. B Biol Sci., 357: 1695–1708.

Snowden, R.J., Treue, S., Erickson, R.G. and Andersen, R.A. (1991) The response of area MT and V1 neurons to transparent motion. J. Neurosci., 11: 2768–2785.

Thiele, A. and Stoner, G.R. (2003) Neural synchrony does not correlate with motion coherence in cortical area MT. Nature, 421: 366–370.

Tong, F. and Engel, S.A. (2001) Interocular rivalry revealed in the human cortical blind-spot representation. Nature, 411: 195–199.

Treisman, A.M. and Gelade, G. (1980) A feature-integration theory of attention. Cognit. Psychol., 12: 97–136.

Valdes-Sosa, M., Cobo, A. and Pinilla, T. (2000) Attention to object files defined by transparent motion. J. Exp. Psychol. Hum. Percept. Perform., 26: 488–505.

Ward, R., Danziger, S., Owen, V. and Rafal, R. (2002) Deficits in spatial coding and feature binding following damage to spatiotopic maps in the human pulvinar. Nat. Neurosci., 5: 99–100.

Whittle, P., Bloor, D.C. and Pocock, S. (1968) Some experiments on figural effects in binocular rivalry. Percept. Psychophys., 4: 183–188.

Wolfe, J.M. (1986) Briefly presented stimuli can disrupt constant suppression and binocular rivalry suppression. Perception, 15: 413–417.

Progress in Brain Research, Vol. 149
ISSN 0079-6123

CHAPTER 17

Anatomical pathways that link perception and action

R.W. Guillery*

Department of Anatomy, School of Medicine, University of Wisconsin, 1300 University Avenue, Madison, WI 53706, USA

Abstract: Pathways linking action to perception are generally presented as passing from sensory pathways, through the thalamus, and then to a putative hierarchy of corticocortical links to motor outputs or to memory. Evidence for more direct sensorimotor links is now presented to show that cerebral cortex rarely, if ever, receives messages representing receptor activity only; thalamic inputs to cortex also carry copies of current motor instructions.

Pathways afferent to the thalamus represent the primary input to neocortex. Generally they are made up of branching axons that send one branch to the thalamus and another to output centers of the brain stem or spinal cord. The information transmitted through the classical "sensory" pathways to the thalamus represents not only information about the environment and the body, but also about instructions currently on their way to motor centers.

The proposed hierarchy of direct corticocortical connections of the sensory pathways is not the only possible hierarchy of cortical connections. There is also a hierarchy of the corticofugal pathways to motor centers in the midbrain, and there are transthalamic corticocortical pathways that may show a comparable hierarchy. The extent to which these hierarchies may match each other, and relate to early developmental changes are poorly defined at present, but are important for understanding mechanisms that can link action and perception in the developing brain.

Introduction

The functional relationship between action and perception has in the past been viewed in two distinct ways. The first looks for the functional links that lead from a sensory event, through several stages of subcortical and cortical perceptual processing to a motor action that is appropriate to that sensory event, or to a record in memory for later action (Fig. 1). This approach can relate neural actions and neural pathways to particular behavioral situations and provide information about the nerve cells that are involved at each stage in the sensory–motor interaction. Examples include neural recordings made at early stages of sensory processing (Mountcastle et al., 1963; Talbot et al., 1968; Hubel and Wiesel, 1977;

Vallbo et al. 1979), but from the point of view of this workshop are most tellingly illustrated by records of neural activity obtained from higher cortical areas in awake animals (Gallant et al., 1998; Cook and Maunsell, 2002 Tsao et al., 2003). In such studies, the relevant cortical areas are generally assumed to lie on a hierarchical chain of corticocortical pathways that leads from the primary receiving areas of cortex to higher areas concerned eventually with memory or motor outputs (Felleman and Van Essen, 1991). This view is based on an initial assumption about the afferent pathways, amply confirmed experimentally (Adrian, 1928; Kuffler, 1953; Perl et al., 1962; Barlow, 2004), that the messages carried to the brain from the eye, the ear, the muscle receptors, the skin etc. function to inform the central sensory pathways about events impinging on peripheral receptors. That is, that they *represent* external events. Churchland et al. (1994), writing critically about

*Tel.: +1-608-263-4763; Fax: +1-608-262-8414;
 E-mail: rguiller@wisc.edu

DOI: 10.1016/S0079-6123(05)49017-2

236

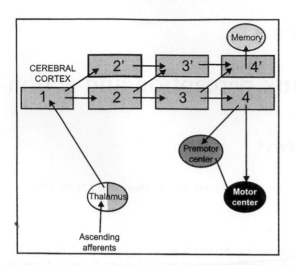

Fig. 1. Schematic, simplified representation of contemporary views of sensory–motor processing within the thalamocortical pathways. Sensory messages enter the thalamus from the ascending afferents, are passed to primary cortical receiving areas and are then passed through a hierarchical, partially parallel series of higher cortical areas, (1,2,3,4//2'.3'.4') far more complicated than illustrated here, either for a motor action from a cortical motor region or for storage in memory. Further details in the text.

such a view of vision, have referred to it as a "theory of pure vision", and one can generalize and think of it as a theory of pure sensation. In this chapter, I argue that such a view, while clearly in accord with known relationships between sensory events and neural activity in ascending pathways to cortex, ignores the fact that the neural activity reaching cortex represents more than merely the information about events that impinge on peripheral receptors. This review shows that it also represents a pattern of instructions that are already on their way to lower motor centers before any of the messages can reach cortex (see Fig. 2 and Section 2; Guillery and Sherman, 2002a; Guillery, 2003).

An alternative view of the relationship between action and perception can be obtained by considering illusory perceptions, misperceptions, or failed perceptions that can lead to inappropriate actions or interpretations (Gibson, 1933; Festinger et al., 1967; Churchland et al., 1994; O'Regan and Noë, 2001). The observations are generally based on subtle experimental approaches to puzzling and often elusive perceptual phenomena or motor actions. These observations serve to illustrate conclusions that

perception is much more closely related to activity in the motor pathways (the "sensorimotor contingencies" of O'Regan and Noë, 2001) than generally recognized by the first view. This second approach, including, for example, that of Helmholtz (see translation by Warren and Warren, 1968) or of Sperry (1952) has, in one way or another, played an important role in accounts that see action as an essential part of perception. However, in general, wherever one looks at evidence of this sort, relating action to perception, the physical links, that is, the anatomical pathways involved, are poorly defined or undefined, except near the periphery (see the motor link from ascending afferents to motor centers in Fig. 2), and these peripheral links are almost invariably ignored by contemporary studies of *sensory* processing.

Churchland et al. (1994) are exceptional in providing a summary of some of the anatomical pathways that might play a role in this second approach to action and perception. Having considered the many back projections that go from cortex not only to the thalamus but also to motor centers such as the superior colliculus and the striatum, they conclude that "the anatomy is consistent with the idea that motor assembly can begin even before sensory signals

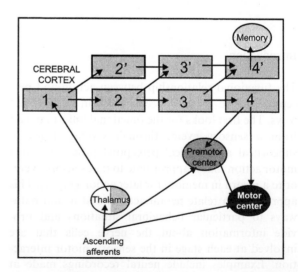

Fig. 2. Simplified schema to show that the messages carried to cortex through the thalamus represent information coming not only from the sensory periphery through the ascending afferents, but also information about the instructions that are concurrently being passed to premotor and motor centers of the brain stem and spinal cord.

reach the highest levels". The pathways summarized in Fig. 2 and mentioned above, show not only that motor assembly *can* begin before the sensory signals reach the highest levels but that the motor and sensory signals are inextricably bound to each other on their way to the thalamus; the motor assembly *must* begin before sensory signals reach the highest levels. This review presents evidence that afferents to the thalamus are commonly made up of branching axons that send one branch to the thalamus for transfer to cortex and another branch to motor or premotor[1] centers for a role in action. That is, these branching axons, which carry the messages to the thalamus for transfer to cortex, are sending to cortex something more than the information about activity in peripheral receptors. They are also providing the cortex with information about the instructions that have already been sent to the motor centers. Currently very little is known about the nature of most of these motor instructions. They may be for preparation, facilitation, or inhibition of movement. The crucial point is that these motor instructions form an essential part of the messages that reach the first stages of cortical perceptual processing. Even though they can be separated in the mind of the neuroscientist who is studying the sensory pathways, they can never be separated by the cortical area in receipt of the messages. Again, very little is known about the functions of these motor collaterals in relation to sensory functions, because they have not been studied from this point of view in the past.

In addition to the motor links shown in Fig. 2, evidence is presented that there are also transthalamic corticocortical pathways (Fig. 3), which provide potentially equally important links between action and perception. As shown in this figure, the message that is passed from one cortical area through the thalamic relay to another cortical area, is commonly (perhaps always) also transmitted by a branch of the corticothalamic axon to a motor or premotor center (Guillery and Sherman, 2002a; Guillery, 2003). These branching axons show that some of the pathways that link one cortical area to another are, like

---

[1]"Premotor" is used here to indicate centers feeding into the final common path of the motor centers in contrast to those that send connections up through the thalamus and to the cortex.

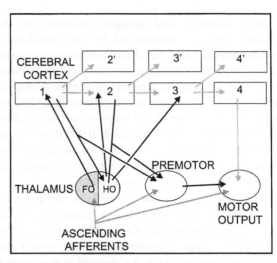

Fig. 3. Simplified schema to show two types of relay in the thalamus, first order relays (FO) which transmit messages to cortex from the ascending pathways, shown as (1), and higher order relays (HO), which transmit to cortex from cortico-thalamocortical pathways, shown as 2 and 3 (Based on Guillery, 1995; Sherman and Guillery, 1996). Thalamic connections for 4 and for the numbers indicated by a superscript prime are not shown in the figure. The question as to whether the sequences of the direct corticocortical connections and the transthalamic corticocortical connections match is not resolved. The pathway to memory has been omitted since it plays no further part in the discussion here.

the ascending pathways to cortex, involved in two intimately related functions that need to be distinguished if one wishes to understand cortical processing. One is to forward messages from one cortical area, through the thalamus, to another cortical area, and the other is to inform one cortical area about the outputs that the other (lower) cortical area is sending to motor or premotor centers of the brain.

"Driver" pathways to the thalamus and their motor branches

There is a basic pattern of organization that is common to the whole of the thalamus, which has been considered in more detail in several earlier publications (Guillery, 1995; Sherman and Guillery, 1996, 2001, 2002; Guillery and Sherman 2002a,b; Sherman, 2005). In summary, all thalamic relays receive a small proportion of afferents that resemble, in their structure and synaptic relationships, the sensory "drivers" represented by the functionally primary inputs from the visual, auditory or somatosensory pathways. Such driver components can also be identified, on the basis of their structure, as coming from the cerebellum and from the mamillary bodies. Although the nature of the message carried by these last two afferents is not as clearly defined as it is for the sensory pathways, there can be no doubt that these are the inputs whose message is transferred through the thalamus to cortex.

A driver input to the thalamus is the one that carries the actual message that is transmitted to the cortex (Sherman and Guillery, 1998), and it differs significantly from a modulatory input, which can modify the way in which the message is transmitted, or can change the nature of the message in particular, often subtle ways. Although the drivers represent considerably less than 10% of the synapses in their thalamic relays, where they have been tested, silencing them produces a loss of the receptive field properties that characterize their thalamic relays.

More than 90% of the synapses in thalamic relays come from modulators that have a variety of different origins. They have a structure distinct from that of the drivers, and also establish distinctive synaptic patterns in the thalamus. For example, the thalamic synapses of corticothalamic axons from cortical layer 6 represent one major population of modulatory afferents. For the lateral geniculate nucleus, the layer 6 axons from visual cortex nucleus represent approximately 30% of the synapses in the nucleus (Erişir et al., 1998) and have distinct and characteristic receptive field properties (Murphy and Sillito, 1996; Murphy et al., 2000). The receptive fields of these cells are not transmitted from the lateral geniculate nucleus back to the cortex. Silencing this cortical input to the lateral geniculate nucleus has subtle effects on transmission to cortex, but does not eliminate the message that is transmitted by the driver input from the retina (Kalil and Chase, 1970; Schmielau and Singer, 1977; Geisert et al., 1981; McClurkin et al., 1994).

The driver axons are the focus for understanding how messages relayed from thalamus to cortex can represent aspects of both perception and action. Many of these axons branch, sending one branch to the thalamus and another branch to a motor or premotor center (Figs. 2 and 3). Some of these driver axons, as for example, those of the medial lemniscus or anterolateral pathway, come from cells that are innervated by axons that send branches to motor centers, so that they represent perception and action on the basis of their innervation, not necessarily on the basis of the branching pattern of their own axons. However, some prethalamic cells that are innervated by axons that send a branch to a motor center also, themselves, have axons that branch, with one branch innervating a motor or premotor center and the other innervating a thalamic relay.

The details of the evidence, that these ascending drivers to the thalamus give off prethalamic branches, have been presented previously (Guillery and Sherman, 2002b) and hence summarized only briefly here.

The somatosensory pathways are fed by dorsal root axons which branch profusely within the spinal cord as do the axons of the dorsal horn cells that lie on the anterolateral pathway (Cajal, 1911; Brown et al., 1977; Brown and Fyffe, 1981; Lu and Willis, 1999). That is, there are local, spinal branches that supply connections to a variety of spinal mechanisms. The messages that are passed to the gracile and cuneate nuclei, or to the ascending anterolateral pathways, represent activity in the peripheral receptors (perception) and also reflect activity that is on its way to spinal motor circuits (action). The gracile and cuneate nuclei send their axons not only to the thalamus for relay to cortex but also to several centers, including the hypothalamus, the superior colliculus, the brain stem reticular formation, and the inferior olive. Some, but probably not all of these axons are branches of the prethalamic axons (Berkley 1975, 1980; Feldman and Kruger, 1980; Berkley et al., 1980; Bull and Berkley, 1984).

These connections tell us that as the infant is learning the significance of a particular dorsal root input, the messages must be understood to represent not just the tactile or proprioceptive changes represented by the discharge of the peripheral receptors, but also a particular pattern of activation of a complex of spinal and supraspinal mechanisms What comes to be regarded, as development proceeds, as a pure sensory experience, probably by the growing infant and almost invariably by the neuroscientist, will continue to carry the burden, or the implications, of all of the other, associated activated pathways.

The visual pathways send branches from many, possibly all of the retinofugal axons that have a relay in the thalamus to the superior colliculus or to the pretectum. These are centers concerned with the control of eye and head movements and with pupil size and accommodation. In rodents all of the retinogeniculate axons have midbrain branches (Chalupa and Thompson 1980; Linden and Perry, 1983; Jhaveri et al., 1991), and the same holds for the cat (Wässle and Illing, 1980; Leventhal et al., 1985; and see summary in Guillery and Sherman, 2002a), where, only for the medium sized X cells, has the demonstration of midbrain branches proved difficult. (Sur et al., 1987; Tamamaki et al., 1994). These branches go to the pretectum and are extremely fine and difficult to demonstrate. The evidence for the monkey clearly shows that many retinothalamic axons have midbrain branches (Bunt et al., 1975; Schiller and Malpeli, 1977; Leventhal et al., 1981; Perry and Cowey, 1984), although there can be some doubt about the parvocellular component, which may represent an unbranched input to the thalamus or, more probably, an input with fine branches to the midbrain, comparable to the X cells of the cat.

The retinofugal terminals in the superior colliculus have in the past been represented as an alternative "sensory" pathway to cortex, acting through colliculopulvinar axons to transfer visual information to higher visual cortical areas. However, receptive field properties of pulvinar cells survive silencing of the colliculus but not of the cortex (Bender 1983; Chalupa, 1991), suggesting that most of the drivers for the pulvinar/posterior complex come from cortex, making the pulvinar a relay in a corticothalamo-cortical route (see later in this section, "corticothalamic drivers"). There is some evidence that axons from the superficial layers of the superior colliculus in the cat may be drivers for a small portion of the pulvinar regions (a part of the lateral posterior nucleus; Kelly et al., 2003)[2], but the essential point

---

[2]Once it is clearly established that there is an ascending transthalamic driver pathway from the superior colliculus through a limited part of the pulvinar region (see Kelly et al., 2003) to extrastriate visual cortex, one can further ask a potentially interesting further question about the axons that make up this pathway. Do the colliculothalamic cells have branches that go to the deep layers of the colliculus?

about these midbrain connections is that the superficial layers of the colliculus act on the deeper layers and are also playing a role in the control of eye movements (Ozen et al., 2000; Schiller and Tehovnik, 2001; Helms et al., 2004). From the point of view of the messages that are being transferred through the lateral geniculate nucleus to area 17, the branching pattern of the retinogeniculate axons indicates that the messages reaching the lateral geniculate nucleus, and thus the visual cortex, represent a downstream motor action as well as the sensory information that is passing upstream. These inputs to the lateral geniculate nucleus do not fit a theory of "pure vision", and, again, the infant learning about the significance of messages that arrive from the retina learns that they relate not only to objects in the visual field but also to particular patterns of stimulation that are fed into the motor centers concerned with head and eye movements.

The auditory pathways are not well documented from the point of view of the branching patterns of the ascending afferents. Axons that innervate brain stem structures for pinna movement or for the auditory startle response are known (Henkel, 1983; Whitley and Henkel, 1984; López et al., 1999) but the published accounts are not clear about the axonal branching patterns. Similarly, although there are rich descending connections from many auditory nuclei, and although the inferior colliculus is known to send axons to the superior colliculus (Harting and Van Lieshout, 2000) and to other centers (Vetter et al., 1993; Shore and Moore, 1998), the extent to which these represent independent pathways or branches of prethalamic axons is not defined. In the past the precise branching patterns of the ascending auditory pathways have not received the attention that the present argument about a dual function for thalamic inputs requires.

The cerebellar pathways from the deep cerebellar nuclei to the ventral lateral thalamic nucleus were shown by Cajal (1911) to give off branches in the midbrain, supplying the red nucleus and other premotor centers, and a number of more recent experiments confirm this (Tsukahara et al., 1967; McCrea et al., 1978; Bentivoglio and Kuypers, 1982; Shinoda et al., 1988).

The mamillothalamictract is made up of axons many of which branch, sending one branch rostrally to the thalamus and another caudally to the mesencephalic and pontine tegmentum (Cajal, 1911; Kölliker, 1896). In view of evidence that lateral mamillary and anterodorsal thalamic cells respond to head orientation signals (Taube, 1995; Stackman and Taube, 1998), it is of some interest to note that some of the caudally directed axons go to the anterior and medial parts of the pontine reticular formation (Guillery, 1957; Cruce, 1977; Torigoe et al., 1986), a region known to be concerned with control of eye movements (Hess et al., 1989). That is, the branches going to the anterior thalamus transmit information about head orientation to the cortex, but also, at the same time transmit information about instructions that have already been passed to oculomotor pathways.

Corticothalamic drivers represent a large and generally unstudied input to the thalamus. Thalamic relays for the major sensory pathways, the cerebellum and the mamillary bodies summarized above, represent less than a half of the thalamus in primates. The rest of the thalamus is largely made up of cell groups that receive driver inputs from layer 5 of the cerebral cortex, and these have been called "higher order" relays (Guillery, 1995; Sherman and Guillery, 2001, 2002). These corticothalamic axons resemble, in their terminal structure and their synaptic relationships, the other driver afferents considered above, and like those they represent less than 10% of the total synapses at their termination[3]. For most of them, for example those in the mediodorsal nucleus that receives drivers from frontal cortex (Schwartz et al., 1991), or those in the center median nucleus that receives layer 5 inputs from motor cortex (Catsman-Berrevoets and Kuypers, 1978; Royce 1983), there is no clear idea about the nature of the message that they are bringing to the thalamus for transfer from one cortical area to another. For some of the inputs to the pulvinar region in cat or monkey it is known that they carry information about complex visual receptive fields that are responsive to motion,

properties that are generally similar to those of the cortical layer 5 cells from which these afferents arise (Chalupa and Abramson, 1989; Casanova, 2003). For inputs to the posterior nucleus in rodents it is known that they carry information about somatosensory receptive fields comparable to those of their cortical cells of origin (Diamond et al., 1992). These two examples are of interest because they relate activity in the thalamic relay to the activity of the layer 5 cells from which the afferents arise, and, more importantly, because in these two situations it has been demonstrated that silencing the cortical origin of the afferents produces a loss of the characteristic receptive field properties of the thalamic cells (Bender, 1983; Chalupa, 1991; Diamond et al., 1992), showing that these are, indeed, the drivers of the relevant thalamic cells. That is, in their action on thalamic activity they differ from the modulatory layer 6 cells (see above).

Many, possibly all of the layer 5 cells that send their axons to the thalamus also have branches that pass to the brain stem or spinal cord. Such a branching pattern has been demonstrated for the pathways from visual, somatosensory and motor cortex for rat, cat and monkey (Casanova, 1993; Deschênes et al., 1994; Bourassa and Deschênes, 1995; Bourassa et al., 1995; Rockland 1998; Veinante et al., 2000; Guillery et al., 2001), suggesting that it may prove to be a pattern for layer 5 corticothalamic axons generally. That is, these branches of the corticothalamic axons shown in Fig. 3 tell us essentially the same thing about the transthalamic corticocortical pathway as Fig. 2 tells us about the branches of the ascending afferents to the thalamus: the thalamus is in the business of sending information to cortex about messages that are already on their way to motor or premotor centers.

Descending axons from cortical layer 5

One issue often overlooked when cortical functions in perceptual processing are being considered is that most, probably all, cortical areas have major outputs from cells in layer 5 to lower brainstem centers (Fig. 4). The roles of these cortical areas in corticocortical perceptual processing will necessarily be closely linked to their other roles, which are more

---

[3]The proportion reported for the pulvinar of the cat is significantly lower than that for the lateral geniculate nucleus (Wang et al., 2002), suggesting that this may represent a difference between first and higher order relays, which may well have modulatory inputs from a greater variety of cortical sources.

closely related to the motor control systems innervated in the brainstem. It is relevant to recall that the surprise generated by early accounts of corticospinal axons arising from cortical areas well beyond the classical motor cortex reflected a conceptual and long believed separation of sensory from motor pathways, which today still often dominates views of perceptual processing. One of the striking conclusions about cortical functions is that there are probably few (if any) cortical areas that function merely as links in cortical processing. They all have other functions related to lower brain stem and spinal centers, and one key to understanding how action and perception relate to each other will be an analysis of how the functions of the corticocortical and descending corticofugal, including corticothalamic, axons from any one cortical area relate to each other. Corticofugal outputs to centers with motor or premotor functions are not limited to the classically recognized motor areas of cortex.

Corticofugal axons that pass to the thalamus arise from cortical layers 5 and 6, and it is the layer 5 axons that are of interest here, because they are the

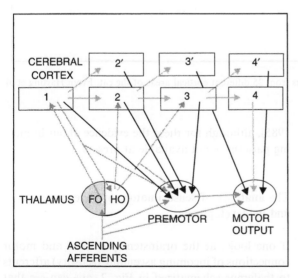

Fig. 4. Simplified, hypothetical schema to show that all cortical areas have a layer 5 output to the brainstem and to raise a question about the distribution of these brain stem branches: does the rough hierarchy described for the direct corticocortical pathways (Felleman and Van Essen, 1991) correspond to the rough hierarchy shown by the brain stem terminals in motor and premotor centers, as seen for example in the corticotectal axons described by Harting et al. (1992, Fig. 5).

ones that branch to innervate lower premotor and motor centers. The layer 6 axons do not pass into subdiencephalic centers, and in the thalamus they represent the modulators discussed on page 238. The layer 5 axons, in contrast, pass to many different regions of the brain stem and spinal cord. That is, it is reasonable to conclude that all corticofugal axons traced into the midbrain or further caudally arise from cells in layer 5. Figure 5, taken from Harting et al., (1992) shows the terminations in the superior colliculus of the cat of corticofugal axons from 25 different, mainly visual, cortical areas. It is worth noting that none of the visual ("sensory") cortical areas studied by Harting et al. lacked a projection to the superior colliculus. This stresses the importance of seeing cortical functions as something more than merely a part of a hierarchy of corticocortical connections concerned with perceptual processing. Each cortical area, while performing its perceptual functions in the cortical hierarchy, also has motor or premotor output to the superior colliculus, and also, though not shown in Fig. 5, many of them have other caudal connections, not only to the thalamus, but also to the pretectum, pons or more caudal regions of the brain stem.

In the superior colliculus the deepest layers shown in Fig. 5[4] relate most directly to the motor outputs concerned primarily with eye movements and head movements, and the most superficial layers receive the retinal afferents. That is, one can regard the deepest layers as being closest to the motor outputs and the superficial layers as being furthest from the motor outputs. When viewed in this light one can see that cortical areas 17 and 18, which are lowest in the visual "sensory-to-motor" hierarchy considered earlier, have the most superficial terminations and the fewest deep terminations. Other cortical areas show two different features: they lose the superficial terminations as they become less obviously "visual-sensory" in their functions, and they gain deeper terminations. That is, one can identify a rough hierarchy of cortical areas, with the "highest" having the fewest superficial and the most deep terminations, and thus being in a position of relatively the most

---

[4]The periventricular grey is closely related to visceral pathways and can be seen as somewhat distinct from the more superficial layers shown in Fig. 5.

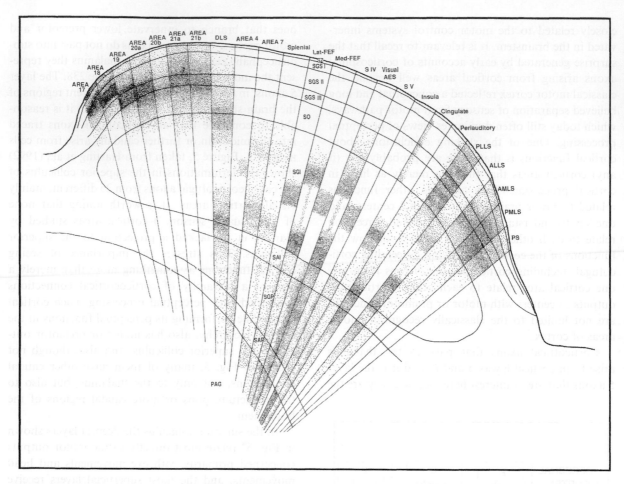

Fig. 5. Representation of terminal distribution of corticotectal axons from 25 different cortical areas of the cat. From Harting et al. (1992), with permission.

direct relationship to motor outputs that relate to vision. The extent to which this rough hierarchy of the motor connections corresponds to the rough hierarchy of corticocortical connections described by Felleman and Van Essen (1991), remains unexplored, although it is easy to see some rough parallels.

It is not known how many of the cortical sites studied for Fig. 5 had a layer 5 cortical input to the thalamus, nor whether such an input was provided by a branching axon that also innervated the superior colliculus. However, it is known that areas 17, 18, and 19 in the cat innervate thalamus and colliculus with branching axons demonstrated for areas 17 and 18 (Guillery et al., 2001) and that several of the "higher" suprasylvian cortical areas also innervate both thalamus and colliculus (Abramson and Chalupa,

1985), although for these the evidence about branching patterns is not available at present.

The anatomy of sensorimotor contingencies and its development

If one looks at the brainstem premotor and motor connections of incoming ascending (sensory) afferents to thalamus schematized in Fig. 2, one can see that they establish connections that are likely to *contribute* to a motor action unless other, higher pathways counteract this action. These connections can be regarded as a first step in the production of the sensorimotor motor contingencies that are basic to our perceptual performance. Helmholtz

(Warren and Warren, 1968), considering how perceptual processing relates to action, made two points that are important for the present discussion. One was that, although the relationship between the physical origin of a sensory stimulus and the neural activity in the afferent pathways is essentially an arbitrary one that depends on the biological structures involved, the relationship must, in general, be constant, in so far as a particular stimulus must produce a consistent neural response.

The second point was that an infant exploring its environment, and making movements that lead to particular new sensory inputs learns, on the basis of its actions, to associate certain limb, eye or head movements with particular perceptual experiences. The first stages of this interplay of action and perception may be barely "exploratory", they may start with relatively uncoordinated movements controlled by ground rules that already exist or are being developed for lower level circuits. These circuits provide the first level of sensorimotor contingencies. It is information about these contingencies that is sent to the thalamus and cortex, and this is the information that has to be learnt as perceptual skills are developed. That is, the infant must learn that certain hand movements produce particular proprioceptive, tactile, or visual, responses, and that certain eye movements produce particular changes in visual inputs etc. It is not enough that a set of sensorimotor contingencies are present early in development, it is necessary that the infant also *learn* about these contingencies. Further, as indicated above, it is equally important to learn that messages coming from the retina have particular actions, probably subtle, possibly inhibitory, upon the centers concerned with movements, and these associations must also be learned. The question that arises from a consideration of the pathways schematized in Figs. 2, 3, and 4 concerns the way in which the pathways that do the learning interact with the pathways that originally underlie (or produce) the contingencies. Here the developmental history of the pathways may provide an important key.

The cerebral cortex develops later than the spinal cord (Windle, 1940; Hamilton et al., 1952). Flechsig's observations (Flechsig, 1920) on the development of human cortical myelinization (Figs. 6–8) showed that on the sensory side, the primary receiving areas V1, S1, A1, myelinate first and that surrounding areas, higher in the "sensory hierarchy" develop their myelin later, during the first years of postnatal life.

Visual skills (Kiorpes and Bassin, 2003) also develop in children during these early post-natal years, but some of these skills continue to develop until about 7 or 8 years of age, and others even continue until the teens. Studies of the growth associated protein GAP43 (Feig, 2004a) have suggested that there is another, potentially interesting developmental hierarchy. GAP 43 is a pre-synaptic protein that is present at high levels in axons and growth cones during growth and synapse formation, and is associated with synaptic modifications in the adult (McGuire et al., 1988; Moya et al., 1992; Biffo et al., 1990; Benowitz and Routtenberg, 1997; Wouters et al., 1998). Transgenic studies have demonstrated that in adult mice the protein can induce axonal sprouting (Aigner et al., 1995; Caroni, 1997), suggesting that the presence of the protein is related to axonal modifications. Feig's (2004a) studies show that this protein is present in all thalamic relays at early developmental stages, but is lost in the first order relays as development proceeds. In contrast to this, the protein continues to be present in adult higher order visual, auditory and somatosensory pathways of rat and monkey (Kruger et al., 1998; Higo et al., 1999; Feig 2004a; and see Figs. 9 and 10). Most importantly from the present point of view, the mRNA for the protein is present in corticothalamic layer 5 cells in adult rats, with more of the RNA in primary than in secondary cortical areas (Fig. 9). Figure 10 illustrates the contrast between the first order relay for the visual pathways (the lateral geniculate nucleus), and a higher order relay (the lateral posterior nucleus) in an adult rat. In general, for thalamic relays, the protein is lost from first order thalamic relays at early post-natal stages, but it is still present in higher order relays in the adult (Feig, 2004b). These results suggest that the higher order corticothalamic circuits maintain more of their plasticity for longer than do the first order circuits, and that there may be a hierarchy of driving afferents to the thalamus, including the corticothalamic drivers from layer 5, with the "lowest" pathways losing their capacity for plastic responses earliest. That is, for the major sensory systems, visual, auditory,

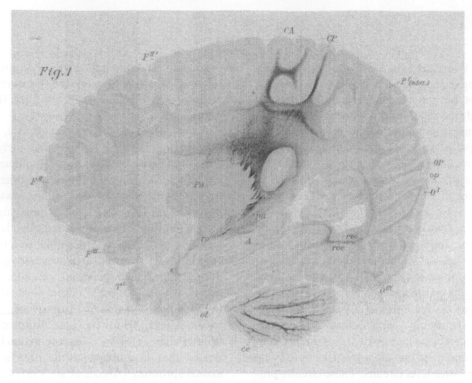

Fig. 6. Distribution of myelin as shown by the Weigert method. New born child. From Flechsig (1920).

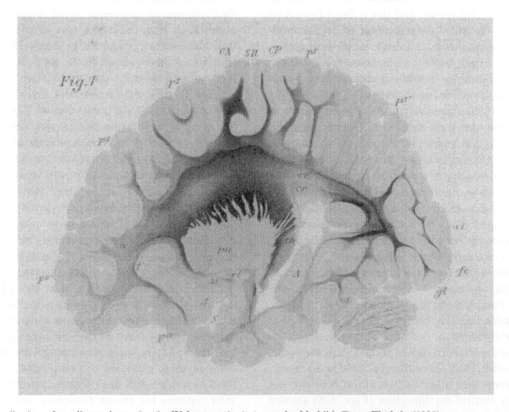

Fig. 7. Distribution of myelin as shown by the Weigert method. 4 month old child. From Flechsig (1920).

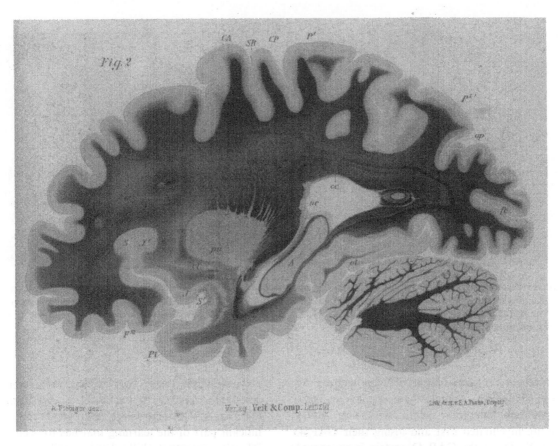

Fig. 8. Distribution of myelin as shown by the Weigert method. Adult. From Flechsig (1920).

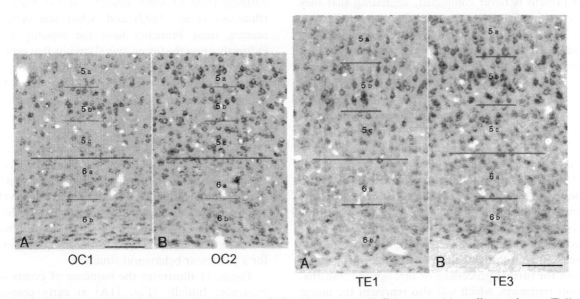

Fig. 9. Distribution of GAP43 mRNA in visual primary (Oc1) and secondary (Oc2) cortex and in auditory primary (Te1) and secondary (Te3) cortex of an adult rat. Layers 5 and 6 are shown, more superficial layers show virtually no GAP 43 mRNA. (From Feig, 2004a, with permission.)

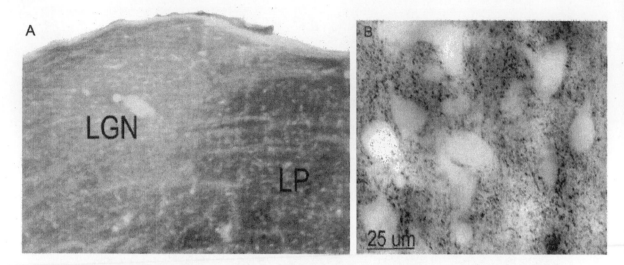

Fig. 10. Transverse section through the thalamus of a rat stained for the GAP 43 protein. A low magnification picture on the left shows the adjacent lateral geniculate and lateral geniculate nuclei, the former with very little protein and the latter with a great deal more. The higher magnification picture on the right shows the punctate distribution of the protein in the lateral posterior nucleus. Figures kindly provided by Dr S Feig.

somatosensory, in terms either of myelinization or of GAP 43 protein content, there appears to be a developmental hierarchy, with the lowest levels becoming myelinated first and losing their GAP 43 earliest. So far as the GAP 43 protein is concerned, for some higher order pathways the loss of the GAP 43 protein is never completed, suggesting that they keep a significant learning capacity.

With this rough sketch of development in mind, one can look, for example, at the way in which sensorimotor relationships are established at different cortical levels. When cortical area S1 is sufficiently mature, the messages it receives from the thalamus relate closely to the dorsal root input, representing information about receptors in (for example) the hand and arm, as well as information transmitted to spinal reflex mechanisms by the spinal branches of dorsal root axons about messages on their way to the spinal ventral horn for motor actions. Once the development of S1 and higher areas is sufficiently advanced this input to S1 cortex, after it has been processed within S1, can be passed to higher cortical areas either through direct corticocortical pathways for further processing or through the transthalamic pathways, which will also represent the motor instructions produced by layer 5 cells in S1. In the

newborn infant the S1 cortex that will receive the ascending messages in the adult is still immature (Flechsig, 1920; Figs. 6–8), and presumably a significant part of the learning that has to occur as the infant's perceptual skills develop will be occurring here as this cortical area matures. The transthalamic pathway from S1 sends branches to the brain stem (Bourassa et al., 1995) and, when this system is mature, these branches have the capacity to act indirectly upon the lower, spinal circuits that establish the first sensorimotor contingencies. Although at present nothing is known about the nature of the action produced by the descending branches, information about the instructions leading to this action is a part of the message that is passed from S1 to higher cortical areas. That is, information about the instructions in the descending branches becomes a part of the sensorimotor contingencies "seen" by the higher somatosensory cortical areas. As development proceeds, each cortical area passes to higher cortical areas information about the contribution that it is making to the sensorimotor contingencies for a particular behavioral situation.

Figure 11 illustrates the sequence of events schematically. Initially (Fig. 11A) at early post-natal developmental stages, the relevant dorsal root

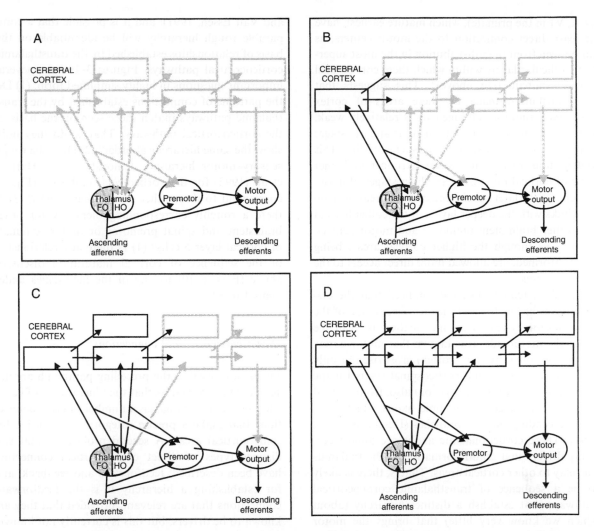

Fig. 11. Schema to show the sequence of development of the connections illustrated in Fig. 3. A–D show a chronological sequence, with black lines indicating mature and grey lines indicating immature pathways.

afferents will innervate lower premotor and motor centers, and may reach the thalamus, but the thalamocortical pathways will be relatively immature and will play a minimal role or no role in the sensory–motor interactions that develop. As development proceeds the primary cortical areas become involved; they then receive information about the sensorimotor contingencies established at spinal and brainstem levels, and will develop their intrinsic circuitry, producing a layer 5 output that goes through higher order thalamic relays to higher cortical areas and also to brainstem premotor centers (Fig. 11B). The circuits shown in black in Fig. 11B impose a cortical

component upon the lower level circuits of Fig. 11A, and that cortical component then becomes a part of the sensorimotor contingencies that are passed to the next level of cortical development through the higher order thalamic relay (Fig. 11C). There are likely to be several levels of corticothalamic circuitry, not shown in Fig. 11, each of them adding further to the complexity of the sensory motor contingencies that define the inputs to higher cortical areas.

No matter how the brain learns about the sensorimotor contingencies, one relationship seems to be clear from the evidence for the visual pathways. The first stages of cortical processing (cortical areas 17, 18 in cat, V1 in the primate), which mature earliest, have the least direct connection to the motor centers, as can be seen from their distribution in the most superficial collicular layers within which these corticofugal axons terminate (see above)[5]. This suggests that the contribution made by these areas of cortex to the sensorimotor contingencies is relatively weak, or distant from the motor instructions at early stages of processing, and also at early stages of life. This contribution appears to become stronger at higher levels of cortical processing and later stages of development, as the later developing cortical areas develop their links with the deeper layers of the colliculus and with other brain stem premotor and motor centers. It looks as though the higher cortical areas, being better informed, are allowed more direct access to the motor systems.

The alert reader must have noticed that the discussion so far has focused on the sensory side of the sensorimotor system. Less information is available about the motor side. It is known that motor cortex (as well as somatosensory cortex) gives rise not only to the corticobulbar and corticospinal tracts for the innervation of motor circuitry, but also, from cortical layer 5 cells, to corticothalamic axons which have long descending (motor) branches (Deschênes et al., 1994). These corticothalamic axons are almost certainly drivers that send information to the thalamus for relay to other cortical areas. That is, there is likely to be a sequence of transthalamic corticocortical pathways that establish a distinct hierarchy (about which we know very little) that brings the motor pathways into close relation with the "sensory" hierarchies considered above. When one is looking at the anatomical basis of sensorimotor contingencies, these pathways are certain to prove important.

The hierarchies of cortical functions and pathways

The cortical areas concerned with vision have been described as forming a rough hierarchy on the basis of the direct corticocortical connections (Felleman

and Van Essen, 1991), and it is possible that a comparable rough hierarchy will be identifiable on the basis of relationships established by the transthalamic corticocortical pathways. Figures 3–10 raise several important questions in highly simplified form: (1) Do the patterns of connections established by the transthalamic pathways match those seen on the basis of the corticocortical pathways? That is, do they both show the same hierarchical order? (2) Does the rough sensory–motor hierarchy demonstrated by Harting et al. (1992) for the corticotectal pathways (Fig. 5) correspond to these other cortical hierarchies? (3) Is there a roughly corresponding hierarchy for other brainstem and spinal premotor or motor terminals of cortical layer 5 cells? (4) Is there any relationship of the sequence of cortical maturation discussed above (Figs. 6–10) to any of the hierarchies under items 1 to 3?

Direct corticocortical connections

The issues raised in the preceding paragraph are not simple. One problem is that the "hierarchy" of corticocortical connections has a number of cross connections that make a precise categorization elusive for some cortical areas. A second problem is that two distinct types of direct corticocortical connection have been described, feedforward and feedback, and for establishing a hierarchy it is the feedforward connections that are relevant, provided that they are known to be drivers, but this is currently not known. Although early distinctions of the feedforward from feedback pathways were clearly based on connections for early visual areas (V1, V2, etc.; 17, 18, 19, etc.), where the previously established hierarchical position of the cortical areas provided a key for interpreting a corticocortical pathway as either feedforward or feedback (Rockland and Pandya, 1979; Rockland, 1989; Rockland and Virga, 1989; Shipp and Zeki, 1989), the distinction for other, higher cortical areas was often based on an extrapolation of these observations to areas where the hierarchy was not established by other means (Maunsell and Van Essen, 1983; Felleman and Van Essen, 1991).

Essentially, the identification of a pathway as either feedforward or feedback has often been based

---

[5]I have focused on the discussion of the collicular connections for the sake of simplicity. It should, however, be noted that many of the cortical areas shown in Fig. 3 also send axons to other brain stem centers such as the pontine nuclei, the reticular nuclei, the pretectum, and other premotor centers.

on anatomical evidence about the cortical layers from which the pathways arise and in which they terminate. The actual function of the pathways as drivers or modulators remains largely unexplored (see Lamme et al., 1998 for a discussion of some of the problems). Records of neural activity at the several stages of the presumed corticocortical hierarchy can show how activity in any one cell group relates to the sensory or motor components of particular situations or experimental tasks, but they generally do not *demonstrate* the cortical pathways that are involved in linking sensory events to each other, nor do most such studies show the cortical layers involved, or provide experimental evidence that can link sensory to motor events along a proposed corticocortical hierarchy. That is, the pathways for any one experimental situation are generally postulated. It can be argued that there is anatomical evidence for the existence of most or all the pathways that have been proposed for linking particular functions, but such a claim generally fails to be a convincing demonstration that any one set of corticocortical pathways actually plays a crucial role in a particular sensorimotor behavior (or that the corticothalamocortical pathways play no role).

One reason for uncertainty about particular corticocortical pathways playing a role in any one functional link is that there is a plethora of corticocortical links (Felleman and Van Essen, 1991; Scannel et al., 1995), so that there are several alternative possibilities. A second reason is that for most corticocortical pathways no information is available about the type of message that they carry. Are they drivers or modulators? What is the message that they convey to the nerve cells they innervate?

The problem can be illustrated by considering cortical layer 6 cells that give rise to a modulatory pathway to the lateral geniculate nucleus (see p. 238). It is clear that although these cells can show responses that relate closely to the details of a sensory situation, with well defined receptive field properties, those properties are not necessarily transmitted from the cortex to the next synaptic station. That is, the message that the layer 6 cells transmit to the thalamic relay cells is not transmitted through the lateral geniculate nucleus to cortex. The basic message the geniculate relay cells are sending to cortex survives silencing these layer 6 cells, and the receptive field properties

of cells in layer 6 are more complex than those of geniculate relay cells.

Comparable evidence is not available about the nature of the message that is passed along any one particular corticocortical pathway, or about the effects of silencing any direct corticocortical pathway but sparing the transthalamic ones. Still it is important to stress that without clear evidence that particular pathways carry particular messages and deliver them from one cortical area to another, for transfer along the proposed hierarchy, schemes of corticocortical pathways based on anatomical studies alone do not provide the functional evidence that is needed to understand corticocortical circuitry; they only provide an essential first step, by showing possible routes. Arguments about the number of cells involved in the transthalamic as opposed to the direct corticocortical pathways (Van Essen, 2005, this volume), help to focus attention on how little is known about the nature of the messages that are passed from one cortical area to another along either route. Once the nature of these messages is understood, it may be possible to understand, the significance of the numbers. The numbers in themselves can put limits on the amount of information that can be passed from one cortical area to another, but until further information about the nature of the messages and the way that the information is coded is available, the numbers cannot tell what each pathway may be doing.

There is a distinct level of uncertainty about the exact functional significance of laminar origins and terminations when used as the major, or often sole criterion for identifying a corticocortical pathway as feedforward or feedback and thus establishing an otherwise undefined hierarchy. That is, there is a circuitous element in the identification of the higher levels of the hierarchy: the known hierarchy at low levels defines the interpretation of the connectivity patterns (see pp. 248–249), and at higher levels the connectivity patterns define the hierarchy.

Transthalamic corticocortical connections

When one considers how the organization of the transthalamic pathways relates to that of the direct corticocortical pathways, one has to recognize that the corticothalamic pathway from layer 5 is functionally quite distinct from that coming from layer 6. The layer 6 pathway is often predominantly a reciprocal feedback pathway, with, as has been noted, a modulatory action in the thalamic relay. The layer 5 thalamic input is a driver and has to be regarded as a feedforward pathway, serving to send messages from one (lower) cortical area to another (higher) one[6]. Shipp (2001, 2003) has proposed that, in accord with what he calls the "replication principle", the organization of the two way connections between visual cortical areas and the pulvinar nucleus of the monkey can be interpreted as showing that the pattern of corticocortical (feedforward?) connections is replicated in the pattern of corticothalamic interconnections. However, his evidence was based on connectional studies that generally labeled large populations of neurons. The cited experiments, included thalamocortical as well as corticothalamic axons in some experiments and in none of the experiments distinguished between the connections established by the modulatory cells of layer 6 (largely feedback) and the drivers of layer 5 (almost certainly feedforward). These are, as has been observed, not only functionally and structurally quite distinct pathways, but they also establish distinct corticothalamic projection patterns.

For the lateral posterior/pulvinar complex of the cat, to take an example where connections are more clearly established than in the pulvinar of the monkey, areas 17 and 18 send layer 5 (driver) afferents to the lateral posterior nucleus (lateral part), but send essentially no layer 6 afferents to that same region, whereas area 19 sends both types of axon to the same region, and also to the pulvinar nucleus itself, which receives no afferents from areas 17 and 18. In addition, this lateral part of the lateral posterior nucleus receives afferents from layer 5 of suprasylvian cortex (Abramson and Chalupa, 1985). The well localized, small terminal arbors of layer 5 cells from

several different cortical areas lie intermingled within any one small part of this nucleus (Guillery et al., 2001), and at present it is not known how the thalamocortical outputs to several of the same cortical areas are organized in relation to the inputs. The question has to be resolved at the single cell level. That is, currently little is known whether single thalamic relay cells can receive corticothalamic axons coming from layer 5 of two different cortical areas. Possibly there are extensive interactions among corticothalamic pathways from different cortical areas within the higher order relays of the thalamus. However, possibly the intermingling of the terminals within the thalamic nucleus explains nothing about their interaction. They may be like the retinogeniculate pathways of the cat, where functionally distinct axon terminals (for example, the X and Y cells, or the on-center and off center cells) mingle in the thalamic relay but there is little significant functional interaction. These important issues are unresolved. It is too early for sweeping generalizations about how the direct and the transthalamic corticocortical pathways relate to each other, or "replicate" each other in terms of their supposed hierarchical arrangements, or how these, in turn relate to the distribution of the motor and premotor terminals of layer 5 cells or to sequence of the development of the several pathways. These are important issues for study in the future.

Conclusions

This study has considered pathways that demonstrate close ties between sensory processing on the one hand and involvement in motor instructions on the other. These are ties provided by branching axons, indicating that for most pathways afferent to the thalamus, and thus for most inputs to the cerebral cortex, the two functions are inextricably linked. As shown in Fig. 12, most messages relayed through the thalamus, possibly all of them, bring information of these two sorts to the cortex. The anatomy of the pathways does not allow for a separation of the two functions, and an analysis of perceptual processing that ignores the motor links will necessarily be incomplete. In order to understand the full implications of a message carried along pathways 4 and 6

---

[6]Layer 5 provides the proposed origin of a feedback pathway in the direct corticocortical pathway (Felleman and Van Essen, 1991). The possibility that layer 5 gives rise to transthalamic corticocortical feedforward connections and direct corticocortical feedback connections suggests that there may be some important functional links between these two systems.

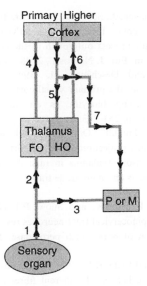

Fig. 12. Schema of the main pathways that have been considered in the text, applicable to any first or higher order thalamic relay. M, premotor or motor center; FO, first order thalamic relay; HO, higher order thalamic relay. Pathway 1, this is the sensory input pathway. Pathway 2, this is the sensory input pathway that carries a copy of a motor instruction (a copy of pathway 3). One could call this a corollary path, or an efference copy of pathway 3, but this would tend to lose sight of the important point that pathway 2 leads to perception and memory storage. Whereas it would obviously not be wrong to see this pathway as a part of a very complicated piece of motor machinery, and whereas this pathway probably originated in phylogeny as an efference copy, it is more useful now to see it as a sensory pathway that leads to perceptual and memory processes, and to recognize the extent to which these processes relate to the functions of efference copies. Pathway 3 is a motor or premotor pathway. Pathway 4 is a thalamocortical pathway. Pathway 5 is a corticothalamic driver innervating a higher order thalamic relay. Pathway 6 is like 4, a thalamocortical pathway. Pathway 7 is like 3 a motor or premotor pathway. From the point of view of the cortex, pathway 6 is like pathway 4 and pathway 5 is like pathway 2.

of Fig. 12 it is important to learn more about the functional nature of the motor links represented by pathways 3 and 7.

The pathway labeled "1" can be treated as a classical sensory input pathway, but pathway 2 differs in that it also carries a copy of concurrent motor instructions. This can be treated as a corollary path (or an efference copy) of pathway 3, which is a premotor or motor link, but I have avoided this terminology in order to stress that pathway 2 is the classical sensory pathway that leads to perceptual processing and memory functions. It is likely that pathway 2 arose in phylogeny as an efference copy, and it can clearly be regarded as part of a complex piece of motor machinery. However, treating it as such would lose sight of the major role that pathway 2 plays in sensory/perceptual processing. It may be strategically more challenging for sensory physiology to ask about the motor functions that are implicit in the messages passing along pathway 2, and to enquire how these contribute to the whole set of functional properties that characterize the "sensory" pathway. Pathway 4 is a thalamocortical pathway going to cortical layers 3 and 4 and transmitting the message carried by pathway 2. Pathway 5 is a corticothalamic driver, arising from cells in cortical layer 5 and providing the main driver afferent to higher order thalamic relay cells. These relay cells in turn send their axons in pathway 6, which is functionally like pathway 4. Pathway 7 is like pathway 3, carrying messages to motor or premotor centers, and giving pathway 5 the functional characteristics that allow it to be seen as an efference copy. The extent to which the messages that pass through higher order thalamic relays are best analyzed as a part of a sensory system leading to perceptual processing, or as efference copies of cortical outputs to lower centers, will depend upon the particular aims of an experimental investigation and, to some extent, on the hierarchical position of the pathway.

For the sake of simplicity, the corticocortical pathways shown in Figs. 1–4 are not included in Fig. 12, nor does Fig. 12 include the array of corticofugal pathways shown in Fig. 4. I have argued that for each group of pathways except for those leading to first order thalamic relays, it may be possible to recognize the possibility of a hierarchical order. That is, the direct corticocortical, the transthalamic corticocortical and the layer 5 corticofugal efferents to premotor and motor centers, may all be arranged in a hierarchical order. The issue arises, first, as to the extent to which such hierarchical order can be rigorously established for any one of the group of pathways and, second, whether the hierarchical orders can be matched for the direct corticocortical, the transthalamic corticocortical and corticofugal pathways to motor centers. Further, we need to know how these hierarchical orders, if they can be established, relate to the development of the relevant corticofugal pathways.

Acknowledgments

The author thanks Murray Sherman, Keith Kluender, and Art Glenberg for comments on an earlier draft and Sherry Feig for Figs. 9 and 10.

References

Abramson, B.P. and Chalupa, L.M. (1985) The laminar distribution of cortical connections with the tecto- and cortico-recipient zones of the cat's lateral posterior nucleus. Neuroscience, 15: 81–95.

Adrian, E.D. (1928) The Basis of Sensation, the Action of the Sense Organs. W.W. Norton & Company, Inc., New York, pp. 1–122.

Aigner, L., Arber, S., Kapfhammer, J.P., Laux, T., Schneider, C., Botteri, F., Brenner, H. and Caroni, P. (1997) Overexpression of the neural growth-associated protein GAP-43 induces nerve sprouting in tha adulte nervous system of transgenic mice. Cell, 83: 269–278.

Barlow, H. (2004) The role of single unit analysis in the past and future of neurobiology. In: Chalupa, L.M. and Werner, J.S. (Eds.), The Visual Neurosciences. MIT press, Cambridge.

Bender, D.B. (1983) Visual activation of neurons in the primate pulvinar depends on cortex but not colliculus. Brain Res., 279: 55–65.

Benowitz, L.I. and Routtenberg, A. (1997) GAP-43: An intrinsic determinant of neuronal development and plasticity. Trends in Neurosci., 20: 84–90.

Bentivoglio, M. and Kuypers, H.G.M. (1982) Divergent axon collaterals from rat cerebellar nuclei to diencephalon, mesencephalon, medulla oblongata and cervical cord. A fluorescent double retrograde labeling study. Exp. Brain Res., 46: 339–356.

Berkley, K.J. (1975) Different targets of different neurons in nucleus gracilis of the cat. J. Comp. Neurol., 163: 285–303.

Berkley, K.J. (1980) Spatial relationships between the terminations of somatic sensory motor pathways in the rostral brainstem of cats and monkeys. II. Cerebellar projections compared with those of the ascending somatic sensory pathways in lateral diencephalon. J. Comp. Neurol., 220: 229–251.

Berkley, K.J., Blomqvist, A., Pelt, A. and Fink, R. (1980) Differences in the collateralization of neuronal projections from the dorsal column nuclei and lateral cervical nucleus to the thalamus and tectum in the cat: An anatomical study using two different double-labeling techniques. Brain Res., 202: 273–290.

Biffo, S., Verhaagen, J., Schrama, L.H., Schotman, P., Danho, W. and Margolis, F.L. (1990) B-50/GAP43 expression correlates with process outgrowth in the embryonic mouse nervous system. Eur. J. Neurosci., 2: 487–499.

Bourassa, J. and Deschênes, M. (1995) Corticothalamic projections from the primary visual cortex in rats: A single fiber study using biocytin as an anterograde tracer. Neuroscience, 66: 253–263.

Bourassa, J., Pinault, D. and Deschênes, M. (1995) Corticothalamic projections from the cortical barrel field to the somatosensory thalamus in rats: A single fibre study using biocytin as an anterograde tracer. Eur. J. Neurosci., 7: 19–30.

Brown, A.G., Rose, P.K. and Snow, P.J. (1977) The morphology of spinocervical tract neurones revealed by intracellular injection of horseradish peroxidase. J. Physiol., 270: 747–764.

Brown, A.G. and Fyffe, R.E. (1981) Direct observations on the contacts made between Ia afferent fibres and alpha-motoneurones in the cat's lumbosacral spinal cord. J. of Physiol., 313: 121–140.

Bull, M.S. and Berkley, K.J. (1984) Differences in the neurones that project from the dorsal column nuclei to the diencephalon, pretectum, and tectum in the cat. Somatosens. Res., 1: 281–300.

Bunt, A.H., Hendrickson, A.E., Lund, J.S., Lund, R.D. and Fuchs, A.F. (1975) Monkey retinal ganglion cells: Morphometric analysis and tracing of axonal projections, with a consideration of the peroxidase technique. J. Comp. Neurol., 164: 265–285.

Cajal, S. and Ramòn, Y. (1911) Histologie du Système Nerveux de l'Homme et des Vertébrés. Maloine, Paris.

Caroni, P. (1997) Intrinsic neuronal determinants that promote axonal sprouting and elongation. Bio. Essays, 19: 767–775.

Casanova, C. (1993) Response properties of neurons in area 17 projecting to the striate recipient zone of of the cat's lateralis posterior-pulvinar complex: A comparison with corticotectal cells. Exp. Brain Res., 96: 247–259.

Casanova, C. (2003) The visual functions of the pulvinar. In: Chalupa, L.M. and Werner, J.S. (Eds.), Visual neurosciences. Vol. 2, Mit Press, Boston, pp. 592–608.

Catsman-Berrevoets, C.E. and Kuypers, H.G. (1978) Differential laminar distribution of corticothalamic neurons projecting to the VL and the center median. An HRP study in the cynomolgus monkey. Brain Res., 154: 359–365.

Chalupa, L.M. (1991) Visual function of the pulvinar. In: Leventhal, A.G. (Ed.), The Neural Basis of Visual Function. CRC Press, Boca Raton, pp. 140–159.

Chalupa, L.M. and Abramson, B.P. (1989) Visual receptive fields in the striate-recipient zone of the lateral posterior-pulvinar complex. J. Neurosci., 9: 347–357.

Chalupa, L.M. and Thompson, I.D. (1980) Retinal ganglion cell projections to the superior colliculus of the hamster demonstrated by the horseradish peroxidase technique. Neurosci. Letters, 19: 13–19.

Cook, E.P. and Maunsell, J.H. (2002) Dynamics of neuronal responses in macaque MT and VIP during motion detection. Nature Neurosci., 5: 985–994.

Churchland, P.S., Ramachandran, V.S. and Sejnowski, T.J. (1994) A critique of pure vision. In: Koch, C. and Davis, J.L. (Eds.), Large Scale Neuronal Theories of the Brain. MIT Press, Cambridge.

Cruce, J.A. (1977) An autoradiographic study of the descending connections of the mamillary nuclei in the rat. J. Comp. Neurol., 176: 631–644.

Deschênes, M., Bourassa, J. and Pinault, D. (1994) Corticothalamic projections from layer 5 cells in rat are collaterals of long range corticofugal axons. Brain Res., 664: 215–219.

Diamond, M.E., Armstrong-James, Budway, M.J. and Ebner, F.F. (1992) Somatic sensory responses in the rostral sector of the posterior group (Pom) and in the ventral posterior medial nucleus (VPM) of the rat thalamus: Dependence on the barrel field cortex. J. Comp. Neurol., 319: 66–84.

Erişir, A., Van Horn, S.C. and Sherman, S.M. (1998) Distribution of synapses in the lateral geniculate nucleus of the cat: Differences between laminae A and A1 and between relay cells and interneurons. J. Comp. Neurol., 390: 247–255.

Feig, S.L. (2004a) Corticothalamic cells in layers 5 and 6 of primary and secondary sensory cortex express GAP-43 mRNA in the adult rat. J. Comp. Neurol., 468: 96–111.

Feig, Sl (2004b) Excitatory and inhibitory pathways express GAP 43 in first and higher order thalamic nuclei of the adult rat. (Submitted).

Feldman, S.G. and Kruger, L. (1980) An axonal transport study of the ascending projection of medial lemniscal neurons in the rat. J. Comp. Neurol., 192: 427–454.

Felleman, D.J. and Van Essen, D.C. (1991) Distributed hierarchical processing in the primate cerebral cortex. Cerebral Cortex, 1: 1–47.

Festinger, L., Burnham, C.A., Ono, H. and Bamber, D. (1967) Efference and the conscious experience of perception. J. Exp. Psychol. Monogr., 74: 1–36.

Flechsig, P.E. (1920) Anatomie des menschlichen Gehirn und Rückenmarks, auf myelogenetischer Grundlage. G. Thieme, Leipzig.

Geisert, E.E., Langsetmo, A. and Spear, P.D. (1981) Influence of the corticogeniculate pathway on the response properties of cat lateral geniculate neurons. Brain Res., 208: 409–415.

Gallant, J.L., Connor, C.E. and Van Essen, D.C. (1998) Neural activity in areas V1, V2 and V4 during free viewing of natural scenes compared to controlled viewing. Neuroreport, 9: 2153–2158.

Gibson, J.J. (1933) Adaptation after-effect and contrast in the perception of curved lines. J. Exp. Psychol., 16: 1–31.

Guillery, R.W. (1957) Degeneration in the hypothalamic connections of the albino rat. J. Anat., 91: 91–115.

Guillery, R.W. (1995) Anatomical evidence concerning the role of the thalamus in corticocortical communication. J. Anat., 187: 583–592.

Guillery, R.W. (2003) Branching thalamic afferents link action to perception. J. Neurophysiol., 90: 539–548.

Guillery, R.W. and Sherman, S.M. (2002a) The thalamus as a monitor of motor outputs. Phil. Trans. Roy. Soc. B, 357: 1809–1821.

Guillery, R.W., Feig, S.L. and Van Lieshout, D.P. (2001) Connections of higher order visual relays in the thalamus: A study of corticothalamic pathways in cats. J. Comp. Neurol., 438: 66–85.

Guillery, R.W. and Sherman, S.M. (2002b) Thalamic relay functions and their role in corticocortical communication: Generalizations from the visual system. Neuron, 33: 1–20.

Hamilton, W.J., Boyd, J.D. and Mossman, H.W. (1952) Human Embryology. William and Wilkins Co., Baltimore, pp. 1–432.

Harting, J.K., Updyke, B.V. and Van Lieshout, D.P. (1992) Corticotectal projections in the cat: Anterograde transport studies of twentyfive cortical areas. J. Comp. Neurol., 324: 379–414.

Harting, J.K. and Van Lieshout, D.P. (2000) Projections from the rostral pole of the inferior colliculus to the cat superior colliculus. Brain Res., 881: 244–247.

Henkel, C.K. (1983) Evidence of sub-collicular auditory projections to the medial geniculate nucleus in the cat: An autoradiographic and horseradish peroxidase study. Brain Res., 259: 21–30.

Helms, M.C., Ozen, G. and Hall, W.C. (2004) Organization of the intermediate gray layer of the superior colliculus. I. Intrinsic vertical connections. J. Neurophysiol., 91: 1706–1715.

Hess, B.J., Blanks, R.H., Lannou, J. and Precht, W. (1989) Effects of kainic acid lesions of the nucleus reticularis tegmenti pontis on fast and slow phases of vesitbulo-ocular and optokinetc reflexes in pigmented rat. Exp. Brain Res., 74: 63–79.

Higo, N., Oishi, T., Yamashita, A., Matsuda, K. and Hayashi, M. (1999) Quantitative non-radioactive in situ hybridization study of GAP-43 and SCG10 mRNAs in the cerebral cortex of adult and infant macaque monkeys. Cerebral Cortex, 9: 317–331.

Hubel, D.H. and Wiesel, T.N. (1977) Ferrier lecture. Functional architecture of macaque monkey visual cortex. Proc. Roy. Soc. B, 198: 1–59.

Jhaveri, S., Edwards, M.A. and Schneider, G.E. (1991) Initial stages of retinofugal axon development in the hamster: Evidence for two distinct stages of growth. Exp. Brain Res., 87: 371–382.

Kalil, R.E. and Chase, R. (1970) Corticofugal influence on activity of lateral geniculate neurons in the cat. J. Neurophysiol., 33: 459–474.

Kelly, L.R., Li, J., Carden, W.B. and Bickford, M.E. (2003) Ultrastructure and synaptic targets of tectothalamic terminals in the cat lateral posterior nucleus. J. Comp.Neurol., 464: 472–486.

Kiorpes, L. and Bassin, S.A. (2003) Development of contour integration in macaque monkeys. Visual Neurosci., 20: 567–575.

Kölliker, A. (1896). Handbuch der Gewebelehre des Menschen. Nervensystem des Menschen und der Thiere. 6th edition, volume 2. W Engelmann, Leipzig.

Kruger, K., Tam, A.S., Lu, C. and Sretavan, D.W. (1998) Retinal ganglion cell axon progression from the optic chiasm to initiate optic tract development requires cell autonomous function of GAP-43. J. Neurosci., 18: 5692–5706.

Kuffler, S.W. (1953) Discharge patterns and functional organization of mammalian retina. J. Neurophysiol., 16: 37–68.

Lamme, V.A.F., Supèr, H. and Spekreijse, H. (1998) Feedforward, horizontal and feedback processing in the visual cortex. Current Opin. Neurobiol., 8: 529–535.

Leventhal, A.G., Rodieck, R.W. and Dreher, B. (1981) Retinal ganglion cell classes in the Old World monkey: Morphology and central projections. Science, 213: 1139–1142.

Leventhal, A.G., Rodieck, R.W. and Dreher, B. (1985) Central projections of retinal ganglion cells. J. Comp. Neurol., 237: 216–226.

Linden, R. and Perry, V.H. (1983) Massive retinotectal projection in rats. Brain Res., 272: 145–149.

López, D.E., Saldaňa, E., Nodal, F.R., Merchán, M.A. and Warr, W.B. (1999) Projections of cochlear root neurons, sentinels of the rat auditory pathway. J. Comp. Neurol., 415: 160–174.

Lu, G.W. and Willis, W.D. Jr. (1999) Branching and/or collateral projections of spinal dorsal horn neurons. Brain Res. Reviews, 29: 50–82.

Maunsell, J.H.R. and Van Essen, D.C. (1983) The connections of the middle temporal visual area (MT) and their relationship to a cortical hierarchy in the macaque monkey. J. Neurosci., 3: 2563–2586.

McClurkin, J.W., Optican, L.M. and Richmond, B.J. (1994) Cortical feedback increases visual information transmitted by monkey parvocellular lateral geniculate relay neurons. Vis. Neurosci., 11: 601–617.

McCrea, R.A., Bishop, G.A. and Kitai, S.T. (1978) Morphological and electrophysiological characteristics of projection neurons in the nucleus interpositus of the cat cerebellum. J. Comp. Neurol., 181: 397–419.

McGuire, C.B., Snipes, G.J. and Norden, J.J. (1988) Light-microscopic immunolocalization of the growth- and plasticity-associated protein GAP-43 in the developing rat brain. Dev. Brain Res., 41: 277–291.

Mountcastle, V.B., Poggio, G.F. and Werner (1963) The relation of thalamic cells response to peripheral stimuli varies over an intensive continuum. J. Neurophysiol., 26: 807–834.

Moya, K.L., Benowitz, L.I., Sabel, B.A. and Schneider, G.E. (1992) Changes in rapidly transported proteins associated with development of abnormal projections in the diencephalon. Brain Res., 586: 265–272.

Murphy, P.C. and Sillito, A.M. (1996) Functional morphology of the feedback pathway from area 17 of the cat visual cortex to the lateral geniculate nucleus. J. Neurosci., 16: 1180–1192.

Murphy, P.C., Duckett, S.G. and Sillito, A.M. (2000) Comparison of the laminar distribution of input from areas 17 and 18 of the visual cortex to the lateral geniculate nucleus of the cat. J. Neurosci., 20: 845–853.

O'Regan, J.K. and Noe, A. (2001) A sensorimotor account of vision and visual consciousness. Noë Behavioral and Brain Sci., 24: 939–973.

Ozen, G., Augustine, G.J. and Hall, W.C. (2000) Contribution of superficial layer neurons to premotor bursts in the superior colliculus. J. Neurophysiol., 84: 460–470.

Perl, E.R., Whitlock, D.G. and Gentry, J.R. (1962) Cutaneous projection to second-order neurons of the dorsal column system. J. Neurophysiol., 25: 337–358.

Perry, V.H. and Cowey, A. (1984) Retinal ganglion cells that project to the superior colliculus and pretectum in the macaque monkey. Neuroscience, 12: 1125–1137.

Rockland, K.S. and Pandya, D.N. (1979) Laminar origins and terminations of cortical connections of the occipital lobe in the rhesus monkey. Brain Res., 179: 3–20.

Rockland, K.S. (1989) Bistratified distribution of terminal arbors of individual axons projecting from area V1 to middle temporal area (MT) in the macaque monkey. Visual Neuroscience 3: 155–170.

Rockland, K.S. and Virga, A. (1989) Terminal arbors of individual "feedback" axons projecting from area V2 to V1 in the macaque monkey: A study using immunohistochemistry of anterogradely transported Phaseolus vulgaris-leucoagglutinin. J. Comp. Neurol., 285: 54–72.

Rockland, K.S. (1998) Convergence and branching patterns of round, type 2 corticopulvinar axons. J. Comp. Neurol., 390: 515–536.

Rockland, K.S. and Knutson, T. (2000) Feedback connections from area MT of the squirrel monkey to areas V1 and V2. J. Comp. Neurol., 425: 345–368.

Royce, G.J. (1983) Cortical neurons with collateral projections to both the caudate nucleus and the centromedian-parafascicular thalamic complex: A fluorescent retrograde double labeling study in the cat. Exp. Brain Res., 50: 157–165.

Scannell, J.W., Blakemore, C. and Young, M.P. (1995) Analysis of connectivity in the cat cerebral cortex. J. Neurosci., 15: 1463–1483.

Schiller, P.H. and Tehovnik, E.J. (2001) Look and see: How the brain moves your eyes about. Prog. Brain Res., 134:

127–142.

Schiller, P.H. and Malpeli, J.G. (1977) Properties and tectal projections of monkey retinal ganglion cells. J. Neurophysiol., 40: 428–445.

Schmielau, F. and Singer, W. (1977) The role of visual cortex for binocular interactions in the cat lateral geniculate nucleus. Brain Res., 120: 354–361.

Schwartz, M.L., Dekker, J.J. and Goldman-Rakic, P.S. (1991) Dual mode of corticothalamic synaptic termination in the mediodorsal nucleus of the rhesus monkey. J. Comp. Neurol., 309: 289–304.

Sherman, S.M. (2005) Thalamic relays and cortical functioning. This volume.

Sherman, S.M. and Guillery, R.W. (1996) The functional organization of thalamocortical relays. J. Neurophysiol., 76: 1367–1395.

Sherman, S.M. and Guillery, R.W. (1998) On the actions that one nerve cell can have on another: Distinguishing "drivers" from "modulators". Proc. Natl. Acad. Sci. USA, 95: 7121–7126.

Sherman, S.M. and Guillery, R.W. (2001) Exploring the Thalamus. Academic Press, San Diego.

Sherman, S.M. and Guillery, R.W. (2002) The role of the thalamus in the flow of information to cortex. Phil. Trans. R Soc. B, 357: 1695–1708.

Shinoda, Y., Futami, T., Mitoma, H. and Yokota, J. (1988) Morphology of single neurones in the cerebello-rubrospinal system. Behav. Brain Res., 28: 59–64.

Shipp, S. (2003) The functional logic of cortico-pulvinar connections. Phil. Trans.Roy. Soc. B, 358: 1605–1624.

Shipp, S. (2001) Corticopulvinar connections of areas V5, V4, and V3 in the macaque monkey: A dual model of retinal and cortical topographies. J. Comp. Neurol., 439: 469–490.

Shipp, S. and Grant, S. (1991) Organization of reciprocal connections between area 17 and the lateral suprasylvian area of cat visual cortex. Visual Neurosci., 6: 339–355.

Shipp, S. and Zeki, S. (1989) The organisation of connections between areas V1 and V5 in macaque monkey visual cortex. Eur. J. Neurosci., 1: 309–332.

Shore, S.E. and Moore, J.K. (1998) Sources of input to the cochlear granule cell region in the guinea pig. Hearing Res., 116: 33–42.

Sperry, R.W. (1952) Neurology and the mind-brain problem. American Scientist, 40: 291–312.

Stackman, R.W. and Taube, J.S. (1998) Firing properties of rat lateral mamillary single units: Head direction, head pitch and angular head velocity. J. Neurosci., 18: 9020–9037.

Sur, M., Esguerra, M., Garraghty, P.E., Kritzer, M.F. and Sherman, S.M. (1987) Morphology of physiologically identified retinogeniculate X- and Y-axons in the cat. J. Neurophysiol., 58: 1–32.

Talbot, W.H., Darian-Smith, I., Kornhuber, H.H. and Mountcastle, V.B. (1968) The sense of flutter-vibration: Comparison of the human capacity with response patterns of mechanoreceptive afferents from the monkey hand. J. Neurophysiol., 31: 301–334.

Tamamaki, N., Uhlrich, D.J. and Sherman, S.M. (1994) Morphology of physiologically identified X and Y axons in the cat's thalamus and midbrain as revealed by intra-axonal injection of biocytin. J. Comp. Neurol., 354: 583–607.

Taube, J.S. (1995) Head direction cells recorded in the anterior thalamic nucleus of freely moving rats. J. Neurosci., 15: 70–86.

Torigoe, Y., Blanks, R.H. and Precht, W. (1986) Anatomical studies on the nucleus reticularis tegmenti pontis in the pigmented rat.II subcortical afferents demonstrated by the retrograde transport of horseradish peroxidase. J. Comp. Neurol., 243: 88–105.

Tsao, D.Y., Vanduffel, W., Sasaki, Y., Fize, D., Knutsen, T.A., Mandeville, J.B., Wald, L.L., Dale, A.M., Rosen, B.R., Van Essen, D.C., Livingstone, M.S., Orban, G.A. and Tootell, R.B. (2003) Stereopsis activates V3A and caudal intraparietal areas in macaques and humans. Neuron 39: 555–568.

Tsukahara, N., Toyama, K. and Kosaka, K. (1967) Electrical activity of red nucleus investigated with intracellular micro-electrodes. Exp. Brain Res., 4: 18–33.

Vallbo, Å.B., Hagbarth, K.E., Torebjörk, H.E. and Wallin, B.G. (1979) Somatosensory, proprioceptive, and sympathetic activity in human peripheral nerves. Physiol. Rev., 59: 919–957.

Van Essen, D (2005) Dynamic aspects of cortico-cortical information flow: Who's in control? (This volume).

Veinante, P., Lavallé, P. and Deschênes, M. (2000) Corticothalamic projections from layer 5 of the vibrissal barrel cortex in the rat. J. Comp. Neurol., 424: 197–204.

Vetter, D.E., Saldana, E. and Mugnaini, E. (1993) Input from the inferior colliculus to the medial olivocochlear neurons in the rat: A double label study with PHA-l and cholera toxin. Hearing Res., 70: 173–186.

Wang, S., Eisenback, M.A. and Bickford, M.E. (2002) Relative distribution of synapses in the pulvinar nucleus of the cat: Implications regarding the "driver/modulator" theory of thalamic function. J. Comp. Neurol., 454: 482–494.

Warren, R.M. and Warren, R.P. (1968) Helmholtz on Perception: Ist Physiology and Development. Wiley, New York.

Wässle, H. and Illing, R.B. (1980) The retinal projection to the superior colliculus in the cat: a quantitative study with HRP. J. Comp. Neurol. 190: 333–356.

Windle, W.F. (1940) Physiology of the Fetus. Saunders, Philadelphia, pp. 1–249.

Whitley, J.M. and Henkel, C.K. (1984) Topographical organization or the inferior collicular projection and other connections of the ventral nucleus of the lateral lemniscus in the cat: A quantitative study with HRP. J. Comp. Neurol., 229: 257–270.

Wouters, B.C., Brock-Samson, S., Little, K. and Norden, J.J. (1998) Up-regulation of fast-axonally transported proteins in retinal ganglion cells of adult rats with optic-peroneal nerve grafts. Mol. Brain Res., 53: 53–68.

Progress in Brain Research, Vol. 149
ISSN 0079-6123

CHAPTER 18

The importance of modulatory input for V1 activity and perception

Michael A. Paradiso*, Sean P. MacEvoy, Xin Huang and Seth Blau

Department of Neuroscience, Brown University, Providence, RI 02912, USA

Abstract: To conduct well-controlled studies of visual processing in the laboratory, deviations from natural visual situations must generally be employed. In some regards, the reduced visual paradigms typically used are adequate for providing an accurate description of visual representations. However, the use of fixation paradigms and stimuli isolated within a receptive field may underestimate the richness of visual processing in area V1. Experiments ranging from lightness encoding and perception to paradigms involving natural scenes and saccades used to examine the relationship between V1 activity and perception are reviewed in this chapter. Using more complex and natural visual stimulation, V1 responses have been detected that are significantly different from responses obtained in more reduced paradigms. A feature common to the findings of different experiments is that the scale of the activated neural population and circuitry appears to play a key role in the correlation between V1 activity and perception. More complex and natural visual stimulation brings into play extra-receptive field modulatory input not involved with stimulation localized to the receptive field. The results suggest that rather than subtly sculpting the response, modulatory input coming from intra- and/or intercortical sources is fundamental in establishing perceptual response patterns in natural visual situations.

Introduction

A principal goal of visual neuroscience research is to understand the computations that take place in the human brain under natural visual conditions. To reach this goal, one approximation frequently made is the use of animals as human surrogates. At present there is no alternative for the examination of neural processing at the single-cell level. Other simplifications are also typically made in the type of visual stimuli employed and the visual behavior of the animal. Rather than complex real-world scenes, animals are presented with unnatural stimuli such as 2D Gabor patches or small bars of light. Rather than

exploring a scene for the purpose of foraging, an animal fixates for an extended period of time while a stimulus is flashed on its peripheral retina. Without a doubt, a tremendous amount has been learned about vision and the brain with the reductionist approach. However, there is that nagging tacit assumption behind virtually all experiments that in natural visual situations, neurons would act the same as in reduced laboratory paradigms.

No one has seriously suggested that everything we know about visual neuroscience from simplified experiments is wrong. However, there are studies that have examined both stimulus complexity and visual behavior that hint that there is more to V1 processing than the reduced paradigms reveal.

Complex stimuli often uncover effects of context that are missed with small stimuli on a blank background. A large literature exists on the effects of

*Corresponding author. Tel.: +1-401-863-1159;
Fax: +1-401-863-1074; E-mail: Michael_Paradiso@brown.edu

DOI: 10.1016/S0079-6123(05)49018-4

context, both perceptual and neural. Demonstrations, some dating back hundreds of years, show that the lightness, color, motion, and other perceived properties of objects are powerfully influenced by the attributes of neighboring objects. Well known examples are color and motion contrast effects. Neural activity also shows powerful contextual influences. A considerable number of experiments have shown that the response of a neuron to a stimulus in its receptive field can be strongly modulated by other stimuli located outside the receptive field (Allman et al., 1985; MacEvoy et al., 1998; Albright and Stoner, 2002). For example, uniform illumination outside the receptive field (RF) suppresses responses to a stimulus in the receptive field (MacEvoy et al., 1998; Rossi and Paradiso, 1999). This is consistent with the suppressive effect seen perceptually in which a gray patch looks dimmer if it is surrounded by a brighter patch. If an optimal bar stimulus is in the receptive field, the response is modulated by the orientation of a bar or grating outside the receptive field (Blakemore and Tobin, 1972; Maffei and Fiorentini, 1976; Fries et al., 1977). This sort of line contrast effect seen in neurons may be related to perceptual effects including figure–ground segregation (Lamme, 1995; Zipser et al., 1996), popout (Knierim and Van Essen, 1992; Nothdurft et al., 1999) and tilt illusions (Paradiso, 1988; Gilbert and Wiesel, 1990). These contextual influences coming from beyond the receptive field presumably arise from lateral or feedback connections. Despite the large number of studies of perceptual and neural contextual effects, there are relatively few cases where it has been established that there is a direct relationship between the two. The contextual studies do not imply that measurements obtained with stimuli confined to the receptive field are incorrect. Rather, the simplified experiments may miss some of the richness of natural processing.

It also appears that visual behavior influences neural coding. A small number of studies have used free viewing paradigms to study receptive fields without enforcing prolonged fixations at specific locations in the visual field. In one study of area IT, free viewing elicited responses indistinguishable from those of fixation paradigms (DiCarlo and Maunsell, 2000). However, there are hints from other experiments that in natural visual situations

brain activity in V1 may be different from what is typically seen in the laboratory. Livingstone et al. (1996) found that it was surprisingly difficult to discern a V1 receptive field from the firing of a neuron during free viewing. To locate a receptive field it was necessary to use a burst filter tailored to the neuron under study. In a series of experiments, Gallant and his coworkers have examined the effects that free viewing has on responses in V1 and later areas. They found that responses in free viewing are often lower and more sparse compared to common flashed-stimulus paradigms (Gallant et al., 1998; Vinje and Gallant, 2000, 2002).

Introducing complex visual stimuli and more natural visual behavior into experiments pose great challenges, but several labs have taken up this challenge. The initial forays into this realm suggest that reduced paradigms may underestimate or mischaracterize neural computations in natural situations (Livingstone et al., 1996; Vinje and Gallant, 2000; David et al., 2004). This may be particularly true in early cortical areas that can appear to be entirely driven by feedforward input (Ferster, 1986; Reid and Alonso, 1995; Kara et al., 2002). The experiments described here are examples from our research showing that neural responses sometimes change significantly as stimulus or behavioral complexity is increased and made more natural. Indeed, in some cases this complexity may be essential for making the V1 response perceptually correlated. The findings have implications for the role and importance of recurrent or modulatory connections in visual cortex. The findings are discussed in terms of their implications for the circuitry underlying perception and the importance of modulatory input to V1 neurons.

Spatial integration and lightness constancy

The great majority of experiments in primary visual cortex employ stimuli that place high contrast features in receptive fields. Indeed, most textbook descriptions state that this is a requirement for evoking a significant response. While this is true for many cells, for many others significant responses can be elicited when the receptive field is covered by a patch of uniform luminance (Kayama et al., 1979; Komatsu et al., 1996; Rossi et al., 1996; Rossi and Paradiso, 1999; Wachtler et al., 2003). The significance of this observation relates to the importance of surface lightness and color in object recognition.

Of particular interest is the finding that many V1 neurons actually respond in a manner better correlated with perceived lightness than with luminance (Rossi and Paradiso, 1999; Kinoshita and Komatsu, 2001; MacEvoy and Paradiso, 2001). It appears that the basis for this neural correlate of perception in primary visual cortex is spatial integration arising from lateral and/or feedback interactions (MacEvoy et al., 1998; Rossi et al., 2001).

There is ample evidence that stimuli located outside the classical receptive field modulate the response to stimuli within the receptive field. For example, the response to an optimally oriented bar in the RF is generally greater when surrounding bars outside the RF are orthogonal and less when the surrounding stimuli are parallel (Blakemore and Tobin, 1972; Gilbert and Wiesel, 1990). Significant surround interactions are also found when the stimuli are surfaces rather than lines (Schein and Desimone, 1990; MacEvoy et al., 1998; Wachtler et al., 2003). One indication of the potential importance of these interactions is the numerous lightness and color illusions that are based on context (e.g., simultaneous contrast). Most often when a uniform patch covers a receptive field, light in the surrounding area has a suppressive effect, though there are cells for which surrounding light enhances the response. The range of the spatial interactions can be quite large, often extending many times the size of the classical receptive field (MacEvoy et al., 1998; Wachtler et al., 2003). This large range is consistent with the large scale over which perceptual interactions occur.

A reasonable hypothesis is that the extensive spatial integration observed in V1 serves some valuable purpose and perceptual illusions are a harmless side effect. It appears that lightness constancy may be one such purpose. Over the course of a day and across the seasons of the year, the illumination coming from the sun varies considerably. Humans, and animals that have been tested, perceive the lightness of objects to be stable despite large variations in illumination. This perceptual constancy for lightness, and related color constancy, was presumably of great evolutionary value. For example, in the absence of perceptual constancies, there might not be reliable cues upon which to select ripe fruits to consume.

Experiments were conducted in cat V1 to test responses for lightness constancy (MacEvoy and Paradiso, 2001). Stimuli consisted of monochromatic patches (i.e., a monochromatic "Mondrian" stimulus) on a computer monitor simulating surfaces with a wide range of reflectances (Fig. 1A). One patch of the stimulus encompassed the receptive field and the rest composed the background. Changes in the luminance values of the patches were made in a manner either consistent (illumination conditions) or inconsistent (control conditions) with overall changes in illumination. Comparisons were made between the two situations when the patches covering the receptive field in each case were identical.

In control conditions only the luminance of the patch covering the receptive field increased, a situation in which the perceived lightness of the patch increases with luminance. By contrast, in the illumination conditions the lightness percept is stable. While there is considerable cell-to-cell variability, on average the responses of V1 neurons to identical stimuli in their receptive field are significantly different in the two conditions (Fig. 1B, C). In the control condition the average V1 response correlates with the luminance of the RF patch. Since perceived lightness also correlates with the luminance, the neural response also correlates with lightness. In marked contrast, in the illumination conditions there is essentially no change in the average V1 response as the luminance of the RF patch increases. This mirrors the perceptual constancy of the patch. These results are reminiscent of the constancy demonstrations of Land (Land and McCann, 1971; Land, 1986). In these demonstrations, the color of patches in a Mondrian were shown to be constant when the overall illumination was varied, but viewing any single patch in isolation (for instance, through a tube) revealed that the patch luminance changed dramatically. The context provided by the changes in the larger area is essential to normalize the local percept. In our physiological studies, in both the illumination and control conditions the response correlates with lightness, but only in the illumination conditions does the response exhibit lightness constancy.

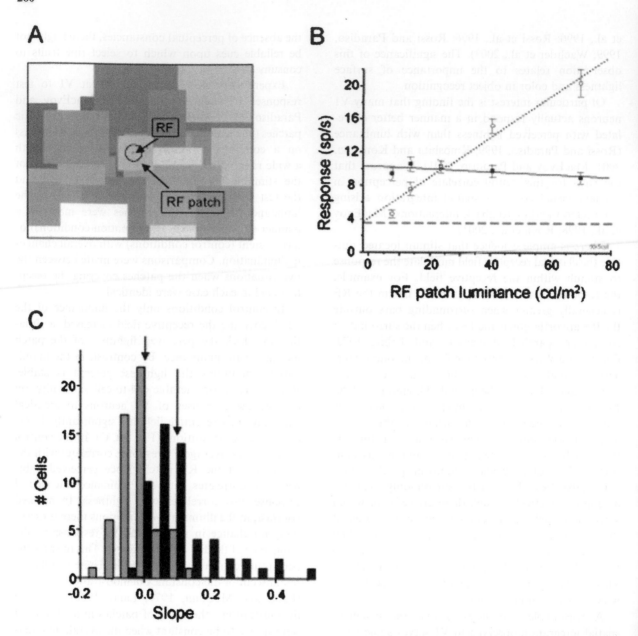

Fig. 1. V1 response to lightness constant stimuli. A. The receptive field was positioned on one patch of a monochromatic Mondrian pattern. B. The dashed line shows that the response of one neuron increases as the luminance of the RF patch increases. When the luminance of all Mondrian patches increases in a manner consistent with an illumination change, the response is unchanged (solid symbols and line). C. Using plots as in 1B, slopes were computed for each cell in illumination and control conditions. The average slope in the control condition was 0.11 indicating that the average response increases with RF patch luminance (black bars). In the illumination condition the average slope was −0.01, nearly invariant (gray bars).

A likely basis for the response invariance in the illumination conditions is the predominant surround suppression seen with uniform patches of light (Schein and Desimone, 1990; MacEvoy et al., 1998; Wachtler et al., 2003). Evidently in the illumination conditions the increased response of the neuron that comes from more light in the RF is counterbalanced by increased suppression from the surround. What is somewhat surprising is that on average the net input to V1 neurons balances the added RF drive with increased surround suppression.

The effects of natural scenes and saccades on V1 activity

The results described above suggest that in the domain of lightness, modulatory inputs from lateral or feedback connections play an important role in making V1 activity lightness constant. Although Mondrian's paintings can be viewed in museums, flashing similar pictures to a fixating animal can hardly be considered a natural visual situation. Visual stimulation in the real world typically involves complex arrangements of light, color, and contrast, quite unlike the simple stimuli usually used in the laboratory. Moreover, natural stimuli fill the visual field whereas many experiments are conducted with small RF stimuli isolated on a large blank display. Another obvious difference between typical experiments and natural vision is behavioral. In a natural setting, the eyes move to bring new stimuli into view; typical fixations are about 300 ms with brief intervening saccades. In most experiments, animals are trained to hold fixation (or anesthetized) while stimuli are flashed into the receptive field.

To explore the significance of stimulus complexity and saccades on V1 responses, we conducted an experiment in alert macaques in which the same stimulus was presented to a neuron under four different conditions, varying with respect to how natural the visual situation was. In the first condition, the animal fixated a point on an otherwise gray visual display and a small bar was flashed into the receptive field. In the second condition the animal fixated the same point and the bar was flashed, but in this case the background was a grayscale outdoor scene (van der Schaaf and van Hateren, 1996) with the same

mean luminance as the gray background. In the third and fourth conditions the background image was a uniform gray or a grayscale photo, respectively. However, in these conditions the fixation of the animal was guided such that a saccade brought the bar stimulus into the receptive field rather than it being flashed on.

It was found that the response to a bar stimulus in the receptive field is influenced by both stimulus complexity and the method by which the stimulus comes into the RF (flash or saccade). Examples are shown in Fig. 2. The cell illustrated in Fig. 2A shows

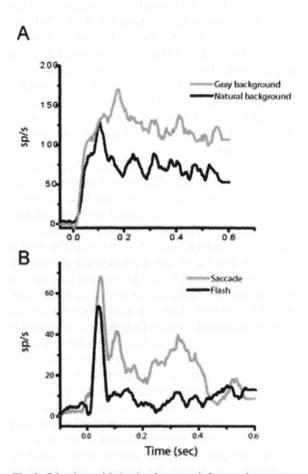

Fig. 2. Stimulus and behavioral context influence the response of a V1 neuron. A. After similar initial responses, a small bar in the receptive field gives a greater response on a uniform gray background (gray curve) than on a grayscale natural image background. B. Responses to the same stimulus are initially similar whether the bar appears in the RF by being flashed or swept in via saccade. After a delay the saccade response is significantly greater.

262

the difference in response associated with the gray and natural scene backgrounds. The response to a small bar is significantly higher when the background is a uniform gray than when it is a grayscale picture. In this case the response was roughly 50% greater when the bar was presented on a gray background compared to a natural scene. This response difference is found regardless of whether a saccade or flash introduced the bar into the receptive field. Also interesting is the delay in the separation of the two curves. The initial response with gray and natural backgrounds is similar but after about 50 ms there is a reduction in the natural scene response. It is not possible to say why the response differs between the two conditions, but the natural scene obviously has contrast and structure not present with the gray background. Previous studies have reported the suppressive effect of contrast outside the receptive field (Allman et al., 1985) and the present result can be interpreted in that context. The delay in the background effect suggests that different circuitry may be involved.

More surprising is the influence of presentation method shown in Fig. 2B. When a saccade brought the bar stimulus into the receptive field the initial response was similar to a flashed stimulus, but after about 50 ms the response in the saccade condition was much larger (more than 100% greater). The neuron shown in this figure has a particularly pronounced difference, but even in the population average, the saccade response with the natural scene background was 15% higher than the flash response on the same background. Several factors were considered to account for the response difference when a stimulus appeared in the receptive field via saccade versus flash. For example, we considered the possibility that the stimulus present in the receptive field prior to the saccade might affect response magnitude. While there was a hint of this in some cells, it could not account for most of the response difference. We also considered the possibility that stimuli swept across the receptive field during the saccade might make the saccade response greater. Again, this was not able to account for the response difference. These and other factors were considered (MacEvoy et al., 2002), and while several factors have small effects on response rate, no single factor has yet been found that can account for the bulk of the response difference.

The combined (and opposed) effects of scene complexity and saccades suggest that it is impossible to predict responses in natural situations from responses to small stimuli flashed into the receptive field.

Background changes and delayed form information

The experiments in which saccades on a natural scene brought stimuli into receptive fields represent a more natural visual situation than flashing a bar isolated to a receptive field. However, the use of complex scenes and saccades complicates interpretation of the results. For example, natural scenes had a suppressive effect on V1 activity relative to a uniform gray background, but the scene complexity made it difficult to ascertain what aspect(s) of the picture was responsible for the suppression.

In a parallel series of experiments, a somewhat less natural visual paradigm was used in order to gain greater control over the effects of image complexity and saccades (Huang and Paradiso, 2000). When an animal makes a saccade while viewing a natural scene, the "contents" of a V1 receptive field change. Perhaps a flower was initially in the receptive field and afterwards the branch of a tree. At the same time that a new local feature is introduced, the background or context usually changes. When the branch of the tree sweeps into the receptive field, adjacent areas in the RF and outside the RF might "see" other vegetation. In the present study, this natural sort of visual stimulation is simulated in the context of a well-controlled fixation paradigm. Macaques fixated a point on the visual display and bars of light or Gabor patches were presented in the receptive field. On some trials the background was static as in most visual physiology experiments. On other trials the background luminance or pattern changed simulating what would occur with a saccade. Comparisons of neural responses were made when identical stimuli were within and beyond the RF in the static and changing background trials. The only difference between the conditions was the stimulus *before* the bar and background used for response measurements.

It was found that when context changes with the introduction of a local feature (the changing background condition), the response pattern is

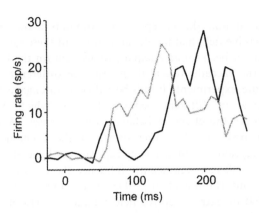

Fig. 3. The temporal response pattern and timing of feature information in a V1 neuron change with contextual changes. When a bar stimulus is flashed on a static background the response has a single peak (gray curve). To mimic the effect of a saccade the same stimulus and background were shown, but preceded by a different background. In this changing background condition the response has two peaks (black curve). With the static background, orientation is reflected in the amplitude of the initial response and contrast is anticorrelated with response latency. With the changing background the initial response carries little orientation or contrast information. Instead, these attributes are represented in the amplitude and latency of the second peak.

qualitatively and quantitatively different than the standard static background situation. An example of this is shown in Fig. 3. When a bar was introduced on a static background, the response typically showed one peak. In this case, orientation selectivity and contrast sensitivity were represented in the amplitude and latency of the earliest response, respectively. The response is quite different in the changing background situation. The data shown in Fig. 3 were obtained when a bar stimulus appeared simultaneously with a change in background luminance, but similar results were obtained with an isoluminant background pattern change. The early response in the changing background condition appears similar to that in the static condition. However, there tended to be response suppression after the initial transient followed by rebound to a higher firing rate. In other words, the average response in the changing background condition showed two peaks rather than one. Of particular interest is the observation that form information is no longer represented in the initial transient as in the static background condition. Instead, orientation and contrast sensitivity are reflected in the amplitude and latency of the delayed

second response peak. This peak occurred about 20–50 ms after the initial peak, suggesting that in the changing background condition, form information was delayed by this amount of time. Other neurons showed only this late response component.

The response differences recorded in the static and changing background conditions suggest that there might be a temporal difference in the brain's access to form information. This hypothesis was tested in a series of human psychophysics experiments (Huang et al., 2001). Bar stimuli were briefly presented and followed by a masking stimulus at various stimulus onset asynchronies (SOAs) to limit the duration of visual processing (Breitmeyer, 1984). As predicted by the physiology data, it appears that perceptual access to form information (orientation and contrast) is delayed when a background change (luminance or pattern) accompanies the presentation of a bar of light. In Fig. 4A orientation discrimination improves significantly as SOA increases with either static or changing background. However, performance saturates at much shorter SOAs with the static background. This suggests that the orientation information is present earlier in that condition. The psychophysics experiments also showed that in the changing background situation observers are able to detect that the scene has changed well before (about 20 ms) they are able to discriminate orientation (Fig. 4B). This suggests that in the changing background condition the early response signals that the scene has changed but does not carry the bulk of the information about the details of the stimulus.

Discussion

The experiments discussed above demonstrate that neural activity in area V1 can be well correlated with visual perception. While this may not be surprising in the general sense that visual activity across the brain must play some role in perception, the correlations with perceptual constancy, detection and discrimination appear more intimate. For example, it was observed that the temporal response patterns, not just the average firing rates, in V1 predict temporal aspects of human detection and discrimination. It is also surprising that lightness constancy appears to be present in V1, as response invariance, such as scale or rotation invariance in inferotemporal neurons

A

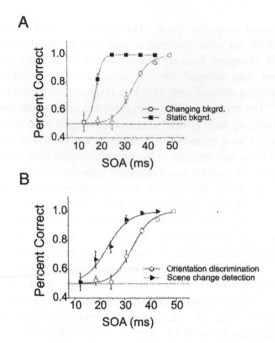

B

Fig. 4. Human detection and discrimination in a masking paradigm with the same stimuli used on neurons in Fig. 3. A. With a static (solid symbols) or changing (open symbols) background, orientation discrimination improves as the SOA between stimulus and mask increases. Performance saturates with the static background at shorter SOAs than with the changing background. B. With a changing background, performance at scene-change detection (solid symbols) asymptotes at shorter SOAs than orientation discrimination (open symbols).

(Logothetis et al., 1995; Booth and Rolls, 1998), is often taken as a hallmark of "higher" processing.

The data also indicate the significant extent to which an animal's behavior and the stimulus context can alter V1 responses. The influence of behavior (i.e., using a saccade to bring a stimulus into a receptive field rather than flashing the stimulus) is intriguing and presently inexplicable. Other experiments have shown that attentional shifts associated with saccades enhance responses to visual stimuli (Motter, 1993) or alter the spatial sensitivity within a receptive field (Tolias et al., 2001) in V4, but the present experiments reveal differences even when attention is not directed to the object in the receptive field. Details of the visual stimulation associated with saccades may partly account for the effect. For example, it was found that the recent stimulation history of the

neuron and the sweep of the stimulus across the receptive field had minor influences, but these factors had not been found adequate to account for the bulk of the saccade versus flash response difference. In future experiments it will be valuable to engage the animal in different behavioral tasks, which may amplify the effect of behavior on responses. While not precisely the same thing, in the domain of perceptual learning, recent experiments have shown that task can significantly influence the response of neurons (Ghose et al., 2002; Yang and Maunsell, 2004) or extra-receptive field interactions (Li et al., 2004).

The finding that stimulus context influences neural responses in more natural situations may not seem surprising. This sounds like the earlier finding that extra-receptive field stimuli modulate the response to stimuli in the receptive field (Allman et al., 1985; Albright and Stoner, 2002). However, findings of extra-RF interactions have frequently been disso- ciated from any perceptual consequence or signifi- cance. The results presented here show not only that extra-RF influences exist, but also that they may be of critical importance for normal vision. When the luminance of an isolated patch increases, perceived brightness and the neural response both also increase. However, when the luminance of surrounding areas increases with the patch in a manner consistent with an illumination change, the response (averaged across V1) and perception are constant. Perceptually the area surrounding a patch is critical for normalizing the local percept. Neuronally a similar contextual normalization appears to occur. Presumably, mod- ulatory input must be used to reach the proper interpretation of the direct (feedforward) input to a cell. For example, in the absence of contextual inter- actions, responses of neurons in V1 may be correlated with perceived brightness (Komatsu et al., 1996; Rossi et al., 1996; Rossi and Paradiso, 1999; Kinoshita and Komatsu, 2001), but they are not lightness constant (MacEvoy and Paradiso, 2001). This is consistent with the lack of perceived constancy found with isolated stimuli. When luminance values change in a manner consistent with illumination, there are con- textual effects in neurons and perceptual constancy is found (Land and McCann, 1971; Land, 1986). More to the point for present purposes, in natural situations V1 neurons would have stimuli outside their receptive fields and the contextual interactions would be crucial for establishing a lightness constant representation in V1. In this sense, V1 activity would commonly only correlate with normal perception in the situation where contextual interactions occurred.

Also, normal vision involves background context changes (from saccades) and the results presented here suggest that data obtained without such changes may misrepresent the normal timing of form information. Form information is delayed in a situation that mimics the effects of saccades. If a stimulus isolated to the receptive field is shown, a neuron's response will show one temporal response pattern and form information is available in the earliest response (Vogels and Orban, 1991; Celebrini et al., 1993). However, if a contextual background change occurs when the focal stimulus appears, there is a different temporal response pattern and form information is delayed by about 20–50 ms. This is particularly interesting because there are perceptual changes in humans that parallel the change in the temporal responses of macaque V1 neurons. Also, in the present experiments actually using saccades, the responses in saccade and flash conditions diverged after a comparable delay.

The delay of information in the more natural situation is long enough (about 20–50 ms) that it probably results from intracortical or feedback inputs to the cell. A similar conclusion has been reached in experiments on figure–ground segregation in which a late component of the V1 response correlates with an object being perceived as figure or ground (Lamme, 1995; Zipser et al., 1996; but see Rossi et al., 2001). In V1 it has also been reported that the response to a gray patch covering the receptive field is initially the same whether the surrounding area is light or dark. However, the later part of the response correlates with perceived brightness and registers the influence of the surround (Kinoshita and Komatsu, 2001). In a different brain area, inferotemporal cortex, it has been reported that global information (e.g., is the stimulus a monkey face?) is present early in the response and detailed information (e.g., what is the facial expression of the monkey?) came about 50 ms later (Sugase et al., 1999). All of these experiments in which some perceptual information is delayed can be taken as consistent with psychophysical masking experiments. The fact that backward masking

experiments work (i.e., that a later stimulus can make a preceding one imperceptible), suggests that perception may sometimes require more than the feedforward sweep of information (Lamme and Roelfsema, 2000).

Three factors suggest that the reduced paradigms typically used in experiments may underestimate the brain circuitry involved in generating form-specific V1 responses. First, many of the findings presented here result from contextual input, whether from a Mondrian stimulus or a natural scene. As others have pointed out (e.g., Angelucci et al., 2002), the scale of perceptual interactions implicates feedback from extrastriate areas. Second, several experiments have reported that the influence of stimuli outside a receptive field is greatest when the stimulus in the receptive field is not optimal (Levitt and Lund, 1997; Hupe et al., 1998; Bullier et al., 2001). In contrast to the stimulus optimization used in many experiments, the analysis of responses associated with free viewing suggests that the great majority of the time, suboptimal stimuli are in receptive fields. Thus, the normal operating domain is one in which contextual effects may be pronounced. Third, the present data indicate that contextual effects are delayed from the initial response. When simple stimuli are flashed into the receptive field, orientation information is found in the earliest response (Vogels and Orban, 1991; Celebrini et al., 1993; Huang and Paradiso, 2000) whereas in the paradigm simulating saccades, form information is delayed by about 20–50 ms. The rapid representation of form information is consistent with the arrangement of afferents reaching V1 from the LGN, but the delay found in this study suggests that additional circuitry is involved.

Intracellular recordings show that the extent and type of visual stimulation can have a large effect on the signals reaching V1 neurons, particularly the inhibitory input (Douglas and Martin, 1991). The present results suggest that to record the natural timing of feature information in V1, stimulation of lateral and/or feedback inputs may be critical. The "canonical circuit" for natural vision may involve more widespread V1 activation, greater inhibition, and more potent contextual input. Lateral or feedback input may be called "modulatory", but this modulation is a crucial component of the normal visual response and representation.

266

Acknowledgments

The authors wish to thank Amber Pierce and Lisa Hurlburt Kinsella for technical assistance. This research was supported by the National Eye Institute.

References

Albright, T.D. and Stoner, G.R. (2002) Contextual influences on visual processing. Annu. Rev. Neurosci., 25: 339–379.

Allman, J., Miezin, F. and McGuinness, E. (1985) Stimulus specific responses from beyond the classical receptive field. Annual Review of Neuroscience, 8: 407–430.

Angelucci, A., Levitt, J.B., Walton, E.J., Hupe, J.M., Bullier, J. and Lund, J.S. (2002) Circuits for local and global signal integration in primary visual cortex. J. Neurosci., 22. 8633 8646.

Blakemore, C. and Tobin, E.A. (1972) Lateral inhibition between orientation detectors in the cat's visual cortex. Experimental Brain Research, 15: 439–440.

Booth, M.C. and Rolls, E.T. (1998) View-invariant representations of familiar objects by neurons in the inferior temporal visual cortex. Cereb. Cortex, 8: 510–523.

Breitmeyer, B.G. (1984). Visual Masking: An Integrative Approach. Oxford University Press, New York.

Bullier, J., Hupe, J.M., James, A.C. and Girard, P. (2001) The role of feedback connections in shaping the responses of visual cortical neurons. Prog. Brain Res., 134: 193–204.

Celebrini, S., Thorpe, S., Trotter, Y. and Imbert, M. (1993) Dynamics of orientation coding in area V1 of the awake primate. Vis. Neurosci., 10: 811–825.

David, S.V., Vinje, W.E. and Gallant, J.L. (2004) Natural stimulus statistics alter the receptive field structure of v1 neurons. J. Neurosci., 24: 6991–7006.

DiCarlo, J.J. and Maunsell, J.H. (2000) Form representation in monkey inferotemporal cortex is virtually unaltered by free viewing. Nat. Neurosci., 3: 814–821.

Douglas, R.J. and Martin, K.A. (1991) A functional microcircuit for cat visual cortex. J. Physiol., 440: 735–769.

Ferster, D. (1986) Orientation selectivity of synaptic potentials in neurons of cat primary visual cortex. J. Neurosci., 6: 1284–1301.

Fries, W., Albus, K. and Creutzfeldt, O.D. (1977) Effects of interacting visual patterns on single cell responses in cats striate cortex. Vision Res., 17: 1001–1008.

Gallant, J.L., Connor, C.E., and Van Essen, D.C. (1998). Neural activity in areas V1, V2 and V4 during free viewing of natural scenes compared to controlled viewing [corrected and republished article originally printed in Neuroreport 1998 Jan 5;9(1):85–90]. Neuroreport, 9: 2153–2158.

Ghose, G.M., Yang, T. and Maunsell, J.H. (2002) Physiological correlates of perceptual learning in monkey V1 and V2. J. Neurophysiol., 87: 1867–1888.

Gilbert, C.D. and Wiesel, T.N. (1990) The influence of contextual stimuli on the orientation selectivity of cells in primary visual cortex of the cat. Vision Research, 30: 1689–1701.

Huang, X., and Paradiso, M.A. (2000). Form information represented in delayed responses of macaque V1 neurons. Invest. Ophthalmol. Vis. Sci. 41:533.

Huang, X., Blau, S. and Paradiso, M.A. (2001) Aspects of human detection and discrimination correlate with macaque V1 physiology. Journal of Vision, 1: 201.

Hupe, J.M., James, A.C., Payne, B.R., Lomber, S.G., Girard, P. and Bullier, J. (1998) Cortical feedback improves discrimination between figure and background by V1, V2 and V3 neurons. Nature, 394: 784–787.

Kara, P., Pezaris, J.S., Yurgenson, S. and Reid, R.C. (2002) The spatial receptive field of thalamic inputs to single cortical simple cells revealed by the interaction of visual and electrical stimulation. Proc. Natl. Acad. Sci. USA, 99: 16261–16266.

Kayama, Y., Riso, R.R., Bartlett, J.R. and Doty, R.W. (1979) Luxotonic responses of units in macaque striate cortex. Journal of Neurophysiology, 42: 1495–1517.

Kinoshita, M. and Komatsu, H. (2001) Neural representation of the luminance and brightness of a uniform surface in the macaque primary visual cortex. J. Neurophysiol., 86: 2559–2570.

Knierim, J.J. and Van Essen, D.C. (1992) Neuronal responses to static texture patterns in area V1 of the alert macaque monkey. Journal of Neurophysiology, 67: 961–980.

Komatsu, H., Murakami, I. and Kinoshita, M. (1996) Surface representation in the visual system. Brain Res. Cogn. Brain Res, 5: 97–104.

Lamme, V.A.F. (1995) The neurophysiology of figure-ground segregation in primary visual cortex. Journal of Neuroscience, 15: 1605–1615.

Lamme, V.A.F. and Roelfsema, P.R. (2000) The distinct modes of vision offered by feedforward and recurrent processing. Trends in Neuroscience, 23: 571–579.

Land, E.H. (1986) Recent advances in retinex theory. Vision Research, 26: 7–21.

Land, E.H. and McCann, J.J. (1971) Lightness and retinex theory. Journal of the Optical Society of America, 61: 1–11.

Levitt, J.B. and Lund, J.S. (1997) Contrast dependence of contextual effects in primate visual cortex. Nature, 387: 73–76.

Li, W., Piech, V. and Gilbert, C.D. (2004) Perceptual learning and top-down influences in primary visual cortex. Nat. Neurosci., 7: 651–657.

Livingstone, M.S., Freeman, D.C. and Hubel, D.H. (1996) Visual responses in V1 of freely viewing monkeys. Cold Spring Harb. Symp. Quant. Biol., 61: 27–37.

Logothetis, N.K., Pauls, J. and Poggio, T. (1995) Shape representation in the inferior temporal cortex of monkeys. Curr. Biol., 5: 552–563.

MacEvoy, S.P., Hanks, T.D. and Paradiso, M.A. (2002) Responses of macaque V1 neurons with natural scenes and saccades. Society for Neuroscience.

MacEvoy, S.P. and Paradiso, M.A. (2001) Lightness constancy in primary visual cortex. Proc. Natl. Acad. Sci. USA, 98: 8827–8831.

MacEvoy, S.P., Kim, W. and Paradiso, M.A. (1998) Integration of surface information in primary visual cortex. Nature Neuroscience, 1: 616–620.

Maffei, L. and Fiorentini, A. (1976) The unresponsive regions of visual cortical receptive fields. Vision Research, 16: 1131–1139.

Motter, B.C. (1993) Focal attention produces spatially selective processing in visual cortical areas V1, V2, and V4 in the presence of competing stimuli. J. Neurophysiol., 70: 909–919.

Nothdurft, H.C., Gallant, J.L. and Van Essen, D.C. (1999) Response modulation by texture surround in primate area V1, correlates of "popout" under anesthesia. Vis. Neurosci., 16: 15–34.

Paradiso, M.A. (1988) A theory for the use of visual orientation information which exploits the columnar structure of striate cortex. Biol. Cybern., 58: 35–49.

Reid, R.C. and Alonso, J.M. (1995) Specificity of monosynaptic connections from thalamus to visual cortex. Nature, 378: 281–284.

Rossi, A.F. and Paradiso, M.A. (1999) Neural correlates of perceived brightness in the retina, lateral geniculate nucleus, and striate cortex. Journal of Neuroscience, 19: 6145–6156.

Rossi, A.F., Rittenhouse, C.D. and Paradiso, M.A. (1996) The representation of brightness in primary visual cortex. Science, 273: 1391–1398.

Rossi, A.F., Desimone, R. and Ungerleider, L.G. (2001) Contextual modulation in primary visual cortex of macaques. J. Neurosci., 21: 1698–1709.

Schein, S.J. and Desimone, R. (1990) Spectral properties of V4 neurons in the macaque. Journal of Neuroscience, 10: 3369–3389.

Sugase, Y., Yamane, S., Ueno, S. and Kawano, K. (1999) Global and fine information coded by single neurons in the temporal visual cortex. Nature, 400: 869–873.

Tolias, A.S., Moore, T., Smirnakis, S.M., Tehovnik, E.J., Siapas, A.G. and Schiller, P.H. (2001) Eye movements modulate visual receptive fields of V4 neurons. Neuron, 29: 757–767.

van der Schaaf, A. and van Hateren, J.H. (1996) Modelling the power spectra of natural images: statistics and information. Vision Res, 36: 2759–2770.

Vinje, W.E., and Gallant, J.L. (2000). Sparse coding and decorrelation in primary visual cortex during natural vision. Science, 287:1273–1276.

Vinje, W.E. and Gallant, J.L. (2000) Sparse coding and decorrelation in primary visual cortex during natural vision. Science, 287: 1273–1276.

Vinje, W.E. and Gallant, J.L. (2002) Natural stimulation of the nonclassical receptive field increases information transmission efficiency in V1. J. Neurosci., 22: 2904–2915.

Vogels, R. and Orban, G.A. (1991) Quantitative study of striate single unit responses in monkeys performing an orientation discrimination task. Exp. Brain. Res., 84: 1–11.

Wachtler, T., Sejnowski, T.J. and Albright, T.D. (2003) Representation of color stimuli in awake macaque primary visual cortex. Neuron, 37: 681–691.

Yang, T. and Maunsell, J.H. (2004) The effect of perceptual learning on neuronal responses in monkey visual area V4. J. Neurosci., 24: 1617–1626.

Zipser, K., Lamme, V.A. and Schiller, P.H. (1996) Contextual modulation in primary visual cortex. J. Neurosci., 16: 7376–7389.

Progress in Brain Research, Vol. 149
ISSN 0079-6123

CHAPTER 19

Dual routes to action: contributions of the dorsal and ventral streams to adaptive behavior

Melvyn A. Goodale[1,]*, Grzegorz Króliczak[2] and David A. Westwood[3]

[1]*Department of Psychology, University of Western Ontario, London, ON N6A 5C2, Canada*
[2]*Neuroscience Program, Department of Psychology, University of Western Ontario, London, ON N6A 5C2, Canada*
[3]*School of Health and Human Performance, Dalhousie University, Halifax, NS B3H 3J5, Canada*

Abstract: More than a decade ago, Goodale and Milner proposed that our perceptual experience of the world depends on visual processing that is fundamentally distinct from that mediating the moment-to-moment visual control of our actions. They mapped this distinction between vision-for-perception and vision-for-action onto the two prominent visual pathways that arise from early visual areas in the primate cerebral cortex: a ventral "perception" pathway projecting to inferotemporal cortex and a dorsal "action" pathway projecting to posterior parietal cortex. In the years since these ideas were first put forward, visual neuroscience has advanced rapidly on several fronts. In this chapter, we examine the perception-action distinction in the light of some of these developments, giving particular emphasis to the differences in the way the two streams process visual information and the way they interact in the production of adaptive behavior.

Introduction

In the last decade, research into the neural substrates of perception, particularly visual perception, has made enormous strides. Much of this progress has been driven by the development of high resolution neuroimaging in humans, which has not only revealed a good deal about the topographical organization of visual areas in the human cerebral cortex, but has also provided new insights into how our brain enables us to perceive, think, and make decisions. In all the excitement, however, it is sometimes forgotten that the ultimate reason we have brains is not so much to perceive the world as it is to act upon it. Brains evolved to enable us to move — and (eventually) to reproduce. Our percepts (and the thoughts that they

engender) can affect the world only insofar as they affect our actions. This basic fact about the function of the brain was highlighted in a recent review by Guillery (2003), in which he observed that perception and action are "inexorably linked at all levels, from the peripheral input to the higher cortical areas".

In fact, it can be argued that the evolution of sensory systems, including vision, was not driven by the need to perceive the world at all but rather by the need to direct movements with respect to that world. After all, a frog does not have to "perceive" the fly; it simply has to catch it. Vision as "perception", in which some sort of inner representation of the outside world is constructed, is a relative newcomer on the evolutionary landscape. The emergence of perception, however, has enabled animals to carry out complex cognitive operations on mental representations of the world — operations that greatly increase the potential for flexible, adaptive behavior. According

*Corresponding author. Tel.: +1-519-661-2070;
Fax: +1-519-661-3961; E-mail: mgoodale@uwo.ca

DOI: 10.1016/S0079-6123(05)49019-6

269

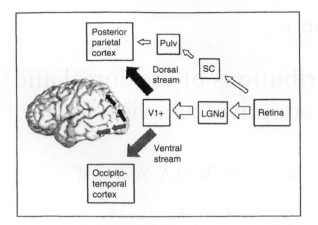

Fig. 1. The two streams of visual processing in human cerebral cortex. The retina sends projections to the lateral geniculate nucleus (pars dorsalis) in the thalamus (LGNd), which projects in turn to primary visual cortex (V1). Within the cerebral cortex, the ventral stream arises from early visual areas and projects to regions in the occipito-temporal cortex. The dorsal stream also arises from early visual areas but projects instead to the posterior parietal cortex. The posterior parietal cortex also receives visual input from the superior colliculus (SC) via the pulvinar (Pulv).

to a proposal put forward by Goodale and Milner in 1992, the informational requirements and the operating characteristics of the more recently evolved "vision-for-perception" system are quite different from those of the more ancient "vision-for-action" system. Indeed, according to Goodale and Milner (1992, 2004; Milner and Goodale, 1995), it is this duplex nature of vision that drove the emergence of distinct visual pathways in the primate cerebral cortex: a dorsal "action" stream, projecting from early visual areas and the superior colliculus (via the pulvinar) to the posterior parietal cortex and a ventral "perception" stream projecting from primary visual cortex to the temporal lobe (Fig. 1). The dorsal stream provides flexible and real time control of motor acts while the ventral stream provides the rich and detailed representation of the world required for cognitive operations such as recognition, identification, and planning.

This might sound rather like Cartesian dualism — the existence of a conscious mind separate from a reflexive machine. But the division of labour between the two streams has nothing to do with the kind of dualism that Descartes proposed. Although the

two kinds of visual processing are separate, both are embodied in the hardware of the brain. Moreover, there is a complex but seamless interaction between the ventral and the dorsal streams in the production of adaptive behavior. For example, the selection of appropriate goal objects depends on the perceptual machinery of the ventral stream, while the execution of a goal-directed action is mediated by dedicated on-line control systems in the dorsal stream and associated motor areas. Indeed, as argued later in this chapter, the integration of processing in the two streams goes well beyond this. The dorsal stream may allow us to reach out and grasp objects with exquisite ease and precision, but it is trapped in the present. Evidence from the behavior of both neurological patients and normal observers shows that, by itself, the encapsulated visuomotor mechanisms in the dorsal stream can deal only with objects that are visible when the action is being programmed. The perceptual machinery in the ventral stream, however, allows us to escape the present and bring to bear information from the past — including information about the function of objects, their intrinsic properties, and their location with reference to other objects in the world. Ultimately then, both streams contribute to the production of goal-directed actions albeit in different ways and on different time scales.

In this chapter, some of the recent evidence from human neuroimaging and monkey neurophysiology that speaks to the idea of two complementary but interacting cortical visual systems have been reviewed first. Next evidence from a range of behavioral studies in normal observers that is consistent with the notion that object-directed actions depend on the integrated activity of two distinct visual systems has been examined.

Neuropsychology meets neuroimaging

Patients with lesions in the dorsal stream, particularly in the region of the intraparietal sulcus (IPS) in the posterior parietal cortex, can have problems using vision to form their grasp or to direct an aiming movement towards objects presented outside foveal vision. This deficit is often described as *optic ataxia* (Bálint, 1909). Despite their problems with the visual control of hand and limb movements, many of these patients can describe the orientation or relative position of the target objects quite accurately (Perenin and Vighetto, 1988). Typically, these patients have no difficulty using input from other sensory systems, such as proprioception or audition, to guide their movements. In short, their deficit is neither "purely" visual nor "purely" motor. It is instead a *visuomotor* deficit.

The nature of the visuomotor deficits observed following damage to the posterior parietal cortex can vary from patient to patient. Some individuals with damage to this region are unable to use visual information to control their hand postures but have no difficulty controlling the direction of their grasp; others show the reverse pattern. Some patients are unable to foveate a target object, but have no difficulty directing a well formed grasp in its direction; others may show no evidence of an oculomotor deficit but be unable to guide their hand towards an object under visual control. Indeed, depending upon the size and locus of the lesion, a patient can demonstrate any combination of these visuomotor deficits (review, see Milner and Goodale, 1995). Different subregions of the posterior parietal cortex, it appears, are critical for the visual control of different motor outputs. In fact, neurophysiological studies have shown that there are specialized visuomotor areas for the control of eye movements, head movements, reaching, and grasping in the monkey posterior parietal cortex, with most of these areas located in or around the IPS. A similar story is emerging in the human neuroimaging literature — separate areas in the IPS and neighboring regions also appear to be specialized for different kinds of visuomotor transformations, and these areas appear to be largely homologous with those in the monkey (Culham and Kanwisher, 2001). A particular motor act, such as reaching out and grasping an object, presumably requires the orchestration of activity in a number of these different areas, including those involved in the control of saccades, visual pursuit, reaching with the limb, and grasping movements of the hands and fingers. Damage to the posterior parietal cortex could interfere with the function of all or any combination of these different regions. But again, even though patients with damage to these dorsal stream regions might experience a devastating loss in visuomotor control, they could at the same time continue to describe (and thus perceive) the intrinsic visual features and location of the very object they cannot acquire.

Quite the opposite pattern of deficits and spared visual abilities has been reported in patients with *visual form agnosia,* where the brain damage is concentrated in the ventral stream. The most compelling example of such a case is patient DF, a young woman who suffered irreversible brain damage in 1988 as a result of anoxia from carbon monoxide poisoning (Milner et al., 1991). Even though DF is unable to indicate the size, shape, and orientation of an object, either verbally or manually, she shows normal pre-shaping and rotation of her hand when reaching out to grasp that object (Goodale et al., 1991; Milner et al., 1991). The initial MR images of DF's brain (Milner et al., 1991), which were acquired just over a year after her accident, suggested that her brain damage is largely confined to the ventrolateral regions of the occipital lobe, in regions that are now known to be part of the human ventral stream. This tentative conclusion was confirmed in a recent high-resolution structural MRI study (James et al., 2003), which revealed that the lateral occipital complex (LOC), a structure in the ventral stream that has been implicated in object recognition (for review, see Grill-Spector, 2003; Hasson et al., 2003) is severely damaged on both sides of DF's brain. The damage is largely localized to area LO (Malach et al., 1995), in the more lateral aspect of LOC, leaving much of the fusiform gyrus and the parahippocampal gyrus quite intact. This sparing of more medial regions of LOC and other parts of the ventral stream may help to explain why DF's perceptual deficit is form specific in that she has great difficulty reporting the geometrical structure of objects but can still accurately describe their surface properties, such as colour and visual texture.

The data from a recent functional MRI study of DF also converges nicely on the earlier neuropsychological observations (James et al., 2003). Thus, when DF was presented with line drawings of common objects, where form provided the only cue as to the identity of the object, none of LOC, even the regions in the fusiform gyrus outside the lesion in area LO, was activated. The lack of activation with line drawings was mirrored in DF's poor performance in identifying the objects in the drawings. Healthy control subjects, who of course had no difficulty identifying the drawings, showed robust activation in the LOC, particularly in area LO. With coloured and greyscale images of common objects, stimuli that DF identified more accurately than line drawings, DF did show some ventral-stream activation, particularly in the fusiform gyrus although the activation was more widely distributed than that seen in controls — and did not include area LO.

In DF's dorsal stream, the structural MRI revealed shrinkage of cortical tissue within the intraparietal sulcus (IPS), a region that has been implicated in visuomotor control (Goodale and Humphrey, 1998; Culham and Kanwisher, 2001; Cohen and Andersen, 2002; Simon et al., 2002; Andersen and Buneo, 2003). Nevertheless, when DF grasped objects that varied in size and orientation, she displayed relatively normal activation in the anterior intraparietal sulcus (AIP), an area that has been shown to play a critical role in the visual control of grasping in both humans (Binkofski et al., 1998; Culham et al., 2003; Jeannerod and Farne, 2003; Culham, 2004) and monkeys (Taira et al., 1990; Sakata and Taira, 1994; Sakata, 2003). Taken together, these findings provide additional support for the idea that perception and action are mediated by separate visual pathways in the cerebral cortex, and confirm the respective roles of the ventral and dorsal visual streams in these functions.

Evidence from monkey neurophysiology

A broad range of neurophysiological studies in the monkey lend considerable support to the distinction outlined in the previous section. Since the pioneering studies of Gross and his colleagues (1972) on the monkey ventral stream, for example, there has been a long history of single-unit work showing that cells in inferotemporal cortex (IT) and neighbouring regions of the superior temporal sulcus are tuned to specific objects and object features (Logothetis and Sheinberg, 1996; Tanaka, 2003) — with some cells maintaining their selectivity irrespective of viewpoint, retinal image size, and even color. Moreover, the responses of these cells are not affected by the animal's motor behavior but are instead sensitive to the reinforcement history and significance of the visual stimuli that drive them. It is important to note, however, that monkeys with IT lesions can orient their fingers in a precision grip to grasp morsels of food embedded in small slots placed at different orientations — even though their ability to discriminate between different orientations is profoundly impaired (Glickstein et al., 1998). In short, monkeys with IT lesions appear to have a similar pattern of deficits and spared abilities as DF.

It has been suggested that IT cells might also play a role in the mnemonic coding of visual objects, acting as one (albeit important) node in a network that includes medial temporal structures and prefrontal regions (Miyashita and Hayashi, 2000). In fact, sensitivity to particular objects can be created in ensembles of IT cells simply by training the animals to discriminate between different objects (Logothetis et al., 1995). There is also evidence for a specialization within separate regions of the ventral stream for the coding of certain categories of objects, such as faces and hands, which are of particular social significance to the monkey (Perrett et al., 1995). Finally, recent studies, using a binocular rivalry paradigm, in which competing images are presented at the same time to different eyes, have shown that cells in IT are tuned to what the monkey reports seeing on a particular trial, not simply to what is present on the two eyes (Logothetis, 1998). But neurons earlier in the visual system, like area V1, do not show these correlations. The neurons in this early visual area respond in the same way no matter what the monkey indicates that it sees. Even in intermediate areas of the ventral stream such as area V4 the correlations are relatively weak. These results provide indirect support for the claim that the ventral stream plays a critical role in delivering the contents of our conscious percepts (insofar as activity in the monkey's inferotemporal cortex reflects what the monkey indicates that it sees). These and other studies too numerous to cite here lend considerable support to the suggestion that the object-based descriptions provided by the ventral stream form the basic raw material for visual perception, recognition memory and other long-term representations of the visual world.

In sharp contrast to the activity of cells in the ventral stream, the responses of many cells in the dorsal stream are dependent on the current motor behavior of the animal. Over thirty years ago, work in the alert behaving monkey demonstrated that the responses of neurons in the posterior parietal cortex are typically modulated both by visual stimuli and by the movements made by the animal (Hyvärinen and Poranen, 1974; Mountcastle et al., 1975). As Andersen (1987) puts it, most neurons in this region "exhibit both sensory-related and movement-related activity". Moreover, the motor modulation is quite specific; some neurons are modulated by visual fixation, by pursuit eye movements, or by saccades; still others by visually guided reaching or by the manipulation of objects. Experiments in Andersen's laboratory have shown, for example, that visual cells in the posterior parietal cortex that code the spatial location of a target for a saccadic eye movement are located in a region (the lateral intraparietal sulcus or LIP) that is anatomically distinct from another region (the socalled parietal reach region or PRR) containing cells that code the spatial location of that same target for a manual aiming movement (Snyder et al., 1997; Cohen and Andersen, 2002). Experiments in other laboratories have found grasp-modulated cells in the anterior intraparietal region of parietal cortex (area AIP) that are sensitive to intrinsic object features, such as size and orientation, that determine the posture of the hand and fingers during the execution of a grasping movement (Taira et al., 1990; Sakata and Taira, 1994). Lesions in this region of the posterior parietal cortex produce deficits in the visual control of reaching and grasping similar in many respects to those seen in humans following damage to the homologous region (Ettlinger, 1977; Glickstein et al., 1998). In one study, small reversible pharmacological lesions were made directly in area AIP in monkey (Gallese et al., 1994). When this region was inactivated, there was a selective interference with pre-shaping of the hand as the monkey reached out to grasp an object, a deficit that is remarkably similar to that seen in humans with discrete lesions in the anterior part of the intraparietal sulcus, an area thought to be homologous with monkey AIP (Binkofski et al., 1998). Finally, it should be noted that the posterior parietal cortex is intimately linked with premotor cortex, the superior colliculus, and pontine nuclei — brain areas that have been implicated in various aspects of the visual control of eye, limb, and body movements. In short, the networks in the dorsal stream have the functional properties and interconnections that one might expect to see in a system concerned with the moment-to-moment control of visually guided actions. [Of necessity, this review of the monkey literature is far from complete. For more details, see Andersen and Buneo (2003), Sakata (2003), and Tanaka (2003).]

The metrics and timing of perception and action

According to the two visual system model put forward by Goodale and Milner, the dorsal and ventral streams both process information about the structure of objects and about their spatial locations, but they transform this information into quite different outputs (Goodale and Milner, 1992, 2004; Milner and Goodale, 1995; Goodale and Humphrey, 1998; James et al., 2002; Ganel and Goodale, 2003). Because the visuomotor systems of the dorsal stream are responsible for the control of highly skilled actions, it is imperative that these systems compute the absolute metrics of target objects in a frame of reference centered on specific effectors, that is, in egocentric coding (Goodale and Humphrey, 1998; Henriques et al., 2002). Indeed, evidence from single-unit studies of the dorsal stream in the monkey suggests that this is the case, and that the different visuomotor areas in this region may, at least, initially share a common frame of reference, one that is centered on the eye, (Cohen and Andersen, 2002). This oculocentric frame of reference may serve as the *lingua franca* of the posterior parietal cortex, allowing the different visuomotor areas in this region to coordinate their activities.

Because observers and goal objects rarely stay in a static relationship with one another, the required coordinates for action are most effectively computed immediately before the movements are initiated; i.e., in *real time*. A corollary of real time visuomotor transformation is that neither the coordinates for a particular action nor the resulting motor program need to be stored in memory — indeed such storage could create interference between competing action programs for multiple objects in the visual array, or between action programs to the same object following a change in the spatial relationship between target and actor.

In contrast to the visual control of action, visual perception has no requirement for absolute metrics or egocentric coding. In fact, object recognition depends on the ability to see beyond the absolute metrics of a particular visual scene; for example, one must be able to recognize a particular object independent of its size and its momentary orientation and position. Encoding an object in a scene-based frame of reference (sometimes called an allocentric frame of reference) permits a representation of the object that preserves the relations between the object parts and its surroundings without requiring precise information about absolute size of the object or its exact position with respect to the observer (Goodale and Humphrey, 1998; Goodale and Milner, 2004). Visual perception also operates over a much longer time scale than that used in the visual control of action. In fact, object recognition would not be possible unless perceptual information about previously encountered objects were stored in memory — and an allocentric representation system is ideal for storing this information.

Many recent psychophysical findings support the general notion that perception and action are mediated by independent visual systems that carry out quite different computations on the information present on the retina. Early evidence that visuomotor control depends on processing distinct from that underlying conscious perception came from a study by Goodale et al. (1986) in which participants reached to visual targets that changed position during a concurrent saccadic eye movement (i.e., a double-step reaching task). Although participants demonstrated no conscious awareness of any change in the target's location (in a two-alternative forced choice task), the endpoints of their reaching movements reflected the new rather than original target position (Bridgeman et al., 1979). More recent work suggests that even if participants are aware of the target perturbation, this awareness does not necessarily influence the movement of their hand (Fecteau et al., 2001) — a finding that is consistent with Pisella et al.'s (2000) proposal that fast corrections to reaching movements are under the guidance of an "automatic pilot" in the posterior parietal cortex (see also Castiello et al., 1991; Desmurget et al., 1999; Desmurget et al., 2001) that, once engaged, is refractory to conscious intervention. Using a variety of tasks and responses, other investigators (Burr et al., 2001; Brown et al., 2002; Dubrowski and Carnahan, 2002; Churchland et al.,

2003; Kerzel and Gegenfurtner, 2003; Whitney et al., 2003) have shown important differences between the perception of visual stimuli and the control of actions towards those stimuli, underscoring the view that perception and action engage quite different visual mechanisms. In addition, a number of experiments (Goodale et al., 1994; Hu and Goodale, 2000; Westwood and Goodale, 2003) have shown that actions, such as grasping, that are initiated *after* the goal object has been removed from view are qualitatively different from the actions that are programmed while the object is visible — even if, in both cases, the goal is not visible during the execution of the movement. These findings suggest that the control of actions to remembered objects may depend heavily on processing in the ventral stream — processing that does not typically intrude on the control of visually guided actions (Goodale et al., 2003).

Neuropsychological evidence from patients with visual form agnosia and those with optic ataxia provides important converging support for the contention that there are two distinct modes of control for object-directed action. Thus, DF (who has visual form agnosia from ventral stream damage) is able to scale her grasp to visible goal objects, but is unable to do so when the goal object has been removed from view for only a few seconds (Goodale et al., 1994). Conversely, patients with optic ataxia from dorsal stream damage will often show a paradoxical improvement in performance if they are encouraged not to respond immediately when the target is presented but to delay their actions until the object is no longer visible (Milner et al., 1999; Milner et al., 2001; Revol et al., 2003; Rossetti et al., 2003). All of this suggests the real time mode of control depends on the visuomotor networks in the dorsal stream, whereas off-line mode control depends, at least in part, on the perceptual mechanisms in the ventral stream.

Of course, the two systems are not hermetically sealed from one another. Indeed, as Guillery (2003) has pointed out, perception and action are intimately linked. After all, many actions, which are mediated by mechanisms in the dorsal stream, are conditional upon the presence of complex stimuli that can be interpreted only by mechanisms in the ventral perceptual stream. Indeed, this may explain why a number of neurophysiological experiments have found neurons in the posterior parietal cortex that are sensitive to stimulus features such as colour (Toth and Assad, 2002), shape (Sereno and Maunsell, 1998), duration (Shadlen and Newsome, 2001), or motion (Leon and Shadlen, 2003) in paradigms where these stimulus dimensions are arbitrarily mapped onto object-directed actions. In other words, the selectivity of the neurons in the dorsal stream for particular visual stimuli is related to the required response rather than to the perceptual processing of the stimulus as such. It should also not be forgotten that our understanding of the actions of others may also depend in part on some of the same machinery our brain uses to generate these same actions in ourselves (Rizzolatti and Matelli, 2003). But even in this case, object-based perceptual machinery has to be initially engaged to parse the scene in which the action is embedded. That is, the activation of premotor "mirror neurons" when observing the actions of others likely depends on the earlier activation of neurons in visual regions of the ventral stream (such as the superior temporal sulcus) responsible for the analysis of the gestural input (Vaina et al., 2001).

Priming and the two streams

Our ability to recognize objects and access their semantic associations can be greatly facilitated by recent encounters with those objects, even when these encounters cannot be explicitly recalled; i.e., priming (Biederman and Gerhardstein, 1993; Thompson-Schill and Gabrieli, 1999; for a review of the related literature on priming and the brain, see Schacter and Buckner, 1998). Can actions directed towards objects benefit in the same way from prior visual information? To the extent that the dorsal "action" system computes the required metrics for motor responses de novo on the basis of currently available visual information, one might predict that actions would not be sensitive to earlier vision of the target stimulus or related stimuli.

In apparent contrast to this prediction, Craighero et al. (1996) reported that the onset of grasping could be reduced by presenting a "priming" stimulus 100 ms before the action was cued, but only if the prime had the same (as compared to different or neutral) orientation as the goal object. Although this result

was interpreted as evidence of "visuomotor priming", the nature of the task used by Craighero et al. suggests that only certain classes of motor responses can be primed by pre-movement visual information. As it turns out, the orientation of the goal object was specified by a verbal cue at the beginning of each trial, but the object was *never visible* to the participants at any point during the experiment. As such participants would have had to plan their movement on the basis of a mental representation of the goal object rather than visual information gleaned from the retina. Since actions based on memory for target information depend on a perceptual representation of the object's features, it is perhaps not surprising that the motor responses in Craighero et al. study could be primed given the susceptibility of the perceptual system to priming effects.

Cant et al. (2005) directly compared priming of memory-driven and visually guided grasping using a paradigm similar to that employed by Craighero et al. (1996). In trials where the target object was occluded from view after seeing a prime stimulus, grasping movements were initiated more quickly for congruent as compared to incongruent primes — much like the results of Craighero et al. (1996). When the target object was visible at the time of response initiation, however, no evidence of priming was found. Presumably the fast visuomotor networks in the dorsal stream were engaged for control of grasping when the target was visible at response cueing but not when the target had to be remembered. In the former case, no priming was observed because of the real time nature of dorsal stream action control. In the latter case, the perceptual representation of the target object used to program the memory-driven action was likely primed by the visual features of the prime object. In another experiment, Cant et al. showed that, under identical stimulation and timing parameters, naming but not grasping responses could be primed by previously viewed objects — provided the goal object was visible at the time the response was requested.

In the Craighero et al. (1996) and Cant et al. (in press) studies discussed above, goal objects always required the same basic action (i.e., grasping) although tailored to match the particular orientation of the target on each trial. Accurate performance

276

thus required the visuomotor system to merely transform low level visual object features into an appropriately calibrated motor response; presumably this transformation neither requires nor benefits from prior knowledge about the target object since all the information necessary for the task is available on the retina. But what if the target was a functional object that required the selection of a particular sort of action? In this case, perceptual mechanisms would need to be engaged to identify the object and determine the appropriate type of hand posture; disaster would quickly ensue if a handgun was picked up by the business end rather than the handle.

In a series of elegant experiments Creem and Proffitt (2001) demonstrated that the functional components of the grasp are processed independently of the metrical aspects of grip scaling and wrist rotation. Participants in their experiment were asked to pick up tools and implements (such as a hammer, a toothbrush, and a screwdriver) with the handle turned away from them. As expected, the participants still reached out and grabbed each tool by its handle even though this meant adopting an uncomfortable hand posture. If, however, they were asked to do this while they simultaneously tried to recall words they had learned earlier in a paired associate task, the participants now picked up the tool as if blind to its functional semantics. But even though they grasped the objects inappropriately, they still picked them up deftly, showing well-calibrated grasps. The dorsal stream, it seemed, was still doing its job as well as ever — it was just the functional aspects of the grasp that were missing. Presumably, the concurrent paired-associate task overloaded the semantic systems needed to retrieve the functional properties of the object and thus the appropriate grasp to use. Indeed, Creem and Proffitt showed in another experiment that tasks which did not have a large semantic component but which nevertheless demanded the participants'' attention interfered much less with the functional aspects of their grasps.

Because the appropriate grasping of functional objects requires perceptual and semantic processing, one might suspect that such actions could be primed. In a recent study, therefore, Garofeanu et al. (2004) compared the effects of priming on the grasping of functional objects and the naming of these same

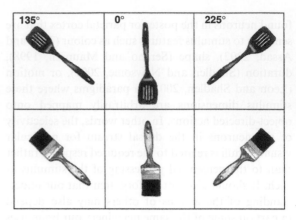

Fig. 2. Examples of the objects and the different orientations used in the Garofeanu et al. (2004) study. Real objects were used and were placed in different orientations on a tabletop in front of the participants.

objects in a repetition-priming paradigm (i.e., prime stimuli are viewed first in a study session then in a test session mixed in with new stimuli). In such paradigms priming is operationalized as decreased latency to respond primed versus new stimuli in the test phase, presumably reflecting implicit memory of the previous encounter since no explicit reference is made to the prior study session and participants are never instructed to memorize the studied objects. In the Garofeanu et al. experiments, a two by two design was used in which functional objects (Fig. 2) were either named or grasped in the study and test phases. In some experiments, the orientation of the objects was changed between the study phase and the test phase. Independent of whether participants grasped or named the prime objects at study, grasps were initiated no faster for primed versus new objects in the test phase (Fig. 3). In other words, there was no evidence of priming for grasping. As expected, there was robust repetition priming for naming, irrespective of whether the orientation of the object was maintained or changed from study to test (supporting the idea that object identification and discrimination can be view-independent; e.g., Biederman and Gerhardstein, 1993; James et al., 2002; Cant et al., 2005), and irrespective of whether primes were named or grasped during the study phase.

The complete absence of visuomotor priming in the Garofeanu et al. study was unexpected given that

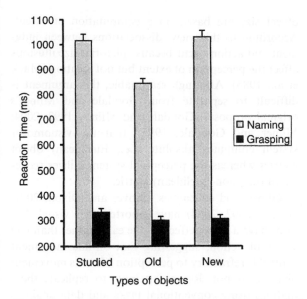

Fig. 3. Reaction time for naming and grasping of studied objects and "old" and "new" objects during later testing (Garofeanu et al., 2004). Reaction times are averaged over all the different combinations of study and test phases (naming–naming, naming–grasping, grasping–naming, and grasping–grasping). Note that there was robust priming of naming: participants named old objects (ones that they had studied earlier) faster than new objects. There was no evidence of visuomotor priming, although participants were faster overall during testing than during study.

the objects to be grasped were tools and implements — objects that are associated with particular functions and thus particular hand postures. Presumably participants would have had to engage semantic processing in order to complete the grasping task — semantic processing that shows robust priming effects. Why then were functional grasps not facilitated by prior exposure to the prime objects? Although the answer to this question is not clear, it seems likely that response selection and the specification of response kinematics do not proceed in a simple serial manner. It is possible that response selection processes were actually facilitated by repetition priming, but this advantage might not have been observable in the time to initiate the action since the kinematic specification of the response might not yet have been complete. In other words, response selection and response specification might proceed in a parallel manner, and there could even be an

information processing bottleneck at the interface between the two processes.

Visual illusions: demonstrating a dissociation between perception and action

A particularly intriguing but controversial line of evidence in support of the perception–action hypothesis comes from studies looking at the influence of perceptual illusions on the control of object-directed actions such as saccades, reaching movements, and manual prehension (Carey, 2001). Early on, it was shown that the final endpoints of saccadic eye movements are insensitive to a dot-in-frame illusion in which the perception of a target's location is shifted opposite to the displacement of a large visual frame (Bridgeman et al., 1981; Wong and Mack, 1981). This result is consistent with the idea, discussed earlier, that visuomotor systems make use of egocentric frames of reference (at least in real time) whereas perception uses allocentric or scene-based frames of reference. Recent single-unit studies in the monkey have shown that prefrontal cortex neurons can code both kinds of frames of reference simultaneously when the monkey is performing a dot-in-frame task, presumably reflecting both dorsal- and ventral-stream processing (Lebedev et al., 2001).

Nearly ten years ago, Aglioti et al. (1995) demonstrated that the scaling of grip aperture was insensitive to the Ebbinghaus illusion, a robust perceptual illusion in which a target surrounded by smaller circles appears to be larger than the same target surrounded by larger circles. At the same time, of course, grip aperture remained exquisitely sensitive to real changes in the size of the target object. Grip aperture is refractory to a size-contrast illusion even when the hand and target are occluded during the action (Haffenden and Goodale, 1998), indicating that on-line visual feedback during grasping is not required to "correct" an initial perceptual bias induced by the illusion. Again, these findings suggest that objects are processed differently by perceptual and visuomotor systems, consistent with the perception–action model (Goodale and Milner, 1992, 2004; Milner and Goodale, 1995; Goodale and Humphrey, 1998).

A number of recent findings, however, have challenged the notion that perceptual illusions do not impact the control of object-directed actions. These challenges fall into several categories from non-replication (Franz et al., 2000), to the contention that early studies did not adequately match action and perception tasks for various input, attention and output demands (Vishton et al., 1999; Bruno, 2001; Smeets and Brenner, 2001), or the idea that action tasks involve multiple stages of processing from purely perceptual to more "automatic" visuo-motor control (Glover and Dixon, 2001; Glover, 2002, 2004). Most of these challenges can readily be accommodated within the basic framework of the perception–action hypothesis, yet each provides important new insight into the nature of the processing mechanisms underlying perception versus action.

Franz and colleagues (Franz et al., 2000), have failed to replicate the early results of Aglioti et al. (1995), and have argued that visually guided actions and perceptual judgments are mediated by the same underlying visual processing mechanisms. Such an account, however, cannot explain why the majority of illusion studies find evidence for a dissociation between perception and action (Carey, 2001). Nor can it explain the dissociations observed in patients with optic ataxia or visual form agnosia — nor for that matter, the extensive neurophysiological and behavioral work on the ventral and dorsal streams in the macaque monkey that supports a distinction between vision-for-perception and vision-for-action (Goodale and Milner, 1992, 2004; Milner and Goodale, 1995; Goodale and Humphrey, 1998). One possible reason that Franz et al. find an effect on grasping with the Ebbinghaus illusion is that, depending on the particular arrangement of the illusory display, the visuomotor system can sometimes treat the surrounding disks as obstacles. As a consequence grip aperture may be affected by the display, not because of a perceived illusion, but because the visuomotor system is attempting to avoid having the fingers collide with an apparent obstacle near the target (Haffenden and Goodale, 2000; Haffenden et al., 2001; de Grave et al., 2004).

Smeets and colleagues (Smeets and Brenner, 2001; Smeets et al., 2002), have argued that the control of grasping is based on the computed locations of points on the object's surface, whereas judgments of

object size are based on a computation of extent. According to this view, dissociations between judgment and action occur because pictorial size illusions affect the perception of extent but not location (Mack et al., 1985). Although reasonable, this argument is difficult to separate from Goodale and Milner's original proposal (Goodale and Milner, 1992, 2004; Milner and Goodale, 1995), that the visuomotor system computes absolute (i.e., Euclidean) object metrics whereas the perceptual system utilizes scene-based (i.e., non-Euclidean) metrics.

Glover and colleagues (Glover and Dixon, 2001; Glover, 2002, 2004) have reported that visual illusions have a larger effect on the early rather than late stages of action, suggesting that on-line movement control is refractory to perception whereas movement planning is not. Recent attempts to replicate these findings using conventional tasks and data analyses have failed (Danckert et al., 2002; Franz, 2003), and neuropsychological evidence does not support the contention that the early and late stages of actions access different visual processing (Milner et al., 2003). Nevertheless, there is good reason to believe that perceptual mechanisms are important for the guidance of action in clearly circumscribed situations; Glover's notion of "action-planning" can be easily subsumed under this framework.

Two recent lines of evidence have helped to clarify the relation between object perception and object-directed action in the context of visual illusions. Dyde and Milner (2002) showed that the orientation of the grasping hand is sensitive to a simultaneous tilt (ST) illusion — similar to that used by Glover and colleagues (Glover and Dixon, 2001), but not a rod-and-frame (RF) illusion, even though the two visual displays have equivalent effects on judgments of target orientation. Dyde and Milner (2002), argue that the sensitivity of action to a perceptual illusion can be understood in terms of the illusion's presumed neural origins. Illusions that presumably arise from "early" (i.e., area V1, area V2) stages of visual processing, such as the ST illusion, should affect both action and perception since the dorsal and ventral visual pathways share this input (Milner and Dyde, 2003). Illusions like the RF that presumably arise from later stages of processing (i.e., in inferotemporal cortex) should not affect action, since the dorsal stream does not have direct access to this processing.

Similar accounts have been put forward to explain the fact that there are reliable directional anisotropies in the perception of the direction of motion even though such anisotropies are not present in smooth pursuit eye movements (Churchland et al., 2003), and the observation that fast reaching movements are sensitive to target mislocalization errors induced by distant visual motion signals (Whitney et al., 2003).

A number of recent studies have highlighted the importance of timing in determining whether or not perceptual illusions will affect action. Thus, perceptual illusions have been shown to influence the control of actions when the programming of those actions is based on a memory of the target stimuli (Wong and Mack, 1981; Gentilucci et al., 1996; Bridgeman et al., 1997; Rossetti, 1998; Hu and Goodale, 2000; Westwood et al., 2000a,b). These findings are consistent with the argument developed earlier that the control of action after a delay depends upon a memory trace of the target object that was originally delivered by the perceptual mechanisms in the ventral stream. Recently, Westwood and Goodale (2003) found that a size-contrast illusion influenced grip aperture when vision of the target was occluded at the moment the response was cued; in contrast, the illusion did not have any effect on grip aperture on other trials in which target vision was not occluded until the movement was initiated. In other words, if vision was available during the programming of the movement, grip aperture reflected the real not the apparent size of the target. This finding underscores once more the idea that the visuomotor networks in the dorsal stream operate in real time and are not engaged unless the target object is visible at the exact moment the response is required.

Future directions

Evidence from a wide range of studies continues to support and extend the idea that the dorsal and ventral streams of visual processing play different but complementary roles in the control of action. Perceptual mechanisms in the ventral stream allow us to recognize objects and access the semantic knowledge necessary to appreciate their causal relations; as such, these ventral stream mechanisms deliver the information that allows us to choose goals and plan courses of action. When it comes time to implement a chosen course of action, however, dedicated visuomotor mechanisms in the dorsal stream are engaged to transform current visual information about the goal object into a calibrated motor response. But actions whose goal is a remembered rather than a visible object must make use of perceptual processing in the ventral stream.

But one of the important issues that remain to be solved is how the two visual streams work together in the control of our behavior. For example, once a target has been identified using ventral stream processing, how is this information communicated to the visuomotor systems in the dorsal stream? One suggestion has been that the communication involves the prominent recurrent projections that could convey a focus of activity in the ventral stream back to primary visual cortex and other early visual areas (Lamme and Roelfsema, 2000). If a target has been "flagged" on retinotopic maps in these early visual areas by recurrent projections, the location of that target can then be relayed to the dorsal stream for action. There is certainly evidence from single-unit studies that when a monkey pays attention to a visual stimulus in a particular location, the activity of neurons corresponding to that location is enhanced in early visual areas, including primary visual cortex (Super et al., 2001). The actual shifting of attention from one stimulus to another may involve mechanisms in the dorsal stream, particularly area LIP. This region, which has been shown to be involved in the voluntary control of saccadic eye movements to visual targets, has been implicated in the shifting of attention to biologically important or salient visual stimuli (Bisley and Goldberg, 2003). But again it is not clear how the loop is closed so that attention is shifted to the "right" stimulus and remains there. Nevertheless, the answers to these questions will no doubt emerge over the next few years as methods and theory-building in visual neuroscience will become more and more sophisticated. In particular, transcranial magnetic stimulation (TMS) promises to be a valuable tool in this endeavor, since it can be used to disrupt the transmission of information between brain regions in a precisely controlled temporal manner.

280

References

Aglioti, S., DeSouza, J.F. and Goodale, M.A. (1995) Size-contrast illusions deceive the eye but not the hand. Curr. Biol., 5: 679–685.

Andersen, R.A. (1987) Inferior parietal lobule function in spatial perception and visuomotor integration. In: Mountcastle, V.B, Plum, F. and Geiger, S.R. (Eds.), Handbook of Physiology Section 1: The Nervous System, Volume V: Higher Functions of the Brain, Part 2, Amer. Physiol. Assoc., Bethesda MD, pp. 483–518.

Andersen, R.A. and Buneo, C.A. (2003) Sensorimotor integration in posterior parietal cortex. Adv. Neurol., 93: 159–177.

Bálint, R. (1909) Seelenlämung des "Schauens", optische Ataxie, räumliche Störung der Aufmerksamkeit. Monatsch. Psychiatr. Neurolog., 25: 51–81.

Biederman, I. and Gerhardstein, P.C. (1993) Recognizing depth-rotated objects: Evidence and conditions for three-dimensional viewpoint invariance. J. Exp. Psychol. Hum. Percept. Perform, 19: 1162–1182.

Binkofski, F., Dohle, C., Posse, S., Stephan, K.M., Hefter, H., Seitz, R.J. and Freund, H.J. (1998) Human anterior intraparietal area subserves prehension: A combined lesion and functional MRI activation study. Neurology, 50: 1253–1259.

Bisley, J.W. and Goldberg, M.E. (2003) The role of the parietal cortex in the neural processing of saccadic eye movements. Adv. Neurol., 93: 141–157.

Bridgeman, B., Lewis, S., Heit, G. and Nagle, M. (1979) Relation between cognitive and motor-oriented systems of visual position perception. J. Exp. Psychol. Hum. Percept. Perform, 5: 692–700.

Bridgeman, B., Kirch, M. and Sperling, A. (1981) Segregation of cognitive and motor aspects of visual function using induced motion. Percept. Psychophys., 29: 336–342.

Bridgeman, B., Peery, S. and Anand, S. (1997) Interaction of cognitive and sensorimotor maps of visual space. Percept. Psychophys., 59: 456–469.

Brown, L.E., Moore, C.M. and Rosenbaum, D.A. (2002) Feature-specific perceptual processing dissociates action from recognition. J. Exp. Psychol. Hum. Percept. Perform, 28: 1330–1344.

Bruno, N. (2001) When does action resist visual illusions? Trends Cogn. Sci., 5: 379–382.

Burr, D.C., Morrone, M.C. and Ross, J. (2001) Separate visual representations for perception and action revealed by saccadic eye movements. Curr. Biol., 11: 798–802.

Cant, J.S., Westwood, D.A., Valyear, K.F. and Goodale, M.A. (2005) No evidence for visuomotor priming in a visually guided action task. Neuropsychologia, 43: 216–226.

Carey, D.P. (2001) Do action systems resist visual illusions? Trends Cogn. Sci., 5: 109–113.

Castiello, U., Paulignan, Y. and Jeannerod, M. (1991) Temporal dissociation of motor responses and subjective awareness. A study in normal subjects. Brain, 114: 2639–2655.

Churchland, A.K., Gardner, J.L., Chou, I., Priebe, N.J. and Lisberger, S.G. (2003) Directional anisotropies reveal a functional segregation of visual motion processing for perception and action. Neuron, 37: 1001–1011.

Cohen, Y.E. and Andersen, R.A. (2002) A common reference frame for movement plans in the posterior parietal cortex. Nat. Rev. Neurosci., 3: 553–562.

Craighero, L., Fadiga, L., Umilta, C.A. and Rizzolatti, G. (1996) Evidence for visuomotor priming effect. Neuroreport, 8: 347–349.

Creem, S.H. and Proffitt, D.R. (2001) Grasping objects by their handles: A necessary interaction between cognition and action. J. Exp. Psychol. Hum. Percept. Perform, 27: 218–228.

Culham, J. (2004) Human brain imaging reveals a parietal area specialized for grasping. In: Kanwisher, N. and Duncan, J. (Eds.), Attention and Performance XX. Functional Neuroimaging of Visual Cognition, Oxford University Press, Oxford, pp. 415–436.

Culham, J.C. and Kanwisher, N.G. (2001) Neuroimaging of cognitive functions in human parietal cortex. Curr. Opin. Neurobiol., 11: 157–163.

Culham, J.C., Danckert, S.L., De Souza, J.F., Gati, J.S., Menon, R.S. and Goodale, M.A. (2003) Visually guided grasping produces fMRI activation in dorsal but not ventral stream brain areas. Exp. Brain Res., 153: 180–189.

Danckert, J.A., Sharif, N., Haffenden, A.M., Schiff, K.C. and Goodale, M.A. (2002) A temporal analysis of grasping in the Ebbinghaus illusion: Planning versus online control. Exp. Brain Res., 144: 275–280.

de Grave, D.D.J., Biegstraaten, M., Brenner, E. and Smeets, J.B.J. (2004). The Ebbinghaus figure is more than a size illusion [Abstract]. J. Vision, 4:836a.

Desmurget, M., Epstein, C.M., Turner, R.S., Prablanc, C., Alexander, G.E. and Grafton, S.T. (1999) Role of the posterior parietal cortex in updating reaching movements to a visual target. Nat. Neurosci., 2: 563–567.

Desmurget, M., Grea, H., Grethe, J.S., Prablanc, C., Alexander, G.E. and Grafton, S.T. (2001) Functional anatomy of nonvisual feedback loops during reaching: A positron emission tomography study. J. Neurosci., 21: 2919–2928.

Dubrowski, A. and Carnahan, H. (2002) Action-perception dissociation in response to target acceleration. Vision Res., 42: 1465–1473.

Dyde, R.T. and Milner, A.D. (2002) Two illusions of perceived orientation: One fools all of the people some of the time; the other fools all of the people all of the time. Exp. Brain Res., 144: 518–527.

Ettlinger, G. (1977) Parietal cortex in visual orientation. In: Rose, F.C. (Ed.), Physiological Aspects of Clinical Neurology, Blackwell, Oxford, pp. 93–100.

Printed and bound by CPI Group (UK) Ltd, Croydon, CR0 4YY

03/10/2024

01040328-0015

Fecteau, J.H., Chua, R., Franks, I. and Enns, J.T. (2001) Visual awareness and the on-line modification of action. Can. J. Exp. Psychol., 55: 104–110.

Franz, V.H. (2003). Planning versus online control: dynamic illusion effects in grasping? Spat. Vis., 16:211–223..

Franz, V.H., Gegenfurtner, K.R., Bulthoff, H.H. and Fahle, M. (2000) Grasping visual illusions: No evidence for a dissociation between perception and action. Psychol. Sci., 11: 20–25.

Gallese, V., Murata, A., Kaseda, M., Niki, N. and Sakata, H. (1994) Deficit of hand preshaping after muscimol injection in monkey parietal cortex. Neuroreport, 5: 1525–1529.

Ganel, T. and Goodale, M.A. (2003) Visual control of action but not perception requires analytical processing of object shape. Nature, 426: 664–667.

Garofeanu, C., Króliczak, G., Goodale, M.A. and Humphrey, G.K. (2004) Naming and grasping common objects: A priming study. Exp. Brain Res., 159: 55–64.

Gentilucci, M., Chieffi, S., Deprati, E., Saetti, M.C. and Toni, I. (1996) Visual illusion and action. Neuropsychologia, 34: 369–376.

Glickstein, M., Buchbinder, S. and May 3rd, J.L. (1998) Visual control of the arm, the wrist and the fingers: Pathways through the brain. Neuropsychologia, 36: 981–1001.

Glover, S. (2002) Visual illusions affect planning but not control. Trends Cogn. Sci., 6: 288–292.

Glover, S. (2004) Separate visual representations in the planning and control of action. Behav. Brain Sci., 27: 3–78.

Glover, S.R. and Dixon, P. (2001) Dynamic illusion effects in a reaching task: Evidence for separate visual representations in the planning and control of reaching. J. Exp. Psychol. Hum. Percept. Perform, 27: 560–572.

Goodale, M.A., Pelisson, D. and Prablanc, C. (1986) Large adjustments in visually guided reaching do not depend on vision of the hand or perception of target displacement. Nature, 320: 748–750.

Goodale, M.A., Milner, A.D., Jakobson, L.S. and Carey, D.P. (1991) A neurological dissociation between perceiving objects and grasping them. Nature, 349: 154–156.

Goodale, M.A. and Milner, A.D. (1992) Separate visual pathways for perception and action. Trends Neurosci., 15: 20–25.

Goodale, M.A., Jakobson, L.S. and Keillor, J.M. (1994) Differences in the visual control of pantomimed and natural grasping movements. Neuropsychologia, 32: 1159–1178.

Goodale, M.A. and Humphrey, G.K. (1998) The objects of action and perception. Cognition., 67: 181–207.

Goodale, M.A. and Milner, A.D. (2004). Sight Unseen: An Exploration of Conscious and Unconscious Vision. Oxford: Oxford Univ. Press.

Goodale, M.A., Westwood, D.A. and Milner, A.D. (2003) Two distinct modes of control for object-directed action. Prog. Brain Res., 144: 131–144.

Grill-Spector, K. (2003) The neural basis of object perception. Curr. Opin. Neurobiol., 13: 159–166.

Gross, C.G., Rocha-Miranda, C.E. and Bender, D.B. (1972) Visual properties of neurons in inferotemporal cortex of the Macaque. J. Neurophysiol., 35: 96–111.

Guillery, R.W. (2003) Branching thalamic afferents link action and perception. J. Neurophysiol., 90: 539–548.

Haffenden, A.M. and Goodale, M.A. (1998) The effect of pictorial illusion on prehension and perception. J. Cogn. Neurosci., 10: 122–136.

Haffenden, A.M. and Goodale, M.A. (2000) Independent effects of pictorial displays on perception and action. Vision Res., 40: 1597–1607.

Haffenden, A.M., Schiff, K.C. and Goodale, M.A. (2001) The dissociation between perception and action in the Ebbinghaus illusion: Nonillusory effects of pictorial cues on grasp. Curr. Biol., 11: 177–181.

Hasson, U., Harel, M., Levy, I. and Malach, R. (2003) Large-scale mirror-symmetry organization of human occipito-temporal object areas. Neuron, 37: 1027–1041.

Henriques, D.Y., Medendorp, W.P., Khan, A.Z. and Crawford, J.D. (2002) Visuomotor transformations for eye-hand coordination. Prog. Brain Res., 140: 329–340.

Hu, Y. and Goodale, M.A. (2000) Grasping after a delay shifts size-scaling from absolute to relative metrics. J. Cogn. Neurosci., 12: 856–868.

Hyvärinen, J. and Poranen, A. (1974) Function of the parietal associative area 7 as revealed from cellular discharges in alert monkeys. Brain, 97: 673–692.

James, T.W., Culham, J., Humphrey, G.K., Milner, A.D. and Goodale, M.A. (2003) Ventral occipital lesions impair object recognition but not object-directed grasping: An fMRI study. Brain, 126: 2463–2475.

James, T.W., Humphrey, G.K., Gati, J.S., Menon, R.S. and Goodale, M.A. (2002) Differential effects of viewpoint on object-driven activation in dorsal and ventral streams. Neuron, 35: 793–801.

Janssen, P., Vogels, R. and Orban, G.A. (1999) Macaque inferior temporal neurons are selective for disparity-defined three–dimensional shapes. Proc. Natl. Acad. Sci., 96: 8217–8222.

Janssen, P., Vogels, R. and Orban, G.A. (2000) Selectivity for 3D shape that reveals distinct areas within macaque inferior temporal cortex. Science, 288: 2054–2056.

Jeannerod, M. and Farne, A. (2003) The visuomotor functions of posterior parietal areas. Adv. Neurol., 93: 205–217.

Kerzel, D. and Gegenfurtner, K.R. (2003) Neuronal processing delays are compensated in the sensorimotor branch of the visual system. Curr. Biol., 13: 1975–1978.

Lamme, V.A. and Roelfsema, P.R. (2000) The distinct modes of vision offered by feedforward and recurrent processing. Trends Neurosci., 23: 571–579.

Le, S., Cardebat, D., Boulanouar, K., Henaff, M.A., Michel, F., Milner, D., Dijkerman, C., Puel, M. and Demonet, J.F. (2002) Seeing, since childhood, without ventral stream: a behavioral study. Brain, 125: 58–74.

Lebedev, M.A., Douglass, D.K., Moody, S.L. and Wise, S.P. (2001) Prefrontal cortex neurons reflecting reports of a visual illusion. J. Neurophysiol., 85: 1395–1411.

Lee, J.H. and van Donkelaar, P. (2002) Dorsal and ventral visual stream contributions to perception-action interactions during pointing. Exp. Brain Res., 143: 440–446.

Leon, M.I. and Shadlen, M.N. (2003) Representation of time by neurons in the posterior parietal cortex of the macaque. Neuron, 38: 317–327.

Logothetis, N.K. (1998) Single units and conscious vision. Philos. Trans. R Soc. Lond. B Biol. Sci., 353: 1801–1818.

Logothetis, N.K., Pauls, J. and Poggio, T. (1995) Shape representation in the inferior temporal cortex of monkeys. Curr. Biol., 5: 552–563.

Logothetis, N.K. and Sheinberg, D.L. (1996) Visual object recognition. Ann. Rev. Neurosci., 19: 577–621.

Mack, A., Heuer, F., Villardi, K. and Chambers, D. (1985) The dissociation of position and extent in Muller-Lyer figures. Percept. Psychophys., 37: 335–344.

Malach, R., Reppas, J.B., Benson, R.R., Kwong, K.K., Jiang, H., Kennedy, W.A., Ledden, P.J., Brady, T.J., Rosen, B.R. and Tootell, R.B. (1995) Object-related activity revealed by functional magnetic resonance imaging in human occipital cortex. Proc. Natl. Acad. Sci. USA, 92: 8135–8139.

Milner, A.D., Perrett, D.I., Johnston, R.S., Benson, P.J., Jordan, T.R., Heeley, D.W., Bettucci, D., Mortara, F., Mutani, R., Terazzi, E. and Davidson, D.L.W. (1991) Perception and action in "visual form agnosia". Brain, 114: 405–428.

Milner, A.D., Dijkerman, H.C., McIntosh, R.D., Pisella, L. and Rossetti, Y. (2003) Delayed reaching and grasping in patients with optic ataxia. Prog. Brain Res., 142: 225–242.

Milner, D. and Dyde, R. (2003) Why do some perceptual illusions affect visually guided action, when others don't? Trends Cogn. Sci., 7: 10–11.

Milner, A.D. and Goodale, M.A. (1995). The Visual Brain in Action. Oxford Univ Press, Oxford.

Milner, A.D., Paulignan, Y., Dijkerman, H.C., Michel, F. and Jeannerod, M. (1999) A paradoxical improvement of misreaching in optic ataxia: New evidence for two separate neural systems for visual localization. Proc. R Soc. Lond. B Biol. Sci., 266: 2225–2229.

Milner, A.D., Dijkerman, H.C., Pisella, L., McIntosh, R.D., Tilikete, C., Vighetto, A. and Rossetti, Y. (2001) Grasping the past. Delay can improve visuomotor performance. Curr. Biol., 11: 1896–1901.

Miyashita, Y and Hayashi, T. (2000) Neural representation of visual objects: Encoding and top-down activation. Curr. Opin. Neurobiol., 10: 187–194.

Mountcastle, V.B., Lynch, J.C., Georgopoulos, A., Sakata, H. and Acũna, C. (1975) Posterior parietal association cortex of the monkey: Command functions for operations within extrapersonal space. J. Neurophysiol., 38: 871–908.

Pascual-Leone, A., Walsh, V. and Rothwell, J. (2000) Transcranial magnetic stimulation in cognitive neuroscience–virtual lesion, chronometry, and functional connectivity. Curr. Opin. Neurobiol., 10: 232–237.

Perenin, M.-T. and Vighetto, A. (1988) Optic ataxia: A specific disruption in visuomotor mechanisms. I. Different aspects of the deficit in reaching for objects. Brain, 111: 643–674.

Perrett, D., Benson, P.J., Hietanen, J.K., Oram, M.W. and Dittrich, W.H. (1995) When is a face not a face? In: Gregory, R., Harris, J., Heard, P. and Rose, D. (Eds.), The Artful Eye, Oxford University Press, Oxford, U.K., pp. 95–124.

Pisella, L., Grea, H., Tilikete, C., Vighetto, A., Desmurget, M., Rode, G., Boisson, D. and Rossetti, Y. (2000) An "automatic pilot" for the hand in human posterior parietal cortex: Toward reinterpreting optic ataxia. Nat. Neurosci., 3: 729–736.

Revol, P., Rossetti, Y., Vighetto, A., Rode, G., Boisson, D. and Pisella, L. (2003) Pointing errors in immediate and delayed conditions in unilateral optic ataxia. Spat. Vis., 16: 347–364.

Rizzolatti, G. and Matelli, M. (2003) Two different streams form the dorsal visual system: Anatomy and function. Exp. Brain Res., 153: 146–157.

Rossetti, Y., Pisella, L. and Vighetto, A. (2003) Optic ataxia revisited: Visually guided action versus immediate visuomotor control. Exp. Brain Res., 153: 171–179.

Sakata, H. (2003) The role of the parietal cortex in grasping. Adv. Neurol., 93: 121–139.

Sakata, H. and Taira, M. (1994) Parietal control of hand action. Curr. Opin. Neurobiol., 4: 847–856.

Schacter, D. and Buckner, R. (1998) Priming and the brain. Neuron, 20: 185–195.

Sereno, A.B. and Maunsell, J.H. (1998) Shape selectivity in primate lateral intraparietal cortex. Nature, 395: 500–503.

Shadlen, M.N. and Newsome, W.T. (2001) Neural basis of a perceptual decision in the parietal cortex (area LIP) of the rhesus monkey. J. Neurophysiol., 86: 1916–1936.

Simon, O., Mangin, J.F., Cohen, L., Le Bihan, D. and Dehaene, S. (2002) Topographical layout of hand, eye, calculation, and language-related areas in the human parietal lobe. Neuron, 33: 475–487.

Smeets, J.B.J. and Brenner, E. (2001). Action beyond our grasp. Trends Cogn. Sci., 5: 287.

Smeets, J.B., Brenner, E., de Grave, D.D. and Cuijpers, R.H. (2002) Illusions in action: Consequences of inconsistent processing of spatial attributes. Exp. Brain. Res., 147: 135–144.

Snyder, L.H., Batista, A.P. and Andersen, R.A. (1997) Coding of intention in the posterior parietal cortex. Nature, 386: 167–170.

Super, H., Spekreijse, H. and Lamme, V.A. (2001) Two distinct modes of sensory processing observed in monkey primary visual cortex(V1). Nat. Neurosci., 4: 304–310.

Rossetti, Y. (1998) Implicit short-lived motor representations of space in brain damaged and healthy subjects. Conscious. Cogn., 7: 520–558.

Taira, M., Mine, S., Georgopoulos, A.P., Murata, A. and Sakata, H. (1990) Parietal cortex neurons of the monkey related to the visual guidance of hand movement. Exp. Brain Res., 83: 29–36.

Tanaka, K. (2003) Columns for complex visual object features in the inferotemporal cortex: Clustering of cells with similar but slightly different stimulus selectivities. Cereb. Cortex, 13: 90–99.

Tanaka, K., Saito, H., Fukada, Y. and Moriya, M. (1991) Coding visual images of objects in the inferotemporal cortex of the macaque monkey. J. Neurophysiol., 66: 170–189.

Thompson-Schill, S.L. and Gabrieli, J.D.E. (1999) Priming of visual and functional knowledge on a semantic classification task. J. Exp. Psychol. Learn Mem. Cogn., 25: 41–53.

Toth, L.J. and Assad, J.A. (2002) Dynamic coding of behaviorally relevant stimuli in parietal cortex. Nature, 415: 165–168.

Vaina, L.M., Solomon, J., Chowdhury, S., Sinha, P. and Belliveau, J.W. (2001) Functional neuroanatomy of biologi-cal motion perception in humans. Proc. Natl. Acad. Sci. USA, 98: 11656–11661.

Vishton, P.M., Rea, J.G., Cutting, J.E. and Nunez, L.N. (1999) Comparing effects of the horizontal-vertical illusion on grip scaling and judgment: Relative versus absolute, not perception versus action. J. Exp. Psychol. Hum. Percept. Perform., 25: 1659–1672.

Westwood, D.A., Chapman, C.D. and Roy, E.A. (2000) Pantomimed actions may be controlled by the ventral visual stream. Exp. Brain Res., 130: 545–548.

Westwood, D.A., Heath, M. and Roy, E.A. (2000) The effect of a pictorial illusion on closed-loop and open-loop prehension. Exp. Brain Res., 134: 456–463.

Westwood, D.A. and Goodale, M.A. (2003) Perceptual illusion and the real-time control of action. Spat. Vis., 16: 243–254.

Whitney, D., Westwood, D.A. and Goodale, M.A. (2003) The influence of visual motion on fast reaching movements to a stationary object. Nature, 423: 869–873.

Wong, E. and Mack, A. (1981) Saccadic programming and perceived location. Acta Psychol., 48: 123–131.

283

Progress in Brain Research, Vol. 149
ISSN 0079-6123

CHAPTER 20

A neurophilosophical slant on consciousness research

Patricia Smith Churchland*

UC President's Professor of Philosophy, Philosophy Department 0119, UCSD, La Jolla, CA 92093, USA

Abstract: Explaining the nature and mechanisms of conscious experience in neurobiological terms seems to be an attainable, if yet unattained, goal. Research at many levels is important, including research at the cellular level that explores the role of recurrent pathways between thalamic nuclei and the cortex, and research that explores consciousness from the perspective of action. Conceptually, a clearer understanding of the logic of expressions such as "causes" and "correlates", and about what to expect from a theory of consciousness are required. The logic of some terms, such as "qualia" and "reductionism", continues to generate misunderstandings about the scientific possibilities and limits. Experimentally, a deeper understanding of the role of the thalamus in coordinating activity across cortical levels, and a readiness to reconsider the orthodox approach to thalamocortical organization are also required.

The problem

The nature of consciousness is a problem at the interface of a range of disciplines: philosophy, psychology, neuroscience, anesthesiology, genetics, ethology, and evolutionary biology. Psychology helps us understand phenomena such as attention, conscious sensation, and declarative memory at the macrolevels. It has, for example, helped us learn that eye movements, made nonconsciously, nonetheless exhibit strategy and planning. On its own, however, psychological investigation is not enough, for we need also to understand mechanisms at the network and neuronal levels. Nonhuman animal studies, both behavioral and neurobiological, are essential to discerning which conscious capacities are shared and which not, and wherein lie the neurobiological differences.

The problem of consciousness in the 21st century is not the mind–body problem Descartes struggled with. The classical mind–body problem was how the nonphysical stuff that makes up the immaterial soul can causally interact with the material stuff that is the body. No one, including of course Descartes, made the slightest progress in solving that problem. But we can see now that interaction is a pseudo problem, like the problem of how the crystal spheres of the heavens daily rotate, or how the heart concocts animals spirits. Compelling evidence implies the extreme improbability that thinking, feeling, and experiencing are events in a nonphysical soul. Rather, they are events of the entirely physical brain. Because one party to the alleged interaction almost certainly does not exist, interactionism is a nonproblem.

The contemporary mind/brain problem, therefore, is a nest of empirical questions about the brain: for example, what are the differences in the brain between being awake and being in deep sleep, and which of these differences explain being conscious when awake and not being conscious in deep sleep? How does that condition compare to the brain during absence seizures or during complex partial seizures? How much of decision-making is conscious, and what are

*Tel.: +1-858-822-1655; Fax: +1-858-534-8566;
 E-mail: pschurchland@ucsd.edu

DOI: 10.1016/S0079-6123(05)49020-2

286

the differences between conscious and nonconscious stages of decision-making? What is the nature and origin of top–down attention and how does it work? What exactly happens in the brain when early skill acquisition slowly becomes a polished skill, performed automatically? This is, evidently, a partial and open-ended list, a list some of whose missing items may be unimagined, and perhaps unimaginable, given the current state of science. A truncated version of the contemporary problem is this: how can psychological phenomena be explained in neurobiological terms? Traditionally in philosophy of science, this is considered roughly equivalent to this question: how can psychology be reduced to neuroscience?

What is reductionism?

Disconnected from its root meaning, the word, "reductionism" has come to be freighted with plethora of very diverse, and often incompatible, emotional meanings. For example, it is sometimes used to mean that a research strategy must proceed "from the bottom up". That is not part of its classical meaning. Rather than sort all that out, this section explains what is meant by reduction from the author's point of view, and why that old bruised and misused word still has traction and utility (Churchland, 2002).

Reduction is a relation between scientific theories. To a first approximation, a science has achieved a reduction when the causal powers described at the macrolevel are explained as the outcome of events and processes at the lower level. Classically, reductions involve identifying functional macrocomponents that map onto structural microcomponents. Next, one assembles and tests hypotheses about how the components interact to produce the large scale effect. Explanation is considered achieved to the degree that the hypotheses survive tough experimental testing, and are consilient with other parts of well established science. That scenario may be repeated when the functions of the microcomponents are themselves decomposed into yet lower level structural constituents and their nanoactivities.

Thus thermodynamics is said to be reduced to statistical mechanics because temperature is explained in terms of the motion of the constituent molecules.

Theory of optics was reduced to theory of electromagnetic radiation, as we came to understand that light is, in fact, electromagnetic radiation, and inhabits the same explanatory framework as radio waves, micro-waves and X-rays. Typically, macro and micro-level theories co-evolve through time, as each provides tests, problems, and ideas for the other. Nature permitting, the two theories may come to knit together more closely, until the explanatory connections are so rich that scientists write their textbooks detailing the relevant range of macrophenomena as explanatorily brought to heel. In the 20th century, this was the profile of macro and microgenetics, and we see it robustly in progress in the co-evolution of embryology and molecular biology. The co-evolution of the cognitive sciences and the neurosciences, though in a very early stage, is filling the journals with remarkable, and often puzzling, discoveries.

One particular aspect of co-evolution of theories is worth dwelling on. As discoveries are made, it is inevitable that the descriptions of various phenomena are upgraded to reflect the discoveries. Consequently the meanings of the words in the descriptions undergo a parallel semantic evolution. As Francis Crick was fond of pointing out, the meaning of the word "gene" in 2000 is much richer and much different from its meaning in 1950. Depending on how the science goes, the semantic evolution mirroring the scientific evolution may be very dramatic. In such instances, people often speak of conceptual revolution. Thus one might well say that in the period from about the 1960 through to 1980 genetics underwent a conceptual revolution. This also marked geology as it came to appreciate that the continents drift on a surface of magma. The idea that heat was not caloric fluid, or any kind of stuff at all, but merely the *motion* of molecules, was a conceptual revolution that occurred in the 19th century. More generally, as the explanatory exoskeleton emerges — that is, as the basic principles are discovered and put into the theoretical framework — quite radical changes can occur. For this is the period when folk ideas are gradually replaced by scientific ideas, and in turn, early scientific ideas are replaced by more mature hypotheses. This is the period when the ostensibly obvious gets wrecked on the shoals of scientific discovery.

One simple example of semantic evolution concerns fire. In the middle ages, formulating a precise definition of "fire" was not possible, since physicists did not know what it really was. Certainly no scientists could say that is was rapid oxidation, since nothing was known as about oxygen as an element or about its role in the burning of wood. Had a kind alien left a message on a monk's pillow, "guess what — burning is rapid oxidation", no one would have known what the message could possibly mean. Such precision as there was in defining "fire" consisted in grouping together a range of phenomena, all considered paradigmatic instances of fire: the sun, comets, burning of wood, lightning, northern lights, and fireflies. The criteria were drawn from what seemed observably obvious: they all emit light or heat or both. As it happened, burning of carbon material was the first to be understood, thanks to Lavosier and Priestly.

The reality behind what was supposed to be observably obvious turned out to be surprising: the items in the list are fundamentally different from each other and are subsumed by very different scientific subfields. The heat and light from the sun is the result not of oxidation, but of nuclear fusion; lightning is actually thermal emission; the fireflies" display is based on biophosphorescence; comets are balls of ice reflecting sunlight; northern lights are the result of spectral emission. These items are not part of the same family at all. From the vantage point of 21st century science, the medieval categorization might seem a bit foolish. Because we learn contemporary science as children, that current science becomes second nature to us — it seems dead obvious. The medieval category was not owed to foolishness but merely to ignorance. When you do not really understand the nature of a phenomenon, you try to do justice to what you think is observably obvious.

In terms of scientific maturity, neuroscience is still wet behind the ears. More exactly, neuroscience is still in search of its basic explanatory exoskeleton — of the fundamental principles that explain how nervous systems work. Although an enormous amount is known about the molecular aspects of individual neurons (their structure and their function), the fundamentals characterizing how macro effects emerge from populations of neurons are still largely mysterious.

Can we expect conceptual revolutions? The progress of science is impossible to predict with much accuracy, but given the history of science, simple prudence suggests that we currently misconceptualize many problems because we do not have the scientific understanding to generate and render precise the appropriate concepts. My hunch is that consciousness is probably a case in point. For example, it sometimes seems observably obvious that consciousness is a single, unitary phenomenon, that you either have it or you do not, that it is like a light — it is either off or on. But these seemingly obvious ideas may turn out to be quite wrong. With an even higher degree of uncertainty, it is conjectured that as we come to understand how *time* is managed and represented and used, and to understand the function of the many emerging and fading intrinsic rhythms displayed by individual neurons and by populations of neurons, some of the explanatory exoskeleton will begin to be discernible (Jahnsen and Llinas, 1984; Sherman and Guillery, 2001; Massimini et al., 2004). Were a kindly alien to leave a message on one's pillow concerning the true neurobiological nature of conscious phenomena, one doubtless could not make much sense of the message.

What are the target phenomena?

The list of phenomena commonly rated as instances of "consciousness" turns out to be diverse and somewhat puzzling. Someone in coma following an epileptic seizure or a blow to the head, for example, is not conscious; someone not paying attention to a mild hunger is not conscious of that hunger; someone in deep sleep is not conscious in the way that he is conscious when awake. Stupor differs from coma in that patients can be aroused from unresponsiveness with vigorous stimuli; patients in persistent vegetative state (PVS) show sleep–wake cycles but are totally nonresponsive to external stimuli, however vigorous; coma patients are totally nonresponsive and exhibit no sleep–wake cycles. Evidently, these are quite different ways of being "not conscious" (Plum and Posner, 1982). Correlatively, being awake, paying attention, explicitly remembering, emerging from anesthesia, smelling mint, regaining awareness following an absence seizure, regaining awareness following a complex partial seizure, being aroused from sedation, dreaming and hallucinating, are, quite possibly, different ways of being conscious.

Executing an intentional action, such as picking up a hammer and pounding in a nail seems to involve consciousness of the action, though many aspects of the action sequence are conscious in one sense, but not in another. For the skilled carpenter, less attention is paid to the details of the hammering movement, and more to planning and organizing the next set of complex actions. Automatized skills are exercised consciously, but not in the way that the novice is conscious of his unskilled action. How formed our decisions are when we become aware of them (and think of ourselves as "creating" them), is unclear. For example, it is known that nonconscious antecedents to an intention, as indicated by the "readiness potential" measured by the EEG, precede a "freely-chosen" action by up to a second and a half (Libet, 1985).

We are aware of emotions, such as being angry or sad, of drives, such as sexual lust, hunger, and curiosity; of the passage of time and of spatial depth and layout. We are aware that a scene is unfamiliar, that we feel dizzy, that we are falling, that we need to pass water. Efference copy allows one to be aware that a movement is one's movement, not the world's movement (Churchland, 2002). Normally, we are aware of our body as our own (Damasio, 1999). Normally we are aware of our thoughts as our own; on one hypothesis, schizophrenic patients lack this sense of ownership, and attribute their thoughts to external agents, such as God, the devil, or the FBI (Frith, 1992).

Why stress the diversity of conscious phenomena? For several reasons. First, because much of the literature assumes without discussion that at bottom there is only one basic phenomenon, with various features that come and go (Chalmers, 1996). From a neural point of view, that assumption may be quite wrong. Like the medieval physicists thinking about fire, we just do not know enough to put much confidence in the "single thing" assumption about consciousness. There may be a set of inter-related but semi-independent processes, some may share some background conditions, but not others. Just as coma is different from persistent vegetative state, so paying attention is likely to be different from waking from deep sleep or emerging from an absence seizure.

The second reason for stressing varieties of conscious phenomena is that the set and its diverse subsets remind us that there are many entry points to the puzzle and many ways of attacking the problem. At this early stage, it may be unwise to assume that one subset is more paradigmatic, more privileged and prototypical, and more accessible to scientific investigation, than others. It may be unrewarding to assume that some items in the list are really only background conditions, not consciousness per se. Visual experiences, for example, have sometimes been regarded as prototypically conscious. Not enough is known about how the brain works to give this idea unquestioned approval, and "intuitions" are neither reliable nor uniform across scientists. And of course some humans are completely blind, and some species, such as the star-nosed mole, have no vision whatever. Where the breakthroughs will come is anyone's guess; efference copy, for example, may be a more promising entry point than visual perception. Consequently, diverse research strategies targeting distinct items on the list, with some attempts to coordinate across approaches, is probably appropriate at this stage.

What counts as a theory of conscious phenomena?

The word "theory" can be used in many ways, from something that is a loose hunch about the causes of a poorly defined phenomena (e.g., the "theory", circa 1950 that autism is caused by cold mothering), to fact-based speculations about a moderately well-defined phenomena (Wegener's postulation of continental drift) to theories that specify mechanism and either mesh with other parts of established science or else testably challenge other parts of science (the Hodgkin–Huxley theory of the action potential in a neuron; the theory of how proteins get produced).

For the purposes at hand, it is useful to adopt the convention that something will be considered a theory of consciousness if, like the theory of how a neuron produces an action potential, it explains the main properties in sufficient detail that the following are satisfied: (1) we understand how macroevents emerge from the properties and organization of the microevents, (2) novel phenomena can be predicted, (3) the system can be manipulated, and (4) it is clear at what level of brain organization the phenomenon resides.

According to this convention, therefore, we assume that a genuine explanation of the properties of conscious phenomena must characterize neurobiological mechanisms. A theory satisfying the four desiderata will not be solely a psychological level account relating various cognitive functions (i.e., not just an array of boxes, labeled as cognitive, with arrows connecting the boxes). Boxology at the psychological level is a crucially important step, but it does not explain the neurobiological bases for the functions in the boxes. Likewise, an explanatory theory will not just consist of detailed anatomical maps of what projects to what, though such maps are also essential to the solution. It is also assumed that finding correlations — perhaps via fMRI or single cell recordings — for certain conscious events does not as such constitute a theory, because such correlations do not, ipso facto, explain mechanism. Notice, moreover, that X can be correlated with Y for a range of reasons: X causes Y, Y causes X, they have a common cause, or X and Y are actually the same thing under different descriptions; i.e., X = Y. Discovery of identities (i.e., that X = Y) is typically needed to make the crucial step towards theoretical authority. Correlating events using different measuring instruments, such as fMRI and behavioral reports, can be extremely useful, certainly, but a roster of correlations does not constitute a theory.

The semantic convention proposed entails a fairly strong requirement for "theory-hood". It is meant to be strong in order to emphasize the importance of testability, predictability, and consilience with other parts of science in general and neuroscience in particular. It is meant to require a theory of consciousness to be comparably powerful to the theory that light is electromagnetic radiation, or the theory of the action potential or the theory that DNA codes for proteins. Without this sort of guideline, just about everybody and his dog lay claim to a theory of consciousness.

In this strong sense, neuroscience has not yet produced a theory of any of the various conscious phenomena aforementioned. What has emerged over the last ten years, however, are fruitful prototheories regarding some aspect or other that highlight some feature(s) at some level of brain organization as being fundamental. Other names for prototheory might be "general approach" or "line of attack".

Prototheories are more speculative, and harbor dark regions where explanation is merely hand-waving. This is not only tolerated but applauded in the hope that prototheories will mature into explanatorily competent theories as they are prodded, pushed, pounded, and goaded into experimental test (For a range of prototheories, see articles in Baars et al., 2003).

Two philosophical objections

Two further matters should be addressed concerning what we can expect from a theory. First, a common philosophical complaint is that any neurobiological theory of consciousness will always leave something out – something crucial. It will always leave out the feeling itself — the feeling of what it is like to be aware, to see blue, smell mint, and so on (Nagel, 1974; Chalmers, 1996). These are so-called qualia — the experiences themselves — and these are what are important about consciousness. Pursuing this point further, the philosopher may go on to conclude that no science can ever really explain qualia because it cannot demonstrate what it is like to see blue if you have never seen blue; consciousness is forever beyond the reach of scientific understanding.

What is the merit in this objection? It is lacking merit, for if you look closely, you will find that it rests on a misunderstanding. The argument presumes that if a conscious phenomenon, say smelling mint, were genuinely explained by a scientific theory, then a person who understood that theory should be *caused to have that experience*; e.g., should be caused to smell mint. Surely, however, the expectation is unwarranted. Why should anyone expect that understanding the theory must result in the production of the phenomenon the theory addresses? Consider an analogy. If a student really understands the nature of pregnancy by learning all there is to know about the causal nature of pregnancy, no one would expect the student to become pregnant thereby. If a student learns and really understands Newton's laws, we should not expect the student, like Newton's fabled apple, to thereby fall down. [1] To smell mint, a certain range of neuronal activities have to obtain,

---

[1] This example is owed to Ed Hubbard.

particularly, let us assume, in olfactory cortex. Understanding that the olfactory cortex must be activated in manner β will not itself activate the olfactory cortex in manner β. We are asking too much of a neuroscientific theory if we ask it not only to explain and predict, but also to *cause* its target phenomenon, namely the smell of mint, simply by virtue of understanding the theory.

A second and related complaint raised by certain philosophers is that even if neuroscience were to discover with what brain states being aware of a burning pain on one's left ear is identical, we would still not understand why just *those* brain states are identical with precisely *that* sensation, as opposed, say, to feeling a desire to void. Neuroscience, it will be averred, will never be able to explain why conscious states Y = brain states X, rather than say, brain state Z. For those who are keen on qualia as metaphysical simples forever beyond the scope of science, the next step may be to infer that we cannot ever hope to understand that identity in neurobiological terms (Chalmers, 1996). Awareness, the claim goes, will always be ineffable and metaphysically basic. This means neuroscience cannot ever really explain consciousness.

This complaint too rests on a misunderstanding. What is an example where a science — any subfield of science — explains why X = Y? Not how we *know* or why we *believe* that X = Y, but why X *is* identical to Y, rather than to Z. Using the examples already at hand, the corresponding questions would be these: why is temperature mean molecular kinetic energy, rather than, say, caloric fluid or something else entirely? Why is visible light actually electromagnetic radiation rather than, say, something else entirely, say, "intrinsic photonicness"? By and large science does not offer explanations for fundamental identities. Rather, the discovery is that two descriptions refer to one and the same thing — or that two different measuring instruments are in fact measuring one and the same thing. Why is that thing, the thing it is? It just is. Science discovers fundamental identities, but the identities it discovers just are the way things are. There is no fundamental set of laws from which to derive that temperature is mean molecular kinetic energy or light is electromagnetic radiation.

Reflection shows this logical point to be acknowledged in an everyday setting. If someone discovers

that The Morning Star (Venus) is identical to The Evening Star (Venus), he will explain why he believes this by citing his evidence. But if asked, "why is The Morning Star (Venus) identical to The Evening Star (Venus)", no answer is appropriate; that is just the way the world is. The question itself is based on the false assumption that identities ought to follow from general laws. But they don't. We may get an explanation of why people mistakenly thought what they saw in the dusk was not the same as the planet they saw in the dawn, and how they came to realize that what they saw in the dusk is identical to what they saw in the dawn. There is, however, no explanation of why Venus is Venus; of why the Morning Star is identical to the Evening Star. It just is. Or, to put it as the medieval philosophers sagely noted, everything is what it is, and not another thing. Correspondingly, assuming we discover that a certain pattern of activity Naj is identical to smelling mint, there will be no further explanation of why *that* pattern of activity is identical to smelling mint (why Naj = C).

Such merit as there is in the complaints probably comes merely to this: given the current state of neuroscience, it is very hard to predict what the explanation of conscious phenomena will look like — *very* hard. But so what? It is always hard to predict the course of a science, and especially hard to predict what an immature science will look like when it matures.

Theories of consciousness: Where is the action?

During the last decade, research targeting the problems of consciousness has intensified. By and large, the efforts have been directed toward cortical regions, cortical pathways, and cortical activity. Under the characterization, "seeking the *neural* correlates of consciousness", the research has largely been looking for the *cortical* correlates of consciousness. Clinical studies of human patients with cortical lesions have inspired this line of attack, owing to suggestive correlations between deficits in specific kind of experiences and region-specific lesions. Correlations such as (a) middle temporal lesions and loss of visual experience of motion, (b) ventral stream lesions resulting in the inability visually to detect shapes, and (c) fusiform lesions resulting in prosopagnosia, have been extremely important in providing a guidance for this research. The ease of imaging cortical activity with fMRI has probably also played some role in the focus on the cortex. Finally, because humans have proportionally more cortex than our closest relative, and because humans regard themselves as conscious beings *par excellence*, it may seem to follow that the cortex holds the answers.

True enough, human cortex is really big, relative to the thalamus, striatum, etc. But the logic in the "it must be cortex" argument is seriously flawed. Almost seventy years ago, neurosurgeons Wilder Penfield and Edwin Boldrey made a cautionary point regarding the exclusive focus on the cortex: "All parts of the brain may well be involved in normal conscious processes, but the indispensable substratum of consciousness lies outside of the cerebral cortex, probably in the diencephalon [thalamus]" (1937, p. 241).

One drawback to cortical chauvinism is that it tends concentrate on conscious *perception*, to the neglect of the perspective of behavior. This focus tends to blind us to the root "motocentric" basis of conscious phenomena. Animals are movers, and nervous systems earn their keep by servicing movement. Other things being equal (and there are a lot of other things), the better and faster the brain's predictive capacities relative to the animal's *modus vivendi*, the better the organism's behavioral portfolio in the cut-throat competition to survive and reproduce. (Churchland, et al., 1994; Allman, 1999; Damasio, 1999; Llinas, 2001; Guillery, this volume). Hence we do well to keep in mind that moving, planning, deciding, executing plans in behavior, and, more generally, keeping the body alive, is the fundamental business of the brain. Cognition and consciousness are what they are, and have the nature they have, because of their role in servicing behavior. Evolution just works that way.

Broadly speaking, the solution found by evolution to the problem of prediction is to modify motor programs (or fixed action patterns) by sensory information. The value of the sensory impact is greater if it can signal *me-relevant* causal regularities between events. To achieve this, the system needs neural populations, interposed between sensory receptors and motor neurons, to find and embody higher-order causal regularities. The richer the interposed

neuronal resources, the more sophisticated the statistical capacities and the greater the isomorphisms achievable between the brain's categorical/causal maps and the world's categorical/causal structures (Churchland and Churchland, 2002). Importantly, much of the brain's input is consequent upon the organism's own movements, exploratory and otherwise. This dynamical loop extracts vastly more information, in a given time interval, about the causal properties of the external world than could a purely passive system.

To acquire predictive prowess is to acquire skills regarding the causal structure of the world. And the essential thing about causal knowledge, is that *time* is at its heart.[2] Predicting durations, interception intervals, velocities, and speeds of the agent's own various body movements are everywhere critical. Hence memory of durations, velocities, and self-movement parameters are everywhere critical. On one construal, the most fundamental problem for a nervous system, is *how to get the timing right*; that is, how to interact with the world so as to succeed in the four Fs: feeding, fleeing, fighting, and reproducing.[3]

Skill in these functions is not a matter of passive observation but of interaction with the world, and prediction of what will happen next can be greatly improved by having access to the just-issued motor commands. Efference copy, given this perspective, is one of evolution's clever solutions to tuning the timing. What is inspiring about the Sherman and Guillery approach (2001; Guillery and Sherman, 2002), is their insight that efference copy is essential information relied upon to tune up the synapses to get the timing right. Efference copy is crucial to enabling the brain to get beyond the fixity of "fixed action patterns", to flexibility and adaptivity in planning, interacting and predicting. This insight entails, among other things, that we seriously rethink efference copy — where the signals go, how they modify sensory processing, how they prepare the nervous system for what's next, and how they contribute to conscious phenomena.

---

[2] I owe much of the discussion on time and temporal properties to the insights of Rick Grush.
[3] As Paul Maclean puts it.

According to the Guillery and Sherman hypothesis, all messages to the thalamus and cortex, including the ostensibly "pure" sensory signals, carry information about ongoing instructions to motor structures. At first this may sound puzzling, accustomed as we are to the conventional wisdom that "the sensory pathways are *purely* sensory". However, the hypothesis is profoundly right. Simplified, part of the point is this: axons from the sensory periphery have collateral branches that go to motor structures. Consequently, as a developing organism begins to interact with the world, a sensory signal becomes also a prediction about what movement will happen next; thus, as the animal learns the consequences of *that* movement, it learns about what in the world will probably happen next, and hence what it might do after that.

Loops between thalamic and cortical structures are probably the substrate for embodying ("ensynapsing", one might say) the temporal/causal properties of the world, and also the temporal/causal portfolio of one's own body. Eyes move faster than legs, head movements are faster than whole body movements, and some of these parameters can change a little or a lot with maturation, practice, anticipation, and changes in emotional state. The thalamus, given its connectivity to all cortical structures and to other subcortical structures, and given the physiology of purported driver and modulator cells, looks particularly well-suited to negotiate temporality in all its diverse aspects — in learning, ongoing prediction, attentional shifts to different sensory — motor tasks, calling up stored timing information — to getting the timing right.

The temporal is endemic to all conscious phenomena, probably because the temporal is the *sine qua non* of movement. Consequently, it is suspected that the secrets of consciousness are embodied in the thalamocortical, thalamostriatal, thalamo-brainstem loops. (See also Groenewegen and Berendse, 1994; Purpura and Schiff, 1997; Damasio, 1999; Llinas, 2001). Admittedly, this anatomical vista includes a lot of brain territory, but with a revision of the prevailing assumptions concerning "pure vision" and "visual hierarchies," the deeply inobvious may become experimentally quite accessible. (Guillery and Sherman, 2002).

Concluding remarks

Conscious phenomena are under study at many different levels of brain organization, using many different lines of attack. So far, however, no explanatorily competent theory has yet emerged. One obstacle is that most efforts are essentially visuocentric. Another is that exploration is typically limited to cortex, disregarding subcortical activity as merely part of the background conditions. This may be like missing the significance of finding fossils on a mountaintop or the difference in color between arterial and venus blood.

Until the *known* anatomy and physiology of thalamocortical connections are better appreciated, and until more of the *unknown* anatomy and physiology is revealed, neuroscientists are unlikely to see the advantages of addressing conscious phenomena from the perspective of the motor organization. In particular, we need to determine the significance of the vast number of projections from cortical layer 5 to the thalamus (Guillery and Sherman, 2002). By shifting perspective from "visuocentricity" to "motor–sensory-centricity", the singular importance of temporality takes center stage. (See also Casagrande, this volume; Colby, this volume.) In turn, this shift engenders the hunch that "time management", for want of a better term, is the key to the complex job portfolio of thalamic nuclei, and very probably the key to a range of conscious phenomena as well.

References

Allman, J.M. (1999) Evolving Brains. Scientific American Library, New York.

Baars B., Banks, W. and Newman, J. (Eds.) (2003) Essential Sources in the Scientific Study of Consciousness. MIT Press, Cambridge, MA.

Casagrande, V. (2005) Constructing visual reality: the impact of attention and motor planning on the lateral geniculate nucleus. Prog. Br. Res., (this volume).

Chalmers, D. (1996) The Conscious Mind: In Search of a Fundamental Theory. Oxford University Press, New York.

Churchland, P.S. (2002) Brain-Wise: Studies in Neurophilosophy. MIT Press, Cambridge, MA.

Churchland, P.S. and Churchland, P.M. (2002) Neural worlds and real worlds. Nature Reviews Neuroscience, 3: 903–907.

Churchland, P.S., Ramachandran, V.S. and Sejnowski, T.J. (1994) A critique of pure vision. In: Koch, C. and Davis, J.L. (Eds.), Large-Scale Neuronal Theories of the Brain. MIT Press, Cambridge, MA, pp. 23–60.

Colby, C. (2005) Corollary discharge and spatial updating; when the brain is split is space still unified? Prog. Br. Res., (this volume).

Damasio, A.R. (1999) The Feeling of What Happens. Harcourt Brace, New York.

Frith, C.D. (1992) The Cognitive Neuropsychology of Schizophrenia. Lawrence Erlbaum and Assoc., Hillsdale, N.J.

Groenewegen, H.J. and Berendse, H.W. (1994) The specificity of the "nonspecific" midline and intralaminar thalamic nuclei. Trends in Neurosci., 17: 52–57.

Guillery, R.W. and Sherman, S.M. (2002) The thalamus as a monitor of motor outputs. Philos. Trans. R Soc. Lond. B Biol. Sci., 357: 1809–1821.

Jahnsen, H. and Llinas, R. (1984) Electrophysiological properties of guinea pig thalamic neurones: An in vitro study. Journal of Physiology (London), 349: 205–226.

Libet, B. (1985) Unconscious cerebral initiative and the role of conscious will in voluntary action. Behavioral and Brain Sciences, 8: 529–566.

Llinas, R.R. (2001) I of the Vortex: From Neurons to Self. MIT Press, Cambridge, MA.

Massimini, M., Huber, R., Ferrarelli, F., Hill, S. and Tononi, G. (2004) The sleep slow oscillation as a traveling wave. The Journal of Neuroscience, 24: 6862–6870.

Nagel, T. (1974) What is it like to be a bat? Philosophical Review, 83: 435–450.

Penfield, W. and Boldrey, E. (1937) Somatic, Motor and Sensory Representation in the Cerebral Cortex of Man as Studied by Electrical Stimulation. J. Bale, Sons & Curnow, London.

Plum F. and Posner, J. (1981) The Diagnosis of Stupor and Coma, 3rd Edition. Oxford University Press, New York.

Purpura, K.P. and Schiff, N.D. (1997) The thalamic intralaminar nuclei: A role in visual awareness. The Neuroscientist, 3: 8–15.

Sherman, S.M. and Guillery, R.W. (2001) Exploring the Thalamus. Academic Press, San Diego, CA.

Index

300